Rick Steves

BEST OF

FRANCE

Rick Steves & Steve Smith

Contents

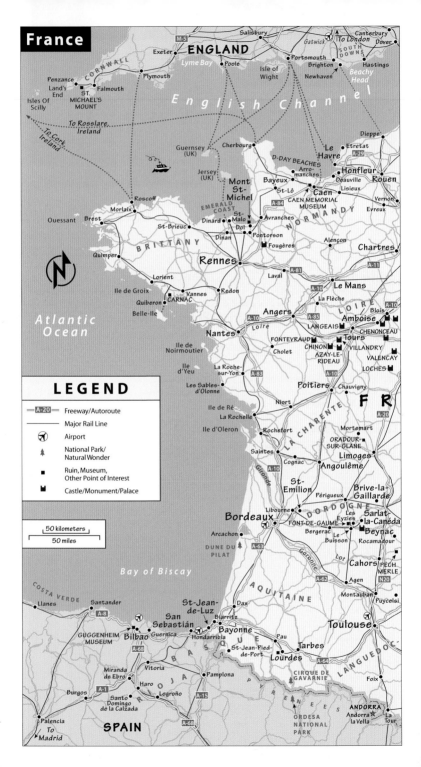

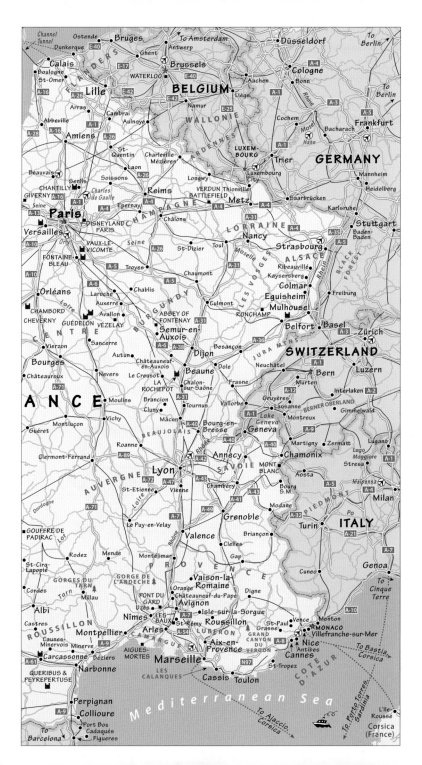

Introduction

France is a place of gentle beauty, where the play of light transforms the routine into the exceptional. Here, you'll discover a dizzying array of artistic and architectural wonders—soaring cathedrals, chandeliered châteaux, and museums filled with the cultural icons of the Western world. Gaze dreamy-eyed at Monet's water lilies, rejoice amid the sunflowers that so moved Van Gogh, and roam the sunny coastlines that inspired Picasso and Matisse.

There are two Frances: Paris...and the rest of the country. France's cultural energy has always been centered in Paris, resulting in an overwhelming concentration of world-class museums, cutting-edge architecture, and historic monuments. The other France venerates land, tradition, and a slower pace of life. *Le terroir* (the soil) brings the flavor to food and wine and nourishes the life the French enjoy. Although the country's brain resides in Paris, its soul lives in its villages—and that's where you'll feel the pulse of France.

L'art de vivre—the art of living—is not just a cute expression. France demands that you slow down and savor the finer things. Come with an appetite to understand and a willingness to experience. Linger in sidewalk cafés, make unplanned stops a habit, and surrender to the play of light as the Impressionists did.

France is Europe's most diverse, tasty, and most exciting country. *Bienvenue!* You've chosen well.

THE BEST OF FRANCE

In this selective book, I recommend France's top destinations—a mix of the most interesting cities and intimate villages, from jet-setting beach resorts to the traditional heartland.

Paris is the queen of culture. Coastal Normandy features romantic Honfleur, historic Bayeux, the stirring D-Day beaches, and the surreal island abbey of Mont St-Michel. The lovely Loire offers *beaucoup de châteaux* in all shapes and sizes. Go back in time in the Dordogne to visit prehistoric cave art and cliff-hanging medieval castles. You won't need a year in Provence to enjoy down-to-earth Arles, elegant Avignon, and the Côtes du Rhône wine road. On the French Riviera, choose your favorite coastal resort and become an expert in the art of relaxation. Wine connoisseurs savor Burgundy. In some cases, when there are interesting sights or towns near my top destinations, I cover these briefly (as "Near" sights), to help you enjoyably fill out a free day or a longer stay.

Beyond the major destinations, I also cover the Best of the Rest—great destina-

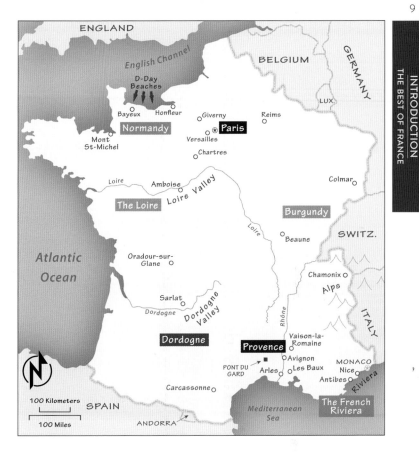

tions that don't quite make my top cut, but are worth seeing if you have more time or specific interests: Reims (with Champagne *caves*), Carcassonne (with medieval walls), Chamonix (with alpine wonders), and Col-mar (with Germanic flair).

To help you link the top stops, I've designed a two-week itinerary (see page 26), with tips to help you tailor it to your interests and time.

THE BEST OF PARIS

Paris is the grand-dame of art, culture, and fine living. Climb up the Arc de Triopmphe, saunter down the Champs-Elysées, cruise the Seine, and zip to the top of the Eiffel Tower. Savor France's greatest selection of cuisine, and explore the City of Light at night, when Paris sparkles.

❶ Versailles' colorful gardens lead into a vast park with ponds, fountains, and a royal retreat.

❷ The **Rodin Museum'**s iconic statue, The Thinker, ponders in the garden.

❸ The best time to enjoy a **Seine riverboat cruise** is at sunset.

❹ Paris' oldest and most appealing square, **Place des Vosges,** is in the Marais district.

❺ The **grand view** from Notre-Dame Cathedral stretches from the Seine River to the Eiffel Tower.

❻ The **Eiffel Tower** is loveliest at night when it's floodlit.

❼ The **Louvre Museum'**s pyramid entrance glistens at twilight.

❽ Notre-Dame Cathedral
The French are rebuilding historic Notre-Dame Cathedral, which lost its roof to a 2019 fire but retained its structure, bell towers, and facade.

THE BEST OF NORMANDY

Sweeping coastlines, half-timbered towns, and thatched roofs decorate the rolling green hills of Normandy. Its rugged coast harbors, enchanting fishing villages like Honfleur, and memories of a WWII battle that changed the course of history remain timeless. And on its western border, the island abbey of Mont St-Michel rises serene and majestic, oblivious to the tides of tourists.

❶ *Rising dramatically from the sea,* **Mont St-Michel** *has long attracted pilgrims and travelers.*

❷ *In picturesque* **Bayeux,** *a stone building on the riverbank sports an old water mill.*

❸ *In a series of scenes, the* **Bayeux Tapestry** *depicts* William the Conqueror's victory over England in 1066.

❹ *At* **Pointe du Hoc,** *US Army Rangers heroically scaled cliffs under Nazi fire on D-Day, June 6, 1944.*

❺ *The* **American Cemetery,** *which lies above* **Omaha Beach,** *makes a powerful pilgrimage.*

❻ *Creamy cheeses, including locally made* **Camembert,** *tempt buyers at cheese shops.*

❼ *Charming,* **half-timbered buildings** *dot townscapes throughout Normandy.*

❽ **Honfleur***'s harbor is lined with skinny, soaring homes from the 16th and 17th centuries.*

THE BEST OF THE LOIRE

The Loire Valley is crisscrossed by rivers, laced with rolling hills, and dotted with inviting towns like Amboise. Thanks to a strategic location, it's also home to more than a thousand castles and palaces. Admire Chenonceau's dreamy elegance, be dazzled by the sheer scale of Chambord, and appreciate the homey intimacy of Cheverny.

Pavés
d'Amboise

Macarons

Nougat
de Tours

Pâté
de Pâques

Pains
Spéciaux

❶ *Arcing over the Cher River, the graceful* **Château de Chenonceau** *is the toast of the Loire.*

❷ *The rooftop of massive* **Château de Chambord** *is a pincushion of spires and towers.*

❸ *Bigot's Pâtisserie and Salon de Thé offers the best chocolate and desserts in* **Amboise.**

❹ *The defense-minded* **Château de Chaumont** *features palatial luxury, fine gardens, and state-of-the-art stables.*

❺ *The many hunting dogs at* **Château de Cheverny** *prove that hunting is still the rage here.*

❻ *The gardens at the* **Château de Villandry** *are the most elaborate and decorative in the Loire.*

THE BEST OF THE DORDOGNE

Sunflowers, walnut orchards, and tobacco plants decorate the Dordogne River Valley's floor, while stone fortresses patrol the cliffs above. The joys of the Dordogne include lazy canoe rides, thriving market towns, and mouth-watering local cuisine. But it's most famous for its cache of prehistoric cave paintings.

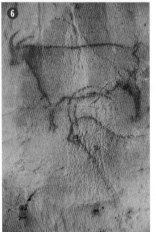

❶ *Floating down the lazy **Dordogne River** is the best way to appreciate this glorious region.*

❷ *The locally quarried stone, used here for a church in **Domme,** exudes a timeless warmth.*

❸ *In summer, radiant fields of **sunflowers** brighten large swaths of the Dordogne.*

❹ *Classic delicacies of the region are **pâtés and fois gras**—worth loosening your belt for.*

❺ *It's dinnertime on the main square of **Sarlat,** one of France's most pedestrian-friendly towns.*

❻ *Colorful paintings from **Grottes de Cougnac** are testament to the artistry of prehistoric people.*

❼ *The brooding **Château de Castlenaud** was an English stronghold during the Hundred Years' War.*

THE BEST OF PROVENCE

Provence features lively cities, adorable hill-capping villages, scenic vineyards, and some of Europe's best Roman ruins. Like Van Gogh, enjoy a starry, starry night in Arles. In Avignon, wander the brooding Palace of the Popes. Then sample the wines and splendid scenery of the Côtes du Rhône.

❶ *Fragrant samples of* **lavender** *are a common sight in Provence's shops and restaurants.*

❷ *In* **Arles,** *the Place du Forum is lined with cafés and filled with ambience.*

❸ *The* **Pont du Gard** *aqueduct is one of the world's most magnificent Roman monuments.*

❹ *Provençal* **outdoor markets** *are France's best, offering the most fun and greatest range of products.*

❺ **Boules,** *popular in Provence, is a social-yet-serious sport that's entertaining to watch or play.*

❻ *The powerful* **Palace of the Popes** *evokes medieval*

memories of when the popes ruled from **Avignon.**

❼ *Easels featuring scenes from* **Van Gogh***'s time in Arles illustrate the artist's unique vision.*

❽ *Provence is littered with brilliant* **Roman structures** *like this arena—nearly 2,000 years old—in Arles.*

THE BEST OF THE FRENCH RIVIERA

Stunning beaches, appealing towns, and intriguing museums lie along the French Riviera. Seductive Nice has world-class museums and an irresistible beachfront promenade. Lovely little Villefranche-sur-Mer charms visitors, the lively port of Antibes offers silky beaches, and Monaco extends a royal welcome. Balmy evenings on the Riviera are made for strolling.

❶ *Nice, the Riviera's capital, offers an engaging mix of urban sightseeing and seaside relaxation.*

❷ *The French Riviera's **Italianate character** is revealed in old-town centers.*

❸ ***Monte Carlo**'s elegant casino lies between a lush park and the Mediterranean.*

❹ *A refreshing **salade niçoise** makes an ideal lunch or light dinner on warm days.*

❺ *The **Picasso Museum** in **Antibes**, housed in a fine stone building, showcases a memorable collection of his work.*

❻ *Renting a lounge chair is the perfect antidote to **Nice's rocky beaches.***

THE BEST OF BURGUNDY

Burgundy welcomes wine lovers with open doors and scenic drives. The compact capital of Beaune features a colorful medieval hospital, full-bodied wines, and pedestrian-friendly strolls. Exploring the nearby villages and vineyards—by car or by bike—is a delight.

❶ The courtyard of **Beaune**'s medieval hospital dazzled its patients 500 years ago and dazzles travelers today.

❷ **Market days** in Burgundy offer a chance to sample what's fresh and to meet the producer.

❸ Traditional **wine tastings** in Burgundy come with pewter wine cups and candlelight.

❹ The **Château de la Rochepot** is beautifully situated in the hills above Beaune.

❺ Only the French can make a snail taste good. Be sure to sample **escargots.**

THE BEST OF THE REST

With extra time, add any of these destinations to your itinerary. A short trip east of Paris, **Reims** offers a historic cathedral and sparkling champagne cellars. Farther east, Germanic Alsace is home to half-timbered buildings and the charming town of **Colmar.** A few hours southeast of Paris, **Chamonix** delivers grand alpine panoramas. Europe's greatest fortress city, **Carcassonne,** guards its perch in southern France.

❶ The mountains just above **Chamonix** are laced with scenic hiking trails for all levels of ability.

❷ **Reims'** magnificent cathedral gleams at night with 800 years of history.

❸ The feudal fortress of **Carcassonne** is a romantic's dream come true.

❹ **Colmar's** lovely half-timbered, pastel buildings proudly show off its Germanic heritage.

TRAVEL SMART

Approach France like a veteran traveler, even if it's your first trip. Design your itinerary, get a handle on your budget, make advance arrangements, and follow my travel strategies on the road. For my best advice on sightseeing, accommodations, restaurants, and transportation, see the Practicalities chapter.

Designing Your Itinerary

Decide when to go. Late spring and fall generally have decent weather and lighter crowds. Summer brings festivals, good weather, and tourists. Crowds hit their peak from mid-July to mid-August, but they concentrate primarily on the Alps, the Riviera, and Dordogne. June is generally quiet outside of Paris. Winter travel is fine for Paris and Nice, but smaller cities are buttoned up tight. The weather is gray, milder in the south, and wetter in the north. Sights and tourist information offices keep shorter hours.

Choose your top destinations. My itinerary (described later) gives you an idea of how much you can reasonably see in 14 days, but you can adapt it to fit your timeframe and choice of destinations.

Suave, classy Paris is a must for anyone, especially for art and history lovers. WWII buffs storm the Normandy beaches while sun worshippers bask on the Riviera. Fans of opulent architecture explore luxurious Loire châteaux. Wine devotees meander along the wine roads of Provence and Burgundy. If you like your art prehistoric, linger in the Dordogne, but if it's ancient Roman ruins you're after, focus on Provence. Hikers love to go a'wandering in the French Alps, and photographers want to go just about everywhere.

Draft a rough itinerary. Figure out how many destinations you can comfortably fit in the time you have. Don't overdo it—few travelers wish they'd hurried more. Allow enough days per stop: Count on at least two days for major destinations (and at least three days for sights-packed Paris and spread-out Normandy).

Staying in a home base (like Paris, Arles, or Nice) and making day trips can be more time-efficient than changing locations and hotels. Minimize one-night stands, especially consecutive ones; it can be worth taking a drive (or train ride) after dinner to get settled into a town for two nights.

Connect the dots. Link your destinations into a logical route. Determine which cities in Europe you'll fly into and out of; begin your search for transatlantic flights at Kayak.com.

Decide if you'll be traveling by car, public transportation, or a combination. Regions that are ideal to explore by car—Normandy's D-Day beaches, the Loire, the Dordogne, and Provence—usually offer minivan tours, buses, or taxis for nondrivers. A car is useless in big cities (park it). If relying on public transportation, the bigger cities are easy to visit, and well-connected by trains, but buses reach some places that trains can't.

Even if you're flying into Paris, you don't need to start your trip there. You could drive or take the train to Bayeux in Normandy for a gentler small-town start, and let Paris be the finale, when you're rested and ready to tackle the big city. Or you could fly into Nice and out of Paris; many find the easygoing Mediterranean city of Nice easier than Paris as a starting point.

Allot sufficient time for transportation in your itinerary. Whether you travel by car, train, or bus, it'll take a half-day to get between most destinations.

To determine approximate transportation times, study the driving chart (on page 435) or train schedules (at www.bahn.com or www.sncf.com). If France is part of a bigger trip, consider budget flights; check Skyscanner.com for intra-European flights.

Plan your days. Fine-tune your itinerary; write out a day-by-day plan of where you'll be and what you want to see. To help make the most of your time, I've suggested day plans for destinations. But check the opening hours of sights; avoid visiting a town on the one day a week that your must-see sight is closed. Research whether any holidays or festivals will fall during your trip—these attract crowds and can close sights (for the latest, visit France's tourist website, http://us.france.fr).

Give yourself some slack. Nonstop sightseeing can turn a vacation into a blur.

Every trip—and every traveler—needs downtime for doing laundry, picnic shopping, relaxing, people-watching, and so on. Pace yourself. Assume you will return.

Ready, set... You've designed the perfect itinerary for the trip of a lifetime.

Trip Costs Per Person

Run a reality check on your dream trip. You'll have major transportation costs in addition to daily expenses.

Flight: A basic round-trip flight from the US to Paris or Nice costs about $1,000-2,000, depending on where you fly from and when (cheaper in winter).

Public Transportation: If you're following my two-week itinerary, allow $525 per person for buses and second-class trains ($600 for first class). Buying train tickets as you go can be fine for short rides, but expensive for long ones. To save money, buy a rail pass and make seat reservations (note that rail passes must be purchased outside of Europe), or lock in reserved tickets with advance-purchase discounts. In some cases, a short flight can be cheaper than taking the train. Make good use of bus companies such as Ouibus and Flixbus.

Car Rental: Allow roughly $250 per week, not including tolls, gas, parking, and insurance. Rentals and leases (an economical way to go if you need a car for at least three weeks) are cheaper if arranged from the US.

Budget Tips: Cut your daily expenses by taking advantage of the deals you'll

THE BEST OF FRANCE IN 2 WEEKS

This unforgettable trip will show you the very best France has to offer. It's geared for drivers, but can be traveled by public transportation.

DAY	PLAN	SLEEP IN
	Arrive in Paris, orient to your neighborhood	Paris
1	Sightsee Paris	Paris
2	Paris	Paris
3	Drivers rent a car in Paris and head for Normandy's Bayeux (3 hours by train), stopping in Honfleur en route (easier for drivers)	Bayeux
4	D-Day beaches (by car, taxi, or minivan tour)	Bayeux
5	Morning for Bayeux, afternoon travel to Mont St-Michel (2.5 hours with a train-and-bus combination)	Mont St-Michel
6	Travel to Loire Valley (5 hours by train), visit Amboise in afternoon	Amboise
7	Explore the Loire Valley (by car, shuttle bus, minivan tour, taxi, or bike)	Amboise
8	Travel to Sarlat-le-Canéda (6 hours by train); drivers visit Oradour-sur-Glane en route	Sarlat
9	Explore the Dordogne (by car, taxi, minivan tour, canoe, or bike)	Sarlat
10	More Dordogne, then travel to Carcassonne (6 hours by train)	Carcassonne
11	Travel to Arles (3 hours by train)	Arles
12	Explore Provence (by car, bus, train, minivan tour, or bike)	Arles
13	Travel to Nice (4 hours by train); drivers drop off car in Nice	Nice
14	Explore the Riviera (by train and bus)	Nice
	Fly out of Nice	

Customize this itinerary. If history doesn't interest you, neither would the D-Day beaches (skip Day 4). You could trim a day by overnighting in Arles on Day 10 rather than Carcassonne.

Adding Burgundy

Wine lovers can add this extension, and end up with a grand finale in Paris.

DAY	PLAN	SLEEP IN
15	Travel from Nice to Beaune in Burgundy (7 hours by train)	Beaune
16	Explore Beaune and nearby vineyards	Beaune
17	Return to Paris (2.5 hours by train); drivers drop off car in Dijon, then catch train	Paris
	Fly home	

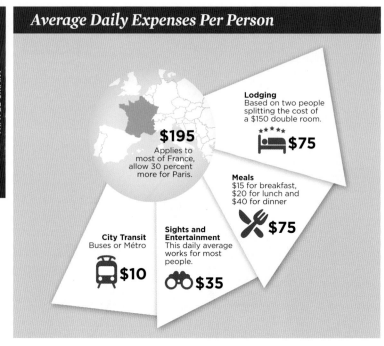

Average Daily Expenses Per Person

$195
Applies to
most of France,
allow 30 percent
more for Paris.

Lodging
Based on two people
splitting the cost of
a $150 double room.

$75

Meals
$15 for breakfast,
$20 for lunch and
$40 for dinner

$75

City Transit
Buses or Métro

$10

**Sights and
Entertainment**
This daily average
works for most
people.

$35

find throughout France and mentioned in this book.

Some businesses—especially hotels and walking-tour companies—offer discounts to my readers (look for the RS% symbol in the hotel listings in this book).

Book your rooms directly with the hotel. Some hotels offer a discount if you stay three nights or more (check online or ask). Or check Airbnb-type sites for deals.

It's easy to eat cheap in France. You can get tasty, inexpensive meals at bakeries (sandwiches, quiche, and mini-pizzas), cafés, créperies, department-store cafeterias, and takeout stands. Cultivate the art of picnicking in atmospheric settings.

City transit passes (for multiple rides or all-day usage) decrease your cost per ride in Paris: Buy a carnet of 10 Métro tickets or a Passe Navigo (which covers Paris as well as trips to outlying châteaux and the airports).

Avid sightseers buy combo-tickets or passes that cover multiple museums (like the worthwhile Paris Museum Pass). If a

town doesn't offer deals, visit the sights that interest you most, and seek out free sights and experiences (people-watching counts).

When you splurge, choose an experience you'll always remember, such as a concert in Paris' Sainte-Chapelle or an alpine lift to panoramic views. Minimize souvenir shopping—how will you get it all home? Focus instead on collecting wonderful memories.

Before You Go

You'll have a smoother trip if you tackle a few things ahead of time. For more information on these topics, see the Practicalities chapter (and www.ricksteves.com, which has helpful tips and travel talks).

Make sure your passport is valid. If it's due to expire within six months of your ticketed date of return, you need to renew it. Allow up to six weeks to renew or get a passport (www.travel.state.gov).

Arrange your transportation. Book your international flights early. Figure

🎧 Stick This Guidebook in Your Ear!

My free Rick Steves Audio Europe app makes it easy for you to download my audio tours of many of Europe's top attractions and listen to them offline during your travels. For France, these include my Historic Paris and Rue Cler walks, and tours of the Louvre and Orsay museums, the Palace of Versailles, and Père Lachaise Cemetery. Sights covered by audio tours are marked in this book with this symbol: 🎧. The app also offers insightful travel interviews from my public radio show with experts from France and around the globe. It's all free! You can download the app via Apple's App Store, Google Play, or Amazon's Appstore. For more info, see www.ricksteves.com/audioeurope.

out your main form of transportation within France: You can buy train tickets as you go, get a rail pass, rent a car, or book a cheap flight. Train travelers: You're required to make seat reservations for high-speed trains (your only option on some routes); book these as early as possible, particularly if using a rail pass, because trains can fill up and pass-holder reservations are limited.

Book rooms well in advance, especially if your trip falls during peak season or any major holidays or festivals.

Reserve or buy tickets ahead for major sights, saving you from long ticket-buying lines. Book an entry time online for the Eiffel Tower several months in advance (see Paris chapter). Some prehistoric caves in the Dordogne region take online reservations. For the greatest cave, Font-de-Gaume, there are no reservations; book a tour guide with tickets as far ahead as possible (at least six months).

Hire guides in advance. Popular guides can get booked up. If you want a specific guide, reserve by email as far ahead as possible—especially important for Paris, the D-Day beaches, Provence, and Burgundy's wine country.

Consider travel insurance. Compare the cost of the insurance to the cost of your potential loss. Check whether your existing insurance (health, homeowners, or renters) covers you and your possessions overseas.

Call your bank. Alert your bank that you'll be using your debit and credit cards in Europe. Ask about transaction fees, and get the PIN number for your credit card. You don't need to bring euros for your trip; you can withdraw euros from cash machines in Europe.

Use your smartphone smartly. Sign up for an international service plan to reduce your costs, or rely on Wi-Fi in Europe instead. Download any apps you'll want on the road, such as maps, translation, transit schedules, and Rick Steves Audio Europe (see sidebar).

Pack light. You'll walk with your luggage more than you think. Bring a single carry-on bag and a daypack. Use the packing checklist in Practicalities as a guide.

Travel Strategies on the Road

If you have a positive attitude, equip yourself with good information (this book), and expect to travel smart, you will.

Read—and reread—this book. To have an "A" trip, be an "A" student. Note opening hours of sights, closed days, crowd-beating tips, and whether reservations are required or advisable. Check the latest at www.ricksteves.com/update.

Be your own tour guide. As you travel, get up-to-date info on sights, reserve tickets and tours, reconfirm hotels and travel arrangements, and check transit connections. Upon arrival in a new town, lay the groundwork for a smooth departure; confirm the train, bus, or road you'll take when you leave.

Give local tours a spin. Your appreciation of a city or region and its history can increase dramatically if you take a walking tour in any big city or even hire a private guide. If you want to learn more about any aspect of France, you're in the right place with experts happy to teach you.

Outsmart thieves. Pickpockets abound in crowded places where tourists congregate. Treat commotions as smokescreens for theft. Keep your cash, credit cards, and passport secure in a money belt tucked under your clothes; carry only a day's spending money in your front pocket. Don't set valuable items down on counters or café tabletops where they can be quickly stolen or easily forgotten.

Minimize potential loss. Keep expensive gear to a minimum. Bring photocopies of important documents (passport and cards) to aid in replacement if the originals are lost or stolen. Back up photos frequently.

Guard your time and energy. Taking a taxi can be a good value if it saves you a long wait for a cheap bus or an exhausting walk across town. To avoid long lines, follow my crowd-beating tips in this book, such as making advance reservations or sightseeing early or late.

Be flexible. Even if you have a well-planned itinerary, expect changes, strikes, closures, sore feet, bad weather, and so on. Your Plan B could turn out to be even better. And if problems arise, keep things in perspective. You're on vacation in a beautiful country.

Attempt the language. The French appreciate your effort. If you learn even just a few phrases, you'll get more smiles and make more friends. Practice the survival phrases near the end of this book and bring a phrase book.

Connect with the culture. Interacting with locals carbonates your experience. Enjoy the friendliness of the French people. Ask questions; most locals are happy to point you in their idea of the right direction. Set up your own quest for the best croissant, sidewalk café, hill town, or the château you'd like to call home. When an opportunity pops up, make it a habit to say *"oui."*

France...here you come!

Welcome to Rick Steves' Europe

Travel is intensified living—maximum thrills per minute and one of the last great sources of legal adventure. Travel is freedom. It's recess, and we need it.

I discovered a passion for European travel as a teen and have been sharing it ever since—through my tours, public television and radio shows, and travel guidebooks. Over the years, I've taught thousands of travelers how to best enjoy Europe's blockbuster sights—and experience "Back Door" discoveries that most tourists miss.

Written with my talented co-author, Steve Smith, this book offers you a balanced mix of France's lively cities and cozy towns, from the traditional heartland to jet-setting beach resorts. It's selective—rather than listing dozens of beautiful châteaux in the Loire region, we cover only the top five. And it's in-depth: Our self-guided museum tours, city walks, and driving tours provide insight into France's vibrant history and today's living, breathing culture.

We advocate traveling simply and smartly. Take advantage of our money- and time-saving tips on sightseeing, transportation, and more. Try local, characteristic alternatives to pricey chain hotels and famous restaurants. In many ways, spending more money only builds a thicker wall between you and what you traveled so far to see.

We visit France to experience it—to become temporary locals. Thoughtful travel engages us with the world, as we learn to appreciate other cultures and new ways to measure quality of life.

Judging from the positive feedback we receive from readers, this book will help you enjoy a fun, affordable, and rewarding vacation—whether it's your first trip or your tenth.

Bon voyage! Happy travels!

Rick Steves

Paris

Paris has been a beacon of culture for centuries. As a world capital of art, fashion, food, literature, and ideas, it stands as a symbol of all the fine things human civilization can achieve, with a splash of romance and joie de vivre.

Paris offers sweeping boulevards, chatty crêpe stands, chic boutiques, and world-class art galleries. Sip decaf with deconstructionists at a sidewalk café, then step into an Impressionist painting in a tree-lined park. Pay homage to beloved Notre-Dame, recovering from a devastating fire. Master the Louvre and Orsay museums, and save some after-dark energy for this romantic city.

PARIS IN 3 DAYS

Day 1: Follow my Historic Paris Walk, featuring Ile de la Cité, Notre-Dame, the Latin Quarter, and Sainte-Chapelle. In the afternoon, tour the Louvre. Late in the day, enjoy the Place du Trocadéro scene and a twilight ride up the Eiffel Tower.

Day 2: Stroll the Champs-Elysées from the Arc de Triomphe (ascend for the view) to the Tuileries Garden, then tour the Orsay Museum.

Day 3: Head to Versailles. Catch RER/Train-C by 8:00 to arrive early. Tour the château's interior, then either visit the vast gardens, or return to Paris for more sightseeing.

On any evening: Take a nighttime tour by cruise boat, taxi/Uber, or bus. Or enjoy dinner on Ile St. Louis, then a floodlit walk by Notre-Dame. For a free skyline view, head to the rooftop of the neighboring Galeries Lafayette or Printemps department stores.

With extra time: Choose from Montmartre (Sacré-Cœur Basilica), the Army Museum and Napoleon's Tomb, the Rodin or Orangerie museums, the Marais neighborhood (Picasso Museum and Pompidou Center), or the Opéra Garnier (near the department stores).

ORIENTATION

Central Paris is circled by a ring road and split in half by the Seine River, which runs east-west. As you look downstream, the Right Bank (Rive Droite) is on your right, and the Left Bank (Rive Gauche) on your left. The bull's-eye on your map is Notre-Dame, on an island in the middle of the Seine.

Twenty arrondissements (administrative districts) spiral out from the center, like an escargot shell. If your hotel's zip code is 75007, you know (from the last two digits) that it's in the 7th arrondissement. The city is peppered with Métro stops, and most Parisians locate addresses by the closest stop. So in Parisian jargon, the Eiffel Tower is on la Rive Gauche (the Left Bank) in the 7ème (7th arrondissement), zip code 75007, Mo: Trocadéro (the nearest Métro stop).

The major sights cluster in convenient zones. Grouping your sightseeing, walks, dining, and shopping thoughtfully can save you lots of time and money.

Paris Neighborhoods

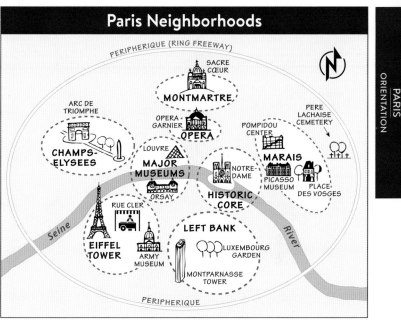

Historic Core: This area centers on the Ile de la Cité ("Island of the City"), located in the middle of the Seine. On the Ile de la Cité, you'll find Paris' oldest sights, from Roman ruins to the medieval Notre-Dame and Sainte-Chapelle churches.

Major Museums Neighborhood: Located just west of the historic core, this is where you'll find the Louvre, Orsay, Orangerie, and Tuileries Garden.

Champs-Elysées: The greatest of the many grand, 19th-century boulevards on the Right Bank, the Champs-Elysées runs northwest from Place de la Concorde to the Arc de Triomphe.

Eiffel Tower Neighborhood: Dominated by the Eiffel Tower, this area also boasts the colorful Rue Cler, the Army Museum and Napoleon's Tomb, and the Rodin Museum.

Opéra Neighborhood: Surrounding the Opéra Garnier, this classy area on the Right Bank is home to a series of grand boulevards, monuments, and high-end shopping.

Left Bank: Anchored by the large Luxembourg Garden, the Left Bank is the traditional neighborhood of Paris' intellectual, artistic, and café life.

Marais: Stretching eastward to Bastille along Rue de Rivoli/Rue St. Antoine, this neighborhood has lots of recommended restaurants and hotels, shops, the delightful Place des Vosges, and artistic sights such as the Pompidou Center and Picasso Museum.

Montmartre: This hill, topped by the bulbous white domes of Sacré-Cœur, hovers on the northern fringes of your Paris map.

Tourist Information

Paris' "TIs" can provide useful information but may have long lines. TIs sell Museum Passes and individual tickets to sights, but charge a small fee and may have longer lines than the museums.

The main TI is located at the **Hôtel de Ville** (daily 9:00-19:00, Nov-April from 10:00, 29 Rue de Rivoli—located on the north side of the Hôtel de Ville City Hall). You may find smaller TIs at **Gare du Nord**

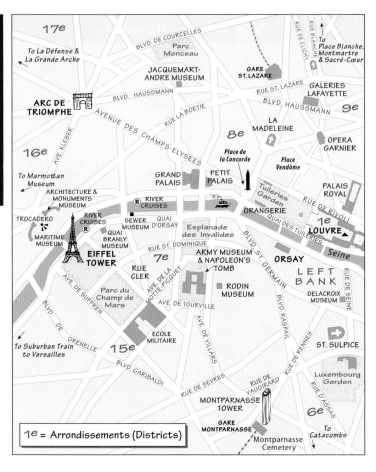

1e = Arrondissements (Districts)

(daily 8:00-18:00), **Gare de l'Est** (Mon-Sat 8:00-19:00, closed Sun), and at the **Puces St. Ouen** flea market (Sat-Mon 10:00-13:00 & 14:00-17:00, closed Tue-Fri, 120 Rue des Rosiers, tel. 01 58 61 22 90). In summer, TI kiosks may pop up in the squares in front of Notre-Dame and Hôtel de Ville. Both **airports** have handy TIs with long hours.

Event Listings: The weekly *L'Officiel des Spectacles* (available at any newsstand) is in French only but has easy-to-decipher listings of the most up-to-date museum hours, art exhibits, concerts, festivals, plays, movies, and nightclubs. The *Paris Voice,* with snappy English-language reviews of concerts, plays, and current

events, is available online-only at www. parisvoice.com.

Sightseeing Passes: In Paris there are two classes of sightseers—those with a **Paris Museum Pass,** and those who stand in line. The pass admits you to many of Paris' most important sights, and it allows you to skip most ticket-buying lines (but not security lines)—which can save hours of waiting, especially in summer. Another benefit is that you can pop into lesser sights that otherwise might not be worth the expense. For more info, visit www. parismuseumpass.com.

Buy the pass in person upon arrival in Paris (it's not worth the cost or hassle to

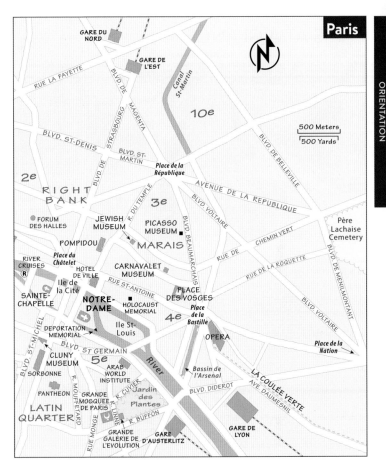

buy the pass online). The pass is sold at participating museums, monuments, TIs (small fee added)—including TIs at Paris airports—and some souvenir stores near major sights. Don't buy the pass at a major museum (such as the Louvre), where the supply can be spotty and lines long.

Rick's Tip: Don't buy the Paris Museum Pass for children and teens, *as most museums are free or discounted for those under age 18 (teenagers may need to show ID as proof of age). If parents have a Museum Pass, kids can usually skip the ticket lines as well. But a few places (Arc de Triomphe, Army Museum) require everyone—even passholders—to stand in line to collect free tickets for their children.*

Avoid lines like these by making an advance reservation for the Eiffel Tower.

PARIS AT A GLANCE

▲▲▲Notre-Dame Cathedral Paris' beloved church, badly damaged in a fire in 2019. Rebuilding the roof is a massive undertaking that will take years, during which time the church will be closed, though its exterior—from its impressive facade to its graceful flying buttresses—may remain viewable.

▲▲▲Sainte-Chapelle Gothic cathedral with peerless stained glass. **Hours:** Daily 9:00-19:00, Oct-March until 17:00. See page 49.

▲▲▲Louvre Europe's oldest and greatest museum, starring *Mona Lisa* and *Venus de Milo.* **Hours:** Wed-Mon 9:00-18:00, Wed and Fri until 21:45, closed Tue. See page 54.

▲▲▲Orsay Museum Nineteenth-century art, including Europe's greatest Impressionist collection. **Hours:** Tue-Sun 9:30-18:00, Thu until 21:45, closed Mon. See page 61.

▲▲▲Eiffel Tower Paris' soaring exclamation point. **Hours:** Daily mid-June-Aug 9:00-24:45, Sept-mid-June 9:30-23:45. See page 68.

▲▲▲Champs-Elysées Paris' grand boulevard. See page 75.

▲▲▲Versailles The ultimate royal palace (Château), with a Hall of Mirrors, vast gardens, and a grand canal, plus a queen's playground (Trianon Palaces and Domaine de Marie-Antoinette). **Hours:** Château April-Oct Tue-Sun 9:00-18:30, Nov-March until 17:30; Trianon/Domaine April-Oct Tue-Sun 12:00-18:30, Nov-March until 17:30; gardens generally April-Oct daily 8:00-20:30, Nov-March until 18:00; entire complex closed Mon year-round except the Gardens. See page 116.

▲▲Orangerie Museum Monet's water lilies and modernist classics in a lovely setting. **Hours:** Wed-Mon 9:00-18:00, closed Tue. See page 66.

▲▲Army Museum and Napoleon's Tomb The emperor's imposing tomb, flanked by museums of France's wars. **Hours:** Daily 10:00-18:00, Nov-March until 17:00; tomb also open July-Aug until 19:00, tomb and

Louis XIV-Napoleon I wing open April-Sept Tue until 21:00; Charles de Gaulle exhibit closed Mon year-round. See page 71.

▲▲**Rodin Museum** Works by the greatest sculptor since Michelangelo, with many statues in a peaceful garden. **Hours:** Tue-Sun 10:00-17:45, closed Mon. See page 72.

▲▲**Marmottan Museum** Art museum focusing on Monet. **Hours:** Tue-Sun 10:00-18:00, Thu until 21:00, closed Mon. See page 73.

▲▲**Cluny Museum** Medieval art with unicorn tapestries. **Hours:** Wed-Mon 9:15-17:45, closed Tue. See page 73.

▲▲**Arc de Triomphe** Triumphal arch marking the start of Champs-Elysées. **Hours:** Exterior always viewable; interior daily 10:00-23:00, Oct-March until 22:30. See page 77.

▲▲**Opéra Garnier** Grand belle époque theater with a modern ceiling by Chagall. **Hours:** Generally daily 10:00-16:30, mid-July-Aug until 18:00. See page 78.

▲▲**Picasso Museum** World's largest collection of Picasso's works. **Hours:** Tue-Fri 10:30-18:00, Sat-Sun from 9:30, closed Mon. See page 80.

▲▲**Pompidou Center** Modern art in colorful building with city views. **Hours:** Permanent collection open Wed-Mon 11:00-21:00, closed Tue. See page 81.

▲▲**Père Lachaise Cemetery** Final home of Paris' illustrious dead. **Hours:** Mon-Fri 8:00-18:00, Sat from 8:30, Sun from 9:00, until 17:30 in winter. See page 85.

▲▲**Sacré-Cœur Basilica and Montmartre** White basilica atop Montmartre with spectacular views. **Hours:** Daily 6:00-22:30; dome climb daily 9:30-19:00, Oct-April until 17:00. See page 86.

Helpful Hints

Theft Alert: Paris is safe in terms of violent crime but is filled with thieves and scammers who target tourists. Don't be paranoid; just be smart. Wherever there are crowds (especially of tourists) there are thieves at work. They thrive near famous monuments and on Métro and train lines that serve airports and high-profile tourist sights. It's smart to wear a money belt, put your wallet in your front pocket, loop your day bag over your shoulders, and keep a tight hold on your purse or shopping bag.

Muggings are rare, but they do occur. If you're out late, avoid dark riverfront embankments and any place with dim lighting and few pedestrians.

Tourist Scams: Be aware of the latest tricks, such as the "found ring" scam (a con artist pretends to find a "pure gold" ring on the ground and offers to sell it to you) or the "friendship bracelet" scam (a vendor asks you to help with a demo, makes a bracelet on your arm that seems like it can't easily be removed, and then asks you to pay for it). Don't be intimidated. They are removed with the pull of a string.

Distractions by a stranger—sometimes a "salesman," an "activist," or even someone posing as a deaf person—can all be tricks that function as a smokescreen for theft. As you try to wriggle away from the pushy stranger, an accomplice picks your pocket. For reports from my readers on the latest scams, go to https://community.ricksteves.com/travel-forum/tourist-scams.

Rick's Tip: *For many sights,* **you can buy advance tickets at the sight's website or through a third party** *(for a fee). Some require you to choose a specific time, including the Eiffel Tower, Louvre, and Catacombs. You can also buy advance tickets that allow you to skip ticket-buying lines for the Orsay and Sainte-Chapelle.*

Closed Days: The Orsay, Rodin, Marmottan, and Picasso museums are closed on Mondays, as are the Catacombs and the palace of Versailles (its gardens are open). Many other sights are closed on Tuesdays, including the Louvre, Orangerie, Cluny, and Pompidou museums.

Useful Apps: Gogo Paris reviews trendy places to eat, drink, relax, and sleep in Paris (www.gogocityguides.com/paris). The **RATP** app can help you plan Métro trips (see "Métro Resources" later in this chapter). ☏ For my free audio tours of some of Paris' best neighborhoods and sights (Historic Paris and Rue Cler, Louvre and Orsay museums, Versailles Palace, and Père Lachaise Cemetery), get the free **Rick Steves Audio Europe** app.

Tobacco Stands *(Tabacs):* These little kiosks—usually just a counter inside a café—sell public-transit tickets, postage stamps (though not all sell international postage), and...oh yeah, cigarettes. To find a kiosk, just look for a *Tabac* sign and the red cylinder-shaped symbol above certain cafés.

Rick's Tip: Parisian drivers are notorious for ignoring pedestrians—*pay attention and don't assume you have the right of way, even in a crosswalk.*

Laundry: Two of my recommended sleeping neighborhoods include handy launderettes. In the Rue Cler, you'll find them on Rue Augereau, on Rue Amélie, and at the southeast corner of Rue Valadon and Rue de Grenelle. Launderettes are also scattered throughout the Marais, including on Impasse Guéménée and on Rue du Petit Musc.

Explore Paris by bike.

Tours

Some tour companies offer a discount when you show this book (indicated in these listings with the abbreviation "RS%").

WALKING TOURS

Paris Walks offers a variety of thoughtful and entertaining two-hour walks, led by British and American guides (€15-20, generally 2/day—morning and afternoon, private tours available, check current offerings online, tel. 01 48 09 21 40, www.paris-walks.com, paris@paris-walks.com).

Context Travel offers "intellectual by design" walking tours geared for serious learners led by well-versed docents (book in advance—groups are limited to six participants; about €100/person, admission to sights extra, generally 3 hours, tel. 09 75 18 04 15, US tel. 800-691-6036, www.contexttravel.com, info@contexttravel.com).

Fat Tire Tours offers high-on-fun and casual walking tours. Their two-hour Classic Paris Walking Tour covers most major sights (usually Mon, Wed, and Fri at 10:00 or 15:00). Their "Skip the Line" tours get you into major sights, including Sainte-Chapelle, the Catacombs, Eiffel Tower, and Versailles. Reservations are required and can be made online, by phone, or in person at their office near the Eiffel Tower (€20-40/person for walking tours, €40-90/person for "Skip the Line" tours; RS%—€2 discount per person, 2-discount maximum; office generally open daily 9:00-18:00 or 19:00, shorter hours in winter, 24 Rue Edgar Faure, Mo: Dupleix, tel. 01 82 88 80 96, www.fattiretours.com/paris).

LOCAL GUIDES

For many, Paris merits hiring a Parisian as a guide (€230-280 half-day, €400-500 day). Try **Thierry Gauduchon** (mobile 06 19 07 30 77, tgauduchon@gmail.com); **Elisabeth Van Hest** (tel. 01 43 41 47 31, mobile 06 77 80 19 89, elisa.guide@gmail.com); **Sylvie Moreau** (tel. 01 74 30 27 46, mobile 06 87 02 80 67, sylvie.ja.moreau@gmail.com); or **Arnaud Servignat** (also does minivan tours of the countryside around Paris, mobile 06 68 80 29 05, www.french-guide.com, arnotour@me.com).

HOP-ON, HOP-OFF BUS TOURS

Several companies offer double-decker bus services connecting Paris' main sights, giving you an easy once-over of the city with a recorded commentary. Buses run from about 9:30-19:00 in high season. **L'OpenTour** has the most options with reasonably frequent service on four routes covering central Paris (1 day-€34, 2 days-€38, 3 days-€42, kids 4-11 pay €17 for 1, 2, or 3 days, tel. 01 42 66 56 56, www.paris.opentour.com). **Big Bus Paris** runs a fleet of buses around Paris on two routes (1 day-€34, 2 days-€38, kids 4-12-€17, €22 night tour, cheaper online, tel. 01 53 95 39 53, www.bigbustours.com), and **City Sightseeing Tours'** red buses run along two routes (11 stops each) and your ticket is valid for 24 or 48 hours from the time you buy it (1 day-€42, 2 days-€47, tickets valid for both routes, 3 buses/hour, 9 Avenue de l'Opèra, https://city-sightseeing.com).

BIKE TOURS

Bike About Tours offers easygoing tours of the eastern half of the city (Marais, Latin Quarter, and Ile de la Cité; RS%—10 percent discount, www.bikeabouttours.com).
Fat Tire Tours offers an extensive program of bike and walking tours (see earlier).

HISTORIC PARIS WALK

Paris has been the cultural capital of Europe for centuries—as a Roman city, a bustling medieval metropolis, the birthplace of the Revolution, the bohemian haunt of the 1920s café scene, and now the glittering City of Light.

We'll start where the city did—on the Ile de la Cité—and make a foray onto the Left Bank. Along the way, we'll step into one of the city's greatest sights, Sainte-Chapelle.

The first two stops of the walk may be affected by reconstruction work on the Notre-Dame Cathedral, damaged in a 2019 fire. Be flexible, know there's a way around, and follow the route as well as you can.

Getting There: The closest Métro stops are Cité, Hôtel de Ville, and St. Michel, each a short walk away.

Length of This Walk: Allow three hours to do justice to this three-mile self-guided walk, beginning at Notre-Dame Cathedral and ending at Pont Neuf; follow the dotted line on the "Historic Paris Walk" map.

Tours: 🎧 Download a free Rick Steves audio version of this walk (see page 29.)

➲ Self-Guided Walk

• *Begin in front of Notre-Dame Cathedral, the physical and historic bull's-eye of your Paris map.*

❶ *Notre-Dame Cathedral*

This beloved, famous church (worth ▲▲▲) is dedicated to "Our Lady" (Notre Dame), Mary. In April 2019, the church caught on fire—the roof fell in, though the structure remained intact. The church is closed to visitors for years during reconstruction and may have scaffolding and barricades when you visit.

Notre-Dame has long been the spiritual heart of Paris. Imagine the faith of the people who built this cathedral. They broke ground in 1163 with the hope

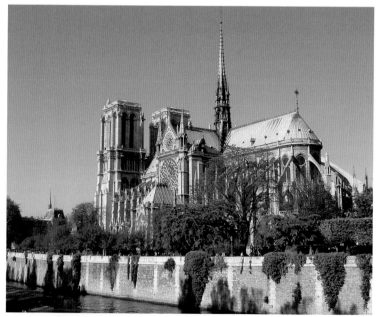

Notre-Dame, before the 2019 fire destroyed the roof and spire.

Notre-Dame's modern altarpiece survived the fire.

Notre-Dame's gargoyles have seen it all.

that someday their great-great-great-great-great-great grandchildren might attend the dedication Mass, which finally took place two centuries later, in 1345. Look up the 200-foot-tall bell towers. Masons supervised, but the people did much of the grunt work themselves for free—hauling the huge stones from distant quarries, and treading like rats on a wheel designed to lift the stones up, one by one. This kind of backbreaking manual labor created the real hunchbacks of Notre-Dame.

Circling the exterior of the church, notice many of the elements of Gothic: pointed arches, the lacy stone tracery of the windows, the gargoyles, and most distinctive of all, the flying buttresses at the back. These 50-foot stone "beams" sticking out of the church help support the structure, freeing up the walls to hold large windows. This is Gothic. Taller and filled with light, Notre-Dame was a major improvement over the earlier Romanesque style. Gothic architects were masters at playing architectural forces against each other to build loftier and brighter churches. The Gothic style was born here in Paris.

Along with a new roof, reconstruction will include a new spire—likely adorned by the former spire's 19th-century sculptures, which had been stored away and were spared by the fire.

Fortunately, Notre-Dame's famous gargoyles escaped the fate of the roof. Picture Quasimodo (the fictional hunchback) limping along the tower balconies among the gargoyles. These grotesque beasts represent souls caught between heaven and earth. Some also function as rainspouts (from the same French root word as "gargle") when there are no evil spirits to battle.

• *Behind Notre-Dame, cross the street and enter through the iron gate into the park at the tip of the island. (If this gate is closed, you can still enter the park 30 yards to the left.) Look for the stairs and head down to reach the...*

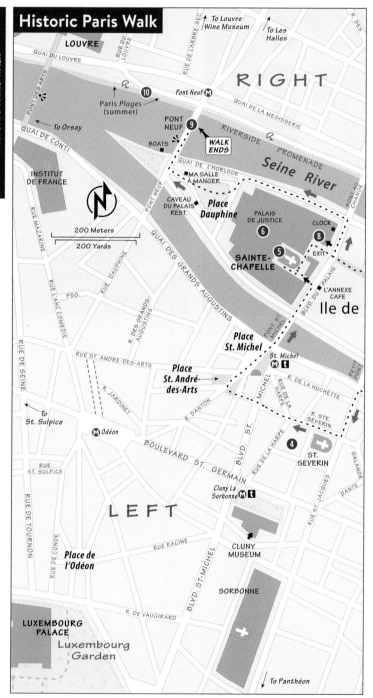

Historic Paris Walk

LOUVRE

QUAI DU LOUVRE

RUE DU LOUVRE

R. DE L'ARBRE-SEC

To Louvre
Wine Museum

To Les
Halles

R. DES

RIGHT

PONT DES ARTS

Paris Plages
(summer)

10

Pont Neuf **M**

QUAI DE LA MÉGISSERIE

To Orsay

QUAI DE CONTI

PONT
NEUF

9

BOATS

WALK
ENDS

RIVERSIDE

PROMENADE

Seine River

QUAI DE L'HORLOGE

PONT AU CHANGE

INSTITUT
DE FRANCE

RUE MAZARINE

200 Meters

200 Yards

MA SALLE
À MANGER

PONT NEUF

CAVEAU
DU PALAIS
REST.

*Place
Dauphine*

PALAIS
DE JUSTICE

6

CLOCK

8

EXIT

QUAI DES GRANDS AUGUSTINS

RUE DAUPHINE

SAINTE-
CHAPELLE

5

BLVD. DU PALAIS

RUE DE SEINE

RUE DE L'ANC. COMÉDIE

PSG

R. DES GRANDS-
AUGUSTINS

RUE ST. ANDRE-DES-ARTS

L'ANNEXE
CAFE

Ile de

*Place
St. Michel*

PONT ST. MICHEL

*Place
St. André-
des-Arts*

R. JARDINET

R. DANTON

St. Michel
M **t**

R. DE LA HUCHETTE

PETIT PONT

To
St. Sulpice

M *Odéon*

BLVD. ST. MICHEL

RUE DE LA HARPE

R. STE.
SEVERIN

RUE ST. JACQUES

GALANDE

BOULEVARD   ST.   GERMAIN

4

ST.
SEVERIN

RUE
ST. SULPICE

RUE DE TOURNON

RUE DE CONDE

*Cluny La
Sorbonne* **M** **t**

LEFT

RUE RACINE

CLUNY
MUSEUM

DANTE

*Place de
l'Odéon*

SORBONNE

R. DE VAUGIRARD

BLVD. ST-MICHEL

LUXEMBOURG
PALACE

Luxembourg
Garden

To Panthéon

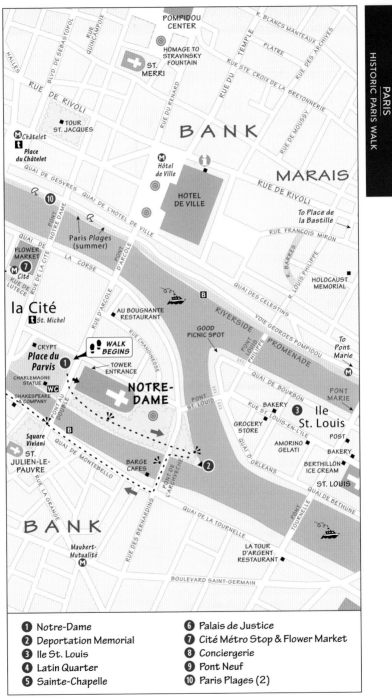

POMPIDOU CENTER

R BLANCS MANTEAUX

R. QUINCAMPOIX

RUE DU TEMPLE

PLATRE

RUE DES ARCHIVES

HALLES

BLVD DE SEBASTOPOL

HOMAGE TO STRAVINSKY FOUNTAIN

ST. MERRI

RUE STE. CROIX DE LA BRETONNERIE

RUE DE RIVOLI

RUE DU RENARD

RUE DE MOUSSY

B A N K

TOUR ST. JACQUES

M Châtelet
Place du Châtelet

Hôtel de Ville

MARAIS

QUAI DE GESVRES

QUAI DE L'HOTEL DE VILLE

HOTEL DE VILLE

RUE DE RIVOLI

To Place de la Bastille

PONT NOTRE DAME

RUE FRANCOIS MIRON

QUAI DE

FLOWER MARKET

Paris Plages (summer)

LA CORSE

PONT D'ARCOLE

R. BARRES

R. DU LONG PHILIPPE

HOLOCAUST MEMORIAL

M Cité

RUE DE LUTECE

RUE DE LA CITE

la Cité

St. Michel

QUAI DES CELESTINS

RIVERSIDE

VOIE GEORGES POMPIDOU

AU BOUGNANTE RESTAURANT

RUE D'ARCOLE

RUE CHANOINESSE

GOOD PICNIC SPOT

PROMENADE

To Pont Marie

CRYPT

Place du Parvis

WALK BEGINS

TOWER ENTRANCE

NOTRE-DAME

PONT LOUIS PHILIPPE

QUAI DE BOURBON

PONT MARIE

M

CHARLEMAGNE STATUE

WC

SHAKESPEARE COMPANY

PONT ST. LOUIS

RUE ST. LOUIS-EN-L'ILE

BAKERY

Ile St. Louis

POST

PONT AU DOUBLE

Square Viviani

B

GROCERY STORE

AMORINO GELATI

BAKERY

ST. JULIEN-LE-PAUVRE

QUAI DE MONTEBELLO

BARGE CAFES

PONT DE L'ARCHEVECHE

QUAI D'ORLEANS

BERTHILLON ICE CREAM

ST. LOUIS

QUAI DE BETHUNE

RUE DE LA GRANGE

QUAI DES BERNARDINS

QUAI DE LA TOURNELLE

PONT DE LA TOURNELLE

B A N K

Maubert-Mutualité
M

LA TOUR D'ARGENT RESTAURANT

BOULEVARD SAINT-GERMAIN

1 Notre-Dame
2 Deportation Memorial
3 Ile St. Louis
4 Latin Quarter
5 Sainte-Chapelle

6 Palais de Justice
7 Cité Métro Stop & Flower Market
8 Conciergerie
9 Pont Neuf
10 Paris Plages (2)

Affording Paris' Sights

Paris is an expensive city for tourists, with lots of pricey sights, but—fortunately—lots of freebies, too. Smart, budget-minded travelers begin by buying and getting the most out of a Paris Museum Pass, then considering these frugal sightseeing options.

Free (or Almost Free) Museums: Many of Paris' famous museums offer free entry on the first Sunday of the month, including the Orsay, Cluny, and Pompidou Center. These sights are free on the first Sunday of off-season months: the Louvre, Rodin Museum, and Arc de Triomphe (all Oct-March), and Versailles (Nov-March). Expect big crowds on free days. You can usually visit the Orsay Museum for free right when the ticket booth stops selling tickets. For just €4, the Rodin Museum garden lets you enjoy many of Rodin's finest works in a lovely outdoor setting.

Other Freebies: Many sights don't charge an entry fee, including the Notre-Dame Cathedral, Père Lachaise Cemetery, Deportation Memorial, Sacré-Cœur Basilica, and St. Sulpice Church (with organ recital). Paris' many glorious, entertaining parks are free.

Reduced Prices: Several sights offer a discount if you enter later in the day, including the Orsay, the Orangerie, and the Army Museum and Napoleon's Tomb (after 17:00 or 16:00 off-season). The Eiffel Tower costs less if you restrict your visit to the two lower levels—and even less if you use the stairs.

Good-Value Tours: At €15-20, Paris Walks' tours are a good value. The Seine River cruises (allow €15), best after dark, are also worthwhile.

Pricey...But Worth It? Certain big-ticket items—primarily the top of the Eiffel Tower, the Louvre, and Versailles—are expensive and crowded, but offer once-in-a-lifetime experiences. All together they amount to less than the cost of a ticket to Disneyland—only these are real.

❷ Deportation Memorial (Mémorial de la Déportation)

This ▲ memorial to the 200,000 French victims of the Nazi concentration camps (1940-1945) draws you into their experience. France was quickly overrun by Nazi Germany, and Paris spent the war years under Nazi occupation. Jews and dissidents were rounded up and deported—many never returned.

Cost and Hours: Free, Tue-Sun 10:00-19:00, Oct-March until 17:00, closed Mon year-round, may randomly close at other times, free 40-minute audioguide may be available; at the east tip of Ile de la Cité, behind Notre-Dame and near Ile St. Louis (Mo: Cité); tel. 01 46 33 87 56.

Visiting the Memorial: As you descend the steps, the city around you disappears. Surrounded by walls, you have become a prisoner. Your only freedom is your view of the sky and the tiny glimpse of the river below. Enter the dark, single-file chamber up ahead. Inside, the circular plaque in the floor reads, "They went to the end of the earth and did not return."

The hallway stretching in front of you is lined with 200,000 lighted crystals, one for each French citizen who died. Flickering at the far end is the eternal flame of hope. The tomb of the unknown deportee lies at your feet. Above, the inscription reads, "Dedicated to the living memory of the 200,000 French deportees shrouded by the night and the fog, exterminated in the Nazi concentration camps." The side

Deportation Memorial   *Shakespeare and Company bookstore*

rooms are filled with triangles—reminiscent of the identification patches inmates were forced to wear—each bearing the name of a concentration camp. Above the exit as you leave is the message you'll find at many other Holocaust sites: "Forgive, but never forget."

• Back on street level, look across the river (north) to the island called...

❸ Ile St. Louis

If Ile de la Cité is a tugboat laden with the history of Paris, it's towing this classy little residential dinghy, laden only with high-rent apartments, boutiques, characteristic restaurants, and famous ice cream shops. Ile St. Louis wasn't developed until much later than Ile de la Cité (17th century). What was a swampy mess is now harmonious Parisian architecture and one of Paris' most exclusive neighborhoods.

Ile St. Louis is a lovely place for an evening stroll. If you won't have time to come back later, consider taking a brief detour across the pedestrian bridge, Pont St. Louis, to explore this little island.

• From the Deportation Memorial, cross the bridge to the Left Bank. Turn right and walk along the river until you reach the Pont au Double (the bridge leading to the facade of Notre-Dame). Carefully cross the street

and continue on Quai de Montebello past a park until you see a cobbled lane on the left that leads to **Shakespeare and Company,** an atmospheric reincarnation of the original 1920s bookshop and a good spot to page through books (37 Rue de la Bûcherie). Before returning to the island, walk a block behind Shakespeare and Company, and take a spin through...

❹ The Latin Quarter

This area (worth ▲) has a touristy fame relating to its intriguing, artsy, bohemian character. This was perhaps Europe's leading university district in the Middle Ages, when Latin was the language of higher education. The neighborhood's main boulevards (St. Michel and St. Germain) are lined with cafés—once the haunts of great poets and philosophers, now the hangouts of tired tourists. Exploring a few blocks up or downriver from here gives you a better chance of feeling the pulse of what survives of Paris' classic Left Bank. For colorful wandering and café-sitting, afternoons and evenings are best.

Although it may look more like the Greek Quarter today (cheap gyros abound), this area is the Latin Quarter, named for the language you'd have heard on these streets if you walked them in

The Latin Quarter

the Middle Ages. The University of Paris (founded 1215), one of the leading educational institutions of medieval Europe, was (and still is) nearby. Walking along Rue St. Séverin, you can still see the shadow of the medieval sewer system. The street slopes into a central channel of bricks. In the days before plumbing and toilets, when people went to the river or neighborhood wells for their water, flushing meant throwing it out the window. At certain times of day, maids on the fourth floor would holler, *"Garde de l'eau!"* ("Watch out for the water!") and heave it into the streets, where it would eventually wash down into the Seine.

Consider a visit to the **Cluny Museum** for its medieval art and unicorn tapestries (see page 73). The **Sorbonne**—the University of Paris' humanities department—is also nearby; visitors can ogle at the famous dome, but aren't allowed to enter the building (two blocks south of the river on Boulevard St. Michel).

Don't miss **Place St. Michel.** This square is the traditional core of the Left Bank's artsy, liberal, hippie, bohemian

district of poets, philosophers, winos, and *baba cools* (neo-hippies). In less commercial times, Place St. Michel was a gathering point for the city's malcontents and misfits. In 1830, 1848, and again in 1871, the citizens took the streets from the government troops, set up barricades *Les Miz*-style, and fought against royalist oppression. During World War II, the locals rose up against their Nazi oppressors (read the plaques under the dragons at the foot of the St. Michel fountain). Even today, whenever there's a student demonstration, it starts here.

• *From Place St. Michel, look across the river and find the prickly steeple of the Sainte-Chapelle church. Head toward it. Cross the river on Pont St. Michel and continue north along the Boulevard du Palais. On your left, you'll see the doorway to Sainte-Chapelle (usually with a line of people).*

❺ *Sainte-Chapelle*

This triumph of Gothic church architecture, worth ▲▲▲, is a cathedral of glass like no other. It was speedily built between 1242 and 1248 for King Louis IX—the only

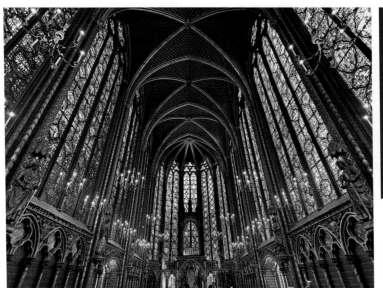

Sainte-Chapelle is a cathedral of stained glass like no other.

French king who is now a saint—to house the supposed Crown of Thorns. Its architectural harmony is due to the fact that it was completed under the direction of one architect and in only six years—unheard of in Gothic times. By contrast, Notre-Dame took more than 200 years.

Cost and Hours: €10, €15 combo-ticket with Conciergerie, free for those under age 18, covered by Museum Pass, advance tickets sold on church website and at FNAC department stores; open daily 9:00-19:00, Oct-March until 17:00; audioguide-€3, 4 Boulevard du Palais, Mo: Cité, tel. 01 53 40 60 80, www.sainte-chapelle.fr. For info on upcoming church concerts, see page 91.

Avoiding Crowds: Security lines are shortest first thing in the morning (be in line by 9:00, or arrive at 10:00 after the early rush subsides) and on weekends (when the courts are closed). They're longest on Tuesday and daily 13:00-14:00 (when staff takes lunch). To avoid this line, it may be worth rearranging the order of the walk: See Sainte-Chapelle first, then walk over to Notre-Dame (5 minutes away). Or see Sainte-Chapelle at the end of the day—being the last person in the chapel is an experience you'll never forget.

Visiting the Church: Though the inside is beautiful, the exterior is basically functional. The muscular buttresses hold up the stone roof, so the walls are essentially there to display stained glass. The lacy spire is Neo-Gothic—added in the 19th century. Inside, the layout clearly shows an *ancien régime* approach to worship. The low-ceilinged basement was for staff and other common folk—worshipping under a sky filled with painted fleurs-de-lis, a symbol of the king. Royal Christians worshipped upstairs. The paint job, a 19th-century restoration, helps you imagine how grand this small, painted, jeweled chapel was. (Imagine Notre-Dame painted like this.) Each capital is playfully carved with a different plant's leaves.

Climb the spiral staircase to the Chapelle Haute. Fill the place with choral music, crank up the sunshine, face the top of the altar, really believe that the Crown

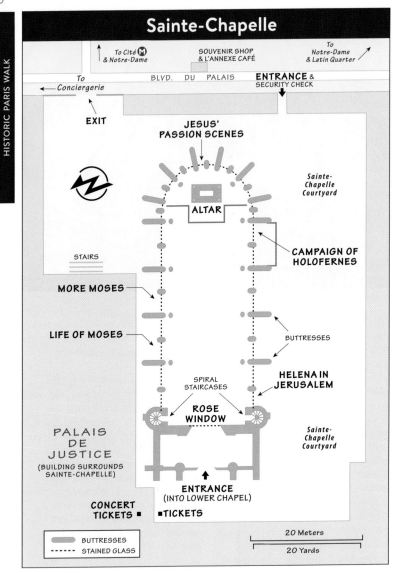

Sainte-Chapelle

To Cité M
& Notre-Dame

SOUVENIR SHOP
& L'ANNEXE CAFÉ

To
Notre-Dame
& Latin Quarter

To
← Conciergerie

BLVD. DU PALAIS

ENTRANCE &
SECURITY CHECK

EXIT

JESUS'
PASSION SCENES

ALTAR

Sainte-
Chapelle
Courtyard

CAMPAIGN OF
HOLOFERNES

STAIRS

MORE MOSES

LIFE OF MOSES

BUTTRESSES

HELENA IN
JERUSALEM

SPIRAL
STAIRCASES

ROSE
WINDOW

Sainte-
Chapelle
Courtyard

PALAIS
DE
JUSTICE
(BUILDING SURROUNDS
SAINTE-CHAPELLE)

ENTRANCE
(INTO LOWER CHAPEL)

CONCERT
TICKETS ■

■TICKETS

20 Meters

20 Yards

BUTTRESSES
STAINED GLASS

of Thorns is there, and this becomes one awesome space.

Fiat lux. "Let there be light." From the first page of the Bible, it's clear: Light is divine. Light shines through stained glass like God's grace shining down to earth. Gothic architects used their new technology to turn dark stone buildings into lanterns of light. The glory of Gothic shines brighter here than in any other church.

The altar was raised up high to better display the Crown of Thorns, which cost King Louis more than three times as much as this church. Today, the relic is kept by the Notre-Dame Treasury (though it's occasionally brought out for display).

• *Exit Sainte-Chapelle. Back outside, as you walk around the church exterior, look down to see the foundation and take note of how much Paris has risen in the 750 years since Sainte-Chapelle was built. As you head toward the exit of the complex, you'll pass by the...*

❻ Palais de Justice

Sainte-Chapelle sits within a huge complex of buildings that has housed the local government since ancient Roman times. It was the site of the original Gothic palace of the early kings of France. The only surviving medieval parts are Sainte-Chapelle and the Conciergerie prison.

Most of the site is now covered by the giant Palais de Justice, built in 1776, home of the French Supreme Court. The motto *Liberté, Egalité, Fraternité* over the doors is a reminder that this was also the headquarters of the Revolutionary government. Here they doled out justice, condemning many to imprisonment in the Conciergerie downstairs—or to the guillotine.

• *Now pass through the big iron gate to the noisy Boulevard du Palais. Cross the street to the wide, pedestrian-only Rue de Lutèce and walk about halfway down.*

❼ Cité "Metropolitain" Métro Stop

Of the 141 original early-20th-century subway entrances, this is one of only a few survivors—now preserved as a national art treasure. (New York's Museum of Modern Art even exhibits one.) It marks Paris at its peak in 1900—on the cutting edge of Modernism, but with an eye for beauty. The curvy, plantlike ironwork is a textbook example of Art Nouveau, the style that rebelled against the erector-set squareness of the Industrial Age. Other similar Métro stations in Paris are Abbesses and Porte Dauphine.

The flower and plant market on Place Louis Lépine is a pleasant detour. On Sundays this square flutters with a busy bird market.

• *Pause here to admire the view. Sainte-Chapelle is a pearl in an ugly architectural oyster. Double back to the Palais de Justice, turn right onto Boulevard du Palais, and enter the Conciergerie (free with Museum Pass; pass holders can sidestep the ticket-buying line bottleneck).*

Cité Métro entrance

Conciergerie prison

❽ *Conciergerie*

Though barren inside, this former prison echoes with history. The Conciergerie was the last stop for the many victims of the guillotine, including France's last *ancien régime* queen, Marie-Antoinette. Before then, kings had used the building to torture and execute failed assassins. (One of its towers along the river was called "The Babbler," named for the pain-induced sounds that leaked from it.) When the Revolution (1789) toppled the king, the progressive Revolutionaries proudly unveiled a modern and more humane way to execute people—the guillotine. The Conciergerie was the epicenter of the Reign of Terror—the year-long period of the Revolution (1793-94) during which Revolutionary fervor spiraled out of control and thousands were killed. It was here at the Conciergerie that "enemies of the Revolution" were imprisoned, tried, sentenced, and marched off to Place de la Concorde for decapitation.

Cost and Hours: €9, €15 combo-ticket with Sainte-Chapelle, covered by Museum Pass, daily 9:30-18:00, videoguide-€6.50, 2 Boulevard du Palais, Mo: Cité, tel. 01 53 40 60 80, www.paris-conciergerie.fr.

Visiting the Conciergerie: Pick up a free map and breeze through the one-way, well-described circuit. You'll start in the spacious, low-ceilinged Hall of Men-at-Arms (Room 1), originally a guards' dining room warmed by four big fireplaces (look up the chimneys). During the Reign of Terror, this large hall served as a holding tank for the poorest prisoners. Then they were taken upstairs (in an area not open to visitors), where the Revolutionary tribunals grilled scared prisoners on their political correctness. Continue to the raised area at the far end of the room (Room 4, today's bookstore). This was the walkway of the executioner, who was known affectionately as "Monsieur de Paris."

Upstairs is a memorial room with the names of the 2,780 citizens condemned to death by the guillotine, including ex-King Louis XVI, Charlotte Corday (who murdered the Revolutionary writer Jean-Paul Marat in his bathtub), and—oh, the irony—Maximilien de Robespierre, the head rabble-rouser of the Revolution, who himself sent so many to the guillotine.

Just past the courtyard look up and notice the spikes still guarding from above.

Pont Neuf crosses the widest part of the Seine.

On October 16, 1793, Marie-Antoinette was awakened at 4:00 in the morning and led away. She walked the corridor, stepped onto the cart, and was slowly carried to Place de la Concorde, where she had her date with "Monsieur de Paris."

• *Back outside, turn left on Boulevard du Palais, then left again onto Quai de l'Horloge and walk along the river, past "The Babbler" tower.*

The bridge up ahead is the Pont Neuf, where we'll end this walk. At the first corner, veer left into a sleepy triangular square called Place Dauphine. It's amazing to find such coziness in the heart of Paris. From the equestrian statue of Henry IV, turn right onto Pont Neuf. Pause at the little nook halfway across.

❾ Pont Neuf and the Seine

This "new bridge" is now Paris' oldest. Built during Henry IV's reign (about 1600), its arches span the widest part of the river. Unlike other bridges, this one never had houses or buildings growing on it. The turrets were originally for vendors and street entertainers. In the days of Henry IV, who promised his peasants "a chicken in every pot every Sunday," this would have been a

lively scene. From the bridge, look downstream (west) to see the next bridge, the pedestrian-only Pont des Arts. Ahead on the Right Bank is the long Louvre museum. Beyond that, on the Left Bank, is the Orsay.

• *Our walk is finished. From here, you can tour the Seine by boat (the departure point for Seine River cruises offered by Vedettes du Pont Neuf is through the park at the end of the island), continue to the Louvre, or head to the...*

❿ Riverside Promenades and Paris Plages

There's one traffic-free expanse on the Left Bank between the Eiffel Tower and the Orsay, and another on the Right Bank between the Louvre and the end of Ile St. Louis. Worth ▲▲, these areas are ideal for strolling, biking, having fun with the kids, dining (in pop-up drinking and eating establishments or at extravagant picnics complete with tablecloths and champagne)—or, simply dangling one's feet over the water and being in the moment. In balmy weather, the embankment takes on a special energy. Each summer, the Paris city government trucks in potted palm trees, hammocks,

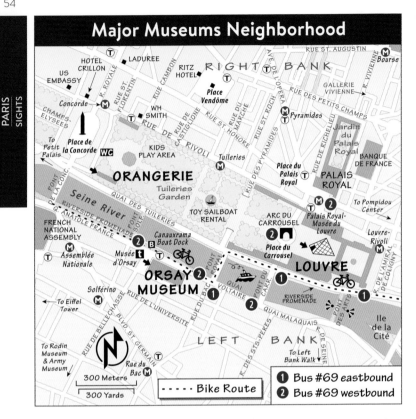

Major Museums Neighborhood

Bus #69 eastbound
Bus #69 westbound
- - - - Bike Route

300 Meters
300 Yards

and lounge chairs to create colorful urban beaches—the Paris *Plages*.

Cost and Hours: Free, promenades always open, *Plages* run mid-July-mid-Aug daily 8:00-24:00, on Right Bank of Seine, just north of Ile de la Cité, between Pont des Arts and Pont de Sully.

SIGHTS

Major Museums Neighborhood

Paris' grandest park, the Tuileries Garden, was once the private property of kings and queens. Today it links the Louvre, Orangerie, and Orsay museums, all of which are within pleasant strolling distance of one another.

▲▲▲LOUVRE (MUSEE DU LOUVRE)

This is Europe's oldest, biggest, greatest, and second-most-crowded museum (after the Vatican). Housed in a U-shaped, 16th-century palace (accentuated by a 20th-century glass pyramid), the Louvre is home to *Mona Lisa, Venus de Milo,* and hall after hall of Greek and Roman masterpieces, medieval jewels, Michelangelo statues, and paintings by the greatest artists from the Renaissance to the Romantics.

Touring the Louvre can be overwhelming, so be selective. Focus on the Denon wing, with Greek sculptures, Italian paintings (by Raphael and Leonardo), and, of course, French paintings (Neoclassical and Romantic), and the adjoining Sully wing, with Egyptian artifacts and more French paintings. For extra credit, tackle the Richelieu wing, displaying works from ancient Mesopotamia, as well as French, Dutch, and Northern art.

Cost and Hours: €15, includes special exhibits, free on first Sun of month Oct-March, covered by Museum Pass, timed-entry tickets available in advance at the website below; Wed-Mon 9:00-18:00, Wed and Fri until 21:45 (except on holidays), closed Tue, galleries start shutting 30 minutes before closing, last entry 45 minutes before closing; several cafés.

Information: Tel. 01 40 20 53 17, recorded info tel. 01 40 20 51 51, www.louvre.fr.

Rick's Tip: Crowds can be miserable on Sun, Mon (the worst day), Wed, and in the morning *(arrive 30 minutes before opening to secure a good place in line). Evening visits are quieter, and the glass pyramid glows after dark.*

Buying a Museum Pass or Advance Ticket: With a Museum Pass or advance ticket, you can avoid long ticket-buying lines, and minimize the line for the security check. If you don't already have a Museum Pass, the **"Museum Pass Tabac"** (a.k.a. La Civette du Carrousel) sells them for no extra charge, plus individual tickets to the Louvre, Orsay, and Versailles (cash only). It's just outside the Louvre entrance in the Carrousel du Louvre mall—to find it, follow *Museum Pass* signs inside the mall.

Timed-entry tickets are available **online** in advance (enter at the pyramid up to 30 minutes before your allotted time)—see the Louvre website for details.

Buying Tickets at the Louvre: Inside the Louvre, tickets are sold in a side room under the pyramid—just line up for the next available self-service machine (machines accept bills, coins, and credit cards with a PIN) or ticket window.

Getting There: Métro stop Palais Royal-Musée du Louvre is the closest. From the station, you can either exit above ground to go in the pyramid entrance, or stay underground to use the Carrousel du Louvre entrance. Eastbound bus #69 stops along the Seine River; the best stop is labeled Quai François Mitterrand. Westbound #69 stops in front of the pyramid.

Getting In: There are two entrances. Everyone must pass through security at the entrances.

Main Pyramid Entrance: There is no grander entry than through the main entrance at the pyramid in the central courtyard. The security line here can be very long, but if you have a ticket or a pass, you can use the VIP line.

Underground Mall Entrance: The less crowded underground entrance is accessed through the Carrousel du Louvre shopping mall. Enter the mall at 99 Rue de Rivoli (the door with the shiny metal awning) or directly from the Métro stop Palais Royal-Musée du Louvre (stepping off the train, exit to *Musée du Louvre-Le Carrousel du Louvre*). Once inside

PARIS
SIGHTS

Under the Louvre's pyramid entrance

The Louvre and its pyramid glows at night.

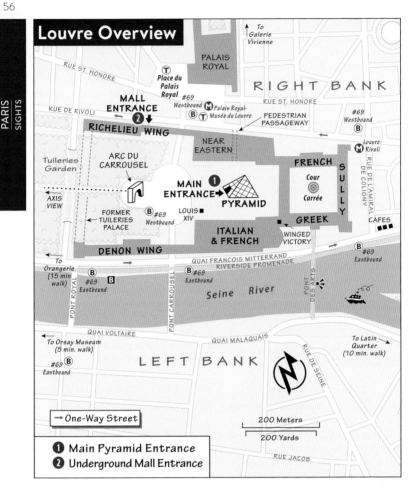

Louvre Overview

To Galerie Vivienne

PALAIS ROYAL

RUE ST. HONORE

T Place du Palais Royal

RIGHT BANK

RUE ST. HONORE

MALL ENTRANCE
2 ↓

#69 Westbound

M Palais Royal-Musée du Louvre
B **T**

#69 Westbound
B

RUE DE RIVOLI

RICHELIEU WING

PEDESTRIAN PASSAGEWAY

Louvre-Rivoli **M**

NEAR EASTERN

FRENCH

S U L L Y

Tuileries Garden

ARC DU CARROUSEL

MAIN ENTRANCE→ **1**

Cour Carrée

RUE DE L'AMIRAL DE COLIGNY

AXIS VIEW

PYRAMID

FORMER TUILERIES PALACE

B #69 Westbound

LOUIS XIV ■

GREEK

CAFES ■■■

ITALIAN & FRENCH

WINGED VICTORY

B #69 Eastbound

DENON WING

QUAI FRANCOIS MITTERRAND
RIVERSIDE PROMENADE

To Orangerie (15 min walk)

B
#69 Eastbound **B**

B #69 Eastbound

PONT DES ARTS

PONT ROYAL

PONT CARROUSEL

Seine River

QUAI VOLTAIRE

To Orsay Museum (5 min. walk)

#69 **B** Eastbound

QUAI MALAQUAIS

RUE DE SEINE

To Latin Quarter (10 min. walk)

L E F T   B A N K

N

→ One-Way Street

200 Meters
200 Yards

RUE JACOB

1 Main Pyramid Entrance
2 Underground Mall Entrance

the mall, continue toward the inverted pyramid next to the Louvre's security entrance. There's no priority security line for Museum Pass holders here, but lines are generally shorter than the main pyramid entrance. (Don't follow signs to the *Passholders* entrance, which is at the pyramid, a long detour away.)

Once Inside: Once past security, everyone proceeds to the grand space beneath the glass pyramid with all the services. If you already have a ticket or Museum Pass, go directly to the galleries. Otherwise, you can buy a ticket (see "Buying Tickets at the Louvre," above).

Tours: Ninety-minute English-language **guided tours** leave twice daily from the *Accueil des Groupes* area, under the pyramid (normally at 11:00 and 14:00, possibly more often in summer; €12 plus admission, tour tel. 01 40 20 52 63). **Videoguides** (€5) provide commentary on about 700 masterpieces.

🎧 Download my free Louvre Museum **audio tour.**

Baggage Check: It's free to store your bag in slick self-service lockers under the pyramid. Consider checking whatever you don't need—even if it's just a small bag—to make your visit more pleasant.

➲ SELF-GUIDED TOUR

With more than 30,000 works of art, the Louvre is a full inventory of Western civilization. To cover it all in one visit is impossible. Let's focus on the Louvre's specialties—Greek sculpture, Italian painting, and French painting.

• *We'll start in the Sully wing, in Salle 16. To get there from the pyramid entrance, first enter the Denon wing, ascend several flights of escalators, and follow the crowds—then get out your map or ask for directions to the* Venus de Milo.

THE GREEKS

Venus de Milo *(Aphrodite)*, late 2nd century BC: This goddess of love created a sensation when she was discovered in 1820 on the Greek island of Melos. The Greeks pictured their gods in human form (meaning humans are godlike), telling us they had an optimistic view of the human race. Venus' well-proportioned body captures the balance and orderliness of the Greek universe. The twisting pose gives a balanced S-curve to her body (especially noticeable from the back view) that Golden Age Greeks and succeeding generations found beautiful. Most "Greek" statues are actually later Roman copies. This is a rare Greek original.

• *Now head to Salle 6, behind* Venus de Milo.

Parthenon Friezes, mid-5th century BC: These stone fragments once decorated the exterior of the greatest Athenian temple of the Greek Golden Age. The temple glorified the city's divine protector, Athena, and the superiority of the Athenians, who were feeling especially cocky, having just crushed their archrivals, the Persians. A model of the Parthenon shows where the panels might have hung.

• *About 50 yards away, find a grand staircase. Climb it to the first floor and the...*

Winged Victory of Samothrace *(Victoire de Samothrace)*, c. 190 BC: This woman with wings, poised on the prow of a ship, once stood on an island hilltop to commemorate a naval victory. Her

Venus de Milo

clothes are windblown and sea-sprayed, clinging close enough to her body to win a wet T-shirt contest. Originally, her right arm was stretched high, celebrating the victory like a Super Bowl champion, waving a "we're number one" finger. This is the *Venus de Milo* gone Hellenistic, from the time after the culture of Athens was spread around the Mediterranean by Alexander the Great (c. 325 BC).

• *Facing* Winged Victory, *turn right (entering the Denon wing), and proceed to the large Salle 3.*

THE MEDIEVAL WORLD (1200-1500)

Cimabue, *The Madonna and Child in Majesty Surrounded by Angels (La Vierge et l'Enfant en Majesté Entourés de Six Anges)*, c. 1280: During the Age of Faith (1200s), almost every church in Europe had a painting like this one. Mary was a cult figure—even bigger than the late-20th-century Madonna—adored and prayed to by the faithful for bringing Baby Jesus into the world. These holy figures are laid flat on a gold background like cardboard cutouts, existing in a golden never-never

land, as though the faithful couldn't imagine them as flesh-and-blood humans inhabiting our dark and sinful earth.

Giotto, *St. Francis of Assisi Receiving the Stigmata (Saint François d'Assise Recevant les Stigmates),* c. 1295-1300: Francis of Assisi (c. 1181-1226), a wandering Italian monk of renowned goodness, kneels on a rocky Italian hillside, pondering the pain of Christ's torture and execution. Suddenly, he looks up, startled, to see Christ himself, with six wings, hovering above. Christ shoots lasers from his wounds to the hands, feet, and side of the empathetic monk, marking him with the stigmata. Francis' humble love of man and nature inspired artists like Giotto to portray real human beings with real emotions, living in a physical world of beauty.

• *Room 3 spills into the long Grand Gallery. Find the following paintings in the Gallery, as you make your way to the* Mona Lisa *(midway down the gallery, in the adjoining Salle 6—just follow the signs and the people).*

ITALIAN RENAISSANCE (1400-1600)

Leonardo da Vinci, *The Virgin and Child with St. Anne (La Vierge à l'Enfant Jésus avec Sainte-Anne),* c. 1510: Three generations—grandmother, mother, and child—are arranged in a pyramid, with Anne's face as the peak and the lamb as the lower right corner. It's as orderly as the geometrically perfect universe created by the Renaissance god. There's a psychological kidney punch in this happy painting. Jesus, the picture of childish joy, is innocently playing with a lamb—the symbol of his inevitable sacrificial death. The Louvre has the greatest collection of Leonardos in the world—five of them. Look for the neighboring *Virgin of the Rocks* and *John the Baptist.*

Raphael, *La Belle Jardinière,* c. 1507: Raphael perfected the style Leonardo pioneered. This configuration of Madonna, Child, and John the Baptist is also a balanced pyramid with hazy grace and beauty. The interplay of gestures and gazes gives the masterpiece both intimacy and cohesiveness, while Raphael's blended

Ⓐ Winged Victory of Samothrace

Ⓑ *Giotto,* St. Francis Receiving the Stigmata

Ⓒ *Leonardo da Vinci,* Mona Lisa

brushstrokes varnish the work with an iridescent smoothness. With Raphael, the Greek ideal of beauty—reborn in the Renaissance—reached its peak.

Leonardo da Vinci, *Mona Lisa,* a.k.a. *La Joconde,* 1503-1506: Leonardo was already an old man when François I invited him to France. Determined to pack light, he took only a few paintings with him. One was a portrait of Lisa del Giocondo, the wife of a wealthy Florentine merchant.

Mona may disappoint you. She's smaller than you'd expect, darker, engulfed in a huge room, and hidden behind a glaring pane of glass. The famous smile attracts you first, but try as you might, you can never quite see the corners of her mouth. The overall mood is one of balance and serenity, but there's also an element of mystery. *Mona*'s smile and long-distance beauty are subtle and elusive, tempting but always just out of reach. *Mona* doesn't knock your socks off, but she winks at the patient viewer.

Paolo Veronese, *The Marriage at Cana (Les Noces de Cana),* 1562-1563: Venetian artists like Veronese painted the good life of rich, happy-go-lucky Venetian merchants. In a spacious setting of Renaissance architecture, colorful lords and ladies, decked out in their fanciest duds, feast on a great spread of food and drink. But believe it or not, this is a religious work showing the wedding celebration in which Jesus turned water into wine. With true Renaissance optimism, Venetians pictured Christ as a party animal, someone who loved the created world as much as they did.

Ⓐ *Raphael,* La Belle Jardinière
Ⓑ *Veronese,* The Marriage at Cana
Ⓒ *Ingres,* La Grande Odalisque
Ⓓ *Delacroix,* Liberty Leading the People

• *Exit behind* Mona *into the Salle Denon (Room 76). Turn right for French Neoclassicism (Salle Daru, David and Ingres); then backtrack through the Salle Denon for French Romanticism (Room 77, Géricault and Delacroix).*

FRENCH PAINTING (1780-1850)

Jacques-Louis David, *The Coronation of Emperor Napoleon (Sacre de l'Empereur Napoléon),* 1806-1807: Napoleon holds

aloft an imperial crown. This common-born son of immigrants is about to be crowned emperor of a "New Rome." He has just made his wife, Josephine, the empress, and she kneels at his feet. Seated behind Napoleon is the pope, who journeyed from Rome to place the imperial crown on his head. But Napoleon feels that no one is worthy of the task. At the last moment, he shrugs the pope aside.

Jean-Auguste-Dominique Ingres, *La Grande Odalisque,* 1814: Take *Venus de Milo,* turn her around, lay her down, and stick a hash pipe next to her, and you have the *Grande Odalisque.* Using clean, polished, sculptural lines, Ingres (ang-gruh) exaggerates the S-curve of a standing Greek nude. As in the *Venus de Milo,* rough folds of cloth set off her smooth skin. Ingres gave the face, too, a touch of *Venus'* idealized features, taking nature and improving on it. Ingres preserves *Venus'* backside for posterior—I mean, posterity.

Théodore Géricault, *The Raft of the Medusa (Le Radeau de la Méduse),* 1819: Clinging to a raft is a tangle of bodies and lunatics sprawled over each other. The scene writhes with agitated, ominous motion—the ripple of muscles, churning clouds, and choppy seas. The bodies rise up in a pyramid of hope, culminating in a flag wave. They signal frantically, trying to catch the attention of the tiny ship on the horizon, their last desperate hope... which did finally save them. Géricault uses rippling movement and powerful colors to catch us up in the excitement. (This painting was based on the actual sinking of the ship *Medusa* off the coast of Africa in 1816.)

Eugéne Delacroix, *Liberty Leading the People (La Liberté Guidant le Peuple),* 1831: The year is 1830. Parisians take to the streets to fight royalist oppressors. Leading them on through the smoke and over the dead and dying is the figure of Liberty, a strong woman waving the French flag. Does this symbol of victory look familiar? It's the *Winged Victory,* wingless and topless.

Michelangelo's Slave *sculptures*

To stir our emotions, Delacroix uses only three major colors—the red, white, and blue of the French flag. France is the symbol of modern democracy, and this painting has long stirred its citizens' passion for liberty.

• *Exit the room at the far end (past the Café Mollien) and go downstairs, where you'll bump into...*

MORE ITALIAN RENAISSANCE

Michelangelo, *Slaves (Esclaves),* 1513-1515: These two statues by the earth's greatest sculptor are a bridge between the ancient and modern worlds. Michelangelo, like his fellow Renaissance artists, learned from the Greeks. The perfect anatomy, twisting poses, and idealized faces appear as if they could have been created 2,000 years earlier.

The *Dying Slave* twists listlessly against his T-shirt-like bonds, revealing his smooth skin. This is probably the most sensual nude that Michelangelo, the master of the male body, ever created. The *Rebellious Slave* fights against his bondage. His shoulders rotate one way, his head and leg turn the other. He even seems to be trying to release himself from the rock he's made of. Michelangelo said that his purpose was to carve away the marble to reveal the figures God put inside. This slave shows the agony of that process and the ecstasy of the result.

• *Tour over! But, of course, there's so much more. After a break (or on a second visit), consider a stroll through a few rooms of the Richelieu wing, which contain some of the Louvre's most ancient pieces.*

Rick's Tip: *Across from the Louvre (to the north) are the* **lovely courtyards of the stately Palais Royal** *(always open and free, entrance off Rue de Rivoli).* **Bring a picnic** *and create your own quiet break, or have a drink at one of the outdoor cafés at the courtyard's northern end.*

▲▲▲ORSAY MUSEUM (MUSÉE D'ORSAY)

The Musée d'Orsay houses French art of the 1800s and early 1900s (specifically, 1848-1914), picking up where the Louvre's art collection leaves off. For us, that means Impressionism, the art of sun-dappled fields, bright colors, and crowded Parisian cafés. The Orsay houses the best general collection anywhere of Manet, Monet, Renoir, Degas, Van Gogh, Cézanne, and Gauguin.

Cost and Hours: €12, €9 Tue-Wed and Fri-Sun after 16:30 and Thu after 18:00, free on first Sun of month and often right when the ticket booth stops selling tickets (Tue-Wed and Fri-Sun at 17:00, Thu at 21:00; they won't let you in much after that), covered by Museum Pass, combo-ticket with Orangerie Museum (€16) or Rodin Museum (€18). Museum open Tue-Sun 9:30-18:00, Thu until 21:45, closed Mon, last entry one hour before closing (45 minutes before on Thu), Impressionist galleries start shutting 45 minutes before closing, cafés and restaurant.

Information: Tel. 01 40 49 48 14, www. musee-orsay.fr.

Avoiding Lines: While everyone must wait to go through security, avoid the long ticket-buying lines with a Museum Pass, a combo-ticket, or by purchasing tickets in advance on the Orsay website; any of these entitle you to use a separate entrance. You can also buy tickets and Museum Passes (no mark-up; tickets valid 3 months) at the newspaper kiosk just outside the Orsay entrance (along Rue de la Légion d'Honneur).

Getting There: The museum, at 1 Rue de la Légion d'Honneur, sits above the RER/Train-C Musée d'Orsay stop; the nearest Métro stop is Solférino, three blocks southeast of the Orsay.

Getting In: As you face the entrance, pass and ticket holders enter on the right (Entrance C). Ticket purchasers enter on the left (Entrance A). Security checks slow down all entrances.

Rick's Tip: *If you're planning to* **get a combo-ticket for the Orsay Museum** *with either the Orangerie or the Rodin Museum, start at one of those museums instead, as they have shorter lines.*

Tours: Audioguides cost €5. English **guided tours** usually run daily at 11:30 (€6/1.5 hours, none on Sun, tours may also run at 14:30—inquire when you arrive).

🎧 Download my free Orsay Museum **audio tour.**

◯ SELF-GUIDED TOUR

This former train station, the Gare d'Orsay, barely escaped the wrecking ball in the 1970s, when the French realized it'd be a great place to house the enormous collections of 19th-century art scattered throughout the city. The ground floor (level 0) houses early-19th-century art, mainly conservative art of the Academy and Salon, plus Realism. On the top floor is the core of the collection—the Impressionist rooms. If you're pressed for time, go directly there.

Remember that the museum rotates its large collection often, so find the latest arrangement on your current Orsay map, and be ready to go with the flow.

CONSERVATIVE ART

In the Orsay's first few rooms, you're surrounded by visions of idealized beauty—nude women in languid poses, Greek mythological figures, and anatomically perfect statues. This was the art adored by 19th-century French academics and the middle-class (bourgeois) public.

Jean-Auguste-Dominique **Ingres**' The Source (1856) is virtually a Greek statue on canvas. Like Venus de Milo, she's a balance of opposite motions. Alexandre **Cabanel** lays Ingres' The Source on her back. His Birth of Venus (1863) is a perfect fantasy, an orgasm of beauty.

REALISM

The French Realists rejected idealized classicism and began painting what they saw in the world around them. For Honoré **Daumier,** that meant looking at the stuffy bourgeois establishment that controlled the Academy and the Salon. In the 36 bustlets of Celebrities of the Happy Medium (1835), Daumier, trained as a political cartoonist, exaggerates each subject's most distinct characteristic to capture with vicious precision the pomposity and self-righteousness of these self-appointed arbiters of taste (most were members of the French parliament).

Jean-François **Millet**'s The Gleaners (1867) shows us three gleaners, the poor women who pick up the meager leftovers after a field has already been harvested for the wealthy. Here he captures the innate dignity of these stocky, tanned women who bend their backs quietly in a large field for their small reward. This is "Realism" in two senses. It's painted "realistically," not prettified. And it's the "real" world—not the fantasy world of Greek myth, but the harsh life of the working poor.

For a Realist's take on the traditional Venus, find Edouard **Manet**'s Olympia (1863). Compare this uncompromising nude with Cabanel's idealized, pastel, Vaseline-on-the-lens beauty in The Birth of Venus. In Olympia, the sharp outlines and harsh, contrasting colors are new and shocking. Manet replaced soft-core porn with hard-core art.

Gustave **Courbet**'s The Painter's Studio (1855) takes us backstage, showing us the

The Orsay Museum occupies an early-20th-century railway station.

gritty reality behind the creation of pretty pictures. We see Courbet himself in his studio, working diligently on a Realistic landscape, oblivious to the confusion around him. Milling around are ordinary citizens, not Greek heroes.

At the far end of the gallery, you'll find the Opéra Exhibit—a **glass floor** over a model of Paris with the 19th-century, green-domed Opéra Garnier at the center.

TOULOUSE-LAUTREC DETOUR

The Henri de **Toulouse-Lautrec** paintings in Room 10 rightly belong with the Post-Impressionist works on level 2, but since you're already here, enjoy his paintings incarnating the artist's love of nightlife and show business. Every night, Toulouse-Lautrec put on his bowler hat and visited the Moulin Rouge to draw the crowds, the can-can dancers, and the backstage action. He worked quickly, creating sketches in paint that serve as snapshots of a golden era. In *Jane Avril Dancing* (1891), he depicts the slim, graceful, elegant, and melancholy dancer, who stood out above the rabble. Her legs keep dancing while her mind is far away.

IMPRESSIONISM

The Impressionist collection is scattered randomly through Rooms 29-36 on the top floor. Look for masterworks by these artists:

Edouard **Manet**'s *Luncheon on the Grass* (*Le Déjeuner sur l'Herbe,* 1863) shocked Paris. It isn't the nudity, but the presence of the men in ordinary clothes that suddenly makes the nudes look naked.

You can see that a new revolutionary movement was starting to bud—Impressionism. Notice the background: the messy brushwork of trees and leaves, the play of light on the pond, and the light that filters through the trees onto the woman who stoops in the haze. Also note the strong contrast of colors (white skin, black clothes, green grass).

Edgar **Degas** blends classical lines and Realist subjects with Impressionist

Ⓐ *Cabanel,* Birth of Venus

Ⓑ *Millet,* The Gleaners

Ⓒ *Manet,* Olympia

Ⓓ *Toulouse-Lautrec,* Jane Avril Dancing

64

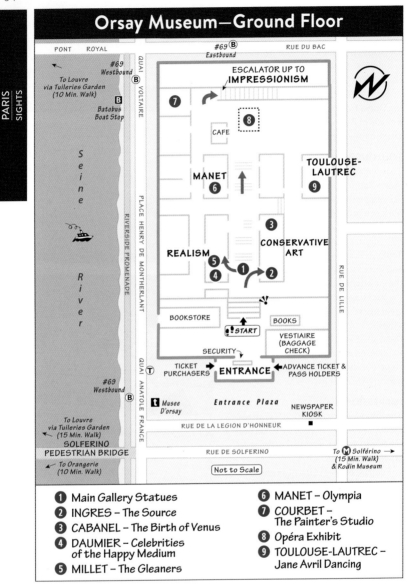

Orsay Museum—Ground Floor

1. **Main Gallery Statues**
2. **INGRES – The Source**
3. **CABANEL – The Birth of Venus**
4. **DAUMIER – Celebrities of the Happy Medium**
5. **MILLET – The Gleaners**
6. **MANET – Olympia**
7. **COURBET – The Painter's Studio**
8. **Opéra Exhibit**
9. **TOULOUSE-LAUTREC – Jane Avril Dancing**

color, spontaneity, and everyday scenes from urban Paris. He loved the unposed "snapshot" effect, catching his models off guard. Dance students, women at work, and café scenes are approached from odd angles that aren't always ideal but make the scenes seem more real. He

gives us the backstage view of life. For instance, a dance rehearsal let Degas capture a behind-the-scenes look at bored, tired, restless dancers (*The Dance Class, La Classe de Danse*, c. 1873-1875). In the painting *In a Café (Dans un Café*, 1875-1876), a weary lady of the evening meets

POST-IMPRESSIONISM

Post-Impressionism—the style that employs Impressionism's bright colors while branching out in new directions—is scattered all around the museum. You'll get a taste of the style with Paul Cézanne on the top floor, with much more on level 2.

Paul **Cézanne** (say-zahn) brought Impressionism into the 20th century. After the color of Monet and the warmth of Renoir, Cézanne's rather impersonal canvases can be difficult to appreciate (see *The Card Players, Les Joueurs de Cartes,* 1890-1895). Where the Impressionists built a figure out of a mosaic of individual brushstrokes, Cézanne used blocks of paint to create a more solid, geometrical shape. These chunks are like little "cubes." It's no coincidence that his experiments in reducing forms to their geometric basics inspired the...Cubists. Because of his style (not the content), he is often called the first modern painter.

Like Michelangelo, Beethoven, and a select handful of others, Vincent **van Gogh** put so much of himself into his work that art and life became one. In the Orsay's collection of paintings (level 2), you'll see both Van Gogh's painting style and his life unfold, from his early days soaking up the Impressionist style (for example, see how he might build a bristling brown beard using thick strokes of red, yellow, and green side by side) to his richly creative but wildly unstable stint in the south of France (*Van Gogh's Room at Arles, La Chambre de Van Gogh à Arles,* 1889). Don't miss his final self-portrait (1889), showing a man engulfed in a confused background of brushstrokes that swirl and rave. Perhaps his troubled eyes know that in only a few months, he'll take a pistol and put a bullet through his chest.

Nearby are the paintings of Paul **Gauguin,** who got the travel bug early in childhood and grew up wanting to be a sailor. Instead, he became a stockbroker. At the age of 35, he got fed up with it all, quit his job, abandoned his wife (her stern

Degas, The Dance Class

morning with a last, lonely, nail-in-the-coffin drink in the glaring light of a four-in-the-morning café.

You'll see various paintings by Claude **Monet,** the father of Impressionism. In the 1860s, Monet (along with Renoir) began painting landscapes in the open air. He studied optics and pigments to know just the right colors he needed to reproduce the shimmering quality of reflected light. The key was to work quickly, when the light was just right, creating a fleeting "impression" of the scene.

Pierre-Auguste **Renoir** started out as a painter of landscapes, along with Monet, but later veered from the Impressionist's philosophy and painted images that were unabashedly "pretty." His best-known work is *Dance at the Moulin de la Galette* (*Bal du Moulin de la Galette,* 1876). On Sunday afternoons, working-class folk would dress up and head for the fields on Butte Montmartre (near Sacré-Cœur basilica) to dance, drink, and eat little crêpes (galettes) till dark. Renoir liked to go there to paint the common Parisians living and loving in the afternoon sun.

A *Renoir,* Dance at the Moulin de la Galette
B *Cézanne,* The Card Players
C *Van Gogh,* Van Gogh's Room at Arles
D *Gauguin,* Arearea

portrait bust may be nearby) and family, and took refuge in his art.

Gauguin traveled to the South Seas in search of the exotic, finally settling on Tahiti. His best-known works capture an idyllic Tahitian landscape peopled by exotic women engaged in simple tasks and making music (*Arearea,* 1892). The style is intentionally "primitive," collapsing the three-dimensional landscape into a two-dimensional pattern of bright colors. Gauguin wanted to communicate to his "civilized" colleagues back home that he'd found the paradise he'd always envisioned.

FRENCH SCULPTURE

The open-air mezzanine of level 2 is lined with statues. Stroll the mezzanine, enjoying the work of great French sculptors, including Auguste **Rodin.**

Born of working-class roots and largely self-taught, Rodin combined classical solidity with Impressionist surfaces to become one of the greatest sculptors since the Renaissance. Rodin's *St. John the Baptist Preaching* (bronze, 1881) captures the mystical visionary who was the precursor to Christ, the man who would announce the coming of the Messiah. Rodin's inspiration came in the form of a shaggy peasant—looking for work as a model—whose bearing caught the artist's eye. Coarse and hairy, with both feet planted firmly, if oddly, on the ground, this sculpture's rough, "unfinished" look reflects light in the same way the rough Impressionist brushwork does—making the statue come alive, never quite at rest in the viewer's eye.

Rodin's sculptures capture the groundbreaking spirit of much of the art in the Orsay Museum. With a stable base of 19th-century stone, he launched art into the 20th century.

▲▲ORANGERIE MUSEUM (MUSEE DE L'ORANGERIE)

Located in the Tuileries Garden and drenched by natural light from skylights,

Monet's Water Lilies *at the Orangerie Museum*

the Orangerie (oh-rahn-zhuh-ree) is the closest you'll ever come to stepping right into an Impressionist painting. Start with the museum's claim to fame: Monet's *Water Lilies*. Then head downstairs to enjoy the manageable collection of select works by Utrillo, Cézanne, Renoir, Matisse, and Picasso.

Cost and Hours: €9, €6.50 after 17:00, free for those under age 18, €16 combo-ticket with Orsay Museum, €20 combo-ticket with Monet's Garden and House at Giverny, covered by Museum Pass; Wed-Mon 9:00-18:00, closed Tue; audioguide-€5, English guided tours usually Mon and Thu at 14:30 and Sat at 11:00, located in Tuileries Garden near Place de la Concorde (Mo: Concorde), 15-minute stroll from the Orsay, tel. 01 44 77 80 07, www.musee-orangerie.fr.

Visiting the Museum: On the main floor you'll find the main attraction, Monet's *Water Lilies (Nymphéas),* floating dreamily in oval rooms. These eight mammoth, curved panels immerse you in Monet's garden. We're looking at the

pond in his garden at Giverny—dotted with water lilies, surrounded by foliage, and dappled by the reflections of the sky, clouds, and trees on the surface. But the true subject of these works is the play of reflected light off the surface of the pond.

Working at his home in Giverny, Monet built a special studio with skylights and wheeled easels to accommodate the canvases. For 12 years (1914-1926), Monet worked on these paintings obsessively. Monet completed all the planned canvases, but he didn't live to see them installed here. In 1927, the year after his death, these rooms were completed and the canvases put in place. Some call this the first "art installation"—art displayed in a space specially designed for it in order to enhance the viewer's experience.

In the underground gallery are select works of other Impressionist heavyweights well worth your time. The museum is small enough to enjoy in a short visit, but complete enough to show the bridge from Impressionism to Modernism. And it's all beautiful.

Eiffel Tower and Nearby

▲▲▲EIFFEL TOWER
(LA TOUR EIFFEL)

Built on the 100th anniversary of the French Revolution (and in the spirit of the Industrial Revolution), the tower was the centerpiece of a World Expo designed simply to show off what people could build in 1889. For decades it was the tallest structure the world had ever known, and though it's since been eclipsed, it's still the most visited monument. Ride the elevators to the top of its 1,063 feet for expansive views that stretch 40 miles. Then descend to the two lower levels, where the views are arguably even better, since the monuments are more recognizable.

Cost and Hours: €25 to ride all the way to the top, €16 for just the two lower levels, €10 to climb the stairs to the first or second level, €19 to climb the stairs to the second level and take the elevator to the summit—must purchase summit elevator before entering tower, 50 percent cheaper for those under 25, 75 percent cheaper for those under 12, not covered by Museum Pass; open daily mid-June-Aug 9:00-24:45, Sept-mid-June 9:30-23:45, last ascent to top at 22:30 and to lower levels at 23:00 all year (elevator or stairs); cafés and great view restaurants, Mo: Bir-Hakeim or Trocadéro, RER/Train-C: Champ de Mars-Tour Eiffel (all about a 10-minute walk away).

The Eiffel Tower stands more than 1,000 feet tall.

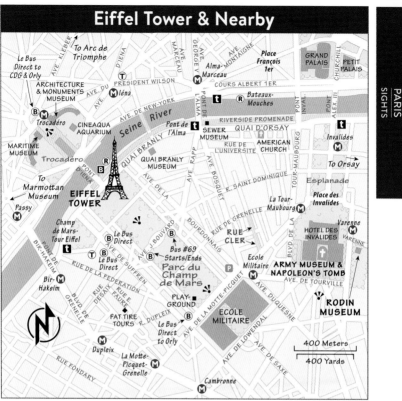

Eiffel Tower & Nearby

Information: Recorded information tel. 08 92 70 12 39, www.toureiffel.paris.

Reservations Smart: It's wise to make a reservation well in advance of your visit. At www.toureiffel.paris, you can book a time slot for your ascent; this allows you to skip the long initial entry line.

Online ticket sales open up about three months before any given date (at 8:30 Paris time). Be sure of your date, as reservations are nonrefundable. To go all the way to the top, select "Lift entrance ticket with access to the summit" as your ticket type. You can either print your tickets (follow the specifications carefully) or download e-tickets to your phone. Note that email or text confirmations alone will not get you in; you must have a printed or electronic ticket showing the bar code.

If no slots are available, try buying a "Lift entrance ticket with access to 2nd floor"—the view from the second floor is arguably better anyway. Or, try the website again about a week before your visit—last-minute spots sometimes open up.

Rick's Tip: No reservation for the Eiffel Tower? *Get in line 30 minutes before it opens. Going late is the next-best bet (after 19:00 May-Aug). You can bypass some (but not all) lines if you have a reservation at either of the tower's view restaurants (Le Jules Verne or 58 Tour Eiffel).*

When to Go: For the best of all worlds, arrive with enough light to see the views, then stay as it gets dark to see the lights. The views are grand whether you ascend

Open-Air Markets

Several traffic-free street markets overflow with flowers, produce, fish vendors, and butchers. Shops are open daily except Sunday afternoons, Monday, and lunchtime throughout the week (13:00 to 15:00 or 16:00).

Rue Cler—a wonderful place to sleep and dine as well as shop—is like a refined street market, serving an upscale neighborhood near the Eiffel Tower (Mo: Ecole Militaire).

Rue Montorgueil and **Rue Montmartre** are thriving, locally popular café-lined streets that run parallel just north of Les Halles (Mo: Etienne Marcel).

Rue Mouffetard is a happening market street by day and does double-duty as restaurant row at night. Hiding several blocks behind the Panthéon, it starts at Place Contrescarpe and ends below at St. Médard Church (Mo: Censier Daubenton). The upper stretch is pedestrian and touristic; the bottom stretch is purely Parisian.

or not. At the top of the hour, a five-minute display features thousands of sparkling lights (best viewed from Place du Trocadéro or the grassy park below).

Getting In: The perimeter of the tower is surrounded by glass walls for security purposes. So, while it's free to enter the area directly under the tower, you must first pass through an airport-like security check (allow 30 minutes or more at busy times). **If you have a reservation,** arrive at the tower 30 minutes before your entry time and look

for either of the two entrances with green signs showing *Visiteurs avec Reservation* (Visitors with Reservation), where attendants scan your ticket and put you on the first available elevator. **Without a reservation,** follow signs for *Individuels* or *Visiteurs sans Tickets* (avoid lines selling tickets only for *Groupes*). The stairs entrance (usually a shorter line) is at the south pillar (next to Le Jules Verne restaurant entrance).

Security Check: Bags larger than 19" × 8" × 12" are not allowed, but there is no baggage check. All bags are subject to a security search. No knives, glass bottles, or cans are permitted.

BACKGROUND

The first visitor to the Paris World's Fair in 1889 walked beneath the "arch" formed by the newly built Eiffel Tower and entered the fairgrounds. This event celebrated both the centennial of the French Revolution and France's position as a global superpower. Bridge builder Gustave Eiffel (1832-1923) won the contest to build the fair's centerpiece by beating out rival proposals such as a giant guillotine.

The tower was nothing but a showpiece, with no functional purpose except to demonstrate to the world that France had the wealth, knowledge, and can-do spirit to erect a structure far taller than anything the world had ever seen. The original plan was to dismantle the tower as quickly as it was built after the celebration ended, but it was kept by popular demand.

The tower, including its antenna, stands 1,063 feet tall, or slightly higher than the 77-story Chrysler Building in New York. Its four support pillars straddle an area of 3.5 acres. Despite the tower's 7,300 tons of metal and 60 tons of paint, it is so well-engineered that it weighs no more per square inch at its base than a linebacker on tiptoes.

VISITING THE TOWER

There are three observation platforms, at roughly 200, 400, and 900 feet. If you want to see the entire tower, from top to bottom, then see it...from top to bottom.

There isn't a single elevator straight to the top *(le sommet).* To get there, you'll first ride an elevator (or hike up the stairs) to the second level. (For the hardy, there are 360 stairs to the first level and another 360 to the second). Once on the second level, immediately line up for the next elevator, to the top. Enjoy the views from the "summit," then ride back down to the second level. When you're ready, head to the first level via the stairs (no line and can take as little

as five minutes) or take the elevator down. Explore the shops and exhibits on the first level. To leave, you can line up for the elevator, but it's quickest and most memorable to take the stairs back down to earth.

For a final look, stroll across the river to Place du Trocadéro or to the end of the Champ de Mars and look back for great views. However impressive it may be by day, the tower is an awesome thing to behold at twilight, when it becomes engorged with light, and virile Paris lies back and lets night be on top. When darkness fully envelops the city, the tower seems to climax with a spectacular light show at the top of each hour...for five glorious minutes.

Near the Eiffel Tower

▲▲ARMY MUSEUM AND NAPOLEON'S TOMB (MUSEE DE L'ARMEE)

Napoleon's tomb rests beneath the golden dome of Les Invalides church. In addition to the tomb, the complex of Les Invalides—a former veterans' hospital built by Louis XIV—has various military collections, together called the Army Museum, Europe's greatest military

Army Museum and Napoleon's Tomb

Rodin's Burghers of Calais

Monet's Impression, Sunrise

museum. Visiting the different sections, you can watch the art of war unfold from stone axes to Axis powers.

Cost and Hours: €12, €9 after 17:00 (16:00 Nov-March), free for military personnel in uniform, free for kids but they must wait in line for ticket, covered by Museum Pass, extra fee for special exhibits and evening concerts; open daily 10:00-18:00, Nov-March until 17:00; Napoleon's Tomb also open July-Aug until 19:00; Napoleon's Tomb and Louis XIV-Napoleon I wing open April-Sept Tue until 21:00; Charles de Gaulle exhibit closed Mon year-round; videoguide-€6, cafeteria, tel. 08 10 11 33 99, www.musee-armee.fr.

Getting There: The Hôtel des Invalides is at 129 Rue de Grenelle, a 10-minute walk from Rue Cler (Mo: La Tour Maubourg, Varenne, or Invalides). You can also take bus #69 (from the Marais and Rue Cler), bus #87 (from Rue Cler and Luxembourg Garden area), or bus #63 from the St. Germain-des-Prés area.

Visiting the Museum: At the center of the complex, Napoleon Bonaparte lies majestically dead inside several coffins under a grand dome—a goose-bump-ing pilgrimage for historians. The dome overhead glitters with 26 pounds of thinly pounded gold leaf.

Your visit continues through an impressive range of museums filled with medieval armor, cannons and muskets, Louis XIV-era uniforms and weapons, and

Napoleon's horse—stuffed and mounted.

The best section is dedicated to the two World Wars. Walk through displays well described in English on the trench warfare of World War I, the victory parades, France's horrendous losses, and the humiliating Treaty of Versailles that led to World War II.

The WWII rooms use black-and-white photos, maps, videos, and a few artifacts to trace Hitler's rise, the Blitzkrieg that overran France, America's entry into the war, D-Day, the concentration camps, the atomic bomb, the war in the Pacific, and the eventual Allied victory. There's special insight into France's role (the French Resistance), and how it was Charles de Gaulle that actually won the war.

▲▲RODIN MUSEUM (MUSEE RODIN)

This user-friendly museum with gardens is filled with passionate works by Auguste Rodin (1840-1917), the greatest sculptor since Michelangelo. You'll see *The Kiss, The Thinker, The Gates of Hell,* and many more, well displayed in the mansion where the sculptor lived and worked.

Cost and Hours: €10, free for those under age 18, free on first Sun of the month Oct-March, €4 for just the garden (with several important works on display), €18 combo-ticket with Orsay Museum, both museum and garden covered by Museum Pass; Tue-Sun 10:00-17:45, closed Mon; gardens close at 18:00, Oct-March at 17:00; audioguide-€6, mandatory baggage check, self-service café in garden, 77 Rue de Varenne, Mo: Varenne, tel. 01 44 18 61 10, www.musee-rodin.fr.

Visiting the Museum: Auguste Rodin (1840-1917) was a modern Michelangelo, sculpting human figures on an epic scale, revealing through their bodies his deepest thoughts and feelings. Like many of Michelangelo's unfinished works, Rodin's statues rise from the raw stone around them, driven by the life force. With missing limbs and scarred skin, these are prefab classics, making ugliness noble. Rodin's people are always moving restlessly. Even the famous *Thinker* is moving; while he's plopped down solidly, his mind is a million miles away.

Exhibits trace Rodin's artistic development, explain how his bronze statues were cast, and show some of the studies he created to work up to his masterpiece, the unfinished *Gates of Hell.* Learn about Rodin's tumultuous relationship with his apprentice and lover, Camille Claudel. Mull over what makes his sculptures some of the most evocative since the Renaissance. And stroll the beautiful gardens, packed with many of his greatest works (including *The Thinker*) and ideal for artistic reflection.

▲▲MARMOTTAN MUSEUM (MUSEE MARMOTTAN MONET)

In this private, intimate, and untouristy museum, you'll find the best collection anywhere of works by Impressionist headliner Claude Monet. Follow Monet's life

through more than a hundred works, from simple sketches to the *Impression: Sunrise* painting that gave his artistic movement its start—and a name. The museum also displays some of the enjoyable large-scale canvases featuring the water lilies from his garden at Giverny.

Cost and Hours: €11, not covered by Museum Pass, €20 combo-ticket with Monet's garden and house at Giverny (lets you skip the line at Giverny); Tue-Sun 10:00-18:00, Thu until 21:00, closed Mon; audioguide-€3 (includes temporary exhibits), 2 Rue Louis-Boilly, Mo: La Muette, tel. 01 44 96 50 33, www.marmottan.fr.

Left Bank

Opposite Notre-Dame, on the left bank of the Seine, is the Latin Quarter. (For more about this neighborhood, see the "Historic Paris Walk," earlier).

▲▲CLUNY MUSEUM (MUSEE NATIONAL DU MOYEN AGE)

The Cluny is a treasure trove of Middle Ages (Moyen Age) art. Located on the side of a Roman bathhouse, it offers close-up looks at stained glass, Notre-Dame carvings, fine goldsmithing and jewelry, and rooms of tapestries. The highlights are several original stained-glass windows from Sainte-Chapelle and the exquisite series of six Lady and the Unicorn tapestries: A delicate, as-medieval-as-can-be noble lady introduces a delighted unicorn to the senses of taste, hearing, sight, smell, and

Cluny Museum's Lady and the Unicorn tapestry

Luxembourg Garden

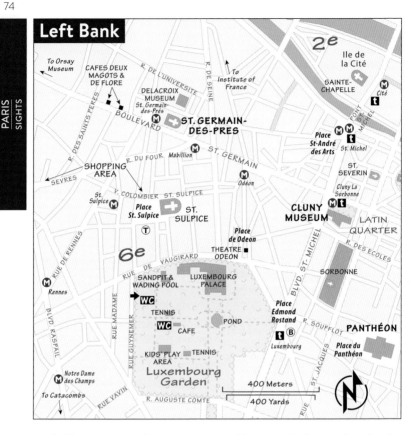

PARIS
SIGHTS

touch. The museum is undergoing a multiyear renovation.

Cost and Hours: €8, includes audioguide, free on first Sun of month, covered by Museum Pass (though pass holders pay €1 for audioguide); Wed-Mon 9:15-17:45, closed Tue; videoguide-€3; near corner of Boulevards St. Michel and St. Germain at 6 Place Paul Painlevé; Mo: Cluny-La Sorbonne, St. Michel, or Odéon; tel. 01 53 73 78 16, www.musee-moyenage.fr.

▲LUXEMBOURG GARDEN (JARDIN DU LUXEMBOURG)

This lovely 60-acre garden is an Impressionist painting brought to life. Slip into a green chair pondside, enjoy the radiant flower beds, go jogging, play tennis or basketball, sail a toy sailboat, or take in a chess game or puppet show. Some of the

park's prettiest (and quietest) sections lie around its perimeter.

Cost and Hours: Free, daily dawn until dusk, Mo: Odéon, RER/Train-B: Luxembourg.

▲CATACOMBS

Spiral down 60 feet below the street and walk a one-mile route through tunnels containing the anonymous bones of six million permanent Parisians. Lines to get in can be several hours long; it's essential to book online in advance. Once inside, allow an hour if you dawdle.

You'll descend 130 steps and land in a room with English posters describing 45 million years of ancient geology, then walk for 10 minutes through tunnels to reach the bones. Appreciate that some of these tunnels were originally built sans

Looking down the Champs-Elysées from the Arc de Triomphe

mortar. The sign, "Halt, this is the empire of the dead," announces your arrival at the bones. From here, shuffle along passageways of artfully arranged, skull-studded tibiae; admire 300-year-old sculptures cut into the walls of the catacombs; and see more cheery signs: "Happy is he who is forever faced with the hour of his death and prepares himself for the end every day." The highlight for me is the Crypt of the Passion (a.k.a. "the Barrel"), where bones are meticulously packed in a barrel shape hiding a support pillar.

Cost and Hours: €13, not covered by Museum Pass, Tue-Sun 10:00-20:30, closed Mon; purchase a timed-entry ticket online in advance at the website below or consider Fat Tire Tours' "Skip the Line" ticket (see page 41); otherwise arrive by 9:30 or after 18:00 to minimize wait; ticket booth closes at 19:30, come no later than 19:00 or risk not getting in; well-done audioguide-€5, pick up English visitors guide for explanations of key stops, tel. 01 43 22 47 63, www.catacombes.paris.fr.

Getting There: It's at 1 Place Denfert-Rochereau. Take the Métro to Denfert-Rochereau and follow *Sortie 1,* then find the lion in the big traffic circle; if he looked left rather than right, he'd stare right at the green entrance to the Catacombs.

Champs-Elysées and Nearby
▲▲▲CHAMPS-ELYSEES

This famous boulevard is Paris' backbone, with its greatest concentration of traffic (although it's delightfully traffic-free on the first Sunday of each month). From the Arc de Triomphe down Avenue des Champs-Elysées, all of France seems to converge on Place de la Concorde, the city's largest square. And though the Champs-Elysées has become as international as it is Parisian, a walk down the two-mile boulevard is still a must.

In 1667, Louis XIV opened the first section of the street, and it soon became *the* place to cruise in your carriage. (It still is today.) By the 1920s, this boulevard was

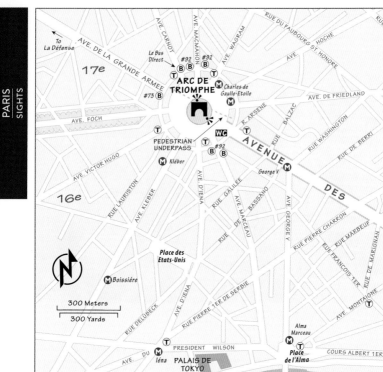

pure elegance—fancy residences, rich hotels, and cafés. Today it's home to big business, celebrity cafés, glitzy nightclubs, high-fashion shopping, and international people-watching. People gather here to celebrate Bastille Day (July 14), World Cup triumphs, and the finale of the Tour de France.

● **Self-Guided Walk:** Start at the Arc de Triomphe (Mo: Charles de Gaulle-Etoile; if you're planning to tour the Arc, do it before starting this walk, described next) and head downhill on the left-hand side. The arrival of McDonald's (at #140) was an unthinkable horror, but these days dining chez MacDo has become typically Parisian, and this branch is the most prof-

itable McDonald's in the world.

The Lido (#116) is Paris' largest burlesque-type cabaret (and a multiplex cinema). Across the boulevard is the flagship store of leather-bag maker Louis Vuitton (#101). Fouquet's café (#99) is a popular spot for French celebrities, especially movie stars—note the names in the sidewalk in front. Enter if you dare for a €10 espresso. Ladurée café (#75) is also classy but has a welcoming and affordable takeout bakery.

Continuing on, you pass international-brand stores, such as Sephora, Disney, and the Gap. Car buffs should park themselves at the sleek café in the Renault store (#53, open noon-midnight). The car exhibits change regularly, but a Formula

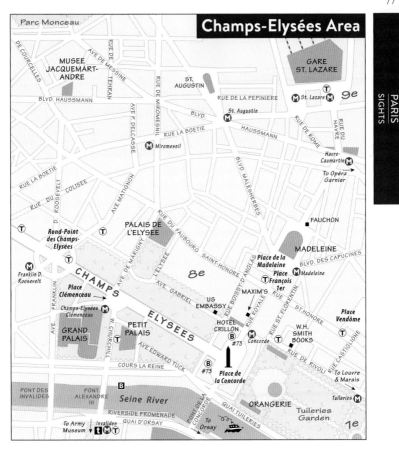

Champs-Elysées Area

One racecar made from 300,000 Legos is usually on display.

You can end your walk at the round Rond Point intersection (Mo: Franklin D. Roosevelt) or continue to obelisk-studded Place de la Concorde, Paris' largest square.

▲▲ARC DE TRIOMPHE

Napoleon had the magnificent Arc de Triomphe commissioned to commemorate his victory at the 1805 battle of Austerlitz. The foot of the arch is a stage on which the last two centuries of Parisian history have played out—from the funeral of Napoleon to the goose-stepping arrival of the Nazis to the triumphant return of Charles de Gaulle after the Allied liberation. Examine the carvings on the pillars,

featuring a mighty Napoleon and excitable Lady Liberty. Pay your respects at the Tomb of the Unknown Soldier. Then climb the 284 steps to the observation deck up top, with sweeping skyline panoramas and

Arc de Triomphe

Opéra Garnier

Chagall ceiling at the Opéra Garnier

a mesmerizing view down onto the traffic that swirls around the arch.

Cost and Hours: Free to view exterior; steps to rooftop-€12, free for those under age 18, free on first Sun of month Oct-March, covered by Museum Pass; daily 10:00-23:00, Oct-March until 22:30, last entry 45 minutes before closing; Place Charles de Gaulle, use underpass to reach arch, Mo: Charles de Gaulle-Etoile, tel. 01 55 37 73 77, www.paris-arc-de-triomphe.fr.

Avoiding Lines: A Museum Pass lets you bypass the slooow underground ticket line, unless you need to get free tickets for kids. You can tour much of the base of the Arc sans ticket, but you need one for the climb to the top (in a line you can't avoid). Lines disappear after 17:00—come for sunset.

Opéra Neighborhood

The glittering Garnier opera house anchors this neighborhood of broad boulevards and grand architecture. This area is also nirvana for high-end shoppers, with the opulent Galeries Lafayette and Printemps stores, and the sumptuous shops that line Place Vendôme and Place de la Madeleine. For a self-guided shopping stroll and a map of this area, see page 89.

▲▲OPERA GARNIER
(OPERA NATIONAL DE
PARIS—PALAIS GARNIER)

A gleaming grand theater of the belle époque, the Palais Garnier was built for Napoleon III and finished in 1875. From Avenue de l'Opéra, once lined with Paris'

most fashionable haunts, the facade suggests "all power to the wealthy." To see the interior, you have several choices: Take a guided tour (your best look), tour the public areas on your own (using the audioguide), or attend a performance. Its golden decor (mostly gold paint, not gilding) features statues, columns, and chandeliers, all set off by colorful ceiling paintings. Note that the auditorium is sometimes off-limits due to performances and rehearsals.

Cost and Hours: €11, not covered by Museum Pass, generally daily 10:00-16:30, mid-July-Aug until 18:00, closes for rehearsals and performances—most reliably open 10:00-13:00; 8 Rue Scribe, Mo: Opéra, RER/Train-A: Auber, www.operadeparis.fr/en/visits/palais-garnier.

Tours: The €5 audioguide gives a good self-guided tour. Guided tours in English run July-Aug at 11:30 and 14:30 daily; Sept-June Wed, Sat, and Sun only; check website below for off-season tours and to confirm times year-round, arrive 30 minutes early for security screening (€15.50, includes entry, 1.5 hours, tel. 01 40 01 17 89 or 08 25 05 44 05, www.cultival.fr/en).

Rick's Tip: *Across the street from the Opéra Garnier is the illustrious* **Café de la Paix** *(on Place de l'Opéra). It's been a meeting spot for the local glitterati for generations. If you can afford the coffee, this spot offers a delightful break.*

Baron Georges-Eugène Haussmann

The elegantly uniform streets that make Paris so Parisian are the work of Baron Haussmann (1809-1891), who oversaw the modernization of the city in the mid-19th century. He cleared out the cramped, higgledy-piggledy, unhygienic medieval cityscape and replaced it with broad, straight boulevards lined with stately buildings and linked by modern train stations.

The quintessential view of Haussmann's work is from the pedestrian island immediately in front of the Opéra Garnier. You're surrounded by Paris circa 1870, when it was the capital of the world. Gaze down the surrounding boulevards to find the column of Place Vendôme in one direction, and the Louvre in another. Haussmann's uniform, cohesive buildings are all five stories tall, with angled, black slate roofs and formal facades. The balconies on the second and fifth floors match those of their neighbors, creating strong lines of perspective as the buildings stretch down the boulevard.

But there was more than aesthetics to the plan. In pre-Haussmann Paris, angry rioters would take to the narrow streets, setting up barricades to hold back government forces (as made famous in Victor Hugo's *Les Misérables*). With Haussmann's new design, government troops could circulate easily and fire cannons down the long, straight boulevards. A whiff of "grapeshot"—chains, nails, and other buckshot-type shrapnel—could clear out any revolutionaries in a hurry.

Marais Neighborhood and Nearby

Naturally, when in Paris you want to see the big sights—but to experience the city, you also need to visit a vital neighborhood. The Marais fits the bill, with trendy boutiques and art galleries, edgy cafés, narrow streets, leafy squares, Jewish bakeries, aristocratic mansions, and fun nightlife—and it's filled with real Parisians. It's the perfect setting to appreciate the flair of this great city.

Place des Vosges and West
▲▲PLACE DES VOSGES

Henry IV built this centerpiece of the Marais in 1605 and called it "Place Royale." As he'd hoped, it turned the Marais into Paris' most exclusive neighborhood. Walk to the center, where Louis XIII, on horseback, gestures, "Look at this wonderful square my dad built." Study the architecture: nine pavilions (houses) per side. The two highest—at the front and back—were for the king and queen (but were never used). Warm red brickwork—some real, some fake—is topped with sloped slate roofs, chimneys, and another quaint relic of a bygone era: TV antennas.

The insightful writer **Victor Hugo** lived at #6 from 1832 to 1848. (It's at the southeast corner of the square, marked by the French flag.) This was when he wrote much of his most important work, including his biggest hit, *Les Misérables.* Inside this free museum you'll wander through eight plush rooms, enjoy a fine view of the square, and find good WCs (free, Tue-Sun 10:00-18:00, closed Mon; tel. 01 42 72 10 16, http://maisonsvictorhugo.paris.fr).

Sample the flashy art galleries ringing the square (the best ones are behind Louis). Ponder a daring new piece for that blank wall at home. Or consider a pleasant break at one of the recommended eateries on the square.

Relaxing at the Place des Vosges

Picasso Museum

▲▲PICASSO MUSEUM (MUSEE PICASSO)

Whatever you think about Picasso the man, as an artist he was unmatched in the 20th century for his daring and productivity. The Picasso Museum has the world's largest collection of his work—some 400 paintings, sculptures, sketches, and ceramics—spread across five levels of this mansion in the Marais. A visit here walks you through the full range of this complex man's life and art.

Cost and Hours: €12.50, covered by Museum Pass, free on first Sun of month and for those under age 18 with ID; open Tue-Fri 10:30-18:00, Sat-Sun from 9:30, closed Mon, last entry 45 minutes before closing; audioguide-€5, 5 Rue de Thori-gny, Mo: St. Sébastien-Froissart, St-Paul, or Chemin Vert, tel. 01 42 71 25 21, www. museepicassoparis.fr.

Visiting the Museum: The museum's fine audioguide is updated with each change to the exhibit. Floors 1 and 2 are the core of the museum with selections from its permanent collection. Floor 3 always features paintings from Picasso's personal collection—works of his that he never sold, and paintings by contemporaries (such as Miró, Matisse, Cézanne, and Braque) who inspired him.

Early Years and Early Cubism: In 1900, Picasso set out to make his mark in Paris. The brash Spaniard quickly became a poor, homesick foreigner, absorbing the styles of many painters while searching for his own artist's voice. When his best friend committed suicide, Picasso plunged into a **Blue Period,** painting emaciated beggars, hard-eyed pimps, and himself, bundled up against the cold, with eyes all cried out (*Autoportrait,* 1901).

In 1904, Picasso got a steady girlfriend, and suddenly saw the world through rose-colored glasses (the **Rose Period,** though the museum has very few works from this time). With his next-door neighbor, Georges Braque, Picasso invented Cubism, a fragmented, "cube"-shaped style. He'd fracture a figure (such as the musician in *Man with a Mandolin,* 1911) into a barely recognizable jumble of facets. Picasso sketched reality from every angle, then pasted it all together, a composite of different views.

Cubist Experiments: Modern art was being born. The first stage had been so-called Analytic Cubism: breaking the world down into small facets, to "analyze" the subject from every angle. Now it was time to "synthesize" it back together with the real world (Synthetic Cubism). Picasso created "constructions" that were essentially still-life paintings (a 2-D illusion) augmented with glued-on, real-life materials—wood, paper, rope, or chair caning (the real 3-D world). In a few short years, Picasso had turned painting in the direction it would go for the next 50 years.

During the gray and sad years of World War II, Picasso stayed in Paris. His beloved mother had died, and he endured an endless, bitter divorce while juggling his two longtime, feuding mistresses—as well as the occasional fling.

Later Years: At war's end, Picasso left Paris and all that emotional baggage behind, finding fun in the sun in the south of France. Sixty-five-year-old Pablo Picasso was reborn, enjoying worldwide fame. Picasso's Riviera works set the tone for the rest of his life—sunny, light-hearted, childlike, experimenting in new media, and using motifs of the sea, Greek mythology (fauns, centaurs), and animals (birds, goats, and pregnant baboons). Picasso was fertile to the end, still painting with bright thick colors at age 91.

▲▲POMPIDOU CENTER (CENTRE POMPIDOU)

One of Europe's greatest collections of far-out modern art is housed in the Musée National d'Art Moderne, on the fourth and fifth floors of this colorful exoskeletal building. Created ahead of its time, the modern and contemporary art in this collection is still waiting for the world to catch up.

The Pompidou Center and the square that fronts it are lively, with lots of people, street theater, and activity inside and out—a perpetual street fair. Kids of any age enjoy the fun, colorful fountain (an homage to composer Igor Stravinsky) next to the Pompidou Center.

Cost and Hours: €14, free on first Sun of month, Museum Pass covers permanent collection and escalators to sixth-floor panoramic views (plus occasional special exhibits); permanent collection open Wed-Mon 11:00-21:00, closed Tue, ticket counters close at 20:00; rest of the building open until 22:00 (Thu until 23:00); arrive after 17:00 to avoid crowds (mainly for special exhibits); free "Centre Pompidou" app, café on mezzanine, pricey view restaurant on level 6, Mo: Rambuteau or Hôtel de Ville, tel. 01 44 78 12 33, www.centrepompidou.fr.

Visiting the Museum: The Pompidou's "permanent" collection...isn't. But while

Ⓐ *Pompidou Center*

Ⓑ *Otto Dix,* Portrait of Journalist Sylvia von Harden

Ⓒ *Joan Miró,* Le Catalan

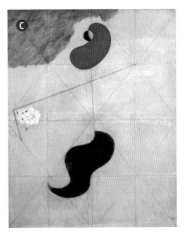

Marais Neighborhood & Nearby

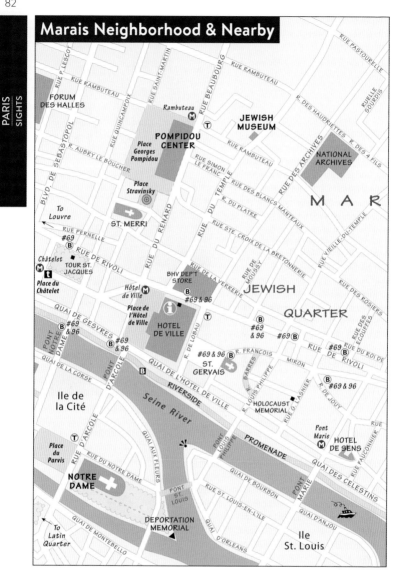

the paintings (and other pieces) change, the museum generally keeps the artists and various styles in a set order. You'll find this general scheme: ground floor—all services; basement—always photography exhibits and always free; floors 1 and 6—temporary exhibits (galleries 1-4); floors 4 and 5—the museum (what you're likely

here for). The museum starts on floor 5 with a one-way route, with the collection displayed in chronological order filling rooms in numerical order. It's that easy.

Use the museum's floor plans (posted on the wall) to find specific artists. See the classics—Picasso, Matisse, etc.—but be sure to leave time to browse the

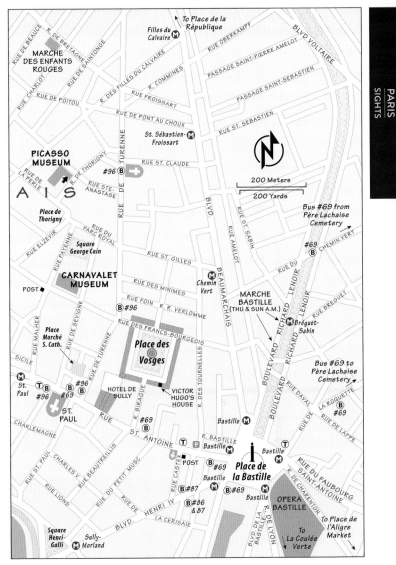

thought-provoking and fun art of more recent artists.

As you tour the Pompidou, remember that most of the artists, including foreigners, spent their formative years in Paris. In the 1910s, funky Montmartre was the mecca of Modernism—the era of Picasso, Braque, and Matisse. In the 1920s, the center shifted to the grand cafés of Montparnasse, where painters mingled with American expats such as Ernest Hemingway and Gertrude Stein. During World War II, it was Jean-Paul Sartre's Existentialist scene around St. Germain-des-Prés. After World War II, the global art focus moved to New York, but by the late 20th

Best Views over the City of Light

The brilliance of the City of Light is best appreciated by rising above it all. Many of the viewpoints listed here are free or covered by the Museum Pass; otherwise, expect to pay €8-20.

Eiffel Tower: It's hard to find a grander view of Paris than from the tower's second level (for most, it's better than from the top level). Go around sunset and stay after dark to see the tower illuminated; or go in the early morning to avoid the midday haze and crowds (not covered by Museum Pass, see page 68).

Arc de Triomphe: Without a doubt, this is the perfect place to see the glamorous Champs-Elysées (if you can manage the 284 steps). It's great during the day, but even greater at night, when the boulevard positively glitters (covered by Museum Pass, see page 77).

Steps of Sacré-Cœur: Join the party on Paris' only hilltop. Walk uphill, or take the funicular or Montmartrobus, then hunker down on Sacré-Cœur's steps to enjoy the sunset and territorial views over Paris. Stay in Montmartre for dinner, then see the view again after dark (free, see page 86).

Galeries Lafayette or **Printemps:** Take the escalator to the top floor of either department store (they sit side by side) for a stunning overlook of the old Opéra district (free, see page 78).

Pompidou Center: Take the escalator up and admire the beautiful cityscape along with the exciting modern art (the sixth floor is the top, but the fifth-floor outdoor terrace is more enjoyable). There may be better views over Paris, but this is the best one from a museum (covered by Museum Pass, see page 81).

Place du Trocadéro: This square, a 20-minute walk from the Eiffel Tower, is *the* place to see the tower. Come for a look at Monsieur Eiffel's festive creation day or night (when the tower is lit up), before or after your tower visit.

Arab World Institute: This building near Ile St. Louis has 180-degree views over the river from its roof terrace (free for views, Tue-Sun 10:00-18:00, closed Mon; for terrace view don't wait in special exhibit line—ask for entrance for *"la terrasse";* 1 Rue des Fossés Saint-Bernard, Place Mohammed V, Mo: Jussieu, tel. 01 40 51 38 38, www.imarabe.org).

Père Lachaise Cemetery

century, Paris had reemerged as a cultural touchstone for the world of modern art.

Rick's Tip: *The sixth floor of the Pompidou has* **stunning views of the Paris cityscape.** *Your Pompidou ticket or Museum Pass gets you there, or you can buy the €5 View of Paris ticket (good for the sixth floor only; doesn't include museum entry).*

East of Place des Vosges
▲▲PERE LACHAISE CEMETERY (CIMETIERE DU PERE LACHAISE)

Littered with the tombstones of many of the city's most illustrious dead, this is your best one-stop look at Paris' fascinating, romantic past residents. More like a small city, the cemetery is big and confusing, but it holds the graves of Frédéric Chopin, Molière, Edith Piaf, Oscar Wilde, Gertrude Stein, Jim Morrison, Héloïse and Abélard, and many more.

Cost and Hours: Free, Mon-Fri 8:00-18:00, Sat from 8:30, Sun from 9:00, until 17:30 in winter; two blocks from Mo: Gambetta (do not go to Mo: Père Lachaise) and two blocks from bus #69's last stop; tel. 01 55 25 82 10, searchable map available at unofficial website: www.pere-lachaise.com.

Visiting the Cemetery: Enclosed by a massive wall and lined with 5,000 trees, the peaceful, car-free lanes and dirt paths of Père Lachaise cemetery encourage parklike meandering. Named for Father *(Père)* La Chaise, whose job was listening to Louis XIV's sins, the cemetery is relatively new, having opened in 1804 to accommodate Paris' expansion. Today, this 100-acre city of the dead (pop. 70,000) still accepts new residents, but real estate prices are sky high (a 21-square-foot plot costs more than €11,000).

This cemetery, with thousands of graves and tombs crammed every which way, has only a few pedestrian pathways to help you navigate. The map available from a nearby florist can also help guide you. I recommend taking a one-way tour through the cemetery, starting from the convenient Métro/bus stops at Place Gambetta, connecting a handful of graves from some of this necropolis' best-known residents, and taking a last bow at either the Père Lachaise or Philippe Auguste Métro stops, or a nearby bus #69 stop.

🎧 Download my free Père Lachaise Cemetery audio tour.

Rick's Tip: *To* **beat the crowds at Montmartre,** *come on a weekday or early on weekend mornings.*

Montmartre

Paris' highest hill, topped by Sacré-Cœur Basilica and rated ▲▲, is best known as the home of cabaret nightlife and bohemian artists. Struggling painters, poets, dreamers, and drunkards came here for cheap rent, untaxed booze, rustic landscapes, and views of the underwear of high-kicking cancan girls at the Moulin Rouge. These days, the hill is equal parts charm and kitsch—still vaguely village-like but mobbed with tourists and pickpockets on sunny weekends. Come for a bit of history, a getaway from Paris' noisy boulevards, and the view.

▲SACRE-CŒUR

You'll spot Sacré-Cœur, the Byzantine-looking white basilica atop Montmartre, from most viewpoints in Paris. Though only 130 years old, it's impressive and iconic, with a climbable dome, and marks Paris' highest natural point (430 feet). The church was finished only a century ago by Parisians humiliated by German invaders. Roman Catholics built it as a kind of penance for how the surrounding neighborhood sowed rebelliousness and division. Many French people were disgusted that in 1871 their government actually shot its own citizens, the Communards, who held out here on Montmartre after the French leadership surrendered to the Prussians.

Cost and Hours: Church-free, daily 6:00-22:30; dome-€6, not covered by Museum Pass, daily 9:30-19:00, Oct-April until 17:00; modest dress required, tel. 01 53 41 89 00, www.sacre-coeur-montmartre.com.

Getting There: You can take the Métro to the Anvers stop (to avoid the stairs up to Sacré-Cœur, use one more Métro ticket and ride up on the funicular). Alternatively, from Place Pigalle, you can take the "Montmartrobus," a city bus that drops you right by Sacré-Cœur (Funiculaire stop, costs one Métro ticket, 4/hour). A taxi from near the Seine saves time and avoids sweat (about €20, €25 at night).

Visiting the Church: The Sacré-Cœur (Sacred Heart) Basilica's exterior, with its onion domes and bleached-bone pallor, looks ancient, but it was finished only a century ago by Parisians humiliated by German invaders. The five-domed, Roman-Byzantine-looking basilica took 44 years to build (1875-1919). It stands on a foundation of 83 pillars sunk 130

Sacré-Cœur

feet deep, necessary because the ground beneath was honeycombed with gypsum mines. The exterior is laced with gypsum, which whitens with age.

Take a clockwise spin around the crowded interior to see impressive mosaics, a statue of St. Thérèse, a scale model of the church, and three stained-glass windows dedicated to Joan of Arc. Pause near the Stations of the Cross mosaic to give St. Peter's bronze foot a rub. For an unobstructed panoramic view of Paris, climb 260 feet (300 steps) up the tight and claustrophobic spiral stairs to the top of the dome.

EXPERIENCES

Seine Cruises

Several companies run one-hour boat cruises on the Seine. For a fun experience, cruise at twilight or after dark. The first three companies are convenient to Rue Cler hotels, and run daily year-round (April-Oct 10:00-22:30, 2-3/hour; Nov-March shorter hours, runs hourly). Check their websites for discounts.

Bateaux-Mouches departs from Pont de l'Alma's right bank and has the biggest open-top, double-decker boats (higher up means better views). But this company caters to tour groups, making their boats jammed and noisy (€13.50, kids 4-12-€6, tel. 01 42 25 96 10, www.bateaux-mouches.fr). **Vedettes de Paris** boats also anchor below the Eiffel Tower and offer better outdoor seating on most of their boats (€15 standard one-hour cruise, €12 one-way, €16 round-trip with stop at Notre-Dame, www.vedettesdeparis.fr). **Vedettes du Pont Neuf** offers essentially the same one-hour tour as the other companies with smaller boats; it starts and ends at Pont Neuf. The boats feature a live guide whose delivery (in English and French) may be as stiff as a recorded narration (€14, kids 4-12-€7, tip requested, nearly 2/hour, daily 10:30-22:30, tel. 01 46 33 98 38, www.vedettesdupontneuf.com).

Bus Restaurants

Dine to soft jazz as you glide along Paris' most famous boulevards and around its greatest monuments on an elegant double-decker bus restaurant. Dining is on the upper deck well above cars below, affording great views and glimpses into Parisian apartments. Buses are designed from scratch for this purpose with a kitchen, drink holders, big windows, toilets, and more. They move slowly, making drinking and dining a breeze. Two companies offer these tours: **Bus Toqué** (€56 for lunch, €90 for dinner, mobile 06 21 40 20 41, www.bustoque.fr) and **Bustronome** (tel. 09 54 44 45 55, www.bustronome.com).

Shopping

Wandering among elegant boutiques provides a break from the heavy halls of the Louvre, and, if you approach it right, a little cultural enlightenment. Even if you don't intend to buy anything, budget some time for window shopping, or, as the French call it, *faire du lèche-vitrines* ("window licking").

Before you enter a Parisian store, remember the following points:

In small stores, always say, *"Bonjour, Madame* or *Mademoiselle* or *Monsieur"* when entering. And remember to say *"Au revoir, Madame* or *Mademoiselle* or *Monsieur"* when leaving.

The customer is not always right. In fact, figure the clerk is doing you a favor by waiting on you.

Except in department stores, it's not normal for the customer to handle clothing. Ask first before you pick up an item: *"Je peux?"* (zhuh puh), meaning, "Can I?"

Saturday afternoons are *très* busy, but stores are generally closed on Sunday. Exceptions include the Galeries Lafayette store near the Opéra Garnier, the Carrousel du Louvre (underground shopping mall at the Louvre with a Printemps department store), and some shops near Sèvres-Babylone, along the Champs-Elysées, and in the Marais.

Don't feel obliged to buy. If a shop-keeper offers assistance, say, *"Je regarde, merci."* (Just looking, thank you.)

For information on VAT refunds and customs regulations, see the Practicalities chapter.

Department Stores (Les Grands Magasins)

Parisian department stores begin with their showy perfume and purse sections, almost always central on the ground floor. Helpful information desks are usually located at the main entrances near the perfume section (with floor plans in English). Stores generally have affordable restaurants (some with view terraces) and a good selection of fairly priced souvenirs and toys. Opening hours are customarily Monday through Saturday from 10:00 to 19:00 or 20:00. The major stores are open on Sundays and later on Thursdays, and all are jammed on Saturdays. You'll find both Galeries Lafayette and Printemps stores in several neighborhoods. The most convenient and most elegant sit side by side behind the Opéra Garnier, complementing that monument's similar, classy ambience (Mo: Chaussée d'Antin-La Fayette, Havre-Caumartin, or Opéra).

Boutique Strolls

Most shops are closed on Sunday, which is the perfect day to head for the **Marais,** where many shops remain open on Sunday (and close on Saturday) and most of the neighborhood is off-limits to cars. For eclectic, avant-garde boutiques, peruse the artsy shops between Place des Vosges and the Pompidou Center.

➔ PLACE DE LA MADELEINE TO PLACE DE L'OPERA

The ritzy streets connecting several high-priced squares—Place de la Madeleine, Place de la Concorde, Place Vendôme, and Place de l'Opéra—form a miracle mile of gourmet food shops, glittering jewelry stores, posh hotels, exclusive clothing

Sampling perfume

boutiques, and people who spend more on clothes in one day than I do in a year. To trace this route, see the "Opéra Neighborhood" map.

Start at Eglise de la Madeleine (Mo: Madeleine). In the northeast corner at #24 is the black-and-white awning of **Fauchon.** Founded on this location in 1886, this bastion of over-the-top edibles became famous around the world, catering to the refined tastes of the rich and famous. **Hédiard** (#21, northwest corner of the square) is older than Fauchon, and it's weathered the tourist mobs a bit better, though it may be closed for renovation during your visit. Hédiard's small red containers—of mustards, jams, coffee, candies, and tea—make great souvenirs.

Step inside tiny **La Maison des Truffe** (#19) to get a whiff of the product—truffles, those prized, dank, and dirty cousins of mushrooms. Check out the tiny jars in the display case. The venerable **Mariage Frères** (#17) shop demonstrates how good tea can smell and how beautifully it can be displayed. At **Caviar Kaspia** (#16), you can add caviar, eel, and vodka to your truffle collection.

Continue along, past **Marquise de Sévigné chocolates** (#11) and Fauchon's new razzle-dazzle hotel, then cross to the island in the middle of **Boulevard Malesherbes.** When the street officially opened in 1863, it ushered in the Golden Age of this neighborhood. Continue across Boulevard Malesherbes. Straight

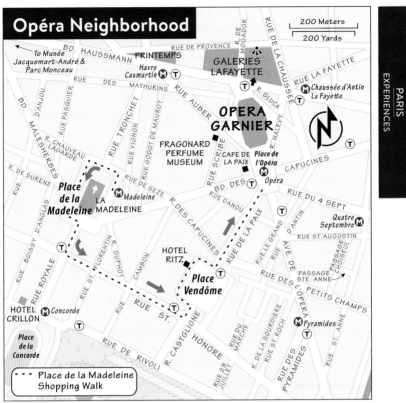

Opéra Neighborhood

ahead is **Patrick Roger Chocolates** (#3), famous for its chocolates, and even more so for M. Roger's huge, whimsical, 150-pound chocolate sculptures of animals and fanciful creatures.

Turning right down **Rue Royale,** there's Dior, Chanel, and Gucci. At Rue St. Honoré, turn left and cross Rue Royale, pausing in the middle for a great view both ways. Check out **Ladurée** (#16) for an out-of-this-world pastry break in the busy 19th-century tea salon, or to just pick up some world-famous macarons. Continue east down **Rue St. Honoré.** The street is a three-block parade of chic boutiques—L'Oréal cosmetics, Jimmy Choo shoes, Valentino, and so on. Looking for a €1,000 handbag? This is your spot.

Find the shortcut on the left at #362 or turn left on Rue de Castiglione to reach

Place Vendôme. This octagonal square is *très* elegant—enclosed by symmetrical Mansart buildings around a 150-foot column. On the left side is the original Hôtel Ritz, opened in 1898. The square is also known for its upper-crust jewelry and designer stores—Van Cleef & Arpels, Dior, Chanel, Cartier, and others (if you have to ask how much...).

Leave Place Vendôme by continuing straight, up **Rue de la Paix**—strolling by still more jewelry, high-priced watches, and crystal—and enter **Place de l'Opéra:** You're in the middle of Right Bank glamour. Here you'll find the Opéra Garnier (described under Sights). If you're shopping until you're dropping, the Galeries Lafayette and Printemps department stores are located a few blocks up Rue Halévy.

SEVRES-BABYLONE TO ST. SULPICE

This Left Bank shopping area lets you sample smart clothing boutiques and clever window displays—and be tempted by tasty treats—while enjoying one of Paris' more attractive and boutique-filled neighborhoods (see "Left Bank" map, earlier).

Start at the Sèvres-Babylone Métro stop (take the Métro). You'll find the **Bon Marché,** Paris' oldest department store. Continue along Rue de Sèvres, working your way to Place St. Sulpice and making detours left and right as the spirit moves you. You'll pass some of Paris' smartest boutiques and coolest cafés, such as **Hermès** (at #17), and **Au Sauvignon Café** (at #10). Make a short detour up Rue du Cherche-Midi and find Paris' most celebrated bread—beautiful round loaves with designer crust—at the low-key **Poilâne** at #8. At the end of your walk, spill into Place St. Sulpice, with its big, twin-tower church. **Café de la Mairie** is a great spot to sip a *café crème,* admire the lovely square, and consider your next move. If you'd like more shopping options, you're in the heart of boutique shopping. As for me, stick a *fourchette* in me—I'm done.

Nightlife

Paris is brilliant after dark. Save energy from your day's sightseeing and experience the City of Light lit. Whether it's a concert at Sainte-Chapelle, a boat ride on the Seine, a walk in Montmartre, a hike up the Arc de Triomphe, or a late-night café, you'll see Paris at its best.

Jazz and Blues Clubs

With a lively mix of American, French, and international musicians, Paris has been an internationally acclaimed jazz capital since World War II. You'll pay €12-25 to enter a jazz club (may include one drink; if not, expect to pay €5-10 per drink; beer is cheapest). See *L'Officiel des Spectacles* under "Concerts" for listings, or, even better, the *Paris Voice* website. You can also check each club's website (all have English versions), or drop by the clubs to check out the calendars posted on their front doors. Music starts after 21:00 in most clubs. Some offer dinner concerts from about 20:30 on. Here are several good bets:

Caveau de la Huchette: This fun, characteristic old jazz/dance club fills an ancient Latin Quarter cellar with live jazz and frenzied dancing every night (admission about €15, €10 for those under 25, drinks from €7, daily from 21:30, no reservations needed, buy tickets at the door, 5 Rue de la Huchette, Mo: St. Michel, tel. 01 43 26 65 05, www.caveaudelahuchette.fr).

Autour de Midi et Minuit: This Old World bistro sits at the foot of Montmartre, above a *cave à jazz.* Eat upstairs if you like, then make your way down to the basement to find bubbling jam sessions Tuesday through Thursday and concerts on Friday and Saturday nights (no cover, €5 minimum drink order Tue-Thu; €20-25 cover Fri-Sat includes one drink; jam sessions at 21:30, concerts usually at 22:00; no music Sun-Mon; 11 Rue Lepic, Mo: Blanche or Abbesses, tel. 01 55 79 16 48, www.autourdemidi.fr).

Other Venues: For a spot teeming with late-night activity and jazz, go to the two-block-long Rue des Lombards, at Boulevard Sébastopol, midway between the river and the Pompidou Center (Mo: Châtelet). **Au Duc des Lombards** is one of the most popular and respected jazz clubs in Paris, with concerts nightly in a great, plush, 110-seat theater-like setting (€30-55, €60-90 with dinner, buy online and arrive early for best seats, reasonable drink prices, shows usually at 19:30 and 21:30, 42 Rue des Lombards, tel. 01 42 33 22 88, www.ducdeslombards.fr). **Le Sunside** is just a block away. The club offers two little stages (ground floor and downstairs): "Le Sunset" stage tends toward contemporary world jazz; "le Sunside" stage features more traditional and acoustic jazz (concerts €20-30, a few are free; 60 Rue des Lombards, tel. 01 40 26 46 60, www.sunset-sunside.com).

Paris churches host frequent concerts.

Extend your sightseeing into the night.

Classical Concerts

For classical music on any night, consult *L'Officiel des Spectacles* magazine (check "Classique" under "Concerts" for listings), and look for posters at tourist-oriented churches. From March through November, these churches regularly host concerts: St. Sulpice, St. Germain-des-Prés, La Madeleine, St. Eustache, St. Julien-le-Pauvre, and Sainte-Chapelle.

Sainte-Chapelle: Enjoy the pleasure of hearing Mozart, Bach, or Vivaldi, surrounded by 800 years of stained glass (unheated—bring a sweater). The acoustical quality is surprisingly good. There are usually two concerts per evening, at about 19:00 and 20:30; specify which one you want when you buy or reserve your ticket. VIP tickets get you a seat in rows 3-10 (about €55), Prestige tickets cover the next 10 rows (€45), and Normal tickets are the last five rows (€35). Seats are unassigned within each section, so arrive at least 30 minutes early to get through the security line and snare a good view.

You can book at the box office, by phone, or online. Several companies sell tickets online. The small box office (with schedules and tickets) is to the left of the chapel entrance gate (8 Boulevard du Palais, Mo: Cité), or call 01 42 77 65 65 or 06 67 30 65 65 for schedules and reservations. You can leave your message in English—just speak clearly and spell your name. You can check schedules and buy your ticket at www.euromusicproductions.fr or www.ticketac.com).

Other Venues: Look also for daytime concerts in parks, such as the Luxembourg Garden. Even the Galeries Lafayette department store offers concerts. Many of these concerts are free *(entrée libre)*, such as the Sunday atelier concert sponsored by the American Church (generally Sept-June at 17:00 but not every week and not in Dec, 65 Quai d'Orsay, Mo: Invalides, RER/Train-C: Pont de l'Alma, tel. 01 40 62 05 00, www.acparis.org). The Army Museum offers inexpensive afternoon and evening classical music concerts all year round (for programs—in French only—see www.musee-armee.fr). There are also concerts at the Louvre's auditorium (www.louvre.fr/en/auditorium-louvre/music).

Night Walks

Go for an evening walk to best appreciate the City of Light. Break for ice cream, pause at a café, and enjoy the sidewalk entertainers as you join the post-dinner Parisian parade. (Avoid poorly lit areas and stick to main thoroughfares.)

Trocadéro and Eiffel Tower: Worth ▲▲▲, this is one of Paris' most spectacular views at night. Take the Métro to the Trocadéro stop and join the party on Place du Trocadéro for a magnificent view of the glowing Eiffel Tower. It's a festival of hawkers, gawkers, drummers, and entertainers.

Champs-Elysées and the Arc de Tri-omphe: The ▲▲ Avenue des Champs-Elysées is best after dark. Start at the Arc de Triomphe (open late), then stroll down Paris' glittering grand promenade.

Ile St. Louis and Notre-Dame: This ▲▲ stroll features floodlit views of Notre-Dame and a taste of the Latin Quarter. Find your way to the east end of Rue St. Louis-en-l'Ile, stopping for dinner—or at least a Berthillon ice cream (at #31) or Amorino Gelati (at #47). At the west end of Ile St. Louis, cross Pont St. Louis to Ile de la Cité, with a view of Notre-Dame (undergoing construction). Cross the bridge to the Left Bank to stroll through the lively Latin Quarter.

EATING

Entire books (and lives) are dedicated to eating in Paris. There is no "Parisian cuisine" to speak of (only French onion soup is truly Parisian), but it draws from the best of France.

My restaurant recommendations are mostly centered on the same great neighborhoods as my hotel listings; you can come home exhausted after a busy day of sightseeing and find a good selection of eateries right around the corner. Serious eaters looking for even more sugges-tions should consult the always appe-tizing www.parisbymouth.com, an eat-ing-and-drinking guide to Paris.

To save piles of euros, go to a bakery for takeout, or stop at a café for lunch. Cafés and brasseries are happy to serve a *plat du jour* (plate of the day, about €16-24) or a chef-like salad (about €12-16) day or night. To save even more, consider picnics (tasty takeout dishes available at charcuteries). Try eating your big meal at lunch, when many fine restaurants offer their dinnertime fixed-price *menus* at a reduced price.

Linger longer over dinner—restau-rants expect you to enjoy a full meal. Most restaurants I've listed have set-price *menus* between €26 and €40. In most cases, the few extra euros you pay are well spent and open up a variety of better choices. Remember that a service charge is included in the prices (so little or no tip-ping is expected).

Rue Cler Neighborhood
On Rue Cler
(Mo: Ecole Militaire)

$ Café du Marché boasts the best seats on Rue Cler. The owner's philosophy: Brasserie on speed—crank out good enough food at fair prices to appreciative locals and savvy tourists. It's high-energy, with young waiters who barely have time to smile...*très* Parisian. The chalkboard lists your choices: good, hearty salads or more filling *plats du jour*. Arrive before 19:00 to avoid waiting (serves continuously, daily 11:00-23:00, no reservations, at the corner of Rue Cler and Rue du Champ de Mars, 38 Rue Cler, tel. 01 47 05 51 27).

$ Le Petit Cler is an adorable and popular little bistro with long leather booths, a vintage interior, tight ranks of tiny and cramped tables—indoors and out, and simple, tasty, inexpensive dishes such as €10 omelets and €9 soups. Eating outside here with a view of the Rue Cler action can be marvelous (delicious *pots de crème*, daily, opens early for dinner, arrive early or call in advance, 29 Rue Cler, tel. 01 45 50 17 50).

Close to Ecole Militaire
(Mo: Ecole Militaire)

$$ Café le Bosquet is a contemporary Parisian brasserie where you'll dine for a decent price inside or outside on a broad sidewalk. Come here for standard café fare—salad, French onion soup, *steak-frites*, or a *plat du jour*. Lanky owner "Jeff" offers three-course meals and *plats* (serves nonstop, closed Sun, corner of Rue du Champ de Mars at 46 Avenue Bosquet, tel. 01 45 51 38 13, www.bosquetparis.com).

$$$ La Terrasse du 7ème is a sprawling, happening café with grand outdoor seating and a living room-like interior with comfy love seats. Chairs face the street, as a meal here is like dinner theater—and the show is slice-of-life Paris (good *salades*, French onion soup, and foie gras, nonstop service daily until at least 24:00, tel. 01 45 55 00 02).

West of Avenue Bosquet
(Mo: Ecole Militaire)

$$$$ Les Fables de la Fontaine is a fine place to relax over a gourmet dinner with appealing seating inside or out on a picturesque square. It has a Michelin star yet maintains fair prices and friendly staff. While the chef's specialty is fish, he also serves a few meat dishes (€75 tasting *menu*, less for à la carte, book ahead on weekends, daily, 131 Rue St. Dominique, tel. 01 44 18 37 55, www.lesfablesdelafontaine.net).

$$$ La Fontaine de Mars, a longtime favorite and neighborhood institution, is charmingly situated on a tiny, jumbled square with tables jammed together for the serious business of eating. Reserve in advance for a table on the ground floor or square, and pass on the upstairs room (superb foie gras and desserts, daily, 129 Rue St. Dominique, tel. 01 47 05 46 44, www.fontainedemars.com).

$$ Le P'tit Troquet is a petite eatery taking you back to the Paris of the 1920s. Anna serves while hubby José cooks a tasty range of traditional choices. The homey charm of the tight little dining room makes this place a delight (€36 three-course dinner *menu* available for €25 at lunch, dinner service from 18:30, closed Sun, reservations smart, 28 Rue de l'Exposition, tel. 01 47 05 80 39, www.leptittroquet.fr).

$ Le Royal is a tiny neighborhood fixture offering the cheapest meals in the area. This humble time-warp place comes with prices and decor from another era. Parisians dine here because "it's like eating at home." Gentle Guillaume is a fine host (closed Sat-Sun, 212 Rue de Grenelle, tel. 01 47 53 92 90).

Marais
On or Near Romantic Place des Vosges
(Mo: St-Paul, Bastille, or Chemin Vert)

$$$ La Place Royale offers an exceptional location on the square with comfortable seating inside or out, and is

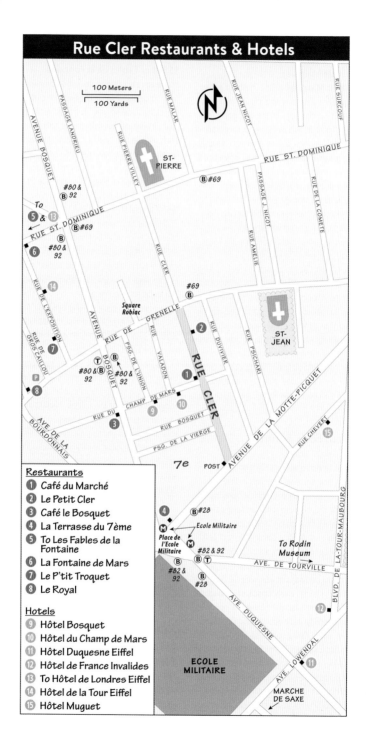

Rue Cler Restaurants & Hotels

Restaurants
1. Café du Marché
2. Le Petit Cler
3. Café le Bosquet
4. La Terrasse du 7ème
5. To Les Fables de la Fontaine
6. La Fontaine de Mars
7. Le P'tit Troquet
8. Le Royal

Hotels
9. Hôtel Bosquet
10. Hôtel du Champ de Mars
11. Hôtel Duquesne Eiffel
12. Hôtel de France Invalides
13. To Hôtel de Londres Eiffel
14. Hôtel de la Tour Eiffel
15. Hôtel Muguet

good for a relaxed lunch or dinner. The hearty cuisine is priced well and served nonstop all day, and the lengthy wine list is reasonable. The €42 dinner *menu* comes with three courses, a half-bottle of wine per person, and coffee; or just order a salad—or split one before a main course—and call it good (lunch specials, daily, reserve ahead to dine outside under the arcade, 2 bis Place des Vosges, tel. 01 42 78 58 16).

$$$ **Chez Janou,** a Provençal bistro, tumbles out of its corner building and fills its broad sidewalk with happy eaters. Don't let the trendy and youthful crowd intimidate you: It's relaxed and charming, with helpful and patient service. The curbside tables are inviting, but I'd sit inside (with very tight seating) to immerse myself in the happy commotion (daily—book ahead or arrive when it opens at 19:00, 2 blocks beyond Place des Vosges at 2 Rue Roger Verlomme, tel. 01 42 72 28 41, www.chezjanou.com).

$$$ **Le Petit Marché,** popular with tourists, delivers a cozy bistro experience inside and out with friendly service and a tasty cuisine that blends French classics with a slight Asian influence (daily, 9 Rue du Béarn, tel. 01 42 72 06 67).

Near Place de la Bastille
(Mo: Bastille)

$$$ **Brasserie Bofinger,** an institution for over a century, specializes in seafood and traditional cuisine with Alsatian flair. You'll eat in a sprawling interior, surrounded by brisk, black-and-white-attired waiters. Come here for the one-of-a-kind ambience in the elaborately decorated ground-floor rooms, reminiscent of the Roaring Twenties. Reserve ahead to dine under the grand 1919 *coupole*—avoid eating upstairs—(open daily for lunch and dinner, fun kids' menu, 5 Rue de la Bastille, don't be confused by the lesser "Petite" Bofinger across the street, tel. 01 42 72 87 82, www.bofingerparis.com).

$$$ **Le Temps des Cerises** is a warm place with wads of character, a young and lively vibe, tight inside seating, and a couple of outdoor tables. (There are a few more upstairs that I'd avoid.) Come for a glass of wine at the small zinc bar, and stay for a very tasty dinner. Owner Ben takes good care of his guests and serves generous portions (reasonable wine list, daily, at the corner of Rue du Petit Musc and Rue de la Cerisaie, tel. 01 42 72 08 63).

In the Heart of the Marais
(Mo: St-Paul)

$$$ **Chez Mademoiselle**'s country-elegant, candlelit decor recalls charming owner Alexia's previous career as a French *comédienne*. Enjoy a French-paced (a.k.a. slow) dinner in a relaxing atmosphere (tables have generous spacing) inside or at a sidewalk table. Let Alexia share her enthusiasm for her seasonal dishes before you choose (good wine list, daily from 19:30, 16 Rue Charlemagne, tel. 01 42 72 14 16).

$$ **Le Metropolitan** is a tiny, easygoing bistro serving top-quality cuisine to those in the know. The young chef's dishes are creative and delicious. Come early (opens at 19:00) or book ahead (closed Sun, 8 Rue de Jouy, tel. 09 81 20 37 38, www.metroresto.fr).

$$ **On Place du Marché Ste. Catherine:** This small, romantic square, just off Rue St. Antoine, is cloaked in extremely Parisian, leafy-square ambience. It feels like the Latin Quarter but classier. On a balmy evening, this is a neighborhood favorite, with a handful of restaurants offering mediocre cuisine (you're here for the setting). It's also family-friendly: Most places serve French hamburgers, and kids can dance around the square while parents breathe. You'll find three French bistros with similar features and menus: **Le Marché, Chez Joséphine,** and **Le Bistrot de la Place** (all open daily, cheaper for lunch, tight seating on simple chairs indoors and out).

Marais Restaurants & Hotels

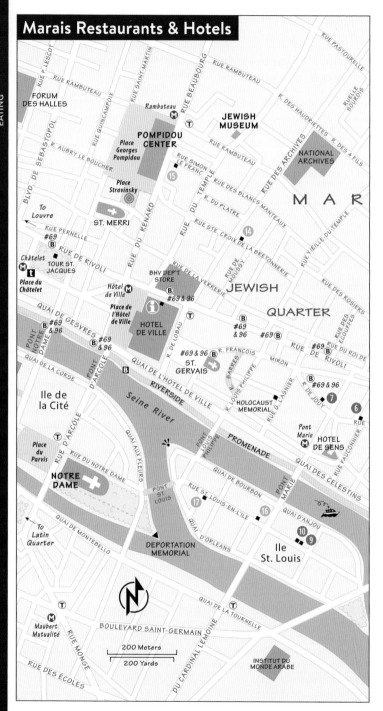

FORUM
DES HALLES

RUE P. LESCOT

RUE RAMBUTEAU

RUE QUINCAMPOIX

RUE SAINT-MARTIN

RUE RAMBUTEAU

RUE BEAUBOURG

RUE PASTOURELLE

RUELLE
SOURDIS

R. DES HAUDRIETTES

R. DES 4 FILS

Rambuteau

POMPIDOU
CENTER

Place
Georges
Pompidou

BLVD. DE SEBASTOPOL

R. AUBRY LE BOUCHER

JEWISH
MUSEUM

RUE RAMBUTEAU

RUE DES ARCHIVES

NATIONAL
ARCHIVES

M A R

Place
Stravinsky

ST. MERRI

RUE SIMON
LE FRANC

RUE DES BLANCS MANTEAUX

RUE DU TEMPLE

R. DU PLATRE

RUE STE. CROIX DE LA BRETONNERIE

RUE VIEILLE-DU-TEMPLE

15

14

To
Louvre

RUE PERNELLE
#69
B

Châtelet

RUE DE RIVOLI

RUE DU RENARD

BHV DEP'T
STORE

RUE DE LA VERRERIE

RUE DE
MOUSSY

RUE DES ROSIERS

TOUR ST.
JACQUES

Place du
Châtelet

Hôtel
de Ville

Place de
l'Hôtel
de Ville

HOTEL
DE VILLE

JEWISH

QUARTER

#69 & 96

B
#69
& 96

#69 B

RUE DES
ECOUFFES

B
#69
& 96

B

RUE DE RIVOLI

QUAI DE GESVRES

B #69
& 96

B #69
& 96

PONT
NOTRE
DAME

QUAI DE LA CORSE

R. DE LOBAU

QUAI DE L'HOTEL DE VILLE

#69 & 96 B
ST.
GERVAIS

R. FRANCOIS
MIRON

B
#69 B

RUE DU ROI DE

RIVERSIDE

Seine River

D'ARCOLE

PONT

B

Ile de
la Cité

R. BARRES

R. LOUIS PHILIPPE

HOLOCAUST
MEMORIAL

RUE G. LASNIER

RUE DE JOUY

#69 & 96

7

6

RUE

Place
du
Parvis

RUE D'ARCOLE

RUE DU NOTRE DAME

QUAI AUX FLEURS

Pont
Marie

PROMENADE

HOTEL
DE SENS

RUE FAUCONNIER

QUAI DES CELESTINS

NOTRE
DAME

PONT
ST.
LOUIS

PONT
LOUIS
PHILIPPE

QUAI DE BOURBON

RUE ST. LOUIS-EN-L'ILE

PONT
MARIE

QUAI D'ANJOU

17

16

To
Latin
Quarter

QUAI DE MONTEBELLO

DEPORTATION
MEMORIAL

QUAI D'ORLEANS

Ile
St. Louis

10
9

N

BOULEVARD SAINT-GERMAIN

QUAI DE LA TOURNELLE

Maubert
Mutualité

RUE MONGE

RUE DES ECOLES

200 Meters
200 Yards

DU CARDINAL LEMOINE

INSTITUT DU
MONDE ARABE

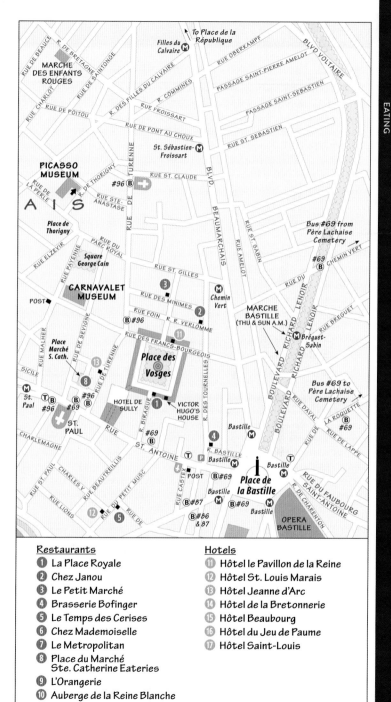

Restaurants
1 La Place Royale
2 Chez Janou
3 Le Petit Marché
4 Brasserie Bofinger
5 Le Temps des Cerises
6 Chez Mademoiselle
7 Le Metropolitan
8 Place du Marché
   Ste. Catherine Eateries
9 L'Orangerie
10 Auberge de la Reine Blanche

Hotels
11 Hôtel le Pavillon de la Reine
12 Hôtel St. Louis Marais
13 Hôtel Jeanne d'Arc
14 Hôtel de la Bretonnerie
15 Hôtel Beaubourg
16 Hôtel du Jeu de Paume
17 Hôtel Saint-Louis

The Paris Food Scene

Food Tours

Note that several of the listings under Cooking Classes below also offer food tours.

Paris by Mouth offers well-respected yet casual small-group tours, with a maximum of seven foodies per group (€110/3 hours, includes tastings, www.parisbymouth.com, tasteparisbymouth@gmail.com).

At **Edible Paris,** friendly Canadian Rosa Jackson designs personalized itineraries based on your interests (unguided itineraries-€125-200, guided tours-€300 for 1-2 people, larger groups welcome, mobile 06 81 67 41 22, www.edible-paris.com, rosa@rosajackson.com).

Cooking Classes

At **Les Secrets Gourmands de Noémie,** charming and knowledgeable Noémie shares her culinary secrets with hands-on fun in the kitchen. Courses tackle savory and sweet dishes with the possibility of an add-on market tour (€65-130, 92 Rue Nollet, Mo: La Fourche, mobile 06 64 17 93 32, www.lessecretsgourmandsdenoemie.com).

Cook'n with Class gets rave reviews for its range of convivial cooking classes from breads to *macarons* to croissants to wine and cheese. There's a maximum of six students (€85-200, 6 Rue Baudelique, Mo: Jules Joffrin or Simplon, mobile 06 31 73 62 77, www.cooknwithclass.com/paris).

La Cuisine Paris has a great variety of classes in English, reasonable prices, and a beautiful space in central Paris (€70-100, €160 for 4-hour class with market tour, also offers gourmet visit to Versailles, 80 Quai de l'Hôtel de Ville, tel. 01 40 51 78 18, www.lacuisineparis.com).

REED is the creation of Catherine Reed, who also runs a restaurant with the same name a few blocks from Rue Cler. Classes are limited to eight students and focus on practical skills—from basic techniques to classic French gastronomy (€145, Sun and Wed at 10:30, 11 Rue Amelie, tel. 01 45 55 88 40, www.reedrestaurant.com).

If you're looking for an upscale demonstration course, you'll find it at **Le Cordon Bleu** (tel. 01 53 68 22 50, www.lcbparis.com) or **Ritz Escoffier Ecole de Gastronomie** (tel. 01 43 16 30 50, www.ritzparis.com).

Wine Tasting

Ô Château is decisively wine-centric, though it also has a respectable restaurant. Their team of sommeliers teach wine-tasting classes in fluent English while you sit in the 18th-century residence of Madame de Pompadour. Classes range from an introductory tasting (€59), to wine-tasting lunches (€75), or three-course dinners with wine pairings (€99). Each tasting lasts about two hours and is usually limited to 12 people; register online using code "RS2019" for a 10-percent discount, or check the website for last-minute deals (68 Rue Jean-Jacques Rousseau, Mo: Louvre-Rivoli or Etienne Marcel, tel. 01 44 73 97 80, www.o-chateau.com).

Ile St. Louis
(Mo: Pont Marie)

$$$ L'Orangerie is an inviting, rustic-yet-elegant place with soft lighting, comfortable, spacious seating, and a hushed ambience. The cuisine blends traditional with modern touches (closed Mon, 28 Rue St. Louis-en-l'Ile, tel. 01 46 33 93 98).

$$ Auberge de la Reine Blanche—woodsy, cozy, and tight—welcomes diners willing to rub elbows with their neighbors. Earnest owner Michel serves basic French cuisine at reasonable prices. Along with like-mother-made-it comfort food, he serves good dinner salads (closed Wed, 30 Rue St. Louis-en-l'Ile, tel. 01 46 33 07 87).

On the Left Bank
Near the Odéon Theater
(Mo: Odéon)

$$$ Brasserie Bouillon Racine takes you back to 1906 with an Art Nouveau carnival of carved wood, stained glass, and old-time lights reflected in beveled mirrors. It's like having dinner with Gustav Klimt and a bunch of tourists. The over-the-top decor and energetic waiters give it an inviting conviviality. Check upstairs before choosing a table (daily, serves nonstop, 3 Rue Racine, tel. 01 44 32 15 60, www.bouillon-racine.com).

$$$ La Méditerranée is all about seafood from the south served in a pastel and dressy setting...with similar clientele. The scene and the cuisine are sophisticated yet accessible, and the view of the Odéon is *formidable* (daily, reservations smart, facing the Odéon at 2 Place de l'Odéon, tel. 01 43 26 02 30, www.la-mediterranee.com).

$$ L'Avant Comptoir and **L'Avant Comptoir de la Mer** are two stand-up-only hors d'oeuvres bars sitting next door to the mothership restaurant. They serve an array of both French-Basque tapas and seafood tapas on sleek zinc counters. At the walk-up counters outside, you can get top quality sandwiches, crêpes, or seafood to go (for less and with less commotion). But step inside for the foodie bar and it's another world (daily 12:00-23:00, 3 Carrefour de l'Odéon).

$$$ Brasserie Lipp is the place to experience an unspoiled yet famous brasserie. The cool two-level interior is awash with worn leather booths and faded decor that looks like it dates to when the place opened in 1880. Come for the ambience and good-enough cuisine (daily, 151 Boulevard St. Germain, tel. 01 45 48 72 93).

Between the Panthéon and the Cluny Museum
(Mo: Cluny-La Sorbonne ; RER/Train-B: Luxembourg)

$$$ At Les Papilles, you'll dine surrounded by bottles of wine in a warm, woody bistro and eat what's offered...and you won't complain. It's one *menu*, no choices, and no regrets. Choose your wine from the shelf or ask for advice from the burly, rugby-playing owner, then relax and let the food arrive. Reserve ahead and make sure that you're OK with what he's cooking (closed Sun-Mon, 30 Rue Gay Lussac, tel. 01 43 25 20 79, www.lespapillesparis.fr).

$$ Le Pré Verre, a block from the Cluny Museum, is a welcoming wine bistro. Hands-on owner Jean-François serves imaginative, modern cuisine at fair prices (inside and out), and packs his place with locals (good wine list, closed Sun-Mon, 8 Rue Thénard, reservations necessary, tel. 01 43 54 59 47, www.lepreverre.com).

$$ Restaurant La Mosquée transports diners to Morocco with its dazzling Arabic ambience and cuisine at fair prices. It's tucked into the back of the Grande Mosquée de Paris and serves tasty baked goods, teas, and even tastier meals—including several varieties of couscous and tagine (daily 9:00-late, 39 Rue Geoffroy-Saint-Hilaire, tel. 01 43 31 38 20).

SLEEPING

I've focused my recommendations on three safe, handy, and colorful neighborhoods: the village-like Rue Cler (near the Eiffel Tower); the artsy and trendy Marais (near Place de la Bastille); and the historic island of Ile St. Louis (next door to Notre-Dame).

Rue Cler Neighborhood

(7th arr., Mo: Ecole Militaire, La Tour Maubourg, Invalides)

Rue Cler is so French that when I step out of my hotel in the morning, I feel like I must have been a poodle in a previous life. This is a neighborhood of wide, tree-lined boulevards, stately apartment buildings, and lots of Americans. Hotels here are a fair value, considering the elegance of the neighborhood. And for sightseeing, you're within walking distance of the Eiffel Tower, Army Museum, Seine River, Champs-Elysées, and Orsay and Rodin museums.

In the Heart of Rue Cler

Many of my readers stay in the Rue Cler neighborhood. If you want to disappear into Paris, choose a hotel elsewhere. The following hotels are within Camembert-smelling distance of Rue Cler.

$$$ Hôtel Bosquet* is an exceptionally good hotel in an ideal location, with comfortable public spaces and well-configured rooms that are large by local standards and feature effective darkness blinds. The staff is politely formal (RS%—use code "RSDEAL"; good but pricey breakfast buffet with eggs and sausage, 19 Rue du Champ de Mars, tel. 01 47 05 25 45, www.hotel-paris-bosquet.com, hotel@relaisbosquet.com).

$$ Hôtel du Champ de Mars* is a top choice, brilliantly located barely 10 steps off Rue Cler. This plush little hotel has a small-town feel from top to bottom. The adorable rooms are snug but lovingly kept by hands-on owners Françoise and Stéphane, and single rooms can work as tiny doubles. It's popular, so book well ahead (continental breakfast only, 30 yards off Rue Cler at 7 Rue du Champ de Mars, tel. 01 45 51 52 30, www.hotelduchampdemars.com, hotelduchampdemars@gmail.com).

Near Ecole Militaire Métro Stop

$$$ Hôtel Duquesne Eiffel,* a few blocks farther from the action, is handsome and hospitable. It features a welcoming lobby, a street-front terrace, comfortable rooms (some with terrific Eiffel Tower views), and connecting rooms that work well for families (RS%, big, hot breakfast—free for Rick Steves readers, 23 Avenue Duquesne, tel. 01 44 42 09 09, www.hde.fr, contact@hde.fr).

$$ Hôtel de France Invalides is a fair midrange option run by a brother-sister team (Alain and Marie-Hélène). It has contemporary decor and 60 rooms, some with knockout views of Invalides' golden dome (but with some traffic noise and no air-con). Rooms on the courtyard are quieter, smaller, and cheaper (RS%, connecting rooms possible, first breakfast free for Rick Steves readers—maximum of two per party, 102 Boulevard de la Tour Maubourg, tel. 01 47 05 40 49, www.hoteldefrance.com, contact@hoteldefrance.com).

Closer to Rue St. Dominique (and the Seine)

$$$ Hôtel de Londres Eiffel* is my closest listing to the Eiffel Tower and the Champ de Mars park. Here you get immaculate, warmly decorated but tight rooms (several are connecting for families), comfy public spaces, and a terrific staff that can't do enough to help. It's less convenient to the Métro (10-minute walk), but very handy to buses #69, #80, and #92, and to RER/Train-C: Pont de l'Alma (some Eiffel Tower view rooms, 1 Rue Augereau, tel. 01 45 51 63 02, www.hotel-paris-londres-eiffel.com, info@londres-eiffel.com, helpful Cédric and Arnaud).

$ Hôtel de la Tour Eiffel** is a solid value on a quiet street near several of my favorite restaurants. The rooms are well-designed and comfortable with air-conditioning (but no breakfast). The six sets of connecting rooms are ideal for families (RS%, 17 Rue de l'Exposition, tel. 01 47 05 14 75, www.hotel-toureiffel.com, hte7@wanadoo.fr).

Near La Tour Maubourg Métro Stop

$$$ Hôtel Muguet*** is quiet, well-located, well-run, and reasonable, with tastefully appointed rooms and a helpful staff (some view rooms, strict 7-day cancellation policy, 11 Rue Chevert, tel. 01 47 05 05 93, www.hotelparismuguet.com, contact@hotelparismuguet.com).

Marais

Those interested in a more central, diverse, and lively urban locale should make the Marais their Parisian home. This is jumbled, medieval Paris at its finest, where classy stone mansions sit alongside trendy bars, antique shops, and fashion-conscious boutiques. The streets are an intriguing parade of artists, students, tourists, immigrants, and baguette-munching babies in strollers. The Marais is also known as a hub of the Parisian gay and lesbian scene.

Near Place des Vosges

(3rd and 4th arr., Mo: Bastille, St-Paul, or Hôtel de Ville)

$$$$ Hôtel le Pavillon de la Reine,***** 15 steps off the beautiful Place des Vosges, merits its stars with top service and comfort and exquisite attention to detail, from its melt-in-your-couch lobby to its luxurious rooms (free access to spa and fitness room, parking, 28 Place des Vosges, tel. 01 40 29 19 19, www.pavillon-de-la-reine. com, contact@pavillon-de-la-reine.com).

$$$ Hôtel St. Louis Marais*** is an intimate and sharp little hotel that sits on a quiet street a few blocks from the river.

The handsome rooms have character... and spacious bathrooms (skip their 3 annex rooms, 1 Rue Charles V, Mo: Sully-Morland, tel. 01 48 87 87 04, www. saintlouismarais.com, marais@saint louis-hotels.com).

$$ Hôtel Jeanne d'Arc*** is a lovely hotel that's ideally located for connoisseurs of the Marais who don't need air-conditioning. Here, artful decor meets stone walls and oak floors, rooms are thoughtfully appointed, and corner rooms are wonderfully bright in the City of Light. Rooms on the street can have some noise until the bars close (family rooms, some view rooms, 3 Rue de Jarente, Mo: St-Paul, tel. 01 48 87 62 11, www.hoteljeannedarc. com, information@hoteljeannedarc.com).

Near the Pompidou Center

(4th arr., Mo: St-Paul, Hôtel de Ville, or Rambuteau)

$$ Hôtel de la Bretonnerie*** makes a fine Marais home. Located three blocks from the Hôtel de Ville, it has a warm, welcoming lobby and helpful staff. Its 30 good-value rooms are on the larger side with an antique, open-beam warmth (family rooms, free breakfast for Rick Steves readers who book direct, no air-con, between Rue Vieille du Temple and Rue des Archives at 22 Rue Ste. Croix de la Bretonnerie, tel. 01 48 87 77 63, www. hotelparismaraisbretonnerie.com, hotel@ bretonnerie.com).

$$ Hôtel Beaubourg*** is a top value on a small street in the shadow of the Pompidou Center. The place is surpris-

ingly quiet, and the 28 plush and traditional rooms are well appointed (bigger doubles are worth the extra cost, 11 Rue Simon Le Franc, Mo: Rambuteau, tel. 01 42 74 34 24, www.hotelbeaubourg.com, reservation@hotelbeaubourg.com).

Ile St. Louis
(4th arr., Mo: Pont Marie)
The peaceful, residential character of this river-wrapped island, with its brilliant location and homemade ice cream, has drawn Americans for decades. There are no budget deals here—all of the hotels are three-star or more—though prices are respectable considering the level of comfort and wonderful location.

$$$$ Hôtel du Jeu de Paume**** occupies a 17th-century tennis center. Its magnificent lobby and cozy public spaces make it a fine splurge. Greet Lemon (luh-moe), *le chien,* then take a spin in the glass elevator for a half-timbered treehouse experience. The 30 rooms are carefully designed and tasteful, though not particularly spacious (you're paying for the location and public areas). Most rooms face a small garden courtyard; all are pin-drop peaceful (apartments for 4-6 people, 54 Rue St. Louis-en-l'Ile, tel. 01 43 26 14 18, www.jeudepaumehotel.com, info@jeudepaumehotel.com).

$$$ Hôtel Saint-Louis*** blends character with modern comforts. The sharp rooms come with cool stone floors and exposed beams. Rates are reasonable...for the location (some rooms with balcony, iPads available for guest use, 75 Rue St. Louis-en-l'Ile, tel. 01 46 34 04 80, www.saintlouisenlisle.com, isle@saint-louis-hotels.com).

Apartment Rentals
Consider this option if you're traveling as a family, in a group, or staying at least a few nights. Intrepid travelers around the world are accustomed to using Airbnb and VRBO when it comes to renting a vacation apartment; search for places in my recommended hotel neighborhoods. In Paris, you have many additional options among rental agencies, and I've found the following to be the most reliable. Their websites are good and essential to understanding your choices: **Paris Perfect,** www.parisperfect.com; **Adrian Leeds Group,** www.adrianleeds.com; **France Homestyle,** www.francehomestyle.com; **Home Rental Service,** www.homerental.fr; **Haven in Paris,** www.haveninparis.com; **Paris Home,** www.parishome2000.com; **Cobblestone Paris Rentals,** www.cobblestoneparis.com; **Paris for Rent,** www.parisforrent.com; and **Cross-Pollinate,** www.cross-pollinate.com.

Bed-and-Breakfasts
Several agencies can help you go local by staying in a private home in Paris. While prices and quality can range greatly, most rooms have a private bath and run from €85 to €150. Most owners won't take bookings for fewer than two nights. To limit stair-climbing, ask whether the building has an elevator. These agencies have a good selection: **Alcôve & Agapes** (www.bed-and-breakfast-in-paris.com) and **Meeting the French** (http://en.meetingthefrench.com).

TRANSPORTATION
Getting Around Paris
Paris is easy to navigate. Your basic choices are Métro (in-city subway), suburban train (commonly called RER, rapid

Métro ticket machines

Transit Basics

- The same tickets are good on the Métro, suburban trains (within the city), and city buses.
- Save money by buying a *carnet* of 10 discounted tickets or a Passe Navigo.
- Beware of pickpockets, and don't buy tickets from people roaming the stations.
- Find your train by its end-of-the-line stop.
- Insert your ticket into the turnstile, retrieve it, and keep it until the end of your journey.
- Safeguard your belongings; avoid standing near the train doors with luggage.
- At a stop, the door may open automatically. If it doesn't, open the door by either pushing a square button (green or black) or lifting a metal latch.
- Transfers (*correspondances*) between the Métro and suburban trains are free (but not between Métro/suburban trains and bus).
- Trash or tear used tickets after you complete your ride and leave the station (not before).

transit tied into the Métro system), public bus, tram, Uber, and taxi.

You can buy tickets and passes at Métro stations and at many *tabacs.* Staffed ticket windows in stations are being replaced by ticket machines, so expect some stations to have only machines and an information desk. Some machines accept only credit cards and coins, though key stations always have machines that take small bills of €20 or less and chip-and-PIN cards (some American cards are accepted—try). These machines work logically with easy-to-follow instructions in English.

Information: The Métro, suburban train, and public bus systems share a helpful website: www.ratp.fr.

Public-Transit Tickets: The Métro, suburban trains (lines A-K), trams, and buses all work on the same tickets. A **single ticket** costs €2. You can buy a **carnet** (kar-nay) of 10 tickets for about €15 (50 percent cheaper for ages 4-10). *Carnets* can be shared among travelers. Plans call for paper tickets to be replaced with plastic travel cards, including the **Navigo Easy** (best for tourists, can be shared and reloaded); the rollout may have started by the time you visit.

Passe Navigo: The weekly version of this pass covers all forms of transit from Monday to Sunday (expiring on Sunday, even if you buy it on, say, a Thursday). This chip-embedded card costs a one-time €5 fee (plus another €5 for the required photo; photo booths are in major Métro stations). The weekly unlimited pass (Navigo Semaine) costs about €23 and is good for all zones in the Paris region. You can buy your Passe Navigo at any Métro station in Paris.

Passe Navigo or *Carnet*? The Navigo covers a far greater area than *carnet* tickets, including your trip from the airport (a €10.50 value alone), but cannot be shared. It's a great deal for visitors who use it for regional trips, or stay a full week (and start their trip early in the week). Two 10-pack *carnets*—enough for most travelers staying a week—cost €30, are shareable, and don't expire, but are only valid in the center of Paris and may soon be replaced with plastic travel cards.

By Métro

In Paris, you're never more than a 10-minute walk from a Métro station. Europe's best subway system allows you to hop from sight to sight quickly and cheaply (runs 5:30-1:00 in the morning, Fri-Sat until 2:00 in the morning). Learn to use it.

Using the Métro System: To get to your destination, determine the closest

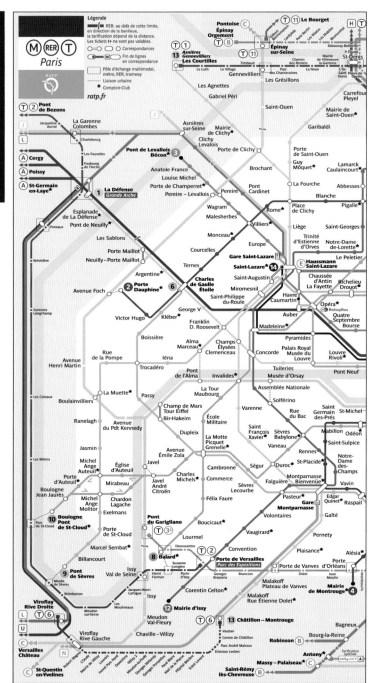

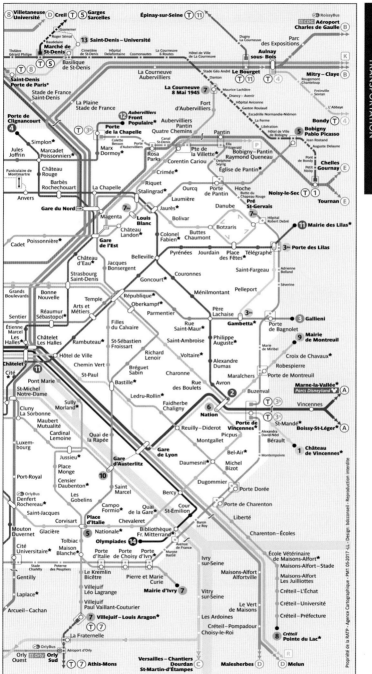

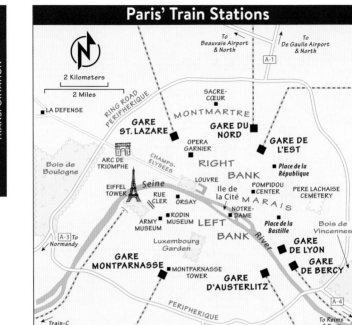

Paris' Train Stations

Key Destinations Served by Train Stations

GARE DU NORD
Auvers-sur-Oise, Chantilly-Gouvieux, Brussels, Bruges, Amsterdam, Berlin, Koblenz, London

GARE MONTPARNASSE
Chartres, Amboise, Pontorson/Mont St-Michel, Dinan, Bordeaux, Sarlat, Toulouse, Albi, Tours, Hendaye

GARE DE LYON
Fontainebleau, Disneyland, Beaune, Dijon, Chamonix, Annecy, Lyon, Avignon, Arles, Nice, Carcassonne, Zürich, Venice, Rome, Bern, Interlaken, Barcelona

GARE DE L'EST
Vaux-le-Vicomte, Colmar, Strasbourg, Reims, Verdun, Interlaken, Zürich, Frankfurt, Munich, Berlin

GARE ST. LAZARE
Giverny, Pontoise, Rouen, Le Havre, Honfleur, Bayeux, Caen, Pontorson/Mont. St-Michel

GARE D' AUSTERLITZ
Orly Airport, Versailles, Amboise, Sarlat, Cahors

GARE DE BERCY
Southbound non-TGV trains

"Mo" stop and which line or lines will get you there. Lines are color-coded and numbered. You can tell their direction by the end-of-the-line stops. For example, the La Défense/Château de Vincennes line, also known as line 1 (yellow), runs between La Défense, on its west end, and Vincennes on its east end. Once in the

Métro station, you'll see the color-coded line numbers and/or blue-and-white signs directing you to the train going in your direction (e.g., *direction: La Défense*). Insert your ticket in the turnstile, reclaim your ticket, pass through, and keep it until you exit the system (some stations require you to pass your ticket through a turnstile to

Scenic Buses for Tourists

Of Paris' many bus routes, these are some of the most scenic. They provide a great, cheap, and convenient introduction to the city.

Bus #69 runs east-west between the Eiffel Tower and Père Lachaise Cemetery by way of Rue Cler, Quai d'Orsay, the Louvre, Ile St. Louis, and the Marais.

Bus #87 runs east-west from Invalides to Orsay Museum, St. Germain-des-Prés, St. Michel, Cluny Museum, Ile St. Louis, Bastille, Gare de Lyon, and Gare de Bercy, ending at Porte de Reuilly.

Bus #63 is another good east-west route, connecting the Marmottan Museum, Trocadéro (Eiffel Tower), Pont de l'Alma, Orsay Museum, St. Sulpice Church, Luxembourg Garden, Latin Quarter/Panthéon, and Gare de Lyon.

Bus #73 is one of Paris' most scenic lines, starting at the Orsay Museum and running westbound around Place de la Concorde, then up the Champs-Elysées, around the Arc de Triomphe, and down Avenue Charles de Gaulle to La Défense.

exit). Fare inspectors regularly check for cheaters, accept absolutely no excuses, and have portable credit card machines to fine you on the spot: Keep that ticket or pay a minimum fine of €45.

Transfers are free and can be made wherever lines cross, provided you do so within 1.5 hours and don't exit the station. When you transfer, follow the appropriately colored line number and end-of-the-line stop to find your next train, or look for *correspondance* (connection) signs that lead to your next line.

When you reach your destination, blue-and-white *sortie* signs point you to the exit. Before leaving the station, check the helpful *plan du quartier* (map of the neighborhood) to get your bearings. At stops with several *sorties,* you can save time by choosing the best exit.

Métro Resources: Métro maps are free at Métro stations and included on freebie Paris maps at your hotel. For an interactive map of Paris' sights and Métro lines, with a trip-planning feature and information about each sight and station's history, see www.metro.paris. The free RATP mobile app can estimate Métro travel times, help you locate the best station exit, and tell you when the next bus will arrive (in English).

By Suburban Train

The suburban train is an arm of the Métro, serving outlying destinations such as Versailles, Disneyland Paris, and the airports. Traditionally called RER (which you may see on signage), the line is undergoing a name change to simply "Train." These routes are indicated by thick lines on your subway map and identified by the letters A-K. Throughout this chapter, you'll see it referred to as "RER/Train."

Within the city center, the suburban train works like the Métro and can be speedier if it serves your destination directly, because it makes fewer stops. Métro tickets are good on the suburban train; you can transfer between the Métro and suburban train systems with the same

ticket. But to travel outside the city (to Versailles or the airport, for example), you'll need a separate, more expensive ticket. The Passe Navigo card covers all suburban train trips, including to the airport and Versailles. Unlike the Métro, not every train stops at every station along the way; check the sign or screen over the platform to see if your destination is listed as a stop (*"toutes les gares"* means it makes all stops along the way), or confirm with a local before you board. For suburban trains, you may need to insert your ticket in a turnstile to exit the system.

By City Bus

Paris' excellent bus system is worth figuring out. Buses require less walking and fewer stairways than the Métro, and you can see Paris unfold as you travel.

Bus Stops: Stops are everywhere, and most come with a good city bus map, route maps for each bus that stops there, a frequency chart and schedule, live screens showing the time the next two buses will arrive, a *plan du quartier* map of the immediate neighborhood, and a *soirées* map explaining night service, if available (there are even phone chargers at some locations). Bus-system maps are also available in any Métro station (and in the *Paris Pratique par Arrondissement* booklet sold at newsstands).

Using the Bus System: Buses use the same tickets and passes as the Métro and suburban trains. One Zone 1 ticket buys you a bus ride anywhere in central Paris within the freeway ring road *(le périphérique)*. Use your Métro ticket or buy one on board for €0.10 more. These tickets are *sans correspondance,* which means you can't use them to transfer to another bus.

When a bus approaches, it's wise to wave to the driver to indicate that you want to be picked up. Board your bus through the front door. (Families with strollers can use any doors—the ones in the center of the bus are wider. To open the middle or back doors on long

buses, push the green button located by those doors.) Validate your ticket in the machine (stripe up) and reclaim it. With a Passe Navigo, scan it on the purple touchpad. Keep track of which stop is coming up next by following the onboard diagram or listening to recorded announcements. When you're ready to get off, push the red button to signal you want a stop, then exit through the central or rear door. Even if you're not certain you've figured out the system, do some joyriding. I always check the bus stop near my hotel to see if it's convenient to my plans.

More Bus Tips: Avoid rush hour (Mon-Fri 8:00-9:30 & 17:30-19:30), when buses are jammed and traffic doesn't move. While the Métro shuts down at about 1:00 in the morning (even later Fri-Sat), some buses continue much later (called *Noctilien* lines, www.vianavigo.com). Not all city buses are air-conditioned, so they can become rolling greenhouses on summer days. *Carnet* ticket holders—but not those buying individual tickets onboard—can transfer from one bus to another on the same ticket (within 1.5 hours, revalidate your ticket on the next bus). However, you can't do a round-trip or hop on and off on the same line using the same ticket. You can use the same ticket to transfer between buses and trams, but you can't transfer between the bus and Métro/suburban train systems (it'll take two tickets).

By Uber

Uber works in Paris like it does at home, and in general works better than taxis in Paris (www.uber.com). One downside is that Uber drivers can't use the taxi/bus lanes during rush hour, so your trip may take longer at busy times than it would in a cab.

By Taxi

Parisian taxis are reasonable, especially for couples and families. The meters are tamper-proof. Fares and supplements (described in English on the rear windows) are straightforward and tightly regulated. Cabbies are legally required to accept four passengers, though they don't always like it. If you have five in your group, you can book a larger taxi in advance (your hotelier can call), or try your luck at a taxi stand. A surcharge may be applied for a fifth rider.

Rates: The meter starts at €2.60 with a €7 minimum charge. A typical 20-minute ride (such as Bastille to the Eiffel Tower) costs about €25 (versus about €1.45/person using a *carnet* ticket on the Métro or bus, or about €15 via Uber). Taxis charge higher rates at rush hour, at night, all day Sunday, and for extra passengers. To tip, round up to the next euro (at least €0.50). The A, B, or C lights on a taxi's rooftop sign correspond to hourly rates, which vary with the time of day and day of the week (for example, the A rate of €32.50/hour applies Mon-Sat 10:00-17:00). Tired travelers need not bother with the subtle differences in fares—if you need a cab, take it.

How to Catch *un Taxi*: You can try waving down a taxi, but it's often easier to ask someone for the nearest taxi stand (*"Où est une station de taxi?"*; oo ay ewn stah-see-ohn duh tahk-see). Taxi stands are indicated by a circled "T" on good city maps and on many maps in this chapter. To order a taxi in English, call the reservation line for the G7 cab company (tel. 01 41 27 66 99), or ask your hotelier or waiter to call for you. When you summon a taxi by phone, a set fee of €4 is applied for an immediate booking or €7 for reserving in advance (this fee will appear on the meter when they pick you up). You can also book a taxi using the cab company's app, which provides approximate wait times (surcharge similar to booking by phone). To download an app, search for either "Taxi G7" or "Taxis Bleus" (the two major companies, both available in English; note when entering your mobile number, you must include the international access code and your country code—use "+1" before the area code for a US/Canadian

phone number).

If you need to catch an early morning train or flight, book a taxi the day before (especially for weekday departures; your hotelier can help). Some taxi companies require a €5 reservation fee by credit card for weekday morning rush-hour departures (7:00-10:00) and have a limited number of reservation spots.

By Bike

Paris is surprisingly easy by bicycle. The city is flat, and riders have access to more than 370 miles of bike lanes and many of the priority lanes for buses and taxis (be careful on these). You can rent from a bike-rental shop or use a city-operated bike-share program.

Though I wouldn't use bikes to get around routinely (traffic is a bit too intense), they're perfect for a joyride away from busy streets, especially on the riverside promenades. A four-mile stretch runs from near the Eiffel Tower to below the Bastille; the round-trip ride makes a wonderful hour-or-so long experience. (It could be much longer if you succumb to the temptations of the lounge chairs, hammocks, outdoor cafés, and simple delights of riverside Parisian life.) Bike-rental shops have good route suggestions.

TIs have a helpful "Paris à Vélo" map, which shows all the dedicated bike paths. Many other versions are available for sale at newsstand kiosks, some bookstores, and department stores.

Bike About Tours is your best bet for bike rental, with good information and kid-friendly solutions such as baby seats, tandem attachments, and kid-sized bikes. Their office/coffee shop, called Le Peloton Café, offers bikes, tours, and artisan coffee (bike rental-€20/day during office hours, €25/24 hours, includes lock and helmet; Thu-Tue 9:30-17:30, closed Wed and Dec-Jan; shop/café at 17 Rue du Pont Louis Philippe, Mo: St-Paul, mobile 06 18 80 84 92, www.bikeabouttours.com).

Fat Tire Tours has a limited supply of

Bike tours can be fun and informative.

bikes for rent, so call ahead to check availability (€4/hour, €25/24 hours, includes lock and helmet, photo ID and credit-card imprint required for deposit; RS%—€2/day rental discount with this book, 2-discount maximum; office open daily 9:00-18:30, bike rental only after 11:00 as priority is given to those taking a tour, near the Eiffel Tower at 24 Rue Edgar Faure—see the "Eiffel Tower & Nearby" map, Mo: Dupleix, tel. 01 82 88 80 96, www.fattiretours.com/paris).

The city's **Vélib'** bike-share program (from *vélo* + *libre* = "bike freedom") scatters bikes across town. Best for quick one-way rides, Vélib' bikes are accessible 24/7 and are free for the first half-hour. The system is being overhauled to offer lighter bikes, electric bikes, and an easier booking process; see www.velib-metropole.fr for updates.

Arriving and Departing

Budget plenty of time to reach your departure point. Paris is a big, crowded city, and getting across town or from terminal to terminal on time is a goal you'll share with millions of others. Factor in traffic delays and walking time through huge stations and vast terminals. Always keep your luggage safely near you. Thieves prey on jet-lagged and confused tourists using public transportation.

By Plane
CHARLES DE GAULLE AIRPORT
Paris' main airport (airport code: CDG, www.charlesdegaulleairport.co.uk) has three terminals: T-1, T-2, and T-3. Most flights from the US use T-1 or T-2. You can travel between terminals on the free CDGVAL shuttle train (departs every 5 minutes, 24/7) or by shuttle bus (on the arrivals level). Allow 30 minutes to travel between terminals and an hour for total travel time between your gates at T-1 and T-2. All three terminals have access to ground transportation.

When leaving Paris, make sure you know which terminal you are departing from (if it's T-2, you'll also need to know which hall you're leaving from—they're labeled *A* through *F*). Plan to arrive at the airport three hours early for an overseas flight, and two hours for flights within Europe (particularly on budget airlines, which can have especially long check-in lines). For airport and flight info, visit www. parisaeroport.fr.

Services: All terminals have Paris Tourisme information desks, where you can get city maps, buy a Paris Museum Pass, and get tickets for the RoissyBus or suburban RER/Train-B to Paris—a terrific time- and hassle-saver (to buy a Passe Navigo card, you must go to the airport train station). You'll also find ATMs *(distributeurs),* free (but slow) Wi-Fi, shops, cafés, and bars. If you're returning home and want a VAT refund, look for tax-refund centers in the check-in area.

Getting Downtown: Buses, suburban trains, airport vans, and taxis link the airport's terminals with central Paris. Total travel time to your hotel should be around 1.5 hours by bus and Métro, one hour by train and Métro, and 50 minutes by taxi. For more information, check the "Getting There" tab at www. charlesdegaulleairport.co.uk.

Rick's Tip: *When deciding how to get from Charles de Gaulle airport into Paris, keep in mind that* **using buses and taxis requires shorter walks than taking suburban trains.** *Also remember that transfers to Métro lines often involve stairs.*

The **RoissyBus** drops you off at the Opéra Métro stop in central Paris (€12, runs 6:00-23:00, 3-4/hour, 50 minutes; buy ticket at airport Paris Tourisme desk, ticket machine, or on bus; tel. 3246, www.ratp.fr). The bus arrives on Rue Scribe; to get to the Métro entrance or nearest taxi stand, turn left as you exit the bus and walk counter-clockwise around the lavish Opéra building to its front. A taxi to any of my listed hotels costs about €15 from here. **Le Bus Direct** has several routes that drop travelers at convenient points in and near the city, though it's a bit slower (€17 one-way, €30 round-trip, runs 5:45-22:30, 2/hour, Wi-Fi and power outlets, toll tel. 08 92 35 08 20, www.lebusdirect.com). You can book tickets online (must print out and bring with you), buy at ticket machines or

ticket windows at stops (credit card only, availability varies by stop), or pay the driver (cash only, see www.lebusdirect.com for round-trip and group discount details).

Paris' **suburban commuter train,** RER/ Train-B, is the fastest public transit option for getting between the airport and the city center (€10.50, runs 5:00-24:00, 4/ hour, about 35 minutes; you may still see maps and signage referring to these trains only by their old name, "RER"). RER/ Train-B runs directly to well-located RER/ Train-B/Métro stations (including Gare du Nord, Châtelet-Les Halles, St. Michel, and Luxembourg); from there, you can hop the Métro to get exactly where you need to go. RER/Train-B is handy and cheap, but it can require walking with your luggage through big, crowded stations— especially at Châtelet-Les Halles, where a transfer to the Métro can take 10-15 minutes and may include stairs. For step-by-step instructions on taking RER/Train-B into Paris, see www.parisbytrain.com (see the options under "Airport").

To return to the airport on RER/Train-B from central Paris, allow plenty of time to get to your departure gate (plan for a 15-minute Métro or bus ride to the closest RER/Train-B station, a 15-minute wait for your train, a 35-minute train ride, plus walking time through the stations and airport). Your Métro or bus ticket is not valid on RER/Train-B to the airport (but a Passe Navigo is). When you catch your train, make sure the sign over the platform shows *Aéroport Roissy-Charles de Gaulle* as a stop served. (The line splits, so not every RER/Train-B serves the airport.) If you're not clear, ask another rider, *"Air-o-por sharl duh gaul?"*

Shuttle vans carry passengers to and from their hotels, with stops along the way to drop off and pick up other riders. Shuttles require you to book a precise pickup time in advance—even though you can't know if your flight will arrive on time. For that reason, they work best for trips *from* your hotel to the airport. Though not as fast as taxis, shuttle vans are a good value for single travelers and big families (about €30 for one person, per-person price decreases the more you have in your party; have hotelier book at least a day in advance). Several companies offer shuttle service; I usually just go with the one my hotel uses. For groups of three or four, take a taxi or Uber instead.

Taxis charge a flat rate into Paris (€55 to the Left Bank, €50 to the Right Bank). Taxis can carry three people with bags comfortably, and are legally required to accept a fourth passenger (though they may not like it; beyond that, there's an extra passenger supplement). Don't take an unauthorized taxi from cabbies greeting you on arrival. Official taxi stands are well signed. For taxi trips from Paris to the airport, have your hotel arrange it. Specify that you want a real taxi *(un taxi normal),* not a limo service that costs €20 more (and gives your hotel a kickback). For weekday-morning departures (7:00-10:00), reserve at least a day ahead (€7 reservation fee payable by credit card). **Uber** offers Paris airport pickup and drop-off for the same rates as taxis, but since they can't use the bus-only lanes (normal taxis can), expect some added time.

The professional **Paris Webservices** car service works well from the airport because your driver meets you inside the terminal and waits if you're late (two people-€90 one-way, €5-10/extra person up to 7, tel. 01 45 56 91 67 or 09 52 06 02 59, www.pariswebservices.com). They also offer guided tours.

ORLY AIRPORT

This easy-to-navigate airport (airport code: ORY, www.airport-orly.com) feels small, but it has all the services you'd expect at a major airport. Orly is good for rental-car pickup and drop-off, as it's closer to Paris and easier to navigate than Charles de Gaulle Airport.

Orly has two terminals: Ouest (west) and Sud (south). At both terminals, arriv-

als are on the ground level (level 0) and departures are on level 1. You can connect the two terminals with the free Orlyval shuttle train (well signed).

Services: Both terminals have Paris Tourisme desks in the arrivals area (a good spot to buy the Paris Museum Pass and tickets for public transit into Paris) and offer free Wi-Fi.

Getting Downtown: Shuttle buses *(navettes),* suburban trains, airport vans, and taxis connect Paris with either terminal. Bus stops and taxis are centrally located at arrivals levels and are well signed.

Bus bays are found in the Sud terminal outside exits L and G, and in the Ouest terminal outside exit D. **Le Bus Direct** route #1 runs to Gare Montparnasse, Eiffel Tower, Trocadéro, and Arc de Triomphe/Etoile stops (all stops have connections to Métro lines). For Rue Cler hotels, take Le Bus Direct to the Eiffel Tower stop (20 Avenue de Suffren—see "Eiffel Tower & Nearby" map), then walk 15 minutes across the Champ de Mars park to your hotel. Buses depart from the arrivals level—Ouest exit B-C or Sud exit L; look for signs to *navettes* (€12 one-way, €20 round-trip, 4/hour, 40 minutes to the Eiffel Tower, buy ticket from driver or book online). See www.lebusdirect. com for details on round-trip and group discounts.

For the cheapest (but slow) access to central Paris (best for the Marais area), take **tram line 7** from outside the Sud terminal (direction: Villejuif-Louis Aragon) to the Villejuif station to catch Métro line 7 (you'll need one Métro ticket for the tram and one for the Métro—buy a *carnet* of 10 tickets at the Paris Tourisme desk in the terminal, 4/hour, 45 minutes to Villejuif Métro station, then 15-minute Métro ride to the Marais).

The next two options take you to **RER/ Train-B,** with access to the Luxembourg Garden area, Notre-Dame Cathedral, handy Métro line 1 at the Châtelet stop,

Gare du Nord, and Charles de Gaulle Airport. The **Orlybus** goes directly to the Denfert-Rochereau Métro and RER/Train-B stations (€8, 3/hour, 30 minutes). The pricier but more frequent—and more comfortable—**Orlyval shuttle train** takes you to the Antony RER/Train-B station (€12.05, 6/hour, 40 minutes, buy ticket to Paris—not just to Antony—before boarding, smart to purchase your 10-ticket *carnet* for the Métro here, too). The Orlyval train is well signed and leaves from the departure level at both Orly terminals. Once at the RER/Train-B station, take the train in direction: Mitry-Claye or Aéroport Charles de Gaulle to reach central Paris.

For access to Left Bank neighborhoods (including Rue Cler) via **RER/Train-C,** take the bus marked *Go C Paris* five minutes to the Pont de Rungis station (€2 shuttle only, €6.25 combo-ticket includes RER/Train-C), then catch RER/Train-C to St. Michel, Musée d'Orsay, Invalides, or Pont de l'Alma (direction: Versailles Château Rive Gauche or Pontoise, 4/hour, 35 minutes).

By **airport van,** figure about €23 for one person or €30 for two (less per person for larger groups and kids).

Taxis are outside the Ouest terminal exit B, and to the far right as you leave the Sud terminal at exit M. Allow 30 minutes for a taxi ride into central Paris (fixed fare: €30 for Left Bank, €35 for Right Bank). **For Uber,** head toward exit B, following signs for *Pre-Ordered Vehicles.* Meet your Uber driver in the lot labeled *Parking Pro* (same fixed rate as taxis for central Paris).

BEAUVAIS AIRPORT

Budget airlines such as Ryanair use this small airport with two terminals (T-1 and T-2), offering dirt-cheap airfares but leaving you 50 miles north of Paris. Still, this airport has direct buses to Paris and is handy for travelers heading to Normandy or Belgium (car rental available). The airport is basic, waiting areas can be crowded, and services sparse (airport code: BVA, toll tel. 08 92 68 20 66, www.aeroportparisbeauvais.com).

Getting Downtown: Buses depart from a stop between the two terminals (€17 one-way, 2/hour, 1.5 hours to Paris, buy ticket online to save time, http://tickets.aeroportbeauvais.com). Buses arrive at Porte Maillot on the west edge of Paris (where you can connect to Métro line 1 and RER/Train-C); the closest taxi stand is next door at the Hôtel Hyatt Regency Paris Etoile. To head back to Beauvais Airport from Porte Maillot, catch the bus in the parking lot on Boulevard Pershing next to the Hyatt Regency.

Trains connect Beauvais' city center and Paris' Gare du Nord (20/day, 1.5 hours). To reach the Beauvais train station, take the Hôtel/Aéroport Navette shuttle or local bus #12 (each hourly, 25 minutes).

Taxis run from Beauvais Airport to the Beauvais train station or city center (€20), or to central Paris (allow €150 and 1.5 hours).

By Train

Paris is Europe's rail hub, with six major stations and one minor station, and trains heading in different directions: **Gare du Nord** (northbound trains); **Gare Montparnasse** (west- and southwest-bound trains); **Gare de Lyon** (southeast-bound trains); **Gare de l'Est** (eastbound trains); **Gare St. Lazare** (northwest-bound trains); **Gare d'Austerlitz** (southwest-bound trains); and **Gare de Bercy** (smaller station with non-TGV trains mostly serving cities in Burgundy).

The main train stations all have free Wi-Fi, banks or currency exchanges, ATMs, train information desks, cafés, newsstands, and clever pickpockets (pay attention in ticket lines—keep your bag firmly gripped in front of you). Not all have baggage checks. Any train station has schedule information, can make reservations, and can sell tickets for any destination, although it may be handier to buy tickets from a neighborhood SNCF office.

Each station offers two types of rail service: long distance to other cities, called Grandes Lignes (major lines, TGV—also called "InOui"—or TER trains); and commuter service to nearby areas, called Banlieue, Transilien, or suburban trains lines A-K. You also may see ticket windows identified as *Ile de France*. These are for Transilien trains serving destinations outside Paris in the Ile de France region (usually no more than an hour from Paris). When arriving by Métro, follow signs for *Grandes Lignes-SNCF* to find the main tracks. Métro and suburban train lines A-K, as well as buses and taxis, are well marked at every station.

Budget plenty of time before your departure to factor in ticket lines and making your way through large, crowded stations. Paris train stations can be intimidating, but if you slow down, take a deep breath, and ask for help, you'll find them manageable and efficient. Bring a pad of paper and a pen for clear communication at ticket/info windows. It helps to write down the ticket you want. For instance: "28/05/19 Paris-Nord→Lyon dep. 18:30." All stations have a central information booth *(accueil)*; bigger stations have roving helpers, usually wearing red or blue vests. They're capable of answering rail questions more quickly than the staff at the information desks or ticket windows. I make a habit of confirming my track number and departure time with these helpers (all rail staff speak English). To make your trip go more smoothly, be sure to review the train tips in the Practicalities chapter.

GARE DU NORD

The granddaddy of Paris' train stations serves cities in northern France and international destinations north of Paris, including Copenhagen, Amsterdam, and the Eurostar to London. The station is undergoing a €600-million renovation that won't be finished until 2024—expect changes and construction disruptions.

Key Destinations Served by Gare du Nord Banlieue/Suburban Lines: Charles de Gaulle Airport (4/hour, 35 minutes, track 41-44).

GARE MONTPARNASSE

This big, modern station covers three floors, serves lower Normandy and Brittany, and has TGV service to the Loire Valley and southwestern France, as well as suburban service to Chartres. Trains to Chartres usually depart from tracks 18-24.

Key Destinations Served by Gare Montparnasse: Chartres (14/day, 1 hour), **Amboise** (8/day in 1.5 hours with change in St-Pierre-des-Corps, requires TGV reservation; non-TGV trains leave from Gare d'Austerlitz), **Pontorson/Mont St-Michel** (5/day, 5.5 hours, via Rennes or Caen), and **Sarlat** (4/day, 5 hours, change in Bordeaux).

GARE DE LYON

This huge, bewildering station offers TGV and regular service to southeastern France, Italy, Switzerland, and other international destinations.

Le Bus Direct coaches—to Gare Montparnasse (easy transfer to Orly Airport) and direct to Charles de Gaulle Airport—stop outside the station's main entrance. They are signed *Navette-Aéroport.*

Key Destinations Served by Gare de Lyon: Beaune (roughly hourly at rush hour but few midday, 2.5 hours, most require change in Dijon; direct trains from Paris' Bercy station take an hour longer), **Chamonix** (7/day, 5.5-7 hours, some change in Switzerland), **Avignon** (hourly direct, 2.5 hours to Avignon TGV station; 5/day in 3.5 hours to Avignon Centre-Ville Station, more connections with change—3-4 hours), **Arles** (hourly, 4 hours, transfer in Avignon or Nîmes), **Nice** (hourly, 6 hours, may require change), and **Carcassonne** (8/day, 5.5 hours, 1 change usually in Bordeaux).

GARE DE L'EST

This two-floor station (with underground Métro) serves northeastern France and international destinations east of Paris.

Key Destinations Served by Gare de l'Est: Colmar (12/day with TGV, 2.5 hours, 3 direct, others change in Strasbourg) and **Reims** Centre station (8/day by direct TGV, 45 minutes).

GARE ST. LAZARE

This compact station serves upper Normandy, including Rouen and Giverny.

Key Destinations Served by Gare St. Lazare: Giverny (train to Vernon, 8/day Mon-Sat, 6/day Sun, 45 minutes), **Honfleur** (13/day, 2-3.5 hours, via Lisieux, Deauville, or Le Havre, then bus), **Bayeux** (9/day, 2.5 hours, some change in Caen), **Pontorson/Mont St-Michel** (2/day, 4-5.5 hours, via Caen; more trains from Gare Montparnasse).

GARE D'AUSTERLITZ

This small station currently provides non-TGV service to the Loire Valley, southwestern France, and Spain.

Key Destinations Served by Gare d'Austerlitz: Orly Airport (via RER/Train-C, 4/hour, 35 minutes), **Versailles** (via RER/Train-C, 4/hour, 35 minutes), **Amboise** (3/day direct in 2 hours, more with transfer; faster TGV connection from Gare Montparnasse), and **Sarlat** (1/day, 6.5 hours, requires change to bus in Souillac, 3 more/day via Gare Montparnasse).

GARE DE BERCY

This smaller station mostly handles southbound non-TGV trains, but some TGV trains do stop here in peak season (Mo: Bercy).

By Bus

Buses generally provide the cheapest—if less comfortable and more time-consuming—transportation to major European cities. Eurolines is the old standby; two relative newcomers (Ouibus and Flixbus) are cutting prices drastically, adding more destinations, and ramping up onboard comfort with Wi-Fi and snacks. These companies provide service usually between train stations and airports within France and to many international destinations. If the schedule works for you, it's a handy and cheap way to connect Paris airports with other French destinations (Tours/Loire, Rouen, and Caen, for example) and skip central Paris train stations.

OuiBus has routes mostly within France but serves some European cities as well (central Paris stop is at Gare de Bercy, Mo: Bercy, easy online booking, toll tel. 08 92 68 00 68, www.ouibus.com). German-run **FlixBus** connects key cities within France and throughout Europe, often from secondary airports and train stations (central Paris stop is near Porte Maillot at 16 Boulevard Pershing, Mo: Porte Maillot, handy eticket system and easy-to-use app, tel. 01 76 36 04 12, www.flixbus.com). **Eurolines'** buses depart from Paris' Gare Routière du Paris-Gallieni in the suburb of Bagnolet (28 Avenue du Général de Gaulle, Mo: Gallieni, toll tel. 08 92 89 90 91; from the US, dial 011 33 1 41 86 24 21, www.eurolines.com).

NEAR PARIS

Efficient trains bring dozens of day trips within the grasp of temporary Parisians. Europe's best palace at Versailles, the awesome cathedral of Chartres, and Monet's flowery gardens at Giverny await the traveler looking for a refreshing change from urban Paris.

Versailles

Every king's dream, Versailles (vehr-"sigh") was the residence of French monarchs and the cultural heartbeat of Europe for about 100 years—until the Revolution of 1789 changed all that.

Versailles offers three blockbuster sights. The main attraction is the palace itself, the **Château.** Here you walk through dozens of lavish, chandeliered rooms once inhabited by Louis XIV and his successors. Next come the expansive **Gardens,** a landscaped wonderland crossed with footpaths and dotted with statues and fountains. The pastoral **Trianon Palaces and Domaine de Marie-Antoinette,** designed for frolicking blue bloods and featuring

several small palaces, is perfect for getting away from the mobs at the Château.

Getting There

The town of Versailles is 35 minutes southwest of Paris. Take **RER/Train-C** from any of these Paris stations: Gare d'Austerlitz, St. Michel, Musée d'Orsay, Invalides, Pont de l'Alma, or Champ de Mars. Buy a round-trip ticket to "Versailles Rive Gauche/Château" (€7.10 round-trip, 4/hour). If the ticket machine doesn't immediately offer a Versailles option, try pressing "Ile de France." Insert your ticket in the turnstile to enter the system (as you would with the Métro). Then check the departure board, which will list the next train to "Versailles Rive Gauche/Château" and its track.

On all Versailles-bound trains, Versailles Rive Gauche/Château is the final stop. Once you arrive, exit through the turnstiles (you may need to insert your ticket). To reach the Château, follow the flow: Turn right out of the station, then

The Neptune fountain at Versailles

Louis XIV and Versailles

Around 1700, Versailles was the cultural heartbeat of Europe, and French culture was at its zenith. Throughout Europe, when you said "the king," you were referring to the French king—Louis XIV. Every king wanted a palace like Versailles. Everyone learned French. French taste in clothes, hairstyles, table manners, theater, music, art, and kissing spread across the Continent. That cultural dominance continued, to some extent, right up to the 20th century.

Louis XIV was a true Renaissance Man, a century after the Renaissance: athletic, good-looking, a musician, dancer, horseman, statesman, patron of the arts, and lover. He called himself the Sun King because he gave life and warmth to all he touched. He was also thought of as Apollo, the Greek god of the sun. For 70 years he was the perfect embodiment of the absolute monarch. He summed it up best himself with his famous expression—"L'état, c'est moi!": "The state, that's me!"

left at the first boulevard, and walk 10 minutes.

By **taxi**, the 30-minute ride (without traffic) between Versailles and Paris costs about €65.

Drivers should get on the *périphérique* freeway that circles Paris, and take the toll-free A-13 autoroute toward Rouen. Exit at Versailles, follow signs to *Versailles Château*, and avoid the hectic Garden lots by parking in the big pay lot at the foot of the Château on Place d'Armes (€4/hour).

Day Plan

Versailles merits a full sightseeing day. In general, allow 1.5 hours each for the Château, the Gardens (includes time for lunch), and the Trianon/Domaine. Add another two hours for round-trip transit, and you're looking at nearly an eight-hour day.

Rick's Tip: *Buy either a* **Paris Museum Pass** *or a* **Versailles Le Passeport Pass,** *both of which give you access to the most important parts of the complex and allow you to skip ticket-buying lines. Ideally, buy your pass (or ticket) before arriving at the palace.*

Orientation

Cost: Château—€18, includes audio-guide; **Trianon Palaces and Domaine de Marie-Antoinette**—€12, no audio-guide; **Gardens**—free Wed-Thu and Nov-March, and on other days when there are no Spectacles (see "Spectacles in the Gardens," later). You can purchase Versailles tickets at any Paris TI, FNAC department store (small fee), or at www.chateauversailles.fr.

Passes: The Paris Museum Pass (see page 36) covers the Château and the Trianon/Domaine area and is the best solution for most. It doesn't include the Gardens on Spectacle days. The **Le Passeport** pass (€20) covers the Château and the Trianon/Domaine area (on Spectacle days, it's €27).

Hours: The **Château** is open April-Oct Tue-Sun 9:00-18:30, Nov-March Tue-Sun until 17:30, closed Mon year-round. The **Trianon Palaces and Domaine de Marie-Antoinette** are open April-Oct Tue-Sun 12:00-18:30, Nov-March until 17:30, closed Mon year-round, last entry 45 minutes before closing. The **Gardens** are open April-Oct daily 8:00-20:30, Nov-March until 18:00.

Crowd-Beating Strategies: Versailles is packed May-Sept 9:30-13:00, so come early or late. Avoid Sundays, Tuesdays, and Saturdays (in that order), when the place is jammed all day. To skip the ticket-buying line, buy a pass or ticket in advance, or book a guided tour. Everyone must go through the same two (often slow) security checkpoints: at the Château's courtyard entry and again at the Château entrance (longest lines 10:00-12:00).

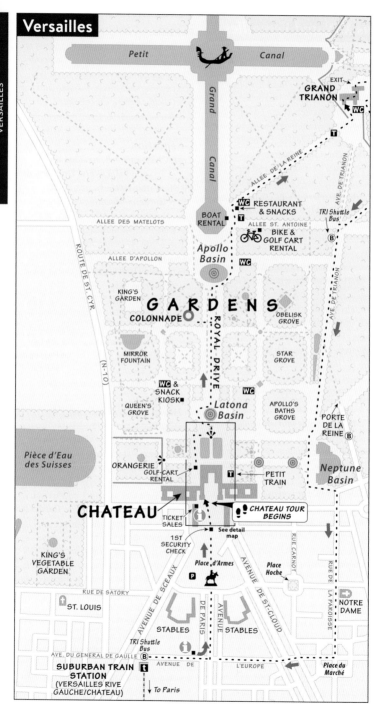

Versailles

Petit   Canal

Grand Canal

EXIT

GRAND TRIANON

WC

T

ALLEE DE LA REINE

AVE. DE TRIANON

WC **RESTAURANT & SNACKS**

BOAT RENTAL

ALLEE DES MATELOTS

ALLEE ST. ANTOINE

TRI Shuttle Bus

BIKE & GOLF CART RENTAL

B

T

Apollo Basin

ALLEE D'APOLLON

WC

ROUTE DE ST. CYR

KING'S GARDEN

GARDENS

COLONNADE

OBELISK GROVE

AVE. DE TRIANON

(N-10)

MIRROR FOUNTAIN

ROYAL DRIVE

STAR GROVE

WC & SNACK KIOSK

QUEEN'S GROVE

WC

Latona Basin

APOLLO'S BATHS GROVE

PORTE DE LA REINE B

Pièce d'Eau des Suisses

ORANGERIE

GOLF-CART RENTAL

T   **PETIT TRAIN**

Neptune Basin

CHATEAU

TICKET SALES

i

CHATEAU TOUR BEGINS

See detail map

1ST SECURITY CHECK

Place d'Armes

Place Hoche

RUE CARNOT

RUE DE LA PAROISSE

NOTRE DAME

KING'S VEGETABLE GARDEN

P

RUE DE SATORY

ST. LOUIS

AVENUE DE SCEAUX

DE PARIS

AVENUE

AVENUE DE ST-CLOUD

RUE DE

STABLES

STABLES

TRI Shuttle Bus B

AVE. DU GENERAL DE GAULLE

i

SUBURBAN TRAIN STATION T

(VERSAILLES RIVE GAUCHE/CHATEAU)

↓ To Paris

AVENUE DE

L'EUROPE

Place du Marché

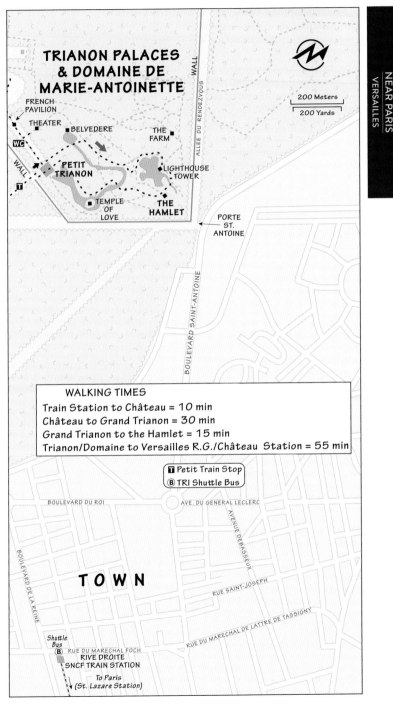

TRIANON PALACES & DOMAINE DE MARIE-ANTOINETTE

FRENCH PAVILION

THEATER

BELVEDERE

THE FARM

WC

WALL

PETIT TRIANON

LIGHTHOUSE TOWER

T

TEMPLE OF LOVE

THE HAMLET

WALL

ALLEE DU RENDEZVOUS

200 Meters

200 Yards

PORTE ST. ANTOINE

BOULEVARD SAINT-ANTOINE

WALKING TIMES

Train Station to Château = 10 min
Château to Grand Trianon = 30 min
Grand Trianon to the Hamlet = 15 min
Trianon/Domaine to Versailles R.G./Château Station = 55 min

T Petit Train Stop
B TRI Shuttle Bus

BOULEVARD DU ROI

AVE. DU GENERAL LECLERC

AVENUE DEBASSEUX

BOULEVARD DE LA REINE

TOWN

RUE SAINT-JOSEPH

RUE DU MARECHAL DE LATTRE DE TASSIGNY

Shuttle Bus
B RUE DU MARECHAL FOCH
RIVE DROITE
SNCF TRAIN STATION
To Paris
(St. Lazare Station)

Information: Check the excellent website for updates and special events—www.chateauversailles.fr. The palace's general contact number is tel. 01 30 83 78 00. The information office at the Château is to the left as you face the palace (WCs).

Tours: The 1.5-hour English **guided tour** gives you access to a few extra rooms and lets you skip the regular security line (€7). Book in advance on the palace's website, or reserve immediately upon arrival at the guided-tours office (to the right of the Château). Tours can sell out by 13:00.

🎧 Download my free Versailles **audio tour.**

Baggage Check: Free and located just after Château entry security. Large bags and baby strollers are not allowed in the Château and the two Trianons.

Eating: To the left of the Château, the **$ Grand Café d'Orléans** offers good-value self-service meals (sandwiches and small salads, great for picnicking in the Gardens). In the Gardens, you'll find several cafés and snack stands with fair prices.

Spectacles in the Gardens: The Gardens and fountains at Versailles come alive at selected times, offering a glimpse into Louis XIV's remarkable world. The Sun King had his engineers literally reroute a river to fuel his fountains and feed his plants. Even by today's standards, the fountains are impressive. Check the Versailles website for current hours and ticket prices.

⊙ *Self-Guided Tour*

On this self-guided tour, you'll see the Château (the State Apartments of the king as well as the Hall of Mirrors), the landscaped Gardens in the "backyard," and the Trianon Palaces and Domaine de Marie-Antoinette, located at the far end of the Gardens. If your time is limited, skip the Trianon/Domaine, which is a hefty 30-minute hike from the Château.

THE CHATEAU

• *Stand in the huge courtyard and face the palace. The golden Royal Gate in the center of the courtyard—nearly 260 feet long and decorated with 100,000 gold leaves—is a replica of the original.*

The section of the palace with the clock is the original château, once a small hunting lodge where little Louis XIV spent his happiest boyhood years. Naturally, the Sun King's private bedroom (the three arched windows beneath the clock) faced the rising sun.

• *As you finally enter the Château, you'll find an information desk (get a map) and bag check. Follow the crowds directly across the courtyard, where you'll go back inside for your free (and worth-the-wait) audioguide. Now make your way to the start of our tour.*

On the way, you'll pass through a dozen ground-floor rooms. Climb the stairs and keep following the flow. You'll eventually reach a palatial golden-brown room, with a doorway that overlooks the Royal Chapel. Let the tour begin.

Royal Chapel: Every morning at 10:00, the organist and musicians struck up the music, these big golden doors opened, and Louis XIV and his family stepped onto the balcony to attend Mass. While Louis looked down on the golden altar, the lowly nobles on the ground floor knelt with their backs to the altar and looked up—worshipping Louis worshipping God.

• *Enter the next room.*

Hercules Drawing Room: Pleasure ruled. The main suppers, balls, and receptions were held in this room. Picture elegant partygoers in fine silks, wigs, rouge, lipstick, and fake moles (and that's just the men) as they dance to the strains of a string quartet.

• *From here on it's a one-way tour—getting lost is not allowed.*

The King's Wing: The names of the rooms generally come from the paintings on the ceilings. For instance, the **Venus Room** was the royal make-out space, where couples would cavort beneath the

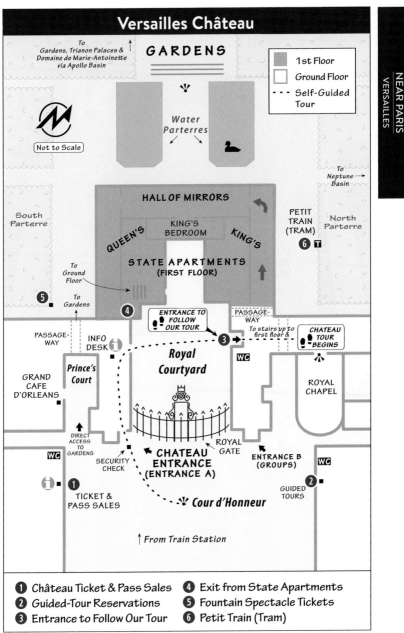

Versailles Château

Louis XIV attended Mass in Versailles' Royal Chapel.

The vast painted ceiling of the Hercules Drawing Room

goddess of love floating on the ceiling. In the **Diana Room,** Louis and his men played pool on a table that stood in the center of the room, while ladies sat surrounding them on Persian-carpet cushions, and music wafted in from next door.

Also known as the Guard Room (as it was the room for Louis' Swiss bodyguards), the **Red Room** is decorated with a military flair. The **Mercury Room** may have served as Louis' official (not actual) bedroom, where the Sun King would ritually rise each morning to warm his subjects.

The **Apollo Room** was the grand throne room. Louis held court from a 10-foot-tall, silver-and-gold canopied throne on a raised platform placed in the center of the room. Even when the king was away, passing courtiers had to bow to the empty throne.

The final room of the King's Wing is the **War Room,** depicting Louis' victories—in marble, gilding, stucco, and paint.

• *Next you'll visit the magnificent...*

Hall of Mirrors: No one had ever seen anything like this hall when it was opened. Mirrors were still a great luxury at the time, and the number and size of these monsters

was astounding. The hall is nearly 250 feet long. There are 17 arched mirrors, matched by 17 windows letting in that breathtaking view of the Gardens. Imagine this place lit by the flames of thousands of candles, filled with ambassadors, nobles, and guests dressed in silks and powdered wigs. At the far end of the room sits the king, on the canopied throne moved in temporarily from the Apollo Room.

In another age altogether, Germany and the Allies signed the Treaty of Versailles, ending World War I (and, some say, starting World War II) right here, in the Hall of Mirrors.

• *Midway down the Hall of Mirrors, you'll be routed to the left through the heart of the palace, to the...*

King's Bedroom and Council Rooms: Louis XIV's bedroom is elaborately decorated, and the decor changed with the season. Look out the window and notice how this small room is at the exact center of the immense horseshoe-shaped building, overlooking the main courtyard and—naturally—facing the rising sun in the east. It symbolized the exact center of power in France.

• *This ends our tour of the Chateau.*

A *Hall of Mirrors*

B *A royal bedchamber*

C *Louis XIV, the Sun King*

D *Domaine de Marie-Antoinette*

Getting Around the Gardens

On Foot: It's a 45-minute walk from the palace, down to the Grand Canal, past the two Trianon palaces, to the far end of Domaine de Marie-Antoinette.

By Bike: A bike-rental station is by the Grand Canal. It's fun pedaling around the greatest royal park in Europe (about €8/hour or €18/half-day).

By *Petit Train*: The slow-moving hop-on, hop-off tram leaves from behind the Château (north side) and makes a one-way loop, stopping at the Petit and Grand Trianons (entry points to Domaine de Marie-Antoinette), then the Grand Canal before returning to the Château (€7.50 round-trip, €4 one-way, free for kids 10 and under, 4/hour).

By Shuttle Bus: Phébus runs an hourly "TRI" shuttle bus between the train station (Versailles Rive Gauche/Château, leaves from curb directly in front of station) and the Trianon/Domaine (doesn't stop at the Château). It's ideal if you're visiting the Trianon/Domaine first, before the Château, or if you want to return to the station straight from the Trianon/Domaine (€2—pay driver, or one Métro ticket, mid-April-Oct only, check current schedule for "Ligne TRI" at www.phebus.tm.fr).

THE GARDENS

Louis XIV was a divine-right ruler. One way he proved it was by controlling nature like a god. These lavish grounds—elaborately planned, pruned, and decorated—showed everyone that Louis was in total command. Louis loved his gardens and, until his last days, presided over their care. He personally led VIPs through them and threw his biggest parties here. With their Greco-Roman themes and incomparable beauty, the gardens illustrated his immense power.

TRIANON PALACES AND DOMAINE DE MARIE-ANTOINETTE

Versailles began as an escape from the pressures of kingship. But in a short time, the Château became as busy as Paris ever was. Louis XIV needed an escape from his escape, so he built a smaller palace out in the boonies.

Delicate, pink, and set amid gardens, the **Grand Trianon** was the king's private residence away from the main palace. Louis XIV usually spent a couple of nights a week here (more in the summer) to escape the sniping politics, strict etiquette, and 24/7 scrutiny of official court life.

Nearby is the fantasy world of palaces, ponds, pavilions, and pleasure gardens called the **Domaine de Marie-Antoinette.** Here you'll find the **Hamlet,** where Marie-Antoinette built a complex of 12 thatched-roof buildings fronting a lake as her own private "Normand" village, and the Petit Trianon, her preferred home base.

Chartres

Chartres, about 50 miles southwest of Paris, gives travelers a pleasant break in a lively, midsize town. But the big reason to come to Chartres (shar-truh) is to see its famous cathedral—arguably Europe's best example of pure Gothic.

Day Plan

Upon arrival in Chartres, head for the cathedral. Allow an hour to savor the church on your own as you follow my self-guided tour. But don't miss the mesmerizing cathedral tour led by Malcolm Miller (details below). Take another hour or two to wander the appealing old city.

Orientation

The spires of the cathedral dominate the town and make a handy landmark.

Tourist Information: The TI is in the historic Maison du Saumon building (open daily, 8 Rue de la Poissonnerie, tel. 02 37 18 26 26, www.chartres-tourisme.com).

Getting There

Chartres is a one-hour ride from Paris' Gare Montparnasse (14/day, about €16 one-way). From the Chartres **train** station, it's a 10-minute walk up Avenue Jehan de Beauce to the cathedral. The free minibus, called the Filibus, gets you near the cathedral (line: Relais des Portes, 3/hour, Mon-Sat 8:30-19:00), or you can take a taxi for about €7.

If arriving **by car,** you'll find pay underground parking on Place des Epars and

Chartres' old town straddles the Eure River.

Place Châtelet, both a short walk from the cathedral.

Sights

▲▲▲CHARTRES CATHEDRAL

Chartres' old church burned to the ground on June 10, 1194. Some of the children who watched its destruction were actually around to help rebuild the cathedral and attend its dedication Mass in 1260. Having been built so quickly, the cathedral has a unity of architecture, statuary, and stained glass that captures the spirit of the Age of Faith like no other church.

The church is (at least) the fourth one on this spot dedicated to Mary, the mother of Jesus, who has been venerated here for some 1,700 years. In 876, the church acquired the torn veil (or birthing gown) supposedly worn by Mary when she gave birth to Jesus. The 2,000-year-old veil (now on display) became the focus of worship at the church.

Cost and Hours: Free, open daily 8:30-19:30, www.cathedrale-chartres.org.

The park behind Chartres Cathedral offers fine views.

Tours: Malcolm Miller has dedicated his life to studying this cathedral (riveting 1.25-hour tours, no reservation needed, €10—cash only, €5 for students, Easter-mid-Oct Mon-Sat at 12:00; no tours last half of Aug, on religious holidays, or if fewer than 12 people show up). Tours begin just inside the church at the *Visites de la Cathédrale* sign. He also offers private tours (millerchartres@aol.com).

Charming American expat **Anne-Marie Woods** is equally passionate about the cathedral (worthwhile 1.5-hour tours daily at 14:45, meet inside gift shop, tel. 02 37 21 75 02).

You can rent a **videoguide** to the right as you enter the cathedral (€7, 70 minutes).

Rick's Tip: Binoculars *are a big help for studying the cathedral art (rent at souvenir shops around the cathedral).*

Visiting the Cathedral: Chartres is a picture book of the entire Christian story, told through its statues, stained glass, and architecture.

Main Entrance (West Facade): Chartres' soaring (if mismatched) steeples announce to pilgrims that they've arrived. Compare the **towers.** The right (south) tower, with a Romanesque stone steeple, survived the fire in 1194, but the left (north) tower lost its wooden steeple. In the 1500s, it was topped with the flamboyant Gothic steeple we see today.

Nave: The place is huge—the nave is 427 feet long, 20 feet wide, and 120 feet high. Try to picture the church in the Middle Ages—painted in greens, browns, and golds. It was packed with pilgrims, and was a rough cross between a hostel, a soup kitchen, and a flea market.

Labyrinth: The broad, round labyrinth inlaid in black marble on the floor (midway up the nave) is a spiritual journey. Labyrinths like this were common in medieval churches. Pilgrims enter from the west rim, by foot or on their knees, and wind around, meditating, on a metaphorical journey to

Blue Virgin window

Cathedral statuary

Jerusalem. About 900 feet later, they hope to meet God in the middle.

Rose Windows: The three big, round "rose" (flower-shaped) windows over the entrances receive sunlight at different times of day. All three are predominantly blue and red, but each has different "petals," and each tells a different part of the Christian story in a kaleidoscope of fragmented images.

Blue Virgin Window: Mary, dressed in blue on a rich red background, cradles Jesus, while the dove of the Holy Spirit descends on her. This very old window (mid-12th century) was the central window behind the altar of the church that burned in 1194. Mary's glowing dress is an example of the famed "Chartres blue," a sumptuous color made by mixing cobalt oxide into the glass.

Mary's Veil: This veil (or tunic), in the Chapel of the Sacred Heart of Mary, was supposedly worn by Mary when she gave birth to Jesus. In the frenzy surrounding the fire of 1194, the veil mysteriously disappeared, only to reappear three days later (recalling the Resurrection). This was interpreted by church officials and the townsfolk as a sign from Mary that she wanted a new church, and thus the building began.

Flying Buttresses: Outside on the south side, six flying buttresses (the arches that stick out from the upper walls) push against six pillars lining the nave inside, helping to hold up the heavy stone ceiling and sloped, lead-over-wood roof. The result is a tall cathedral held up by slender pillars buttressed from the outside, allowing the walls to be opened up for stained glass.

Eating

$$ Café Bleu offers a great view terrace and classic French fare (closed Tue, 1 Cloître Notre-Dame). **$ La Picoterie** is inexpensive and cozy (daily, 36 Rue des Changes). **$ Maison Monarque** offers decadent pastries and light lunches with a cathedral view (closed Mon-Tue, 49 Rue des Changes).

Giverny

Claude Monet spent his last (and most creative) years cultivating his garden and his art at Giverny (zhee-vayr-nee), 50

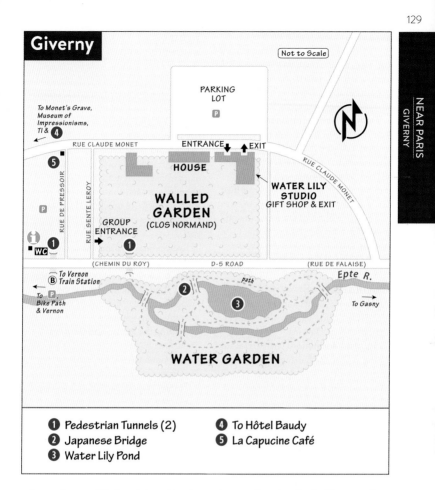

Giverny

Not to Scale

PARKING LOT

To Monet's Grave,
Museum of
Impressionisms,
TI & 4

RUE CLAUDE MONET

ENTRANCE ↓ ↑ EXIT

HOUSE

RUE CLAUDE MONET

5

RUE DE PRESSOIR

RUE SENTE LEROY

WALLED
GARDEN
(CLOS NORMAND)

WATER LILY
STUDIO
GIFT SHOP & EXIT

GROUP
ENTRANCE
1

WC

(CHEMIN DU ROY)

D-5 ROAD

(RUE DE FALAISE)

To Vernon
B Train Station

Path

Epte R.

To P;
Bike Path
& Vernon

2

3

To Gasny

WATER GARDEN

1 Pedestrian Tunnels (2)
2 Japanese Bridge
3 Water Lily Pond

4 To Hôtel Baudy
5 La Capucine Café

miles northwest of Paris and the spiritual home of Impressionism. Visiting the Marmottan and/or the Orangerie museums in Paris before your visit here heightens your appreciation of these gardens.

Day Plan

Minivan and big bus tours take groups to Giverny, and the trip is doable in a half-day by car. Trains will get you there, but they're infrequent—be prepared for a six-hour excursion if you go by rail.

Once in Giverny, give yourself a full hour or more to view the picturesque gardens, and another hour to tour the house. Afterward, pay your respects at Mon-

et's grave, then drop by the Museum of Impressionisms, which has picnic-pleasant gardens in front.

Getting There

Big **bus tour companies** do a Giverny day trip from Paris for around €50 (5 hours, includes entry, get details at your hotel or www.pariscityvision.com).

From Paris' périphérique ring road, **drivers** should follow A-13 toward Rouen, exit at Sortie 14 to Vernon, and follow Centre Ville signs, then signs to Giverny. You can park right at Monet's house or at one of several nearby lots.

The Rouen-bound **train** from Paris Gare

St. Lazare Station stops at Vernon, about four miles from Giverny (45 minutes, about €30 round-trip). The train that leaves Paris at around 8:15 is ideal for this trip, with departures about every two hours after that (8/day Mon-Sat, 6/day Sun).

From the Vernon Station to Giverny: A Vernon-Giverny **bus** makes the 15-minute run to Giverny (timetable at www.giverny.org/transpor). **Taxis** wait in front of the station (€15 one-way for up to 3 people). Another option is to rent a **bike** at L'Arrivée de Giverny café (opposite the station) and take a 30-minute ride along a well-signed, paved bike path that's also open to **walkers** (4 level miles, about 1.5 hours on foot).

Orientation

All of Giverny's sights and shops string along Rue Claude Monet, which runs in front of Monet's house.

Tourist Information: The TI is located by the WCs in the parking lot near the road to Vernon (daily April-Sept, closed off-season, 80 Rue Claude Monet).

Sights

▲MONET'S GARDEN AND HOUSE

There are two gardens, split by a busy road, plus the house, which displays Monet's prized collection of Japanese prints. The gardens are always flowering with something; they're at their most colorful April through July.

Cost and Hours: €10.50, €17 combo-tickets available with nearby Museum of Impressionisms, €20 with Paris' Orangerie or Marmottan Museums; daily April-Oct 9:30-18:00, closed Nov-March; tel. 02 32 51 90 31, http://fondation-monet.com.

Crowd-Beating Tips: Minimize crowds by arriving a little before 9:30, when it opens, or come after 16:00 and stay until it closes. Advance ticket and combo-ticket holders skip the ticket-buying line and use the nifty group entrance.

Visiting the House and Gardens: There are two parts to the gardens—the Walled Garden (next to the house) and the Water Garden (across the road).

For the **Walled Garden,** Monet cleared

Monet's kitchen

Wisteria drapes the Japanese bridge in Monet's Water Garden.

the land of pine trees and laid out symmetrical beds, split down the middle by a "grand alley" covered with iron trellises of climbing roses. The **Water Garden,** with Monet's famous pond and lilies, leaves artists aching for an easel. Find a bench and linger for a while. Monet landscaped like he painted—he built an Impressionist pattern of blocks of color. After he planted the gardens, he painted them, from every angle, at every time of day, in all kinds of weather.

End your visit with a wander through Monet's charming **home,** with pretty furnishings, Japanese prints, and old photos. The gift shop at the exit is the actual skylighted studio where Monet painted his masterpiece water-lily series (displayed at the Orangerie Museum in Paris).

MUSEUM OF IMPRESSIONISMS
(MUSEE DES IMPRESSIONNISMES)

This bright, modern museum, dedicated to the history of Impressionism and its legacy, houses temporary exhibits of Impressionist art.

Cost and Hours: €7.50, €17 comboticket with Monet's Garden and House, daily April-Oct 10:00-18:00, closed Nov-March; to reach it, turn left after leaving Monet's place and walk 200 yards; tel. 02 32 51 94 00, www.mdig.fr.

CLAUDE MONET'S GRAVE

Monet's grave is a 15-minute walk from his door. Turn left from his house, walk down Rue Claude Monet, and find it in the backyard of the white church Monet attended (Eglise Sainte-Radegonde). Look for flowers, with a cross above. The inscription says: *Here lies our beloved Claude Monet, born 14 November 1840, died 5 December 1926; missed by all.*

Eating

Your best lunch option is a block to the left at **$ La Capucine,** a self-serve restaurant. The rose-colored **$$ Hôtel Baudy,** once a hangout for American Impressionists, offers an appropriately pretty setting for lunch or dinner (81 Rue Claude Monet).

BEST OF THE REST

Reims

With its Roman gate, Gothic cathedral, Champagne *caves,* and vibrant pedestrian zone, Reims (pronounced "rance") feels both historic and youthful. And thanks to the TGV bullet train, it's less than an hour's ride from Paris.

Day Plan

You can see Reims' essential sights either as a day trip from Paris or as a stop en route to or from Paris. Take a morning train and explore the cathedral and city center before lunch, then spend your afternoon below ground, in a cool, chalky Champagne cellar or *cave* (pronounced "kahv"). You can be back at your Parisian hotel by dinner.

Orientation

Reims' hard-to-miss cathedral marks the city center and makes an easy orientation landmark. Most sights of interest are within a 15-minute walk from the Reims-Centre train station.

Tourist Information: The main TI is one block from the cathedral at 6 Rue Rockefeller (daily, tel. 03 26 77 45 00, www.reims-tourisme.com). A smaller TI lies just outside the Reims-Centre train station (closed Sun off-season).

Rick's Tip: *Either of Reims' TIs will* **call a taxi** *(about €10) to get you to any* **Champagne cave** *that you book. TIs also have information on* **minivan excursions** *into the vineyards and Champagne villages.*

Getting There

From Paris' Gare de l'Est station, take the **direct TGV** to the Reims-Centre station (12/day, 50 minutes). Trains also run directly from Charles de Gaulle Airport to the Champagne-Ardenne TGV station five miles away from Reims-Centre station (4/day, 45 minutes).

By **car,** day-trippers should follow *Cathédrale* signs, and park in metered

Reims Cathedral

Palais du Tau

spots on or near the cathedral or in the well-signed Parking Cathédrale structure.

To get around town, Reims has an integrated network of colorful buses, trams, and an electric shuttle bus (www.citura.fr, French only, but excellent maps).

Sights

▲▲▲REIMS CATHEDRAL

The cathedral of Reims is a glorious example of Gothic architecture and one of Europe's greatest churches. (Expect to see scaffolding during ongoing restoration work.) It celebrated its 800th birthday in 2011. Clovis, the first Christian king of the Franks, was baptized at a church on this site in AD 496, establishing France's Christian roots, which still hold firm today. Since Clovis' baptism, Reims Cathedral has served as *the* place for the coronation of 26 French kings, giving it a more important role in France's political history than Notre-Dame Cathedral in Paris. This cathedral is to France what Westminster Abbey is to England.

And there's a lot of history here. A self-assured Joan of Arc led a less-assured Charles VII to be crowned here in 1429. Thanks to Joan, the French rallied

around their new king to push the English out of France and finally end the Hundred Years' War. During the French Revolution, the cathedral was converted to a temple of reason (as was Paris' Notre-Dame). After the restoration of the monarchy, the cathedral hosted the crowning of Charles X in 1825—the last coronation here.

During World War I about 300 shells hit the cathedral, damaging statues and windows and destroying the roof, but the structure survived. Then, during the 1920s, it was completely rebuilt, thanks in large part to financial support from John D. Rockefeller Jr.

Luckily, World War II spared the church, and since then it has come to symbolize reconciliation. French and German plaques set in the pavement just in front celebrate the belief that another war today between these two nations would be unthinkable.

Cost and Hours: Free, daily 7:30-19:15, helpful information boards in English throughout the church (www.reims-cathedral.culture.fr).

Cathedral Tower: An escorted one-hour tour climbs the 250 steps of the tower to explore the rooftop and get a

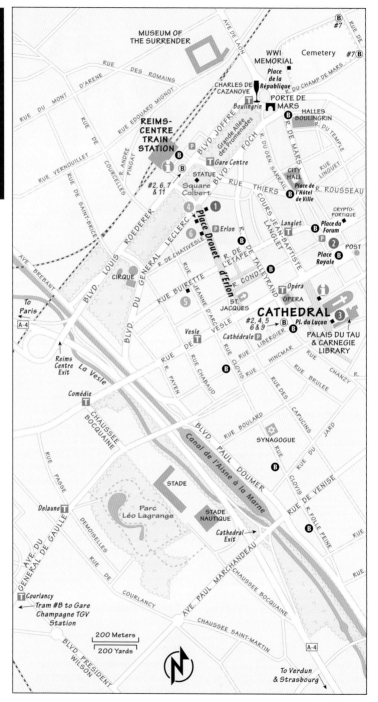

MUSEUM OF
THE SURRENDER

AVE. DE LAON

B
#7

RUE DE

WWI
MEMORIAL

Cemetery   #7 **B**

*Place
de la
République*

R. DU CHAMP DE MARS

RUE   DES   ROMAINS

CHARLES DE
CAZANOVE

D'ARENE

PORTE DE
MARS

Boulingrin

HALLES
BOULINGRIN

RUE   DU   MONT

RUE EDOUARD MIGNOT

BLVD. JOFFRE

R. DE MARS

R. DU TEMPLE

**REIMS-
CENTRE
TRAIN
STATION**

*Grande Allée
des Promenades*

RUE

DE

R. ANDRE PINGAT

R. DU GEN. SARRAIL

FOCH

RUE
LINGUET

P

B
Gare Centre

CITY
HALL

R. ROUSSEAU

RUE DE COURCELLES

#2, 6, 7
& 11

i
B

STATUE
**Square
Colbert**

BLVD.

RUE   THIERS

*Place de
l'Hôtel
de Ville*

CRYPTO-
PORTIQUE

RUE VERNOUILLET

4   **1**

Place Drouet d'Erlon

P *Erlon*

Langlet

T

*Place du
Forum*

P

2

RUE DE SAINT-BRICE

6

COURS JEAN-BAPTISTE LANGLET

R. DE L'ETAPE

POST

*Place
Royale*   **B**

BLVD. LOUIS ROEDERER

BLVD. DU GENERAL LECLERC

R. DE CHATIVESLE

RUE JEANNE D'ARC

RUE BUIRETTE

RUE

CONDORCET

CIRQUE

AVE. BREBANT

5

ST.
JACQUES

B

T   *Opéra*

OPERA

i   **P**

To
Paris

A-4

Vesle

T

Cathédrale   **P**

#2, 4, 5
6 & 9   ➤ *Pl. du Luçon*
B

CATHEDRAL   3

**PALAIS DU TAU
& CARNEGIE
LIBRARY**

Reims
Centre
Exit

La Vesle

RUE   DE   VESLE

RUE LIBERGIER

HINCMAR

RUE

RUE   CHANZY

R.

Comédie

T

RUE CLOVIS

RUE   CHABAUD

R. PAYEN

B

RUE   DES

RUE BRULEE

CAPUCINS

JARD

CHAUSSEE
BOCQUAINE

BLVD. PAUL DOUMER

RUE BOULARD

SYNAGOGUE

RUE DU

RUE   DE   VENISE

Delaune   T

Canal de l'Aisne à la Marne

STADE

B

RUE CLOVIS

R. FOLIE PEINE

AVE. DU GENERAL DE GAULLE

RUE PASSE

DEMOISELLES

RUE   DE

**Parc
Léo Lagrange**

STADE
NAUTIQUE

*Cathedral
Exit* ➤

B

RUE

T *Courlancy*

➤ Tram #B to Gare
Champagne TGV
Station

COURLANCY

AVE. PAUL MARCHANDEAU

CHAUSSEE BOCQUAINE

200 Meters

200 Yards

CHAUSSEE SAINT-MARTIN

A-4

BLVD. PRESIDENT WILSON

N

*To Verdun
& Strasbourg*

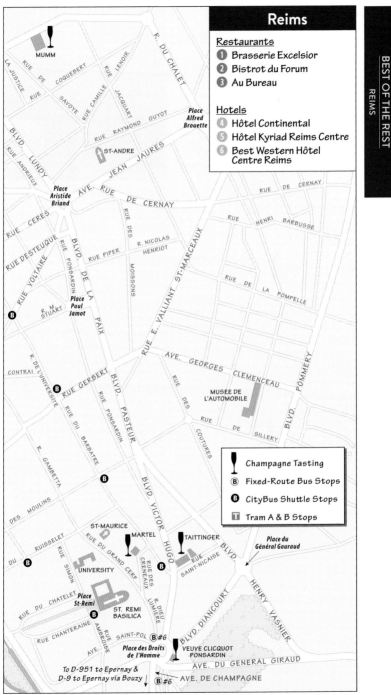

Reims

Restaurants
1. Brasserie Excelsior
2. Bistrot du Forum
3. Au Bureau

Hotels
4. Hôtel Continental
5. Hôtel Kyriad Reims Centre
6. Best Western Hôtel Centre Reims

Legend:
- Champagne Tasting
- Ⓑ Fixed-Route Bus Stops
- Ⓑ CityBus Shuttle Stops
- Ⓣ Tram A & B Stops

To D-951 to Epernay &
D-9 to Epernay via Bouzy

close-up look at the Gallery of Kings statuary (€8, €11 combo-ticket with Palais du Tau; reserve tickets on cathedral website on day of your visit, get hours at TI or Palais du Tau, where you'll pick up tickets and meet escort).

Cathedral Sound-and-Light Show (Rêve de Couleurs): For a memorable experience, join the crowd in front of the cathedral for a free, 25-minute sound-and-light show on most summer evenings. The show generally starts when it's dark—between 21:30 and 23:00 (TI has the schedule, nightly except Mon July-Aug, Wed-Sun only in June).

PALAIS DU TAU

This former Archbishop's Palace, named after the Greek letter *T (tau)* for its shape, houses artifacts from the cathedral next door and a pile of royal goodies. You'll look into the weathered eyes of original statues from the cathedral's facade, and see precious tapestries, coronation jewels, and more.

Cost and Hours: €8, €11 combo-ticket includes cathedral tower tour, Tue-Sun 9:30-18:30, Sept-April Tue-Sun 9:30-12:30 & 14:00-17:30, closed Mon year-round. The €3 audioguide is overkill for most (tel. 03 26 47 81 79, www.palais-du-tau.fr).

▲CARNEGIE LIBRARY (BIBLIOTHEQUE CARNEGIE)

The legacy of the Carnegie Library network, funded generously by the 19th-century American millionaire Andrew Carnegie and his steel fortune (notice the American flag above the main entrance on the left), extends even to Reims. Carnegie built several thousand such libraries around the world (he dedicated $200,000 for the one in Reims). Built in 1921 in the flurry of interwar reconstruction, this beautiful Art Deco building still houses the city's public library. Considering that admission is free and it's just behind the cathedral, it's worth a quick look.

Cost and Hours: Free; Tue-Wed and Fri-Sat 10:00-13:00 & 14:00-19:00 except

Museum of the Surrender

Sat until 18:00, Thu 14:00-19:00 only, closed Sun-Mon; Place Carnegie.

▲MUSEUM OF THE SURRENDER (MUSEE DE LA REDDITION)

Anyone interested in World War II will enjoy visiting the place where US General Dwight Eisenhower and the Allies received the unconditional surrender of all German forces on May 7, 1945. The news was announced the next day, turning May 8 into Victory in Europe (V-E) Day. There's an extensive collection of artifacts, but the most thrilling sight is the war room (or Signing Room), where Allied operations were managed.

Cost and Hours: €5, Wed-Mon 10:00-18:00 (may close at lunchtime—check hours locally), closed Tue, 12 Rue Franklin Roosevelt, tel. 03 26 47 84 19, www.musees-reims.fr.

Champagne Caves

Reims, the capital of the Champagne region, offers many opportunities to visit its ▲▲ world-famous chalk Champagne cellars *(caves)*. The oldest were dug by the Romans as they mined chalk and salt in the 1st century BC. Hundreds of years later, Champagne producers converted the *caves*—with their perfect and constant temperatures—into wine storage.

All charge entry fees, most have several daily English tours, and most require a reservation (only Taittinger allows

Mumm's cave

on tasting level, includes cellar tour, can reserve ahead online, April-mid-Nov daily; mid-Nov-March closed Sat-Sun; 9 Place St. Niçaise, www.taittinger.fr).

MARTEL

This small operation with less extensive *caves* offers a homey contrast, and it's a great deal. Call to set up a visit and expect a small group that might be yours alone (€16, one-hour tour and tasting, daily, reservations advised, TI can call ahead for you, 17 Rue des Créneaux, www.champagnemartel.com).

VEUVE CLICQUOT PONSARDIN

Because it's widely exported in the US, Veuve Clicquot is inundated with American travelers willing to pay the high price to visit their cellars. Reservations are required and fill up three weeks in advance, so book before your trip on their website (figure €28-60 for tour and tasting, Place des Droits de l'Homme, www.veuve-clicquot.com).

Eating

Consider **$$$ Brasserie Excelsior,** with a woody brasserie interior (96 Place Drouet d'Erlon); the informal **$$ Bistrot du Forum,** with a cool zinc bar (6 Place Forum); or **$$ Au Bureau,** on Cathedral Square—worth it if you grab a table outside (9 Place du Cardinal Luçon).

Sleeping

Try **$$$ Hôtel Continental****** on lively Place d'Erlon (RS%, 93 Place Drouet d'Erlon, www.continental-hotel.fr); **$ Hôtel Kyriad Reims Centre***** (29 Rue Buirette, www.kyriad.com/en/hotels/kyriad-reims-centre); or **$ Best Western Hôtel Centre Reims***** (75 Place Drouet d'Erlon, www.hotel-centre-reims.fr).

drop-in visits). Call, email, or visit the website for the schedule and to secure a spot on a tour.

MUMM

Mumm ("moome") is one of the easiest *caves* to visit, as it's a short walk from the central train station. Reservations are essential, especially on weekends (€20-50 depending on tasting level, includes one-hour tour; tours daily March-Oct, some closed days in off-season; 34 Rue du Champ de Mars—go to the end of the courtyard and follow *Visites des Caves* signs; www.mumm.com).

CHARLES DE CAZANOVE

If you're in a rush and not too concerned about quality, Cazanove is closest to the train station and has a cheap and basic tasting (€15, includes "tour" with 3 tastings; daily, 5-minute walk from the station up Boulevard Joffre to 8 Place de la République, www.champagnedecazanove.com).

TAITTINGER

One of the biggest, slickest, and most renowned of Reims' *caves,* Taittinger (tay-tan-zhay) runs morning and afternoon tours in English through their vast and historic cellars (€19-45 depending

Normandy

The long coast of Normandy (Normandie) shelters romantic villages, a church with a precious tapestry, the historic D-Day beaches, and the iconic island abbey of Mont St-Michel. Parisians call Normandy "the 21st arrondissement." It's their nearest beach escape.

Despite the peacefulness you sense today, the region's history is filled with war. Normandy was founded by Viking Norsemen who invaded from the north, settled here in the ninth century, and gave the region its name. A couple of hundred years later, William the Conqueror invaded England from Normandy. His victory is commemorated in a remarkable tapestry at Bayeux. A few hundred years after that, France's greatest cheerleader, Joan of Arc (Jeanne d'Arc) was convicted of heresy here and burned at the stake by the English, against whom she rallied France during the Hundred Years' War. And in 1944, Normandy was the site of a WWII battle that changed the course of history.

This large region is ideal for exploring by car. Travelers without a car can rely on taking a combination of trains, buses, and minivan tours.

NORMANDY IN 3 DAYS

You'll want a full day for the D-Day beaches and a half-day each for Honfleur, Bayeux, and Mont St-Michel.

On your first day, if you're driving between Paris and Bayeux, Honfleur makes a good day stop.

Use your second day to tour the D-Day beaches. Drive to Arromanches, then work your way west and end at Ste-Mère Eglise. Return to Bayeux for the night.

On the third day, see the sights at Bayeux, then travel in the afternoon to Mont St-Michel, which must be seen early or late to avoid the masses of midday tourists (it's best to arrive late in the day and spend the night). Leave the next morning for your next destination—likely the Loire Valley.

With extra time: Drivers coming from Paris could add a visit to Giverny en route and overnight in lovely Honfleur, then continue to Bayeux the next day.

Without a car: Take the train (3 hours) from Paris to Bayeux (skip Honfleur unless you'd like to overnight there). On the second day, take a minivan tour from Bayeux of the D-Day beaches, then return to Bayeux. On the third day, visit Mont St-Michel: Either take a shuttle-van day trip from Bayeux, or take a six-hour train-and-bus trip to Mont St-Michel and spend the night.

Getting Around Normandy

By Car: Normandy is best explored by car, which gives you the freedom to stop at the region's sights for as long as you want.

By Train and Bus: Trains from Paris serve Bayeux, Caen, and Mont St-Michel (via Pontorson or Rennes). Mont St-Michel is a headache by train, but enterprising businesses in Bayeux run **shuttle vans** between Bayeux and Mont St-Michel—a great help to those without cars.

Buses link Honfleur, Arromanches, and Mont St-Michel to train stations in nearby towns (less frequent on Sundays). To plan ahead, visit the websites for **Bus Verts** (for Honfleur, Bayeux, Arromanches, and Caen, www.busverts.fr) and **Keolis** (for Mont St-Michel, https://keolis-armor.com).

By Minivan Tour: For specifics on your many options for touring the D-Day beaches, see page 164.

HONFLEUR

Gazing at its cozy harbor lined with skinny, soaring houses, it's easy to overlook the historic importance of Honfleur (ohn-flur). For more than a thousand years, sailors have enjoyed this port's ideal location, where the Seine River greets the English Channel. William the Conqueror received supplies shipped from Honfleur. Samuel de Champlain sailed from here in 1603 to North America, where he founded Quebec City. The charming town was also a favorite of 19th-century Impressionists who were captivated by Honfleur's unusual light—the result of its river-meets-sea setting. The 19th-century artist Eugène Boudin lived and painted in Honfleur, attracting Monet and other creative types from Paris. In some ways, modern art was born in the fine light of idyllic little Honfleur.

Honfleur escaped the bombs of World War II, and today offers a romantic port enclosed on three sides by sprawling outdoor cafés. Long eclipsed by the gargantuan port of Le Havre just across the Seine, Honfleur happily uses its past as a bar stool...and sits on it.

Orientation

Honfleur is popular—expect crowds on weekends and during summer. All of Honfleur's appealing lanes and activities are within a short stroll of its old port, the Vieux Bassin. The Seine River flows just east of the center, the hills of the Côte de

Artists have found inspiration in Honfleur for generations.

NORMANDY AT A GLANCE

▲▲▲**D-Day Beaches** Atlantic coastline—stretching from Utah Beach in the west to Sword Beach in the east—dotted with WWII museums, monuments, and cemeteries left in tribute to the Allied forces who successfully carried out the largest amphibious military operation in history: D-Day. See page 162.

▲▲▲**Mont St-Michel** Pretty-as-a-mirage island abbey that once sent pilgrims' spirits soaring—and does the same for tourists today. See page 179.

▲▲**Honfleur** Picturesque port town, located where the Seine greets the English Channel, which has shimmering light that once captivated Impressionist painters. See page 141.

▲▲**Bayeux** Six miles from the D-Day beaches and the first city liberated after the D-Day landings, worth a visit for its famous medieval tapestry, enjoyable town center, and awe-inspiring cathedral, illuminated at night. See page 153.

Grâce form its western limit, and Rue de la République slices north-south through the center to the port. Honfleur has two can't-miss sights—the harbor and St. Catherine Church—and a handful of other intriguing monuments. But really, the town itself is its best sight.

Tourist Information: The TI is in the glassy public library *(Mediathéque)* on Quai le Paulmier, two blocks from the Vieux Bassin (Mon-Sat 9:30-19:00, Sun 10:00-17:00; Sept-June Mon-Sat until 18:30 and closed daily for lunch 12:30-14:00; closed Sun afternoon Nov-Easter; free WCs, tel. 02 31 89 23 30, www.ot-honfleur.fr). Here you can rent a €5 audioguide for a self-guided town walk, pick up regional bus and train schedules, and get limited information on the D-Day beaches.

Museum Pass: The €13 museum pass, sold at participating museums, covers the Eugène Boudin Museum, Maisons Satie, and other sights (www.musees-honfleur.fr).

Market Day: The area around St. Catherine Church becomes a colorful open-air market every Saturday (9:00-13:00). A smaller organic-food-only market takes place here on Wednesday mornings, and a flea market takes center stage here the first Sunday of every month and also on Wednesday evenings in summer.

Laundry: Lavomatique is a block behind the TI, toward the port (self-service only, open daily, 4 Rue Notre-Dame). **La Lavandière** has handy drop-off service (closed Sun, two blocks from the harbor at 41 Rue de la République).

◑ Honfleur Walk

For good exercise and a bird's-eye view of Honfleur and the Normandy Bridge (worth ▲), go for an uphill 30-minute walk (or quick drive) up to the Côte de Grâce—best in the early morning, late afternoon, or at sunset.

From St. Catherine Church, **walk** up Rue du Puits and then follow the blue-on-white *Rampe du Mont Joli* signs to reach the splendid view over Honfleur and the

Normandy Bridge at the top. This viewpoint alone justifies the climb.

Drivers should head up Rue Brulée and make a right on Rue Eugène Boudin, then take a hard left at Rue de Puits and follow *Côte de Grâce* signs.

At the top, walkers and drivers can continue past the viewpoint for about 300 yards along a country lane to the **Chapel of Notre-Dame de Grâce,** built in the early 1600s by the mariners and people of Honfleur (open daily 8:30-17:30). Model boats hang from the ceiling, pictures of boats balance high on the walls, and several stained-glass windows are decorated with images of sailors at sea praying to the Virgin Mary. Find the 23 church bells hanging on a wood rack 20 steps to the right as you leave the church and imagine the racket they make (the bells ring four times an hour). Below the chapel, a lookout offers a sweeping view of super-industrial Le Havre and the Seine estuary where the river hits the Manche (English Channel).

Sights

▲▲ VIEUX BASSIN (OLD PORT)

If you're an early riser, you can watch the morning light at it shines brilliantly on Honfleur's harbor. Take a prebreakfast walk to savor the quiet scene that Monet would have loved.

No matter when you go, start by standing near the water facing Honfleur's square

Vieux Bassin

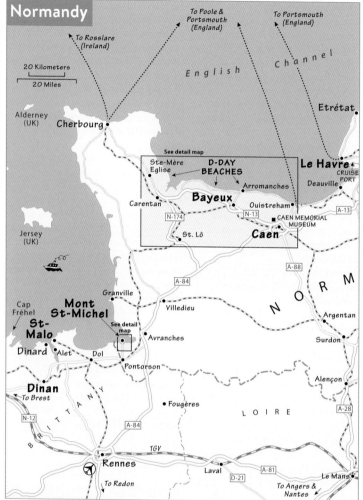

harbor, with the merry-go-round across the lock to your left, and survey the town. The word "Honfleur" is Scandinavian, meaning the shelter (*fleur*) of Hon (a Viking warlord). This town has been sheltering residents for about a thousand years. During the Hundred Years' War (14th century), the entire harbor was fortified by a big wall with twin gatehouses (the one surviving gatehouse, La Lieutenance, is on your right). A narrow channel allowing boats to pass was protected by a heavy chain.

After the walls were demolished around 1700, those skinny houses on the right side were built for the town's fishermen. How about a room on the top floor, with no elevator? Imagine moving a piano or a refrigerator into one of these units today. The spire halfway up the left side of the port belongs to Honfleur's oldest church. The port, once crammed with fishing boats, now harbors sleek sailboats.

Walk toward the Lieutenance gatehouse. In front of the barrel-vaulted arch

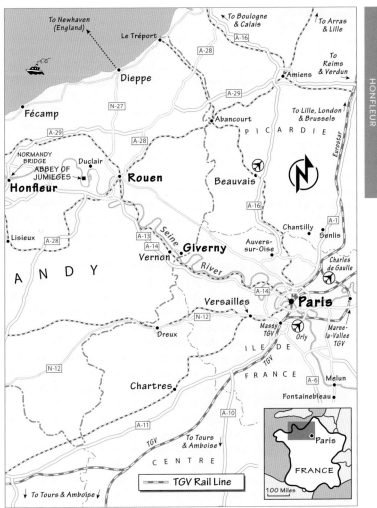

To Newhaven (England)

Le Tréport

To Boulogne & Calais

To Arras & Lille

A-16

A-28

Dieppe

Amiens

To Reims & Verdun

N-27

Fécamp

A-29

Abancourt

To Lille, London & Brussels

P I C A R D I E

A-29

NORMANDY BRIDGE

A-28

Duclair

ABBEY OF JUMIEGES

Rouen

Beauvais

Eurostar

Honfleur

A-16

A-1

Chantilly

Senlis

Lisieux

A-28

Seine

A-13

A-14

Giverny

Auvers-sur-Oise

Charles de Gaulle

Vernon

River

A N D Y

A-14

Versailles

Paris

N-12

Massy TGV

Orly

Marne-la-Vallee TGV

Dreux

I L E   D E

N-12

TGV

F R A N C E

A-6

Melun

Chartres

Fontainebleau

A-10

A-11

TGV

To Tours & Amboise

Paris

C E N T R E

FRANCE

TGV Rail Line

100 Miles

To Tours & Amboise

(once the entry to the town), you can see a bronze bust of Samuel de Champlain—the explorer who, 400 years ago, sailed with an Honfleur crew—famous for their maritime skills—to make his discoveries in the New World.

Turn around to see various tour and fishing boats and the masts of the high-flying Normandy Bridge (described later) in the distance. Fisherfolk catch flatfish, scallops, and tiny shrimp daily to bring to the Marché au Poisson, located

100 yards to your right (look for white metal structures with blue lettering). Wednesday through Saturday, you may see fishermen's wives selling *crevettes* (shrimp) and more. You can buy them *cuites* (cooked) or *vivantes* (alive and wiggly). They are happy to let you sample one (rip off the cute little head and tail, and pop what's left into your mouth—*délicieuse!*), or buy a cupful to go for a few euros.

You'll probably see artists sitting at

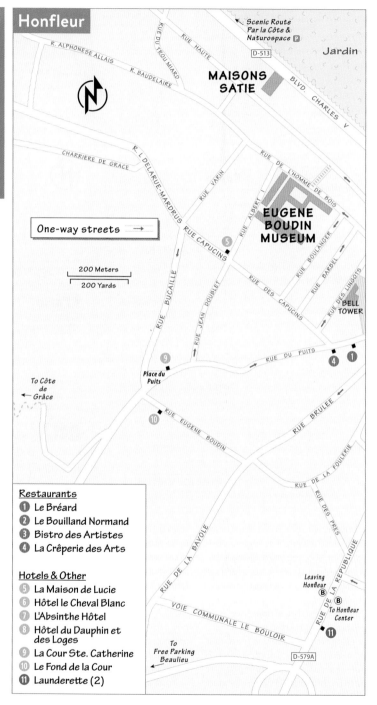

Honfleur

Scenic Route
Par la Côte &
Naturospace 🅿

Jardin

D-513

MAISONS
SATIE

BLVD CHARLES V

R. ALPHONESE ALLAIS

R. BAUDELAIRE

R. DU TROU MIARD

RUE HAUTE

CHARRIERE DE GRACE

R. L DELARUE-MARDRUS

RUE VARIN

RUE DE L'HOMME DE BOIS

EUGENE
BOUDIN
MUSEUM

RUE ALBERT I

RUE CAPUCINS

RUE BOULANGER

RUE BARBEL

RUE DES LINGOTS

One-way streets →

RUE BUCAILLE

RUE JEAN DOUBLET

RUE DES CAPUCINS

BELL
TOWER

200 Meters
200 Yards

5

9

Place du
Puits

RUE DU PUITS

4   1

To Côte
de
← Grâce

10

RUE EUGENE BOUDIN

RUE BRULEE

RUE DE LA FOULERIE

RUE DES PRES

RUE DE LA BAVOLE

Restaurants
1 Le Bréard
2 Le Bouilland Normand
3 Bistro des Artistes
4 La Crêperie des Arts

Hotels & Other
5 La Maison de Lucie
6 Hôtel le Cheval Blanc
7 L'Absinthe Hôtel
8 Hôtel du Dauphin et
   des Loges
9 La Cour Ste. Catherine
10 Le Fond de la Cour
11 Launderette (2)

VOIE COMMUNALE LE BOULOIR

Leaving
Honfleur
🅑   🅑
To Honfleur
Center

RUE DE LA REPUBLIQUE

11

To
Free Parking
Beaulieu

D-579A

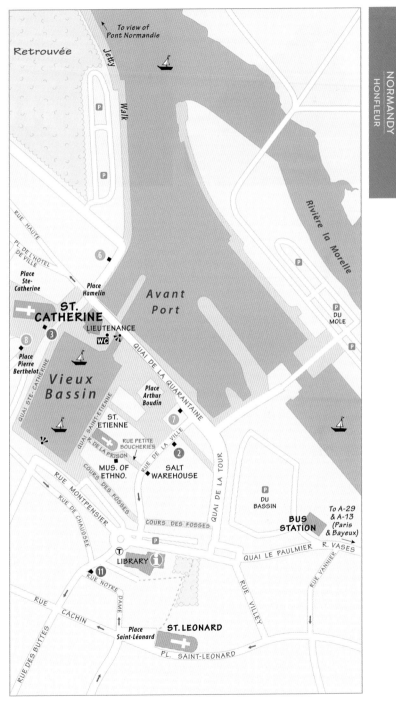

To view of
Pont Normandie

Retrouvée

Jetty

Walk

P

P

RUE HAUTE

PL DE L'HOTEL
DE VILLE

Place
Ste-
Catherine

Place
Hamelin

6

Avant
Port

ST.
CATHERINE

LIEUTENANCE

WC

8

Place
Pierre
Berthelot

QUAI STE-CATHERINE

Vieux
Bassin

3

Place
Arthur
Boudin

7

QUAI DE LA QUARANTAINE

Rivière la Morelle

P

P
DU
MOLE

P

ST.
ETIENNE

QUAI SAINT-ETIENNE

R. DE LA PRISON

RUE PETITE
BOUCHERIES

RUE DE LA VILLE

2

MUS. OF
ETHNO.

SALT
WAREHOUSE

QUAI DE LA TOUR

P
DU
BASSIN

BUS
STATION

To A-29
& A-13
(Paris
& Bayeux)

COURS DES FOSSES

RUE MONTPENSIER

RUE DE CHAUSSEE

COURS DES FOSSES

P

T
LIBRARY

i

11

RUE NOTRE DAME

RUE

CACHIN

RUE DES BUTTES

Place
Saint-Léonard

ST. LEONARD

PL. SAINT-LEONARD

RUE VILLEY

RUE VANNIER

QUAI LE PAULMIER

R. VASES

La Lieutenance gatehouse

Ste. Catherine Church

easels around the harbor, as Boudin and Monet did. Many consider Honfleur the birthplace of 19th-century Impressionism. This was a time when people began to revere the out-of-doors, and pretty towns like Honfleur and the nearby coast made perfect subjects (and still do), thanks to the unusual luminosity of the region. And with the advent of new railway lines in the late 1800s, artists could travel to the best light like never before. Monet came here to visit the artist Boudin, a hometown boy, and the battle cry of the Impressionists—"Out of the studio and into the light!"—was born. Artists set up their easels along the harbor to catch the light playing on the line of buildings, slate shingles, timbers, geraniums, clouds, and reflections in the water—much as they still do today.

▲▲ ST. CATHERINE CHURCH (EGLISE STE. CATHERINE)

St. Catherine's replaced an earlier stone church, destroyed in the Hundred Years' War. In those chaotic times, the town's money was spent to fortify its walls, leaving only enough funds to erect a wooden church. The unusual wood-shingled exterior suggests that this church has a different story to tell than most. In the last months of World War II, a bomb fell through the church's roof—but didn't explode—leaving this unique church

intact for you to visit today.

Walk inside. You'd swear that if it were turned over, the building would float—the legacy of a community of sailors and fishermen, with loads of talented boat-builders (and no church architect). When workers put up the first (left) nave in 1466, it soon became apparent that more space was needed—so a second was built in 1497 (on the right). Because it felt too much like a market hall, they added side aisles.

The oak columns were prepared as if the wood was meant for a ship—soaked in seawater for seven years and then dried for seven years. Notice some pillars are full-length and others are supported by stone bases. Trees come in different sizes, yet each pillar had to be the same length.

Cost and Hours: Free, daily 9:00-18:30, Sept-June until 17:15, Place Ste-Catherine.

Bell Tower: The church's bell tower was built away from the church to avoid placing too much stress on the wooden church's roof, and to help minimize fire hazards. Notice the funky shingled chestnut beams that run from its squat base to support the skinny tower, and find the small, faded wooden sculpture of a tiny St. Catherine over the door. Until recently the bell ringer lived in the bell tower. (The tower interior may be open to visit on summer weekends.)

Eugène Boudin (1824-1898)

Born in Honfleur, Boudin was the son of a harbor pilot. As an amateur teenage artist, he found work in an art-supply store that catered to famous artists from Paris (such as landscapists Corot and Millet) who came to paint the seaside. Boudin himself studied in Paris and his work was exhibited there, but he kept his hometown roots.

At age 30 Boudin met the teenage Claude Monet. Monet had grown up in nearby Le Havre and, like Boudin, sketched the world around him—beaches, boats, and small-town life. Boudin encouraged him to don a scarf, set up his easel outdoors, and paint the scene exactly as he saw it. Today, we say: "Well, duh!" But "open-air" painting was unorthodox for artists trained to thoroughly study their subjects in the perfect lighting of a controlled studio setting. Boudin didn't teach Monet as much as give him the courage to follow his artistic instincts.

In the 1860s and 1870s, Boudin spent summers at his farm (St. Siméon) on the outskirts of Honfleur, hosting Monet, Edouard Manet, and other hangers-on. They taught Boudin the Impressionist techniques of using bright colors and building a subject with many individual brushstrokes. Boudin adapted those "strokes" to build subjects with "patches" of color. In 1874, Boudin joined the renegade Impressionists at their "revolutionary" exhibition in Paris.

Boudin, Beach at Trouville

Rick's Tip: *As you walk around Honfleur, take time to enjoy today's art, too. The* **best art galleries** *are along the streets between St. Catherine Church and the port.*

▲EUGENE BOUDIN MUSEUM

Eugène Boudin established Honfleur's artistic tradition in the 1800s. This pleas-ing little museum opened in 1869 and has several interesting floors with many paintings of Honfleur and the surround-ing countryside, giving you a feel for Hon-fleur in the 1800s. Look for the *Peintures du 19eme Siècle* room, a small gallery of 19th-century paintings. Focus your time here. Boudin's artwork is shown alongside that of his colleagues and contemporaries (usually Claude Monet and Gustave Courbet), letting you see how those masters took Boudin's approach to the next level.

Cost and Hours: €8, covered by museum pass; May-Sept Wed-Mon 10:00-12:00 & 14:00-18:00, no lunchtime closure July-Aug, shorter hours Oct-April, closed Tue year-round; good but skippable audioguide-€2, elevator, Rue de l'Homme de Bois, tel. 02 31 89 54 00, www.musees-honfleur.fr.

▲MAISONS SATIE

If Honfleur is over-the-top cute, this museum, housed in composer Erik Satie's birthplace, is a burst of witty charm—just like the musical genius it honors. As you wander from room to room with your included audioguide, infrared signals transmit bits of Satie's dreamy music, along with a first-person story. As if you're living as an artist in 1920s Paris, you'll drift through a weird and whimsical series of old-school installations—winged pears, strangers in windows, and small girls with green eyes. The finale—performed by you—is the Laboratory of Emotions pedal-go-round, a self-propelled carousel where your feet create the music (pedal softly). For a relaxing finale, enjoy the 12-minute movie (plays by request, French only) featuring modern dance springing from Parade, Satie's collaboration with Pablo Picasso and Jean Cocteau. You'll even hear the boos and whistles that greeted these ballets' debuts. If you like Satie's music, this is a delight—a

Normandy Bridge

1920s "Yellow Submarine." If not, it can be a ho-hum experience. Allow an hour for your visit.

Cost and Hours: €6.30, includes audioguide, covered by museum pass; May-Sept Wed-Mon 10:00-19:00, off-season 11:00-18:00, closed Jan-mid-Feb and Tue year-round; last entry one hour before closing, 5-minute walk from harbor at 67 Boulevard Charles V, tel. 02 31 89 11 11, www.musees-honfleur.fr.

BOAT EXCURSIONS

Boat trips in and around Honfleur depart from various docks between Hôtel le Cheval Blanc and the opposite end of the outer port (Easter-Oct usually about 11:00-17:00). The tour boat *Calypso* takes good 45-minute spins around Honfleur's **harbor** (€8, Jetée de la Lieutenance, mobile 06 71 64 50 46). Other cruises run to the **Normandy Bridge**—the longest cable-stayed bridge in western Europe—which, unfortunately, means two boring trips through the locks (€11/1.5 hours). Choose between *Jolie France* (near Park-

Maisons Satie

Normandy's Cuisine Scene

Normandy is known as the land of the four C's: Calvados, Camembert, cider, and *crème*. The region specializes in cream sauces, organ meats (sweetbreads, tripe, and kidneys—the gizzard salads are great), and seafood (*fruits de mer*). You'll see *crêperies* offering inexpensive and good-value meals everywhere. A galette is a savory buckwheat crêpe enjoyed as a main course; a crêpe is sweet and eaten for dessert.

Dairy products are big, too. Local cheeses are Camembert (mild to very strong), Brillat-Savarin (buttery), Livarot (spicy and pungent), Pavé d'Auge (spicy and tangy), and Pont l'Evêque (earthy).

What, no local wine? *Eh oui,* that's right. Here's how to cope. Fresh, white Muscadet wines are made nearby (in western Loire); they're cheap and a good match with much of Normandy's cuisine. But Normandy is proud of its many apple-based beverages. You can't miss the powerful Calvados apple brandy or the Bénédictine brandy (made by local monks). The local dessert, *trou Normand,* is apple sorbet swimming in Calvados. The region also produces three kinds of alcoholic apple ciders: *Cidre* can be *doux* (sweet), *brut* (dry), or *bouché* (sparkling—and the strongest). You'll also find bottles of Pommeau, a tasty blend of apple juice and Calvados (sold in many shops), as well as *poiré,* a tasty pear cider. And don't leave Normandy without sampling a *kir Normand,* a mix of crème de cassis and cider. Drivers in Normandy should be on the lookout for *Route du Cidre* signs (with a bright red apple); this tourist trail leads you to small producers of handcrafted cider and brandy.

ing du Môle, Jetée du Transit, mobile 06 71 64 50 46, www.promenade-en-bateau-honfleur.fr) or *L'Evasion* (near Hôtel le Cheval Blanc, Quai des Passagers, mobile 06 31 89 21 10).

Eating

Eat seafood, crêpes, or cream sauces here. Choose between an irresistible waterfront table at one of many lookalike places lining the harbor, or finer dining elsewhere in town. It's best to call ahead to reserve (particularly on weekends). While I wouldn't blame you for enjoying a forgettable meal in an unforgettable setting on the harborfront, consider these better alternatives a couple of blocks away.

$$$$ Le Bréard is a fine place to dial it up a little and eat very well for a fair price. The decor is low key but elegant, the cuisine is inventive, delicious, and not particularly *Normand,* and the service is excellent (closed Mon, 7 Rue du Puits, tel. 02 31 89 53 40).

$$ Le Bouilland Normand hides a block off the port on a pleasing square and offers true *Normand* cuisine at reasonable prices. Annette, Claire, and chef-hubby Bruno provide quality dishes and enjoy serving travelers (closed Wed and Sun, dine inside or out, 7 Rue de la Ville, tel. 02 31 89 02 41).

Rick's Tip: *If you're in Honfleur on a clear morning,* **enjoy the ambience of breakfast on the port,** *where several cafés offer* petit déjeuner. *Morning sun and views are best from the high side of the harbor.*

$$ Bistro des Artistes is a two-woman operation with a pleasant 10-table dining room (call ahead for a window table). Hardworking Anne-Marie cooks up huge portions; one course is plenty...and maybe a dessert (great salads, closed Wed, 30 Place Berthelot, tel. 02 31 89 95 90).

$ La Crêperie des Arts serves up crêpes in a comfortable setting with a huge fireplace, and is a good, centrally located budget option (closed Tue-Wed, 13 Rue du Puits, tel. 02 31 89 14 02).

Sleeping

Though Honfleur is popular in summer, it's busiest on weekends and holidays (blame Paris). English is widely spoken (blame vacationing Brits).

Hotels

$$$ La Maison de Lucie*** is a fine *Normand* splurge and greets its guests with a garden courtyard, sumptuous lounges, and rooms filled with thoughtful touches and fine furnishings (suites available, 44 Rue des Capucines, tel. 02 31 14 40 40, www.lamaisondelucie.com, info@lamaisondelucie.com).

$$$ Hôtel le Cheval Blanc*** is an impersonal waterfront splurge with port views from all of its 35 plush and pricey rooms (many with queen beds), plus a rare-in-this-town elevator and a spa, but no air-conditioning—noise can be a problem with windows open (family rooms, pay parking, 2 Quai des Passagers, tel. 02 31 81 65 00, www.hotel-honfleur.com, info@hotel-honfleur.com).

$$ L'Absinthe Hôtel*** offers 11 tasteful rooms with king-size beds in two locations. The traditional rooms in the main (reception) section come with wood-beamed decor and share a cozy public lounge with a fireplace. Six rooms are located above their next-door restaurant and have views of the modern port and three-star, state-of-the-art comfort. There are minimal hotel services as the focus is their restaurant (includes breakfast, air-con in both buildings, private pay parking, 1 Rue de la Ville, tel. 02 31 89 23 23, www.absinthe.fr, reservation@absinthe.fr).

$$ Hôtel du Dauphin et des Loges*** combines two hotels in adjacent locations and delivers very central and fairly priced rooms. The main building (Hôtel du Dauphin with reception) has narrow stairs (normal in Honfleur), an Escher-esque floor plan, and Wi-Fi in the lobby only. The Hôtel des Loges is more comfortable with larger rooms, Wi-Fi in all rooms, and slightly higher rates (RS%, a stone's throw from St. Catherine Church at 10 Place Pierre Berthelot, tel. 02 31 89 15 53, www.hoteldudauphin.com, info@hotelhonfleur.com).

Chambres d'Hotes

The TI has a long list of Honfleur's many *chambres d'hôtes* (rooms in private homes), but most are too far from the town center. Those listed here are good values.

$$ La Cour Ste. Catherine is an enchanting bed-and-breakfast with six big, tasteful rooms—each with a separate sitting area—surrounding a perfectly *Normand* courtyard with fine plantings and small sitting areas placed just so. There's a cozy lounge area ideal for cool evenings and a gourmet, home-cooked dinner (€32, must book ahead). They also have free loaner bikes and serve light snacks, wine, and other drinks all day (includes good breakfast, cash only, pay parking, 200 yards up Rue du Puits from St. Catherine Church at #74, tel. 02 31 89 42 40, www.coursaintecatherine.com, coursaintecatherine@orange.fr).

$$ Le Fond de la Cour, kitty-corner to La Cour Ste. Catherine and run by British expats Amanda and Craig, offers a good mix of crisp, modern, and comfortable accommodations around a peaceful courtyard. They have cottages that can sleep four, and four comfortable doubles (doubles include English-style breakfast, free street parking nearby, limited private pay parking, 29 Rue Eugène Boudin, mobile 06 72 20 72 98, www.lefonddela-cour.com, amanda.ferguson@orange.fr).

Transportation
Arriving and Departing
BY CAR

Follow *Centre-Ville* signs, then find your hotel and unload your bags (double-parking is OK for a few minutes). Parking is a headache in Honfleur, especially on summer and holiday weekends. Some hotels offer pay parking (worth considering); otherwise, your hotelier knows where you can park for free. If you don't mind paying for convenience, Parking du Bassin across from the TI is central (€3/hour, €24/24 hours). To save piles of euros, find Parking du Môle or Parking Bassin de l'Est (€5/day). Free parking is available farther out at the Naturospace Museum (15-minute walk up Boulevard Charles V, near the beach), and at Parking Beaulieu (take Rue St-Nichol to Rue Guillaume de Beaulieu). Street parking, metered during the day, is free from 20:00 to 8:00. See the "Honfleur" map for parking locations.

BY BUS

Get off at the small bus station (*gare routière*), and confirm your departure at the information counter. To reach the TI

and Old Town, turn right as you exit the station and walk five minutes up Quai le Paulmier. Note that the bus stop on Rue de la République is closer to some accommodations (see the "Honfleur" map). If you need a taxi, call 06 08 60 17 98.

Leaving Honfleur: There's no direct train service to Honfleur, so you must connect by bus or car. Buses #39 (express) and #20 (local) link Honfleur with train service in Caen and Deauville. Some trips also run to Le Havre on these lines. Bus #50 runs between Le Havre, Honfleur, and Lisieux. Although train and bus service usually is coordinated, confirm your connection with the helpful staff at Honfleur's bus station (English info desk open Mon-Fri 9:30-12:00 & 13:15-18:00, in summer also Sat-Sun, tel. 02 31 89 28 41, www.busverts.fr). If the station is closed, you can get schedules at the TI. Rail-pass holders will save money by connecting through Deauville, as bus fares increase with distance.

From Honfleur by Bus and/or Train to: Caen (bus #39 2/day, 1 hour; slower bus #20 12/day Mon-Sat, 7/day Sun, 2 hours); **Bayeux** (bus #39 or #20 to Caen, then 20-minute train to Bayeux); **Paris'** Gare St. Lazare (13/day, 2-3.5 hours, by bus to Caen, Lisieux, Deauville, or Le Havre, then train to Paris; buses from Honfleur meet most Paris trains).

BAYEUX

Only six miles from the D-Day beaches, Bayeux was the first city liberated after the landing on June 6, 1944. Incredibly, the town was spared the bombs of World War II. The Allied Command needed an intact town from which to administer the push to Berlin. And after a local chaplain made sure London knew that his city was neither strategically important nor a German headquarters, a scheduled bombing raid was canceled—making Bayeux the closest city to the D-Day landing site not destroyed. Even without its famous medi-

Water mill and mill pond in Bayeux

eval tapestry and proximity to the D-Day beaches, Bayeux would be worth a visit for its enjoyable town center and awe-inspiring cathedral, beautifully illuminated at night. Its location and manageable size (pop. 14,000) make Bayeux an ideal home base for visiting the area's sights, particularly if you lack a car. You can day-trip to the D-Day beaches on a minivan tour (see "D-Day Beaches," later in this chapter) or to Mont St-Michel by shuttle van (see Bayeux's "Transportation," later).

Orientation

Tourist Information: The information-packed TI is on a small bridge two blocks north of the cathedral. Ask for bus schedules to the beaches and inquire about special events, concerts, and short tours of local sights. They have an excellent—and free—D-Day booklet (*Normandy, Land of Liberty*), but WWII buffs may prefer the D-Day maps (€5-8) showing troop deployments and more (June-Aug daily 9:00-19:00, April-May and Sept-Oct Mon-Sat 9:30-12:30 & 14:00-18:00, Sun 10:00-13:00 & 14:00-18:00; shorter hours off-season; on Pont St. Jean leading to Rue St. Jean, tel. 02 31 51 28 28,

www.bessin-normandie.com). For a **self-guided walking tour**, pick up the map called *Découvrez Vieux Bayeux* at the TI, which corresponds to bronze info plates embedded in sidewalks around town.

Helpful Hints

Sightseeing Tips: Bayeux's three main museums—the Bayeux Tapestry, Battle of Normandy Memorial Museum, and MAHB—offer combo-tickets that save you money if you see more than one sight. A combo-ticket covering two sights is €12; for all three it's €15 (buy at the first sight you visit). Note that many sights close in January.

Market Days: The Saturday open-air market on Place St. Patrice is Bayeux's best, though the Wednesday market on pedestrian Rue St. Jean is pleasant. Both end by 13:00.

Laundry: A launderette is a block behind the TI, on Rue Maréchal Foch. Another launderette is near Place St. Patrice, at 69 Rue des Bouchers (both open daily).

Bike Rental: These two places rent both electric and standard bikes. **Vélos Location** is across from the TI and delivers to outlying hotels (daily 8:00-20:30, closes earlier off-season, inside grocery store at Impasse de Islet, tel. 02 31 92 89 16, www.velosbayeux.com). **Maison du Vélo** is near the train station at 4 Rue de la Résistance (tel. 02 31 21 52 50, www.lamaisonduvelobayeux.fr).

Sights

▲▲▲BAYEUX TAPESTRY (TAPISSERIE DE BAYEUX)

Made of wool embroidered onto linen cloth, this historically precious document is a mesmerizing 70-yard-long cartoon. The tapestry tells the story of William the Conqueror's rise from duke of Normandy to king of England, and shows his victory over England's King Harold at the Battle of Hastings in 1066. Long and skinny, the tapestry was designed to hang in the nave of Bayeux's cathedral as a reminder for locals of their ancestor's courage. The terrific museum that houses the tapestry is an unusually good chance to teach your kids about the Middle Ages. Models, mannequins, a movie, and more make it an engaging, fun place to visit.

Cost and Hours: €9.50, covered by Bayeux museums combo-ticket, includes excellent audioguide for adults and special kids' version; daily May-Aug 9:00-19:00, March-April and Sept-Oct until 18:30; Nov-Dec and Feb 9:30-12:30 & 14:00-18:00, closed Jan; last entry 45 minutes before closing, 13 bis Rue de Nesmond, tel. 02 31 51 25 50, www.bayeuxmuseum.com. Photography of the actual tapestry is not allowed, but you can take pictures of a replica.

Planning Your Visit: It's busiest in August, and most crowded from 10:00 to 17:00. Arrive before 10:00, during lunch, or late in the day (lunchtime is most reliably quiet). As the audioguide cannot be paused, you're limited to 25 minutes with the tapestry. It's a strict one-way route. Allow at least a full hour for your complete museum visit.

Film: When buying your ticket, get the schedule for the English version of the 16-minute battle film (runs every 40 minutes). Because you can watch the film only after viewing the tapestry, and the last show time is about an hour before closing, arriving late means no film.

Visiting the Museum: Your visit starts with the actual **tapestry,** accompanied by an included audioguide that gives a top-notch, fast-moving, 25-minute scene-by-scene narration complete with period music (no pausing or rewinding—if you lose your place, find subtitles in Latin).

Appreciate the fun details—such as the bare legs in scene 4 or Harold's pouting expressions in various frames—and look for references to places you may have visited (like Dinan). Pay strict attention to scene 23, where Harold takes his oath to William; the importance of keeping one's word is the point of the tapestry. Get close and (almost) feel the tapestry's texture. The most famous scene is Harold's death: This marks the end of the intense battle—and victory for William.

Next, you'll climb upstairs into a room

Viewing the Bayeux Tapestry

King Harold's death depicted in tapestry

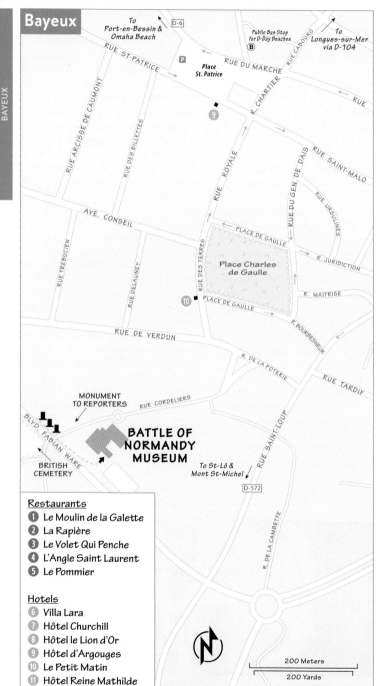

Bayeux

To
Port-en-Bessin &
Omaha Beach

D-6

Public Bus Stop
for D-Day Beaches

B

RUE CABOURG

To
Longues-sur-Mer
via D-104

RUE ST-PATRICE

P

Place
St. Patrice

RUE DU MARCHE

R. CHARTIER

RUE

RUE ARCISSE DE CAUMONT

RUE DES BILLETTES

9

RUE ROYALE

RUE SAINT-MALO

RUE DU GEN. DE DAIS

AVE. CONSEIL

RUE TREBUCIEN

RUE DELAUNEY

RUE DES TERRES

PLACE DE GAULLE

RUE URSULINES

Place Charles
de Gaulle

R. JURIDICTION

10

PLACE DE GAULLE

R. MAITRISE

R BOURBESNEUR

RUE DE VERDUN

R. DE LA POTERIE

RUE TARDIF

MONUMENT
TO REPORTERS

RUE CORDELIERS

BLVD. FABIAN WARE

RUE SAINT-LOUP

BATTLE OF
NORMANDY
MUSEUM

BRITISH
CEMETERY

To St-Lô &
Mont St-Michel

D-572

R. DE LA CAMBETTE

Restaurants
1 Le Moulin de la Galette
2 La Rapière
3 Le Volet Qui Penche
4 L'Angle Saint Laurent
5 Le Pommier

Hotels
6 Villa Lara
7 Hôtel Churchill
8 Hôtel le Lion d'Or
9 Hôtel d'Argouges
10 Le Petit Matin
11 Hôtel Reine Mathilde

N

200 Meters

200 Yards

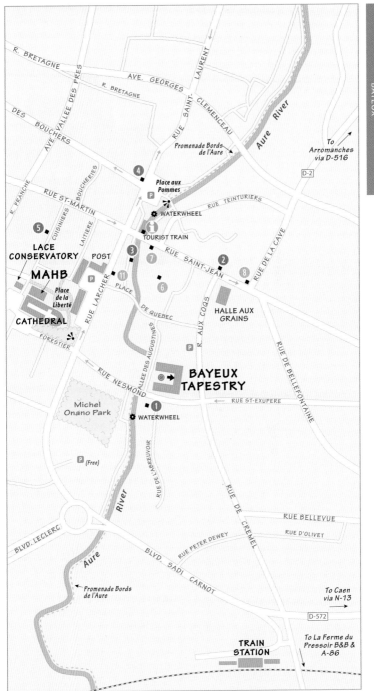

R. BRETAGNE

AVE. GEORGES

RUE SAINT-LAURENT

R. BRETAGNE

AVE. VALLÉE DES PRÉS

DES BOUCHERS

Aure River

Promenade Bords
de l'Aure

To
Arromanches
via D-516

D-2

R. FRANCHE

RUE ST-MARTIN

RUE DES BOUCHERIES

❹

Place aux
Pommes

P

⚙ WATERWHEEL

RUE TEINTURIERS

❺

CUISINIERS

LAITIÈRE

ℹ

TOURIST TRAIN

❸

❼

RUE SAINT-JEAN

❷

RUE DE LA CAVE

LACE
CONSERVATORY

POST

❽

MAHB

P

❶❶

PLACE

DE QUÉBEC

R. AUX COQS

HALLE AUX
GRAINS

Place
de la
Liberté

RUE LARCHER

❻

CATHEDRAL

FORESTIER

ALLÉE DES AUGUSTINES

P

RUE DE BELLEFONTAINE

RUE NESMOND

Michel
Onano Park

⚙ WATERWHEEL

BAYEUX
TAPESTRY

❶

RUE ST-EXUPÈRE

P (Free)

RUE DE L'ABREUVOIR

RUE DE CRÉMEL

River

RUE BELLEVUE

RUE D'OLIVET

BLVD. LECLERC

Aure

BLVD. SADI CARNOT

RUE PETER DEWEY

To Caen
via N-13

Promenade Bords
de l'Aure

D-572

To La Ferme du
Pressoir B&B &
A-86

TRAIN
STATION

filled with engaging **exhibits,** including a full-size replica of a Viking ship much like the one William used to cross the Channel (Normans inherited their weaponry and seafaring skills from the Norsemen). You'll also see mannequins (find William looking unmoved with his new crown), a replica of the Domesday Book (an inventory of noble's lands as ordered by William), and models of castles (who knew that the Tower of London was a Norman project?).

Your visit finishes with a **film** that ties it all together one last time (in the cinema upstairs, skippable if you're pressed for time). Just before the theater you reach a full-sized replica of the tapestry (which you are welcome to photograph).

▲BAYEUX CATHEDRAL

This massive building, as big as Paris' Notre-Dame, dominates the small town of Bayeux. Make a point to enjoy the cathedral rising over the town late in the afternoon, when the facade is bathed in light, or after dark, when the entire church is illuminated.

Cost and Hours: Free, daily July-Aug 8:30-19:00, Sept-June until 18:00, 4 Rue du Général de Dais.

Visiting the Cathedral: To start your visit, find the small **square** opposite the front entry (info board about the cathedral facade in rear corner). Notice the two towers—originally Romanesque, they were capped later with tall Gothic spires. The cathedral's west facade is structurally Romanesque, but with a decorative Gothic "curtain" added.

Now step inside the cathedral. The magnificent view of the **nave** from the top of the steps shows a mix of Romanesque (ground floor) and soaring Gothic (upper floors). Historians believe the Bayeux tapestry originally hung here. Imagine it draped halfway up the big Romanesque arches. Try to visualize this scene with the original, richly colored stained glass in all those upper windows. Rare 13th-century stained-glass bits are in the high central window above the altar; the other glass (below) is from the 19th and 20th centuries.

Bayeux Cathedral

Walk down the nave and notice the areas between the big, round **arches.** That busy zigzag patterning characterizes Norman art in France as well as in England. These 11th-century Romanesque arches are decorated with a manic mix of repeated geometric shapes: half-circles, hash marks, full circles, and diagonal lines. Notice also the creepy faces eyeing you, especially the ring of devil heads lining the third arch on the right.

More 13th-century Norman Gothic is in the **choir** (the fancy area behind the central altar). Here, simple Romanesque carvings lie around Gothic arches with characteristically tall, thin lines, which add a graceful verticality to the interior.

For maximum 1066 atmosphere, step into the beautifully lit **crypt** (beneath the central altar), which originally was used as a safe spot for the cathedral's relics.

▲MAHB (MUSEE D'ART ET D'HISTOIRE BARON GERARD)

For a break from D-Day and tapestries, MAHB offers a modest review of European art and history in a beautiful display space within what was once the Bayeux bishop's palace. The 14 rooms on two

The Battle of Hastings

Because of this pivotal battle, the most memorable date of the Middle Ages is 1066. England's king, Edward the Confessor, was about to die without an heir. The big question: Who would succeed him—Harold, an English nobleman and the king's brother-in-law, or William, duke of Normandy and the king's cousin? Edward chose William, and sent Harold to Normandy to give William the news. On the journey, Harold was captured. To win his release, he promised he would be loyal to William and not contest the decision. To test his loyalty, William sent Harold to battle for him in Brittany. Harold was successful, and William knighted him. To further test his loyalty, William had Harold swear on the relics of the Bayeux cathedral that when Edward died, he would allow William to ascend the throne. Harold returned to England, Edward died...and Harold grabbed the throne.

William, known as William the Bastard, invaded England to claim the throne. Harold met him in southern England at the town of Hastings, where their forces fought a fierce 14-hour battle. Harold was killed, and his Saxon forces were routed. William—now "the Conqueror"—marched to London, claimed his throne, and became king of England (though he spoke no English).

The advent of a Norman king of England muddied the political waters and set in motion 400 years of conflict between England and France—not to be resolved until the end of the Hundred Years' War (1453). The Norman conquest of England brought that country into the European mainstream (but Brexit might reverse the flow). The Normans established a strong central English government. Historians speculate that had William not succeeded, England would have remained on the fringe of Europe (like Scandinavia), and French culture (and language) would have prevailed in the New World—which would have meant no communication issues for us in France. Hmmm.

floors are laid out in chronological order (prehistory, ancient Rome, medieval, and early modern) and descriptions are translated into English. Bayeux was born during the Roman Empire and you'll see ample evidence of that. In the stern Court of Justice—a courtroom from French revolutionary times (1793)—a bust of Lady Liberty (Marianne) presides over the tribunal like a secular goddess, backed by some Napoleonic stained glass (1806). You'll see a fine little collection of 18th- and 19th-century paintings donated by Baron Henri-Alexandre Gérard more than a century ago. Notable are an early work— *Le Philosophe (The Philosopher)*—by Neo-classical master Jacques-Louis David and,

by Antoine-Jean Gros, *Sappho*—a moon-lit version of the Greek poetess' suicide that influenced Géricault and Delacroix. Lace lovers will enjoy several rooms of exquisite lace with drawers full of bobbins and artful creations. Your visit is capped with an exhibit dedicated to the ceramics of Bayeux.

Cost and Hours: €7.50, covered by Bayeux museums combo-ticket, daily May-Sept 9:30-18:30, shorter hours off-season, near the cathedral at 37 Rue du Bienvenu, tel. 02 31 92 14 21, www.bayeuxmuseum.com.

BATTLE OF NORMANDY
MEMORIAL MUSEUM
(MUSÉE MÉMORIAL DE LA
BATAILLE DE NORMANDIE)

This museum provides a manageable overview of WWII's Battle of Normandy. With its many maps and timelines of the epic battle to liberate northern France, it's aimed at military history buffs. You'll get a good briefing on the Atlantic Wall (the German fortifications stretching along the coast—useful before visiting Longues-sur-Mer), learn why Normandy was selected as the landing site, understand General Charles de Gaulle's contributions to the invasion, and realize the key role played by aviation. You'll also appreciate the challenges faced by doctors, war correspondents, and civil engineers (who had to clean up after the battles—the gargantuan bulldozer on display looks useful).

Cost and Hours: €7.50, covered by Bayeux museums combo-ticket, daily May-Sept 9:30-18:30, Oct-Dec and mid-Feb-April 10:00-12:30 & 14:00-18:00, closed Jan-mid-Feb, last entry one hour before closing, on Bayeux's ring road, 20 minutes on foot from center on Boulevard Fabian Ware, free parking, tel. 02 31 51 25 50, www.bayeuxmuseum.com.

Film: A 25-minute film with original footage gives a good summary of the Normandy invasion from start to finish, and highlights the slog that continued even after the beaches were liberated (normally shown in English May-Sept at 10:30, 12:00, 14:00, 15:30, and 17:00; Oct-April at 10:30, 14:45, and 16:15).

Nearby: A right out of the museum leads along a footpath to the **Monument to Reporters,** a grassy walkway lined with white roses and stone monuments listing, by year, the names of reporters who have died in the line of duty from 1944 to today.

The path continues to the **British Military Cemetery,** decorated with 4,144 simple gravestones marking the final resting places of these fallen soldiers.

Eating

You'll find many restaurants along Rue St. Jean, a traffic-free street lined with cafés, *crêperies,* and inexpensive dining options. As there's more demand for good restaurants than supply in Bayeux, you're smart to book a day ahead for the $$$ listings below.

$ Le Moulin de la Galette is like eating in an Impressionist painting. Enjoy a big selection of tasty crêpes, salads, and *plats* at good prices in a dreamy setting right on the small river. There's fine seating inside, but the place is very popular so book ahead or come when it opens at 18:00 (effective heaters, closed Wed, 38 Rue de Nesmond, tel. 02 31 22 47 75).

$$$ La Rapière is a wood-beamed eatery—calm and romantic—filled with locals enjoying a refined meal and a rare-these-days cheese platter for a finale. Reservations are wise (closed Sun, 53 Rue St. Jean, tel. 02 31 21 05 45, www.larapiere.net, charming Linda).

$ Le Volet Qui Penche is a fun-loving, wine-shop-meets-bistro run by playful, English-speaking Pierre-Henri and Stéphane. They serve salads, escargot, charcuterie-and-cheese platters, and a small selection of meaty à la carte dishes as well as a vast selection of wines and cider by the glass (food service 18:00-21:00 most days—making early dinners easy, closed Sun, near the TI at 3 Passage de l'Islet, tel. 02 31 21 98 54).

$$$ L'Angle Saint Laurent is a tasteful and elegant place run by a husband-and-

wife team (Caroline speaks English and manages the floor while Sébastien cooks). Come here for a special meal of *Normand* specialties done in a contemporary gourmet style. The selection is limited and changes with the season (good wine list, closed Mon, 2 Rue des Bouchers, reserve in advance, tel. 02 31 92 03 01, www.langle-saintlaurent.com).

$$ Le Pommier, with street appeal inside and out, is a good place to sample regional products with clever twists in a relaxed yet refined atmosphere. Owner Thierry mixes old and new in his cuisine and decor, and focuses on organic food (good vegetarian *menu,* open daily, 38 Rue des Cuisiniers, tel. 02 31 21 52 10, www.restaurantlepommier.com).

Sleeping

$$$$ Villa Lara***** owns the town's most luxurious accommodations smack in the center of Bayeux. Most of the 28 American-size, spacious rooms have brilliant views of the cathedral (best after dark), and a few have small terraces. Hands-on owner Rima and her attentive staff take top-notch care of their guests (pricey but excellent breakfast, elevator, exercise room, comfortable lounges, free and secure parking, between the tapestry museum and TI at 6 Place de Québec, tel. 02 31 92 00 55, www.hotel-villalara.com, info@hotel-villalara.com).

$$$ Hôtel Churchill,*** on a traffic-free street across from the TI, could not be more central. The hotel has 46 plush-and-pricey rooms—some with traditional furnishings, and others quite modern. All have big beds and surround convivial public spaces peppered with historic photos of Bayeux's liberation (family rooms, no elevator, 14 Rue St. Jean, tel. 02 31 21 31 80, www.hotel-churchill.fr, info@hotel-churchill.fr).

$$ Hôtel le Lion d'Or,*** General Eisenhower's favorite hotel in Bayeux, draws a loyal American and British clientele who love the historic aspect of staying here. It has an atmospheric Old World bar, 31 stylish rooms, and a responsive staff (no elevator, no air-con, limited pay parking, restaurant with fair prices, 71 Rue St. Jean, tel. 02 31 92 06 90, www.liondor-bayeux.fr, info@liondor-bayeux.fr).

$$ Hôtel d'Argouges*** (dar-goozh) is named for its builder, Lord d'Argouges. This tranquil retreat has a mini château feel with classy public spaces, lovely private gardens, and 28 standard-comfort rooms. The hotel is impeccably run by Frederic and his staff (big family rooms, good breakfast, no air-con, no elevator, secure free parking, just off Place St. Patrice at 21 Rue St. Patrice, tel. 02 31 92 88 86, www.hotel-dargouges.com, info@hotel-dargouges.com).

$$ Le Petit Matin, run by friendly Pascal, is a central, kid-friendly, and handsome bed-and-breakfast with good public spaces, five stylish rooms with big bathrooms, and a magnifique back garden with play toys and tables (breakfast included, on Place Charles de Gaulle at 9 Rue des Terres, tel. 02 31 10 09 27, www.lepetitmatin.fr, lepetitmatin@hotmail.fr).

$ Hôtel Reine Mathilde** is a solid, centrally located value with 16 sharp rooms above an easygoing brasserie, and 10 pricier and larger rooms with three-star comfort in two annexes nearby (family rooms, some rooms with air-con, no elevator, reception one block from TI at 23 Rue Larcher, tel. 02 31 92 08 13, www.hotel-bayeux-reinemathilde.fr, info@hotel-bayeux-reinemathilde.fr).

Transportation
Arriving and Departing
BY CAR

A handy ring road circles Bayeux with well-signed parking and hotels. Look for the cathedral spires and follow signs for *Centre-Ville,* and then signs for the *Tapisserie* or your hotel. Day-trippers will find pay parking lots in the town center (including at the Hôtel de Ville near the TI; and at Place St. Patrice, 3-hour limit,

free parking 12:00-14:00 & 19:00-21:00).
You can park for free along the ring road
below the station and at a few lots in the
city (the TI has a map of free parking, or
ask your hotelier).

Rick's Tip: **Don't park your car overnight on Place St. Patrice on Friday,** *as it will be towed early Saturday for market day.*

If you need to **rent a car,** Bayeux offers
two choices. **Hertz** allows you to drop
off in a different city and is open daily,
but it's not very central—you'll need to
take a cab (Mon-Fri 8:00-20:00, Sat-Sun
8:00-12:00 & 14:00-17:00, at the Total gas
station on Route de Cherbourg, tel. 02
31 92 03 26). **Renault Rent** is just below
the train station on the ring road at the
Renault dealership, but you must return
your car here (Mon-Sat 7:30-19:30,
closed Sun, 16 Boulevard Sadi Carnot,
tel. 02 31 51 18 51). Allow about €50-70/
day with a 200-kilometer limit, which is
sufficient to see the key sights from Arromanches to Utah Beach—you'll drive
about 180 kilometers.

BY TRAIN AND BUS
Trains and buses share the same station
(no bag check). It's a 15-minute **walk**
from the station to the Bayeux Tapestry museum, and 15 minutes from the
tapestry to Place St. Patrice. To reach
the tapestry, the cathedral, and recommended hotels, cross the major street
in front of the station and follow Rue de
Cremel toward *l'Hôpital,* then turn left on
Rue Nesmond. Find signs to the *Tapisserie*
(tapestry) or continue on to the cathedral.
Taxis usually wait at the station—allow
€9 to any recommended hotel or sight
in Bayeux, and €21 to Arromanches (€32
after 19:00 and on Sundays, taxi tel. 02 31
92 92 40 or mobile 06 70 40 07 96).

From Bayeux by Train to: Paris' Gare
St. Lazare (9/day, 2.5 hours, some change
in Caen), **Amboise** (4/day, 5 hours, change
in Caen and Tours' St-Pierre-des-Corps),

Caen (20/day, 20 minutes), **Honfleur** (2/
day, 20-minute train to Caen, then 1-hour
express bus #39; or train to Caen and
slower bus #20, 12/day Mon-Sat, 7/day Sun,
2 hours; bus info tel. 02 31 89 28 41, www.
busverts.fr), **Pontorson/Mont St-Michel**
(2/day, 6 hours, train to Pontorson, then
bus to Mont St-Michel; also consider faster
shuttle vans described below).

By Shuttle Van to Mont St-Michel:
Two services run shuttle-van day trips to
Mont St-Michel for €65 round-trip (about
1.5 hours each way, plus at least 3 hours
at Mont St-Michel): **Hôtel Churchill**
(small discount for hotel guests, www.
hotel-churchill.fr) and **Bayeux Shuttle**
(includes skip-the-line abbey ticket, www.
bayeuxshuttle.com). Either trip is a terrific
deal, as you'll get a free tour of Normandy
along the way from your knowledgeable
driver. Both run morning and afternoon
trips when demand justifies.

D-DAY BEACHES

The 54 miles of Atlantic coast north of
Bayeux—stretching from Utah Beach in
the west to Sword Beach in the east—are
littered with WWII museums, monuments, cemeteries, and battle remains
left in tribute to the courage of the British,
Canadian, and American armies that successfully carried out the largest amphibious invasion in history: D-Day. (It's called
Jour J in French.) It was on these serene
beaches, at the crack of dawn on June
6, 1944, that the Allies (roughly one-
half Americans and one-half British and
Canadians) finally gained a foothold in
France. From this moment, Nazi Europe
was destined to crumble.

*The first 24 hours of the invasion will be
decisive... The fate of Germany depends
on the outcome... For the Allies, as well
as Germany, it will be the longest day.*
—Field Marshal Erwin Rommel to
his aide, April 22, 1944

Utah Beach memorial

June 6, 2019, was the 75th anniversary of the landings. It was a particularly poignant commemoration, given how very few D-Day veterans are still alive. Locals talk of the last visits of veterans with heartfelt sorrow; they have adored seeing the old soldiers in their villages and fear losing the firsthand accounts of the battles. All along this rambling coast, locals will never forget what the troops and their families sacrificed all those years ago. A warm regard for Americans has survived political disputes, from de Gaulle to Trump. This remains particularly friendly soil for Americans—a place where US soldiers are still honored and the image of the US as a force for good remains largely untarnished.

Orientation

I've listed the prime D-Day sites from east to west, starting with Arromanches (the British sector) and then the American sectors (with a stop-by-stop tour of Omaha Beach and its related sights, followed by Utah Beach). Finally, I backtrack east to cover the Caen Memorial Museum. In the British and Canadian sectors, urban sprawl makes it harder to envision the events of June 1944, but the American sector looks today very much as it did 75 years ago. To best appreciate the beaches, avoid visiting at high tide if you can. For more information on touring the D-Day beaches, www.normandie-tourisme.fr is a useful resource.

Rick's Tip: *The free* **D-Day Normandy: Land of Liberty** *booklet gives succinct reviews of area D-Day museums and sites with current opening times. It's available at TIs, but you usually need to ask for it (or you can download it yourself from www.normandie-tourisme.fr).*

D-Day Sites in One Day

If you have only one day, spend it visiting the exciting sites and impressive museums along the beaches, and skip the Caen Memorial Museum (but to squeeze in the museum, visit it on your way to or from the area).

If you're traveling by car, begin on the cliffs above Arromanches. From there, visit the Port Winston artificial harbor and the D-Day Landing Museum, then con-

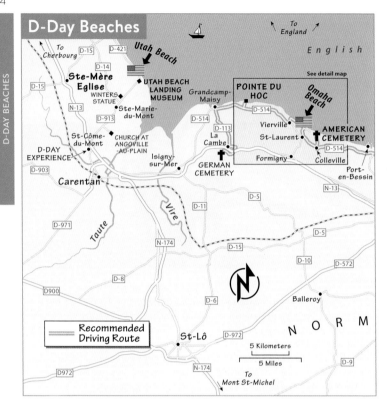

tinue west to Longues-sur-Mer and tour the German gun battery there. Spend your afternoon visiting the American Cemetery and its thought-provoking visitors center, walking on Omaha Beach at Vierville-sur-Mer, and exploring the Pointe du Hoc Ranger Monument. If time allows, consider a quick stop at the impressive Utah Beach sights.

Without a car, take a minivan tour to make the most of your time.

Getting Around the D-Day Beaches
On Your Own
Though the guided minivan excursions listed below teach important history lessons, **renting a car** is a far less expensive way to visit the beaches, particularly for three or more people (for rental sugges-

tions, see Bayeux's "Transportation" section, earlier).

Rick's Tip: *Take advantage of* **guided tours in English at individual sites,** *generally available in high season for free or a very low fee at Arromanches, Longues-sur-Mer, the American Cemetery, Pointe du Hoc, and the Utah Beach Landing Museum. Get times at area TIs, check each site's website, or see www.bayeux-bessin-tourisme.com.*

By Taxi Minivan (Unguided)
Taxi minivans shuttle up to seven people between the key sites at reasonable rates (which vary depending on how far you go). Allow €280 for a six-hour taxi day to visit the top Utah and Omaha Beach sites. No guiding is included; you are pay-

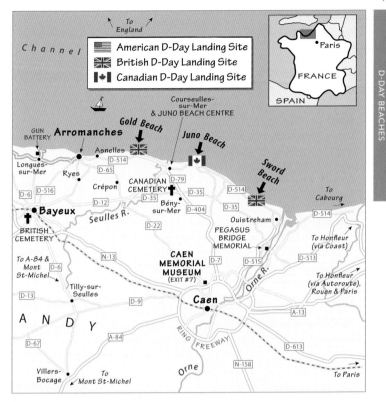

ing strictly for transport. Figure about €22 each way between Bayeux and Arromanches, €37 between Bayeux and the American Cemetery, and €110 for a 2.5-hour visit to Omaha Beach sites from Bayeux or Arromanches (50 percent surcharge after 19:00 and on Sun, taxi tel. 02 31 92 92 40 or mobile 06 70 40 07 96, www.taxis-bayeux.com, taxisbayeux@orange.fr).

Abbeilles Taxis offer D-Day excursions from Caen (about €230/5-hour visit, tel. 02 31 52 17 89, www.taxis-ab-beilles-caen.com).

By Minivan Tour (Guided)

An army of small companies and private guides offers all-day guided excursions (shared or private) to the D-Day beaches. The classic itinerary run by most is Ste-Mère Eglise, Utah Beach, Pointe du Hoc, Omaha Beach, and the American Cemetery.

I've worked hard to find guides who respect the importance of your time and these sights. To land one of these guides, book your tour in advance (3-6 months is best during peak periods). While some companies discourage children, others (including Dale Booth, Normandy Sightseeing Tours, and Sylvain Kast) welcome them.

TOURS IN A SHARED MINIVAN

These tour companies offer shared tours designed for individual sign-ups. Figure about €110/person for a day and €65/person for a half-day. Most tours don't go inside museums, which is a shame. These companies also run private tours.

Bayeux Shuttle's vans come with tablets that show effective video clips as you travel, and their guides are well trained.

Countdown to D-Day

1939

On September 1, Adolf Hitler invades the Free City of Danzig (today's Gdańsk, Poland), sparking World War II.

1940

Germany's Blitzkrieg ("lightning war") quickly overwhelms France, Nazis goose-step down Avenue des Champs-Elysées, and the country is divided into Occupied France (the north) and Vichy France (the south, administered by right-wing French). Just like that, nearly the entire Continent is fascist.

1941

The Allies (Britain, Soviet Union, and others) peck away at the fringes of "Fortress Europe." The Soviets repel Hitler's invasion at Moscow, while the Brits (with American aid) battle German U-boats for control of the seas. On December 7, Japan bombs the US naval base at Pearl Harbor, Hawaii. The US enters the war against Japan and its ally, Germany.

1942

Three crucial battles—at Stalingrad, El-Alamein, and Guadalcanal—weaken the German forces and their ally Japan. The victorious tank battle at El-Alamein in the deserts of North Africa soon gives the Allies a jumping-off point (Tunis) for the first assault on the Continent.

1943

More than 150,000 Americans and Brits, under the command of George Patton and Bernard "Monty" Montgomery, land in Sicily and begin working their way north through Italy. Meanwhile, Germany has to fend off tenacious Soviets on their eastern front.

You can visit their office in Bayeux and usually book at the last minute. All departures are assured (€60 half-day tour, €100 all-day tour, office open daily about 7:45-18:00, across from the Bayeux TI at Impasse de Islet, tel. 09 70 44 49 89, www.bayeuxshuttle.com).

Normandy Sightseeing Tours delivers a French perspective with capable guides and will pick you up anywhere you like—for a price (€70 half-day tour, €100 all-day tour, tel. 02 31 51 70 52, www.normandy-sightseeing-tours.com).

Overlord Tours is also a good choice (www.overlordtour.com).

The **Caen Memorial Museum** runs a busy program of half- and full-day tours covering the American and Canadian sectors in combination with a visit to the museum (handy for those with limited time—see museum listing on page 178).

TOURS WITH A PRIVATE GUIDE

Costs are about the same for all guides listed here. Private groups should expect to pay €500-650 for up to eight people

1944

On June 6, 1944, the Allies launch "Operation Overlord," better known as D-Day. The Allies amass three million soldiers and six million tons of *matériel* in England in preparation for the biggest fleet-led invasion in history—across the English Channel to France, then eastward toward Berlin. The Germans, hunkered down in northern France, know an invasion is imminent, but the Allies keep the details top secret. On the night of June 5, more than 180,000 soldiers board ships and planes in England, not knowing where they are headed until they're under way. Each one carries a note from General Dwight D. Eisenhower: "The tide has turned. The free men of the world are marching together to victory."

At 6:30 on June 6, 1944, Americans spill out of troop transports into the cold waters off a beach in Normandy, code-named Omaha. The weather is bad, seas are rough, and the prep bombing has failed. The soldiers, many seeing their first action, are dazed, confused, and weighed down by heavy packs. Nazi machine guns pin them against the sea. Slowly, they crawl up the beach on their stomachs. More than a thousand die. They hold on until the next wave of transports arrives.

Americans also see action at Utah Beach, while the British and Canadian troops storm Sword, Juno, and Gold. All day long, Allied confusion does battle with German indecision—the Nazis never really counterattack, thinking D-Day is just a ruse, not the main invasion. By day's end, the Allies have taken all five beaches along the Normandy coast and soon begin building two completely artificial harbors, code-named "Mulberry," providing ports for the reconquest of western Europe. The stage is set for the eventual end to the war.

1945

Having liberated Paris (August 26, 1944), the Allies' march on Berlin bogs down, hit by poor supply lines, bad weather, and the surprising German counterpunch at the Battle of the Bulge. Finally, in the spring, the Americans and Brits cross the Rhine, Soviet soldiers close in on Berlin, Hitler shoots himself, and—after nearly six long years of war—Europe is free.

for an all-day tour and €250-330 for a half-day). The best route for a one-day tour with a private guide is to start in Arromanches and end at Pointe du Hoc or the American Cemetery (request extra time at the cemetery to see the excellent visitors center).

- **Dale Booth Normandy Tours,** led by Dale Booth (tel. 02 33 71 53 76, www.dboothnormandytours.com, dboothholidays@sfr.fr). Dale's wife Debbie provides inexpensive chauffeur service to D-Day sights with an audio

tour (www.visitsinnormandy.com).
- **D-Day Historian Tours,** with Paul Woodadge (mobile 07 88 02 76 57, www.ddayhistorian.com, paul@ddayhistorian.com).
- **First Normandy Battlefield Tours,** offered by Allan Bryson (www.firstnormandybattlefieldtours.com, firstnormandy@sfr.fr).
- **Rodolphe Passera,** owner of American Heroes Tours (mobile 06 30 55 63 39, www.normandyamericanheroes.com, normandyamericanheroes@gmail.com).

- **Sylvain Kast** (mobile 06 17 44 04 46, www.d-day-experience-tours.com, sylvainkast@yahoo.fr).
- **Vanessa Letourneur** can guide anywhere in Normandy (mobile 06 98 95 89 45, www.normandypanorama.com).

Arromanches

This small town—part of Gold Beach (in the British landing zone)—was ground zero for the D-Day invasion. The Allies decided it would be easier to build their own port than to try to take one from the Nazis—and one here would surprise the enemy. And so, almost overnight, Arromanches sprouted the immense harbor Port Winston, which gave the Allies a foothold in Normandy from which to begin their victorious push toward Berlin and the end of World War II.

Today a touristy-but-fun little town that offers a pleasant cocktail of war memories, cotton candy, and trinket shops, Arromanches makes a good home base for drivers touring the D-Day beaches. Here you'll find an evocative beach, rusty hardware with English descriptions scattered around town, a good waterfront museum, a bluff with great views, and a theater with a thrilling little film. The town's seaside promenade is a great place from which to view the port.

Wander the wide beach, sit on the seawall after dark, listen to the surf, and contemplate the events that took place here 75 years ago.

Orientation

Tourist Information: The service-oriented TI in the town center has good D-Day information, bus schedules, and a listing of area hotels and *chambres d'hôtes* (daily mid-June-Aug 9:30-19:00, off-season 10:00-12:00 & 14:00-17:00, 2 Avenue Maréchal Joffre, tel. 02 31 22 36 45, www.bayeux-bessin-tourisme.com). The TI offers short orientation walking tours to the beach and landing museum—call ahead for the schedule.

Services: To get an Arromanches-based **taxi,** call mobile 06 66 62 00 99.

Sights

Arromanches' key sight, the Port Winston artificial harbor, is best seen from two vantage points—above town on the bluff (with the Arromanches 360° theater), and from the seawall in town (near the D-Day Landing Museum).

▲▲▲PORT WINSTON ARTIFICIAL HARBOR

Arromanches is all about its artificial harbor—the remains of which can be seen to this day. Winston Churchill's brainchild, the prefab harbor was made by the British and affectionately nicknamed Port Winston by the troops. To appreciate the massive undertaking of creating this harbor in a matter of days, start on the bluff overlooking the site of the impressive harbor. See the presentation at the cliff-top Arromanches 360° theater then head down to the D-Day Landing Museum and a nearby viewing area.

Getting to the Bluff: Drive two minutes toward Courseulles-sur-Mer and pay to park in the big, can't-miss-it lot overlooking the sea. Your other options are to hike 10 steep minutes from Arromanches' center up the hill behind the town's D-Day Landing Museum, or take the free minibus from the museum (runs every 10 mins daily June-Sept, Sat-Sun only Oct-mid-Nov and April-May, none in winter). I'd take the minibus up and then walk down.

Viewing the Harbor from the Bluff: Survey the coast from the observation platform. To the left is the American sector, with Omaha Beach and then Utah Beach (notice the sheer cliffs typical of Normandy's coastline). Below and to the right lie the British and Canadian sectors (level landscape, no cliffs).

Along the beaches below, the Allies arrived in the largest amphibious attack ever, launching the liberation of Western Europe. On D-Day +1—June 7, 1944—17

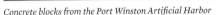

Concrete blocks from the Port Winston Artificial Harbor

old ships sailed 100 miles across the English Channel under their own steam to Arromanches. Their crews sank them so that each bow faced the next ship's stern, forming a sea barrier. Then 500 tugboats towed 115 football-field-size cement blocks (called "Phoenixes") across the channel. These were also sunk (with the ships and Phoenixes making a semicircle). This created a four-mile-long breakwater about a mile offshore. Finally, engineers set up seven floating steel pierheads with extendable legs, then linked these to shore with four floating roads made of concrete pontoons. (You'll see sections of pontoon roads at various locations along the beaches.) Soldiers placed 115 antiaircraft guns on the Phoenixes and pontoons, protecting a port the size of Dover, England. Within just six days of operation, 54,000 vehicles, 326,000 troops, and 110,000 tons of goods had crossed the English Channel. An Allied toehold in Normandy was secure. Eleven months later, Hitler was dead and the war was over.

▲▲ARROMANCHES 360° THEATER

The domed building at the cliff-top houses the powerful film *Normandy's 100 Days.* The screens surrounding you show archival footage and photographs of the endeavor to liberate Normandy (works in any language). In addition to honoring the many Allied and German soldiers who died, it reminds us that 20,000 French civilians were killed in aerial bombardments. The experience is intense—as loud and slickly produced as anything at the D-Day beaches.

Cost and Hours: €6, €22.50 combo-ticket with Caen Memorial Museum; 2 shows/hour (on the hour and half-hour), daily May-Aug 9:30-18:00, April-May and Sept from 10:00, Oct-mid-Nov 10:00-17:30, these are first and last show times, closed most of Jan, Chemin du Calvaire, tel. 02 31 06 06 45, www.arromanches360.com.

▲D-DAY LANDING MUSEUM (MUSEE DU DEBARQUEMENT)

This museum, facing the harbor, makes a worthwhile hour-long visit and is the best way to appreciate how the artificial harbor was built. While gazing through windows at the site of this amazing undertaking, you can study helpful models, videos, and photographs illustrating the construction and use of the prefabricated harbor.

Screens over the first big model show a virtual reconstruction of Port Winston. Those blimp-like objects tethered to the port prevented German planes from getting too close (though the German air force was largely irrelevant by this time). Ponder the overwhelming task of building this harbor in just 12 days, while battles raged. The essential 15-minute film (up the stairs behind the cashier) uses British newsreel footage to illustrate the construction of the port. Another video (7 minutes, far end of ground floor) recalls the night of the first landings.

Cost and Hours: €8, daily May-Aug 9:00-19:00, Sept until 18:00, Oct-Dec and Feb-April 10:00-12:30 & 13:30-17:00, closed Jan, Place du 6 Juin, tel. 02 31 22 34 31, www.arromanches-museum.com.

Viewing the Harbor from near the Museum: Find the round bulkhead on the seawall, near the entrance to the D-Day Landing Museum. Stand facing the sea. Designed to be temporary (it was used for 6 months), the harbor was supposed to wash out to sea over time—which is exactly what happened with its twin harbor at Omaha Beach (which lasted only 12 days, thanks to a terrible storm). If the tide is out, you'll see rusted floats mired on the sand close in—these supported the pontoon roads. Imagine the traffic pouring in past the many antiaircraft guns poised to defend against the invasion.

On the hill beyond the museum, there's a partially viewable Sherman tank, one of 50,000 deployed during the landings. Stroll to the east side of the museum and find a section of a pontoon road with a bulldozer, an antiaircraft gun, and a searchlight. Walk down to the beach and wander among the concrete and rusted litter of the battle—and be thankful that all you hear are birds and surf.

Eating

You'll find cafés, *crêperies,* and shops selling sandwiches to go (ideal for beach-front picnics). The **bakery** next to the Arromanches Militaria store makes good sandwiches, quiches, and tasty pastries. Many restaurants line Rue Maréchal Joffe, the bustling pedestrian zone a block inland. The following restaurants at recommended hotels are also reliable:

$$ Restaurant "Le Pappagall" serves basic café fare in a cheery setting (daily in high season, closed Wed and possibly other days off-season, see Hôtel d'Arromanches listing, later).

$$ Hôtel de la Marine allows you to dine or drink in style—and with good quality cuisine—right on the water (ideal outdoor seating for a drink in nice weather, daily, see hotel listing later).

For evening fun, have a drink at **The Mary Celeste** pub, a block from the beach on Rue Colonel René Michel.

Sleeping

Consider **$$ Hotel Les Villas d'Arromanches***,** perched above the sea (1 Rue du Lieutenant-Colonel de Job, www.lesvillasdarromanches.com); **$$ Hôtel de la Marine***,** with views to the artificial harbor (good restaurant, Quai du Canada, www.hotel-de-la-marine.fr);

$ Hôtel d'Arromanches,* on the main pedestrian drag near the TI (with Restaurant "Le Pappagall," 2 Rue Colonel René Michel, www.hoteldarromanches.fr); and **$ L'Hôtel Ideal de Mountbatten,***** located a long block up from the water (20 Boulevard Gilbert Longuet, www.hotelarromancheslideal.fr).

American D-Day Sites

The American sector, stretching west of Arromanches, is divided between Omaha and Utah beaches. Omaha Beach starts just a few miles west of Arromanches and has the most important sights for visitors. Utah Beach sights are farther away (on the road to Cherbourg), but were also critical to the ultimate success of the Normandy invasion. The American Airborne sector covers a broad area behind Utah Beach and centers on Ste-Mère Eglise.

Omaha Beach Area

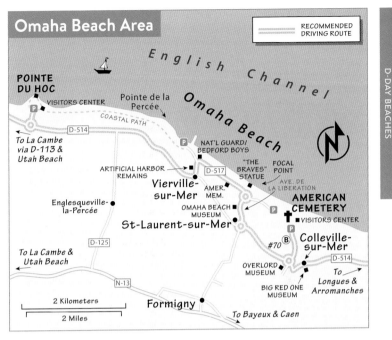

RECOMMENDED
DRIVING ROUTE

English Channel

POINTE
DU HOC

VISITORS CENTER

Pointe de la Percée

Omaha Beach

COASTAL PATH

D-514

To La Combe
via D-113 &
Utah Beach

NAT'L GUARD/
BEDFORD BOYS

ARTIFICIAL HARBOR
REMAINS

D-517

"THE
BRAVES"
STATUE

FOCAL
POINT

Vierville-
sur-Mer

AMER.
MEM.

AVE. DE
LA LIBERATION

Englesqueville-
la-Percée

OMAHA BEACH
MUSEUM

AMERICAN
CEMETERY

St-Laurent-sur-Mer

VISITORS CENTER

D-125

To La Combe &
Utah Beach

#70 ⒷColleville-
sur-Mer

OVERLORD
MUSEUM

D-514

N-13

BIG RED ONE
MUSEUM

To
Longues &
Arromanches

2 Kilometers

Formigny

2 Miles

To Bayeux & Caen

Rick's Tip: *The D-Day landing sites are rural, and you won't find a grocery on every corner.* **Plan ahead if you want to picnic,** *or find groceries in Arromanches or Port-en-Bessin.*

Omaha Beach

Omaha Beach is the landing zone most familiar to Americans. This well-defended stretch was where US troops suffered their greatest losses. Going west from Arromanches, I've listed the most powerful stops.

▲LONGUES-SUR-MER GUN BATTERY

Four German casemates (three with guns intact)—built to guard against seaborne attacks—hunker down at the end of a country road. The guns, 300 yards inland, were arranged in a semicircle to maximize the firing range east and west, and are the only original coastal artillery guns remaining in place in the D-Day region. (Much

was scrapped after the war, long before people thought of tourism.) This battery, staffed by 194 German soldiers, was more defended than the better-known Pointe du Hoc. The Longues-sur-Mer Battery was a critical link in Hitler's Atlantic Wall defense, which consisted of more than 15,000 defensive structures stretching from Norway to the Pyrenees. These guns could hit targets up to 12 miles away with relatively sharp accuracy if linked to good

German gun at Longues-sur-Mer

target information. The Allies had to take them out.

Cost and Hours: Free and always open (and a good spot for a picnic); on-site TI open April-Oct daily 10:00-13:00 & 14:00-18:00. The TI's €5.70 booklet is helpful, and guided tours are offered several times a day (€5, one-hour tour, details at TI, tel. 02 31 21 46 87).

Getting There: You'll find the guns 10 minutes west of Arromanches off D-514 on Rue de la Mer (D-104). Follow *Port-en-Bessin* signs from Arromanches; once in Longues-sur-Mer, turn right at the town's only traffic light and follow *Batterie* signs to the free and easy parking lot (with WC).

▲▲▲WWII NORMANDY AMERICAN CEMETERY AND MEMORIAL

The American Cemetery is a pilgrimage site for Americans visiting Normandy. Crowning a bluff just above Omaha Beach, 9,386 brilliant white, marble tombstones honor and remember the Americans who gave their lives on the beaches below to free Europe. France has given the US permanent free use of this 172-acre site, which is immaculately maintained by the American Battle Monuments Commission.

A fine modern visitors center prepares you for your visit. Plan to spend at least 1.5 hours at this stirring site. If you come late in the day, a moving flag ceremony takes place at 17:00 at the main flagpole.

Cost and Hours: Free, daily 9:00-18:00, mid-Sept-mid-April until 17:00, tel. 02 31 51 62 00, www.abmc.gov. Guided 45-minute tours are offered a few times a day in high season (call ahead to confirm times). The best WC is in the basement of the visitors center.

Getting There: The cemetery is just outside Colleville-sur-Mer, a 30-minute drive northwest of Bayeux. Follow signs on D-514 toward Colleville-sur-Mer; at the big roundabout in town, follow signs leading to the cemetery (plenty of free parking).

Visiting the Cemetery: From the parking lot, stroll in a counterclockwise circle through the lovingly tended, parklike grounds, making four stops: at the visitors center, the bluff overlooking Omaha

American Cemetery at Omaha Beach

Beach, memorials to the fallen and the missing, and finally the cemetery itself.

The low-slung, modern **Visitors Center** is mostly underground. On the arrival level (after security check) are computer terminals providing access to a database containing the Roll of Honor—the name and story of each US serviceman and woman whose remains lie in Europe. Out the window, a rectangular pond points to the infinite sea.

The exhibit downstairs does more than recount the battle. It humanizes the men who fought and died, and are now buried, here. First find a large theater playing the video *Letters,* a touching 16-minute film with excerpts of letters home from the servicemen who now lie at rest here (shown on the half-hour, you can enter late). Next is a smaller, open theater with a moving eight-minute video, *On Their Shoulders.* From here, worthwhile exhibits and more videos (one includes an interview with Dwight Eisenhower) tell the stories of the brave individuals who gave their lives to liberate people they could not know, and show the few possessions they left behind (about 25,000 Americans died in the entire battle for Normandy).

A lineup of informational plaques on the left wall provides a worthwhile and succinct overview of key events from September 1939 to June 5, 1944. Starting with June 6, 1944, the plaques present the progress of the landings in three-hour increments. Omaha Beach was secured within eight hours of the landings; within 24 hours it was safe to jump off your landing vehicle and slog onto the shore.

You'll exit the visitors center through the Sacrifice Gallery, with photos and bios of several individuals buried here, as well as those of some survivors. A voice reads the names of each of the cemetery's permanent residents on a continuous loop.

Next, walk through **a parkway along the bluff** designed to feel like America (with Kentucky bluegrass) to a viewpoint overlooking the piece of Normandy beach called "that embattled shore, the portal of freedom." An orientation table looks over the beach and sea. Gazing at the quiet and peaceful beach, it's hard to imagine the horrific carnage of June 6, 1944. You can't access the beach directly from here (the path is closed for security)—but those with a car can drive there easily. A walk on the beach is a powerful experience.

With your back to the sea, climb the steps to reach the memorial (on the left), overlooking the cemetery.

This striking **memorial** with a soaring statue represents the spirit of American youth. Around the statue, giant reliefs of the Battle of Normandy and the Battle of Europe are etched on the walls. Behind is the semicircular **Garden of the Missing,** with the names of 1,557 soldiers who perished but whose remains were never found. A small bronze rosette next to a name indicates one whose body was eventually recovered.

Finally, wander through the peaceful and poignant sea of **headstones** that surrounds an interfaith chapel in the distance. Names, home states, and dates of death are inscribed on each tombstone, with dog-tag numbers etched into the lower backs. During the campaign, the dead were buried in temporary cemeteries throughout Normandy. After the war, the families of the soldiers could decide whether their loved ones should remain with their comrades or be brought home for burial. (About two-thirds were returned to America.)

Among the notable people buried here are General Theodore Roosevelt Jr., his brother Quentin (who died in World War I but was moved here at the request of the family), and the Niland brothers (whose story inspired *Saving Private Ryan*). There are 33 pairs of brothers lying side by side, 1 father and son, 149 African Americans, 149 Jewish Americans, and 4 women. From the three generals buried here to the youngest casualty (a teen of just 17), each grave is of equal worth.

Visiting the Beach: To visit Omaha Beach itself, return up the long driveway to the roundabout (at the Overlord Museum) and follow signs to St-Laurent-sur-Mer (D-514). Omaha Beach has five ravines (or "draws"), which provided avenues from the beach past the bluff to the interior. These were the goal of the troops that day. You'll drive down one (Avenue de la Libération)—passing the small Omaha Beach Memorial Museum—to reach the beach and two commemorative statues. Then drive west along the beach to the National Guard Memorial before leaving the beach up a second ravine.

▲▲▲POINTE DU HOC RANGER MONUMENT

This point of land was the Germans' most heavily fortified position along the Utah and Omaha beaches. The cliffs are so severe here that the Germans turned their defenses around to face what they assumed would be an attack from inland. Yet US Army Rangers famously scaled the impossibly steep cliffs to disable the gun battery. Pointe du Hoc's bomb-cratered, lunar-like landscape and remaining bun-

kers make it one of the most evocative of the D-Day sites.

Cost and Hours: Free, always open; visitors center open daily 9:00-18:00, mid-Sept-mid-April until 17:00, tel. 02 31 51 62 00, www.abmc.gov/cemeteries-memorials. It's off route D-514, 20 minutes west of the American Cemetery, in Cricqueville-en-Bessin.

Visiting Pointe du Hoc: The visitors center is at the eastern end of the lot. If you have time, stop here for the WCs and to see the eight-minute film explaining the daring Ranger mission from a personal perspective, through interviews with survivors.

Follow either gravel path to the site (both with info panels focusing on individual Rangers). The path to the western end of the site leads past a big French 155mm gun barrel from World War I. While state-of-the-art in 1917, in World War II this gun was still formidable. Six of these were what Pointe du Hoc was all about.

The **craters** you see are the result of 10 kilotons of bombs—nearly the explosive power of the atomic bomb at Hiroshima—but dropped over seven weeks. This was

The landscape at Pointe du Hoc is still pocked by WWII bombing craters.

On Omaha Beach

Walking on Omaha Beach is a powerful ▲▲▲ experience for history buffs. (While the beach is about 300 yards wide at low tide, it disappears at high tide.) Let the modern world melt away here and try to put yourself in those soldiers' combat boots:

You're wasted from lack of sleep and nervous anticipation. Now you get seasick, too, as you're about to land in a small, flat-bottomed boat, cheek-to-jowl with 29 other soldiers. Your water-soaked pack feels like a boulder, and your gun feels even heavier. The boat's front ramp drops open, and you run for your life through water and sand for 500 yards onto this open beach, dodging bullets from above (the landings had to occur at low tide so that mines and obstacles would be visible). Your only protection is the defensive obstacles left by the Germans.

Omaha Beach witnessed by far the most intense battles of any along the D-Day beaches. The hills above were heavily fortified with machine gun and mortar nests. (The aerial, naval, and supporting rocket fire that the Allies poured onto the German defenses failed to put them out of commission.) A single German machine gun could fire 1,200 rounds a minute. That's right—1,200. It's amazing that anyone survived. It's estimated that on the first day of the campaign, the Allies suffered 10,500 casualties (killed, wounded, and missing), 6,000 of whom were Americans. The highest casualty rates occurred at Omaha Beach. More than 4,000 troops were killed and wounded here that day, many of whom drowned after being hit.

If the tide's out, you may notice remains of rusted metal objects just below the surface. Omaha Beach was littered with obstacles to disrupt the landings. Thousands of metal poles and "Czech hedgehogs" (antitank barriers made from Czech steel), miles of barbed wire, and more than six million mines were scattered along this shore. At least 150,000 tons of metal were taken from the beaches after World War II, and they still didn't get it all. They never will.

a jumbo German gun battery, with more than a mile of tunnels connecting its battlements. Its six 155mm guns could fire as far as 13 miles—good enough to hit anything on either beach. For the American D-Day landings to succeed, this nest had to be taken out. So the Allies pulverized it with bombs, starting in April 1944 and continuing until June 6—making this the most intensely bombarded of the D-Day targets. Even so, the heavily reinforced bunkers survived.

Walk around. You can identify the gun placements by the short, circular, concrete walls, sometimes with the rusted remains of a gun support sticking out of the center.

The **Dagger Memorial** represents the Ranger dagger used to help scale the cliffs. Here, it's thrust into the command center of the battery. Exploring the heavily fortified interior of this observation bunker (officers' quarters, enlisted quarters, and command room) with its charred ceiling and battered hardware, you can imagine the fury of the attack that finally took this station.

Walk down the steps to the front of the bunker for the greatest impact. Peer over the cliff and think about the 225 handpicked Rangers who attempted a castle-style assault on the gun battery (they landed on the beach down to the right). They used rocket-propelled grappling hooks connected to 150-foot ropes, and climbed ladders borrowed from London fire departments.

Timing was critical; the Rangers had just 30 minutes to get off the beach before the rising tide would overcome them. Fortunately, the soldiers successfully surprised the Germans and climbed to the top in two hours—the Germans had prepared no defense for an attack up the cliffs. After taking control of the clifftop, the Rangers found that the guns had been moved—the Germans had put telegraph poles in their place as decoys. The Rangers eventually found the operational guns hidden a half-mile inland and destroyed them.

Before you leave, navigate the craters inland about 100 yards to a bunker capped with a **viewing platform.** Climb up top to appreciate the intensity of the blasts that made the craters and disabled phone lines—cutting communication between the command bunker and the guns to render them blind.

Utah Beach

Utah Beach, added late in the planning for D-Day, proved critical. This was where two US paratrooper units (the 82nd and the 101st Airborne Divisions) dropped behind enemy lines the night before the invasion, as dramatized in *Band of Brothers* and *The Longest Day.* Many landed off-target. It was essential for the invading forces to succeed here, then push up the peninsula (which had been intentionally flooded by the Nazis) to the port city of Cherbourg. While the brutality on this beach paled in comparison with the carnage on Omaha Beach, most of the paratroopers missed their targets—causing confusion and worse—and the units that landed here faced a three-week battle before finally taking Cherbourg. Ultimately over 800,000 Americans (and 220,000 vehicles) landed on Utah Beach over a five-month period.

These stops are listed in the order you'll find them coming from Bayeux or Omaha Beach.

▲▲▲UTAH BEACH LANDING MUSEUM (MUSEE DU DEBARQUEMENT)

This is the best museum located on the D-Day beaches, and worth the 45-minute drive from Bayeux. For the Allied landings to succeed, many coordinated tasks had to be accomplished: Paratroopers had to be dropped inland, the resistance had to disable bridges and cut communications, bombers had to soften German defenses by delivering their payloads on target and on time, the infantry had to land safely on the beaches, and supplies had to follow the infantry closely. This thorough yet manageable museum pieces together those many parts together in a series of fascinating exhibits and displays.

Cost and Hours: €8, daily June-Sept 9:30-19:00, Oct-Nov and Jan-May 10:00-18:00, closed Dec, last entry one hour before closing, tel. 02 33 71 53 35, off D-913 at Plage de la Madeleine, www.utah-beach. com. Park in the *"obligitaire"* lot, then walk five minutes to reach the museum.

Visiting the Museum: Built around the remains of a concrete German bunker, the museum nestles in the sand dunes on Utah Beach with floors above and below beach level. Your visit follows a one-way route past rooms of artifacts. It starts with background about the American landings on Utah Beach (over 20,000 troops landed on the first day alone) and the German defense strategy (Rommel was in charge of maintaining the western end of Hitler's Atlantic Wall). See the outstanding 12-minute film, *Victory in the Sand,* which sets the stage.

Highlights of the museum are the displays of innovative invasion equipment with videos demonstrating how it all worked (most were built for civilian purposes and adapted to military use): the remote-controlled Goliath mine, the LVT-2 Water Buffalo and Duck amphibious vehicles, and the wooden Higgins

Utah Beach Landing Museum

landing craft. Next, see a fully restored B-26 bomber with its zebra stripes and 11 menacing machine guns—find the one at the rear, without which the landings would not have been possible (the yellow bomb icons painted onto the cockpit indicate the number of missions a plane had flown).

Upstairs is a large, glassed-in room overlooking the beach. From here, you'll peer over re-created German trenches and get a sense for what it must have been like to defend against such a massive and coordinated onslaught.

Outside the museum, find the beach access where Americans first broke through Hitler's "Atlantic Wall." Pile into the Higgins boat replica (this one is made of steel—those used in the landings were made from plywood). You can hike up to the small bluff, which is lined with monuments to the branches of military service that participated in the fight. A gun sits atop a buried battlement under the flags, part of a vast underground network of German defenses. And all around is the hardware of battle frozen in time.

▲STE-MERE EGLISE

This celebrated village lies 15 minutes west of Utah Beach and was the first village to be liberated by the Americans.

The area around Ste-Mère Eglise was the center of action for American paratroopers, whose objective was to land behind enemy lines before dawn on D-Day and wreak havoc in support of the Americans landing at Utah Beach that day.

For *The Longest Day* movie buffs, Ste-Mère Eglise is a necessary pilgrimage. It was in and near this village that many paratroopers, facing terrible weather and heavy antiaircraft fire, landed off-target—and many landed in the town. American paratrooper Private John Steele dangled from the town's church steeple for two hours (a parachute has been reinstalled on the steeple near where Steele became snagged). Though many paratroopers were killed in the first hours of the invasion, the Americans eventually overcame their poor start and managed to take the town. (Steele survived his ordeal by playing dead). These troops who dropped (or glided) in behind enemy lines in the dark played a critical role in the success of the Utah Beach landings by securing roads and bridges.

Today, the village greets travelers with flag-draped streets (and plenty of pay parking). The 700-year-old **medieval church** on the town square now holds

Ste-Mère Eglise

two contemporary stained-glass windows. One, in the back, celebrates the heroism of the Allies (made in 1984 for the 40th anniversary of the invasion). The window in the left transept features St. Michael, patron saint of paratroopers (made in 1969 for the 25th anniversary).

The **TI** on the square across from the church has loads of information (July-Aug Mon-Sat 8:30-18:00, Sun 10:00-16:00; Sept and April-June closes Mon-Sat 12:00-14:00 and on Sun; shorter hours off-season; 6 Rue Eisenhower, tel. 02 33 21 00 33, www.ot-baieducotentin.fr).

▲AIRBORNE MUSEUM

This four-building collection is dedicated to the daring aerial landings that were essential to the success of D-Day. During the invasion, in the Utah Beach sector alone, 23,000 men were dropped from planes or landed in gliders, along with countless vehicles and tons of supplies.

Your visit to the museum unfolds across four buildings (allow a full hour to visit). In the first building, you'll see a **Waco glider,** one of 104 such gliders flown into Normandy at first light on D-Day to land supplies in fields to support the paratroopers. The second, larger building holds a **Douglas C-47** plane that dropped para-

troops and supplies. A third structure, labeled **Operation Neptune,** puts you into the paratrooper's experience starting with a night flight and jump, then tracks your progress on the ground past enemy fire using elaborate models and sound effects. Don't miss the touching video just before the exit showing the valor of Gen. Theodore Roosevelt Jr. on D-Day. The fourth building houses temporary exhibits and a cushy **theater** showing a good 20-minute film focusing on the airborne invasion.

Cost and Hours: €8.50, daily May-Aug 9:00-19:00, April and Sept 9:30-18:30, shorter hours off-season and closed Jan, 14 Rue Eisenhower, tel. 02 33 41 41 35, www.airborne-museum.org.

Other D-Day Sights

▲▲CAEN MEMORIAL MUSEUM

Caen, the largest city in lower Normandy, has the most thorough (and by far the priciest) WWII museum in France. With thorough coverage of the lead-up to World War II and of the war in both Europe and the Pacific, accounts of the Holocaust and Nazi-occupied France, the Cold War aftermath, and more, it effectively puts the Battle of Normandy into a broader context.

Cost and Hours: €20, ticket valid 24 hours, free for all veterans and kids under 10 (ask about good family rates), €22.50 combo-ticket with Arromanches 360° theater. Open March-Sept daily 9:00-19:00; Oct-Dec and Feb Tue-Sun 9:30-18:00, closed Mon; closed most of Jan, Esplanade Général Eisenhower, tel. 02 31 06 06 44—as in June 6, 1944, www.memorial-caen.fr.

Minivan Tours: The museum offers good-value minivan tours covering the key sites along the D-Day beaches and is a top option for day-trippers from Paris. The all-day "D-Day Tour" package (€131) includes pickup/drop-off at the Caen train station, a tour of the museum followed by lunch, and a five-hour tour of the American sector (there's a similar tour option to Juno Beach). There's also a €95 half-day minivan tour that includes free entry to the museum (no tour) but does not include lunch. It's appropriate to tip if you were satisfied with your tour.

Visiting the Museum: Find *Début de la Visite* signs and begin your museum tour here with a downward-spiral stroll, tracing (almost psychoanalyzing) the path Europe and America followed from the end of World War I to the rise of fascism to World War II. Rooms are decorated to immerse you in the pre-WWII experience.

The **"World Before 1945"** exhibits deliver a thorough description of how World War II was fought—from General Charles de Gaulle's London radio broadcasts to Hitler's early missiles to wartime fashion to the D-Day landings. Videos, maps, and countless displays relate the stories of the Battle of Britain, Vichy France, German death camps, the Battle of Stalingrad, the French Resistance, the war in the Pacific, and finally, liberation. Several powerful displays summarize the terrible human costs of World War II, from the destruction of Guernica in Spain to the death toll (21 million Russians died during the war; Germany lost 7 million; the US lost 300,000). A smaller, separate exhibit (on your way back up to the main hall) cov-

ers D-Day and the Battle of Normandy, though the battle is better covered at other D-Day museums described in this chapter.

Next, don't miss the 25-minute film, *Saving Europe,* an immersive and, at times, graphic black-and-white film covering the agonizing 100 days of the Battle of Normandy (runs every half-hour 10:00-18:00, English subtitles).

At this point, you've completed your WWII history course. Next comes the **"World After 1945"** wing, which sets the scene for the Cold War with photos of European cities destroyed during World War II and insights into the psychological battle waged by the Soviet Union and the US for the hearts and minds of their people until the fall of communism (you'll even see a real Soviet MiG 21 fighter jet). The wing culminates with an important display recounting the division of Berlin and its unification after the fall of the Wall.

Finish your tour with a walk through the **US Armed Forces Memorial Garden** (Vallée du Mémorial). On a visit here, I was bothered at first by the seemingly unaware laughing of lighthearted children, unable to appreciate the gravity of their surroundings. Then I read this inscription on the pavement: "From the heart of our land flows the blood of our youth, given to you in the name of freedom." And their laughter made me happy.

MONT ST-MICHEL

Mont St-Michel, one of the top pilgrimage sites of Christendom through the ages, floats like a mirage on the horizon. For centuries devout Christians endeavored to make a great pilgrimage once in their lifetimes. If they couldn't afford Rome, Jerusalem, or Santiago de Compostela, they came here, earning the same religious merits. Today, several million visitors—and a steady trickle of pilgrims—flood the single street of the tiny island each year. If this place seems built for tourism, in a sense it was. It's accommodated, fed, watered, and sold trinkets to generations of travelers visiting its towering abbey.

Orientation

Mont St-Michel is surrounded by a vast mudflat and connected to the mainland by a bridge. Think of the island as having three parts: the Benedictine abbey soaring above, the spindly road leading to the abbey, and the medieval fortifications below. The lone main street (Grand Rue), with the island's hotels, restaurants, and trinkets, is mobbed in-season from 11:00 to at least 16:00. Though several tacky history-in-wax museums tempt visitors with hustlers out front, these are commercial gimmicks with no real artifacts. The only worthwhile sights are the abbey at the summit and a ramble on the ramparts, which offers mudflat views and an escape from the tourist zone.

The "village" on the mainland side of the causeway (called La Caserne) was built to accommodate tour buses. It consists of a lineup of modern hotels, a handful of shops, vast parking lots, and efficient shuttle buses zipping to and from the island every few minutes.

The tourist tide comes in each morning and recedes late each afternoon. To avoid crowds, arrive late in the afternoon, sleep on the island or nearby on the mainland, and depart early.

Tourist Information: On the mainland, near the parking lot's shuttle stop, look for the helpful **Visitors Center** with convenient WCs (daily April-Sept 9:00-19:00, off-season 10:00-18:00, www.accueilmontsaintmichel.fr). The official **TI** is on the island (just inside the town gate, daily July-Aug 9:15-19:00, March-June and Sept-Oct 9:15-12:30 & 14:00-18:00, shorter hours off-season; tel. 02 33 60 14 30, www.ot-montsaintmichel.com). A post office and ATM are 50 yards beyond the island TI. While either office can inform you about English tour times for the abbey, bus schedules, and tide tables (*horaires des marées*), the Visitors Center at the parking lot is far less crowded.

An Island Again

In 1878, a causeway was built that allowed Mont St-Michel's pilgrims to come and go regardless of the tide. The causeway increased the flow of visitors, but blocked the flow of water around the island. The result: Much of the bay silted up, and Mont St-Michel was gradually becoming part of the mainland.

An ambitious project to keep it an island was completed in 2015. The first phase was the construction of a dam (*barrage*) on the Couesnon River, which traps water at high tide and releases it at low tide, flushing the bay and forcing sediment out to the sea. The dam is an attraction in its own right, with informative panels and great views of the abbey from its sleek and picnic-friendly wood benches. Parking lots at the foot of the island were then removed and a huge mainland parking lot built, with shuttle buses ferrying visitors to the island.

Finally, workers tore down the old causeway and replaced it with the super-sleek, artistically swooping bridge you see today. The bridge allows water to flow freely around Mont St-Michel, preserving its island character. Those wanting to experience Mont St-Michel at its natural best should plan their trip to coincide with high tide (see www.ot-montsaintmichel.com for tide tables).

Rick's Tip: Because Mont St-Michel faces southwest, **morning light from the bridge is eye-popping.** *Take a memorable walk before breakfast. And* **don't miss the illuminated island after dark** *(also best from the bridge).*

Tides: The tides here rise above 50 feet—the largest and most dangerous in Europe. High tides (*grandes marées*) lap against the island TI door, where you should find tide tables posted (also

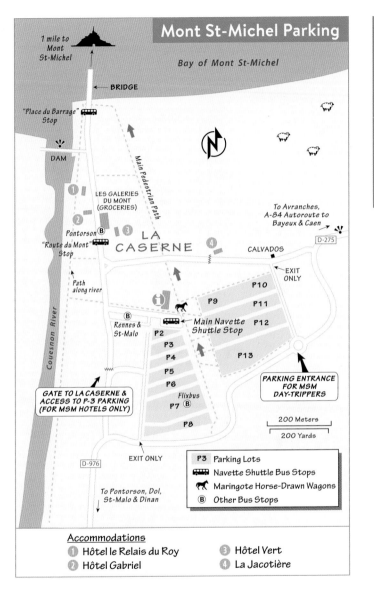

Mont St-Michel Parking

1 mile to
Mont
St-Michel

Bay of Mont St-Michel

← BRIDGE

"Place du Barrage"
Stop

DAM

LES GALERIES
DU MONT
(GROCERIES)

Pontorson Ⓑ
"Route du Mont"
Stop

LA
CASERNE

To Avranches,
A-84 Autoroute to
Bayeux & Caen

D-275

CALVADOS

EXIT
ONLY

Path
along river

Ⓑ
Rennes &
St-Malo

Main Navette
Shuttle Stop

P10
P9   P11
P12
P2
P3
P4   P13
P5
P6
Flixbus Ⓑ
P7
P8

PARKING ENTRANCE
FOR MSM
DAY-TRIPPERS

GATE TO LA CASERNE &
ACCESS TO P-3 PARKING
(FOR MSM HOTELS ONLY)

200 Meters
200 Yards

D-976   EXIT ONLY

To Pontorson, Dol,
St-Malo & Dinan

P3 Parking Lots
Navette Shuttle Bus Stops
Maringote Horse-Drawn Wagons
Ⓑ Other Bus Stops

Accommodations
❶ Hôtel le Relais du Roy   ❸ Hôtel Vert
❷ Hôtel Gabriel   ❹ La Jacotière

posted at parking lot visitors center).
If you plan to explore the mudflats, it's
essential to be aware of the tides—and be
prepared for muddy feet.

Guided Abbey Tours: Between the
information in this chapter and the tours
(and audio tours) available at the abbey, a
private guide is not necessary.

Sights

The island's main street (Grand Rue),
lined with shops and hotels leading to the
abbey, is grotesquely touristy. To avoid
the crowds, veer left as you approach the
island's main entry and walk under the
stone arch of the freestanding building.
Follow the cobbled ramp up to the abbey.

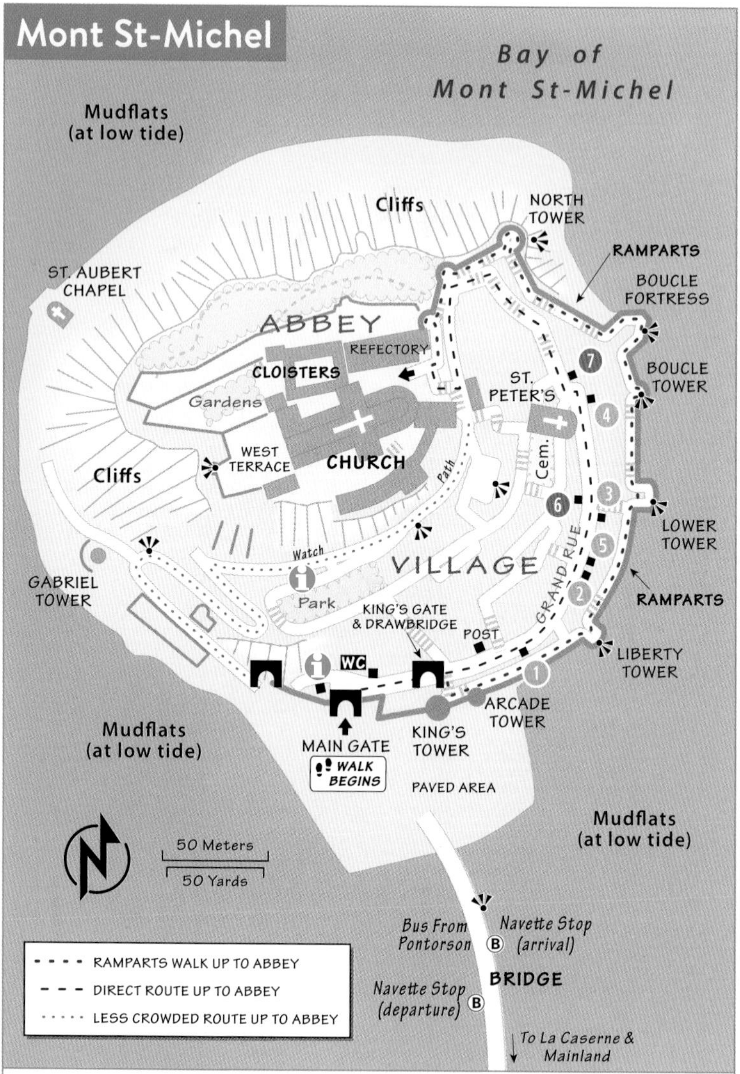

Mont St-Michel

Bay of Mont St-Michel

Mudflats
(at low tide)

Cliffs

NORTH TOWER

RAMPARTS

BOUCLE FORTRESS

ST. AUBERT CHAPEL

ABBEY

REFECTORY

CLOISTERS

Gardens

ST. PETER'S

7

BOUCLE TOWER

4

WEST TERRACE

CHURCH

Path

Cem.

Cliffs

6

3

LOWER TOWER

Watch

VILLAGE

GRAND RUE

5

GABRIEL TOWER

Park

2

RAMPARTS

KING'S GATE & DRAWBRIDGE

POST

1

LIBERTY TOWER

WC

ARCADE TOWER

Mudflats
(at low tide)

MAIN GATE

WALK BEGINS

KING'S TOWER

PAVED AREA

Mudflats
(at low tide)

N

50 Meters

50 Yards

Bus From Pontorson

Navette Stop (arrival)

B

Navette Stop (departure)

B

BRIDGE

To La Caserne & Mainland

- - - - RAMPARTS WALK UP TO ABBEY

- - - DIRECT ROUTE UP TO ABBEY

· · · · LESS CROWDED ROUTE UP TO ABBEY

Hotels and Restaurants

1. Hôtel St. Pierre
2. Hôtel Croix Blanche & Rest.
3. Hôtel le Mouton Blanc & Café La Mère Poulard
4. Hôtel la Vieille Auberge & Restaurant
5. Hôtel du Guesclin & Restaurant
6. Restaurant le St. Michel
7. Les Terrasses Poulard

Mont St-Michel

This is also the easiest route up, thanks to the long ramps, which help you avoid most stairs. To trace the route, see the "Mont St-Michel" map, earlier.

▲▲▲ABBEY OF MONT ST-MICHEL

Mont St-Michel has been an important pilgrimage center since AD 708, when the bishop of Avranches heard the voice of Archangel Michael saying, "Build here and build high." Michael reassured the bishop, "If you build it...they will come." Today's abbey is built on the remains of a Romanesque church, which stands on the remains of a Carolingian church. St. Michael, whose gilded statue decorates the top of the spire, was the patron saint of many French kings, making this a favored site for French royalty through the ages. St. Michael was particularly popular in Counter-Reformation times, as the Church employed his warlike image in the fight against Protestant heresy.

This abbey has 1,200 years of history, though much of its story was lost when its archives were taken to St-Lô for safety during World War II—only to be destroyed during the D-Day fighting. As you climb the stairs, imagine the centuries of pilgrims and monks who have worn down the edges of these same stone steps. Don't expect well-furnished rooms;

those monks lived simple lives with few comforts.

Cost and Hours: €10; May-Aug daily 9:00-19:00, until 24:00 Mon-Sat early July-Aug; Sept-April daily 9:30-18:00; closed Dec 25, Jan 1, and May 1; may close during music festival in late Sept; last entry one hour before closing; allow 20 minutes on foot uphill from the island TI, www.mont-saint-michel.monuments-nationaux.fr. Mass is held Mon-Sat at 12:00 and Sun at 11:15 (www.abbaye-montsaint-michel.com).

When to Go: To avoid crowds, arrive before 10:00 or after 16:00 (the place gets really busy by 11:00). In summer, consider a **nighttime visit.** You'll enjoy the same access with mood-lighting effects (bordering on cheesy) and no crowds (€15, €13 at TI, early July-Aug Mon-Sat 19:00-24:00, last entry one hour before closing, daytime tickets aren't valid for re-entry, but you can visit before 19:00 and stay on). The last shuttle bus leaves the island for the mainland parking lot at midnight.

Tours: The excellent audioguide gives greater detail (€3, €5/2 people). You can also take a 1.25-hour English guided tour (free but tip requested, 2-4 tours/day, first and last tours usually around 11:00 and 15:00, confirm times at TI, meet at top ter-

In the village below the abbey

Abbey at Mont St-Michel

race in front of church). These tours can be good, but come with big crowds. You can start a tour, then decide if it works for you—but I'd skip it, instead following my directions, next.

 Self-Guided Tour: Your visit is a one-way route, so there's no way to get lost—just follow the crowds. You'll climb to the ticket office, then climb some more. Along that final stony staircase, monks and nuns (who live in separate quarters on the left) would draw water from a cistern from big faucets on the right. At the top (just past the WC) is a small view terrace, with a much better one just around the corner.

You've climbed the mount. Stop and look back to the church. Now go through the room marked *Accueil*, with interesting models of the abbey through the ages.

• *Emerging on the other side, find your way to the big terrace, walk to the round lookout at the far end, and face the church.*

West Terrace: In 1776, a fire destroyed the west end of the church, leaving this unplanned grand view terrace. The original extent of the church is outlined with short walls. In the paving stones, notice the stonecutter numbers, which are gen-

erally not exposed like this—a reminder that stonecutters were paid by the piece. The buildings of Mont St-Michel are made of granite stones quarried from the Isles of Chausey (visible on a clear day, 20 miles away). Tidal power was ingeniously harnessed to load, unload, and even transport the stones, as barges hitched a ride with each incoming tide.

As you survey the Bay of Mont St-Michel, notice the polder land—farmland reclaimed by Normans in the 19th century with the help of Dutch engineers. The lines of trees mark strips of land regained in the process. Today, the salt-loving plants covering this land are grazed by sheep, which have salty meat that is considered a local treat. You're standing 240 feet above sea level.

The bay stretches from Normandy (on the right as you look to the sea) to Brittany (on the left). The Couesnon River below marks the historic border between the two lands. Brittany and Normandy have long vied for Mont St-Michel. In fact, the river used to pass Mont St-Michel on the other side, making the abbey part of Brittany. Today, it's just barely—but definitively—on

Norman soil. The new dam across this river was built in 2010. Central to the dam is a system of locking gates that retain water upriver during high tide and release it six hours later, in effect flushing the bay and returning sediment to a mudflat at low tide.

• *Now enter the...*

Abbey Church: Sit on a pew near the altar, under the little statue of the Archangel Michael (with the spear to defeat dragons and evil, and the scales to evaluate your soul). Monks built the church on the tip of this rock to be as close to heaven as possible. The downside: There wasn't enough level ground to support a sizable abbey and church. The solution: Four immense crypts were built under the church to create a platform to support each of its wings. While most of the church is Romanesque (see the 11th-century round arches behind you), the light-filled apse behind the altar was built later, when Gothic arches were the rage. In 1421, the crypt that supported the apse collapsed, taking that end of the church with it. None of the original windows survive (victims of fires, storms, lightning, and the Revolution).

In the chapel to the right of the altar stands a grim-looking 12th-century statue of St. Aubert, the man with the vision to build the abbey. Directly in front of the altar, look for the glass-covered manhole (you'll see it again later from another angle). Take a spin around the apse and find the suspended pirate-looking ship.

• *Follow Suite de la Visite signs to enter the...*

Cloisters: A standard abbey feature, this peaceful zone connected various rooms. Here monks could meditate, read the Bible, and tend their gardens (growing food and herbs for medicine). The great view window is enjoyable today (what's the tide doing?), but was not part of the original design. The more secluded a monk could be, the closer he was to God. (A cloister, by definition, is an enclosed place.) Notice how the columns are staggered. This efficient design allowed the cloisters to be supported with

Cloister of the abbey church

less building material (a top priority, given the difficulty of transporting stone this high up). Carvings above the columns feature various plants and heighten the cloister's Garden-of-Eden ambience. The statues of various saints, carved among some columns, were defaced—literally—by French revolutionaries.

• *Continue on to the...*

Refectory: At its peak, the abbey was home to about 50 monks. This was the dining hall where they consumed both food and the word of God in near silence as one monk read in a monotone from the Bible during meals (pulpit on the right near the far end). The monks gathered as a family here in one undivided space under one big arch (an impressive engineering feat in its day). The abbot ate at the head table; guests sat at the table below the cross. The clever columns are thin but very deep, allowing maximum light and solid support. From 966 until 2001, this was a Benedictine abbey. In 2001, the last three Benedictine monks checked out, and a new order of monks from Paris took over the tradition.

• *Stairs lead down one flight to a...*

Stone Relief of St. Michael: This romanticized scene (carved in 1860) depicts the legend of Mont St-Michel: The archangel Michael wanted to commemorate a hard-fought victory over the devil with the construction of a monumental abbey on a nearby island. He sent his message to the bishop of Avranches—St. Aubert—who saw Michael twice in his dreams. But the bishop didn't trust his dreams until the third time, when Michael drove his thumb into the bishop's head, leaving a mark that he could not ignore. Notice the urgent gesture of Michael's hand and arm as the saint points to the uninhabited mount. The bishop finally got the message, and the first chapel was consecrated in 709.

• *Continue down the stairs another flight to the...*

Guests' Hall: St. Benedict wrote that guests should be welcomed according to their status. That meant that when kings (or other VIPs) visited, they were wined and dined without a hint of monastic austerity. This room once exploded in color, with gold stars on a blue sky across the ceiling. (This room's decoration was said to be the model for Sainte-Chapelle in Paris.) The floor was composed of glazed red-and-green tiles. The entire space was bathed in glorious sunlight, made divine as it passed through a filter of stained glass. The big double fireplace, kept out of sight by hanging tapestries, served as a kitchen—walk under it, imagine an entire wild boar on a spit, and see the light.

• *Hike up the stairs through a chapel to the...*

Hall of the Grand Pillars: Perched on a pointy rock, the huge abbey church had four sturdy crypts like this to prop it up. You're standing under the Gothic portion of the abbey church—this was the crypt that collapsed in 1421. Notice the immensity of the columns (15 feet around) in the new crypt, rebuilt with a determination not to let it fall again. Now look up at the round hole in the ceiling and recognize it as the glass "manhole cover" from the church altar above.

• *To see what kind of crypt collapsed, continue on to the...*

Crypt of St. Martin: This simple 11th-century vault, one of the oldest on the mount, is textbook Romanesque. It has minimal openings, since the walls needed to be solid and fat to support the buildings above. As you leave, notice the thickness of the walls.

• *Walking on, study the barnacle-like unplanned stone construction, added haphazardly over the centuries, yet all integrated. Next, you'll find the...*

Ossuary (identifiable by its big treadwheel): The monks celebrated death as well as life. This part of the abbey housed the hospital, morgue, and ossuary. Because the abbey graveyard was small, it was routinely emptied, and the bones were stacked here.

During the Revolution, monasticism was abolished. Church property was taken by the secular government, and from 1793 to 1863, Mont St-Michel was used as an Alcatraz-type prison. Its first inmates were 300 priests who refused to renounce their vows. (Victor Hugo complained that using such a place as a prison was like keeping a toad in a reliquary.) The big treadwheel from 1820—the kind that did heavy lifting for big building projects throughout the Middle Ages—is from the decades when the abbey was a prison. Teams of six prisoners marched two abreast in the wheel, hamster-style, powering two-ton loads of stone and supplies up Mont St-Michel. Spin the rollers of the sled next to the wheel.

From here, you'll pass through a chapel (with a rare fragment of a 13th-century fresco above), walk up the Romanesque-arched North-South Stairs, pass through the Promenade of the Monks (appreciate the fine medieval stonework, built directly into the granite rock of the island), go under more Gothic vaults, and finally descend into the vast...

Scriptorium Hall (a.k.a. Knights Hall): This important room is where monks decorated illuminated manuscripts and transcribed texts. It faces north so its big windows would let in lots of flat, indirect light, the preference of artists throughout time. You'll then spiral down to the gift shop, exiting out the back door (follow signs to the *Jardins*).

• *You'll emerge into the rear garden. From here, look back from where you just came and up at a miracle (merveille) of medieval engineering.*

The "Merveille": This was an immense building project—a marvel back in 1220. Three levels of buildings were created: the lower floor for storage, the middle floor for work and study, and the top floor for meditation (in the cloister, open to the heavens). It was a medieval skyscraper. The vision was even grander—the place where you're standing was to be built up in similar fashion to support an expansion of the church. But the money ran out, and the project was abandoned. As you leave the garden, notice the tall narrow windows of the refectory on the top floor.

• *Exiting the abbey, you'll pop out midway on the steps you climbed to get here. You could descend here straight into tourist hell. But for a little rampart romance, go down only until you find the short stairway on the left. Climb up the dozen steps and circle right, following a well-fortified outer rampart with a few awe-inspiring viewpoints before heading back down to the King's Gate and the bridge.*

Eating

Puffy omelets (*omelette montoise,* or *omelette tradition*) are Mont St-Michel's specialty. Also look for mussels, seafood platters, and locally raised lamb *pré-salé* (a saltwater-grass diet gives the meat a unique taste, but beware of impostor lamb from New Zealand—ask where your dinner was raised). Muscadet wine (dry, white, and cheap) from the western Loire valley is made nearby and goes well with most regional dishes.

The cuisine served at most restaurants is low quality, similar, and geared to tourists (with *menus* from €18 to €29, cheap crêpes, and full à la carte choices). Pick a

restaurant for its view. Window-shop the places that face the bay from the ramparts walk (several access points—one is across from the post office at the bottom of the village) and arrive early to land a view table. Unless noted, the following restaurants are open daily for lunch and dinner.

$$ Hôtel du Guesclin is the top place for a traditional meal, with white tablecloths and beautiful views of the bay from its inside-only tables (closed Thu, book a window table in advance; see details under "Sleeping—On the Island," later).

$$ Restaurant le St. Michel is lighthearted, reasonable, family-friendly, and run by helpful Patricia (decent omelets, mussels, salads, and pasta; open daily for lunch, open for dinner July-Aug, closed Thu-Fri off-season, test its toilet in the rock, across from Hôtel le Mouton Blanc, tel. 02 33 60 14 37).

$$ Café La Mère Poulard is a stylish three-story café-*crêperie*-restaurant one door up from Hôtel le Mouton Blanc. (Don't confuse it with the Restaurant La Mère Poulard by the drawbridge.) It's worth considering for its upstairs terrace, which offers the best outside table views up to the abbey (when their umbrellas don't block it). **La Vieille Auberge** has a broad terrace with the next-best views to the abbey. **La Croix Blanche** owns a small deck with abbey views and window-front tables with bay views, and **Les Terrasses Poulard** has indoor views to the bay.

Groceries: In La Caserne, **Les Galeries du Mont St-Michel** is stocked with souvenirs and enough groceries to make a credible picnic (daily 9:00-20:00).

Rick's Tip: The small lanes above the main street hide **romantic picnic spots,** *such as the small park at the base of the ancient treadwheel ramp to the upper abbey. Catch late sun by following the ramp that leads through the* gendarmerie *and down behind the island (on the left as you face the main entry to the island).*

Sleeping

Sleep on or near the island so that you can visit Mont St-Michel early and late. What matters is being here before or after the crush of tourists, and seeing the island floodlit after dark. Sleeping on the island—inside the walls—is a memorable experience for medieval romantics who don't mind small and overpriced rooms of average quality, and baggage hassles. To reach a room on the island, you'll need to carry your bags 15 minutes from the *navette* (shuttle) stop. Take only what you need for one night in a smaller bag, but don't leave any luggage visible in your car.

Hotels and *chambres d'hôtes* near the island are a better value (if less romantic). Those listed below are within walking distance of the free and frequent shuttle to the island.

On the Island

Because most visitors day-trip here, finding a room is generally no problem. Though some pad their profits by requesting that guests buy dinner from their restaurant, requiring it is illegal. Higher-priced rooms generally have bay views.

The following hotels, all on Grand Rue, are listed in order of altitude from lowest to highest.

$$$ Hôtel St. Pierre* and **Hôtel Croix Blanche*** sit side by side and share the same owners and reception desk (at St. Pierre). Each provides comfortable rooms at inflated prices, some with good views (family rooms, lower rates at Hôtel Croix Blanche, tel. 02 33 60 14 03, www.auberge-saint-pierre.fr, contact@auberge-saint-pierre.fr).

$$$ Hôtel le Mouton Blanc* delivers a higher price value, with 15 rooms split between two buildings. Rooms in the main building have wood beams and all are freshly renovated with contemporary decor (tel. 02 33 60 14 08, www.lemoutonblanc.fr, contact@lemoutonblanc.fr).

$$ Hôtel la Vieille Auberge is a small place with good rooms at fair prices (pricier but worthwhile view room with deck; check in at their restaurant, but book through Hôtel St. Pierre, listed earlier).

$$ Hôtel du Guesclin has the cheapest and best-value rooms I list on the island and is the only family-run hotel left there. Rooms have simple decor and provide basic comfort (tel. 02 33 60 14 10, www.hotelduguesclin.com, hotel.duguesclin@wanadoo.fr).

On the Mainland

Modern hotels with easy parking and quick shuttle-bus access gather in La Caserne near the bridge to the island.

$$ Hôtel le Relais du Roy* houses small but well-configured and plush rooms above comfy public spaces. Most rooms are on the riverside, with countryside views, and many have small balconies allowing "lean-out" views to the abbey (bar, restaurant, 8 Route du Mont Saint-Michel, tel. 02 33 60 14 25, www.le-relais-du-roy.com, reservation@le-relais-du-roy.com).

$$ Hôtel Gabriel* has 45 modern rooms, with flashy colors and OK rates (includes breakfast, Route du Mont Saint-Michel, tel. 02 33 60 14 13, www.hotelgabriel-montsaintmichel.com, hotelgabriel@le-mont-saint-michel.com).

$ Hôtel Vert provides 54 motel-esque, comfortable rooms at good rates (family rooms, Route du Mont Saint-Michel, tel. 02 33 60 09 33, www.hotelvert-montsaintmichel.com, stmichel@le-mont-saint-michel.com). They also have a small launderette for guests.

Chambres d'Hotes

$ La Jacotière is closest to Mont St-Michel and within easy walking distance of the regional bus stop and the island shuttle buses (allowing you to avoid all parking fees). Welcoming Véronique offers six comfortable rooms and views of the island from the cool backyard garden (studio with great view from private patio, family rooms, includes breakfast, tel. 02 33 60 22 94, www. lajacotiere.fr, la.jacotiere@wanadoo.fr). Drivers coming from Bayeux should keep right well before the main parking lot entry: As the road bends to the left away from the bay, stay straight and look for a Calvados products store standing alone on the right. Follow the small service lane in front of the store signed *sauf véhicule autorisé*—La Jacotière is the next building.

Transportation
Arriving and Departing

Bus and train service to and from Mont St-Michel can be a challenge. You may find that you're forced to arrive and depart early or late—leaving you with too much or too little time on the island. For good explanations of your arrival options by car or train/bus, visit www.accueilmontsaintmichel.fr.

BY CAR

Day-trippers are directed to a sea of parking (remember your parking-area number). Expect parking jams in high season between 10:00 and noon. To avoid extra walking, take your parking ticket with you and pay at the machines near the visitors center (€12/24 hours—no re-entry, €6.50/up to 2.5 hours, machines take cash and US credit cards, parking tel. 02 14 13 20 15). If you arrive after 19:00 and leave before 11:00 the next day, the fee is €4.50.

If you're staying at a hotel on the island or in La Caserne, you'll receive a parking-gate code from your hotel (ending with "V"). As you approach the parking areas, follow wheelchair and bus icon signs until you come to a gate. Those staying on the island turn right here and follow signs for *Parking P3* (the parking is close to the shuttle bus; €12/24 hours). Those staying at the foot of the island in La Caserne should be able to continue straight at the gate (enter your code), then drive right to your hotel (€6.50 fee). Changes to the parking system are possible—ask when booking your hotel.

From the Parking Lot or La Caserne to the Island: You can either **walk** (about 50 level and scenic minutes) or pile onto the free and frequent **shuttle bus** (runs 7:30-24:00, 12-minute trip). The shuttle makes four stops: at the parking lot visitors center, in La Caserne village (in front of the Les Galeries du Mont St-Michel grocery), near the dam at the start of the bridge, and at the island end of the bridge.

BY TRAIN AND BUS

The nearest train station is five miles away in **Pontorson** (called Pontorson/Mont St-Michel). Few trains stop here, and Sunday service is almost nonexistent. Trains are met by buses that take passengers to the foot of the island (€3, 10 buses/day July-Aug, 8/day Sept-June, fewer on Sun, 20 minutes). Or take a taxi to the shuttle stop in the Mont St-Michel parking lot (about €20, €26 after 19:00 and on weekends/holidays; tel. 02 33 60 26 89, mobile 06 32 10 54 06).

Buses connecting with fast trains from **Rennes** and **Dol-de-Bretagne** stations drop you near the shuttle stop in the parking lot. From Bayeux, it's faster by shuttle van.

From Mont St-Michel to Paris: Most travelers take the regional bus from Mont St-Michel's parking lot to Rennes or Dol de Bretagne and connect directly to a high-speed train (4/day via Rennes, about 3 hours total from Mont St-Michel to Paris' Gare Montparnasse via fastest train from Rennes; €15 for bus to Rennes; not covered by rail pass, buy ticket from driver, all explained in English at https://keolis-armor.com). Flixbus runs direct service from Mont St-Michel to Paris' Gare de Bercy.

From Mont St-Michel via Pontorson to: Bayeux (2/day, 6 hours; faster by shuttle van—see page 162).

The Loire

As it glides gently east to west, officially separating northern from southern France, the Loire River has come to define this popular tourist region. The valley's prime location, just south of Paris, has made the Loire a strategic hot potato for more than a thousand years. Today, this region is still the dividing line for the country—for example, weather forecasters say, "north of the Loire...and south of the Loire..."

When a "valley address" became a must-have among 16th-century hunting-crazy royalty, rich Renaissance palaces replaced outdated medieval castles. Hundreds of these castles and palaces are open to visitors, and it's castles that you're here to see. Old-time aristocratic château-owners, struggling with the cost of upkeep, enjoy financial assistance from the government if they open their mansions to the public.

Amboise is the best town to use as a home base, with sights of its own and handy access by car and minivan tour to important châteaux. If you'd rather stay in a village, Chenonceaux is a fine choice.

If you want to sleep in a castle surrounded by a forest, the Loire Valley is the place—you have several choices in all price ranges. Most of my château-hotel recommendations, best for drivers, are located within 15 minutes of Amboise.

Traveling by car is the easiest way to get around, and day rentals are reasonable (in Amboise or at the St-Pierre-des-Corps TGV station just outside the city of Tours). Minivan tours, taxis, trains, a few buses, and bikes allow those without a car to reach the well-known châteaux.

Frequent bullet trains link the Loire to Paris in less than two hours (with a few direct runs to Charles de Gaulle Airport). Some travelers find the Loire can serve as a good first or last stop on their French odyssey.

THE LOIRE IN 2 DAYS

Two full days are sufficient to sample the best châteaux. Don't go overboard. Two châteaux, possibly three, are the recommended maximum per day.

Homebase in (or near) Amboise, and visit its sights the day you arrive. The next morning, drive to my favorite château—graceful Chenonceau—arriving before 9:00 to be one of the first in. Next, drive to Cheverny (40 minutes), with a fun dog-feeding spectacle at 11:30 and good lunch options. End your day at monumental Chambord, a 15-minute drive from Cheverny. To see the dog feeding at Cheverny, you need to stay on task and leave Chenonceau by 10:30—or visit these sights in reverse order, starting with Chambord (arrive close to 9:00 opening), then Cheverny, and ending at Chenonceau (this means more crowds at Chenonceau).

THE LOIRE AT A GLANCE

Amboise

▲**Amboise** Supposed burial place of Leonardo da Vinci, with terrific views over the town. **Hours:** Daily 9:00-18:00, July-Aug until 20:00, shorter hours Nov-March. See page 196.

▲**Clos-Lucé** Leonardo da Vinci's final home and gardens, with models of his creations. **Hours:** Daily 9:00-19:00, July-Aug until 20:00; shorter hours Nov-Jan. See page 204.

Châteaux Beyond Amboise

▲▲▲**Chenonceau** Elegant château arching over the Cher River, with lovely gardens. **Hours:** Daily 9:00-19:30, July-Aug until 20:00, closes earlier off-season. See page 210.

▲▲▲**Chambord** Epic grandeur (440 rooms) and fun rooftop views in an evocative setting surrounded by a forest. **Hours:** Daily 9:00-18:00, Oct-March until 17:00. See page 214.

▲▲**Cheverny** Intimate-feeling château with lavish furnishings and daily feeding of hunting dogs (at 11:30). **Hours:** Daily 9:15-18:30, Nov-March 10:00-17:00. See page 218.

▲▲**Chaumont-sur-Loire** Imposing setting over the Loire River, notable for its historic connections to America and impressive Festival of Gardens. **Hours:** Daily 10:00-20:00, shorter hours Oct-mid-April. See page 220.

▲▲**Villandry** Average palace boasting the best gardens in the Loire—and possibly all of France. **Hours:** Daily 9:00-19:00, March and Oct until 18:00, Nov-Feb until 17:00. See page 222.

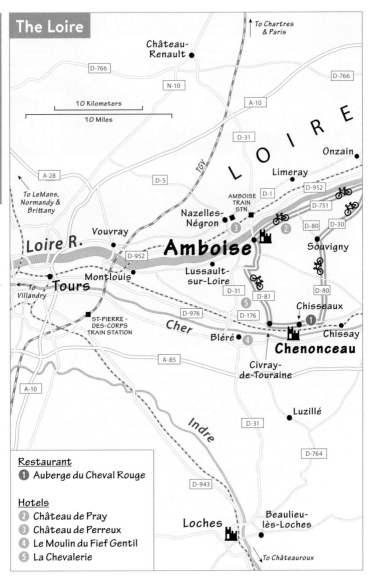

The Loire

To Chartres
& Paris

Château-
Renault

D-766

N-10

D-766

A-10

10 Kilometers

10 Miles

D-31

L O I R E

Onzain

A-28

D-5

TGV

Limeray

D-952

To LeMans,
Normandy &
Brittany

AMBOISE
TRAIN
STN.

D-1

D-751

Nazelles-
Négron

D-80

D-30

Vouvray

Amboise

Souvigny

Loire R.

D-952

Lussault-
sur-Loire

Montlouis

Tours

D-31

D-81

To
Villandry

Chisseaux

ST-PIERRE-
DES-CORPS
TRAIN STATION

D-976

D-80

Cher

D-176

Chissay

A-85

Bléré

Chenonceau

A-10

Civray-
de-Touraine

Indre

D-31

Luzillé

D-764

Restaurant
① Auberge du Cheval Rouge

D-943

Hotels
② Château de Pray
③ Château de Perreux
④ Le Moulin du Fief Gentil
⑤ La Chevalerie

Loches

Beaulieu-
lès-Loches

To Châteauroux

Try to see one château on your drive into (or out of) Amboise. For example, if arriving from the north, visit Chambord or Chaumont; if coming from the west or the south, see Villandry for its gardens.

Without a car: Homebase in Amboise and take a minivan tour of the châteaux. This is easily the best plan for most visitors. If you'd rather use public transportation to reach the châteaux, it's doable but time-consuming; allow an extra day.

Getting Around the Loire

Shuttle services and minivan tours offer affordable transportation from Amboise to many of the valley's châteaux. Taxi

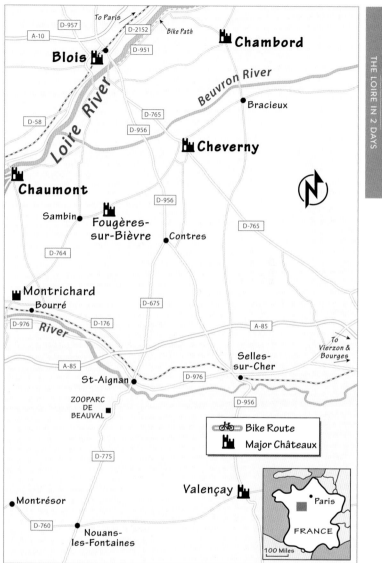

To Paris
Bike Path
D-957
A-10
D-2152
D-951
Chambord
Blois
Loire River
Beuvron River
D-58
D-765
D-956
Bracieux
Cheverny
Chaumont
D-956
Sambin
Fougères-sur-Bièvre
Contres
D-765
D-764
Montrichard
Bourré
D-675
D-976
River
D-176
A-85
To Vierzon & Bourges
A-85
Selles-sur-Cher
St-Aignan
D-976
ZOOPARC DE BEAUVAL
D-956

🚲 Bike Route
🏰 Major Châteaux

D-775

Valençay
Montrésor
D-760
Nouans-les-Fontaines

Paris
FRANCE
100 Miles

excursions can be affordable—particularly when split among several people and especially from Amboise to Chenonceau.

By Shuttle Van: Shuttles connect Amboise and Tours with key châteaux in peak season (€6-20), and minivan tours combine several châteaux into a painless day tour (about €40/person for sched-uled half-day itineraries from Amboise or Tours, €60 for all day; allow €150/person for all-day guided tours that include wine tastings, châteaux visits, and lunch; figure €240 for custom groups of up to 7 for 4 hours, €400 for 8 hours). Most of these services depart from TIs (who can book them for you) and can save you time (in line) and money (on admissions) when you purchase your château ticket at a discounted group rate from the driver.

By Minivan Tour: While on the road, you'll usually get a running commentary—but you're on your own at the sights (discounted tickets available from the driver). Reserve a week ahead by email, or two to three days by phone. (Day-trippers from Paris find these services convenient.) **Acco-Dispo** runs half- and all-day English tours from Amboise and Tours to all the major châteaux (Mon-Sat, half-day tours-€40/person, full-day-€60/person; meet at the TI, small groups of 2-8 people, mobile 06 82 00 64 51, www.accodispo-tours.com). **Touraine Evasion** runs half-day tours daily from Amboise that stop at Chambord and Chenonceau (€40/person) and all-day tours that add Cheverny (€60/person). They also have many château options out of Tours (daily in season, none in winter, mobile 06 07 39 13 31, www.tourevasion.com). **Loire Valley Tours** offers all-day, fully-guided itineraries from Amboise and Tours that include admissions, lunch, and wine tasting (about €160/person, tel. 02 54 33 99 80, www.loire-valley-tours.com).

By Train or Bus to Chenonceaux: Amboise and the village of Chenonceaux are connected by train (6/day, 1 hour, transfer at St-Pierre-des-Corps) and less frequent buses (1-2/day, Mon-Sat only, 25 minutes, stop in Amboise—called Théâtre—is between Place St-Denis and the river on the west side of Avenue des Martyrs de la Résistance, across from the Théâtre de Beaumarchais).

By Taxi: A taxi from Amboise to Chenonceau costs about €29 (€41 on Sun and after 19:00, €7 pickup fee, call 02 47 57 13 53). Most other châteaux are too expensive to visit by cab.

By Bike: Pick up the free bike-path map at any TI, buy the more detailed map available at TIs, or study the route options at www.cycling-loire.com. Travelers with only a day or two may prefer to rent a car

or stick to the châteaux easily reached by buses and minivans.) **Détours de Loire** can help you plan your bike route. They can also deliver rental bikes to most places in the Loire for reasonable rates. They have shops in Amboise and Tours, allowing one-way rentals between these and their partner shops (www.detoursdeloire.com).

AMBOISE

Straddling the widest stretch of the Loire River, Amboise is an inviting town with a pleasing old quarter below its hilltop château. A castle has overlooked the Loire from Amboise since Roman times. Leonardo da Vinci retired here...just one more of his many brilliant ideas.

As the royal residence of François I (r. 1515-1547), Amboise wielded far more importance than you'd imagine from a lazy walk through its center. In fact, its residents are pretty conservative, giving the town an attitude—as if no one told them they're no longer the second capital of France. Locals keep their wealth to themselves; consequently, many grand mansions hide behind nondescript facades.

With or without a car, Amboise is an ideal small-town home base for exploring the best of château country.

Orientation

Amboise (pop. 14,000) covers ground on both sides of the Loire, with the "Golden Island" (Ile d'Or) in the middle. The train station is on the north side of the Loire, but nearly everything else is on the south (château) side. Pedestrian-friendly Rue Nationale parallels the river a few blocks inland and leads from the base of Château d'Amboise through the town center and past the clock tower—once part of the town wall—to the Romanesque Church of St-Denis.

Tourist Information: The information-packed TI is on Quai du Général de Gaulle (April-June and Sept-Oct Mon-Sat

Amboise hugs the bank of the Loire River.

9:30-18:00, Sun 10:00-13:00 & 14:00-17:00; July-Aug Mon-Sat 9:00-19:00, Sun 10:00-18:00; Nov-March shorter hours Mon-Sat, closed Sun; tel. 02 47 57 09 28, www.amboise-valdeloire.com). Pick up the city map, and consider purchasing tickets to key area châteaux (saving money and time in ticket lines). Ask about sound-and-light shows (generally summers only). The TI can recommend local guides. They can also help you organize tours to the châteaux with a shuttle bus or minivan service.

Rick's Tip: **The TI sells tickets in bundles** *of two or more to sights and châteaux around Amboise, saving on entry fees—and time spent in line. You can also get* **discounted tickets** *if you take a minivan tour.*

Helpful Hints

Market Days: Open-air markets are held on Friday (smaller but more local) and Sunday (the big one) in the parking lot behind the TI on the river (both 8:30-13:00).

Baggage Storage: Besides the **Amboise TI,** which stores bags for €2 each, most châteaux offer free storage if you've paid admission.

Laundry: The nearest launderette is at **Supermarket LeClerc,** a half-mile from the TI toward Tours on D-751.

Taxi: There's no taxi station, so you must call for one (tel. 02 47 57 13 53, 06 12 92 70 46, 02 47 57 30 39, or 06 88 02 44 10).

Car Rental: It's easiest to rent cars at the St-Pierre-des-Corps train station (TGV service from Paris), a 15-minute drive from Amboise.

On the outskirts of Amboise, **Désiré Automobile** at the Renault dealership rents cars (closed Sun, about a mile downriver from the TI at 105 Avenue de Tours, tel. 02 47 57 17 92, renault-amboise@orange.fr). **Europcar** is outside Amboise on Route de Chenonceaux at the Total gas station (tel. 02 47 57 07 64, reservation tel. 02 47 85 85 85, www.europcar.com). Figure €10 for a taxi from Amboise to either place.

Local Guides: An expert in all things Loire, **Fabrice Maret** gives an excellent walking tour of Amboise and its sights, or can guide you around the area's châteaux using your rental car (€260/day plus transportation from Blois, tel. 02 54 70 19 59, www.chateauxloire.com, info@

Hot-Air Balloon Rides

In France's most popular regions, you'll find hot-air balloon companies eager to take you for a ride (Burgundy, the Loire, Dordogne, and Provence are best suited for ballooning). It's not cheap, but it's unforgettable—a once-in-a-lifetime chance to sail serenely over châteaux, canals, vineyards, Romanesque churches, and villages. Balloons don't go above 3,000 feet and usually fly much lower than that, so you get a bird's-eye view of France's sublime landscapes.

Most companies offer similar deals and work this way: Trips range from 45 to 90 minutes of air time, to which you should add two hours for preparation, champagne toast, and transport back to your starting point. Deluxe trips add a gourmet picnic, making it a four-hour event. Allow about €200 for a short tour, and about €300 for longer flights. Departures are, of course, weather-dependent, and are usually scheduled first thing in the morning or in early evening. If you've booked ahead and the weather turns bad, you can reschedule your flight, but you can't get your money back. Most balloon companies charge about €25 more for a bad-weather refund guarantee; unless your itinerary is very loose, it's a good idea.

Flight season is April through October. It's smart to bring a jacket for the breeze, though temperatures in the air won't differ too much from those on the ground. Heat from the propane flames that power the balloon may make your hair stand up—I wear a cap. Airsickness is usually not a problem, as the ride is typically slow and even. Baskets have no seating, so count on standing the entire trip. Group (and basket) size can vary from 4 to 16 passengers. Area TIs have brochures. **France Montgolfières** gets good reviews and offers flights in the areas that I recommend (tel. 03 80 97 38 61, US tel. 917/310-0783, www.france-balloons.com). Others are **Aérocom Montgolfière** (tel. 02 54 33 55 00, www.aerocom.fr) and **Touraine Montgolfière** (tel. 02 47 30 10 80, www.touraine-montgolfiere.fr).

chateauxloire.com). To experience the region off the beaten path, consider **Loire Valley à la Carte,** where passionate and longtime resident Catherine Canteau Cohen can organize or guide your day from soup to nuts (tel. 07 81 61 19 58, www.loirevalleyalacarte.com, contact@loireval-leyalacarte.com).

⊖ Amboise Walk

This short walk starts at the banks of the Loire River, winds past the old church of St-Denis, and meanders through the heart of town to a fine little city museum. You'll end near the entrance to Château Royal d'Amboise and Leonardo's house. Use the "Amboise" map to orient yourself.

• *Climb to the top of the embankment over-looking the river from near the bridge.*

Amboise Riverbank: Survey the town, its island, bridge, and castle. If you have a passion for anything French—philoso-phy, history, food, wine—you'll feel it here, along the Loire. This river, the longest in the country and the natural boundary between northern and southern France,

is the last "untamed" river in the country (there are no dams or mechanisms to control periodic flooding). The region's châteaux line up along the Loire and its tributaries, because before trains and trucks, stones for big buildings were best shipped by boat. You may see a few of the traditional flat-bottomed Loire boats moored here. The bridge spanning the river marks a strategic crossing and a long-time political border. That's why the first Amboise castle was built here. In the 15th century, this was one of the biggest forts in France.

The half-mile-long "Golden Island" (Ile d'Or) is the only island in the Loire substantial enough to withstand flooding and to have permanent buildings. It was important historically as the place where northern and southern France came together. Truces were made here.

• *Walk downstream on the footpath above busy Quai du Général de Gaulle. After about a quarter-mile, you'll see a parking lot below and to your right, where farmers markets take place on Friday and Sunday*

Amboise and its Château Royal

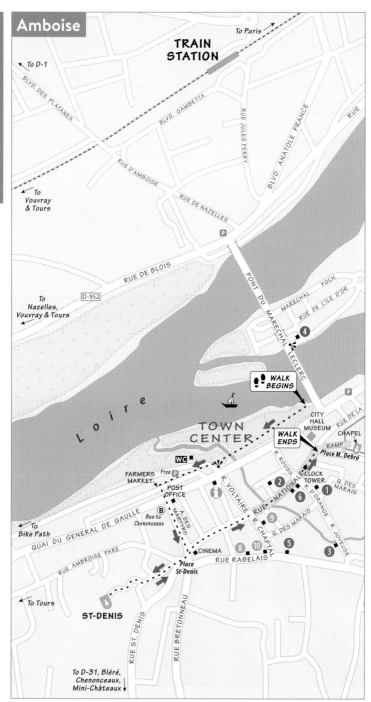

Amboise

To Paris

TRAIN STATION

To D-1

BLVD. DES PLATANES

BLVD. GAMBETTA

RUE JULES FERRY

BLVD. ANATOLE FRANCE

RUE

RUE D'AMBOISE

To Vouvray & Tours

RUE DE NAZELLES

RUE DE BLOIS

D-952

To Nazelles, Vouvray & Tours

PONT DU MARECHAL LECLERC

MARECHAL FOCH

RUE DE L'ÎLE D'OR

4

L o i r e

WALK BEGINS

TOWN CENTER

CITY HALL MUSEUM

RUE DE LA

CHAPEL

WALK ENDS

RAMP

Place M. Debré

WC

Free P

FARMERS MARKET

POST OFFICE

CLOCK TOWER

R. ROUSS.

2

R. VOLTAIRE

RUE NATIONALE

6

R. D'ORANGE

1

Q. DES MARAIS

B Bus to Chenonceaux

To Bike Path

QUAI DU GENERAL DE GAULLE

A. DES MARTYRS

9

R. CHAPTAL

Q. DES MARAIS

R. JOYEUSE

CINEMA

RUE AMBOISE PARE

8 **10** **5** **3**

RUE RABELAIS

Place St-Denis

To Tours

ST-DENIS

RUE ST. DENIS

RUE BRETONNEAU

To D-31, Bléré, Chenonceaux, Mini-Châteaux

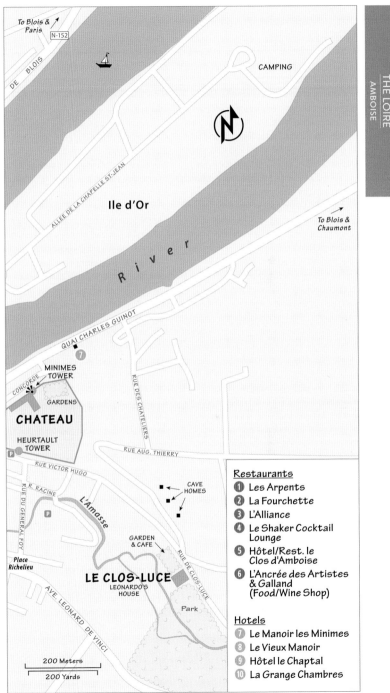

Restaurants
1 Les Arpents
2 La Fourchette
3 L'Alliance
4 Le Shaker Cocktail Lounge
5 Hôtel/Rest. le Clos d'Amboise
6 L'Ancrée des Artistes & Galland (Food/Wine Shop)

Hotels
7 Le Manoir les Minimes
8 Le Vieux Manoir
9 Hôtel le Chaptal
10 La Grange Chambres

mornings. When you spot the post office across the street, cross Quai du Général de Gaulle. Walk up Avenue des Martyrs de la Résistance and turn right at Place St-Denis to find the old church standing proudly on a bluff to the right.

Church of St-Denis (Eglise St-Denis): Ever since ancient Romans erected a Temple of Mars here, this has been a place of worship. According to legend, God sent a bolt of lightning that knocked down the statue of Mars, and Christians took over the spot. The current Romanesque church dates from the 12th century. A cute little statue of St. Denis (above the entry's arch) greets you as you step in. The delightful carvings capping the many columns inside date from Romanesque times. The lovely (but poorly lit) pastel-painted *Deposition* to the right of the choir is restored to its 16th-century brilliance. The medieval stained glass in the windows, likely destroyed in the French Revolution, was replaced with 19th-century glass. A plaque in the rear of the church lists Amboise residents who died in World War I.

From the steps of the church, look out to the hill-capping Amboise château. For a thousand years, it's been God on this hill and the king on that one. It's interesting to ponder how, throughout French history, the king's power generally trumped the Church's, and how the Church and the king worked to keep people down—setting the stage for the French Revolution.
• *Retrace your steps down from the church and across Place St-Denis, go past Amboise's cinema, continue walking straight, and follow Rue Nationale through the heart of town toward the castle.*

Rue Nationale: The broad, pedestrianized Rue Nationale, with its narrow intersecting lanes, survives from the 15th century. At that time, when the town spread at the foot of the king's castle, this was the "Champs-Elysées" of Amboise. Supporting the king and his huge entourage was a serious industry. The French king spilled money wherever he stayed.

As you walk along this spine of the town, spot rare surviving bits of rustic medieval oak in the half-timbered buildings. The homes of wealthy merchants rose from the chaos of this street. Side lanes can be more candid—they often show what's hidden behind modern facades.

Stop when you reach the impressive **clock tower** (Tour de l'Horloge), built into part of the 15th-century town wall. This was once a fortified gate, opening onto the road to the city of Tours. Imagine the hefty wood-and-iron portcullis (fortified door) that dropped from above.
• *At the intersection with Rue François I (where you'll be tempted by the Bigot chocolate shop), turn left a couple of steps to the...*

City Hall Museum: This free museum is worth a quick peek for its romantic interior, town paintings, and historic etchings (a flyer gives some English explanations, inconsistent hours, usually open July-Aug daily 10:00-12:30 & 14:00-19:00, otherwise closed). In the room dedicated to Leonardo da Vinci are his busts and photos of the gripping deathbed painting of him with caring King François I at his side (the original is on loan to the château). In the Salle des Rois (Kings' Room), find portraits of Charles VIII (who coldcocked himself at Amboise's castle) and other nobles; I like to admire their distinct noses.

Upstairs, in the still-functioning city assembly hall (last room), notice how the photo of the current president faces the lady of the Republic. (According to locals, her features change with the taste of the generation, and the bust of France's Lady Liberty is often modeled on famous supermodels of the day.)
• *Retrace your steps along Rue François I to* **Place Michel Debré,** *at the base of the Château Royal d'Amboise and the end of this walk. Here, at one of the most touristy spots in the Loire, tourism's importance to the local economy is palpable. Notice the fat, round 15th-century fortified tower, whose interior ramp was built for galloping*

horses to spiral up to castle level. Beyond the château is Leonardo's last residence at Clos-Lucé.

Sights

▲CHATEAU ROYAL D'AMBOISE

This historic heap, built mostly in the late 15th century, became the favored royal residence in the Loire under Charles VIII. Charles is famous for accidentally killing himself by walking into a door lintel on his way to a tennis match (seriously). Later, more careful occupants include Louis XII (who moved the royal court to Blois) and François I (who physically brought the Renaissance here in 1516, in the person of Leonardo da Vinci).

Cost and Hours: €13, daily 9:00-18:00, July-Aug until 20:00, shorter hours Nov-March, skip the unnecessary audioguide, Place Michel Debré, tel. 02 47 57 00 98, www.chateau-amboise.com.

◐ **Self-Guided Tour:** After climbing the long ramp to the ticket booth and picking up the free and well-done English brochure, your first stop is the petite **chapel** where Leonardo da Vinci is supposedly buried. This flamboyant little Gothic chapel is where the king began and ended each day in prayer. It comes with two fireplaces "to comfort the king" and two plaques "evoking the final resting place" of Leonardo (one in French, the other in Italian). Where he's actually buried, no one seems to know.

Enter the **castle rooms** across from Leonardo's chapel. The three-floor route takes you chronologically from Gothic-style rooms to those from the early Renaissance and on to the 19th century. The first room, **Salle des Gardes,** shows the château's original, much larger size; drawings in the next room give you a better feel for its original look. (The little chapel you just saw was once part of the bigger complex.)

You'll pass the sumptuous **council chambers** (Salle du Conseil) where the king would meet with his key staff (find his throne). King **Henry II's bedroom** is livable. The second son of François I, Henry is remembered as the husband of the ambitious and unscrupulous Catherine de' Medici—and for his tragic death in a jousting tournament.

Château Royal d'Amboise is the town's top sight.

The rose-colored top-floor rooms are well-furnished from the post-Revolutionary 1800s and demonstrate the continued interest among French nobility in this château. Find the classy portrait of King Louis-Philippe, the last Louis to rule France.

The **Minimes Tower** delivers grand views from its terrace. From here, the strategic value of this site is clear: The visibility is great, and the river below provided a natural defense.

The bulky tower climbs 130 feet in five spirals—designed for a mounted soldier in a hurry. Walk a short distance down the spiral ramp and exit into the **gardens.** Each summer, bleachers are set up for sound-and-light spectacles—a faint echo of the extravaganzas Leonardo orchestrated for the court. Modern art decorating the garden reminds visitors of the inquisitive and scientific Renaissance spirit that Leonardo brought to town. The flags are those of France and Brittany—a reminder that, in a sense, modern France was created at the nearby château of Langeais when Charles VIII (who was born here) married Anne of Brittany, adding her domain to the French kingdom.

Spiral down the **Heurtault Tower**. As with the castle's other tower, this was designed to accommodate a soldier on horseback. As you gallop down to the exit, notice the cute little characters and scenes left by 15th-century stone carvers. While they needed to behave when decorating churches and palaces, here they could be a bit racier and more spirited.

Leaving the Château: The turnstile puts you on the road to Château du Clos-Lucé (described next; turn left and hike straight for 10 minutes). Along the way, you'll pass **troglodyte houses**—both new and old—carved into the hillside stone (a type called *tuffeau,* a sedimentary rock). Originally, poor people resided here—the dwellings didn't require expensive slate roofing, came with natural insulation, and could be dug essentially for free, as builders valued the stone quarried in the process. Today wealthy stone lovers are renovating them into stylish digs worthy of *Better Homes and Caves.*

Rick's Tip: *Many of the major* **châteaux have free apps** *that reproduce their rentable audioguides—check château websites for info. The Amboise TI also offers free city guide apps. Download these apps before you leave home to save time and money when you get here.*

▲CHATEAU ROYAL D'AMBOISE SOUND-AND-LIGHT SHOW

This summer-only show is considered one of the best shows of its kind in the area. Although it's entirely in French, you can rent an English audioguide. Over 100 volunteer locals re-create the life of François I with dramatic lighting effects, lavish costumes, battle scenes, and fireworks. Dress warmly.

Cost and Hours: €20 with audioguide, family deals, 1.5-hour show runs several days per week, July 22:30-24:00, Aug 22:00-23:30, tel. 02 47 57 14 47, www. renaissance-amboise.com. Buy tickets online or from the ticket window on the ramp to the château (opens at 20:30).

▲CHATEAU DU CLOS-LUCE AND LEONARDO DA VINCI PARK

In 1516, Leonardo da Vinci packed his bags (and several of his favorite paintings, including the *Mona Lisa*) and left

Henry II's bedroom

Châteaux of the Loire: A Brief History

The Loire River's place in history goes back to the very foundation of France. Traditional flat-bottomed boats romantically moored along embankments are a reminder of the age before trains and trucks, when river traffic safely and efficiently transported heavy loads of stone and timber. With prevailing winds sweeping east from the Atlantic, boats headed upriver; on the way back, they flowed downstream with the current.

With this transportation infrastructure providing access to Paris and the region's thick forests—offering plenty of timber, firewood, and hunting terrain—it's no wonder that castles were built here in the Middle Ages. The first stone fortresses went up a thousand years ago; many of the pleasure palaces you see today rose over the ruins of those original keeps.

The Hundred Years' War (roughly 1336 to 1453) was a desperate time for France. Because of a dynastic dispute, the English had a serious claim to the French throne, and by 1415 controlled much of the country, including Paris. French King Charles VII and his court retreated to the Loire Valley. In 1429, the dispirited king was visited by the charismatic Joan of Arc in his refuge at Chinon. She inspired him to get off his duff and send the English packing.

The French kings continued to live in the Loire region for the next two centuries, having grown comfortable with the château culture of the region. The climate was mild, hunting was good, dreamy rivers made nice reflections, and the location was just close enough to Paris—but still far enough away. Charles VII ruled from Chinon, Charles VIII preferred Amboise, Louis XII reigned from Blois, and François I held court in Chambord and Blois.

With peace and stability, there was no need for fortifications. The most famous luxury hunting lodges were built during this period—including Chenonceau, Chambord, Chaumont, Amboise, and Azay-le-Rideau. Kings (François I), writers (Rabelais), poets (Ronsard), and artists (Leonardo da Vinci) made the Loire a cultural hub.

Because French kings ruled effectively only by being constantly on the move among their subjects, many royal châteaux were used infrequently. The entire court and its trappings were portable. A castle kept empty 11 months of the year would come to life when the king came to town. Royal roadies hung tapestries, unfolded chairs, and wrestled with big trunks in the hours before the royal entourage's arrival.

In 1525, François I moved to his newly built super-palace at Fontainebleau, and political power left the Loire. From then on, châteaux were used as vacation retreats, but became refuges for kings again during the French Wars of Religion (1562-1598). Its conclusion marked the end of an active royal presence on the Loire. With the French Revolution in 1789, symbols of the Old Regime, like the fabulous palaces along the Loire, were ransacked. Fast talking saved some châteaux, especially those whose owners had personal relationships with Revolutionary leaders.

Only in the 1840s did the châteaux of the Loire become appreciated for their historic value. In the 19th century, Romantic writers such as Victor Hugo and Alexander Dumas visited and celebrated the châteaux. The Loire Valley and its historic châteaux found a place in our collective hearts and have been treasured to this day.

an imploding Rome for better wine and working conditions in the Loire Valley. He accepted the position of engineer, architect, and painter to France's Renaissance king, François I. This "House of Light" is the plush palace where Leonardo spent his last three years. (He died on May 2, 1519.) François, only 22 years old, installed the 65-year-old Leonardo here just so he could enjoy his intellectual company.

The house is a kind of fort-château of its own, with a fortified rampart walk and a 16th-century chapel. Two floors of finely decorated rooms are open to the public, but most of the furnishings are neither original nor compelling. Come here to learn about the genius of Leonardo and to see well-explained models of his inventions, displayed inside the house and out in the huge park.

Leonardo attracted disciples who stayed active here, using this house as a kind of workshop and laboratory. The place survived the Revolution because the quick-talking noble who owned it was sympathetic to the cause; he convinced the Revolutionaries that, philosophically, Leonardo would have been on their side.

Cost and Hours: The €16 admission (includes house and gardens) is worth it for Leonardo fans with two hours to fully appreciate this sight. Skip the special exhibit (*Da Vinci et la France,* in the garden) and its €5 supplement. Open daily 9:00-19:00, July-Aug until 20:00, shorter hours Nov-Jan, last entry one hour before closing, tel. 02 47 57 00 73, www.vinci-closluce.com.

Getting There: It's a 10-minute walk uphill at a steady pace from Château Royal d'Amboise, past troglodyte homes (see earlier). If you park in the nearby lot, leave nothing of value visible in your car.

Tours: Follow the helpful free English handout. A free app in English includes background information and audio tours of the château and grounds.

Eating: Several garden cafés, including one just behind the house and others in the park, are reasonably priced and appropriately meditative. For a view over Amboise, choose the terrace *crêperie.*

Visiting the Château and Gardens: Your visit begins with a tour of Leonardo's elegant yet livable Renaissance **home.** This little residence was built in 1450 as a guesthouse for the king's château nearby. Today it re-creates the everyday atmosphere Leonardo enjoyed while he lived here, pursuing his passions to the very end. Find the touching sketch in Leonardo's bedroom of François I comforting his genius pal on his deathbed.

The basement level is filled with **sketches** recording the storm patterns of Leonardo's brain and **models** of his remarkable inventions (inspired by nature and built according to his notes). Helpful descriptions reveal his vision for these way-before-their-time inventions. Imagine Leonardo's résumé letter to kings of Europe: "I can help your armies by designing tanks, flying machines, wind-up cars, gear systems, extension ladders, and water pumps." The French considered him a futurist who never really implemented his visions.

Exit into the rose garden, then find another less-compelling room with 40 small models of his inventions. Don't waste time on the French-only video above the souvenir shop.

Your visit finishes with a stroll through the whimsical and expansive **park**

Château du Clos-Lucé

The Loire Valley's Cuisine Scene

Here in "the garden of France," locally produced food is delicious. Look for seasonal vegetables, such as white and green asparagus, and *champignons de Paris*—mushrooms grown in local caves, not in the capital. Around Chinon, pears and apples are preserved *tapées* (dried and beaten flat for easier storage), rehydrated in alcohol, and served in tasty recipes. Loire Valley rivers yield fresh trout (*truite*), shad (*alose*), and smelt (*éperlan*), which are often served fried (*friture*). Various dishes highlight *rillons*, big chunks of cooked pork,

while *rillettes*, a stringy pile of *rillons*, make for a cheap, mouthwatering sandwich spread (add a baby pickle, called a *cornichon*).

Locally raised pork is a staple, but don't be surprised to see steak, snails, *confit de canard* (a Dordogne duck specialty), and seafood on menus—the Loire borrows much from neighboring regions. The area's wonderful goat cheeses include Crottin de Chavignol (*crottin* means horse dung, which is what this cheese, when aged, resembles), Saint-Maure de Touraine (soft and creamy), and Selles-sur-Cher (mild). For dessert, try a delicious *tarte tatin* (upside-down caramel-apple tart). Regional pastries include *sablés* (shortbread cookies) from Sablé-sur-Sarthe.

grounds, with life-size models of Leonardo's inventions (including some that kids can operate), "sound stations" (in English), and translucent replicas of some of his paintings. The models and explanations make clear that much of what Leonardo observed and created was based on his intense study of nature.

Eating

The epicenter of the city's dining action is along Rue Victor Hugo, between Place Michel Debré and the château. Because selection and seating are limited, it's smart to book a day ahead.

$$ Les Arpents offers inventive and delicious cuisine at reasonable prices. Book ahead, particularly to land a table in the courtyard (reservations smart, closed Sun-Mon, 5 Rue d'Orange, tel. 02 36 20 92 44, https://restaurant-lesarpents.fr).

$ La Fourchette is Amboise's tiny

family diner, with simple décor, a handful of tables inside and out, and fresh food from an open kitchen. Book ahead—the morning of the same day is fine (closed Sun and Wed, on a quiet corner near Rue Nationale at 9 Rue Malebranche, mobile 06 11 78 16 98).

$$$ L'Alliance is a low-key place offering high-quality, fresh French cuisine—and it's open when most other places are closed. Here, you'll get quality ingredients prepared with an original twist (good but pricey cheese tray, closed Tue-Wed for lunch, 14 Rue Joyeuse, tel. 02 47 30 52 13).

$$ Le Shaker Cocktail Lounge is an ideal choice for a light meal on a warm evening. The place is young, lively, and great for kids. The menu and food quality are limited, but the French burgers and ceasar salad are good (daily from 18:30 until later than you'll stay awake, 3 Quai François Tissard).

$$ Hôtel le Clos d'Amboise offers

outside tables overlooking its lovely gardens and excellent cuisine. Prices are fair, and it makes a good choice on Sunday or Monday when most other places are closed—or if you just want an intimate and peaceful evening (daily, for details, see "Sleeping," later).

$ L'Ancrée des Artistes is a reliable, centrally located *crêperie* that's young at heart (three-course crêpe *menus,* good meat dishes grilled on stones—called *pierres,* and casserole-like *cocottes,* daily July-Aug, off-season closed Sun evening and Mon, 35 Rue Nationale, tel. 02 47 23 18 11).

Sleeping

Amboise is busy in the summer, but there are lots of reasonable hotels and *chambres d'hôtes* in and around the city.

In the Town Center

$$$ Le Manoir les Minimes** is a good place to experience the refined air of château life in a 17th-century mansion, with antique furniture and 15 large, modern and luxurious rooms (family rooms, air-con, closed much of winter, three blocks upriver from bridge at 34 Quai Charles Guinot, tel. 02 47 30 40 40, www.manoirlesminimes.com, reservation@manoirlesminimes.com).

$$ Hôtel le Clos d'Amboise** is a smart, urban refuge opening onto beautiful gardens and a small, heated swimming pool. The traditional rooms are well-designed with warm colors and carpets (RS%, family rooms, air-con, elevator, sauna, easy and free parking, 27 Rue Rabelais, tel. 02 47 30 10 20, www.leclosdamboise.com, infos@leclosamboise.com). They also offer meals at their **$$ restaurant**—best experienced on a warm night in the garden (see "Eating," earlier).

$$ Le Vieux Manoir** is an entirely different splurge. American expats Gloria and Bob Belknap beautifully restored this secluded but central one-time convent. The gardens are delightful—as is the atrium-like breakfast room—and its six bedrooms are lovingly decorated. Knowledgeable Gloria is a one-person tourist office (cottages, includes good breakfast, air-con, no TVs, free parking, 13 Rue Rabelais, tel. 02 47 30 41 27, www.le-vieux-manoir.com, le_vieux_manoir@yahoo.com).

$ Hôtel le Chaptal* is a solid, central budget bet with smallish but tastefully designed rooms and air-con (family rooms, 11 Rue Chaptal, tel. 02 47 57 14 46, http://hotel-chaptal.com, infos@hotel-chaptal-amboise.com).

Chambres d'Hôtes

$ La Grange Chambres welcomes with an intimate, flowery courtyard and four comfortable rooms, each tastefully restored with modern conveniences. There's also a common room with a fridge and tables for do-it-yourself dinners (includes breakfast, reserve with credit card but pay in cash only, where Rues Chaptal and Rabelais meet at 18 Rue Chaptal, tel. 02 47 57 57 22, www.la-grange-amboise.com, lagrange-amboise@orange.fr). Adorable Yveline Savin also rents a small two-room cottage and speaks fluent *franglais.*

Near Amboise

The area around Amboise is peppered with accommodations of every shape, size, and price range. This region offers drivers the best chance to experience château life at affordable rates—and my recommendations justify the detour. For locations, see "The Loire" map. Also consider the recommended accommodations in Chenonceaux.

$$$$ Château de Pray** allows you to sleep in a 700-year-old fortified castle with hints of its medieval origins. A few minutes from Amboise, the château's 19 rooms aren't big or luxurious, but they come with character and history—and with tubs in most bathrooms (about half have air-con). A newer annex offers four more-modern rooms (sleeping up to three each) with lofts, terraces, and castle views (3-minute drive upriver from Amboise toward Chaumont on D-751 before the village of Chargé, Rue du Cèdre, tel. 02 47 57 23 67, www.chateaudepray.fr, contact@chateaudepray.fr). The **$$$$ dining room,** cut into the hillside rock in the old *orangerie,* is an OK place to splurge, but I prefer dining outside on a beautiful terrace when the weather agrees (four-course *menus* from €59, reservations required, closed Mon-Tue).

$$$ Château de Perreux*** rents big rooms in a majestic 18th-century castle overlooking a huge park just 10 minutes by car from Amboise. Here, upscale bed-and-breakfast service meets château-hotel ambience with 11 plush and tastefully designed rooms and a pool. A casual €26 dinner is available for guests who book ahead (family rooms, air-con, elevator, Wi-Fi on main floor only, on D-1 between Nazelles and Pocé-sur-Cisse; coming from Amboise, turn left at the *Château de Perreux* sign, 36 Rue de Pocé, tel. 02 47 57 27 47, www.chateaudeperreux.fr, info@chateaudeperreux.fr).

$$ Le Moulin du Fief Gentil is a lovely 16th-century mill house with five large and immaculate rooms set on four acres with a backyard pond, and the possibility of home-cooked dinners by English-speaking owner Florence (includes breakfast, four-course dinner *menu* with wine—must reserve in advance, cash only, Wi-Fi

in mechanical mill room, 3 Rue de Culoison, tel. 02 47 30 32 51, mobile 06 64 82 37 18, www.fiefgentil.com, contact@fiefgentil.com). It's located on the edge of Bléré, a 15-minute drive from Amboise and 7 minutes from Chenonceaux—from Bléré, follow signs toward *Luzillé;* it's on the right.

Transportation
Arriving and Departing
BY CAR

Drivers set their sights on the flag-festooned château that caps the hill. Most parking is free; hotels can help you locate a spot (the big parking area downriver from the TI has lots of free parking, handy for day-trippers).

BY TRAIN

Amboise's train station is birds-chirping peaceful. You can't store bags here, but you can leave them at the TI or at some châteaux. Allow 20 minutes to walk to the TI from the station: Turn left out of the station (you may have to cross under the tracks first), make a quick right, and walk down Rue Jules Ferry five minutes to the end, then turn right and cross the long bridge leading over the Loire River to the town center. It's a €10 taxi ride from the station to central Amboise, but taxis seldom wait at the station (see "Helpful Hints," earlier, for taxi phone numbers).

From Amboise by Train to: Paris Gare Montparnasse (8/day, 1.5 hours with change to TGV at St-Pierre-des-Corps, requires TGV reservation), **Paris Gare d'Austerlitz** (3/day direct, 2 hours, no reservation required, more with transfer), **Sarlat-la-Canéda** (3/day, 6 hours, change at St-Pierre-des-Corps, then TGV to Bordeaux, then train through Bordeaux vineyards to Sarlat), **Pontorson/Mont St-Michel** (5/day, 5.5 hours with several transfers), **Bayeux** (4/day, 5 hours, best requires transfers at St-Pierre-des-Corps and Caen, more with transfer in Paris leaving from Gare St. Lazare), **Beaune** (6/day, 6 hours, transfers at Nevers and/or

St-Pierre-des-Corps; more with multiple connections and reservations).

CHENONCEAU

Château de Chenonceau, rated ▲▲▲, is the toast of the Loire. This 16th-century Renaissance palace arches gracefully over the Cher River and is impeccably maintained, with fresh flower arrangements in the summer and roaring log fires in the winter.

The one-road, sleepy village of Chenonceaux makes a good home base for drivers and a workable base for train travelers who don't mind connections.

Getting There
From Amboise, you can get here by **train** (6/day, 1 hour, transfer at St-Pierre-des-Corps) or faster by **bus,** which drops off at the TI (1-2/day, Mon-Sat only, none on Sun, 25 minutes—see page 196 for details on this bus). There may be **shuttles** running from Amboise; ask at the TI. Minivan **excursions** from Amboise and Tours are also available (see page 196).

You can also take a **taxi** from Amboise (€29 one-way, €41 on Sun and after 19:00, €7 pickup fee; for contact info, see "Taxi"

under "Helpful Hints" for Amboise on page 196).

If **driving,** plan on a 15-minute walk from the parking lot to the château. Don't leave any valuables visible in your car.

---

*Rick's Tip: The **château is packed** in high season. Come early (by 9:00) or late (after 17:00). **Buy advance tickets** (at area TIs) or from the **ticket machines** at the main entry (just follow the prompts; US credit cards work but instructions in English are hit-and-miss—withdraw your card at the prompt "retirez").*

Orientation
Cost and Hours: €14.50, €11.50 for kids under 18, daily 9:00-19:30, July-Aug until 20:00, closes earlier off-season. The château's gardens may stay open later on selected evenings in summer (with music to enjoy as you stroll).

Information: Tel. 02 47 23 90 07, www.chenonceau.com.

Tours: The interior is fascinating—but only if you take advantage of the excellent 20-page **booklet** (included with entry), or rent the wonderful **videoguide** (€4). Pay for

Château de Chenonceau

the guide when buying your ticket (before entering the château grounds), then pick it up just inside the château's door.

Services: WCs are available by the ticket office and behind the old stables.

Eating: A reasonable **$$** cafeteria is next door to the hospital room. Fancy **$$$** meals are served in the *orangerie* behind the stables (Restaurant l'Orangerie). There's a cheap *crêperie*/sandwich shop at the entrance gate. While picnics are not allowed on the grounds, there are picnic tables in a park near the parking lot.

Boat Trips: In summer, the château has rental **rowboats**—an idyllic way to savor graceful château views (€7/30 minutes, July-Aug daily 10:00-19:00, 4 people/boat, not available when the river is low).

Background: Find a riverside view of the château to get oriented. Although earlier châteaux were built for defensive purposes, Chenonceau was the first great pleasure palace. Nicknamed the "château of the ladies," it housed many famous women over the centuries. The original owner, Thomas Bohier, was away on the king's business so much that his wife, Katherine Briçonnet, made most of the design decisions during construction of the main château (1513-1521).

In 1547, King Henry II gave the château to his mistress, Diane de Poitiers, who added an arched bridge across the river to access the hunting grounds. She enjoyed her lovely retreat until Henry II died (pierced in a jousting tournament in Paris); his vengeful wife, Catherine de' Medici, unceremoniously kicked Diane out (and into the château of Chaumont, described later). Catherine added the three-story structure on Diane's bridge. She died before completing her vision of a matching château on the far side of the river, but not before turning Chenonceau into *the* place to see and be seen by the local aristocracy. (Whenever you see a split coat of arms, it belongs to a woman— half her husband's and half her father's.)

➲ Self-Guided Tour

Strut like an aristocrat down the tree-canopied path to the château. You'll cross three moats and two bridges, and pass an old round tower, which predates the main building. Notice the tower's fine limestone veneer, added so the top would better fit the new château.

The main château's original **oak door** greets you with the coats of arms of the first owners. The knocker is high enough to be used by visitors on horseback. The smaller door within the large one could be for two purposes: to slip in after curfew, or to enter during winter without letting out all the heat.

Once inside, you'll tour the château in a clockwise direction. Take time to appreciate the beautiful brick floor tiles and lavishly decorated ceilings. As you continue, follow your pamphlet or videoguide, and pay attention to these details:

In the **guard room,** the best-surviving tiles from the original 16th-century floor are near the walls—imagine the entire room covered with these faience tiles. And though the tapestries kept the room cozy, they also functioned to tell news or recent history (to the king's liking, of course). The French-style joist beams feature Catherine de' Medici's monogram.

The superbly detailed **chapel,** with its original 1521 wood gallery above the entry, survived the vandalism of the Revolution because the fast-thinking lady of the palace filled it with firewood. Angry masses were supplied with mallets and instructions to smash everything royal or religious. While this room was both, all they saw was stacked wood. The hatch door provided a quick path to the kitchen and an escape boat downstairs. The windows, blown out during World War II, are replacements from the 1950s. Look for graffiti in English left behind by the guards who protected Mary, Queen of Scots (who stayed here after her marriage to King François II).

The centerpiece of the **bedroom of Diane de Poitiers** is, ironically, a severe portrait of her rival, Catherine de' Medici, at 40 years old. Notice the various monograms in the room. You've already seen Catherine's Chanel-like double-C insignia. Henri II flaunts his singular H.

The 16th-century tapestries are among the finest in France. Each one took an average of 60 worker-years to make. Study the complex compositions of the *Triumph of Charity* (over the bed) and the violent *Triumph of Force*.

At 200 feet long, the three-story **Grand Gallery** spans the river. The upper stories house double-decker ballrooms and a small museum. Notice how differently the slate and limestone of the checkered floor wear after 500 years. Catherine, a contemporary of Queen Elizabeth I of England, wanted to rule with style. She threw wild parties and employed her ladies to circulate and soak up all the political gossip possible from the well-lubricated Kennedys and Rockefellers of her realm. Parties included grand fireworks displays and mock naval battles on the river. The niches once held statues—Louis XIV took a liking to them, and they now decorate the palace at Versailles.

In summer and during holidays, you can take a quick walk outside for more good palace **views:** Cross the bridge, pick up a re-entry ticket, then stroll the other bank of the Cher (across the river from the château). During World War I, the Grand Gallery served as a military hospital, where more than 2,200 soldiers were cared for—picture hundreds of beds lining the gallery. And in World War II, the river you crossed marked the border between the collaborationist Vichy government and Nazi-controlled France. Back then, Chenonceau witnessed many prisoner swaps, and at night, château staff would help resistance fighters and Jews cross in secret. Because the gallery was considered a river crossing, the Germans had their artillery aimed at Chenonceau, ready to destroy the "bridge" to block any Allied advance.

Double back through the gallery to find the sensational state-of-the-art (in the 16th century) **kitchen** below. It was built near water (to fight the inevitable kitchen fires) and in the basement; because heat rises, it helped heat the palace. Cross the small bridge to find the stove and landing bay for goods to be ferried in and out.

From here, find the **Muse/Three Graces Room**, then visit the King Louis XIV Room.

Back on the main floor, the staircase leading **upstairs** wowed royal guests. It was the first nonspiral staircase they'd seen...quite a treat in the 16th century. When open, the balcony provides lovely views of the gardens, which originally supplied vegetables and herbs. The estate is still full of wild boar and deer—the primary dishes of past centuries. You'll see more lavish bedrooms on this floor. Small side rooms show fascinating old architectural sketches of the château. The walls,

Portrait of Diane de Poitiers

Grand Gallery

20 feet thick, were honeycombed with the flues of 224 fireplaces and passages for servants to do their pleasure-providing work unseen. There was no need for plumbing: Servants fetched, carried, and dumped everything.

Above the Grand Gallery is the **Medici Gallery,** now a minimuseum for the château. Displays in French and English cover the lives of six women who made their mark on Chenonceau. There's also a timeline of the top 10 events in the history of the château and a cabinet of curiosities.

Go to the **top floor** to peek inside the somber bedchamber and mourning room of Louise de Lorraine, widow of Henri III. Perpetually dressed in the then-traditional mourning color, she became known as the White Queen. Take a close look at the silver teardrops that adorn the black walls before paying homage at the 16th-century portrait of Henri III.

To end your visit, escape the hordes by touring the **two gardens** with their postcard-perfect views of the château. Designed in the austere Italian style, the water fountain was revolutionary in its time for its forceful jet.

Military Hospital Room and Traditional Farm: These sights are best seen after you've toured the château and gardens. The military hospital room (with effective English explanations) is located in the château stables and gives an idea of what the Grand Gallery was like when it housed wounded soldiers during World War I. You can taste the owner's wines in the atmospheric **Cave des Dômes** below. Just past the stables you can stroll around a traditional farm. Imagine the production needed to sustain the château while making your way through the vegetable and flower gardens toward the exit.

Eating

The village of Chenonceaux offers a variety of options. Reserve ahead to dine in formal style at the country-elegant and Michelin-starred **$$$$ Auberge du Bon Laboureur** restaurant (€55 and €90 *menus*). **$$$ Hôtel la Roseraie** serves good fixed-price meals in a lovely dining room or on a garden terrace (*menus* for €29 or €34). **$$ Relais Chenonceaux** dishes up savory crêpes, salads, and *plats* in a pleasant interior or on its terrace. The price is right for the basic cuisine at **$ Hostel du Roy,** with an all-you-can-eat salad bar for €10 and a cheap *plat du jour.*

La Maison des Pages has some bakery items, sandwiches, cold drinks to go, and just enough groceries for a modest picnic (closed Wed, on the main drag between Hostel du Roy and Hôtel la Roseraie).

For a French treat and no tourists in sight, book ahead and drive about a mile to Chisseaux and dine at the *très* traditional **$$ Auberge du Cheval Rouge.** You'll enjoy some of the region's fine cuisine at affordable prices, either inside a pretty dining room or on a verdant patio (closed Tue-Wed, 30 Rue Nationale,

Chenonceau's Kitchen

Gardens at Chenonceau

Chisseaux, tel. 02 47 23 86 67, www.auberge-duchevalrouge.com).

Sleeping

Hotels are a good value in Chenonceaux, and there's one for every budget, each with a recommended restaurant. You'll find them *tous ensemble* on Rue du Dr. Bretonneau, all with free and secure parking.

$$$ Auberge du Bon Laboureur**** turns heads with its ivied facade, lush terraces, and stylish indoor lounges and bars. The staff is a tad stiff, but past the formal pleasantries are lovely four-star rooms with every comfort at three-star prices (family rooms and suites, heated pool, air-con, fine gardens, finer restaurant, 6 Rue du Dr. Bretonneau, tel. 02 47 23 90 02, www.bonlaboureur.com, contact@bonlaboureur.com).

$$ Hôtel la Roseraie*** has a flowery terrace, bar, and 22 handsome rooms—request one that overlooks the gardens. Sabine, Jerome, and dog Layla run a good show with fair prices for three-star comfort (air-con, pool, closed mid-Nov-March, 7 Rue du Dr. Bretonneau, tel. 02 47 23 90 09, www.hotel-chenonceau.com, laroseraie-chenonceaux@orange.fr). The traditional dining room and sweet terrace are ideal for a nice dinner—available for guests and nonguests alike who reserve ahead (daily May-Sept 19:00-21:00, closed Tue off-season and mid-Nov-mid-March).

$ Relais Chenonceaux** greets guests with a nice patio and a mix of rooms. The best rooms are in the annex; those in the main building are plain and above a restaurant (family rooms, tel. 02 47 23 98 11, 10 Rue du Dr. Bretonneau, www.chenonceaux.com, info@chenonceaux.com).

CHAMBORD

With its huge scale and prickly silhouette, Château de Chambord, worth ▲▲▲, is the granddaddy of the Loire châteaux. It's surrounded by Europe's largest enclosed forest park, a game preserve defined by a 20-mile-long wall and teeming with wild deer and boar. Chambord (shahm-bor) began as a simple hunting lodge for bored Blois counts and became a monument to the royal sport and duty of hunting. (Hunting was considered important to keep the animal population under control and the vital forests healthy.)

The château's massive architecture is the star attraction—particularly the mind-boggling double-helix staircase. Six times the size of your average Loire castle, the château has 440 rooms and a fireplace for every day of the year. The château is laid out as a keep in the shape of a Greek cross, with four towers and two wings surrounded by stables. The ground floor has reception rooms, the first floor up has the royal apartments, the second floor up houses temporary exhibits and a hunting museum, and the rooftop offers a viewing terrace to plot your next hunting adventure. Because hunters could see best after autumn leaves fell, Chambord was a winter palace (which helps explain the 365 fireplaces). Only 80 of Chambord's rooms are open to the public—but that's plenty.

Rick's Tip: **If you hate crowds, you'll like Chambord.** *Because it's so huge, it's relatively easy to escape the crowds. It helps that there's no one-way, mandatory tour route—you're free to roam like a duke or duchess surveying your domain.*

Getting There

With a car, allow 45 minutes to drive from Amboise, 55 minutes from Chenonceaux, and 15 minutes from Cheverny. You'll pay €6 to park (pay at machines near the lots when you arrive to avoid end-of-day lines, credit cards only, US cards work—except for American Express). If you have trouble with the machine, pay at the ticket office as you approach the château. Without a car, take a minivan excursion from Amboise.

Wines of the Loire

Loire wines are overlooked, and that's a shame—there is gold in them thar grapes. The Loire is France's third-largest producer of wine and grows the greatest variety of any region. Four main grapes are grown in the Loire: two reds (gamay and cabernet franc) and two whites (sauvignon blanc and chenin blanc).

The Loire is divided into four subareas, and the name of a wine (its *appellation*) generally refers to where its grapes were grown. The Touraine subarea covers the wines of Chinon and Amboise. Using 100 percent cabernet franc grapes, growers in Chinon and Bourgeuil are the main (and best) producers of reds. Thanks to soil variation and climate differences year in and out, wines made from a single grape have an intriguing range in taste. The best white wines are the Sancerres (my opinion), made on the less-touristed eastern edge of the Loire. Less expensive, but still tasty, are Touraine Sauvignons and the sweeter Vouvray, whose *chenin blanc* grapes are grown not far from Amboise. Vouvray is also famous for its light and refreshing sparkling wines (called *vins pétillants*)—locals will tell you the only proper way to begin any meal in this region is with a glass of it, and I can't disagree (try the *rosé pétillant* for a fresh sensation). A dry rosé is popular in the Loire in the summer and can be made from a variety of grapes.

You'll pass scattered vineyards as you travel between châteaux, though there's no scenic wine road to speak of (the closest thing is around Bourgueil). It's best to call ahead before visiting a winery.

Orientation

Cost and Hours: €13, daily 9:00-18:00, Oct-March until 17:00. One ticket office is in Chambord's "village" near the main parking area; another is inside the château.

Information: Château tel. 02 54 50 40 00, www.chambord.org.

Tours: This château requires helpful information to make it come alive. The free handout is a start, and most rooms have some explanations. For a lot more context, rent the €6.50 "Histopad" tablet guide inside the château.

Services: The primary ticket office and TI are located together in a flashy building near the closest parking area to the château. Nearby you'll also find a "village" of shops and services, including souvenir shops, a wine-tasting room, and several choices for a quick meal. There's a WC behind the primary ticket office and another at the château itself.

Views: Walk out of the back of the château into the gardens for fine views, or walk straight out the main entrance a few hundred yards for exquisite looks back to the château. On the "village" side, cross the small river in front of the château and turn right for more views.

Background: Starting in 1518, a young François I created this "weekend retreat," employing 1,800 workmen for 15 years. (You'll see his signature salamander symbol everywhere.) François I was an absolute monarch—with an emphasis on absolute. In 32 years of rule (1515-1547), he never once called the Estates-General to session (a rudimentary parliament in *ancien régime* France). This imposing hunting palace was another way to show off his power.

The grand architectural plan of the château—modeled after an Italian church—feels designed as a place to worship royalty. Each floor of the main structure is essentially the same: Four equal arms of

Château de Chambord

a Greek cross branch off a monumental staircase, which leads up to a cupola. From a practical point of view, the design pushed the usable areas to the four corners. This castle, built while the pope was erecting a new St. Peter's Basilica, is like a secular rival to the Vatican.

Construction started the year Leonardo died, 1519. The architect is unknown, but an eerie Leonardo-esque spirit resides here. The symmetry, balance, and classical proportions combine to reflect a harmonious Renaissance vision that could have been inspired by Leonardo's notebooks.

Typical of royal châteaux, this palace of François I was rarely used. Because any effective king had to be on the road to exercise his power, royal palaces sat empty most of the time. In the 1600s, Louis XIV renovated Chambord, but he visited it only six times (for about two weeks each visit). And while the place was ransacked during the Revolution, the greatest harm to Chambord came later, from neglect.

○ Self-Guided Tour

I've covered the highlights, floor by floor.

Ground Floor: This stark level shows off the general plan—four wings, small doors to help heated rooms stay warm, and a massive staircase. In a room just inside the front door, on the left, you can watch a worthwhile, 18-minute video—look for a screen on the side wall for viewing with English subtitles.

The attention-grabbing **double-helix staircase** dominates the open vestibules and invites visitors to climb up. Its two spirals are interwoven, so people can climb up and down and never meet. Find the helpful explanation of the staircase posted on the wall. From the staircase, enjoy fine views of the vestibule action, or just marvel at the playful Renaissance capitals carved into its light tuff stone.

First Floor Up: Here you'll find the most interesting rooms. Starting opposite a big ceramic stove (added in the 18th century), tour this floor basically clockwise. You'll enter the lavish apartments in the **king's wing** and pass through the

ally visited this château only once, in 1871.

The **chapel,** tucked off in a side wing, is interesting only for how unimpressive and remotely located it is. It's dwarfed by the mass of this imposing château—clearly designed to trumpet the glories not of God, but of the king of France.

Second Floor: Beneath beautiful coffered ceilings (notice the "F" for François) is a series of ballrooms that once hosted post-hunt parties. From here, you'll climb up to the rooftop, but first lean to the center of the staircase and look down its spiral.

Rooftop: A pincushion of spires and chimneys decorates the rooftop viewing terrace. From a distance, the roof—with its frilly forest of stone towers—gives the massive château a deceptive lightness. From here, ladies could scan the estate grounds, enjoying the spectacle of their ego-pumping men out hunting. On hunt day, a line of beaters would fan out and work inward from the distant walls, flushing wild game to the center, where the king and his buddies waited. The showy lantern tower of the tallest spire glowed with a nighttime torch when the king was in.

Gaze up at the grandiose tip-top of the tallest tower, capped with the king's fleur-de-lis symbol. It's a royal lily—not a cross—that caps this monument to the power of the French king.

Rick's Tip: Chambord's 45-minute **Medieval Pageantry on Horseback Show,** designed for young children, is **not worth the time or money.**

In the Courtyard: In the far corner, next to the summer café, a door leads to the Rolls-Royce of **carriage rooms** and the fascinating **lapidary rooms.** Here you'll come face-to-face with original stonework from the roof, including the graceful lantern cupola, with the original palace-capping fleur-de-lis. Imagine having to hoist that load. The volcanic tuff stone used to build the spires was soft

Spiral staircase at Chambord

grand bedrooms of Louis XIV, his wife Maria Theresa, and, at the far end after the queen's boudoir, François I (follow *Logis de François 1er* signs). These theatrical bedrooms place the royal beds on raised platforms—getting them ready for some nighttime drama. The furniture in François' bedroom was designed so it could be easily disassembled and moved with him.

A highlight of the first floor is the seven-room **Museum of the Count of Chambord** (Musée du Comte de Chambord). The last of the French Bourbons, Henri d'Artois (a.k.a. the count of Chambord) was next in line to be king when France decided it didn't need one. He was raring to rule—you'll see his coronation outfits and even souvenirs from the coronation that never happened. Watch the short video about the man who believed he should have become King Henry V but who lived in exile from the age of 10. Although he opened the palace to the public and saved it from neglect, he actu-

and easy to work, but not very durable—particularly when so exposed to the elements. Several displays explain the ongoing renovations to François' stately pleasure dome. On the opposite side of the courtyard, find the château **kitchen,** with good English explanations.

CHEVERNY

This stately hunting palace, a ▲▲ sight, is one of the more lavishly furnished Loire châteaux. Because the immaculately preserved Château de Cheverny (shuh-vehr-nee) was built and decorated in a relatively short 30 years, from 1604 to 1634, it has a unique architectural harmony and unity of style. From the start, this château has been in the Hurault family, and Hurault pride shows in its flawless preservation and intimate feel (it was opened to the public in 1922). The charming viscount and his family still live on the third floor (not open to the public, but you'll see some family photos). Cheverny was spared by the French Revolution; the count's relatives were popular then, as today, even among the village farmers.

The château sits alongside a pleasant village, with a small grocery store and cafés offering good lunch options (the town also has a few hotels).

Getting There: You can reach Cheverny by minivan excursion from Amboise or Tours. Drivers can park for free at the château.

Cost and Hours: €12, €16 combo-ticket includes Tintin "adventure" rooms, family deals available; daily 9:15-18:30, Nov-March 10:00-17:00.

Information: Tel. 02 54 79 96 29, www.chateau-cheverny.fr.

Visiting the Château: As you walk across the manicured grounds toward the château, the sound of hungry hounds may follow you. Lined up across the facade are sculpted medallions with portraits of Roman emperors, including Julius Caesar (above the others in the center). As you enter the château, pick up the excellent self-guided tour brochure.

Your visit starts in the lavish **dining room,** decorated with leather walls and a sumptuous ceiling. Next, as you climb the stairs to the private apartments, look out the window and spot the *orangerie*

Co-authors Steve Smith and Rick Steves at Cheverny

Cheverny's dining room

The hounds of Cheverny

across the gardens. It was here that the *Mona Lisa* was hidden (along with other treasures from the Louvre) during World War II.

On the first floor, turn right from the stairs and tour the I-could-live-here **family apartments** with silky bedrooms, kids' rooms, and an intimate dining room. On the other side of this floor is the impressive **Arms Room** with weapons, a sedan chair, and a snare drum from the count of Chambord (who would have been king). In the **King's Bedchamber**, study the fun ceiling art, especially the "boys will be boys" cupids.

On the top floor, peek inside the **chapel** before backtracking down to the ground floor. Browse the left wing and find a family tree going back to 1490, a grandfather clock with a second hand that's been ticking for 250 years, and a letter of thanks from George Washington to this family for their help in booting out the English.

Leaving the château, consider a short stroll through the gardens to the *orangerie,* which today houses a kids' play area and a garden café.

Dog Kennel: Barking dogs remind visitors that the viscount still loves to hunt (he goes twice a week year-round). The kennel (200 yards in front of the château, look for *Chenil* signs) is especially interesting when the 70 hounds are fed (daily at 11:30). The dogs—half English foxhound and half French Poitou—are bred to have big feet and bigger stamina. They're given

food once a day (two pounds each in winter, half that in summer), and the feeding *(la soupe des chiens)* is a fun spectacle that shows off their strict training. Before chow time, the hungry hounds fill the little kennel rooftop and watch the trainer (who knows every dog's name) bring in troughs stacked with delectable raw meat. He opens the gate, and the dogs gather enthusiastically around the food without touching it—yelping hysterically. Only when the trainer says to eat can they dig in. You can see the dogs at any time, but the feeding show is fun to attend.

Near the Kennel: Tintin comic lovers can enter a series of fun rooms designed to take them into a Tintin "adventure" (called *Les Secrets de Moulinsart*—it's in French, ask for English translations); hunters can inspect an antler-filled **trophy room;** and gardeners can prowl the château's fine **kitchen and flower gardens** (free, behind the dog kennel).

Wine Tastings: Opposite the entry to the château sits a slick wine-tasting room, La Maison des Vins. It's run by an association of 32 local vintners. Their mission: to boost the Cheverny reputation for wine (which is fruity, light, dry, and aromatic compared to the heavier, oaky wines made farther downstream). For most, the best approach is to enjoy four free tastes from featured bottles of the day, offered with helpful guidance (€6-11 bottles). Wine aficionados can pay to sample among the 96 bottles by using modern automated dispensers (3 wines—€4, 7 wines—€6.50). Even if just enjoying the free tasting, wander among the spouts. Each gives the specs of that wine in English (daily 11:00-13:15 & 14:15-19:00, open during lunch July-Aug, closed in winter, tel. 02 54 79 25 16, www.maisondesvinsdecheverny.fr).

CHAUMONT-SUR-LOIRE

A castle has been located on this spot since the 11th century; the current version is a ▲▲ sight (▲▲▲ for garden or horse lovers). The first priority at Chaumont (show-mon) was defense; the second, it seems, was gardening. Gardeners will appreciate the elaborate Festival of Gardens that unfolds next to the château every year, and modern-art lovers will enjoy how works have been incorporated into the gardens, château, and stables. If it's cold, you'll also appreciate that the château is heated in winter (rare in this region).

Getting There: The train between Blois and Amboise can drop you (and your bike) in Onzain, a 25-minute roadside walk across the river to the château (14 trains/day, 10 minutes from Amboise). By bike, Chaumont is about 11 level miles from Amboise.

To avoid the hike up, drivers should skip the river-level entrance (closed in winter) and park up top behind the château (open all year). From the river, drive up behind the château (direction: Montrichard); at the first roundabout follow signs to *Château* and *Festival des Jardins.*

Cost and Hours: €18 combo-ticket covers château, stables, and Festival of Gardens; €12 off-season combo-ticket covers château and stables (gardens closed); open daily 10:00-20:00, early Oct until 18:00, mid-Oct-mid-April until 17:00, stables open 11:00-17:00, last entry 45 minutes before closing; audioguide—€4, good English handout and posted explanations.

Information: Tel. 02 54 20 99 22, www.domaine-chaumont.fr.

Festival of Gardens: This annual exhibit, with 25 elaborate gardens arranged around a different theme each year, draws rave reviews from international gardeners. It's as impressive as the Chelsea Flower Show in England, but without the crowds—if you love contemporary garden design, you'll love this. When the festival is on, you'll find several little cafés and reasonable lunch options scattered about the hamlet. Chaumont also hosts a winter garden festival inside several greenhouses.

Background: The Chaumont château you see today was built mostly in the 15th and 16th centuries. Catherine de' Medici forced Diane de Poitiers to swap Chenonceau for Chaumont; you'll see tidbits about both women inside.

There's a special connection to America here. Jacques-Donatien Le Ray, a rich financier who owned Chaumont in the 18th century, was a champion of the

A drawbridge leads into the castle of Chaumont-sur-Loire.

American Revolution. He used his wealth to finance loans in the early days of the new republic (and even let Benjamin Franklin use one of his homes in Paris rent-free for nine years). Unfortunately, the US never repaid the loans in full and eventually Le Ray went bankrupt.

Ironically, the American connection saved Chaumont during the French Revolution. Le Ray's son emigrated to New York and became an American citizen, but returned to France when his father deeded the castle to him. During the Revolution, he was able to turn back the crowds set on destroying Chaumont by declaring that he was now an American—and that all Americans were believers in *liberté, égalité,* and *fraternité.*

Today's château offers a good look at a top defense design from the 1500s: on a cliff with a dry moat, big and small drawbridges with classic ramparts, loopholes for archers, and handy holes through which to dump hot oil on attackers.

◑ **Self-Guided Tour:** The castle's medieval **entry** is littered on the outside with various coats of arms. As you enter, take a close look at the two drawbridges (a new mechanism allows the main bridge to be opened with the touch of a button). Once inside, the heavy defensive feel is replaced with palatial luxury. Peek into the courtyard—during the more stable mid-1700s, the fourth wing, which had enclosed the courtyard, was taken down to give the terrace its river-valley view. The château kitchens are down the steps from the entry, though there's little of interest to see unless you enjoy wild art installations.

Entering the ground floor château rooms, signs direct you along a one-way loop path *(suite de la visite)* through the château's three wings. Catherine de' Medici, who missed her native Florence, brought a touch of Italy to all her châteaux, and her astrologer (Ruggieri) was so important that he had his own (plush)

Fairy-tale towers of the Château of Chaumont-sur-Loire

room—next to hers. **Catherine's bedroom** has a 16th-century throne—look for unicorns holding a shield. The Renaissance-style bed is a reproduction from the 19th century. Peer into the chapel below before leaving her room.

The exquisitely tiled **Salle de Conseil** has a grand fireplace and elaborate tapestries designed to keep this conference room warm. The treasury box in the **guard room** is a fine example of 1600s-era locksmithing. The lord's wealth could be locked up here as safely as possible in those days, with a false keyhole, no handles, and even an extra-secure box inside for diamonds.

The **King's room** offers a fascinating collection of medallions. Look for the case of ceramic portrait busts dating from 1772, when Le Ray invited the Italian sculptor Jean-Baptiste Nini to work for him. In addition to Marie Antoinette, Voltaire, and Catherine the Great, you'll find several medallions depicting Benjamin Franklin.

A big spiral staircase leads up through many unfurnished rooms and galleries of contemporary art. Instead, head downstairs to find rooms decorated in 19th-century style. The **dining room**'s fanciful limestone fireplace is exquisitely carved. Find the food (frog legs, snails, goats for cheese), the maid with the bellows, and even the sculptor with a hammer and chisel at the top (maid and sculptor on the left). Your visit ends with a stroll through the 19th-century

library, the billiards room, and the living room. The porcupines over the fireplace and elsewhere are thanks to the Duke of Orléans, who adopted the porcupine as his emblem in 1394.

In the **courtyard,** study the entertaining spouts and decor on the walls, and remember that this space was originally enclosed on all sides. Chaumont has one of the best château views of the Loire River—rivaling Amboise for its panoramic tranquility.

Veer right, leaving the château to find the **stables** (*écuries*) which were entirely rebuilt in the 1880s. The medallion above the gate reads *pour l'avenir* (for the future), which shows off an impressive commitment to horse technology. Inside, circle clockwise—you can almost hear the clip-clop of horses walking. Notice the deluxe horse stalls, padded with bins and bowls for hay, oats, and water, complete with a strategically placed drainage gutter. The horse kitchen (*cuisine des chevaux*) produced mash twice weekly for the horses, which were named for Greek gods and great châteaux. You'll also see an impressive display of riding harnesses, saddles, and several carriages parked and ready to go.

The **estate** is set in a 19th-century landscape, with woodlands and a fine lawn. More English than French, it has rolling open terrain, follies such as a water tower, and a designer *potager* (vegetable garden) with an imaginative mix of edible and decorative plants. Its trees were imported from throughout the Mediterranean world to be enjoyed—and to fend off any erosion on this strategic bluff.

VILLANDRY

Château de Villandry (vee-lahn-dree) is famous for its extensive gardens, considered to be the best in the Loire Valley, and possibly all of France. Its château is an average Loire palace, but the grounds—arranged in elaborate geometric patterns and immaculately maintained—make it a ▲▲ sight (worth ▲▲▲ for gardeners).

The grounds at Chaumont-sur-Loire

Still, if you're visiting anyway, it's worth the extra euros to tour the château as well.

Getting There: In summer, buses run twice a day from the train station in Tours to Villandry, though the best option for most is to take a minivan excursion from Amboise or Tours (see "Getting Around the Loire" on page 194). Villandry is a popular bike destination.

Drivers will find free parking located across from the entry (hide valuables in your trunk).

Cost and Hours: €11, €7 for gardens only, daily 9:00-19:00, March and Oct until 18:00, Nov-Feb until 17:00.

Information: Tel. 02 47 50 02 09, www.chateauvillandry.fr.

Tours: The excellent handout leads you through the château's 19th-century rooms. Skip the unnecessary audioguide.

Services: Storage lockers are available.

Background: Finished in 1536, Villandry was the last great Renaissance château built on the Loire. It's yet another pet project of a fabulously wealthy finance minister of François I—Jean le Breton. While serving as ambassador to Italy, Jean picked up a love of Italian Renaissance gardens. When he took over this property, he razed the 12th-century castle (keeping only the old tower), put up his own château, and installed a huge Italian-style garden. The château was purchased in 1906 by the present owner's great-grandfather, and the garden—a careful reconstruction of what the original might have been—is the result of three generations of passionate dedication.

Visiting the Château and Gardens: The **château**'s 19th-century rooms feel so lived-in that you'll wonder if the family just stepped out to get their poodle bathed. Don't miss the 15-minute *Four Seasons of Villandry* slideshow just inside the château. With period music and no narration, it delivers a glimpse at the gardens throughout the year in a relaxing little theater (ask at the ticket window or you may miss it). The literal high point of your château visit is the spiral climb to the top of the keep—the only surviving part of the medieval castle—where you'll find a 360-degree view of the gardens, village, and surrounding countryside. The extra cost for visiting the château seems worth it when you take in the panorama.

The lovingly tended **gardens** are well-described by your handout. Follow its recommended route through the four garden types. The 10-acre Renaissance garden, inspired by the 1530s Italian-style original, is full of symbolism and flair. The earliest Loire gardens were practical, grown by medieval abbey monks who needed vegetables to feed their community and medicinal herbs to cure their ailments. And those monks liked geometrical patterns. Later Italian influence brought decorative ponds, tunnels, and fountains. Harmonizing the flowers and vegetables was an innovation of 16th-century Loire châteaux. This example is the closest we have to that garden style.

The 85,000 plants—half of which come from the family greenhouse—are replanted twice a year by 10 full-time gardeners. They use modern organic methods: ladybugs instead of pesticides and a whole lot of hoeing. Stroll under the grapevine trellis, through a good-looking salad zone, and among Anjou pears (from the nearby region of Angers). If all the topiary and straight angles seem too rigid, look for the sun garden in the back of the estate, which has "wilder" perennial borders favored by the Brits.

Villandry's gardens are the best in the Loire.

BETWEEN THE LOIRE AND DORDOGNE

ORADOUR-SUR-GLANE

Lost in lush countryside, two hours north of Sarlat-la-Canéda, Oradour-sur-Glane is a powerful experience—worth ▲▲▲. French children know this town well, as most come here on school trips. **Village des Martyrs,** as it is known, was machine-gunned and burned on June 10, 1944, by Nazi troops. With cool attention to detail, the Nazis methodically rounded up the entire population of 642 townspeople, of whom about 200 were children. The women and children were herded into the town church, where they were tear-gassed and machine-gunned as they tried to escape the burning chapel. Oradour's men were tortured and executed. The town was then set on fire, its victims left under a blanket of ashes.

The reason for the mass killings remains unclear. Some say the Nazis wanted revenge for the kidnapping of one of their officers, but others believe the Nazis were simply terrorizing the pop-ulace in the wake of D-Day. Today, the ghost town, left untouched for more than 70 years (by order of President Charles de Gaulle), greets every pilgrim who enters with only one English word: Remember.

Getting There: For drivers coming from the south, Oradour-sur-Glane is well-signed off the (mostly free) A-20. Those driving from the north should take A-10 to Poitiers, then follow signs toward *Limoges* and turn south at Bellac.

Cost and Hours: Entering the village is free, but the museum costs €9 (audioguide-€2). Both are open daily mid-May-mid-Sept 9:00-19:00, off-season until 17:00 or 18:00, last visit one hour before closing, tel. 05 55 43 04 30, www.oradour.org. Allow two hours for your visit.

◗ Self-Guided Tour: Follow *Village Martyrs* signs to the parking lot and enter at the rust-colored **underground museum** (Centre de la Mémoire). The pricey-for-what-it-offers museum gives a

Preserved destruction at Oradour-sur-Glane

standard timeline of the rise of Hitler and WWII events, shows haunting footage of everyday life in Oradour before the attack, and offers a day-by-day account of the town's destruction. At the bookshop, consider picking up a €3 English map to better navigate the site (which has almost no posted information).

From the museum's back door, you pop out at the edge of the ruined village itself. It's shocking just how big and how ruined it is—a harrowing embodiment of the brutality and pointlessness of war.

Join other hushed visitors to walk the length of Oradour's **main street,** past gutted, charred buildings and along lonely streetcar tracks. *Lieu de Supplice* signs show where the townsmen were tormented and murdered. The plaques on the buildings provide the names and occupations of the people who lived there (*laine* means wool, *sabotier* is a maker of wooden shoes, *couturier* is a tailor, *quincaillerie* is a hardware store, *cordonnier* is shoe repair, *menuisier* is a carpenter, and *tissus* are fabrics). You'll pass several cafés and butcher shops and a hôtel-restaurant. This village was not so different from many you have seen on your trip.

At the end of main street, visit the modest **church,** with its bullet-pocked altar. Then double back through the upper part of the village, bearing right at the long, straight street to the **cemetery.** The names of all who died in the massacre on that June day are etched into the rear wall of the cemetery, around an austere pillar. In front of the pillar, glass cases display ashes of some of the victims. Leaving the cemetery, jog right and cut through the hedges to find the entrance to the easy-to-miss, bunker-like **underground memorial,** where you'll see displays of people's possessions found after the attack: eyeglasses, children's toys, sewing machines, cutlery, pocket watches, and so on.

Nearby: The adorable village of **Mortemart** lies 15 minutes north with a good café (closed Mon) wedged between its ancient market hall and low-slung château (a block off the main road, to the right; wander behind for a sweet scene).

Dordogne

The Dordogne is famous for its prehistoric cave paintings, but also has photogenic villages, thriving market towns, and cliff-topping medieval castles overlooking the Dordogne River.

During much of the on-again, off-again Hundred Years' War, this strategic river—so peaceful today—separated warring England and France. Today's Dordogne River carries more travelers than goods, as the region's economy relies heavily on tourism.

The Dordogne is a joy with a car, and tough without one if you want to visit the caves. Consider renting a car for a day or taking a minivan excursion. Regardless of whether you have a car, renting a canoe is the most fun way to explore the towns along the river.

The best home base for train travelers is the pedestrian-friendly market town of Sarlat-la-Canéda (often shortened to "Sarlat," pronounced sar-lah). Those with a car could consider sleeping in La Roque-Gageac, a beautiful riverside village with good hotels.

If you're serious about visiting the Dordogne's best caves, plan carefully and book ahead when possible (explained on page 252).

THE DORDOGNE IN 2 DAYS

Make your home base in Sarlat. On your first day, enjoy the morning in town (ideally on a market day—Sat or Wed), then take a canoe trip in the afternoon, including stops to explore Castelnaud and Beynac. (If it's not market day in Sarlat, take the canoe trip first.)

Devote the next day to prehistoric cave art—your starting point will depend on whether you've booked in advance. Lacking reservations, start in Les Eyzies-de-Tayac at the Prehistory Welcome Center and the National Museum of Prehistory. From there, head to the fascinating Grotte de Rouffignac (no prebooking, but you can usually get in). If you're here in July or August, start with Rouffignac (rather than the museum). Serious cave dwellers can add Lascaux II or IV replica caves (though you need to book tours ahead).

Without a car: Follow the first day's plan, and on the second day, take a minivan tour or taxi for cave-art activities.

DORDOGNE AT A GLANCE

▲▲▲**Dordogne Scenic Loop** Lovely route for exploring the scenic river valley by car or bike. See page 242.

▲▲▲**Dordogne Canoe Trip** Refreshing way to see (and visit) riverside villages and castles. See page 244.

▲▲▲**La Roque-Gageac** Cute village that looks carved out of the rock between the river and the cliffs. See page 248.

▲▲▲**Beynac** Pretty stone village and home to one of the most imposing castles in France. See page 250.

▲▲▲**Cro-Magnon Caves** Prehistoric caves famous worldwide for their art. See page 252 for a summary.

▲▲**Sarlat-la-Canéda** Regional market town with a seductive tangle of cobblestone streets peppered with beautiful buildings and traffic-free lanes. See page 232.

▲▲**Domme** Busy village town that merits a stop for its stunning view alone. See page 247.

▲▲**Château de Castelnaud** Medieval castle with displays focusing on warfare. **Hours:** Daily July-Aug 9:00-20:00, April-June and Sept 10:00-19:00, Oct and Feb-March until 18:00, shorter hours Nov-Jan. See page 250.

▲▲**Château de Beynac** Cliff-hanging château overlooking the Dordogne River. **Hours:** Daily May-Oct 10:00-19:00, off-season until 18:30. See page 251.

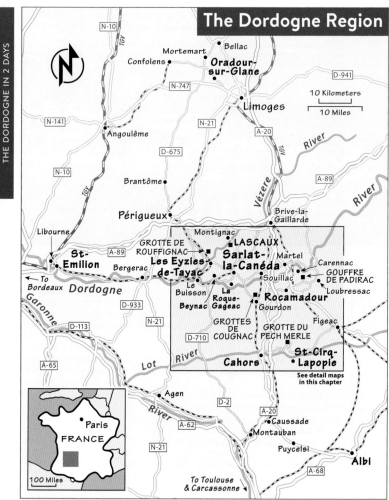

The Dordogne Region

Getting Around the Dordogne

By Car: Roads are small, slow, and scenic. You can rent a car in Sarlat (see page 241). In summer (mid-June–mid-Sept), you'll pay to park in most villages' riverfront lots between 10:00 and 19:00. Leave nothing in your car at night.

By Minivan Tour: Exploreo Tours is run by passionate world traveler (and fluent English speaker) David Lascoux. He offers a variety of half- and full-day minivan trips. Individuals should ask about shared tours (€360/day, €220/half-day, tel. 09 67 72 58 96, www.exploreo24. com, exploreo24@gmail.com). **Caves and Castles** is run by a British couple (Steve and Judie Burman) who offer tours to the area's main sights for a day or more (British mobile 44-789-972-0482, www.cavesandcastles.com).

By Taxi: To taxi from Sarlat-la-Canéda to Beynac or La Roque-Gageac, allow €28 one-way (€39 at night and on Sun); from Sarlat to Les Eyzies-de-Tayac, allow

Dordogne Markets

Markets are a big deal in rural France, and nowhere more so than in the Dordogne. I've listed good markets for every day of the week, so there's no excuse for drivers not to experience one. Here's what to look for:

Strawberries (*fraises*): Available from April to November, they're gorgeous, and they smell even better than they look. Look for *fraises des bois,* the tiny, sweet, and less visually appealing strawberries found in nearby forests.

Cheeses (*fromages*): The region is famous for its Cabécou goat cheese, though often you'll also find Auvergne cheeses (St. Nectaire and Cantal are the most common) from just east of the Dordogne (usually in big rounds) and Tomme and Brebis (sheep cheeses) from the Pyrenees to the south.

Truffles (*truffes*): Truffle season is during off-season (Nov-Feb), when you'll find them at every market. During summer, the fresh truffles you might see are *truffes d'été,* a less desirable and cheaper, but still tasty, species.

Anything with Walnuts (*aux noix*): Pain aux noix is a thick-as-a-brick bread loaf chock-full of walnuts. *Moutarde de noix* is walnut mustard. *Confiture de noix* is a walnut spread. *Gâteaux de noix* are tasty cakes.

Goose or Duck Livers and Pâté (foie gras): This spread is made from geese (better) and ducks (still good) or from a mix of the two. You'll see two basic forms: *entier* and *bloc. Entier* is a piece cut right from the product, whereas *bloc* has been blended. Foie gras is best accompanied by a sweet white wine (such as the locally produced Monbazillac or Sauternes from Bordeaux).

Confit de Canard: At butcher stands, look for chunks of duck smothered in white fat, just waiting for someone to take them home and cook them up.

Dried Sausages (*saucissons secs*): Long tables are piled high with dried sausages covered in herbs or stuffed with local goodies. Some of the variations include *porc, canard* (duck), *fumé* (smoked), *à l'ail* (garlic), *cendré* (rolled in ashes), *aux myrtilles* (with blueberries), *sanglier* (wild boar), and even *âne* (donkey)—and, of course, *aux noix* (with walnuts).

Olive Oil (*huile d'olive*): You'll find stylish bottles of various olive oils, as well as vegetable oils flavored with truffles, walnuts, chestnuts (*châtaignes*), and hazelnuts (*noisettes*)—good for cooking, ideal on salads, and great as gifts. Pure walnut oil, pressed at local mills from nuts grown in the region, is a local specialty.

Brandies and Liqueurs: Armagnac and Cognac (made a few hours away), as well as southwestern fruit-flavored liquors like *pomme verte,* are usually available from a seller or two.

€47 one-way (€68 at night and on Sun). Book your rides (even short transfers) in advance, as there are very few taxis around. **Christoph Kusters** speaks fluent English and also does tours (mobile 06 08 70 61 67, www.taxialacarte.com, taxi-alacarte@gmail.com).

By Boat: Renting a canoe is my favorite way to explore this region. A canoe offers easy access to the river's sights and villages at your own pace, and some canoe companies will pick you up in Sarlat-la-Canéda for no extra charge (based on their schedule). For options, see page 244.

SARLAT-LA-CANEDA

Sarlat–la–Canéda is a pedestrian-filled banquet of a town, serenely set amid forested hills. While there are no block-buster sights, Sarlat delivers a seductive tangle of traffic-free, golden cobblestone lanes peppered with beautiful buildings, lined with foie gras shops, and stuffed with tourists, especially on market days (Wed and Sat). The town is warmly lit at night and ideal for after-dinner strolls. It's the handiest home base for those without a car.

Orientation

Rue de la République slices like an arrow through the circular Old Town. The action lies east of Rue de la République. Sarlat's smaller half has few shops and many quiet lanes.

Tourist Information: The TI is 50 yards to the right of the Cathedral of St. Sacerdos as you face it (generally Mon-Sat 9:00-19:30, Sun 10:00-13:00 & 14:00-18:00, shorter hours and closed Sun off-season; on Rue Tourny, tel. 05 53 31 45 45, www.sarlat-tourisme.com). Ask for information on caves and renting a car, bike, or canoe.

Laundry: Le Lavandou launderette sits across from the recommended Hôtel la Couleuvrine (self-serve daily 24 hours, 10 Place de la Bouquerie, mobile 06 81 30 57 81).

❂ Sarlat Walk

This short self-guided walk, rated ▲▲, starts facing the Cathedral of St. Sacerdos (a few steps from the TI, where you can buy tickets for the panoramic elevator, which we'll visit on the way). The walk works well in the day—when sights are open—but in some ways it's better after dinner, when the gaslit lanes and candlelit

Sarlat's market is a feast for the senses.

restaurants twinkle. See the "Sarlat-la-Canéda" map to help navigate.

• *Start in front of the Cathedral of St. Sacerdos, on the...*

Place du Peyrou: An eighth-century Benedictine abbey once stood where the Cathedral of St. Sacerdos is today. It provided the stability for Sarlat to develop into an important trading city during the Middle Ages. The old Bishop's Palace, built right into the cathedral (on the right, with its top-floor Florentine-style loggia), recalls Sarlat's Italian connection. The Italian bishop was the boyfriend of Catherine de' Medici (queen of France)—a relationship that landed him this fine residence. After a short stint here, he split to Paris with loads of local money. And though his departure scandalized the town, it left Sarlat with a heritage of Italian architecture.

Another reason for Sarlat's Italo-flavored urban design was its loyalty to the king during wartime. Sarlat's glory century was from about 1450 to 1550, after the Hundred Years' War. Loyal to the French cause—through a century of war—Sarlat was rewarded by the French king, who gave the town lots of money to rebuild itself in stone. Sarlat's new nobility needed fancy houses, complete with ego-boosting features. Many of the most impressive buildings date from this prosperous era, when the Renaissance style was in vogue and everyone wanted an architect with an Italian résumé.

• *Take a closer look (opposite the cathedral) at...*

The House of Etienne de la Boëtie: This house was a typical 16th-century merchant's home—family upstairs and open ground floor (its stone arch now filled in) with big, fat sills to display retail goods. Pan up, scanning the crude-but-still-Renaissance carved reliefs. It was a time when anything Italian was trendy (when yokels "stuck a feather in their cap and called it macaroni"). La Boëtie (lah bow-ess-ee), a 16th-century bleeding-heart liberal who spoke and wrote against the rule of tyrannical kings, remains a local favorite.

Notice how the house just to the left arches over the small street. This was a common practice to maximize buildable space in the Middle Ages. Sarlat enjoyed a population boom in the mid-15th century after the Hundred Years' War ended.

• *If you're doing this walk during the day, head into the cathedral now. After hours, skip ahead to the Lantern of the Dead (see below).*

Sarlat's sidewalk cafés are inviting.

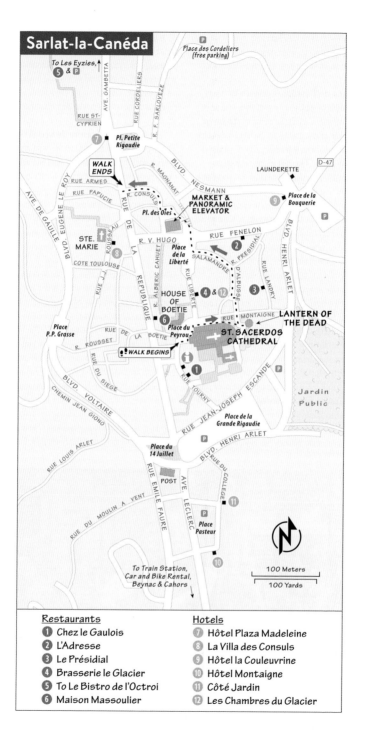

Sarlat-la-Canéda

Restaurants

1 Chez le Gaulois
2 L'Adresse
3 Le Présidial
4 Brasserie le Glacier
5 To Le Bistro de l'Octroi
6 Maison Massoulier

Hotels

7 Hôtel Plaza Madeleine
8 La Villa des Consuls
9 Hôtel la Couleuvrine
10 Hôtel Montaigne
11 Côté Jardin
12 Les Chambres du Glacier

Cathedral of St. Sacerdos: Though the cathedral's facade has a few well-worn 12th-century carvings, most of it dates from the 18th and 19th centuries. Step inside. The faithful believed that Mary delivered them from the great plague of 1348, so you'll find a full complement of Virgin Marys here and throughout the town. The Gothic interiors in this part of France are simple, with clean lines and nothing extravagant. The first chapel on the left is the baptistery. Locals would come here to give thanks after they made the pilgrimage to Lourdes for healing and returned satisfied. The second column on the right side of the nave shows a long list of hometown boys who gave their lives for France in World War I.

• *Exit the cathedral's front door and turn right, walk uphill on the first lane (Rue de Montaigne), then go right again through a short walkway that leads behind the church. Here you'll find a bullet-shaped building ready for some kind of medieval takeoff, known as the...*

Lantern of the Dead (Lanterne des Morts): Dating from 1147, this is the oldest monument in town. In four horrible days, a quarter of Sarlat's population (1,000 out of 4,000) died in a plague. People prayed to St. Bernard of Clairvaux for help. He blessed their bread—and instituted hygiene standards while he was at it, stopping the disease. This lantern was built in gratitude.

• *Facing the church, go back the way you came, toward an adorable house with its own tiny tower. Cross one street and keep straight, turn left a block later on Impasse de la Vieille Poste, make a quick right on Rue d'Albusse, and then take a left onto...*

Rue de la Salamandre: The salamander—unfazed by fire or water—was Sarlat's mascot. Befitting its favorite animal, Sarlat was also unfazed by fire (from war) and water (from floods). Walk a few steps down this "Street of the Salamander" and find the Gothic-framed doorway just below on your right. Step back and notice the tower that housed the staircase. Spiral staircase towers like this (Sarlat has about 20) date from about 1600 (after the wars of religion between the Catholics and Protestants), when the new nobility needed to show off.

• *Continue downhill, passing under the salamander-capped arch, and pause near (or better, sit down at) the café on the...*

House of Etienne de la Boëtie

Lantern of the Dead

Place de la Liberté: This has been Sarlat's main market square since the Middle Ages, though it was expanded in the 18th century. Sarlat's patriotic Town Hall stands behind you (with a café perfectly situated for people-watching). You can't miss the dark **stone roofs** topping the buildings across the square. They're typical of this region: Called *lauzes* in French, the flat limestone rocks were originally gathered by farmers clearing their fields, then made into cheap, durable roofing material (today few people can afford them). The unusually steep pitch of the *lauzes* roofs—which last up to 300 years—helps distribute the weight of the roof (about 160 pounds per square foot) over a greater area. Although most *lauzes* roofs have been replaced by roofs made from more affordable materials, a great number remain. The small windows in the roof are critical: They provide air circulation, allowing the lichen that coat the porous stone to grow—sealing gaps between the stones and effectively waterproofing the roof. Without that layer, the stone would crumble after repeated freeze-and-thaw cycles.

• *Walk right, to the "upper" end of the square. The bulky Church of Ste. Marie, right across from you, today serves as Sarlat's...*

Covered Market and Panoramic Elevator: Once a parish church dedicated to St. Marie, with a massive *lauzes* roof and a soaring bell tower, this building was converted into a gunpowder factory and then a post office before becoming today's **indoor market** (daily 8:30-13:00). Marvel at its tall, strangely modern, seven-ton doors, and imagine the effort it took to deliver and install them in the center of this tight-laned town.

On the opposite side of this building (walk through if it's open, or around if it's closed), you'll find the entrance to a modern, glass-sided **panoramic elevator,** which whisks tourists up through the center of the ancient church's bell tower for bird's-eye views over Sarlat's rooftops. Your elevator operator doubles as a guide, who gives a quick history of Sarlat at the top. If they gather enough English-speakers, the spiel is in English; otherwise, it'll be in French and you'll use the good English handout (feel free to ask questions). Because the elevator

View from the panoramic elevator

is open-air, it doesn't run in the rain (€5, buy timed-entry ticket at machines, chip credit card required, rarely a wait, cash-only tickets available at TI; 5/hour, visit lasts 12 minutes, generally open daily in summer 10:00-14:00 & 17:00-21:00, in spring and fall 10:00-13:00 & 14:00-18:00, shorter hours off-season).

• *When you've returned to earth, double back into Place de la Liberté and climb up the small ramp opposite the market's big doors to meet the "Boy of Sarlat"—a statue marking the best view over Place de la Liberté. Notice the cathedral's tower to the left, with a salamander swinging happily from its spire. Just below you on the stairs are several shops.*

Foie Gras and Beyond: Tourist-pleasing stores line the streets of Sarlat and are filled with the finest local products. The shop near the "boy" sells it all, from truffles to foie gras to walnut wine to truffle liqueur.

• *Turn left behind the boy and trickle like medieval rainwater down the ramp into an inviting square. Here you'll find a little gaggle of geese.*

Place des Oies: Feathers fly when geese are traded on this "Square of the Geese" on market days (Nov-March). Birds have been serious business here since the Middle Ages. Even today, a typical Sarlat menu reads, "duck, duck, goose." Trophy homes surround this cute little square on all sides.

Check out the wealthy merchant's home to the right as you enter the square—the **Manoir de Gisson**—with a tower built big enough to match his ego. The owner was the town counsel, a position that arose as cities like Sarlat outgrew the Middle Ages. Town counsels replaced priests in resolving civil conflicts and performing other civic duties. Touring the interior of the manor reveals how the wealthy lived in Sarlat (study the big poster next to the entry). You'll climb up one of those spiral staircase towers, ogle at several rooms carefully decorated with authentic 16th- to 18th-century furniture,

Manoir de Gisson

and peek inside the impressive *lauzes* roof. It's fun to gaze out the windows and imagine living here, surrounded by 360 degrees of gorgeous cityscape (€8, daily April-Sept 10:00-18:30, until 19:00 July-Aug, closes earlier off-season, borrow English booklet, tel. 05 53 28 70 55, www. manoirdegisson.com).

• *Walk to the right along Rue des Consuls. Just before Le Mirandol restaurant, turn right toward a...*

Fourteenth-Century Vault and Fountain: For generations, this was the town's only source of water, protected by the Virgin Mary (find her at the end of the fountain). Opposite the restaurant and fountain, find the wooden doorway (open late June-Aug only) that houses a massive Renaissance stairway. These showy stairways, which replaced more space-efficient spiral ones, required a big house and a bigger income. Impressive.

• *Follow the curve along Rue des Consuls, and enter the straight-as-an-arrow...*

Rue de la République: This "modern" thoroughfare, known as *La Traverse* to locals, dates from the mid-1800s, when blasting big roads through medieval cities was standard operating procedure (it's traffic-free in afternoons in high season). It wasn't until 1963 that Sarlat's other streets would become off-limits to cars, thanks to France's forward-thinking minister of culture, André Malraux. The law that bears his name has served to preserve and restore important monuments and neighborhoods throughout France. Eager to protect the country's architectural heritage, private investors, cities, and regions worked together to create traffic-free zones, rebuild crumbling buildings, and make sure that no cables or ugly wiring marred the ambience of towns like this. Without the Malraux Law, Sarlat might well have more "efficient" roads like Rue de la République slicing through its old town center.

• *Our walk is over, but make sure you take time for a poetic ramble through the town's quiet side—or, now may also be a good time to find a café and raise a toast to Monsieur Malraux.*

Rick's Tip: Strolling any of Sarlat's lanes after dark is a must. *This is the only town in France illuminated by gas lamps, which cause the warm limestone to glow, turning the romance of Sarlat up even higher.*

Experiences
Market Days
Sarlat has been an important market town since the Middle Ages. Outdoor markets still thrive on Wednesday morning and all day Saturday. Saturday's market swallows the entire town and is best in the morning (produce and food vendors leave around noon). Come before 9:00, have breakfast or coffee on the square, and watch them set up. On Thursday evenings (starting at 18:00), a small organic market enlivens the town's lower side (just south of the old center at Place du 14 Juillet) and a lively bric-a-brac market runs until midnight on Rue de la République. From November to March, a truffle market takes place on Saturday mornings on Rue Fénelon.

Rick's Tip: *If ever you were going to* **spring for a hot-air balloon ride in France,** *the Dordogne is the place to do it.* **Montgolfières du Périgord** *is conveniently based in La Roque-Gageac and offers a variety of flights with well-trained pilots (one-hour flight about €220/person, tel. 05 53 28 18 58, www.montgolfiere-du-perigord. com, perigordballoons@wanadoo.fr).*

Biking
Sarlat is surrounded by beautiful country lanes that would be ideal for biking were it not for all those hills and cars (consider renting an electric bike). Villages along the Dordogne River make good biking destinations, but expect traffic (bike-rental places can advise quieter routes) and some serious ups and downs between Sarlat and the river. There's a lovely 16-mile bike-only lane from Sarlat to Souillac following an old rail right-of-way.

Liberty Cycle rents bikes and offers short bike tours from Sarlat (1 Route de Souillac, Madrazès, daily, delivery to hotel possible, mobile 07 81 24 78 79, www.liberty-cycle.com, guillaume@liberty-cycle.com). **Aquitaine Bike,** run by a British-American couple, can deliver top quality hybrid and road bikes to your hotel in and near Sarlat and provides route advice, customized self-guided tours, and roadside assistance (4-day minimum, tours available, tel. 05 53 30 35 17, mobile 06 32 35 56 50, www.aquitainebike.com, aquitainebike@gmail.com).

Eating
Sarlat is stuffed with restaurants that cater to tourists, but you can still dine well and cheaply. The following places have been reliable. If you have a car, consider driving to Domme, Beynac, or La Roque-Gageac for a riverfront dining experience.

The Dordogne's Cuisine Scene

Gourmets flock to this area for its geese, ducks, and wild mushrooms. The geese produce (involuntarily) the region's famous **foie gras**. Foie gras tastes like butter and is priced like gold. The main duck specialty is *confit de canard* (duck meat preserved in its own fat—sounds terrible, but tastes great). You'll also see *magret de canard* (sautéed duck breast), smoked duck, and anything fried in duck fat on menus.

Pommes de terre sarladaises are mouthwatering, thinly sliced potatoes fried in duck fat and commonly served with *confit de canard*. **Wild truffles** are dirty black mushrooms that grow underground, generally on the roots of oak trees. Farmers traditionally locate them with sniffing pigs and then charge a fortune for their catch (roughly $300 per pound). Local *cèpe* mushrooms are commonly pan-fried with parsley and garlic—look for omelets cooked this way.

Native cheeses are **Cabécou** (a silver-dollar-size, pungent, nutty-flavored goat cheese) and **Echourgnac** (made by local Trappist monks). You'll find walnuts *(noix)* in salads, cakes, liqueurs, salad dressings, and more.

Wines to sample are **Bergerac** (red, white, and rosé), **Pecharmant** (red, must be at least four years old), **Cahors** (a full-bodied red), and **Monbazillac** (sweet dessert wine). The *vin de noix* (sweet walnut liqueur) is delightful before dinner.

$ Chez le Gaulois is a change from the traditional places that line Sarlat's lanes. Pyrenees-raised Olivier and his wife Nora serve a hearty mountain cuisine featuring fondue, raclette, *tartiflette* (roasted potatoes mixed with ham and cheese—comes with a salad), and thinly sliced ham (Olivier spends all evening slicing away). The *cassolette de légumes* (a ratatouille-like dish) and filling *salade plein sud* are also tasty. They have a few sidewalk tables, but the fun is inside where the ceiling is cluttered with ham hocks, and the soundtrack is jazz (closed Sun-Mon except in July-Aug, near the TI at 1 Rue Tourny, tel. 05 53 59 50 64).

$$$ L'Adresse is Sarlat's small, foodie bistro serving delicious cuisine with creative twists. You'll experience an open kitchen and young staff; inside seating is tight but fun, and there's a nice terrace in front. Book ahead, particularly if you want a table on the terrace (well-priced *menus* with good choices, closed Sun-Mon, 10 Rue Fénelon, tel. 05 53 30 56 19).

$$$ Le Présidial is a lovely, formal place for a refined meal of regional cuisine in a historic mansion. The setting is exceptional—you're greeted with beautiful gardens (where you can dine in good weather), and the interior comes with high ceilings, stone walls, and rich wood floors (closed Sun, reservations recommended, 6 Rue Landry, tel. 05 53 28 92 47, www.lepresidial.fr).

$ **Brasserie le Glacier** offers main-square views from its outdoor tables and good-enough café fare served nonstop from 11:00-22:00. Come here for friendly service (Filomena has the big smile), big salads, pizza, or *un plat* (daily, tel. 05 53 29 99 99, also rents rooms—see Les Chambres du Glacier under "Sleeping," later).

$$ **Le Bistro de l'Octroi,** overlooking a busy road a few blocks north of the old town, provides top cuisine and competitive prices. Quality bistro fare (mostly meat dishes) is served on a generous terrace and within the pleasant interior. The three-course *menus* offer many options at good prices—order two starters if you prefer (daily, 111 Avenue des Selves, tel. 05 53 30 83 40, www.lebistrodeloctroi.fr).

$ **Maison Massoulier** is a classy pastry shop with sidewalk tables along Rue de la République, where you can enjoy decadent desserts with a hot drink while people-watching (daily, 33 Rue de la République, tel. 05 53 59 00 85).

Sleeping

Sarlat is the train traveler's best Dordogne home base. Book early here for July and August.

$$$ **Hôtel Plaza Madeleine****** is a central and upscale value with formal service, a handsome pub/wine-bar, stylish public spaces, and 39 very sharp rooms with every comfort. You'll find a pool out back, a sauna, and a whirlpool bath—all free for guests (connecting rooms for families, big breakfast buffet, air-con, elevator, pay garage parking, at north end of ring road at 1 Place de la Petite Rigaudie, tel. 05 53 59 10 41, www.plaza-madeleine.com, contact@plaza-madeleine.com).

$ **La Villa des Consuls,**** a cross between a B&B and a hotel, occupies a 17th-century home buried on Sarlat's quiet side with 11 lovely, spacious rooms, each with a small kitchen and many with a living room. The rooms surround a small courtyard and come with wood floors, private decks, and high ceilings (family rooms, higher prices for 1-night stays, air-con, adorable owners help with hauling bags from the street, reception closed 12:00-15:30 and after 19:00, 3 Rue Jean-Jacques Rousseau, tel. 05 53 31 90 05, www.villaconsuls.fr, villadesconsuls@aol.com).

$ **Hôtel la Couleuvrine*** offers 27 simple rooms with character at fair rates in a historic building with a handy location—across from the launderette and with easy parking (for Sarlat). Some rooms have tight bathrooms, and a few have private terraces (family rooms, elevator, on ring road at 1 Place de la Bouquerie, tel. 05 53 59 27 80, www.la-couleuvrine.com, contact@la-couleuvrine.com). Half-pension is encouraged during busy periods and in the summer—figure €38 per person beyond the room price for breakfast and a good dinner in the classy restaurant.

$ **Hôtel Montaigne,**** a good value located a block south of the pedestrian zone, is run by the hardworking Martinat family. The 28 rooms are simple, comfortable, and air-conditioned. Of the hotels I list, this is the one nearest to the train station (family rooms, elevator, easy parking nearby, Place Pasteur, tel. 05 53 31 93 88, www.hotelmontaigne.fr, contact@hotel-montaigne.fr).

$ Côté Jardin is a fine spread with good rates run by gregarious Michelle. She rents three top-comfort rooms, each with its own terrace, surrounding a large garden. Her breakfast room is beyond cozy (air-con, 13 Rue du Collège, mobile 06 03 11 52 96, www.sarlatcotejardin.com, msimonet24@gmail.com).

$ Les Chambres du Glacier, where kind Monsieur Da Costa and son Bruno offer four cavernous, simple, but surprisingly comfortable rooms above an outdoor café, is in the thick of Sarlat's pedestrian zone (perfect for market days). Rooms come with sky-high ceilings, big and soundproof windows over Sarlat's world, polished wood floors, cheap furnishings, and bathrooms you can get lost in (family rooms, no air-con, includes continental breakfast, Place de la Liberté, tel. 05 53 29 99 99, www.leglacier-sarlat.fr, contact.leglacier@gmail.com).

Transportation
Arriving and Departing
BY CAR

The hilly terrain around Sarlat-la-Canéda creates traffic funnels unusual for a town of this size. Hotels know the best strategies for parking. The closest parking to the center is metered and easy on non-market and off-season days (about €2/hour, free 19:00-9:00). On market days, avoid the center by parking along Avenue du Général de Gaulle (at the north end of town), or in one of the signed lots on the ring road. You'll also find free parking at Place des Cordeliers, a 5-minute walk north of Place de la Petite Rigaudie. To rent a car, try **Europcar** (Le Pontet, at south end of Avenue Leclerc on roundabout, Place du Maréchal de Lattre de Tassigny, tel. 05 53 30 30 40).

BY TRAIN

Sarlat's sleepy train station keeps a lonely vigil (without a shop, café, or hotel in sight). It's a mostly downhill, 20-minute walk to the town center (taxis are about €10, book ahead, mobile 06 08 70 61 67 or tel. 05 53 59 02 43). To walk into town, turn left out of the station and follow Avenue de la Gare as it curves downhill, then turn right at the bottom, on Avenue Thiers, to reach the town center. Some trains (such as those from Limoges and Cahors) arrive at nearby Souillac, which is poorly connected to Sarlat's train station by bus (2-3/day, schedule at www.transperigord.fr).

Sarlat's TI has train schedules. Souillac and Périgueux are the train hubs for points within the greater region. For all the following destinations, you could go west on the Libourne/Bordeaux line (transferring in either city, depending on your connection), or east by infrequent bus to Souillac (bus leaves from Sarlat train station). I've listed the fastest path in each case. For any travel to the southeast, it's easier to take a train from Souillac.

Train Connections from Sarlat-la-Canéda to: Les Eyzies-de-Tayac (2-3/day, 1-2.5 hours, transfer in Le Buisson), **Paris** (4/day, 5 hours, change in Bordeaux), **Amboise** (3/day, 6 hours, via Bordeaux, then TGV to Tours' St-Pierre-des-Corps, then local train to Amboise), **Bourges** (6/day, 7 hours, 2 changes), **Carcassonne** (5/day, 7 hours, 1-2 changes usually in Bordeaux and/or Toulouse).

THE DORDOGNE RIVER VALLEY

The most striking stretch of the Dordogne lies between Carsac and Beynac. Traveling by canoe is the best way to savor the highlights of the Dordogne River Valley, though several scenic sights lie off the river and require a car or bike.

Drivers should allow a minimum of a half-day to sample the river valley. Drive slowly to savor the scenery and to stay out of trouble (there are some narrow, cliff-hanging roads). The area is picnic-

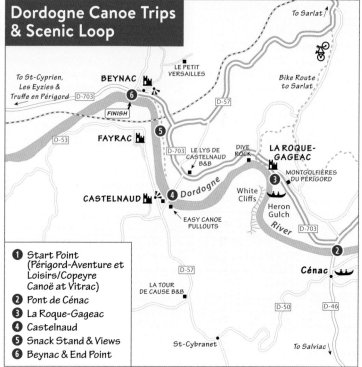

Dordogne Canoe Trips & Scenic Loop

To Sarlat

LE PETIT VERSAILLES

BEYNAC

To St-Cyprien, Les Eyzies & Truffe en Périgord — D-703

Bike Route to Sarlat

D-57

FINISH

D-53

FAYRAC

D-703

LE LYS DE CASTELNAUD B&B

DIVE ROCK

LA ROQUE-GAGEAC

MONTGOLFIÈRES DU PÉRIGORD

CASTELNAUD

Dordogne

White Cliffs

Heron Gulch

River

D-703

EASY CANOE PULLOUTS

D-57

LA TOUR DE CAUSE B&B

Cénac

D-50   D-46

St-Cybranet

To Salviac

To Sarlat

Bike Route to Sarlat

❶ Start Point (Périgord-Aventure et Loisirs/Copeyre Canoë at Vitrac)
❷ Pont de Cénac
❸ La Roque-Gageac
❹ Castelnaud
❺ Snack Stand & Views
❻ Beynac & End Point

perfect, but buy your supplies before leaving Sarlat; pickings are slim in the villages (though view cafés are abundant). Vitrac (near Sarlat) is the best place to park for a canoe ride down the river. La Roque-Gageac, Beynac, and Domme have good restaurants.

In this section I've given distances in kilometers; if you're driving, you can match these with your rental car's odometer. In riverfront villages, you'll pay a small fee to park during the day. Parked cars are catnip to thieves: Take everything out or stow belongings out of sight.

Key villages along these routes are described in detail later in this chapter, under "Dordogne Towns and Sights."

❷ Dordogne Scenic Loop

Following these directions, beginning and ending in Sarlat-la-Canéda, you can see this area by car or bike, a ▲▲▲ experience covering 27 hilly miles. Cyclists can cut seven miles off this distance and still see most of the highlights by following D-704 from Sarlat toward Cahors, then taking the Montfort turnoff (well-signed after the big Leclerc grocery store at the roundabout) and tracking signs to Montfort (see the above map). Once in Montfort, follow the river downstream to La Roque-Gageac.

From Sarlat to Beynac and Back: Leave Sarlat on D-704 following signs toward *Cahors*. You'll soon pass the Rougié foie gras outlet store, then the limestone **quarry** that gives the houses in this area their lemony color.

In about five minutes, be on the lookout for the little signposted turnoff on the right to the *Eglise de Carsac* (Church of Carsac). Set peacefully among cornfields, with its WWI monument, bonsai-like plane trees, and simple, bulky Romanesque exterior, the **Eglise de Carsac**

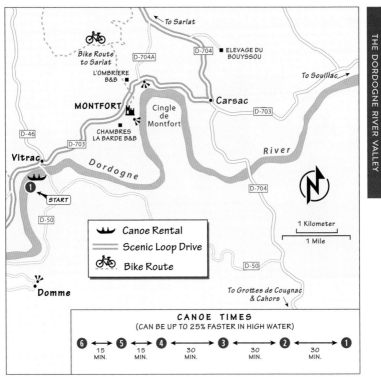

To Sarlat

Bike Route
to Sarlat

D-704

D-704A

ELEVAGE DU
BOUYSSOU

L'OMBRIERE
B&B

To Souillac

MONTFORT

Cingle
de
Montfort

Carsac

D-703

CHAMBRES
LA BARDE B&B

D-46

D-703

River

Vitrac

Dordogne

START

D-50

D-704

N

1 Kilometer

1 Mile

Canoe Rental

Scenic Loop Drive

Bike Route

D-50

Domme

To Grottes de Cougnac
& Cahors

CANOE TIMES
(CAN BE UP TO 25% FASTER IN HIGH WATER)

6		5		4		3		2		1
	15 MIN.		15 MIN.		30 MIN.		30 MIN.		30 MIN.	

church is part of a vivid rural French scene. Take a break here and enter the church (usually open). The stone capitals behind the altar are exquisitely medieval, and the chapel to the left of the altar reminds us how colorful medieval churches were.

Continue on, following signs to *Montfort.* About a kilometer west of Carsac,

Carsac's Romanesque church

pull over to enjoy the scenic viewpoint (overlooking a bend in the river known as Cingle de Montfort). Across the Dordogne River, fields of walnut trees stretch to distant castles, and the nearby hills are covered in oak trees. This area is nicknamed "black Périgord" for its thick blanket of oaks, which stay leafy throughout the winter. The fairy-tale castle you see is **Montfort,** once the medieval home of Simon de Montfort, who led the Cathar Crusades in the early 13th century. Today it's considered mysterious by locals. (It's rumored that the castle is now the home of a brother of the emir of Kuwait.) A plaque on the rock near where you parked honors those who fought Nazi occupiers in this area in 1943.

Pass under Montfort's castle (which you can't tour); its cute little village has a few cafés and restaurants lassoed in a small pedestrian zone. If you're combining

Château at Montfort

a canoe trip with this drive, cross the river following signs to *Domme,* and find my recommended canoe rental on the right side (see "Dordogne Canoe Trip," next).

The touristy *bastide* (fortified village) of **Domme** is well worth a side-trip from Vitrac or La Roque-Gageac for its sensational views (best early in the day). The driving route continues to the more important riverfront villages of **La Roque-Gageac,** then on to **Castelnaud,** and finally to **Beynac** (all described later in this chapter). From Beynac, it's a quick run back to Sarlat.

Dordogne Canoe Trip

For a refreshing break from the car or train, explore the riverside castles and villages of the Dordogne by canoe, a trip worth ▲▲▲. My recommended route is a nine-mile paddle from Vitrac to Beynac. This is the most interesting, scenic, and handy trip if you're based in or near Sarlat. Vitrac, on the river close to Sarlat, is a good starting point. And, with its mighty castle and good cafés and restaurants, Beynac delivers the perfect finale to your journey. Allow 2 hours for this paddle at a

relaxed pace in spring and fall, and up to 2.5 hours in summer when the river is usually at its lowest flow.

Planning Your Trip: The trip is fun even in light rain—but steady, heavy rains can make the current too fast to handle. Prolonged droughts can have the opposite effect. Check river levels before you rent.

Beach your boat wherever it works to take a break—it's light enough that you can drag it up high and dry to go explore. (The canoes aren't worth stealing, as they're cheap and clearly color-coded for their parent company.) It's OK if you're a complete novice—the only whitewater you'll encounter will be the rare wake of passing tour boats...and your travel partner frothing at the views.

Renting a Canoe or Kayak: You can rent plastic boats—hard, light, and indestructible—from many area outfits. Whether a two-person canoe or a one-person kayak, they're stable enough for beginners (canoes are easier to manage in the river and more comfortable).

Some rental places will pick you up at an agreed-upon spot, even in Sarlat, if they aren't too busy and you can give a

Paddling the Dordogne

precise pickup time and location (and be flexible on the return time). Also, consider hiring a taxi/driver to connect your canoe float with a visit to a prehistoric cave (see "Getting Around the Dordogne," earlier).

All companies let you put in anytime between 9:30 and 16:00 (start no later than 15:00 to allow time to linger when the mood strikes; they'll pick you up at about 18:00). They all charge about the same and most accept cash only (two-person canoe–€15-20/person, one-person kayak–€16-26). You'll get a life vest and, for about €2 extra, a watertight bucket in which to store your belongings. (The bucket is bigger than you'd need for just a camera, watch, wallet, and phone; if that's all you have, bring a resealable plastic baggie or something similar for dry storage.) You must have shoes that stay on your feet; travelers wearing flip-flops will be invited to purchase more appropriate footwear (sold at most boat launches for around €10).

Périgord-Aventure et Loisirs has a pullout arrangement in Beynac (to get to their Vitrac put-in base, from the main roundabout in the town of Vitrac, cross the Dordogne, and turn right). They may be able to pick you up in Sarlat for free (RS%—10 percent discount with this book, arrange in advance, return times to Sarlat based on driver availability, tip the driver a few euros for this helpful service; tel. 05 53 28 23 82, mobile 06 83 27 30 06, www.perigordaventureloisirs.com, info@perigordaventureloisirs.com). Allow time to explore Beynac after your river paddle and before the return shuttle trip. Périgord-Aventure also arranges a longer, 14-mile trip from Carsac to Beynac, adding the gorgeous Montfort loop (*Cingle de Montfort*). Ask about their canoe, hike, and bike options, such as the canoe trip to Beynac, followed with a walk along a riverside trail to Castelnaud, and ending with a mountain-bike ride on uneven terrain back to your starting point in Vitrac (€30, no discounts, reserve in advance, start or end the loop wherever you like).

The Nine-Mile Paddle from Vitrac to Beynac: Here's a rundown of the two-hour Vitrac-Beynac adventure: Leave **Vitrac,** paddling at an easy pace through lush, forested land. The fortified hill town of Domme will be dead ahead. Pass through

Heron Gulch, and after about an hour you'll come to **La Roque-Gageac** (one of two easy and worthwhile stops before Beynac).

Paddle past La Roque-Gageac's wooden docks (with the tour boats) to the stone ramp leading up to the town. Do a 180-degree turn and beach thyself, dragging the boat high and dry. From there you're in La Roque-Gageac's tiny town center, with a TI and plenty of cafés, snacks, and ice-cream options. Enjoy the town before heading back to your canoe and into the water.

When leaving La Roque-Gageac, float backward for a bit to enjoy the village view. About 15 minutes farther downstream, you'll approach views of the feudal village and castle of **Castelnaud.** Look for the castle's huge model of medieval catapults silhouetted menacingly against the sky (it's a steep but worthwhile climb to tour this castle). You'll find two grassy pullouts flanking the bridge below the castle. The bridge arches make terrific frames for castle views. Nearby, there's a small market and charcuterie with all you need for a picnic. The local café serves good-enough fare with views (near where you pull out).

Another 15 minutes downstream brings views of **Château de Fayrac** on your left. The lords of Castelnaud built this to spy on Beynac during the Hundred Years' War (1336-1453). It's another 15 minutes to your last stop: **Beynac.** The awesome Beynac castle—looming high above the town— gets more impressive as you approach. Slow down and enjoy the ride (sometimes there's a snack stand with the same views at the bridge on the right). Keep to the right as you approach the Périgord-Aventure depot. You'll see the ramp just before the parking lot and wooden dock (where the tour boats generally tie up). Do another 180-degree turn, and beach yourself hard. The office is right there. Return your boat, and explore Beynac.

Other Canoe Options: All along the river you'll see canoe companies, each with stacks of plastic canoes. Depending on their location and relations with places to pull out, each one works best on a particular stretch of the river. All have essentially the same policies. Below Domme in Cénac, **Dordogne Randonnées** has canoes and kayaks for the scenic two-hour stretch to a pullout just past Beynac (to reach their office coming from Sarlat or Beynac, take the first left after crossing the

View of the Dordogne River from the castle at Castelnaud

bridge to Cénac, tel. 05 53 28 22 01). In La Roque-Gageac, **Canoe-Dordogne** rents canoes for the worthwhile two-hour float to Château des Milandes, allowing canoers to stop in Beynac along the way (tel. 05 53 29 58 50). For a lazier, no-paddle alternative, a boat cruise on the river to Castelnaud and back—either from Beynac or La Roque-Gageac—is great for landlubbers (€10, 1 hour, described in the next section).

Dordogne Towns and Sights

The towns and sights described below coincide with the Dordogne River Valley scenic loop and canoe trip outlined earlier. These villages are a joy to wander early and late in the day. In high season, expect mobs of tourists and traffic in the afternoons. Those with a car can enjoy tranquil rural accommodations at great prices in these cozy villages. Read about the villages below, then make your choice—you can't go wrong.

Montfort

There's more to this castle-topped village than meets the eye—leave most tourists

behind and find a handful of cafés, restaurants, and *chambres d'hôtes,* including these recommended listings (for locations, see the "Dordogne Canoe Trips & Scenic Loop" map).

Sleeping near Montfort: $$ Chambres la Barde has five good rooms in a warm, recently built stone home with friendly French owners, a swimming pool, cozy lounge, big grass yard, communal kitchen, and views to Montfort castle from most rooms' terraces (family rooms, includes breakfast, cash only, well-signed behind Montfort castle at 135 Route de la Plage de Caudon, tel. 05 53 28 24 34, mobile 06 09 63 19 71, www.labardemontfort.com, frederique.drouin5@gmail.com).

$$ L'Ombrière, with four elegant rooms and welcoming German hosts Niels and Lena, is a calm B&B overlooking a walnut grove with many picnic spaces (includes breakfast, attic rooms have air-con, on east edge of Montfort village—watch for signs, tel. 05 53 28 11 38, www.lombriere.com, info@lombriere.com).

Domme

This busy little ▲▲ town merits a stop for its stunning view and is ideal early in the

Backstreet Domme

day. Otherwise, come late, when crowds recede and the light is divine. If you come for lunch or dinner, arrive early enough to savor the cliff-capping setting, and if you come on market day (Thu) expect to hoof it up from a parking lot well below (cars not allowed in old town until the market is over). On other days, follow signs up to *La Bastide de Domme,* and drive right through the narrow gate of the fortified town walls. Park at the pay lot near the view (*Panorama*). You'll find picnic-perfect benches, cafés, and a view you won't soon forget. While the main street is lined with touristy shops that make the town feel greedy, you can lose yourself in some of the unusually picturesque back lanes, where roses climb over rustic doorways.

Eating and Sleeping in Domme: **$$ Hôtel de l'Esplanade***** delivers the valley's most sensational views from many of its 15 comfortable and traditional bedrooms and restaurant tables. If you come for the **$$$** restaurant (closed Mon lunch), book ahead for view seating. Both the hotel and the restaurant are traditional, formal, and a bit stiff (air-con, tel. 05 53 28 31 41, www.esplanade-perigord. com, esplanade.domme@wanadoo.fr).

La Roque-Gageac

Whether you're joyriding, paddling the Dordogne, or taking a hot-air balloon ride, ▲▲▲ La Roque-Gageac (lah rohk-gah-zhahk) is an essential stop—and a strong contender on all the "cutest towns in France" lists. Called by most simply "La Roque" ("The Rock"), it looks sculpted out of the rock between the river and the cliffs. It also is a fine base for drivers touring the region.

At the upstream end of town, you'll find parking and an ATM, the **TI** (closed off-season, tel. 05 53 29 17 01), a WC, swings and slides for kids, canoe rental, and *pétanque (boules)* courts. A small market brightens La Roque-Gageac on Friday mornings in summer. Though busy with day-trippers, the town is tranquil at night.

Visiting La Roque-Gageac: Stand along the river just downstream from the boat ticket office and survey La Roque-Gageac: It's a one-street town stretching along the river. The highest stonework (on the far right) was home to the town's earliest inhabitants in the 10th century. High above (about center), 12th-century cave dwellers built a settlement during the era of Norman (Viking) river raids. Long after the Vikings were tamed, French soldiers used this lofty perch as a barracks while fighting against England in the Hundred Years' War. Sturdy modern supports now reinforce the cave.

Now locate the exotic foliage around the church on the right. Tropical gardens (bamboo, bananas, lemons, cactus, and so on) are a village forte, because limestone absorbs heat. Notice the two church chapels extending over the cliff—when level land is scarce, necessity is the mother of invention.

The wooden boats on the river are modeled after boats called *gabarres,* originally built here to take prized oak barrels filled with local wine down to Bordeaux. Unable to return against the river current, the boats were routinely taken apart for their lumber. Today, tourists, rather than barrels, fill the boats on river cruises. These actual boats (dolled up) were used by Johnny Depp in the movie *Chocolat,* to the delight of viewers and Juliette Binoche alike.

Looking downstream, notice the fanciful castle built in the 19th century by a British aristocrat (whose family still nurtures Joan of Arc dreams in its turrets). The old building just beyond that (downstream end of town) actually is historic—it's the quarantine house, where lepers and out-of-town visitors who dropped by in times of plague would be kept (after their boats were burned).

Walk along the main drag to get a closer look at the village. La Roque-Gageac frequently endures winter floods that would

La Roque-Gageac

leave you (standing where you are now) underwater. When there's a big rain in central France, La Roque-Gageac floods two days later. The first floors of all the riverfront buildings are vacated off-season. The new riverfront wall, finished in 2014, was pushed out into the river, adding 13 feet of width to the street. Notice the openings at sidewalk level allowing water to flow through in heavy rains. A house about five buildings downriver from Hôtel la Belle Etoile has high-water marks engraved on its wall (*inondation* means "flood").

Climb into the town by strolling up the cobbled lane to the right of Hôtel la Belle Etoile. Where the stepped path ends, veer right to find the exotic plants and viewpoint (in front of the simple church). From here you can make out Château de Castelnaud downriver, and the village of Domme capping its hill to the left. A left turn at the end of the stepped path takes you to more views and a nice loop that connects back to the river.

Boat Tours: Tour boats cruise from La Roque-Gageac to Castelnaud and back (one-hour cruise–€10, includes audioguide, 2/hour, April-Nov daily, tel. 05 53 29 40 44).

Hot-Air Balloon Rides: Montgolfières

du Périgord, located in La Roque-Gageac, offers a range of flights (www.mont-golfiere-du-perigord.com).

Sleeping and Eating: Along with Beynac, this is one of the region's most beautiful villages. Park in the lot at the eastern end of town if you're staying in La Roque-Gageac, and take everything of value out of your car.

$$ Manoir de la Malartrie is a wonderful splurge. It has five country-classy rooms and two family apartments with oak-meets-leather public areas, all surrounding a big, heated pool and impeccable terraced gardens (begging for a picnic). Your gentle hostess Ouaffa manages her place with elegance (3-night minimum in summer, air-con, free parking, barely downstream from the village—10-minute walk to town on trail above road, mobile 06 18 61 61 18, www.chambresdhotes-la-malartrie.com, lamalartrie@orange.fr).

$ Hôtel la Belle Etoile,*** a well-managed hotel-restaurant in the center of La Roque-Gageac, is a terrific value. Hostess Danielle and chef Régis (ray-geez) offer good, basic rooms overlooking the river, a nice terrace, and a fine restaurant (air-con, free parking, closed Nov-March, tel. 05 53

29 51 44, www.belleetoile.fr, hotel.belle-etoile@wanadoo.fr). Régis is the third generation of his family to be chef here and he takes his job seriously. Come to the **$$ restaurant** for a memorable dinner of classic French cuisine with modern accents in a romantic setting. The *œufs cocottes* are really good (closed for lunch Wed and all day Mon; book a few days ahead).

Château de Castelnaud

This ▲▲ castle may look a tad less mighty than Château de Beynac (down the river), but it packs a powerful medieval punch. The concise handout escorts you room by room through the castle-museum. The exhibits—which focus on warfare (armor, crossbows, and catapults) are well-organized and slicker than Beynac's, but the castle is also more touristy and lacks personality.

Cost and Hours: €11; daily July-Aug 9:00-20:00, April-June and Sept 10:00-19:00, Oct and Feb-March until 18:00, shorter hours Nov-Jan, last entry one hour before closing; tel. 05 53 31 30 00, www.castelnaud.com.

Getting There: From the river, it's a steep 30-minute hike through the village

Château de Castelnaud

to the castle. Drivers must park in the pay lot (5-minute walk uphill from the castle). You can stop at Castelnaud on your canoe trip or hike an hour from Beynac along a riverside path (although it's tricky to follow in parts—it hugs the river as it passes through campgrounds and farms—determined walkers do fine).

Visiting the Castle: After passing the ticket booth, read your essential handout and follow the *suite de la visite* signs. Start by climbing through the tower. Every room has a story to tell, and many have displays of costumed mannequins, suits of armor, weaponry (including the biggest and most artistic crossbows I've ever seen), and artifacts from the Hundred Years' War. Other rooms show informative videos (with English subtitles)—don't miss the catapult video where you'll learn that the big ones could fire only two shots per hour and required up to 250 men to manage. Kids eat it up, in part thanks to the children's guide with fun puzzles. The upper courtyard has a 150-foot-deep well (drop a pebble). On your way back down, you'll see a sparsely furnished medieval kitchen and an iron forge with an interesting video. The rampart views are as unbeatable as the four siege machines are formidable. A few cafés and fun medieval shops await at the foot of the castle.

Beynac

Four miles downstream from La Roque-Gageac, ▲▲▲ **Beynac** (bay-nak) is the other must-see Dordogne village. It's also home to one of the most imposing castles in France.

This well-preserved medieval village winds like a sepia-tone film set from the castle above to the river below (easy parking at the top avoids the steep climb). The stone village—with cobbled lanes that retain their Occitan (old French) names—is just plain pretty, best late in the afternoon and downright dreamy after dark. For the best light, tour the castle late, or at least walk out to the sensational viewpoint, then have a dinner here.

Orientation: The TI is near the river, across from Hôtel du Château (closed in winter, tel. 05 53 29 43 08). Pick up the *Plan du Village* in English for a simple self-guided walking tour, and get information on hiking and canoes. A few steps down from the TI is the post office (ATM outside). If you need a lift, call Beynac-based Bernard at **Taxi Corinne** (tel. 05 53 29 42 07, mobile 06 72 76 03 32). From mid-June to mid-September, a cute little market sets up on Monday mornings in the river-front parking lot.

Drivers can **park** at pay lots located on the river (busy), way up at the castle (quieter, follow signs to *Château de Beynac*), or halfway between. The same parking ticket works at all three lots (park below, explore the lower village, then drive to the top for the castle).

Château de Beynac: Beynac's brooding, cliff-clinging château, worth ▲▲, soars 500 feet above the Dordogne River (€8, daily 10:00-19:00, off-season until 18:30, last entry 45 minutes before closing, tel. 05 53 29 50 40, www.chateau-beynac. com). Spring for the essential and well-

done €3 audioguide that can be shared by many (no headphones needed). This castle is the ultimate for that top-of-the-world, king-of-the-castle feeling. During the Hundred Years' War, the castle of Beynac housed the French, while the English set up camp across the river at Castelnaud. This authentic, sparsely furnished castle is best for its valley views, but it still manages to evoke a memorable medieval feel. (These castles never had much furniture in any case.) When buying your ticket, notice the list showing the barons of Beynac (*Beynac et Ses Barons*)— Richard the Lionheart (*Coeur de Lion*) spent 10 years here.

You're free to wander on your own. As you tour the castle, swords, spears, and crossbows keep you honest, and two stone WCs keep kids entertained. The furnishings show how soldiers parked their swords and hung their crossbows before sitting down to dinner and drink (soldiers drank over two quarts of wine per day). Circling up through the castle, find your way to the highest crenellated terraces for sensational views. This is the closest look you'll have to a *lauzes* roof.

Château de Beynac and its village

Just down the river, mighty Castelnaud—which seems so imposing from up close—looks like a child's playset.

Walks and Viewpoints: A busy road separates Beynac from its river. Traffic-free lanes climb steeply uphill from the river to the château—the farther you get from the road, the more medieval the village feels. A pedestrian sidewalk runs along the river connecting to a riverfront trail, which begins across from Hôtel Bonnet at the eastern end of town and follows the river toward Castelnaud, offering great views back toward Beynac. For able route-finders, this is a level one-hour hike to the village of Castelnaud. Make time to walk at least a few hundred yards along this trail to enjoy the view to Beynac.

One of the Dordogne's most commanding views lies a short walk from the castle at the **top of the village** (easy parking, not essential if you toured the castle). Step just outside the village's upper end and take the enclosed lane to the right of the little cemetery. Stroll uphill to an odd glass structure. Castelnaud's castle hangs on the hill in the distance straight ahead. Château de Fayrac (owned by a Texan) is just right of the rail bridge and was originally constructed by the lords of Castelnaud to keep a close eye on the castle of Beynac. The Château de Marqueyssac, on a hill to the left, was built by the barons of Beynac to keep a close eye on the boys at Castelnaud—touché. More than a thousand such castles were erected in the Dordogne alone during the Hundred Years' War.

Boat Tours: Boats leave from Beynac's riverside parking lot for relaxing, 50-minute river cruises to Château de Fayrac and back (€10, nearly hourly, departures Easter-Oct daily 10:00-12:30 & 14:00-18:00, more frequent July-Aug, tel. 05 53 28 51 15).

Eating in Beynac: $$ **La Petite Tonnelle,** cut into the rock, has a romantic interior and a fine terrace out front. Locals love it for its tasty cuisine served at fair prices, though the service can be erratic. It's a block up from Hôtel du Château (good *menu* options, closed Sun-Mon, on the road to the castle, tel. 05 53 29 95 18, www.restaurant-petite-tonnelle.fr).

CRO-MAGNON CAVES

The area around the town of Les Eyzies-de-Tayac—about a 30-minute drive from Sarlat or the Dordogne Valley—has a rich history of prehistoric cave art. The paintings you'll see in this area's caves are famous throughout the world for their remarkably modern-looking technique, beauty, and mystery. Les Eyzies-de-Tayac, near most of the caves, offers two good introductory museums for your visit.

While the cave art here is amazing, it can be a headache to strategize. Delicate caves come with strict restrictions, and many of them are in out-of-the-way locations—making it time-consuming to fit a cave visit into your vacation (allow three hours for a typical visit, including transit time from Sarlat). Try to visit a cave on your way in or out of the area—Lascaux is north of Sarlat and Cougnac is to the south. The most famous cave with original art, Font-de-Gaume, is so restricted that getting in is nigh impossible. Some caves (like Lascaux IV) require long visits. But several caves are easier to plan for and visit, and well worth your time, provided you come prepared.

If seeing the very best matters, plan way ahead and book a local guide or transport service to the best cave: Grotte de Font-de-Gaume. If you don't score an entry here, the best alternative is Rouffignac (no reservations available, but you can generally show up and get in without too long a wait—call ahead to see how busy they are). Abri du Cap Blanc is bookable in advance, but it only has carvings, not paintings.

Rick's Tip: *All the prehistoric caves listed here are within* **45 minutes** *of Sarlat. Public transit is not a viable option.* **If you don't have a car, take a guided tour.**

Reserve Ahead or Get Up Early: Be clear on which caves take reservations (see the "Prehistoric Sights at a Glance" sidebar), and try to reserve your choice; other caves are first-come, first-served. That means it's essential to arrive early to secure a ticket, and then find something to do nearby if you have time to kill. How early you need to arrive varies by cave; I've suggested times for caves where you can't make a reservation. July and August are busiest, and rainy weather anytime sends sightseers scurrying for the caves. The caves are quieter from October to April; in high season, Saturdays are best (unless it's a holiday)—but note that Grotte de Font-de-Gaume and Abri du Cap Blanc are closed that day, as is the Prehistory Welcome Center.

Cave Tips: Dress warmly, even if it's hot outside. Tours can last up to an hour, and the caves are all a steady, chilly 55 degrees Fahrenheit, with 98 or 99 percent humidity. Photos, daypacks, big purses, and strollers are not allowed. (You can take your camera—without using it—and check the rest at the site.)

Local Guide: Angelika Siméon is a passionate guide/lecturer eager to teach you about the caves and well worth spending a day with. She handles cave reservations and makes your cave visit easy and educational (book ahead; €195/half-day, €285/day, prices are for two people, tel. 05 53 35 19 30, mobile 06 24 45 96 28, angelika.simeon@wanadoo.fr).

Les Eyzies-de-Tayac

This single-street town is the touristy hub of a cluster of Cro-Magnon caves, castles, and rivers. It merits a stop for its Prehistory Welcome Center, National Museum of Prehistory, and (if you can get in) the Grotte de Font-de-Gaume cave, a 15-minute walk or two-minute drive outside of town. Les Eyzies-de-Tayac is world-famous because it's where the original Cro-Magnon man was discovered in 1870. That breakthrough set of bones was found just behind the hotel of Monsieur Magnon—Hôtel le Cro-Magnon, which is in business to this day on the western end of the main street. The name "Cro-Magnon" translates as "Mr. Magnon's Hole."

Orientation: Les Eyzies-de-Tayac's **TI** is below the museum on the main drag (July-Aug daily 9:30-18:30, closed off-season 12:30-14:00 and Sun afternoons, ask about bike rentals, tel. 05 53 06 97 05, www.lascaux-dordogne.com). The train station is a level 500 yards from the town center (turn right from the station to get into town).

PREHISTORY WELCOME CENTER (POLE INTERNATIONAL DE LA PREHISTOIRE)
You could start your prehistoric explorations at the Pôleo International de la Préhistoire (PIP) as you enter town from the east (Sarlat). This glass-and-concrete facility is a helpful resource for planning a visit to the region's important prehistoric sites. The low-slung building houses timelines, a good eight-minute film (English subtitles), and exhibits that work together to give visitors a primer on the origins of humanity. The English-speaking staff is happy to provide maps of the region and give suggestions on places to visit. Park here (for free), then walk out the center's back door 200 yards on a pedestrian-only lane to the National Museum of Prehistory.

Cost and Hours: Free; Mon-Fri 9:30-18:30, Sun from 10:30, off-season closes one hour earlier, closed Sat except July-Aug; free parking across the street, located east of downtown Les Eyzies-de-Tayac at 30 Rue du Moulin—watch for tall silver *PIP* sign, tel. 05 53 06 06 97, www.pole-prehistoire.com.

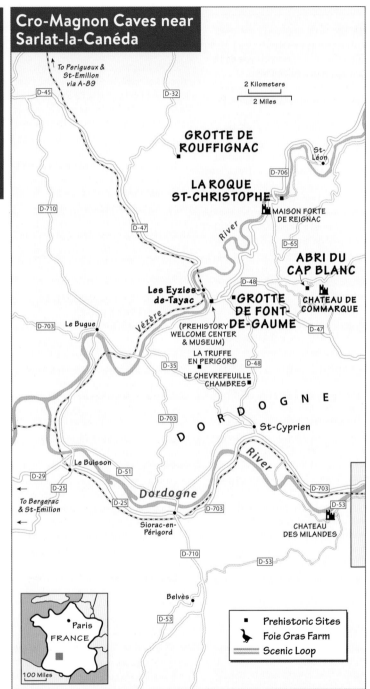

Cro-Magnon Caves near Sarlat-la-Canéda

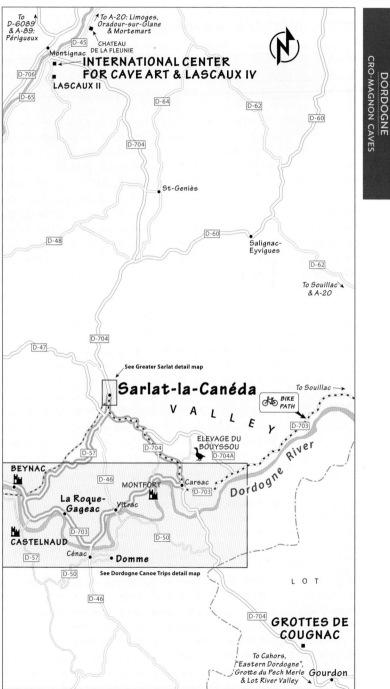

To
D-6089
& A-89:
Périgueux

To A-20: Limoges,
Oradour-sur-Glane
& Mortemart

D-45

CHATEAU
DE LA FLEUNIE

Montignac

INTERNATIONAL CENTER
FOR CAVE ART & LASCAUX IV

D-706

LASCAUX II

D-65

D-64

D-62

D-60

D-704

St-Geniès

D-48

D-60

Salignac-
Eyvigues

D-62

To Souillac
& A-20

D-47

D-704

See Greater Sarlat detail map

Sarlat-la-Canéda

To Souillac

V A L L E Y

BIKE
PATH

D-703

ELEVAGE DU
BOUYSSOU

D-704A

D-57

D-704

Dordogne River

BEYNAC

D-46

MONTFORT

Carsac

D-703

La Roque-
Gageac

Vitrac

CASTELNAUD

D-703

D-50

D-57

Cénac

Domme

D-50

See Dordogne Canoe Trips detail map

L O T

D-46

D-704

GROTTES DE
COUGNAC

To Cahors,
"Eastern Dordogne",
Grotte du Pech Merle
& Lot River Valley

Gourdon

PREHISTORIC SIGHTS AT A GLANCE

You can reserve ahead only for Lascaux II and IV and Abri du Cap Blanc. For the other caves, it's first-come, first-served.

Les Eyzies-de-Tayac

▲**National Museum of Prehistory** More than 18,000 well-displayed artifacts offer good background information for patient students. **Hours:** July-Aug daily 9:30-18:30; closed Tue Sept-June, closed at lunchtime Oct-May. **Reservations:** Not necessary, but reserve if you want a tour. Allow one hour to visit. See page 258.

Prehistory Welcome Center Free, helpful intro to region's important prehistoric sites. **Hours:** Mon-Fri 9:30-18:30, Sun from 10:30, off-season closes one hour earlier; closed all day Sat except July-Aug. **Reservations:** Not necessary. Allow 30 minutes to visit. See page 253.

Caves

▲▲▲**Grotte de Font-de-Gaume** Last prehistoric multicolored paintings open to public, with strict limits on the number of daily visitors. **Hours:** Mid-May-mid-Sept Sun-Fri 9:30-17:30, mid-Sept-mid-May Sun-Fri 9:30-12:30 & 14:00-17:30, closed Sat year-round. **Reservations:** Not available, but some area guides and transport services may be able to secure advance tickets. Without a guide, be in line by 7:30 in summer, 8:30 in spring and fall, and 9:00 in winter. Required 45-minute tour (likely in French). See page 260.

▲▲**International Center for Cave Art at Lascaux** Exact replicas of the world's most famous cave paintings, and an interactive center on cave

art. **Hours:** Lascaux IV—daily July-Aug 9:00-21:00; late March-June and Sept-Nov until 19:00, shorter hours in winter and closed Jan. Lascaux II—shorter hours and closed mid-Nov-late March. **Reservations:** Book in advance online, especially in high season. Required 40-minute tour for Lascaux IV, 75-minute tour for Lascaux II; allow up to 3 hours. See page 262.

▲▲**Grotte de Rouffignac** Etchings and paintings of prehistoric creatures, such as mammoths, in a large cave accessed by a little train. **Hours:** Daily July-Aug 9:00-11:30 & 14:00-18:00, April-June and Sept-Nov 10:00-11:30 & 14:00-17:00, closed Dec-March. **Reservations:** Not available or necessary, arrive by 8:30 in mid-July-Aug, otherwise 30 minutes early. Visit lasts one hour. See page 264.

▲▲**Grottes de Cougnac** Oldest paintings (30,000 years) open to public, showing rust-and-black ibex, mammoths, giant deer, and a few humans, on a tour more focused on cave geology than art. **Hours:** Mid-July-Aug daily 10:00-17:45; April-mid-July and Sept daily 10:00-11:30 & 14:30-17:00; Oct Mon-Sat 14:00-16:00, closed Sun; closed Nov-March. **Reservations:** Not available. Arrive 10 minutes before it opens in summer. Required 70-minute tour (with minimal English explanation). See page 265.

▲**Abri du Cap Blanc** 14,000-year-old carvings that use natural contours of cave to add dimension, but no cave paintings. **Hours:** Mid-May-mid-Sept Sun-Fri 10:00-18:00, mid-Sept-mid-May Sun-Fri 10:00-12:30 & 14:00-18:00, closed Sat year-round, last entry at about 16:15. **Reservations:** Book a tour time by phone, or just show up at the Font-de-Gaume ticket office. Required 45-minute tour (often with some English, usually 6/day); call for times. See page 261.

▲**La Roque St-Christophe** Terraced, shallow cliffside caves where prehistoric people lived. **Hours:** Daily July-Aug 10:00-20:00, April-June and Sept until 18:30, shorter hours off-season. **Reservations:** Not available or necessary. Allow 45 minutes to visit. See page 262.

Cave Art 101

To help you appreciate prehistoric art, my long-time collaborator, Gene Openshaw, offers this background:

From 18,000 to 10,000 BC, long before Stonehenge, before the pyramids, back when mammoths and saber-toothed cats still roamed the earth, prehistoric people painted deep inside limestone caverns in southern France and northern Spain. These are not crude doodles; they're sophisticated, costly, and time-consuming engineering projects planned and executed by dedicated artists supported by a unified and stable culture—the Magdalenians.

The Magdalenians (c. 18,000-10,000 BC): These hunter-gatherers of the Upper Paleolithic period (40,000-10,000 BC) were driven south by the Second Ice Age. The Magdalenians flourished in southern France and northern Spain for eight millennia—long enough to chronicle the evolution and extinction of several animal species. (Think: Egypt lasted a mere 3,000 years; Rome lasted 1,000; America fewer than 250 so far.)

Physically, the people were Cro-Magnons—fully developed *Homo sapiens* who could blend in to our modern population. We know these people by the possessions found in their settlements: stone axes, flint arrowheads, bone needles for making clothes, musical instruments, grease lamps, and cave paintings and sculptures. Many objects are beautifully decorated.

The Magdalenians did not live in the deep limestone caverns they painted (which are cold and difficult to access). But many did live in the shallow cliffside caves that you'll see throughout your Dordogne travels, which were continuously inhabited from prehistoric times until the Middle Ages.

The Paintings: Though there are dozens of caves painted over a span of more than 8,000 years, they're all surprisingly similar. These Stone Age hunters painted the animals they hunted—bison or bulls (especially at Lascaux and

▲NATIONAL MUSEUM OF PREHISTORY (MUSEE NATIONAL DE PREHISTOIRE)

This well-presented, modern museum houses more than 18,000 bones, stones, and crude little doodads that were uncovered locally. It takes you through prehistory—starting 400,000 years ago—and is good preparation for your cave visits. Appropriately located on a cliff inhabited by humans for 35,000 years (above Les Eyzies-de-Tayac's TI), the museum's sleek design is intended to help it blend into the surrounding rock. Inside, the many worthwhile exhibits include videos demonstrating scratched designs, painting techniques, and how spearheads were made. You'll

also see full-size models of Cro-Magnon people and animals that stare at racks of arrowheads. The museum's handheld English explanations require patience to correlate to the exhibits.

Cost and Hours: €6, €8 with temporary exhibits, daily 9:30-18:30, closed Tue Sept-June, closed at lunchtime Oct-May, last entry 45 minutes before closing, tel. 05 53 06 45 65, www.musee-prehistoire-eyzies.fr.

Tours: To get the most out of your visit, consider a private or semiprivate English-language guided tour; for details, call 05 53 06 45 65 or email reservation. prehistoire@culture.gouv.fr.

Visiting the Museum: Pick up the museum layout with your ticket. Notice

Grotte de Font-de-Gaume), mammoths (the engravings at Grotte de Rouffignac), and woolly rhinoceroses (at Grotte de Font-de-Gaume).

The animals stand in profile, with unnaturally big bodies and small limbs and heads. The thick black outlines are often wavy, suggesting the animal in motion. Except for a few friezes showing a conga line of animals running across the cave wall, there is no apparent order or composition. The artists engraved them on the wall by laboriously scratching outlines into the rock with a flint blade. A typical animal might be made using several techniques—an engraved outline that follows the natural contour, reinforced with thick outline paint, then colored in.

No paintbrushes have been found, so artists probably used a sponge-like material made from animal skin and fat. They may have used moss or hair, or maybe even finger-painted with globs of pure pigment. Once they had drawn the outlines, they filled everything in with spray paint—either spit out from the mouth or blown through tubes made of hollow bone.

Dating: Determining exactly how old this art is—and whether it's authentic—is tricky. (Because much of the actual paint is mineral-based with no organic material, carbon-dating techniques are often ineffective.) As different caves feature different animals, prehistorians can deduce which caves are relatively older and younger, since climate change caused various animal species to come and go within certain regions.

Why? No one knows the purpose of the cave paintings. The sites the artists chose were deliberately awe-inspiring, out of the way, and special. They knew their work here would last for untold generations, as had the paintings that came before theirs. Whatever the purpose—religious, aesthetic, or just plain fun—there's no doubt the effect is thrilling.

Turkana Boy, *National Museum of Prehistory*

the timeline shown on the stone wall starting a mere 7 million years ago. Then enter, walking in the footsteps of your ancestors, and greet the 10-year-old Turkana Boy, whose bone fragments were found in Kenya in 1984 by Richard Leakey and date from 1.5 million years ago.

Spiral up the stairs to the first floor, which sets the stage by describing human evolution and the fundamental importance of tools. You'll also see a life-size re-creation of *Megaloceros*—a gigantic deer (with even bigger antlers)—and a skeleton of an oversized steppe bison, both of which appear in some of the area's cave paintings.

The more engaging second floor highlights prehistoric artifacts found in France.

Some of the most interesting objects you'll see are displayed in this order: a handheld arrow launcher, a 5,000-year-old flat-bottomed boat (pirogue) made from oak, prehistoric fire pits, amazing cavewoman jewelry (including a necklace labeled *La Parure de St-Germain-la-Rivière,* made of 70 stag teeth—pretty impressive, given that stags only have two teeth each), engravings on stone (find the unflattering yet impressively realistic female figure), a handheld lamp used to light cave interiors (*lampe façonnée,* found at Lascaux), and beautiful replicas of horses (much like the sculptures at the cave of Abri du Cap Blanc).

Your visit ends on the cliff edge, with a Fred Flintstone-style photo op on a stone ledge (through the short tunnel) that some of our ancient ancestors once called home.

The Caves

▲▲▲GROTTE DE FONT-DE-GAUME

Even if you're not a connoisseur of Cro-Magnon art, you'll dig this cave just east of Les Eyzies-de-Tayac—it's the last one in France with prehistoric multicolored (polychrome) paintings still open to the public. (Lascaux—45 minutes down the road—has replica caves; the other cave paintings open to the public are monochrome.) This cave, made millions of years ago—not by a river, but by the geological activity that created the Pyrenees Mountains—is entirely natural. It contains 15,000-year-old paintings of 230 animals, 82 of which are bison.

On a carefully guided and controlled 100-yard walk, you'll see about 20 red-and-black bison—often in elegant motion—painted with a moving sensitivity. When two animals face each other, one is black, and the other is red. Your guide, with a laser pointer and great reverence, will trace the faded outline of the bison and explain how, 15 millennia in the past, cave dwellers used local minerals and the rock's natural contours to give the paintings dimension. Some locals knew about the cave long ago, when there was little interest in prehistory, but the paintings were officially discovered in 1901 by the village schoolteacher.

Warning: Access to Font-de-Gaume is extremely restricted, and individual reservations are not accepted. The 78 tickets available each day meets only a fraction of the demand. Area guides snap up 26 of these ahead of time; the 52 remaining

The Dordogne is rich in prehistoric cave sites.

spots are given out on a first-come basis (see details below). If you must see Font-de-Gaume, book through a guide service long ahead or line up for tickets early on the morning of the day you want to visit. It would be pretty clear that you're not going to get a ticket if you show up and all 52 spots are already taken. Drivers who can't get a ticket here should try the other interesting caves I recommend. Rouffignac is the best backup (you're already partway there).

Cost and Hours: €10, 17 and under free, includes required 45-minute tour; open mid-May-mid-Sept Sun-Fri 9:30-17:30, mid-Sept-mid-May Sun-Fri 9:30-12:30 & 14:00-17:30, closed Sat year-round; no photography or large bags, tel. 05 53 06 86 00, www.eyzies.monuments-nationaux.fr. Those planning to also visit Abri du Cap Blanc (described next) can reserve and buy tickets here.

Getting Tickets: The 52 tickets for individuals are doled out in person each morning starting at 9:30. In summer, plan to be in line by 7:30, in spring and fall no later than 8:30, and in the dead of winter you should be OK if you arrive by 9:00. Be aware that there are minimal facilities for the ticket queue (no shelters, no food services, etc.) There are 52 numbered seats outside the entrance, so you'll know where you are in line. (Each person can buy only one ticket, so you can't send one member of your party ahead for the whole group.) You must check in at least 20 minutes before your tour time, or you may lose your place to sightseeing vultures waiting to snatch up the spots of late arrivals.

Local guide **Angelika Siméon** (see page 253) may be able to get tickets, but you must reserve at least six months ahead and hire her for a tour.

Tours: English tours are available but limited; expect to visit with a French guide. Depending on the guide, the actual tour can be either illuminating and enthusiastic, or uninspiring. Don't fret if you're not on an English tour—most important is experiencing the art itself. You can buy an informative book afterward.

Getting There: The cave is at the corner of D-47 and D-48, about a two-minute drive (or a 15-minute walk) east of Les Eyzies-de-Tayac (toward Sarlat). There's easy on-site parking. After checking in at the ticket house, walk 400 yards on an uphill path to the cave entrance (where there's a free, safe bag check and a WC).

▲ABRI DU CAP BLANC
In this prehistoric cave (a 10-minute drive from Grotte de Font-de-Gaume), early artists used the rock's natural contours to add dimension to their sculpture. Your guide spends the tour in a single stone room explaining the 14,000-year-old carvings. The small museum helps prepare you for your visit, and the useful English handout describes what the French-speaking guide is talking about (some guides add English commentary). Look for places where the artists smoothed or roughened the surfaces to add depth. Keep in mind that you'll be seeing carvings, not cave paintings. Impressive as these carvings are, their subtle majesty is lost on some.

Cost and Hours: €8, ages 18 and under free; includes required 45-minute tour, 6 tours/day (35 people each), call for tour times and to reserve. The cave is open mid-May to mid-Sept Sun-Fri 10:00-18:00, mid-Sept-mid-May Sun-Fri 10:00-12:30 & 14:00-18:00, closed Sat year-round, last entry at about 16:15, no photos, tel. 05 53 59 60 30.

Getting Tickets: Buy tickets at the sight or book by phone. You can also buy a ticket in person at the Font-de-Gaume ticket office (see previous listing).

Getting There: Abri du Cap Blanc is well-signed and is located about seven kilometers after Grotte de Font-de-Gaume on the road to Sarlat. From the parking lot, walk 200 yards down to the entry. Views of the Château de Commarque are terrific as you arrive.

▲LA ROQUE ST-CHRISTOPHE

Five fascinating terraces carved by the Vézère River have provided shelter to people here for 55,000 years. Although the terraces were inhabited in prehistoric times, there's no prehistoric art on display—the exhibit (except for one small cave) is entirely medieval.

Cost and Hours: €10, daily July-Aug 10:00-20:00, April-June and Sept until 18:30, shorter hours off-season, last entry 45 minutes before closing, lots of steps; eight kilometers north of Les Eyzies-de-Tayac—soon after passing Maison Forte de Reignac—follow signs to *Montignac;* tel. 05 53 50 70 45, www.roque-st-christophe.com.

Background: The official recorded history goes back to AD 976, when people settled here to steer clear of the Viking raiders who would routinely sail up the river. A clever relay of river watchtowers kept an eye out for raiders. When they came, cave dwellers gathered their kids, hauled up their animals (see the big, re-created winch), and pulled up the ladders. Although there's absolutely nothing old here except for the gouged-out rock (with holes for beams, carved out of the soft limestone), it's easy to imagine the entire village—complete with butcher, baker, and candlestick maker—in this family-friendly exhibit. This place is a dream for kids of any age who hold fond tree-house memories.

La Roque St-Christophe

Visiting the Terraces: There's a free parking lot across the stream, with picnic tables, a WC, and, adjacent to the babbling brook, a pondside café (selling salads, sandwiches, and drinks—the nearby pretty village of St-Léon provides more lunch choices). Climb through the one-way circuit, which is slippery when damp. Panels show the medieval buildings that once filled this space; don't miss the English translations on the back side. Allow at least 45 minutes for your visit.

▲▲INTERNATIONAL CENTER FOR CAVE ART (LASCAUX CENTRE INTERNATIONAL DE L'ART PARIETAL)

The region's—and the world's—most famous cave paintings are at Lascaux, 14 miles north of Sarlat-la-Canéda and Les Eyzies-de-Tayac. The Lascaux caves were discovered accidentally in 1940 by four kids and their dog. From 1948 to 1963, more than a million people climbed through the prehistoric wonderland of incredibly vivid and colorful paintings—but the visitors tracked in fungus on their shoes and changed the temperature and humidity with their heavy breathing. In just 15 years, the precious art deteriorated more than during the previous 15,000 years, and the caves were closed to the public.

Today you can only see replicas here. Seeing the real thing at one of the other caves is thrilling, but coming to Lascaux and taking one of the scheduled tours is a great introduction to the region's cave art. Forget that these are copies and enjoy being swept away by the prehistoric majesty of it all.

To plan your visit, know the lingo: **Lascaux I** is the original cave. In 1983, a replica of the cave called **Lascaux II** was built next to the original—accurate to within one centimeter, reproducing the best 40-yard-long stretch, and showing 90 percent of the paintings found in Lascaux. **Lascaux III** is an exhibit designed to travel abroad. And **Lascaux IV** is the newest razzle-dazzle replica—opened

Lascaux II

in 2017, reproducing 100 percent of the original cave, and designed with the latest technology. Visitors can tour Lascaux II or IV—or both—depending on their interest (descriptions below). The Lascaux caves are a constant 56 degrees year-round, so dress warmly.

At the end of your visit, the pleasant town of Montignac is close and worth a wander if you have time to kill.

Cost and Hours: Lascaux IV—€17 includes tour, audioguide, 3-D film, and many exhibits, open daily July-Aug 9:00-21:00, late March-June and Sept-Nov until 19:00, shorter hours in winter and closed Jan, last ticket sold two hours before closing; Lascaux II—€13, includes tour only, open July-Aug 9:00-19:00, late March-June and Sept-early Nov 10:00-12:30 & 14:00-18:00, closed mid-Nov-late March.

Getting Tickets: Reservations for the few daily English tours are essential for either cave (most reliable English tours are usually around 10:00 or 11:00). Book in advance on the Lascaux website at www.lascaux.fr/en. Tickets also sold at the sight.

Information: Located on Avenue de Lascaux in Montignac, reach by traveling northeast from Les Eyzies on D-706; tel. 05 53 50 99 10, www.lascaux.fr/en.

Eating: Lascaux IV has a good cafeteria with fair prices and outdoor seating. The pleasant town of Montignac is less than a mile away with cafés and food shops.

Visiting the Caves: These replica caves each took years to create. The prehistoric reindeer, horses, and bulls of the original Lascaux cave were painstakingly reproduced by talented artists, using the same dyes, tools, and techniques their predecessors used 15,000 years ago.

Lascaux IV gives a thorough overview of the original cave but has a circus-like feel in high season: Groups of 35 are processed every six minutes, and you wade through huge parking lots to get there. It's housed in the International Center for Cave Art, a sight in itself built into the hillside next to the original cave. Your visit to this state-of-the-art center starts with a well-done, 40-minute guided tour of the replica caves. Then you are set free with a tablet to view interactive exhibits that explain the role Lascaux played in prehistory, scientific research analyzing cave art, and the link from cave art to modern art. The thought-provoking, what-do-these-paintings-mean, 3-D film is a fine way to finish your visit. Plan to spend a minimum of 1.5 hours here.

Lascaux II sits a half-mile above Lascaux IV in the woods and offers a more intimate, quiet, and intensive look at the caves on a 75-minute tour with a group of 20 people.

Sleeping and Eating near Lascaux:
$$-$$$ Château de la Fleunie* allows you to bed down in a medieval castle at digestible prices. Built between the 12th and 16th centuries, this castle shares its land with pastures and mountain goats, a big pool (unheated), worn tennis courts, and play toys. Rooms are located in three buildings: the main château, an attached wing, and the modern pavilion. The château's rooms are Old World-worn with musty and dated bathrooms (many big rooms for families), while the pavilion offers contemporary rooms with private view decks (family rooms, half-pension possible—about €40 more/person). Stay-awhile terraces overlook the scene and its riddled-with-character **$$ restaurant** (€30-70 *menus,* cheaper "grill" restaurant open in high season, 10-minute drive north of Montignac on D-45 road toward Aubas, near Condat-sur-Vézère, tel. 05 53 51 32 74, www.lafleunie.com, lafleunie@free.fr).

▲▲GROTTE DE ROUFFIGNAC

At Rouffignac you'll ride a clunky little train down a giant subterranean river-bed, exploring about half a mile of this six-mile-long gallery with black-on-white paintings and engravings. The cave itself was long known to locals, but the 15,000-year-old drawings were officially "discovered" only in 1956. With a little planning, you'll have no trouble getting a ticket to this fascinating cave. Dress warmly as you'll be sitting during your visit.

Cost and Hours: €8, daily July-Aug 9:00-11:30 & 14:00-18:00, April-June and

Grotte de Rouffignac

Sept-Nov 10:00-11:30 & 14:00-17:00, closed Dec-March; essential videoguide-€1.50; one-hour guided tours run 2-3/hour, no reservations; tel. 05 53 05 41 71, www.grottederouffignac.fr.

Getting Tickets: It's really crowded only mid-July-Aug—during these months the ticket office opens at 9:00 and closes when tickets are sold out for the day—usually by noon. Arrive by 8:30 in summer and 30 minutes early at other times of year (you may get an entry time for a bit later in the day). Weekends tend to be quietest, particularly Saturday.

Getting There: Grotte de Rouffignac is well-signed from the route between Les Eyzies-de-Tayac and Périgueux (don't take the first turnoff, for *Rouffignac;* wait for the *Grotte de Rouffignac* sign); allow 25 minutes from Les Eyzies-de-Tayac.

Visiting the Cave: Your tour will be in French (with highlights described in English), but the videoguide explains it all. Before the tour begins, read your videoguide's background sections and the displays in the cave entry area. Once on the tour it's easy to follow along. Here's the gist of what they're saying on the stops of your train ride:

The cave was created by the underground river. It's entirely natural, but it was much shallower before the train-track bed was excavated. As you travel, imagine the motivation and determination of the artists who crawled more than a half-mile into this dark and mysterious cave. They left behind their art...and the wonder of people who crawled in centuries later to see it all.

You'll ride about five minutes before the first stop. Along the way, you'll see crater-like burrows made by hibernating bears long before the first humans drew here. There are hundreds of them—not because there were so many bears, but because year after year, a few of them would return, preferring to make their own private place to sleep (rather than using some other bear's den). After a long winter nap, bears would have one thing on their mind: Cut those toenails. The walls are scarred with the scratching of bears in need of clippers.

Stop 1: The guide points out bear scratches on the right. On the left, images of woolly mammoths etched into the walls can be seen only when lit from the side (as your guide will demonstrate). As the rock is very soft here, these were simply gouged out by the artists' fingers.

Stop 2: Look for images of finely detailed rhinoceroses outlined in black. Notice how the thicker coloring under their tummies suggests the animals' girth. The rock is harder here, so nothing is engraved. Soon after, your guide will point out graffiti littering the ceiling—made by "modern" visitors who were not aware of the prehistoric drawings around them (with dates going back to the 18th century).

Stop 3: On the left, you'll see woolly mammoths and horses engraved with tools in the harder rock. On the right is the biggest composition of the cave: a herd of 10 peaceful mammoths. A mysterious calcite problem threatens to cover the art with ugly white splotches.

Off the Train: When you get off the train, notice how high the original floor was (today's floor was dug out in the 20th century to allow for visitors). Imagine both the prehistoric makers and viewers of this art crawling all the way back here with pretty lousy flashlight substitutes. The artists lay on their backs while creating these 60 images (unlike at Lascaux, where they built scaffolds).

The ceiling is covered with a remarkable gathering of animals. You'll see a fine 16-foot-long horse, a group of mountain goats, and a grandpa mammoth. Art even decorates the walls far down the big, scary hole. When the group chuckles, it's because the guide is explaining how the mammoth with the fine detail (showing a flap of skin over its anus) helped authenticate the drawings: These couldn't be fakes, because no one knew about this anatomical detail until the preserved remains of an actual mammoth were found in Siberian permafrost in modern times. (The discovery explained the painted skin flap, which had long puzzled French prehistorians.)

▲▲GROTTES DE COUGNAC

Located 23 kilometers south of Sarlat-la-Canéda and three well-signed kilometers north of Gourdon on D-704, this cave holds fascinating rock formations and the oldest (20,000-25,000-year-old) paintings and drawings open to the public. Family-run

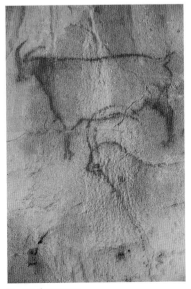

Grottes de Cougnac

and less developed than other sites, it provides a more intimate look at cave art, as guides take more time to explain the caves (your guide should give some explanations in English—ask). The art you see is single-color outlines or silhouettes (in red, yellow, or black). It's just one small part of the full tour, which focuses heavily on the cave's geology and unique formations—you'll see spaghetti-style stalactites, curtain stalactites, and much more.

Cost and Hours: €8.50, includes required 70-minute tour; these hours correspond to first/last tour times: mid-July-Aug daily 10:00-17:45; April-mid-July and Sept daily 10:00-11:30 & 14:30-17:00; Oct Mon-Sat 14:00-16:00, closed Sun; closed Nov-March; free WCs, consider the decent €5 English-language booklet. Tel. 05 65 41 47 54, www.grottesdecougnac.com.

Getting Tickets: Because access is first-come, first-served (and groups are limited to 25), plan your visit carefully. There are no online reservations. You can call right at 9:30 or 14:30 (when the ticket office opens) to check on availability, or show up 20 minutes before the ticket office opens to assure entry. During busy times (in summer and in bad weather), they're most crowded 11:00-12:00 and 15:00-17:00. At quieter times, you can

usually stop by before 11:00 and get in. Outside of July and August, be careful not to arrive too close to the last tour before lunch (11:30)—if that tour is full, you'll have to wait for the 14:30 departure. Note: If you have time to kill, you're only minutes from the town of Gourdon (with shops, restaurants, and a historic center).

Visiting the Cave: The 70-minute tour, likely in French, begins in a cave below the entrance, where the guide explains the geological formations (you'll learn that it takes 70 years for water to make it from the earth's surface into the cave). From this first cave, you'll return to the fresh air and walk eight minutes to a second cave. Inside, you'll twist and twist through forests of stalagmites and stalactites before reaching the grand finale: the drawings you came to see. They are worth the wait. Vivid depictions (about 10) of ibex, mammoths, and giant deer (Megaloceros), as well as a few nifty representations of humans, are outlined in rust or black. The rendering of the giant deer's antlers is exquisite, and many drawings use the cave's form to add depth and movement. The art is subtle—small sketches here and there, rather than the grand canvases of some of the more famous caves—but powerful.

BEST OF THE REST

Carcassonne

Tucked between the Dordogne and Provence, medieval Carcassonne is a 13th-century world of towers, turrets, and cobblestones. This is Europe's ultimate walled fortress city.

Day Plan

Carcassonne is stuffed with tourists—consider yourself warned. But early, late, or off-season, a quieter Carcassonne is an evocative playground for any medievalist. Forget midday—this is one city that can be well seen with a late afternoon arrival. There's only one "sight" to enter, and the majesty of the place can best be enjoyed after-hours.

Orientation

Contemporary Carcassonne is neatly divided into two cities: the magnificent La Cité (the fortified old city) and the lively Ville Basse (modern lower city). Two bridges, the busy Pont Neuf and the traffic-free Pont Vieux, both with great views, connect the two parts.

Tourist Information: The main TI, in **Ville Basse,** is useful only if you're walking to La Cité (28 Rue de Verdun). A far more convenient branch is in **La Cité,** a block to your right (on Impasse Agnès de Montpellier) after entering the main Narbonne Gate (open daily year-round, tel. 04 68 10 24 30, www.carcassonne-tourisme.com).

Getting There

The **train station** is located in Ville Basse, a 30-minute walk or a short **taxi** trip (€12) from La Cité. **Public bus #4** runs to La Cité from the Chénier stop (on Boulevard Omer Sarraut, at the far edge of the park a block from the station, €1, hourly Mon-Sat, none Sun).

Drivers should follow signs to *Centre-Ville,* then *La Cité.* Several huge public pay lots (€10/6 hours) are clustered near the main Narbonne Gate. Leave nothing on display; theft is common in public lots.

Rick's Tip: *Pleasing Place Carnot in Ville Basse hosts a thriving nontouristy* **open-air market** *on Tue, Thu, and Sat mornings until 13:00—Sat is the biggest and worth the detour.*

---

❷ Carcassonne Walk

This self-guided walk, rated ▲▲▲, introduces you to the city with history and wonder. This walk can be done at any hour. It's wonderfully peaceful and scenic early or late in the day, when the sun is low (but the church and castle may be closed).

• *Start outside La Cité's main entrance, the Narbonne Gate (Porte Narbonnaise).*

Narbonne Gate: Pause at the drawbridge and survey this immense fortification. When forces from northern France finally conquered Carcassonne, it was a strategic prize. Not taking any chances, they evicted the residents, whom they allowed to settle in the lower town (Ville Basse)—as long as they stayed across the river. (Though it's called "new," this lower town actually dates from the 13th century.) La Cité remained a French military garrison until the 18th century.

This drawbridge was made crooked to slow attackers' rush to the main gate and has a similar effect on tourists today.

• *After crossing the drawbridge, lose the crowds and walk left between the walls. At the first short set of stairs, climb to the outer-wall walkway.*

Wall View: The Romans built Carcassonne's first wall, upon which the bigger medieval wall was constructed. Identify the ancient Roman bits by looking about

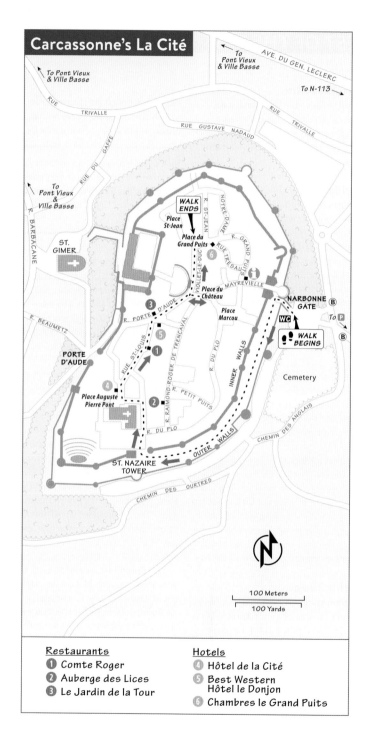

Carcassonne's La Cité

To
Pont Vieux
& Ville Basse

AVE. DU GEN. LECLERC

To Pont Vieux
& Ville Basse

To N-113 →

RUE

TRIVALLE

RUE GUSTAVE NADAUD

RUE

TRIVALLE

RUE DU GAFFE

To
Pont Vieux
&
Ville Basse

R.

R. BARBACANE

ST.
GIMER

NOTRE-DAME

R. ST-JEAN

WALK
ENDS

Place
St-Jean

Place du
Grand Puits

R. GRAND PUITS

RUE TRESAUS

VIOLET-LE-DUC

Place du
Château

MAYREVIELLE

NARBONNE
GATE

B

To P

B

R. PORTE D'AUDE

Place
Marcou

WC

WALK
BEGINS

R. BEAUMETZ

RUE ST-LOUIS

R. RAIMOND-ROGER DE TRENCAVAL

R. DU PLO

INNER WALLS

Cemetery

PORTE
D'AUDE

Place Auguste
Pierre Pont

R. PETIT PUITS

R. DU PLO

OUTER WALLS

CHEMIN DES ANGLAIS

ST. NAZAIRE
TOWER

CHEMIN DES OURTRES

N

100 Meters

100 Yards

Restaurants
1 Comte Roger
2 Auberge des Lices
3 Le Jardin de la Tour

Hotels
4 Hôtel de la Cité
5 Best Western
  Hôtel le Donjon
6 Chambres le Grand Puits

one-third of the way up and finding the smaller rocks mixed with narrow stripes of red bricks (and no arrow slits). The outer wall that you're on was not built until the 13th century (after the French defeated the city), more than a thousand years after the Roman walls went up.

Look over the wall and down at the moat below (now mostly used for parking). Like most medieval moats, it was never filled with water (or even alligators). A ditch like this—which was originally even deeper—effectively stopped attacking forces from rolling up against the wall in their mobile towers and spilling into the city.

• *Stop at the first possible entrance into La Cité, the...*

Inner Wall Tower (St. Nazaire Tower): The tower has the same four gates it had in Roman times. Before entering, notice the squat tower on the outer wall—there's one placed opposite each inner gate for extra protection.

As you breach the wall and enter the old town, study the ornate defenses. Look up to see a slot for the portcullis and the frame for a heavy wooden door. The entry is at an angle (to provide better cover). At

Carcassonne gate

the inner set of doors, you can see centuries-old, rusty parts of the hinge.

• *Opposite the tower stands the...*

St. Nazaire Church (Basilique St. Nazaire): This was a cathedral until the 18th century, when the bishop moved to the lower town. Today, due to the depopulation of the basically dead-except-for-tourism Cité, it's not even a functioning parish church. Step inside. Notice the Romanesque arches of the nave and the delicately vaulted Gothic arches over the altar and transepts. When the lights are off, the interior—lit only by candles and 14th-century stained glass (some of finest in southern France)—is evocatively medieval.

• *The ivy-covered luxury hotel in front of the church entrance is...*

Hôtel de la Cité: This hotel sits where the bishop's palace did 700 years ago. Today, it's a worthwhile detour to see how the privileged few travel. You're welcome to wander in. Find the cozy bar/library (reasonable beer and wine by the glass), and step into the rear garden for super wall views.

• *Leaving the hotel, turn left and take the right fork at the medieval flatiron building. Follow Rue St. Louis for several blocks. Merge right onto Rue de la Porte d'Aude, then look for a small view terrace on your left.*

Château Comtal: Originally built in 1125, Carcassonne's third layer of defense was enlarged in later reconstructions. From this impressive viewpoint you can see the wooden rampart extensions (rebuilt in modern times) that once circled the entire city wall. (Notice the empty peg holes to the left of the bridge.) During sieges, these would be covered with wet animal skins as a fire retardant. Take a stroll through the tranquil garden moat (free).

• *Fifty yards away, opposite the entrance to the castle, is...*

Place du Château: This busy little square sports a modest statue honoring the man who saved the city from deterioration and neglect in the 19th century.

The walls of Carcassonne

Hôtel de la Cité

The bronze model circling the base of the statue shows Carcassonne's walls as they looked before their fanciful 1855 Neo-Gothic reconstruction by architect Eugène Viollet-le-Duc.

• Our walk is finished. If you turn left at the fountain, you'll pop out in the charming, restaurant-lined Place St-Jean.

Night Wall Walk

Save some post-dinner energy for a ▲▲▲ don't-miss walk around the same walls you visited today (great dinner picnic sites as well). The effect at night is mesmerizing: Embedded lights become torches and unfamiliar voices become the enemy. You can enter and exit the old city from two locations: Porte d'Aude, on the west side, or from the main Narbonne Gate, on the east side. From either point you can walk 15 minutes down to the Pont Vieux (old bridge) and find an unforgettable view of the floodlit walled town. Ideally, take one route down and the other back up (see the La Cité map).

Sights

CHATEAU COMTAL AND RAMPART WALK

Your best look at Carcassonne's medieval architecture, worth ▲▲, is a walk through this castle-within-the-castle, followed by a walk atop the city ramparts. Grab the basic flier in English (and rent the €3 audioguide for the full story).

Start your visit in a small theater, where a short video sets the stage. Next is a big model of La Cité (made in 1910 to show the city as it looked in 1300). From here, a self-guided tour with posted English explanations (and your audioguide) leads you around the inner ramparts of Carcassonne's castle. You'll learn all about medieval defense systems.

From the castle you can climb out onto the actual city ramparts and circle about two-thirds of the old town. The north rampart is open all the way to the main Narbonne Gate, but there's no exit and you'll need to backtrack. The west rampart lets you circle all the way to the St. Nazaire Tower, from where you can exit (drop off your audioguide before entering the west rampart). I'd explore both sections.

Cost and Hours: €9, daily 10:00-18:30, Oct-March 9:30-17:00, last entry 45 minutes before closing, tel. 04 68 11 70 70, www.remparts-carcassonne.fr.

Eating

Elegant **$$$ Comte Roger** offers fresh Mediterranean cuisine (closed Sun-Mon, 14 Rue St. Louis). **$$ Auberge des Lices** serves traditional plates (daily July-Aug, closed Tue-Wed Sept-June, 3 Rue Raymond Roger Trencavel). Try **$$ Le Jardin de la Tour** for good cassoulet (closed Sun-Mon, lunch served July-Aug only, 11 Rue de la Porte d'Aude).

Sleeping

Sleeping inside the walls, you'll enjoy reliable luxury at **$$$$ Hôtel de la Cité*****</br>** (Place Auguste-Pierre Pont, www.hoteldelacite.com) and well-appointed rooms in the main building of **$$ Best Western Hôtel le Donjon****** (2 Rue Comte Roger, www.hotel-donjon.fr). For a splendid value, try **$ Chambres le Grand Puits** (cash only, 8 Place du Grand Puits, http://legrandpuits.free.fr).

Provence

This magnificent region is shaped like a giant wedge of quiche. From its sunburned crust, fanning out along the Mediterranean coast, it stretches north along the Rhône Valley. The splendid recipe *provençale* mixes pastel hills, appealing cities, bountiful vineyards, and sweet, hilltop villages.

The Romans were here in force and left many ruins—some of the finest anywhere. Over the centuries, they were followed by seven popes, who resided in a formidable palace in Avignon, and artist Vincent van Gogh, whose work celebrates Provence's sunflowers and starry nights.

The best home bases are Arles and Avignon (plus Vaison-la-Romaine for drivers exploring the Côtes du Rhône wine country). Beyond the towns, the top sights are Les Baux's medieval castle ruins and the ancient Roman aqueduct, Pont du Gard.

A car will come in handy, though towns and sights are connected by public transit. Those traveling *sans* car could take a minivan tour for time-saving efficiency.

PROVENCE IN 2 DAYS

Make Arles or Avignon your sightseeing base. While Francophiles usually pick urban Avignon, Italophiles prefer smaller Arles.

You'll want one day for sightseeing in Arles and Les Baux. Spend most of the day in Arles—try to time your arrival for Wednesday or Saturday, to enjoy the market. Then visit Les Baux in the late afternoon or early evening. On the second day, allow a half-day for Avignon and a half-day for Pont du Gard.

With another day, measure the pulse of rural Provence and spend at least

Provence

To Lyon & Burgundy
Grignan
To Chamonix & Alps
Valréas
Ardèche
Bollène
Nyons
Buis-les-Baronnies
Ardèches Gorges
St. Cécile
Vaison-la-Romaine
Rhône
Rasteau
Séguret
Dentelles de Montmirail
Sablet
Orange
Gigondas
Malaucène
Vacqueyras
Suzette
Gard
Uzès
Châteauneuf-du-Pape
Beaumes-de-Venise
Mont Ventoux
To Gorges du Tarn
PONT DU GARD
Remoulins
Avignon
Isle-sur-la-Sorgue
Nîmes
Durance
Gordes
Joucas
Roussillon
Beaucaire
Tarascon
Oppède
Apt
Les Baux
St-Rémy
Cavaillon
LUBERON
Fontvieille
Arles
Alpilles
Lourmarin
Aigues-Mortes
CAMARGUE
Pertuis
Rhône
To Gorges du Verdon
Saintes-Maries-de-la-Mer
Aix-en-Provence
Petit Rhône
Palette
Martigues
To Nice & Côte d'Azur
Paris
FRANCE
Marseille
Aubagne
Mediterranean Sea
Les Calanques
Cassis
100 Miles
20 Kilometers
20 Miles

one night in a smaller town, such as Vaison-la-Romaine. Exploring the Côtes du Rhône wine country takes about a half-day, but you may want to linger.

Without a car: Explore Arles one day and take a minivan excursion the next. Or, if using public transit, visit Les Baux by bus from Arles on your first day, and on the second day, train to Avignon (for an overnight) and split your time between the town and Pont du Gard (reachable by bus).

PROVENCE AT A GLANCE

Arles

▲▲**Roman Arena** A big amphitheater, once used by gladiators, that hosts summer "bullgames" and occasional bullfights. **Hours:** Daily May-Sept 9:00-19:00, shorter hours off-season. See page 286.

▲▲**St. Trophime Church** Medieval church with exquisite Romanesque entrance. **Hours:** Daily 9:00-12:00 & 14:00-18:30, until 17:00 Oct-March. See page 288.

▲▲**Arlaten Folk Museum** Leading Provencal museum for traditional culture. Due to reopen soon after renovation is complete. **Hours:** Check with TI. See page 292.

▲▲**Ancient History Museum** Filled with models and sculptures, taking you back to Arles' Roman days. **Hours:** Wed-Mon 10:00-18:00, closed Tue. See page 292.

▲**Fondation Van Gogh** Small gallery with works by major contemporary artists paying homage to Van Gogh. **Hours:** Daily 11:00-19:00, July-Aug from 10:00, shorter hours and closed Mon off-season. See page 290.

Avignon

▲▲**Palace of the Popes** A 14th-century Gothic palace built by the popes who made Avignon their home. **Hours:** Daily 9:00-19:00, July-Aug until 20:00, Nov-Feb 9:30-17:45. See page 307.

▲**St. Bénezet Bridge** The "Pont d'Avignon" of nursery-rhyme fame, once connecting the pope's territory to France. **Hours:** Daily 9:00-19:00, July-Aug until 20:00, Nov-Feb 9:30-17:45. See page 306.

▲**Jardin du Rocher des Doms** View park overlooking the Rhône River Valley and Avignon's famous broken bridge. **Hours:** Daily 7:30-20:00, June-Aug until 21:00, Oct-March until 18:00. See page 303.

Nearby

▲▲▲**Pont du Gard** Part bridge and part aqueduct, a huge stone structure heralding the greatness of Rome. **Hours:** Aqueduct—daily May 9:00-21:00, June and Sept until 22:00, July-Aug until 23:00, Feb-April and Oct until 20:00, Nov-Jan until 18:00; museum—daily April-June and Sept 9:00-19:00, July-Aug until 20:00, Oct-Nov and March until 18:00, Dec-Feb until 17:00. See page 311.

▲▲▲**Les Baux** Rock-top village sitting in the shadow of its ruined medieval citadel. **Hours:** Castle—daily 9:00-19:00, July-Aug until 20:00, March and Oct 9:30-18:30, Nov-Feb 10:00-17:00. See page 313.

▲▲**Côtes du Rhône Wine Road Drive** A self-guided drive through picturesque villages and vineyards, unfurling along a scenic wine-tasting route. See page 322.

▲**Vaison-la-Romaine** History-rich town atop a 2,000-year-old Roman site. See page 317.

Getting Around Provence

By Car: The region is made to order for a car, although travel time between some sights will surprise you—thanks, in part, to narrow roads and endless roundabouts. Be wary of thieves: Park only in well-monitored spaces and leave nothing valuable in your car.

By Bus or Train: Frequent trains link Avignon and Arles. From Arles you can catch a bus to Les Baux (high season only). From Avignon, you can bus to Pont du Gard and Vaison-la-Romaine.

By Minivan Tour: Imagine Tours adapt to your interests and your guide can meet you at your hotel (€190/half-day, €315/day, prices for up to 4 people starting from near Avignon or Arles, mobile 06 89 22 19 87, www.imagine-tours.net, imagine.tours@gmail.com).

Visit Provence runs day tours from Arles, Avignon, and more. Tours provide introductory commentary, but no guiding at sights. They use eight-seat, air-conditioned minivans (per person: about €65-80/half-day, €100-125/day). Ask about their cheaper big-bus excursions, or consider hiring a van and driver for your private use (allow about €300/half-day, €500/day, tel. 04 90 14 70 00, www.provence-reservation.com).

Some tour companies focus on wine, such as **Wine Safari** (www.winesafari.net), **Le Vin à la Bouche** (www.levinalabouche.com), and **Avignon Wine Tour** (www.avignon-wine-tour.com).

ARLES

In Roman times, Arles (pronounced "arl") was an important port city. With the first bridge over the Rhône River, it was a key stop on the Roman road from Italy to Spain, the Via Domitia. After reigning as the seat of an important archbishop and a trading center for centuries, Arles became a sleepy backwater of little importance in the 1700s. Vincent van Gogh settled here in the late 1800s, but left only a chunk of his ear. American bombers destroyed much of Arles in World War II as the townsfolk hid out in its underground Roman galleries. But today Arles thrives again, with its evocative Roman Arena, an eclectic assortment of museums, made-for-ice-cream pedestrian zones, and squares that play hide-and-seek with visitors.

Workaday Arles is not a wealthy city and, compared to its neighbor Avignon, it feels unpolished and even a little dirty. But to me, that's part of its charm.

Rick's Tip: *For a helpful overview to your Arles sightseeing,* **start at the Ancient History Museum,** *then head to the city-center sights, linked by my Arles City Walk. Save money by getting one of the city's* **sightseeing passes,** *which cover the ancient monuments and the Ancient History Museum.*

Orientation

Though the town is built along the Rhône, it largely ignores the river. Landmarks hide in Arles' medieval tangle of narrow, winding streets. Hotels have good, free city maps, and helpful street-corner signs point you toward sights and hotels.

Tourist Information

The TI is on the ring road Boulevard des Lices, at Esplanade Charles de Gaulle (daily 9:00-18:45; Oct-March Mon-Sat 9:00-16:45, Sun 10:00-13:00; tel. 04 90 18 41 20, www.arlestourisme.com). The TI sells worthwhile city sightseeing passes.

Roman Arena

Helpful Hints

Sightseeing Passes: The good-value **Pass Liberté** (€12) covers any four monuments and one museum of your choice (I recommend the Ancient History Museum). The **Pass Avantage** (€16) covers all monuments and museums and is worthwhile if you visit two or more museums. Both passes offer a discount at the Fondation Van Gogh. Buy your pass at the TI or any included sight.

Rick's Tip: *In Arles, the* **ancient monuments**—*Roman Arena, Classical Theater, Cryptoporticos, and St. Trophime Cloisters*—**all have the same hours** *(daily 9:00-19:00, April and Oct until 18:00, Nov-March 10:00-17:00).*

Market Days: The big markets are on Wednesdays and Saturdays.

Baggage Storage and Bike Rental: Hôtel Régence will store your bags (€3/bag, daily 7:30-22:00, closed in winter, 5 Rue Marius Jouveau). They also rent bikes (€7/half-day, €15/day, one-way rentals within Provence possible, same hours as baggage storage).

Laundry: A launderette is at 41 Rue du 4 Septembre. Another is near the bus station at 34 Boulevard Georges Clemenceau. Both are open long hours daily.

Local Guides: Charming **Agnes Barrier** offers tours covering Van Gogh and Roman history (€145/3 hours, mobile 06 11 23 03 73, agnes.barrier@hotmail.fr). **Alice Vallat** offers tours of Arles' key sights several days a week (€25/person for 1.5-hour group tour, €145 for 3-hour private tour, mobile 06 74 01 22 54, www.guidearles.com, alice.vallat13@gmail.com).

Arles City Walk

The joy of Arles is how its compact core mixes ancient sights, Van Gogh memories, and a raw and real contemporary scene that is easily covered on foot. All dimensions of the city come together in this self-guided walk. If you enter the sights described (which I recommend, even if briefly), the walk will take most of a day.

Most sights on this walk are covered by the city's sightseeing passes—sold at the TI and included sights. To better understand the ancient sites along this route, visit the Ancient History Museum on the edge of town before taking this walk (see "Sights," later).

Rick's Tip: *While only the Ancient History Museum, Roman Arena, and Arlaten Folk Museum are important to enter, a* **Pass Advantage** *lets you pop into nearly everything.*

Background

The life and artistic times of Dutch artist **Vincent van Gogh** form a big part of Arles' draw, and the city does a fine job of highlighting its Van Gogh connection: Throughout town, about a dozen steel-and-concrete panels, or "easels," provide then-and-now comparisons of the paintings versus the current view.

In the dead of winter in 1888, 35-year-old Van Gogh left big-city Paris for Provence, hoping to jump-start his floundering career and social life. He was as inspired as he was lonely. Coming from the gray skies and flat lands of the north, Vincent was bowled over by everything Provençal—the sun, bright colors, rugged landscape, and raw people. For the next two years he painted furiously, cranking out a masterpiece every few days.

Of the 200-plus paintings that Van Gogh made in the south, none permanently resides in the city that so moved him (though one is usually on loan at the Fondation Van Gogh gallery, which we'll visit on this stroll). But walking the same streets he knew and seeing the places he painted, you can understand how Arles inspired him.

At the Café Van Gogh

Van Gogh "easels" throughout Arles pair the artist's paintings with actual views.

The Rules of Boules

The game of *boules*—also called *pétanque*—is the horseshoes of France. Invented here in the early 1900s, it's a social yet serious sport, and endlessly entertaining to watch—even more so if you understand the rules.

The game is played with heavy metal balls and a small wooden target ball called a *cochonnet* (piglet). Whoever gets his *boule* closest to the *cochonnet* is awarded points. Teams commonly have specialist players: a *pointeur* and a *tireur*. The *pointeur*'s goal is to lob his balls as close to the target as he can. The *tireur*'s job is to blast away opponents' *boules*.

In teams of two, each player gets three *boules*. The starting team traces a small circle in the dirt (in which players must stand when launching their *boules*), and tosses the *cochonnet* about 30 feet to establish the target. The *boule* must be thrown underhand, and can be rolled, launched sky-high, or rocketed at its target. The first *pointeur* shoots, then the opposing *pointeur* shoots until his *boule* gets closer. Once the second team lands a *boule* nearest the *cochonnet,* the first team goes again. If the other team's *boule* is very near the *cochonnet,* the *tireur* will likely attempt to knock it away.

Once all *boules* have been launched, the tally is taken. The team with a *boule* closest to the *cochonnet* wins the round, and they receive a point for each *boule* closer to the target than their opponents' nearest *boule*. The first team to get to 13 points wins. A regulation *boules* field is 10 feet by 43 feet, but the game is played everywhere—just scratch a throwing circle in the sand, toss the *cochonnet,* and you're off.

❍ Self-Guided Walk

• Start at the north gate of the city, just outside the medieval wall on Place Lamartine (100 yards in front of the medieval gate, with the big Monoprix store across the street to the right, beyond the roundabout). A four-foot-tall easel shows Van Gogh's painting.

❶ THE YELLOW HOUSE EASEL

Vincent arrived in Arles on February 20, 1888, to a foot of snow. He rented a small house here on the north side of Place Lamartine. The house was destroyed in 1944 by an errant bridge-seeking bomb, but the four-story building behind it still stands (find it in the painting). The house had four rooms, including a small studio and the cramped trapezoid-shaped bedroom made famous in his paintings. It was painted yellow inside and out, and Vincent named it…"The Yellow House." In

the distance, the painting shows the same bridges you see today.

• Walk to the river. You'll pass, on the right, a monument in honor of two WWII American pilots killed in action during the liberation of Arles; a post celebrating Arles' nine sister cities (left); and a big concrete high school (right).

At the river, find the easel in the wall where ramps lead down.

❷ STARRY NIGHT OVER THE RHONE EASEL

One night, Vincent set up his easel along the river and painted the stars boiling above the city skyline. Vincent looked to the night sky for the divine and was the first to paint outside after dark, adapting his straw hat to hold candles (which must have blown the minds of locals back then). As his paintings progressed, the stars became larger and more animated (like Vincent himself). The lone couple in

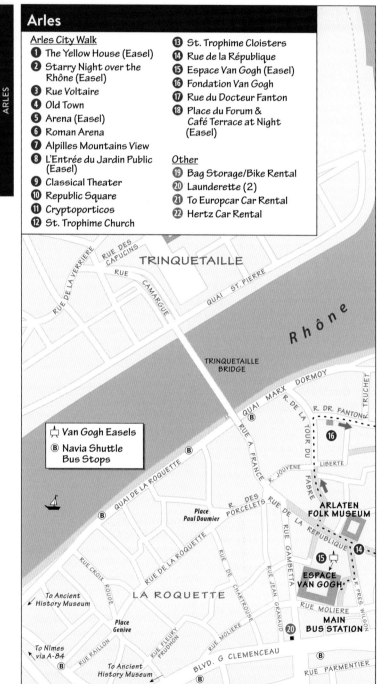

Arles

Arles City Walk

1. The Yellow House (Easel)
2. Starry Night over the Rhône (Easel)
3. Rue Voltaire
4. Old Town
5. Arena (Easel)
6. Roman Arena
7. Alpilles Mountains View
8. L'Entrée du Jardin Public (Easel)
9. Classical Theater
10. Republic Square
11. Cryptoporticos
12. St. Trophime Church
13. St. Trophime Cloisters
14. Rue de la République
15. Espace Van Gogh (Easel)
16. Fondation Van Gogh
17. Rue du Docteur Fanton
18. Place du Forum & Café Terrace at Night (Easel)

Other

19. Bag Storage/Bike Rental
20. Launderette (2)
21. To Europcar Car Rental
22. Hertz Car Rental

Van Gogh Easels

(B) Navia Shuttle Bus Stops

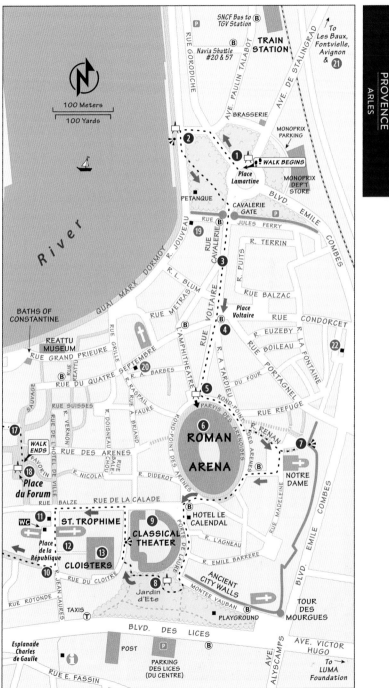

P

SNCF Bus to
TGV Station **B**

RUE GORODICHE

Navia Shuttle
#20 & 57 **B**

RUE PAULIN TALABOT

AVE. DE STALINGRAD

**TRAIN
STATION**

To
Les Baux,
Fontvieille,
Avignon
& **21**

BRASSERIE

MONOPRIX
PARKING

2

1

WALK BEGINS

**Place
Lamartine**

MONOPRIX
DEP'T
STORE

PETANQUE

CAVALERIE
GATE **B**

JULES FERRY

P

BLVD. EMILE COMBES

River

QUAI MARX DORMOY

RUE JOUVEAU

RUE CAVALERIE

19

R. TERRIN

R. PUITS

3

RUE BALZAC

R. L. BLUM

RUE METRAS

RUE VOLTAIRE

**Place
Voltaire**

B

4

R. EUZEBY

RUE BOILEAU

RUE CONDORCET

LA FONTAINE

BATHS OF
CONSTANTINE

REATTU
MUSEUM

RUE GRILLE

RUE GRAND PRIEURE

RUE DU QUATRE SEPTEMBRE

B

RUE REATTU

20

L'AMPHITHEATRE

R. A. BARDES

R. A. TARDIEU

DU FOUR

RUE PORTAGNEL

22

RUE DU QUATRE SEPTEMBRE

B

5

SAUVAGE

RUE SUISSES

R. VERNON

RUE DE L'HOTEL DE VILLE

R. DOISNEAU

R. FAURE

R. BRIAND

R. RASPAIL

PARVIS DES

ROND-POINT DES ARENOBES

RUE REFUGE

6

**ROMAN

ARENA**

R. RENAN

7

NOTRE
DAME

17

**WALK
ENDS**

18

**Place
du Forum**

RUE DES ARENES

R. DOISNEAU

R. CHOUL

R. NICOLAI

R. DIDEROT

ROND-POINT DES ARENES

DES ARENES

B

RUE MADELEINE

BLVD. EMILE COMBES

WC

11

RUE BALZE

RUE DE LA CALADE

B HOTEL LE
CALENDAL

ST. TROPHIME

9

**CLASSICAL
THEATER**

R. L'AGNEAU

12

13

CLOISTERS

10

RUE DU CLOITRE

**Place
de la
République**

8

Jardin
d'Ete

R. EMILE BARRERE

COTE DE L'OURE

MONTEE VAUBAN

**ANCIENT
CITY WALLS**

**TOUR
DES
MOURGUES**

RUE ROTONDE

R. JEAN JAURES

TAXIS **T**

PLAYGROUND **B**

BLVD. DES LICES

**Esplanade
Charles
de Gaulle**

i

POST

P

B

PARKING
DES LICES
(DU CENTRE)

RUE E. FASSIN

AVE. ALYSCAMPS

AVE. VICTOR
HUGO

To
LUMA
Foundation

100 Meters

100 Yards

the painting pops up again and again in his work. (Note: This painting is not the *Starry Night* you're probably thinking of—that one was painted later, in St-Rémy.)

• *With your back to the river, angle right through the scruffy park of plane trees (a kind of sycamore). Continue into town through the park and between the stumpy 14th-century stone towers where the city gates once stood. Walk a block up Rue de la Cavalerie to the decorative (if dry) fountain with the colorful old mosaic.*

❸ RUE VOLTAIRE

Van Gogh first walked into town down this street in 1888. When he saw this fountain, it was just a year old. Its mosaic celebrates the high culture of Provence (she's the winged woman who obviously loves music and reading). But this neighborhood was Arles' 19th-century red light district, and the far-from-home Dutchman spent many lonely nights in its bars and brothels. This street still has a certain edgy local color, with humble shops, bars, and bakeries.

• *Stay left and keep walking to Place Voltaire, a center of this working-class neighborhood (the local Communist Party headquarters is across the square on the left). Stop at the top end of the square under the plane tree in front of Brasserie le Pitchounet.*

❹ OLD TOWN

You've left the bombed-out part of town and entered the old town, with buildings predating World War II. The stony white arches of the ancient Roman Arena ahead mark your destination. As you hike up Rue Voltaire, notice the shutters, which contribute to Arles' character. The old town is strictly protected: These traditional shutters come in a variety of styles but cannot be changed.

• *Keep straight up Rue Voltaire, climb to the Roman Arena, and find the Arena easel at the top of the stairs, to the right.*

❺ ARENA EASEL

All summer long, fueled by sun and alcohol, Vincent painted the town. He loved the bullfights in the arena and sketched the colorful surge of the crowds, spending more time studying the people than watching the bullfights (notice how the bull is barely visible). Vincent had little interest in Arles' antiquity—it was people and nature that fascinated him.

• *At this point you can visit the Roman Arena.*

Arles' old town

Inside the Roman Arena

The Romans in Provence

Many scholars claim the best-preserved ancient Roman buildings are not in Italy, but in France. These ancient stones will be an important part of your sightseeing agenda.

Classical Rome endured from about 500 BC through AD 500—spending about 500 years growing, 200 years peaking, and 300 years declining. Julius Caesar conquered Gaul—which included Provence—during the Gallic Wars (58-51 BC), then crossed the Rubicon River in 49 BC to incite civil war within the Roman Republic. He erected a temple to Jupiter on the future site of Paris' Notre-Dame Cathedral.

The concept of one-man rule lived on with his grandnephew, Octavian (whom he had also adopted as his son). Octavian took the title "Augustus" and became the first in a line of emperors who would control Rome for the next 500 years. Rome morphed from a Republic into an Empire: a collection of many diverse territories ruled by a single man. At its peak (c. AD 117), the Roman Empire had 54 million people—"Rome" didn't just refer to the city, but to the entire civilized Western world.

Provence, with its strategic location, benefited greatly from Rome's global economy and grew to become an important part of its worldwide empire. After Julius Caesar conquered Gaul, Emperor Augustus Romanized it, building and renovating cities in the image of Rome.

When it came to construction, the Romans' magic building ingredient was concrete. Easier to work than stone and longer lasting than wood, concrete served as flooring, roofing, filler, glue, and support. Builders would start with a foundation of brick, then fill it in with poured concrete. They would then cover important structures, such as basilicas, in sheets of expensive marble (held on with nails), or decorate floors and walls with mosaics.

Most cities had a theater, baths, and aqueducts; the most important cities had sports arenas. A typical Roman city (such as Arles) was a garrison town, laid out on a grid plan with two main roads: one running north-south (the *cardus*), the other east-west (the *decumanus*). Approaching the city on your chariot, you'd pass by the cemetery, which was located outside of town for hygienic reasons. You'd enter the main gate and wheel past warehouses and apartment houses to the town square (forum). Facing the square were the most important temples, dedicated to the patron gods of the city. Nearby, you'd find bathhouses; like today's fitness clubs, these served the almost sacred dedication to personal vigor. Also close by were businesses that catered to the citizens' needs: the marketplace, bakeries, banks, and brothels. Aqueducts brought fresh water for drinking, filling the baths, and delighting the citizens with bubbling fountains.

❻ ROMAN ARENA (AMPHITHEATRE)

This well-preserved arena is worth ▲▲ and is still in use today. Nearly 2,000 years ago, gladiators fought wild animals to the delight of 20,000 screaming fans. Now local daredevils still fight wild animals here—"bullgame" posters around the arena advertise upcoming spectacles.

Cost and Hours: €9 combo-ticket with Classical Theater; daily 9:00-19:00, April and Oct until 18:00, Nov-March 10:00-17:00, Rond-point des Arènes, tel. 04 90 49 36 86, www.arenes-arles.com.

Visiting the Arena: After passing the ticket kiosk, find the helpful English display under the second arch, where you can read about the arena's history and renovation. Then climb up and take a seat in the theater. Thirty-four rows of stone bleachers extended all the way to the top of those vacant arches that circle the arena. All arches were numbered to help distracted fans find their seats. The many passageways you'll see (called vomitoires) allowed for rapid dispersal after the games—fights would break out among frenzied fans if they couldn't leave quickly.

Throughout medieval times and until the early 1800s, the stadium became a fortified town with towers added, arches bricked up, and 200 humble homes crammed within its circular defenses. Parts of three of the medieval **towers** survive.

To climb one of the towers and enjoy magnificent **views** over Arles and the arena, find the *"To the Tower"* sign near the ticket booth and exit.

• *Exit at street level and turn right, and after a quarter of the way around, turn left (where the metal fence ends and you hit the little street). Go up the cute stepped lane (Rue Renan). Take three steps and turn around to study the arena.*

The big stones are Roman; the little medieval stones—more like rubble—filling the two upper-level archways are a reminder of the arena's time as a fortified town in the Middle Ages. You can even see rooflines and beam holes where

The well-preserved Roman Arena

the Roman structure provided a solid foundation to lean on.

• *Hike up the pretty, stepped lane through the parking lot, keeping to the left of the stark and stony church to the highest point in Arles. Take in the countryside view.*

❼ ALPILLES MOUNTAINS VIEW

This view pretty much matches what Vincent van Gogh, an avid walker, would have seen. Imagine him hauling his easel into those fields under intense sun, leaning against a ferocious wind, struggling to keep his hat on. Vincent carried his easel as far as the medieval Abbey of Montmajour, that bulky structure on the hill in the distance. The St. Paul Hospital, where he was eventually treated in St-Rémy, is on the other side of the Alpilles mountains, several miles beyond Montmajour.

• *Cross in front of the church to return to the arena, and continue circling it clockwise. At the high point, turn left and walk out Rue de Porte de Laure. (You'll pass the ancient Classical Theater on your right, which we'll visit later.) After a couple of blocks, go right, down the curved staircase into the park. Continue toward the busy street. Take the second right (through the gate and into the park) and find the...*

❽ L'ENTREE DU JARDIN PUBLIC EASEL

Vincent spent many a sunny day painting in the leafy Jardin d'Eté. In another letter to his sister, Vincent wrote, "I don't know whether you can understand that one may make a poem by arranging colors...In a similar manner, the bizarre lines, purposely selected and multiplied, meandering all through the picture may not present a literal image of the garden, but they may present it to our minds as if in a dream."

• *Hike through the park and uphill toward the three-story surviving tower of the Classical Theater. At the ancient tower, follow the white metal fence to the left, enjoying peeks at "le jardin" of stone—a collection of carved bits of a once-grand Roman theater. Go up four steps and around to the right for a fine view of the...*

❾ CLASSICAL THEATER (THEATRE ANTIQUE)

This first-century BC Roman theater once seated 10,000. There was no hillside to provide structural support; instead, this elegant, three-level arena had 27 buttress arches radiating out behind the seats.

Cost and Hours: €9 combo-ticket with Roman Arena, same hours as Arena.

Visiting the Theater: Start with the 10-minute video, which provides background information that makes it easier to imagine the scattered stones back in place (crouch in front to make out the small English subtitles).

Then walk into the theater and pull up a stone seat in a center aisle. Imagine that for 500 years, ancient Romans gathered here for entertainment. The original structure was much higher, with 33 rows of seats covering three levels to accommodate demand. During the Middle Ages, the old theater became a convenient town quarry—much of St. Trophime Church was built from theater rubble. Precious little of the original theater survives—though it still is used for events, with seating for 2,000 spectators.

• *From the theater, walk downhill on Rue de la Calade. Take the first left into a big square.*

❿ REPUBLIC SQUARE (PLACE DE LA REPUBLIQUE)

This square used to be called "Place Royale"...until the French Revolution. The obelisk was the former centerpiece of Arles' Roman Circus (outside of town). The lions at its base are the symbol of the city, whose slogan is (roughly) "the gentle lion." Observe the age-old scene: tourists, peasants, shoppers, pilgrims, children, and street musicians. The City Hall (Hôtel

Classical Theater

de Ville) has a stately facade, built in the same generation as Versailles. Where there's a City Hall, there's always a free WC (if you win the Revolution, you can pee for free at the mayor's home). Notice the flags: The yellow-and-red of Provence is the same as the yellow-and-red of Catalunya, its linguistic cousin in Spain.

• *Today's City Hall sits upon an ancient city center. Inside, find the entrance to an ancient cryptoportico (foundation).*

⓫ CRYPTOPORTICOS (CRYPTOPORTIQUES)

This dark, drippy underworld of Roman arches was constructed to support the upper half of Forum Square. Two thousand years ago, most of this gallery of arches was at or above street level; modern Arles has buried about 20 feet of its history over the millennia. Through the tiny windows high up you would have seen the sandals of Romans on their way to the forum. Other than dark arches and broken bits of forum littering the dirt floor, there's not much down here beyond ancient memories (€4.50, same hours as Arena).

• *The highlight of Place de la République is...*

⓬ ST. TROPHIME CHURCH

Named after a third-century bishop of Arles, this church, worth ▲▲, sports the finest Romanesque main entrance I've seen anywhere. The Romanesque and Gothic interior—with tapestries, relics, and a rare painting from the French Revolution when this was a "Temple of Reason"—is worth a visit.

Cost and Hours: Free, daily 9:00-12:00 & 14:00-18:30, Oct-March until 17:00.

Exterior: Like a Roman triumphal arch, the church **facade** trumpets the promise of Judgment Day. The tympanum (the semicircular area above the door) is filled with Christian symbolism. Christ sits in majesty, surrounded by symbols of the four evangelists: Matthew (the winged man), Mark (the winged lion), Luke (the ox), and John (the eagle). The 12 apostles are lined up below Jesus. It's Judgment

Day...some are saved and others aren't. Notice the condemned (on the right)—a chain gang doing a sad bunny-hop over the fires of hell. For them, the tune trumpeted by the three angels above Christ is not a happy one. Below the chain gang, St. Stephen is being stoned to death, with his soul leaving through his mouth and instantly being welcomed by angels. Study the exquisite detail. In an illiterate world, this was colorfully painted, like a neon billboard over the town square. It's full of meaning, and a medieval pilgrim understood it all.

Interior: Just inside the door on the right, a yellow chart locates the interior highlights and helps explain the carvings you just saw on the tympanum. The tall 12th-century Romanesque nave is decorated by a set of tapestries (typical in the Middle Ages) showing scenes from the life of Mary (17th century, from the French town of Aubusson).

This church is a stop on the ancient pilgrimage route to Santiago de Compostela in northwest Spain. For 800 years pilgrims on their way to Santiago have paused here...and they still do today. Notice the modern-day pilgrimages advertised on the far right near the church's entry.

• *To reach the adjacent peaceful cloister, leave the church, turn left, then left again through a courtyard.*

⓭ ST. TROPHIME CLOISTERS

Worth seeing if you have an Arles sightseeing pass (otherwise €5.50, same hours as Arena), the cloisters' many small columns were scavenged from the ancient Roman theater and used to create an oasis of peace in Arles' center. Enjoy the delicate, sculpted capitals, the rounded Romanesque arches (12th century), and the pointed Gothic ones (14th century). The pretty vaulted hall exhibits 17th-century tapestries showing scenes from the First Crusade to the Holy Land. There's an instructive video and a chance to walk outside along an angled rooftop designed

St. Trophime Church

to catch rainwater: Notice the slanted gutter that channeled the water into a cistern and the heavy roof slabs covering the tapestry hall below.

• *From Place de la République, exit on the far corner (opposite the church and kitty-corner from where you entered) to stroll a delightful pedestrian street.*

⓮ RUE DE LA REPUBLIQUE

Rue da la République is Arles' primary shopping street. Walk downhill, enjoying the scene and popping into shops that catch your interest.

Near the start is **Maison Soulier Bakery.** Inside you'll be tempted by *fougasse* (bread studded with herbs, olives, and bacon bits), *sablés Provençal* (cookies made with honey and almonds), *tarte lavande* (a sweet almond lavender tart), and big crispy meringues. A few doors down is **Restaurant L'Atelier** (with two prized Michelin stars), **L'Occitane en Provence** (local perfumes), **Puyricard Chocolate** (with enticing €1 treats and *calisson,* a sweet almond delight), as well as local design and antique shops. The

fragile spiral columns on the left (just before the tourist-pleasing Lavender Boutique on the corner) show what 400 years of weather can do to decorative stonework. The big Arlaten Folk Museum is up on the right.

• *Take the first left onto Rue Président Wilson. Just after the butcher shop, turn right to find the* **Hôtel Dieu,** *a hospital made famous by one of its patients: Vincent van Gogh.*

⓯ ESPACE VAN GOGH EASEL

In December 1888, shortly after his famous ear-cutting incident (see *Café Terrace at Night* easel, described later), Vincent was admitted into the local hospital—today's Espace Van Gogh cultural center. It surrounds a flowery courtyard (open to the public) that the artist loved and painted when he was being treated for blood loss, hallucinations, and severe depression that left him bedridden for a month. The citizens of Arles circulated a petition demanding that the mad Dutchman be kept under medical supervision. Félix Rey, Vincent's kind doctor, worked out a compromise:

The artist could leave during the day so that he could continue painting, but he had to sleep at the hospital at night. Look through the postcards sold in the courtyard and find a painting of Vincent's ward showing nuns attending to patients in a gray hall (*Ward of Arles Hospital*).

• *Return to Rue de la République. Take a left and continue two blocks downhill. Take the second right up Rue Tour de Fabre and follow signs to Fondation Van Gogh. After a few steps, you'll pass* **La Main Qui Pense** (*The Hand That Thinks*) *pottery shop. A couple of blocks farther down, turn right onto Rue du Docteur Fanton. On your immediate right is the...*

⑯ FONDATION VAN GOGH

This art foundation, worth ▲, delivers a refreshing stop for modern-art lovers and Van Gogh fans, with two temporary exhibits per year in which contemporary artists pay homage to Vincent with thought-provoking interpretations of his works. You'll also see at least one original work by Van Gogh (painted during his time in the region).

Cost and Hours: €9, discount with sightseeing passes; daily 11:00-19:00, July-Aug from 10:00, Oct-March until 17:45, closed Mon off-season; audioguide-€3, 35 Rue du Docteur Fanton, tel. 04 90 49 94 04, www.fondation-vincentvangogh-arles.org.

• *Continue on Rue du Docteur Fanton.*

⑰ RUE DU DOCTEUR FANTON

A string of recommended restaurants is on the left. On the right is the **Crèche**

Municipale. Open workdays, this is a free, government-funded daycare where parents can drop off their infants up to two years old. The notion: No worker should face financial hardship in order to receive quality childcare. At the next corner is the recommended **Soleileïs,** Arles' top ice cream shop.

After the ice cream shop, turn right and step into **Bar El Paseo** at 4 Rue des Thermes, which is run by the Leal family, famous for its bullfighters. The main museum-like room is full of bull—including the mounted heads of three big ones who died in the local arena and a big black-and-white photo of Arles' arena packed to capacity. You're welcome to look around...and to buy a glass of Spanish Rioja wine or sangria.

• *A few steps farther is...*

⑱ FORUM SQUARE (PLACE DU FORUM) AND CAFE TERRACE AT NIGHT EASEL

Named for the Roman forum that once stood here, **Forum Square,** worth ▲, was the political and religious center of Roman Arles. Still lively, this café-crammed square is a local watering hole and popular for a *pastis* (anise-based aperitif). The bistros on the square can put together a passable salad or *plat du jour*—and when you sprinkle on the ambience, that's €14 well spent.

At the corner of Grand Hôtel Nord-Pinus, a plaque shows how the Romans built a foundation of galleries to make the main square level in order to compensate for Arles' slope down to the river. The two columns are all that survive from the

Fondation Van Gogh

A café on Forum Square

upper story of the entry to the forum.

The statue on the square is of **Frédéric Mistral** (1830-1914). This popular poet, who wrote in the local dialect rather than in French, was a champion of Provençal culture. After receiving the Nobel Prize in Literature in 1904, Mistral used his prize money to preserve and display the folk identity of Provence. He founded a regional folk museum (the Arlaten Folk Museum) at a time when France was rapidly centralizing and regions like Provence were losing their unique identities. (The local mistral wind has nothing to do with his name.)

• *Facing the brightly painted yellow café, find your final Van Gogh easel—***Café Terrace at Night.**

In October 1888, lonely Vincent—who dreamed of making Arles a magnet for fellow artists—persuaded his friend Paul Gauguin to come. He decorated Gauguin's room with several humble canvases of sunflowers (now some of the world's priciest paintings), knowing that Gauguin had admired a similar painting he'd done in Paris. Their plan was for Gauguin to be the "dean" of a new art school in Arles, and Vincent its instructor-in-chief. At first, the two got along well. They spent days side by side, rendering the same subjects in their two distinct styles. At night they hit the bars and brothels. Van Gogh's well-known *Café Terrace at Night* captures the glow of an absinthe buzz at Café la Nuit on Place du Forum.

After two months together, the two artists clashed over art and personality differences (Vincent was a slob around the house, whereas Gauguin was meticulous). The night of December 23, they were drinking absinthe at the café when Vincent suddenly went ballistic. He threw his glass at Gauguin. Gauguin left. Walking through Place Victor Hugo, Gauguin heard footsteps behind him and turned to see Vincent coming at him, brandishing a razor. Gauguin quickly fled town. The local paper reported what

happened next: "At 11:30 p.m., Vincent van Gogh, painter from Holland, appeared at the brothel at no. 1, asked for Rachel, and gave her his cut-off earlobe, saying, 'Treasure this precious object.' Then he vanished." He woke up the next morning at home with his head wrapped in a bloody towel and his earlobe missing.

The **bright-yellow café**—called Café la Nuit—was the subject of one of Vincent van Gogh's most famous works in Arles. Although his painting showed the café in a brilliant yellow from the glow of gas lamps, the facade was bare limestone. The café is now a tourist trap that its current owners painted to match Van Gogh's version...and to cash in on the Vincent-crazed hordes who pay too much to eat or drink here.

In spring 1889, the bipolar genius (a modern diagnosis) checked himself into the St. Paul Monastery and Hospital in St-Rémy-de-Provence. He spent a year there, thriving in the care of nurturing doctors and nuns. Painting was part of his therapy, so they gave him a studio to work in, and he produced more than 100 paintings. Alcohol-free and institutionalized, he did some of his wildest work. With thick, swirling brushstrokes and surreal colors, he made his placid surroundings throb with restless energy.

Eventually, Vincent's torment became unbearable. In the spring of 1890, he left Provence to be cared for by a sympathetic doctor in Auvers-sur-Oise, just north of Paris. On July 27, he wandered into a field and shot himself. He died two days later.

• *With this walk, you've seen most of Arles' top sights. The Arlaten Folk Museum is a short walk away; the Ancient History Museum is on the outskirts (both described next). But first, enjoy a drink on the Place du Forum and savor the joy of experiencing the essence of Provence.*

Sights

Many of Arles' city-center sights (such as the Roman Arena and St. Trophime church) are covered on my self-guided walk. Two more sights are worth your time; the first is central, the second is away from the center.

▲▲ARLATEN FOLK MUSEUM (MUSEON ARLATEN)

This is the leading museum in Provence for traditional culture and folklore. After a long closure for renovation, it should be open by the time you visit and is expected to resume its place as one of the top attractions in Arles.

Cost and Hours: Scheduled to reopen soon—check ahead for price and opening hours. Tel. 04 13 31 51 99, www.museon-arlaten.fr.

▲▲ANCIENT HISTORY MUSEUM (MUSEE DEPARTEMENTAL ARLES ANTIQUE)

This museum, just west of central Arles along the river, provides valuable background on Arles' Roman history: Visit it first, before delving into the rest of the city's sights (drivers should stop on the way into town).

Located on the site of the Roman chariot racecourse (the arc of which defines today's parking lot), this air-conditioned, all-on-one-floor museum is full of models and original sculptures that re-create the Roman city, making workaday life and culture easier to imagine.

While the museum's posted descriptions of most of its treasures are only in French, the audioguide does a fine job describing the exhibits in English. For a deeper understanding of Provence's ancient roots, read "The Romans in Provence," earlier.

Cost and Hours: €8, free first Sun of the month, Wed-Mon 10:00-18:00, closed Tue, audioguide-€2, Presqu'île du Cirque Romain, tel. 04 13 31 51 03.

Getting There: Drivers will see signs for the museum at the city's western end. To reach the museum from the city center sans car, take the free **Navia shuttle** (see "Getting Around Arles" under "Transportation," later). The museum is about a 20-minute **walk** from the city center; a **taxi** ride costs about €12.

Visiting the Museum: The permanent

Model of Arles' Classical Theater

collection is housed in a large hall flooded with natural light. Highlights include models of the ancient city and its major landmarks, a 2,000-year-old Roman boat, statues, mosaics, and sarcophagi. Here's what you'll see.

A wall **map** of the region during the Roman era greets visitors and shows the geographic importance of Arles: Three important Roman trade routes—vias Domitia, Grippa, and Aurelia—all converged on or near Arles.

After a small exhibit on pre-Roman Arles you'll come to fascinating **models of the Roman city** and the impressive Roman structures in (and near) Arles. These breathe life into the buildings, showing how they looked 2,000 years ago.

Start with the **model of Roman Arles** and ponder the city's splendor when Arles' population was almost double that of today. Find the forum—it's still the center of town, although only two columns survive (the smaller section of the forum is where today's Place du Forum is built). The next model shows the grandeur of the forum in greater detail.

At the museum's center stands the original **statue of Julius Caesar,** which once graced Arles' ancient theater's magnificent stage wall. To the left of Julius, find a **model of Arles' theater** and its wall, as well as models of the ancient town's other major buildings. Find the arena with its movable cover to shelter spectators from sun or rain, the floating wooden bridge over the widest, slowest part of the river—giving Arles a strategic advantage, and the hydraulic mill of Barbegal with its 16 waterwheels cascading water down a hillside.

Step down into the hall to Julius's right and find the large model of the **chariot racecourse.** Part of the original racecourse was just outside the windows, and although long gone, it likely resembled Rome's Circus Maximus. The rest of this hall is dedicated to the museum's newest and most exciting exhibit: a **Gallo-Roman**

vessel and much of its cargo (English translations on panels). This almost-100-foot-long Roman barge was hauled out of the Rhône in 2010, along with some 280 amphorae and 3,000 ceramic artifacts. It was typical of flat-bottomed barges used to shuttle goods between Arles and ports along the Mediterranean (vessels were manually towed upriver). This one hauled limestone slabs and big rocks—no wonder it sank. A worthwhile 20-minute video about the barge's recovery (with English subtitles) plays continuously in a tiny theater at the end of the hall.

Elsewhere in the museum, you'll see displays of pottery, jewelry, metal, and glass artifacts. You'll also see well-crafted mosaic floors that illustrate how Roman Arles was a city of art and culture. The many **statues** are all original, except for the greatest—the *Venus of Arles,* which Louis XIV took a liking to and had moved to Versailles.

Experiences
▲▲MARKETS

Provençal market days offer France's most colorful and tantalizing outdoor shopping. On Wednesday and Saturday mornings, Arles' ring road erupts into an open-air festival of fish, flowers, produce...and everything Provençal. The main event is on Saturday, with vendors jamming the ring road from Boulevard Emile Combes to the east, along Boulevard des Lices near the TI (the heart of the market),

Wednesday and Saturday are Arles' market days.

and continuing down Boulevard Georges Clemenceau to the west. Wednesday's market runs only along Boulevard Emile Combes, between Place Lamartine and Avenue Victor Hugo; the segment nearest Place Lamartine is all about food, and the upper half features clothing, tablecloths, purses, and so on. On the first Wednesday of the month, a flea market doubles the size of the usual Wednesday market along Boulevard des Lices near the TI. Both markets are open until about 12:30.

▲▲BULLGAMES (COURSES CAMARGUAISES)

Provençal "bullgames" are held in Arles and in neighboring towns. Those in Arles occupy the same seats that fans have used for nearly 2,000 years, and deliver the city's most memorable experience—the *courses camarguaises* in the ancient arena. The nonviolent bullgames are more sporting than bloody bullfights (though traditional Spanish-style bullfights still take place on occasion). The bulls of Arles (who, locals insist, "die of old age") are promoted in posters even more boldly than their human foes. In the bullgame, a ribbon (*cocarde*) is laced between the bull's horns. The *razeteur*, dressed in white and carrying a special hook, has 15 minutes to snare the ribbon. Local businessmen encourage a *razeteur* by shouting out how much money they'll pay for the *cocarde*. If the bull pulls a good stunt, the band plays the famous "Toreador" song from *Carmen*. The following day, newspapers report on the games, including how many *Carmens* the bull earned.

Three classes of bullgames—determined by the experience of the *razeteurs*—are advertised in posters: The *Course de Protection* is for rookies. The *Trophée de l'Avenir* comes with more experience. And the *Trophée des As* features top professionals. During Easter (*Féria de Pâques*) and the fall rice-harvest festival (*Féria du Riz*), the arena hosts traditional Spanish bullfights (look for *corrida*) with outfits, swords, spikes, and the whole gory shebang. (Nearby villages stage *courses camarguaises* in small wooden bullrings nearly every weekend; TIs have the latest schedule.)

Bulls are not harmed in Provençal-style "bullgames."

Provence's Cuisine Scene

The almost extravagant use of garlic, olive oil, herbs, and tomatoes makes Provence's cuisine France's liveliest. To sample it, order anything *à la provençale*. Among the area's spicy specialties are **ratatouille** (a mixture of vegetables in a thick, herb-flavored tomato sauce), **aioli** (a rich, garlicky mayonnaise spread over vegetables, potatoes, fish, or whatever), **tape-
nade** (a paste of pureed olives, capers, anchovies, herbs, and sometimes tuna), *soupe au pistou* (thin yet flavorful vegetable soup with a sauce of basil, garlic, and cheese), and *soupe à l'ail* (garlic soup, called *aigo bouido* in the local dialect). Look for *riz de Camargue* (reddish, chewy, nutty-tasting rice) and *taureau* (bull's meat). The native goat cheeses are *banon de banon* or *banon à la feuille* (dipped in brandy and wrapped in chestnut leaves) and spicy *picodon*. Don't miss the region's prized **Cavaillon melons** (cantaloupes) or its delicious cherries and apricots (often turned into jams and candied fruits).

Wines of Provence: Provence produces some of France's great wines at relatively reasonable prices. Look for wines from **Gigondas, Rasteau, Cairanne, Beaumes-de-Venise, Vacqueyras,** and **Châteauneuf-du-Pape.** For the cheapest but still tasty wines, look for labels showing **Côtes du Rhône Villages** or **Côtes de Provence.** If you like rosé, you win. **Rosés from Tavel** are considered among the best in Provence. For reds, splurge for Châteauneuf-du-Pape or Gigondas, and for a fine aperitif wine or a dessert wine, try the **Muscat** from **Beaumes-de-Venise.**

Bullgame tickets usually run €11-20; bullfights are pricier (€36-100). Schedules for bullgames vary (usually July-Aug on Wed and Fri)—ask at the TI or check www.arenes-arles.com.

BOULES

The local *"bouling* alleys" are by the Alyscamps necropolis (a block outside the ring road and sometimes by the river on Place Lamartine). Watch the old boys congregate for a game of *pétanque* after their afternoon naps (see "The Rules of *Boules"* sidebar in the "Arles City Walk," earlier, for more on this popular local pastime).

Eating

You can dine well in Arles on a modest budget (most of my listings have *menus* for under €25). Sunday is a quiet night for restaurants, though eateries on Place du Forum are open. For a portable snack, try Maison Soulier Bakery (see "Arles City Walk," earlier), and for groceries, use the big Monoprix supermarket/department store on Place Lamartine (closed Sun).

Rick's Tip: *Cafés on the Place du Forum deliver great atmosphere and fair prices (at Le Tambourin and Mon Bar Brasserie), but mediocre food.* **Avoid the garish yellow tourist trap Café la Nuit.** *For serious cuisine, wander away from the square.*

For Lunch or a Light Dinner

$ Cuisine de Comptoir, just off Place du Forum, offers light and cheap dinners of *tartine*—a cross between pizza and bruschetta, served with soup or salad for €11—and offers a fun array of pizza-style *tartine* toppings. This Provençal answer to a pizzeria, run by Vincent, has indoor seating only (closed Sun, off lower end of square at 10 Rue de la Liberté, tel. 04 90 96 86 28).

$ Café Factory République is a youthful, creative, and fun-loving place run by jovial Gilles. He's fun to talk with and serves sandwiches, hearty salads, and a wide variety of drinks. While not really a dinner place, he takes orders until 18:00 (Mon-Sat 8:00-19:00, closed Sun, 35 Rue de la République, tel. 04 90 54 52 23, skinniest WC in France).

$ Le Comptoir du Calendal, in the recommended Hôtel le Calendal, serves light, seasonal fare either curbside overlooking the arena, in its lovely courtyard, or inside the café—order at the counter (delicious and cheap little sandwiches and salads, daily 8:00-20:00, guest computer available, 5 Rue Porte de Laure, tel. 04 90 96 11 89).

Finer Dining

One of France's most recognized chefs, Jean-Luc Rabanel, runs two very different places 50 yards from Place de la République. They sit side by side at 7 Rue des Carmes.

$$$$ L'Atelier is a top-end place with two Michelin stars (contemporary tasting menus only—around €125, closed Mon-Tue, tel. 04 90 91 07 69). And next door is **$$$ A Côté,** a place with all the quality, none of the pretense, and meals at a fraction of the price. It offers a smart wine bar/bistro ambience and fine cuisine. This is a wonderful opportunity to sample the famous chef's talents with the €32 three-course menu (limited selection of wines by the glass, closed Mon-Tue, tel. 04 90 47 61 13, www.rabanel.com).

$$ Le Criquet, possibly the best value in Arles, is a sweet little place two blocks above the arena, serving well-presented and delicious Provençal classics with joy at good prices. Sisters Lili and Charlotte serve while mama and papa run the kitchen. Their mouthwatering €25 *bourride* is the house specialty: a creamy fish soup thickened with aioli and lots of garlic and stuffed with mussels, clams, calamari, and more. They have a lovely dining room and a petite terrace (closed Sun and Wed, 21 Rue Porte de Laure, tel. 04 90 96 80 51).

On Rue du Docteur Fanton

$$$ Le Galoubet is a popular local spot, blending a warm interior, traditional French cuisine, and gregarious service, thanks to owner Frank. It's the most expensive and least flexible place on the street, serving *menus* only. If it's cold, a roaring fire keeps you toasty (closed Sun-Mon, great fries and desserts, at #18, tel. 04 90 93 18 11).

$$ Les Filles du 16 is a warm, affordable place to enjoy a good Provençal two- or three-course dinner. The choices, while tasty, are limited, so check the selection before sitting down (closed Sat-Sun, at #16, tel. 04 90 93 77 36).

$$ Le Plaza la Paillotte buzzes with happy diners enjoying delicious, well-presented Provençal cuisine. Attentive owners Stéphane and Graziela (he cooks, she serves) welcome diners with a comfortable terrace and a smart interior (open daily, at #28, tel. 04 90 96 33 15).

Ice Cream: At **Soleileïs,** Marijtje scoops up fine ice cream made with organic milk, fresh fruit, all-natural ingredients, and creative flavors that fit the season. There's also a shelf of English books for exchange (daily 14:00-18:30, closed in winter, at #9).

Sleeping

Hotels are a great value here—most are air-conditioned, though few have elevators.

$$ Hôtel le Calendal*** is a service-with-a-smile place ideally located between the Roman Arena and Classical Theater. The hotel opens to the street with airy lounges and a lovely palm-shaded courtyard. You'll find snacks and drinks in the café/sandwich bar (daily 8:00-20:00). The soothing rooms show a modern flair and come in all shapes and sizes (some with balcony, family rooms, air-con, free spa for adults, ask about parking deals, 5 Rue Porte de Laure, tel. 04 90 96 11 89, www.lecalendal.com, contact@lecalendal.com).

$ Hôtel du Musée** is a quiet, affordable manor-home hideaway tucked deep in Arles (if driving, call the hotel from the street—they'll open the barrier so you can drive in to drop off your bags). This delightful place comes with 29 tasteful rooms, a flowery courtyard, and comfortable lounges. Lighthearted Claude and English-speaking Laurence are good hosts (family rooms, no elevator, pay parking garage, follow *Réattu Museum* signs to 11 Rue du Grand Prieuré, tel. 04 90 93 88 88, www.hoteldumusee.com, contact@hoteldumusee.com).

$ Hôtel de la Muette** is an intimate, good-value hotel located in a quiet corner of Arles, run by hard-working owners Brigitte and Alain. Its sharp rooms and bathrooms come with tiled floors and stone walls (RS%, family rooms, no elevator, pay private garage, 15 Rue des Suisses, tel. 04 90 96 15 39, www.hotel-muette.com, hotel.muette@wanadoo.fr).

Rick's Tip: *An international photo event* **jams hotels in Arles the second weekend of July,** *while the twice-yearly Féria* **draws crowds over Easter and in mid-September.**

$ Hôtel Régence** is a top budget deal with a riverfront location, comfortable, Provençal rooms, and easy parking. And it's just a 10-minute walk from the train station (family rooms, choose river-view or quieter courtyard rooms, no elevator; from Place Lamartine, turn right after passing between towers to reach 5 Rue Marius Jouveau; tel. 04 90 96 39 85, www.hotel-regence.com, contact@hotel-regence.com). Gentle Valérie and Eric speak English.

$ Hôtel Acacias*** sits just off Place Lamartine and inside the old city walls. It's a modern hotel with small, clean, and comfortable rooms (family rooms, air-con, pay parking garage, 2 Rue de la Cavalerie, tel. 04 90 96 37 88, https://hotel-arles.brithotel.fr, arles@brithotel.fr).

Transportation
Getting Around Arles

In this flat city, everything's within **walking** distance. Only the Ancient History Museum is far enough out to consider a shuttle or taxi ride. The riverside promenade provides a scenic and direct stroll to the Ancient History Museum (as well as to the train station).

The free **Navia shuttle** circles the town, stopping at the train station and along Rue du 4 Septembre, then along the river. It's useful for access to hotels and the Ancient History Museum (2/hour, Mon-Sat 7:00-19:00, none Sun).

Arles' **taxis** charge a set fee of about €12, but nothing except the Ancient History Museum is worth a taxi ride. To call a cab, dial 04 90 96 52 76.

Arriving and Departing

Compare train and bus schedules: For some nearby destinations the bus may be the better choice, and it's usually cheaper.

BY TRAIN

The train station is on the river, a 10-minute walk from the town center. For baggage storage, see "Helpful Hints," earlier (no baggage storage at the station).

To reach the town center or Ancient History Museum from the train station, wait for the free **Navia shuttle** at the glass

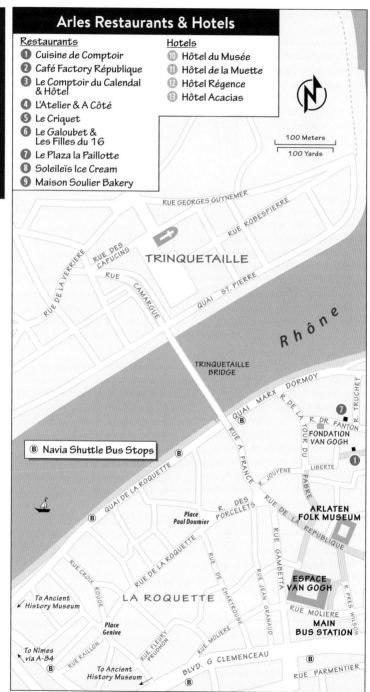

Arles Restaurants & Hotels

Restaurants
1. Cuisine de Comptoir
2. Café Factory République
3. Le Comptoir du Calendal & Hôtel
4. L'Atelier & A Côté
5. Le Criquet
6. Le Galoubet & Les Filles du 16
7. Le Plaza la Paillotte
8. Soleileïs Ice Cream
9. Maison Soulier Bakery

Hotels
10. Hôtel du Musée
11. Hôtel de la Muette
12. Hôtel Régence
13. Hôtel Acacias

100 Meters

100 Yards

RUE GEORGES GUYNEMER

RUE ROBESPIERRE

RUE DES CAPUCINS

RUE DE LA VERRIERE

TRINQUETAILLE

RUE CAMARGUE

QUAI ST. PIERRE

R h ô n e

TRINQUETAILLE BRIDGE

QUAI MARX DORMOY

R. DE LA TOUR DU FABRE

R. TRUCHET

R. DR. FANTON

FONDATION VAN GOGH

RUE A FRANCE

LIBERTE

Ⓑ Navia Shuttle Bus Stops

QUAI DE LA ROQUETTE

R. JOUVENE

R. DES PORCELETS

RUE DE LA REPUBLIQUE

Place Paul Doumier

ARLATEN FOLK MUSEUM

RUE GAMBETTA

RUE DE LA ROQUETTE

RUE DE CHARTROUSE

RUE JEAN GRANAUD

ESPACE VAN GOGH

R. PRES. WILSON

To Ancient History Museum

LA ROQUETTE

RUE CROIX ROUGE

RUE MOLIERE

MAIN BUS STATION

Place Genive

RUE MOLIERE

RUE FLEURY PRUDHON

To Nîmes via A-84

RUE RAILLON

To Ancient History Museum

BLVD. G CLEMENCEAU

RUE PARMENTIER

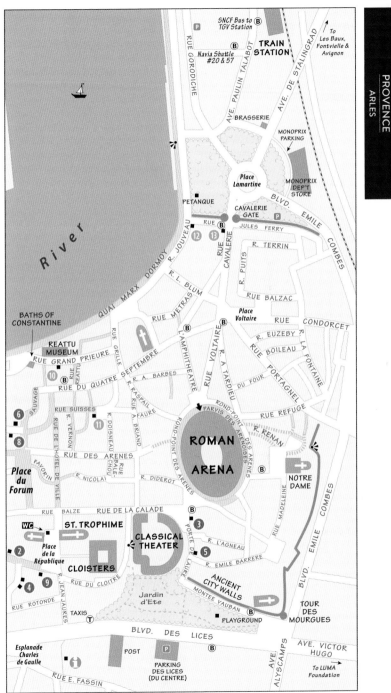

shelter facing away from the station (cross the street and veer left, 2/hour Mon-Sat 7:00-19:00, none Sun). The bus makes a counterclockwise loop around Arles, stopping near most of my recommended hotels. **Taxis** usually wait in front of the station.

From Arles **by Train to: Paris** (hourly, 4 hours, transfer in Avignon or Nîmes; or take the SNCF bus to Avignon TGV Station and train from there), **Avignon Centre-Ville** (hourly, 20 minutes), **Carcassonne** (4/day direct, 2.5 hours, more with transfer in Narbonne, direct trains may require reservations), **Beaune** (hourly, 5 hours, transfer in Lyon), **Nice** (hourly, 4 hours, most require transfer in Marseille).

BY BUS

Arles' main bus station is located on Boulevard Georges Clemenceau, a few blocks from the TI. Most buses to regional destinations depart from here, and most trips cost under €2. Get schedules at the TI or from the bus company (closed Sun, tel. 08 10 00 08 18, www.lepilote.com).

From Arles **Train Station to Avignon TGV Station:** The direct SNCF bus is your best option (€8, 8/day, 1 hour, included with rail pass).

From Arles **by Bus to Les Baux:** Cartreize bus #57 connects Arles to Les Baux (6/day, daily July-Aug, Sat-Sun only in early May-June and Sept, none in off-season; departs from the train station, not the bus station; 35 minutes to Les Baux, then runs to Avignon).

BY CAR

I'd avoid driving in old Arles. Enter on foot after stowing your car (at least temporarily) at Arles' only parking garage, **Parking des Lices,** near the TI on Boulevard des Lices (about €2/hour, €18/24 hours). All of my recommended hotels are within a 10-minute walk of this garage. Most hotels have parking deals for a nearby lot (ask before you arrive).

Lots and curbside parking spots in Arles center are metered 9:00-19:00 every day May-Sept (some limited to 2.5 hours). You'll find metered lots along the city wall at Place Lamartine (except Tue night, when it is restricted). To find these, first follow signs to *Centre-Ville,* then *Gare SNCF* (train station) until you come to the roundabout with a Monoprix department store to the right. The hotels I list are no more than a 15-minute walk from here.

Car Rental: Europcar and **Hertz** are downtown (Europcar is at 61 Avenue de Stalingrad, tel. 04 90 93 23 24; Hertz is closer to Place Voltaire at 10 Boulevard Emile Combes, tel. 04 90 96 75 23).

AVIGNON

Famous for its nursery rhyme, medieval bridge, and brooding Palace of the Popes, contemporary Avignon (ah-veen-yohn) bustles and prospers behind its mighty walls. For nearly 100 years (1309-1403) Avignon was the capital of Christendom, home to seven popes. (And, for a difficult period after that—during the Great Schism when there were two competing popes—Avignon was "the other Rome.") During this time, it grew from a quiet village into a thriving city.

Today, with its large student population and fashionable shops, Avignon is an intriguing blend of medieval history, youthful energy, and urban sophistication. Street performers entertain the international throngs who fill Avignon's ubiquitous cafés and trendy boutiques. And each July the city goes pedal to the metal during its huge theater festival (with about 2,000 performances, big crowds, higher prices, and hotels booked up long in advance).

Orientation

Cours Jean Jaurès, which turns into Rue de la République, runs straight from the Centre-Ville train station to Place de l'Horloge and the Palace of the Popes, splitting Avignon in two. The larger eastern half is where the action is. Climb to the Jardin du Rocher des Doms for the town's best view, tour the pope's immense palace, and go organic in its vibrant market hall.

Tourist Information

The TI is located on the main street linking the Centre-Ville train station to the old town (Mon-Sat 9:00-18:00 except Sat until 17:00 Nov-March, Sun 10:00-17:00 except until 12:00 Nov-March, daily until 19:00 in July, 41 Cours Jean Jaurès, tel. 04 32 74 32 74, www.avignon-tourisme.com). Pick up a map with several good (but tricky to follow) walking tours and ask about guided tours in English.

Helpful Hints

Book Ahead for July: During the July theater festival, rooms are almost impossible to come by—reserve early, or stay in Arles.

Baggage Storage: La Consigne will either be in the Centre-Ville train station or a few blocks away under the modern arcade at 1 Avenue Maréchal de Lattre de Tassigny (€6-10/day; June-Aug daily 8:00-21:00; Sept-May Mon-Sat 9:00-18:00, closed Sun, tel. 09 82 45 20 24, www.consigne-avignon.fr).

Laundry: At **La Blanchisseuse,** you can drop off your laundry and pick it up the same day (daily 7:00-21:00, several blocks west of the TI at 24 Rue Lanterne, tel. 04 90 85 58 80). The launderette at 66 Place des Corps-Saints, where Rue Agricol Perdiguier ends, is handy to most hotels (daily 7:00-20:00).

Bike Rental: Rent pedal and electric bikes and scooters near the train station at **Provence Bike** (April-Oct 9:00-18:30, 7 Avenue St. Ruf, tel. 04 90 27 92 61, www.provence-bike.com), or ask at the TI about other options. You'll enjoy riding on the Ile de la Barthelasse (the TI has bike maps), but biking is better in and around Vaison-la-Romaine.

Local Guides: Isabelle Magny is a good local guide for the city and region (€160/half-day, €330/day, no car, mobile 06 11 82 17 92, isabellemagny@sfr.fr). **Nina Seffusatti** is also good (same prices as Isabelle, mobile 06 14 80 30 37, nina-seffusatti@wanadoo.fr). The **Avignon Gourmet Walking Tour** is a wonderful experience if you like to eat. Charming and passionate Aurélie meets small

PROVENCE AVIGNON

Place de l'Horloge

groups daily (except Sun and Mon) at the TI at 9:00 for a well-designed three-hour, eight-stop walk (€59/person, 2-8 people per group, mobile 06 35 32 08 96, www.avignongourmetours.com). Book in advance on her website.

Avignon Walk

This self-guided walk, worth ▲▲, offers a fine overview of the city and its major sights.

❍ Self-Guided Walk

• *Start this tour where the Romans did, on Place de l'Horloge, in front of City Hall (Hôtel de Ville).*

PLACE DE L'HORLOGE

In ancient Roman times this was the forum, and in medieval times it was the market square. The square is named for the clock tower (now hiding behind the more recently built City Hall) that, in its day, was a humanist statement. In medieval France, the only bells in town rang from the church tower to indicate not the hours but the calls to prayer. With the dawn of the modern age, secular clock towers like this rang out the hours as people organized their lives independent of the Church.

Taking humanism a step further, the City Hall, built after the French Revolution, obstructed the view of the old clock tower while celebrating a new era. The slogan "liberty, equality, and brotherhood" is a reminder that the people supersede the king and the Church. And today, judging from the square's jammed cafés and restaurants, it is indeed the people who rule.

The square's present popularity arrived with the trains in 1854. Facing City Hall, look left down the main drag, Rue de la République. When the trains came to Avignon, proud city fathers wanted a direct, impressive way to link the new station to the heart of the city—so they destroyed existing homes to create Rue de la République and widened Place de l'Horloge.

• *Walk slightly uphill past the neo-Renaissance facade of the theater and the carousel (public WCs behind). Look back to see the late Gothic bell tower. Then veer right at the Palace of the Popes and continue into...*

PALACE SQUARE (PLACE DU PALAIS)

Pull up a concrete stump just past the café. These bollards effectively keep cars from double-parking in areas designed for people. Many of the metal ones slide up and down by remote control to let privileged cars come and go.

Now take in the scene. This grand square is lined with the Palace of the Popes, the Petit Palais, and the cathedral. In the 1300s the entire headquarters of the Roman Catholic Church was moved to Avignon. The Church purchased the city of Avignon and gave it a complete makeover. Along with clearing out vast spaces like this square and building a three-acre palace, the Church erected more than three miles of protective wall (with 39 towers), "appropriate" housing for cardinals (read: mansions), and residences for its entire bureaucracy. The city was Europe's largest construction zone. Avignon's population grew from 6,000 to 25,000 in short order. (Today, only 13,000 people live within the walls.) The limits of pre-papal Avignon are outlined on your city map: Rues Joseph Vernet, Henri Fabre, des Lices, and Philonarde all follow the route of the city's

Palace Square

PROVENCE
AVIGNON

earlier defensive wall (about half the diameter of today's wall).

The imposing facade behind you, across the square from the Palace of the Popes' main entry, was "the papal mint," which served as the finance department for the Holy See. The Petit Palais (Little Palace) seals the uphill end of the square and was built for a cardinal; today it houses medieval paintings.

Avignon's 12th-century Romanesque cathedral, just to the left of the Palace of the Popes, has been the seat of the local bishop for more than a thousand years.

• *You can visit the massive* **Palace of the Popes** *(described later), but it works better to visit that palace at the end of this walk.*

Now is a good time to take in the...

PETIT PALAIS MUSEUM (MUSEE DU PETIT PALAIS)

This former cardinal's palace now displays the Church's collection of (mostly) art. You'll find some English information but not a lot of detail. Still, a visit here before going to the Palace of the Popes helps furnish and populate that otherwise barren building. You'll see bits of statues and tombs—an inventory of the destruction of exquisite Church art that was wrought by the French Revolution (which tackled established French society with Taliban-esque fervor). Then you'll see many rooms filled with religious Italian paintings, organized in chronological order

from early Gothic to late Renaissance. Room 10 holds two paintings by Botticelli.

Cost and Hours: Free, Wed-Mon 10:00-13:00 & 14:00-18:00, closed Tue, ask about summer sound-and-light shows in main courtyard, at north end of Palace Square, tel. 04 90 86 44 58, www.petit-palais.org.

• *From Palace Square, head up to the cathedral (enjoy the viewpoint overlooking the square), and fill your water bottle just past the gate. Now climb the ramp to the top of a rocky hill to where Avignon was first settled. Atop the hill is an inviting café and pond in a park—the Jardin du Rocher des Doms. At the far side is a viewpoint from where you can see Avignon's beloved broken bridge.*

▲ JARDIN DU ROCHER DES DOMS

Enjoy the view from this bluff. On a clear day, the tallest peak you see (far to the right), with its white limestone cap, is Mont Ventoux ("Windy Mountain"). Below and just to the right, you'll spot free passenger ferries shuttling across the river, and—tucked amid the trees on the far side—the recommended restaurant, Le Bercail, a local favorite. The island is the Ile de la Barthelasse, a lush nature preserve where Avignon can breathe. In the distance to the left is the TGV rail bridge.

The Rhône River marked the border of Vatican territory in medieval times. Fort St. André—across the river on the hill—was in the kingdom of France. The fort was built in 1360, shortly after the pope moved to Avignon, to counter the papal incursion into this part of Europe. Avignon's famous bridge was a key border crossing, with towers on either end—one was French, and the other was the pope's. The French one, across the river, is the Tower of Philip the Fair.

Cost and Hours: Free, park gates open daily 7:30-20:00, June-Aug until 21:00, Oct-March until 18:00.

• *Take the walkway down to the left and find the stairs leading down to the tower. You'll catch glimpses of the...*

Petit Palais Museum

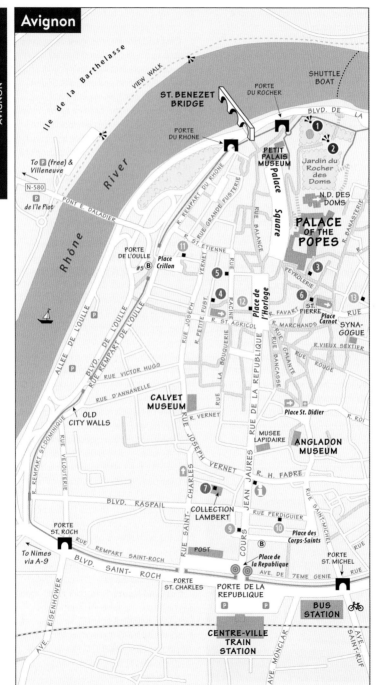

Avignon

Île de la Barthelasse

VIEW WALK

SHUTTLE BOAT

ST. BENEZET BRIDGE

PORTE DU ROCHER

BLVD. DE LA

PORTE DU RHONE

PETIT PALAIS MUSEUM

Jardin du Rocher des Doms

N.D. DES DOMS

Rhône River

To P (free) & Villeneuve

N-580

P de l'Île Piot

PONT E. DALADIER

R. REMPART DU RHONE

RUE GRANDE FUSTERIE

RUE BALANCE

Palace Square

PALACE OF THE POPES

R. BANASTERIE

Rhône

PORTE DE L'OULLE

#5 B Place Crillon

R. ST. ETIENNE

RUE VERNET

11

5

RUE

PEYROLERIE

3

ALLEE DE L'OULLE

BLVD. DE L'OULLE

RUE REMPART DE L'OULLE

RUE VICTOR HUGO

RUE D'ANNANELLE

RUE JOSEPH

R. PETITE FUST.

4

R. ST. AGRICOL

12

Place de l'Horloge

RACINE

RUE FAVART

6

ST. PIERRE

Place Carnot

13

RUE

RUE MARCHANDS

R. MARCHANDS

SYNA-GOGUE

RUE GALANTE

RUE ROUGE

R. VIEUX SEXTIER

RUE DE LA REPUBLIQUE

RUE BANCASSE

CALVET MUSEUM

RUE JOSEPH VERNET

R. VERNET

RUE LA BOUQUERIE

RUE VERNET

OLD CITY WALLS

R. REMPART ST-DOMINIQUE

RUE VELOUTERIE

RUE JOSEPH VERNET

JEAN JAURES

MUSEE LAPIDAIRE

ANGLADON MUSEUM

R. H. FABRE

Place St. Didier

R. ROI

BLVD. RASPAIL

RUE SAINT CHARLES

7

COLLECTION LAMBERT

9

RUE PERDIGUIER

10

RUE SAINT-MICHEL

RUE

Place des Corps-Saints

PORTE ST. ROCH

POST

COURS

B

PORTE ST. MICHEL

To Nimes via A-9

RUE REMPART SAINT-ROCH

BLVD. SAINT- ROCH

Place de la Republique

AVE. DE 7EME GENIE

PORTE ST. CHARLES

PORTE DE LA REPUBLIQUE

P

P

BUS STATION

AVE. EISENHOWER

AVE. MONCLAR

AVE. SAINT-RUF

CENTRE-VILLE TRAIN STATION

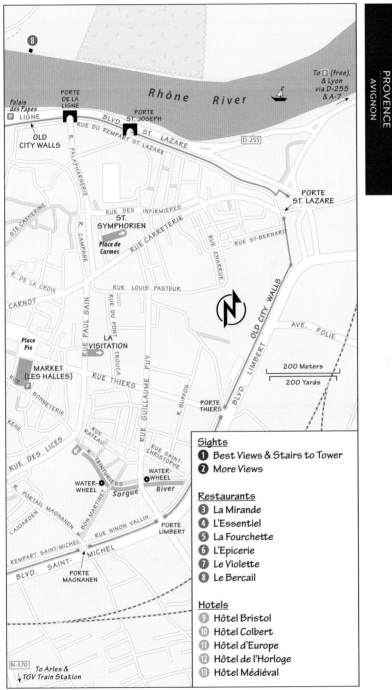

Rhône River

To P (free),
& Lyon
via D-255
& A-7

Palais
des Papes
P LIGNE

PORTE
DE LA
LIGNE

PORTE
ST. JOSEPH

BLVD. ST. LAZARE
RUE DU REMPART ST. LAZARE

D-255

OLD
CITY WALLS

R. PALAPHARNERIE

PORTE
ST. LAZARE

STE. CATHERINE

RUE DES INFIRMIERES

ST.
SYMPHORIEN

R. CAMPANE

RUE CARRETERIE

RUE ST-BERNARD

Place de
Carmes

RUE CHARRUE

R. DE LA CROIX

RUE LOUIS PASTEUR

CARNOT

RUE PAUL SAIN

RUE DU PONT

OLD CITY WALLS

AVE. FOLIE

Place
Pie

LA
VISITATION

TROUCA

BLVD. LIMBERT

200 Meters

200 Yards

MARKET
(LES HALLES)
P

RUE THIERS

RUE GUILLAUME PUY

R. BUFFON

PORTE
THIERS

RUE BONNETERIE

RENE

RUE DES LICES

RUE
RATEAU

R. TEINTURIERS

RUE SAINT-
CHRISTOPHE

WATER-
WHEEL

WATER-
WHEEL

Sorgue

River

R. PORTAIL MAGNANEN

L'AIGARDEN MAGNANEN

R. BON MARTINET

RUE NINON VALLIN

PORTE
LIMBERT

REMPART SAINT-MICHEL

MICHEL

BLVD. SAINT-

PORTE
MAGNANEN

N-570
To Arles &
TGV Train Station

Sights
1 Best Views & Stairs to Tower
2 More Views

Restaurants
3 La Mirande
4 L'Essentiel
5 La Fourchette
6 L'Epicerie
7 Le Violette
8 Le Bercail

Hotels
9 Hôtel Bristol
10 Hôtel Colbert
11 Hôtel d'Europe
12 Hôtel de l'Horloge
13 Hôtel Médiéval

RAMPARTS

The only bit of the rampart you can walk on is accessed from St. Bénezet Bridge (accessible with ticket, see next). Just after the papacy took control of Avignon, the walls were extended to take in the convents and monasteries that had been outside the city. What you see today was partially restored in the 19th century.

• *When you come out of the tower on street level, turn left to walk inside the city wall to the entry to the old bridge.*

▲ST. BENEZET BRIDGE (PONT ST. BENEZET)

This bridge, whose construction and location were inspired by a shepherd's religious vision, is the "Pont d'Avignon" of nursery-rhyme fame. The ditty (which you've probably been humming all day) dates back to the 15th century: *Sur le Pont d'Avignon, on y danse, on y danse, sur le Pont d'Avignon, on y danse tous en rond* ("On the bridge of Avignon, we will dance, we will dance, on the bridge of Avignon, we will dance all in a circle").

And the bridge was a big deal even outside its kiddie-tune fame. Built between 1171 and 1185, it was strategic—one of only three bridges crossing the mighty Rhône in the Middle Ages, important to pilgrims, merchants, and armies. It was damaged several times by floods but always rebuilt. In the winter of 1668, most of it was knocked out for the last time by a disastrous icy flood. The townsfolk decided not to rebuild this time, and for more than a century, Avignon had no bridge across the Rhône. While only four arches survive today, the original bridge was huge: Imagine a 22-arch, half-mile-long bridge extending from Vatican territory across the island to the lonely Tower of Philip the Fair, which marked the beginning of France (see displays of the bridge's original length).

Cost and Hours: €5, includes audioguide, €14.50 combo-ticket includes Palace of the Popes, daily 9:00-19:00, July-Aug until 20:00, Nov-Feb 9:30-17:45, last entry one hour before closing, tel. 04 90 27 51 16.

• *To get to the Palace of the Popes from here, walk away from the river and follow the signs to Palais des Papes.*

St. Bénezet Bridge

▲▲PALACE OF THE POPES (PALAIS DES PAPES)

In 1309 a French pope was elected (Pope Clément V). His Holiness decided that dangerous Italy was no place for a pope, so he moved the whole operation to Avignon for a secure rule under a supportive French king. The Catholic Church literally bought Avignon and built the Palace of the Popes, where the popes resided until 1403. Eventually, Italians demanded a Roman pope, so from 1378 on, there were twin popes—one in Rome and one in Avignon—causing a schism in the Catholic Church that wasn't fully resolved until 1417.

Cost and Hours: €12, includes multimedia Histopad; €14.50 combo-ticket includes St. Bénezet Bridge, daily 9:00-19:00, July-Aug until 20:00, Nov-Feb 9:30-17:45, last entry one hour before closing; tel. 04 90 27 50 00, www.palais-des-papes.com.

Visiting the Palace: Visitors follow a tangled one-way route through mostly massive rooms equipped with an iPad they call the "Histopad." There's a lot of history here, but artifacts are sparse and wall frescos are faint: Without guiding help, it's mostly meaningless. Your visit becomes greatly enriched if you master the included Histopad—the staff is happy to help you with it.

The palace was built stark and strong, before the popes knew how long they'd be staying (and before the affluence and fanciness of the Renaissance and Baroque ages). This was the most fortified palace of the time (remember, the pope left Rome to be more secure). With 10-foot-thick walls, it was a symbol of power.

This largest surviving Gothic palace in Europe was built to accommodate 500 people as the administrative center of the Holy See and home of the pope. Seven popes ruled from here, making this the center of Christianity for nearly 100 years. The last pope checked out in 1403, but the Church owned Avignon until the French Revolution in 1791. During this interim period, the palace still housed Church authorities. Avignon residents, many of whom had come from Rome, spoke Italian for a century after the pope left, making the town a cultural oddity within France.

The palace is pretty empty today—nothing portable survived both the pope's return to Rome and the French Revolution. Just before the gift shop exit, you can climb the tower (Tour de la Gâche) for grand views. The artillery room is now a gift shop channeling all visitors on a full tour of knickknacks for sale.

• *You'll exit at the rear of the palace. To return to Palace Square, make two rights after leaving the palace.*

Experiences

Ile de la Barthelasse Saunter

A free shuttle boat, the **Navette Fluviale,** plies back and forth across the Rhône River from near St. Bénezet Bridge to the Ile de la Barthelasse. This peaceful island offers grassy walks, bike rides, and the recommended riverside restaurant, Le Bercail. For great views, walk the riverside path to Daladier Bridge, and then cross the bridge back into town.

Cost and Hours: Free; 3 boats/hour, daily April-June and Sept 10:00-12:15 & 14:00-18:00, July-Aug 11:00-20:45; Oct-March weekends and Wed afternoons only).

Rick's Tip: *If you stay on the island to eat, check the schedule to make sure you* **don't miss the last return boat (otherwise, it's a 25-minute walk).**

Eating

Skip the crowd-pleasing places on Place de l'Horloge—Avignon is brimming with delightful squares and back streets lined with little restaurants eager to feed you. At the finer places, reservations are smart (especially on weekends).

Fine Dining

$$$$ La Mirande, inside Hôtel la Mirande just behind the Palace of the Popes, transports you into a historic and aristocratic world. What was once a cardinal's palace today is a romantic oasis where you'll dine in 18th-century splendor with elegant service and presentation (dine inside or in the queenly garden, closed Tue-Wed, €50 *plats,* enticing five-course €65 *menu* must be ordered by everyone in your party, 4 Place de l'Amirande, tel. 04 90 14 20 20, www.la-mirande.fr).

$$$ L'Essentiel is modern, spacious, and bright, with traditional French dishes. It has classy presentation and ambience, and seating indoors or outdoors on a romantic back terrace (€36-48 *menus,* closed Sun-Mon, reservations recommended, 2 Rue Petite Fusterie, tel. 04 90 85 87 12, www.restaurantlessentiel.com).

$$$ La Fourchette is an inviting, dressy place graced with warm colors and spacious indoor-only seating. The cuisine mixes traditional French with Provençal. Book ahead for this popular place (closed Sun-Mon, 17 Rue Racine, tel. 04 90 85 20 93, www.la-fourchette.net).

Dining Well on a Moderate Budget

$$$ L'Epicerie sits alone under green awnings on the romantic Place St-Pierre square and is ideal for dinner outside (or in the small but cozy interior). It has an accessible menu with Mediterranean dishes and big, splittable *assiettes* (sample plates), each with a theme (daily, 10 Place St-Pierre, tel. 04 90 82 74 22, Magda speaks English).

$$ Le Violette, in the peaceful courtyard of the Collection Lambert modern art museum, serves fresh modern cuisine and is gorgeous when lit by the museum rooms at night (July-Aug daily, Sept-June closed Sun and Mon, 5 Rue Violette, tel. 04 90 85 36 42).

Rick's Tip: *For a fun* **lunch spot,** *visit the farmers market hall* **Les Halles,** *with its handful of wonderfully characteristic and cheap places serving locals the freshest of food (on Place Pie, closes Tue-Fri at 13:30 and at 14:00 Sat-Sun; closed Mon).*

Local Favorite

$$$ Le Bercail offers a fun opportunity to cross the Rhône River and take in the country air with a terrific riverfront view of Avignon, all while enjoying big portions of Provençal cooking. Make a reservation before trekking out there (daily May-Oct, often closed off-season, tel. 04 90 82 20 22, www.restaurant-lebercail.fr). Take the free shuttle boat (located near St. Bénezet Bridge) to the Ile de la Barthelasse, turn right, and walk five minutes. As the boat usually stops running at about 18:00 (20:45 in July-Aug), you can either taxi back or walk 25 minutes along the pleasant riverside path and over Daladier Bridge.

Sleeping

Hotel values are better in Arles. Drivers should ask about parking discounts through hotels.

Rick's Tip: *During the* **July theater festival,** *rooms are few in Avignon—you must book long ahead and pay inflated prices.* **It's better to stay in Arles.**

Near Centre-Ville Station

$$ Hôtel Bristol** is a big, professionally run place on the main drag, offering spacious public spaces, large rooms, big elevators, and a generous buffet breakfast (family rooms, pay parking—reserve ahead, 44 Cours Jean Jaurès, tel. 04 90 16 48 48, www.bristol-avignon.com, contact@bristol-avignon.com).

$ Hôtel Colbert** is on a quiet lane, with a dozen spacious rooms gathered on four floors around a skinny spiral staircase (no elevator). Patrice decorates each room with a colorful (occasionally erotic) flair. There are warm public spaces and a sweet little patio (some tight bathrooms, rooms off the patio can be musty, closed Nov-March, 7 Rue Agricol Perdiguier, tel. 04 90 86 20 20, www.lecolbert-hotel.com, contact@avignon-hotel-colbert.com).

Near Place de l'Horloge

$$$$ Hôtel d'Europe,*** one of Avignon's most prestigious addresses, lets peasants sleep affordably—but only if they land one of the six reasonable *"classique"* rooms. With formal staff, spacious lounges, and a shady courtyard, the hotel is located on the handsome Place Crillon, near the river (pay garage parking, near Daladier Bridge at 12 Place Crillon, tel. 04 90 14 76 76, www.heurope.com, reservations@heurope.com).

$$$ Hôtel de l'Horloge** is as central as it gets—on Place de l'Horloge. It offers 66 comfortable rooms, some with terraces and views of the city and the Palace of the Popes (1 Rue Félicien David, tel. 04 90 16 42 00, www.hotel-avignon-horloge.com, hotel.horloge@hotels-ocre-azur.com).

$ Hôtel Médiéval,** burrowed deep in the old center a few blocks from the Church of St. Pierre, was built as a cardinal's home. This stone mansion's grand staircase leads to 35 comfortable, pastel rooms (no elevator, kitchenettes, 5 blocks east of Place de l'Horloge, behind Church of St. Pierre at 15 Rue Petite Saunerie, tel. 04 90 86 11 06, www.

hotelmedieval.com, hotel.medieval@wanadoo.fr, run by Régis).

Transportation

Getting Around Avignon

Avignon's walled city is compact, and all the major sights can be visited on foot. The streets are cobbled, so wear comfortable shoes.

If you tire of walking, take advantage of the city's **shuttle vans.** Wave down a **Baladine** electric minivan along its loop route through Avignon, or use **City Zen** minibuses with fixed stops (€0.50, 4/hour for either). City Zen also links remote parking lots with the city center. The TI has route maps. If you want a **taxi,** dial 04 90 82 20 20.

Arriving and Departing

BY TRAIN

Avignon has two train stations: Centre-Ville and TGV (linked to downtown by shuttle trains). Some TGV trains stop at Centre-Ville—verify your station in advance.

The **Centre-Ville station** (*Gare Avignon Centre-Ville*) gets all non-TGV trains (and a few TGV trains). To reach the town center, cross the busy street in front of the station and walk through the city walls onto Cours Jean Jaurès. Baggage storage is close by (see "Helpful Hints," earlier).

From Avignon's Centre-Ville Station to: Arles (roughly hourly, 20 minutes, less frequent in the afternoon), **Carcassonne** (8/day, 7 with transfer in Narbonne or Nîmes, 3 hours).

The **TGV station** (*Gare TGV*), on the outskirts of town, has easy car rental, but no baggage storage. Car rental, buses, and taxis are outside the north exit (*sortie nord*). To reach the city center, take the **shuttle train** from platform A or B to the Centre-Ville station (€1.60, included with rail pass, 2/hour, 5 minutes, buy ticket from machine on platform or at *billeterie* in main hall). A **taxi** ride between the TGV station and downtown Avignon costs about €18.

If you're connecting from the TGV

station to other points, you'll find **buses** to Arles' Centre-Ville station at the second bus shelter (€7.50, 9/day, hourly, included with rail pass, schedule posted on shelter and available at TGV station info booths). If you're **driving** a rental car from the station to Arles or Les Baux, follow signs to *Avignon Sud,* then *La Rocade.* You'll soon see exits to Arles (best for Les Baux, too).

From Avignon's TGV Station to: Nice (hourly, most by TGV, 4 hours, many require transfer in Marseille), **Paris' Gare de Lyon** (hourly direct, 2.5 hours), **Paris' Charles de Gaulle airport** (7/day, 3 hours).

BY BUS

The efficient bus station (*gare routière*) is 100 yards to the right as you exit the Centre-Ville train station, beyond and below Hôtel Ibis (helpful info desk open Mon-Sat 7:00-19:30, closed Sun, tel. 04 90 82 07 35). Nearly all buses leave from this station (a few leave from the ring road outside the station—ask, buy tickets on bus or at bus station). Service is reduced or nonexistent on Sundays and holidays. Verify your destination with the driver.

From Avignon to: Pont du Gard (bus #A15, 5/day Mon-Fri, 3/day Sat-Sun, 1 hour), **Arles train station** (8/day, 1 hour, leaves from TGV station), **Vaison-la-Romaine** (bus #4, 10/day Mon-Sat, 2/day Sun, 2 hours) and **Séguret** (3-6/day; all buses pass through Orange—faster

to take train to Orange, and transfer to bus there).

BY CAR

Avignon is essentially traffic-free in the old center. For the most central parking garage, follow signs to *Centre,* then to the *Centre Historique* and then **P Palais des Papes** (from where, after parking, you'll climb the stairs and arrive at the pope's doorstep, €12 half-day, €20/24 hours).

You can also park for free at the edge of town at lots with complimentary shuttle buses to the center (no shuttles on Sunday). Follow *P Gratuit* signs for **Parking de l'Ile Piot,** across Pont Daladier on Ile de la Barthelasse, with shuttles to Place Crillon; or to **Parking des Italiens,** along the river east of the Palace of the Popes, with shuttles to Place Pie (allow 30 minutes to walk from either parking lot to the center). Street parking is €1-3/hour for a maximum of four hours Mon-Sat 9:00-19:00 (free 19:00-9:00 and all day Sunday).

No matter where you park, leave nothing of value in your car.

Car Rental: The TGV station has counters for all the big companies; only Avis is at the Centre-Ville station.

NEAR ARLES AND AVIGNON

It's a short hop from Arles or Avignon to splendid scenery, Roman sights, warm stone villages, and world-class wine. See the marvelous Roman Pont du Gard aqueduct; explore the ghost town that is ancient Les Baux; and spend time in pleasant Vaison-la-Romaine, a handy hub for the sunny Côtes du Rhône wine road.

Pont du Gard

Throughout the ancient world, aqueducts were like flags of stone that heralded the greatness of Rome. A visit to this impressively preserved ▲▲▲ sight still works to proclaim the wonders of that age.

In the first century AD, the Romans built a 30-mile aqueduct that ran to Nîmes, one of ancient Europe's largest cities. While most of it ran on or below the ground, at Pont du Gard the aqueduct spans a canyon on a massive bridge over the Gardon River—one of the most remarkable surviving Roman ruins anywhere.

Allow about a full four hours for visiting Pont du Gard (including transportation time from Avignon).

Getting There: Pont du Gard is a 30-minute **drive** due west of Avignon (follow N-100 from Avignon, tracking signs to *Nîmes* and *Remoulins,* then *Pont du Gard* and *Rive Gauche*), It's 45 minutes northwest of Arles (via Tarascon on D-6113). **Buses** run to

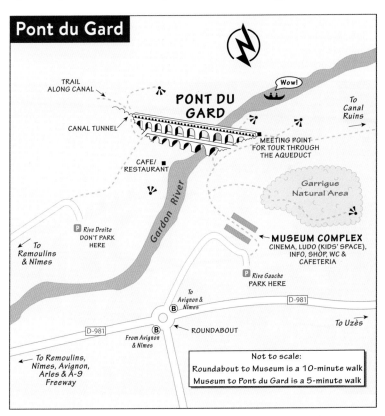

Pont du Gard

TRAIL ALONG CANAL

PONT DU GARD

Wow!

To Canal Ruins

CANAL TUNNEL

MEETING POINT FOR TOUR THROUGH THE AQUEDUCT

CAFE/ RESTAURANT

Gardon River

Garrigue Natural Area

Rive Droite
DON'T PARK HERE

To Remoulins & Nîmes

MUSEUM COMPLEX
CINEMA, LUDO (KIDS' SPACE), INFO, SHOP, WC & CAFETERIA

Rive Gauche
PARK HERE

To Avignon & Nîmes

D-981

To Uzès

D-981

From Avignon & Nîmes

ROUNDABOUT

To Remoulins, Nîmes, Avignon, Arles & A-9 Freeway

Not to scale:
Roundabout to Museum is a 10-minute walk
Museum to Pont du Gard is a 5-minute walk

Pont du Gard from Avignon (#A15, 5/day Mon-Fri, 3/day Sat-Sun, 1 hour).

Orientation

There are two riversides at Pont du Gard: the Left Bank (Rive Gauche) and Right Bank (Rive Droite). Park on the Rive Gauche (parking validated with ticket purchase), where you'll find the museum, ticket booth, and TI. You'll see the aqueduct in two parts: first the informative museum complex, then the actual river gorge spanned by the ancient bridge.

Cost: €8.50 Discovery Pass includes access to the aqueduct and museum; €11.50 Pass Aqueduct also includes a 30-minute tour through the top channel of the aqueduct—book online in advance. Skip the €15.50 Pass Patrimoine.

Hours: Daily from 9:00 until 21:00 or later (confirm online)—closes earlier in off-season; museum open similar hours.

Information: Tel. 04 66 37 50 99, www.pontdugard.fr.

After Hours: During summer months, the site is open late so that people can watch a light show projected on the monument. After the museum closes, you'll pay only €5/person to enter (free for kids under 17). If you don't care to see the museum, seeing Pont du Gard in the evening is dramatic (and cheap).

Rick's Tip: *Pont du Gard is perhaps best enjoyed on your back and* **in the water**—*bring along a swimsuit and flip-flops for the rocks. The best Pont du Gard viewpoints are up steep hills with uneven footing*—**bring good shoes,** *too.*

Visiting the Aqueduct

You'll enter the ▲ **state-of-the-art museum** (well presented in English) to the sound of water and understand the critical role fresh water played in the Roman "art of living." You'll see copies of lead pipes, faucets, and siphons; walk through a mock rock quarry; and learn how they moved

Pont du Gard

those huge rocks into place and how those massive arches were made.

A broad walkway from the museum complex leads in 10 minutes to the aqueduct. Before crossing the bridge, walk to a terrific riverside viewpoint by continuing under the aqueduct on a stony path, then find two staircases about 50 yards apart leading down to an unobstructed view of the world's second-highest standing Roman structure. (Rome's Colosseum is only six feet taller.)

This was the biggest bridge in the whole 30-mile-long aqueduct. The arches are twice the width of standard aqueducts, and the main arch is the largest the Romans ever built—80 feet across (the width of the river). The bridge is about 160 feet high and was originally about 1,200 feet long.

The stones that jut out—giving the aqueduct a rough, unfinished appearance—supported the original scaffolding. The protuberances were left, rather than cut off, in anticipation of future repair needs. The lips under the arches supported wooden templates that allowed the stones in the round arches to rest on something until the all-important keystone was dropped into place. Each stone weighs from two to six tons. The structure stands with no mortar (except at the very top, where the water flowed)—taking full advantage of the innovative Roman arch, made strong by gravity.

Cross to the right bank for a closer look and the best views. Soon find steps leading up a short, steep trail (marked *View Point/Bellevedere*). Follow the short-but-rugged trail with the river to your right to several superb lookouts above the aqueduct.

Back on the museum side, steps lead up to the top of the Rive Gauche side of the aqueduct, where tours meet to enter the water channel. From here you can follow the canal path along a trail (marked with red-and-white horizontal lines) to find remains of the Roman canal (spur trails off this path lead to more panoramic views).

Les Baux

Tucked between Arles and Avignon, the hilltop town of Les Baux and its medieval citadel crown the rugged Alpilles (ahl-pee) mountains. Here, you can imagine the struggles of a strong community that lived a rough-and-tumble life—thankful more for their top-notch fortifications than for their dramatic views.

Day Plan

Savor the castle, then tour—or blitz—the lower town's polished-stone gauntlet of boutiques. It's mobbed with tourists most of the day, but Les Baux rewards those who arrive by 9:00 or after 17:30. Sunsets are dramatic, and the castle is brilliantly illuminated after dark.

Getting There

Les Baux is a 20-minute **drive** from Arles. Follow signs for *Avignon,* then Les Baux. From Arles, Cartreize **bus #57** runs to Les Baux (6/day, 35 minutes, daily July-Aug, early May-June and Sept Sat-Sun only, none in off-season; timetables at www.lepilote.com). From Avignon, ride Cartreize **bus #57** to St-Rémy (12/day Mon-Fri, 6/day Sat-Sun, 45 minutes), then continue to Les Baux on the same bus (described above). Otherwise, continue to Les Baux by taxi.

A demonstration at Les Baux

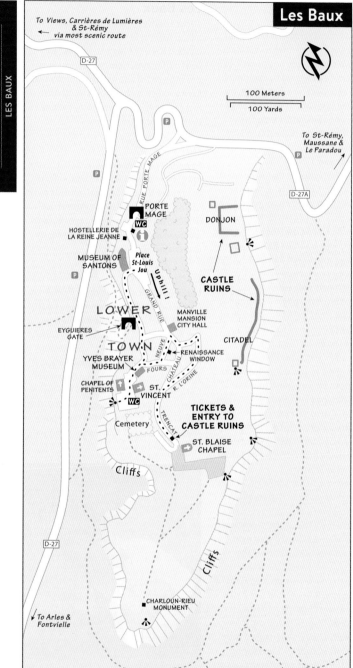

Les Baux

To Views, Carrières de Lumières & St-Rémy
via most scenic route

D-27

100 Meters

100 Yards

To St-Rémy,
Maussane &
Le Paradou

D-27A

RUE PORTE MAGE

PORTE MAGE

WC

HOSTELLERIE DE
LA REINE JEANNE

DONJON

MUSEUM OF
SANTONS

Place
St-Louis
Jou

Uphill !

GRAND RUE

CASTLE
RUINS

LOWER

MANVILLE
MANSION
CITY HALL

CITADEL

EYGUIERES
GATE

TOWN

NEUVE

RENAISSANCE
WINDOW

YVES BRAYER
MUSEUM

FOURS

CHATEAU

R. L'ORME

CHAPEL OF
PENITENTS

ST.
VINCENT

WC

TRENCAT

TICKETS &
ENTRY TO
CASTLE RUINS

Cemetery

ST. BLAISE
CHAPEL

Cliffs

D-27

Cliffs

To Arles &
Fontvielle

CHARLOUN-RIEU
MONUMENT

Orientation

Les Baux is actually two visits in one: castle ruins perched on an almost lunar landscape, and a medieval town below. The town's main drag leads directly to the castle—just keep going uphill (a 10-minute walk).

Tourist Information: The TI is immediately on the left as you enter the village (daily 9:00-18:00, shorter hours and closed Sun in off-season).

Sights

▲▲▲CASTLE RUINS (CHATEAU DES BAUX)

The sun-bleached ruins of the stone fortress of Les Baux are carved into, out of, and on top of a rock 650 feet above the valley floor. Many of the ancient walls of this striking castle still stand as a testament to the proud past of this once-feisty village.

Cost: €9, €11 if there's "entertainment" (described below), €16 Pass Provence combo-ticket with Carrières de Lumières, entry fees include excellent audioguide.

Hours: Daily 9:00-19:00 (July-Aug until 20:00), shorter hours off-season, www.chateau-baux-provence.com.

Rick's Tip: *Château des Baux closes at the end of the day, but once you're inside, you can stay as long as you like. You're welcome to bring a picnic (no food sold inside) and live out your medieval fantasies, all night long.*

Entertainment: Every weekend from April through early September and daily in summer, the castle presents medieval pageantry, tournaments, demonstrations of catapults and crossbows, and jousting matches. Pick up a schedule as you enter (or check online).

Visiting the Castle: Imagine the importance of this citadel in the Middle Ages, when the lords of Baux were notorious warriors, and Les Baux was a powerhouse in southern France, controlling about 80 towns.

View from Château des Baux

Castle ruins at Les Baux

The sight is exceptionally well presented. As you walk on the windblown spur (*baux* in French), you'll pass kid-thrilling medieval siege weaponry (go ahead, try the battering ram). Good displays in English and big paintings in key locations help reconstruct the place. Imagine 4,000 people living up here. Notice the water-catchment system (a slanted field that caught rainwater and drained it into cisterns—necessary during a siege), and find the reservoir cut into the rock below the castle's highest point. Look for post holes throughout the stone walls that reveal where beams once supported floors.

For the most sensational views, climb to the blustery top of the citadel—hold tight if the mistral wind is blowing.

▲LOWER TOWN

After your castle visit, you can shop and eat your way back through the lower town. Or, escape some of the crowds by visiting these minor but worthwhile sights as you descend: There's the **Yves Brayer Museum** (Musée Yves Brayer), with three small floors of luminous paintings (Van Gogh-like Expressionism) by Yves Brayer (1907-1990), who spent his final years in Les Baux (€8, covered by Pass Provence combo-ticket, daily 10:00-12:30 & 14:00-18:30 in season, www.yvesbrayer.com). Next door is **St. Vincent Church**, a 12th-century Romanesque church that was built short and wide to fit the terrain. Lower down, the free and fun **Museum of Santons** displays a collection of popular folk figurines that decorate local Christmas mangers.

▲CARRIERES DE LUMIERES (QUARRIES OF LIGHT)

A 15-minute walk from Les Baux, this colossal quarry-cave with immense vertical walls offers a mesmerizing multimedia experience. Enter a darkened world filled with floor-to-ceiling images and booming music. Wander through a complex of cathedral-like aisles, transepts, and choirs (no seating provided) as you experience the spectacle. The show lasts 40 minutes and runs continuously. Dress warmly, as the cave is cool.

Cost and Hours: €12.50, covered by Pass Provence combo-ticket; daily 9:30-19:30, Nov-March 10:00-18:00; tel. 04 90 54 47 37, www.carrieres-lumieres.com.

Eating

You'll find quiet cafés with views as you walk through Les Baux's lower town.

$ Hostellerie de la Reine Jeanne offers friendly service and good-value meals indoors or out (open daily).

Vaison-la-Romaine

With quick access to vineyards, villages, and Mont Ventoux, this pleasant little ▲ town of 6,000 makes a good base for exploring the Côtes du Rhône region.

Day Plan

Explore Vaison-la-Romaine's lower Roman city (following my self-guided walk, later) and upper medieval village, then set sail along the Côtes du Rhône wine road and visit a winery or wine cooperative.

Orientation

You get two villages for the price of one: Vaison-la-Romaine's "modern" lower city (Ville-Basse) has Roman ruins, a lone pedestrian street, and a lively, café-lined main square. The car-free medieval hill town (Ville-Haute) looms above, with meandering cobbled lanes and a ruined castle. A Roman-era bridge connects the lower and upper towns.

Tourist Information: The TI is in the lower city at Place du Chanoine Sautel (daily except closed Sun mid-Oct-March; tel. 04 90 36 02 11, www.vaison-ventoux-tourisme.com).

Local Guide: Janet Henderson offers enthusiastic and educational walks of Vaison-la-Romaine (€30/person, minimum 3 people or €90, allow 2.5 hours, www.provencehistorytours.com).

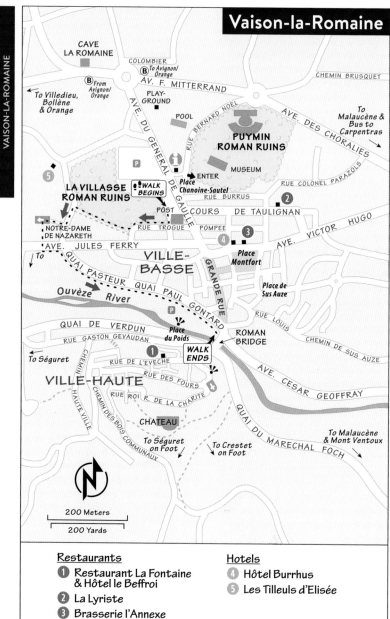

Vaison-la-Romaine

CAVE LA ROMAINE

COLOMBIER

B To Avignon/Orange

B From Avignon/Orange

AV. F. MITTERRAND

CHEMIN BRUSQUET

To Villedieu, Bollène & Orange

PLAY-GROUND

POOL

RUE BERNARD NOEL

PUYMIN ROMAN RUINS

AV. DES CHORALIES

To Malaucène & Bus to Carpentras

P

i

MUSEUM

ENTER

RUE COLONEL PARAZOLS

WALK BEGINS

Place Chanoine-Sautel

LA VILLASSE ROMAN RUINS

5

NOTRE-DAME DE NAZARETH

POST

RUE TROGUE

RUE BURRUS

COURS DE TAULIGNAN

2

POMPEE

3

4

AV. VICTOR HUGO

AVE. JULES FERRY

VILLE-BASSE

Place Montfort

QUAI PASTEUR QUAI PAUL GONTARD

GRANDE RUE

Place de Sus Auze

Ouvèze River

P

RUE LOUIS

QUAI DE VERDUN

RUE GASTON GEVAUDAN

Place du Poids

WALK ENDS

ROMAN BRIDGE

CHEMIN DE SUS AUZE

To Séguret

RUE DE L'EVECHE

1

AV. CESAR GEOFFRAY

VILLE-HAUTE

RUE DES FOURS

RUE ROI R. DE LA CHARITE

HAUTE VILLE

CHEMIN DES BOIS COMMUNAUX

CHATEAU

To Séguret on Foot

To Crestet on Foot

QUAI DU MARECHAL FOCH

To Malaucène & Mont Ventoux

N

200 Meters

200 Yards

Restaurants

1 Restaurant La Fontaine & Hôtel le Beffroi

2 La Lyriste

3 Brasserie l'Annexe

Hotels

4 Hôtel Burrhus

5 Les Tilleuls d'Elisée

Le Mistral

Provence lives with its vicious mistral winds, which blow 30-60 miles per hour, about 100 days out of the year. The mistral clears people off the streets and turns lively cities into ghost towns. You'll likely spend a few hours or days taking refuge. The winds are strongest between noon and 15:00.

When the mistral blows, it's everywhere, and you can't escape. Author Peter Mayle said it could blow the ears off a donkey (I'd include the tail). According to the natives, it ruins crops, shutters, and roofs (look for stones holding tiles in place on many homes).

The mistral starts above the Alps and Massif Central mountains and gathers steam as it heads south, gaining momentum as it screams over the Rhône Valley before exhausting itself when it hits the Mediterranean. And though this wind rattles shutters everywhere in the Riviera and Provence, it's strongest over the Rhône Valley...so Avignon, Arles, and the Côtes du Rhône villages bear its brunt. While wiping the dust from your eyes, remember the good news: The mistral brings clear skies.

Cooking Classes: Charming Barbara Schuerenberg offers cooking classes from her view home (€90, cash only, includes lunch, 4-person maximum, www.cuisinedeprovence.com).

Getting There

Frequent bus (but not train) service connects Vaison-la-Romaine with Avignon (10/day Mon-Sat, 2/day Sun, 2 hours). Bus stops are near the Cave la Romaine winery on the edge of the lower town. Drivers should follow signs to *Centre-Ville,* then *Office de Tourisme,* and park in or near the big lot across from the TI. Parking is free in Vaison-la-Romaine.

Rick's Tip: *Sleep in Vaison-la-Romaine on Monday night, and you'll wake to an* **amazing Tuesday market**. *But avoid parking at market sites, or you won't find your car where you left it.*

Sights

ROMAN RUINS

A modern road splits the town's Gallo-Roman ruins into two well-presented sites, Puymin and La Villasse. The Puymin side has more to see and gives a good introduction to these ruins, thanks to its small museum offering a look at life during the Roman Empire. For helpful background about Roman civilization, read "The Romans in Provence" on page 285.

Cost and Hours: €9 ticket admits you to both sites; daily June-Sept 9:30-18:30, shorter hours off-season, closed Jan-Feb; good audioguide-€3, tel. 04 90 36 50 48, www.vaison-la-romaine.com.

Visiting the Puymin Ruins: Near the entry are the scant but worthwhile ruins of a sprawling mansion. Find the faint remains of a colorful frescoed wall and mosaic floors, as well as a few wells, used before Vaison's two aqueducts were built. Climb the short hill to the good little **museum** (pick up your audioguide here). Artifacts include lead water pipes, well-preserved mosaic floors, and a few models of ancient buildings. Be sure to see the 12-minute **film** (plays in English every other showing) that takes you inside the homes and daily life of wealthy Vaison residents some 2,000 years ago.

A five-minute walk behind the museum brings you to a largely rebuilt (but still used) 6,000-seat **theater**—just enough seats for the whole town (of yesterday and today).

◉ *Walk from Roman Ruins to Roman Bridge*

• *Start this self-guided walk just across from the TI, where there's a parking lot. Lean against the railing there to get a look at the...*

Villasse Ruins: The Roman town extended all the way from where you're standing to the Ouvèze River (to the left, or south). Vaison was a river port, boasting aqueducts, a big theater, baths, a forum, busy shopping streets, and the trophy homes of wealthy businessmen.

When the barbarians arrived in the fifth century AD, the Romans were forced out, and the townspeople fled from their unwalled, unprotected low neighborhoods into the hills.

Make your way to the corner of Rue Trogue Pompée, just behind the post office, and turn right and stop just before reaching the tall arch. Spot the wire mesh that covers parts of a Roman sewer that was used until the 1900s. That tall arch was the centerpiece of a public Roman bath.

The stone-paved street running perpendicularly below you was lined with shops. The columns and remnants on the left side are what's left of two megahomes. You won't see the homes of poorer folks as they were built from materials that did not last.

• *Where the street curves left, continue along the pedestrian walkway that hugs the ruins; at the end of the path, turn left as you leave the ruins behind. You'll pass a lovely garden, then turn right at the first little path you come to. Stop when you reach the back of...*

Notre-Dame de Nazareth Cathedral: As you approach this medieval church, look at its base to find the stubs of Roman columns that form its foundation. The first church built over the Roman ruins was abandoned in the Middle Ages, when residents fled to the relative safety of the upper town; the present building dates from the 11th to 12th century.

• *With your back to the church, walk out to the street and turn left on Avenue Jules Ferry, then veer right on Quai Louis Pasteur. After several blocks, angle through the parking lot and find a spot above the river.*

Medieval Hill Town: Look up to the medieval village. From the fourth century onward, Vaison-la-Romaine was ruled by a prince-bishop. When the sitting prince-bishop came under attack by the count of Toulouse in the 12th century, he built the abandoned castle you see on the top of this rocky outcrop (about 1195). Over time, the townspeople followed, vacating the lower town and building their homes behind the upper town's fortified wall—where they would remain until after the French Revolution.

• *Continue along the river until you reach the...*

Roman Bridge: The Romans cut this sturdy, no-nonsense vault into the canyon rock 2,000 years ago, and it has survived ever since. Until the 20th century, this was the only way to cross the Ouvèze River. A vicious 1992 flood crested well above the bridge. The flood destroyed several other modern bridges downstream, but couldn't budge the 55-foot Roman arch supporting the bridge.

• *Our walk is over. From here, you have two choices:*

Upper Town (Ville-Haute): To reach the upper town, hike across the Roman bridge and up to the right (passing a WWI memorial), looping around and through the medieval gate, under the lone tower. Although there's nothing of particular importance to see in the medieval town, the cobbled lanes and enchanting fountains make you want to break out a sketchpad.

Lower Town (Ville-Basse): From the Roman bridge, do an about-face and walk up the pedestrian-only Grande Rue, Vaison's main shopping street. The modern town centers on café-friendly Place Montfort. Tables line the north side of the square, conveniently sheltered from the prevailing mistral wind while enjoying the generous shade of the ubiquitous plane trees.

Vaison-la-Romaine's ancient theater

▲Hiking and Biking

Stop at the TI for detailed information on hikes into the hills above Vaison-la-Romaine. It's about 1.5 hours to the quiet hill town of Crestet, and there's a five-mile trail to Séguret (allow 2 hours). For either route, consider hiking one way and taking a taxi back (best to arrange a pickup in advance in Vaison-la-Romaine—ask your hotelier). The TI also has details on several manageable bike routes, with good directions in English, as well as information on mountain-biking trails.

Eating

In the upper town, **$$$ Restaurant La Fontaine,** located at the recommended **Hôtel le Beffroi,** serves traditional cuisine in the lovely hotel gardens when the weather agrees (closed Wed). In the lower town, **$$ La Lyriste** is an unpretentious place to experience true Provençal cuisine (closed Sun-Mon, 45 Cours Taulignan). On Place Montfort, the popular **$$ Brasserie l'Annexe** is best (open daily).

Sleeping

Cozy **$$ Hôtel le Beffroi***** hides deep in the upper town (Rue de l'Evêché, www.le-beffroi.com). In the lower town, good choices are **$ Hôtel Burrhus** (1 Place Montfort, www.burrhus.com) and **$ Les Tilleuls d'Elisée** (1 Avenue Jules Mazen, www.vaisonchambres.info).

Côtes du Rhône Wine Road

This self-guided driving tour, worth ▲▲, provides a crash course in Rhône Valley wine, an excuse to meet the locals who make the stuff, and breathtaking scenery. Allow at least a half-day for this 35-mile loop drive. Theft is a problem in this beautiful area—leave absolutely nothing in your car.

● Self-Guided Drive

You can start anywhere along the circular route, but I suggest beginning a bit south of Vaison-la-Romaine, in little Séguret.

❶ SEGURET

Blending into the hillside with a smattering of shops, two cafés, made-to-stroll lanes, and a natural spring, this hamlet is understandably popular. Séguret makes for a good coffee or ice cream stop and has a good café-restaurant.

Séguret's name comes from the Latin word *securitas* (meaning "security"). The town's long bulky entry arch came with a massive gate, which drilled in the message of the village's name. Walk through the arch and up a block. To appreciate how the homes' outer walls provided security in those days, drop down the first passage on your right (near the fountain). These tunnel-like exit passages, or *poternes*, were needed in periods of peace to allow the town to expand below. You will come across La Maison d'Eglantine tucked in here, serving delicious cakes, coffee, and tea in a cozy room with views.

• *Signs near Séguret's upper parking lots lead you up, up, and away to the nearby Domaine de Mourchon.*

❷ DOMAINE DE MOURCHON WINERY

This high-flying winery blends state-of-the-art technology with traditional winemaking methods (a shiny ring of stainless-steel vats holds grapes grown on land plowed by horses). Free and informative English tours of the vineyards are offered from Easter-late September on Wednesdays at 17:00, followed by a tasting (call to verify or to learn of times during other months). You're welcome to taste anytime they're open (winery open

The village of Séguret

Côtes du Rhône Driving Tour

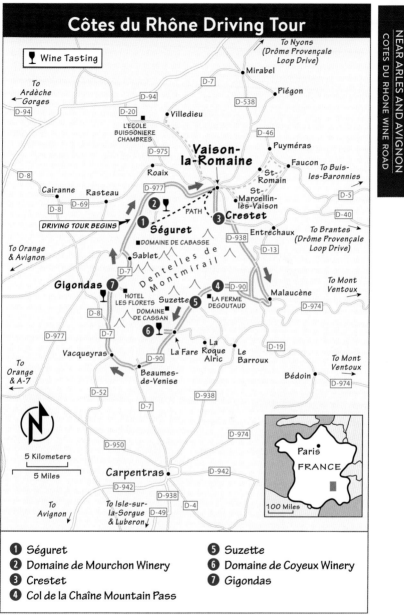

1 Séguret
2 Domaine de Mourchon Winery
3 Crestet
4 Col de la Chaîne Mountain Pass
5 Suzette
6 Domaine de Coyeux Winery
7 Gigondas

Mon-Sat 9:00-18:00, Sun by appointment only; tel. 04 90 46 70 30, www.domained-emourchon.com).

• *Next, drop back down to Séguret, head toward Vaison-la-Romaine, and once past the city follow signs for Carpentras/Malaucène. After passing through "lower" Crestet on the main highway, look for signs for a side road leading up to Le Village. Drivers can park at the second lot on the approach to the town or keep climbing toward Place du Château at the top of town.*

❸ CRESTET

This quiet village—founded after the fall of the Roman Empire, when people banded together in high places like this for protection from marauding barbarians—followed the usual hill-town evolution. The outer walls of the village did double duty as ramparts and house walls. The castle above (from about 850) provided a final safe haven when the village was attacked.

Wander the peaceful lanes and appreciate the amount of work it took to put these stones in place. The bulky Romanesque church is built into the hillside; if it's open, peek in to see the unusual stained-glass window behind the altar. The village's only business, the café-restaurant $$ **Le Panoramic,** has what must be Provence's greatest view tables (closed in bad weather and Dec-March).

❹ COL DE LA CHAINE MOUNTAIN PASS

Get out of your car at the pass (elevation: about 1,500 feet) and enjoy the breezy views. The peaks in the distance—thrusting up like the back of a stegosaurus—are the Dentelles de Montmirail, a small range running just nine miles basically north to south and reaching 2,400 feet in elevation. This region's land is constantly shifting. Those rocky tops were the result of a gradual uplifting of the land, which was then blown bald by the angry mistral wind. The village below the peaks is Suzette (you'll be there soon).

Now turn around and face Mont Ventoux. Are there clouds on the horizon? You're looking into the eyes of the Alps (behind Ventoux), and those "foothills" help keep Provence sunny.

• *Time to push on. With the medieval castle of Le Barroux topping the horizon in the distance (off to the left), drive on to little…*

❺ SUZETTE

Tiny Suzette floats on its hilltop, with a small 12th-century chapel, wine tastings, a handful of residents, and the gaggle of houses where they live. Park in Suzette's lot, then find the big orientation board above the lot. Look out to the broad shoulders of Mont Ventoux. At 6,000 feet, it always seems to have some clouds hanging around. If it's clear, the top looks like it's snow-covered; if you drive up there, you'll see it's actually white stone.

Back across the road from the orientation table is a simple tasting room for **Château Redortier** wines. Good picnic tables lie just past Suzette on our route.

• *Continue from Suzette in the direction of Beaumes-de-Venise. You'll drop down into the lush little village of La Fare. Just after leaving the village is the…*

❻ DOMAINE DE COYEUX WINERY

A private road winds up and up to this impossibly beautiful setting, with the best views of the Dentelles I've found. Le Caveau signs lead to a modern tasting room (you may need to ring the buzzer) within a big winery. The owners and staff are sincere and take your interest in their wines seriously—skip it if you only want a quick taste or are not interested in buying (generally open daily 10:00-12:00 & 14:00-18:00, except closed Sun off-season and no midday closure July-Aug; www.domained-ecoyeux.com, some English spoken).

• *Drive on toward Beaumes-de-Venise. Navigate through Beaumes-de-Venise, following signs for Vacqueyras (a famous wine village with a Thursday market), and then signs for Gigondas and Vaison par la route touristique.*

❼ GIGONDAS

This upscale village produces some of the region's best reds and is ideally situated for hiking, mountain biking, and driving into the mountains. The TI has lists of wineries and tips for good hikes or drives (closed Sun, 5 Rue du Portail, www.gigondas-dm.fr). Take a short walk up through the village lanes to find a good viewing platform over the heart of the Côtes du Rhône vineyards; you'll find even better views a little higher at the church. Several good tasting opportunities lie on the main square (Le Caveau de Gigondas is the best). The **$** restaurant at **Hôtel les Florets** is well worth the price—particularly if you dine on the magnificent terrace (closed Wed, closed Thu for lunch, a half-mile above Gigondas).

• *From Gigondas, follow signs to the circular wine village of Sablet (the TI and wine* coopérative *share a space in the town center)—then back to Séguret, where our tour ends.*

❶ *Wine tasting in the Côtes du Rhône*
❷ *Vineyards of Domaine de Coyeux*
❸ *Côtes du Rhône vineyards*
❹ *Gigondas street scene*

The French Riviera

A hundred years ago, celebrities from London to Moscow flocked to the French Riviera to socialize, gamble, and escape the dreary weather at home. Today, budget vacationers and heat-seeking Europeans fill belle époque resorts at France's most sought-after fun-in-the-sun destination.

Some of the Continent's most stunning scenery and intriguing museums lie along this strip of land—as do millions of sun-worshipping tourists. The Riviera's gateway is urban Nice, with world-class museums, a splendid beachfront promenade, a seductive old town, the best selection of hotels in all price ranges, and good nightlife options.

This sunny sliver of land is well served by public transportation, making day trips by train or bus almost effortless. If you drive here, expect traffic—although you'll be rewarded with sensational views on the coastal routes. If you head east from Nice, you'll find little Villefranche-sur-Mer staring across the bay at exclusive Cap Ferrat. Farther along, Monaco offers a royal welcome and a fairy-tale past. To the west, Antibes has a thriving port and silky sand beaches. Wherever you choose to spend your days, evenings everywhere on the Riviera are radiant—made for a promenade and outdoor dining.

THE FRENCH RIVIERA IN 2 DAYS

My favorite home bases are Nice, Villefranche-sur-Mer, and Antibes. Nice, with convenient train and bus connections to most regional sights, is the most practical base for train travelers. Villefranche-sur-Mer is the romantic's choice, with a peaceful setting and small-town warmth, while midsize Antibes has the best beaches and works best for drivers.

Allow a full day for Nice: Spend your morning sifting through the old city (called Vieux Nice; take my Old Nice Walk) and ascend the elevator up Castle Hill for fine views. Devote the afternoon to the museums (Chagall is best, closed Tue) and strolling the Promenade des Anglais, taking my self-guided walk (best before or after dinner, but anytime is fine).

Save most of your second day for Monaco (tour Monaco-Ville, have lunch, and drop by the famous Monte Carlo casino), then consider a late afternoon or dinner in Villefranche-sur-Mer. With more time, explore Antibes' fine Picasso Museum and sandy old town. Or stop by lush Cap Ferrat, filled with mansions, gardens, and beaches.

THE FRENCH RIVIERA AT A GLANCE

Nice

▲▲▲**Promenade des Anglais** Nice's sun-struck seafront promenade. See page 332.

▲▲▲**Chagall Museum** The world's largest collection of Marc Chagall's work, popular even with people who don't like modern art. **Hours:** Wed-Mon 10:00-18:00, Nov-April until 17:00, closed Tue year-round. See page 340.

▲▲**Vieux Nice** Charming old city offering enjoyable atmosphere and a look at Nice's French-Italian cultural blend. See page 337.

▲**Matisse Museum** Modest collection of Henri Matisse's paintings, sketches, and paper cutouts. **Hours:** Wed-Mon 10:00-18:00, mid-Oct-mid-June from 11:00, closed Tue year-round. See page 341.

▲**Russian Cathedral** Finest Orthodox church outside Russia. **Hours:** Daily 9:30-17:30. See page 342.

▲**Castle Hill** Site of an ancient fort boasting great views. **Hours:** Park closes at 20:00 in summer, earlier off-season. See page 342.

Nearby

▲▲▲**Villefranche-sur-Mer** Romantic pastel-orange beach village with a yacht-filled harbor and small-town ambience. See page 355.

▲▲**Cap Ferrat** Exclusive woodsy peninsula with a family-friendly beach and tourable Rothschild mansion. See page 358.

▲▲**Monaco** Tiny independent municipality known for its classy casino and Grand Prix car race. See page 360.

▲**Antibes** Laid-back beach town with a medieval center, worthwhile Picasso museum, sandy beaches, and view hikes. See page 366.

Getting Around the Riviera

By Bus and Train: Trains and buses do a good job of connecting places along the coast, with bonus views along many routes. Buses are often less expensive and more convenient while trains are faster and pricier.

By Car: This is France's most challenging region to drive in. Beautifully distracting vistas, loads of Sunday-driver tourists, and every hour being lush-hour in the summer make for a dangerous combination. Parking can be exasperating. Bring lots of coins and patience.

By Minivan Tour: Consider **Sylvie Di Cristo** (€600/day, €350/half-day for up to 8 people, mobile 06 09 88 83 83, http://frenchrivieraguides.com, dicristosylvie@gmail.com).

NICE

Nice (sounds like "niece"), with its spectacular Alps-meets-Mediterranean surroundings, is the big-city highlight of the Riviera. Its traffic-free Vieux Nice—the old town—blends Italian and French flavors to create a spicy Mediterranean

dressing, while its big squares, broad seaside walkways, and long beaches invite lounging and people-watching. Nice may be nice, but it's jammed in May, July, and August—reserve ahead and get a room with air-conditioning.

Orientation

Focus your time on the area between the beach and the train tracks (about 15 blocks apart). The city revolves around its grand Place Masséna, where pedestrian-friendly Avenue Jean Médecin meets Vieux Nice and the Promenade du Paillon parkway (with quick access to the beaches). It's a 20-minute walk (or about €15 by taxi) from the train station to the beach, and a 20-minute stroll along the promenade from the fancy Hôtel Negresco to the heart of Vieux Nice.

Tourist Information

Nice has three helpful TIs (tel. 08 92 70 74 07, www.nicetourisme.com), including branches at the **train station** and at **#5 Promenade des Anglais** (both daily 9:00-18:00, July-Aug until 19:00), and by the fountains near **Place Masséna,** called "Pavillon" (May-mid-Sept only, daily

Nice's historic Hôtel Negresco overlooks the Promenade des Anglais.

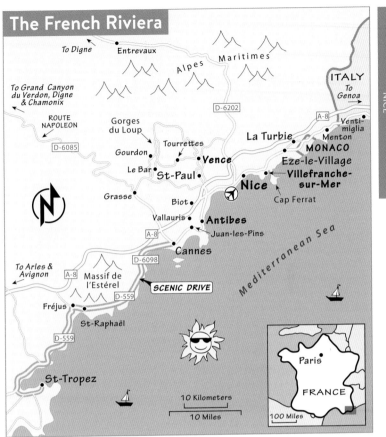

The French Riviera

10:00-20:00). Ask for day-trip information (including details on boat excursions, bus stop locations, and schedules).

Helpful Hints

Theft Alert: Nice has its share of pickpockets (especially at the train station, on the tram, and trolling the beach). Stick to main streets in Vieux Nice after dark.

Sightseeing Tips: Mondays and Tuesdays can frustrate market lovers and museumgoers. Closed on Monday: Nice's Cours Saleya produce and flower market; Antibes' Picasso Museum and market hall (Sept-May). Closed on Tuesday: Chagall and Matisse museums in Nice.

A €10 **combo-ticket for Nice** covers all of the city's museums, except the Chagall Museum (sold at participating sights).

Rick's Tip: The **French Riviera Pass covers many Riviera sights and activities,** *including Nice's Chagall Museum, Monaco's Oceanography Museum (with aquarium), and Villa Ephrussi de Rothschild on Cap Ferrat (€26/24 hours, €38/48 hours, €56/72 hours, sold at TIs and online, tel. 04 92 14 46 14, http://en.frenchrivierapass.com). This pass is worthwhile if you want to do some bigger-ticket items in Nice like the included hop-on, hop-off Le Grand Tour Bus (see "Tours") or the Trans Côte d'Azur cruise (see "Experiences").*

Baggage Storage: You can store your bags inside the train station (€5-10/bag per day) or at the **Bagguys** in Vieux Nice (€8/bag per day, daily 10:00-19:00, 22 Rue Centrale, info@bagguys.fr).

Renting a Bike (and Other Wheels): **Holiday Bikes** has multiple locations, including one across from the train station, and they have electric bikes (www.loca-bike.fr). **Roller Station** is well-situated near the sea and rents bikes, rollerblades, skateboards, and Razor-style scooters (bikes-€5/hour, €10/half-day, €15/day, leave ID as deposit, open daily, 49 Quai des Etats-Unis, tel. 04 93 62 99 05).

Tours

HOP-ON, HOP-OFF BUS

Le Grand Tour Bus provides a useful 14-stop, hop-on, hop-off service on an open-deck bus with good headphone commentary (1-day pass-€23, 2-day pass-€26, buy tickets on bus, 2/hour, daily 10:00-19:00, 1.75-hour loop with Villefranche-sur-Mer, www.nice.opentour.com).

LOCAL GUIDES AND WALKING TOURS

For a guided tour of Nice or the region (using public transit or your rental car), consider **Pascale Rucker** (€160/half-day, €260/day, mobile 06 16 24 29 52, pascalerucker@gmail.com). **Boba Vukadinovic-Millet** is an effective teacher, ideal for those wanting to dive more deeply into the region's history and art (from €250/half-day, from €350/day, mobile 06 27 45 68 39, www.yourguideboba.com, boba@yourguideboba.com). The TI on Prome-nade des Anglais organizes weekly walking tours of Vieux Nice in French and English (€12, Sat at 9:30, 2.5 hours, reservations necessary, departs from TI, tel. 08 92 70 74 07).

Walks in Nice

To get acquainted with Nice, combine the following two self-guided walks. "Promenade des Anglais" covers the sun-drenched seaside that made Nice famous, while "Vieux Nice" takes you through the historic old town of this engaging Franco-Italian city.

❍ *Promenade des Anglais Walk*

This leisurely, level self-guided walk, worth ▲▲▲, is a straight line along this much-strolled beachfront. It begins near the landmark Hôtel Negresco and ends just before Castle Hill. While this one-mile section is enjoyable at any time, the first half makes a great pre- or post-meal stroll (meals served at some beach cafés). If extending this stroll to Castle Hill, it's ideal to time things so you wind up on top of the hill at sunset. Allow one hour at a promenade pace to reach the elevator up to Castle Hill. To trace the route of this walk, see the "Nice" map, later.

• *Start your walk at the pink-domed...*

HOTEL NEGRESCO

Built in 1913, Nice's finest hotel is also a historic monument, offering up the city's most expensive beds and a museum-like interior. The hotel is technically off-limits if you're not a guest, but if you're decently dressed and explain to the doorman that you'd like to get a drink at Negresco's classy-cozy Le Relais bar, you'll be allowed past the registration desk. You can also explain that you want to shop at their store, which also might get you in—*bonne chance.*

If you get in, you can't miss the huge **Salon Royal** ballroom. The chandelier hanging from its dome is made of 16,000 pieces of crystal. It was built in France for the Russian czar's Moscow palace...but

Biking the promenade

thanks to the Bolshevik Revolution in 1917, he couldn't take delivery. Bronze portrait busts of Czar Alexander III and his wife, Maria Feodorovna—who returned to her native Denmark after the revolution—are to the right, facing the shops. Circle the interior of the ballroom and admire the soft light from the glass dome that Gustave Eiffel designed two decades after his more famous tower in Paris, then wander the perimeter to enjoy both historic and modern art. Fine portraits include Emperor Napoleon III and wife Empress Eugénie (who acquired Nice for France from Italy in 1860).

• Across the street from the Hôtel Negresco (to the east) is...

VILLA MASSENA

When Nice became part of France, France invested heavily in what it expected to be the country's new high society retreat—an elite resort akin to Russia's Sochi. This fine palace was built for Jean-Andre Masséna, a military hero of the Napoleonic age. Take a moment to stroll around the lovely garden (free, daily 10:00-18:00).

• From Villa Masséna, head for the beach and begin your Promenade des Anglais stroll. But first, grab a blue chair and gaze out to the...

BAY OF ANGELS (BAIE DES ANGES)

Face the water. The body of Nice's patron saint, Réparate, was supposedly escorted into this bay by angels in the fourth century. To your right is where you might have been escorted into France—Nice's airport, built on a massive landfill. The tip of land beyond the runway is Cap d'Antibes. Until 1860, Antibes and Nice were in different countries—Antibes was French, but Nice was a protectorate of the Italian kingdom of Savoy-Piedmont, a.k.a. the Kingdom of Sardinia. In 1850, the people here spoke Italian or Nissart (a local dialect) and ate pasta. As the story goes, the region was given a choice: Join newly united Italy or join France, which was enjoying prosperous times under the rule of Napoleon III. The majority voted in 1860 to go French...and voilà!

The lower green hill to your left is Castle Hill (where this walk ends). Farther left lie Villefranche-sur-Mer and Cap

The Bay of Angels epitomizes the beauty of the French Riviera.

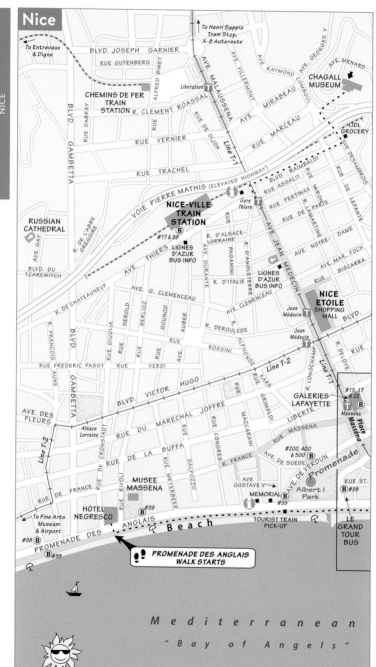

Nice

To Entrevaux & Digne

BLVD. JOSEPH GARNIER

RUE GUTENBERG

To Henri Sappia Tram Stop, A-8 Autoroute

Libération

CHEMINS DE FER TRAIN STATION

R. CLEMENT ROASSAL

AVE. MALAUSSENA

AVE. VILLERMONT

AVE. MIRABEAU

AVE. RAYMOND COMBOUIL

AVE. GEORGES V

AVE. MENARD

CHAGALL MUSEUM

LIDL GROCERY

BLVD. GAMBETTA

RUE DABRAY

ALFRED BINET

RUE VERNIER

RUE DE DIJON

RUE MARCEAU

AVE. DESAMBROIS

AVE. DE LEPANTE

RUE TRACHEL

Line T-1

BLVD. RAIMBALDI

RUSSIAN CATHEDRAL

AVE. GAY

R. DE L'ABBE GREGOIRE

VOIE PIERRE MATHIS (ELEVATED HIGHWAY)

Gare Thiers

RUE ASSALIT

RUE PERTINAX

R. LAMARTINE

RUE DE PARIS

RUE MIRONS

BLVD. DU TZAREWITCH

R. DE CHATEAUNEUF

NICE-VILLE TRAIN STATION

#17 & 98

RUE THIERS

R. D'ALSACE-LORRAINE

RUE DURANTE

PAGANINI

R. D'ANGLETERRE

LIGNES D'AZUR BUS INFO

R. D'ITALIE

AVE. JEAN MEDECIN

AVE. NOTRE-DAME

AVE. MAR. FOCH

BISCARRA

LIGNES D'AZUR BUS INFO

AVE. G. CLEMENCEAU

AVE. CLEMENCEAU

Jean Médecin

NICE ETOILE SHOPPING MALL

BLVD.

R. FRANCOIS

BLVD. GAMBETTA

HEROLD

BERLIOZ

GOUNOD

AUBER

R. DEROULEDE

R. ALPHONSE KARR

ROSSINI

Jean Médecin

R. DELOYE

RUE

RUE FREDERIC PASSY

AUNE

RUE GUGLIA

RUE

VERDI

Line T-2

RUE

RUE LONGCHAMP

Line T-1

AVE. DES FLEURS

BLVD. GAMBETTA

Alsace Lorraine

BLVD. VICTOR HUGO

RUE DU MARECHAL JOFFRE

RUE

RUE GRIMALDI

RUE MACCARANI

GALERIES LAFAYETTE

LIBERTE

#15, 17 & 22

Massena

Place Masséna

Line T-2

RUE DE CRONSTADT

RUE DE LA BUFFA

RUE CONGRES

RUE DALPOZZO

R. FRANCE

RUE MASSENA

AVE. DE SUEDE

#200, 400 & 500

Promenade

RUE ST.

RUE DE FRANCE

RUE RIVOLI

MUSEE MASSENA

RUE MEYERBEER

#98

AVE GUSTAVE V

MEMORIAL

#98

AVE DE VERDUN

Albert I Park

#98

LE GRAND TOUR BUS

HOTEL NEGRESCO

To Fine Arts Museum & Airport

#98

PROMENADE DES ANGLAIS

#98

Beach

TOURIST TRAIN PICK-UP

PROMENADE DES ANGLAIS WALK STARTS

Mediterranean

"Bay of Angels"

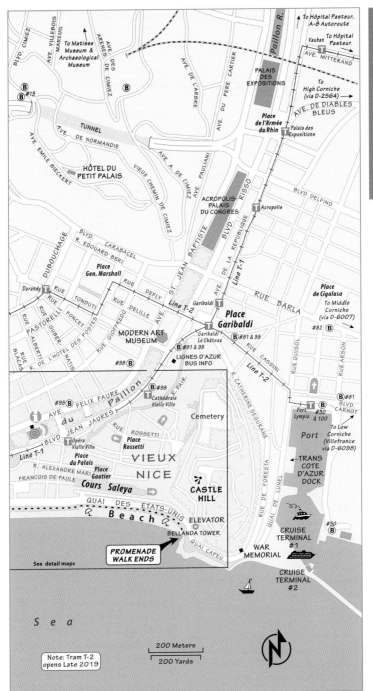

Ferrat (marked by the tower at land's end, and home to lots of millionaires), then Monaco (which you can't see, with more millionaires), then Italy. Behind you are the foothills of the Alps, which trap threatening clouds, ensuring that the Côte d'Azur enjoys sunshine more than 300 days each year.

• *With the sea on your right, begin strolling.*

THE PROMENADE

Nearby sit two fine belle-époque establishments: the West End and Westminster hotels, both boasting English names to help those original guests feel at home. (The West End is now part of the Best Western group...to help American guests feel at home.) These hotels symbolize Nice's arrival as a tourist mecca in the 19th century, when the combination of leisure time and a stable economy allowed visitors to find the sun even in winter.

As you walk, be careful to avoid the bike lane. Find the easel showing a painting of La Jetée Promenade—Nice's elegant pier and first casino, built in 1883. Even a hundred years ago, there was sufficient tourism in Nice to justify its construction. La Jetée Promenade stood east of those white-covered pilings just offshore, until the Germans dismantled it during World War II to salvage its copper and iron. When La Jetée was thriving, it took gamblers two full days to get to the Riviera by train from Paris. The painting shows what an event strolling the Promenade was—it was all about dressing up, being seen, and looking good.

Although La Jetée Promenade is gone, you can still see the striking 1927 Art Nouveau facade of the **Palais de la Méditerranée,** once a magnificent complex housing a casino, luxury hotel, and theater. It became one of the most famous destinations in all of Europe until it was destroyed in the 1980s to make room for a new hotel (the Hyatt Regency). The facade of the grand old building was spared the wrecking ball, but the classy interior was lost forever.

Despite the lack of sand, the pebble beaches here are still a popular draw. You can go local and rent beach gear—about €15 for a *chaise longue* (long chair) and a *transat* (mattress), €5 for an umbrella, and €5 for a towel.

Albert I Park is named after the Belgian king who defied a German ultimatum at the beginning of World War I. While the English came first, the Belgians and Russians were also big fans of 19th-century Nice. That tall statue at the edge of the park commemorates the 100-year anniversary of Nice's union with France.

Continuing along the promenade you'll soon enter the **Quai des Etats-Unis** ("Quay of the United States"). This name was given as a tip-of-the-cap to the Americans for finally entering World War I in 1917. The big, blue chair statue celebrates the inviting symbol of this venerable walk and kicks off the best stretch of beach—quieter and with less traffic. Check out the laid-back couches at the **Plage Beau Rivage** lounge and consider a beachfront drink.

Ahead on the left, the elegant back side of Nice's opera house faces the sea. The tiny bronze Statue of Liberty (right in front of you as you face the opera) reminds all that this stretch of seafront promenade is named for the USA.

The top level of the long, low galleries on the left was British tourists' preferred place for a stroll before the Promenade des Anglais was built. The ground floor served the city's fishermen. Behind the galleries bustles the **Cours Saleya Market**—long the heart and soul of Vieux Nice, with handy WCs under its arches.

Farther along, on the far-right side of the Quai des Etats-Unis (opposite Le Camboda restaurant), find the three-foot-tall white **metal winch** at the ramp to the beach. Long before tourism—and long before Nice dredged its harbor—hard-working fishing boats rather than vacationing tourists lined the beach. The boats were hauled in through the surf by winches like this and tied to the iron rings on either side.

• Your walk is over. From here you can continue 10 minutes along the coast to the port, around the foot of Castle Hill (fine views of the entire promenade and a monumental war memorial carved into the hillside); hike or ride the elevator up to **Castle Hill** *(catch the elevator next to Hôtel Suisse); or head into Vieux Nice (you can follow my "Vieux Nice Walk").*

Rick's Tip: *To make life tolerable on the rocks, swimmers should buy a pair of the cheap plastic* **beach shoes** *sold at many shops.* **Go Sport** *at #13 on Place Masséna is a good bet (open daily).*

● Vieux Nice Walk

This self-guided walk through Nice's old town, worth ▲▲, gives you a helpful introduction to the city's bicultural heritage and its most interesting neighborhoods. For the route, see the "Vieux Nice Restaurants & Hotels" map on page 346. Allow about one hour at a leisurely pace for this level walk from Place Masséna to Place Rossetti. It's best done in the morning (while the outdoor market thrives), and preferably not on a Sunday, when things are quiet. This ramble is also a joy at night, when fountains glow and pedestrians control the streets.

• Start where Avenue Jean Médecin hits the people-friendly Place Masséna—the successful result of a long, expensive city upgrade and the new center of Nice.

PLACE MASSENA

The grand Place Masséna is Nice's drawing room, where old meets new, and where the tramway bends between Vieux Nice and the train station. The square's black-and-white pavement feels like an elegant outdoor ballroom, with the sleek tram waltzing across its dance floor. While once congested with cars, the square today is crossed only by these trams, which swoosh silently by every couple of minutes. The men on pedestals sitting

high above are modern-art additions that arrived with the tram. For a mood-altering experience, return after dark and watch the illuminated figures float yoga-like above. Place Masséna is at its sophisticated best after the sun goes down.

This vast square dates from 1848 and pays tribute to Jean-André Masséna, a French military leader during the Revolutionary and Napoleonic wars. Not just another pretty face in a long lineup of French military heroes, he's considered among the greatest commanders in history—anywhere, anytime. Napoleon called him "the greatest name of my military Empire."

Avenue Jean Médecin, Nice's Champs-Elysées, cuts from here through the new town to the train station. Looking up the avenue, you'll see the tracks, the freeway, and the Alps beyond.

Appreciate the city's Italian heritage—it feels more like Venice than Paris. The portico flanking Avenue Jean Médecin is Italian, not French. The rich colors of the buildings reflect the taste of previous Italian rulers.

Now turn to the fountains and look east to see the **Promenade du Paillon,** a pedestrian-friendly parkway that extends from the sea to the Museum of Modern Art. Past the fountain stands a bronze statue of the square's namesake, Masséna.

Promenade du Paillon

The hills beyond separate Nice from Villefranche-sur-Mer.

To the right of the Promenade du Paillon lies **Vieux Nice,** with its jumbled and colorful facades below Castle Hill. Looking closer and further to the right, the **statue of Apollo** has horsey hair and holds a beach towel (in the fountain) as if to say, "It's beer o'clock, let's go."

• *Walk past Apollo into Vieux Nice (careful of those trams). A block down Rue de l'Opéra you'll see a grouping of rusted girders. Turn left onto Rue St. François de Paule.*

RUE ST. FRANÇOIS DE PAULE

This colorful street leads into the heart of Vieux Nice. On the left is the Hôtel de Ville (City Hall). Peer into the **Alziari olive oil shop** (at #14 on the right). Dating from 1868, the shop produces top-quality stone-ground olive oil. The proud and charming owner, Gilles Piot, claims that stone wheels create less acidity, since grinding with metal creates heat (see photo in back over the door). Locals fill their own containers from the huge vats.

A few awnings down, **La Couqueto** is a colorful shop filled with Provençal fabrics and crafts, including lovely folk characters (*santons*). The *boulangerie* next door is ideal for a cheap lunch and has good outdoor seating.

Next door is Nice's grand **opera house**. Imagine this opulent jewel back in the 19th century. With all the fancy big-city folks wintering here, this rough-edged town needed some high-class entertainment. And Victorians needed an alternative to those "devilish" gambling houses. (Queen Victoria, so disgusted by casinos, would actually close the drapes on her train window when passing Monte Carlo.) The four statues on top represent theater, dance, music, and party poopers.

Across the street, **Pâtisserie Auer**'s grand old storefront would love to tempt you with chocolates and candied fruits. It's changed little over the centuries. The writing on the window says, "Since 1820 from father to son." Wander in for a whiff of chocolate and a dazzling interior.

• *Continue on, sifting your way through a cluttered block of tacky souvenir shops to the big market square.*

COURS SALEYA

Named for its broad exposure to the sun (*soleil*), Cours Saleya (koor sah-lay-yuh)—a commotion of color, sights, smells, and people—has been Nice's main market square since the Middle Ages (flower market all day Tue-Sun, produce market Tue-Sun until 13:00, antiques on Mon). If you're early enough for coffee, pause for a break at **Café le Flore**'s outdoor tables in the heart of the market (a block up on the left).

The first section is devoted to the Riviera's largest **flower market.** In operation

Cours Saleya Market

A movable art gallery

since the 19th century, this market offers plants and flowers that grow effortlessly and ubiquitously in this climate, including the local favorites: carnations, roses, and jasmine. Locals know the season by what's on sale (mimosas in February, violets in March, and so on). Until the recent rise in imported flowers, this region supplied all of France with flowers.

The boisterous **produce section** trumpets the season with mushrooms, strawberries, white asparagus, zucchini flowers, and more—whatever's fresh gets top billing.

The market opens up at Place Pierre Gautier. It's also called Plassa dou Gouvernou—you'll see bilingual street signs here that include the old Niçois language, an Italian dialect. This is where farmers set up stalls to sell their produce and herbs directly.

From the steps, look up to the **hill** that dominates to the east. In the Middle Ages, a massive castle stood there with soldiers at the ready. Over time, the city sprawled down to where you are now. With the river guarding one side (running under today's Promenade du Paillon parkway) and the sea the other, this mountain fortress seemed strong—until Louis XIV leveled it in 1706. Nice's medieval seawall ran along the line of two-story buildings where you're standing.

Now, look across Place Pierre Gautier to the large "palace." The **Ducal Palace** was where the kings of Sardinia, the city's Italian rulers until 1860, resided when in Nice. (For centuries, Nice was under the rule of the Italian capital of Turin.) Today, the palace is the local police headquarters. The land upon which the Cours Saleya sits was once the duke's gardens and didn't become a market until Nice's union with France.

• *Continue down Cours Saleya. The faded golden building that seals the end of the square is where Henri Matisse spent 17 years. I imagine he was inspired by his view. The* **Café les Ponchettes** *is perfectly posi-*

tioned for you to enjoy the view, too, if you want a coffee break. At the café, turn onto...

RUE DE LA POISSONNERIE

Look up at the first floor of the first building on your right. **Adam and Eve** are squaring off, each holding a zucchini-like gourd. This scene represents the annual rapprochement in Nice to make up for the sins of a too-much-fun Carnival (Mardi Gras, the pre-Lenten festival). Residents of Nice have partied hard during Carnival for more than 700 years.

Next, check out the small **Baroque church** (Notre-Dame de l'Annonciation, closed 12:00-14:30) dedicated to St. Rita, the patron saint of desperate causes and desperate people (see display in window). She holds a special place in locals' hearts, making this the most popular church in Nice. Drop in for a peek at the dazzling Baroque decor. The first chapel on the right is dedicated to St. Erasmus, protector of mariners.

• *Turn right on the next street, where you'll pass one of Vieux Nice's most happening bars* **(Distilleries Ideales)**. *Pause at the next corner and study the classic Vieux Nice scene. Now turn left on Rue Droite and enter an area that feels like Little Naples.*

RUE DROITE

In the Middle Ages, this straight, skinny street provided the most direct route from river to sea within the old walled town. Pass the recommended restaurant Acchiardo. Notice stepped lanes leading uphill to the castle. Pop into the Jesuit **Eglise St-Jacques** church (also called Eglise du Gésu) for an explosion of Baroque exuberance hidden behind that plain facade.

• *Make a left on Rue Rossetti; shortly you'll cross Rue Benoît Bunico.*

In the 18th century, this street served as a **ghetto** for Nice's Jews. At sunset, gates would seal the street at either end, locking people in until daylight. To identify Jews as non-Christians, the men were required to wear yellow stars and the women to wear yellow scarves. Wander a few steps up the street to find the white columns and archway across from #19 that mark what was the synagogue until 1848, when revolution ended the notion of ghettos in France.

• *Continue down Rue Rossetti to...*

PLACE ROSSETTI

The most Italian of Nice's piazzas, Place Rossetti comes alive after dark—in part because of the **Fenocchio gelato shop,** popular for its many innovative flavors.

Check out the **Cathedral of St. Réparate**—an unassuming building for a big-city cathedral. It was relocated here in the 1500s, when Castle Hill was temporarily converted to military use. The name comes from Nice's patron saint, a teenage virgin named Réparate, whose martyred body floated to Nice in the fourth century accompanied by angels. The beautiful interior is worth a wander.

• *This is the end of our walk. From here you can hike up* **Castle Hill** *(from Place Rossetti, take Rue Rossetti uphill). Or you can have an ice cream and browse the colorful lanes of Vieux Nice...or grab Apollo and hit the beach.*

Sights

Some of Nice's top attractions—the Promenade des Anglais, the beach, and the old town—are covered earlier in my self-guided walks. But Nice offers some additional worthwhile sights, covered here. A €10 combo-ticket (sold at participating sights) covers all of Nice's museums, except the Chagall Museum, which requires a separate admission (and is well worth it).

Rick's Tip: Visit the Chagall and Matisse museums together, *but* not on Tuesday, *when they're closed.*

The Chagall and Matisse museums are a long walk northeast of Nice's city center. Because they're in the same direction and served by the same bus line, try to visit them on the same trip. From Place Masséna, the Chagall Museum is a 10-minute bus ride, and the Matisse Museum is a few stops beyond that.

▲▲▲CHAGALL MUSEUM (MUSEE NATIONAL MARC CHAGALL)

Even if you don't get modern art, this museum—with the world's largest collection of Marc Chagall's work in captivity—is a delight. Between 1954 and 1967, he painted a cycle of 17 large murals designed for, and donated to, this museum. These paintings, inspired by the biblical books of Genesis, Exodus, and the Song of Songs, make up the "nave," or core, of what Chagall called the "House of Brotherhood."

Cost and Hours: €8, €2 more during frequent special exhibits; Wed-Mon 10:00-18:00, Nov-April until 17:00, closed Tue year-round; ticket includes helpful audioguide idyllic **$** garden café (salads and *plats*), tel. 04 93 53 87 20, http://en.musees-nationaux-alpesmaritimes.fr.

Getting There: The museum is located on Avenue Docteur Ménard. **Taxis** from the city center cost about €15. **Buses** connect the museum with downtown Nice. From downtown, catch bus #15 (Mon-Sat

Eglise St-Jacques

Place Rossetti

6/hour, Sun 3/hour, 10 minutes). Catch the bus from the east end of the Galeries Lafayette department store, near the Masséna tram stop, on Rue Sacha Guitry. Watch for a *Musée Chagall* sign on the bus shelter where you'll get off (on Boulevard de Cimiez).

Visiting the Museum: It takes about one hour to see this small museum.

In the **main hall** you'll find the core of the collection (Genesis and Exodus scenes). Each painting is a lighter-than-air collage of images that draws from Chagall's Russian folk-village youth, his Jewish heritage, the Bible, and his feeling that he existed somewhere between heaven and earth. He believed that the Bible was a synonym for nature, and that both color and biblical themes were key for understanding God's love for his creation. Chagall's brilliant blues and reds celebrate nature, as do his spiritual and folk themes. Notice the focus on couples. To Chagall, humans loving each other mirrored God's love of creation.

The adjacent **octagonal room** houses five more paintings. The paintings in this room were inspired by the Old Testament Song of Songs. Chagall was one of the few "serious" 20th-century artists to portray unabashed love. Where the Bible uses the metaphor of earthly, physical, sexual love to describe God's love for humans, Chagall uses unearthly colors and a mystical ambience to celebrate human love. These red-toned canvases are hard to interpret literally, but they capture the rosy spirit of a man in love with life.

Back near the entry, the wall **mosaic** (which no longer reflects in the filthy reflecting pond) evokes the prophet Elijah in his chariot of fire (from the Second Book of Kings)—with Chagall's addition of the 12 signs of the zodiac, which he used to symbolize time.

The **auditorium** is worth a peaceful moment to enjoy three Chagall stained-glass windows depicting the seven days of creation. This is also where you'll find a wonderful film (52 minutes) on Chagall, which plays at the top of each hour (not available during special exhibits).

▲MATISSE MUSEUM (MUSEE MATISSE)

This small, underachieving museum fills an old mansion in a park surrounded by scant Roman ruins, and houses a limited sampling of works from the various periods of Henri Matisse's artistic career. The museum offers an introduction to the artist's many styles and materials, both shaped by Mediterranean light and by fellow Côte d'Azur artists Picasso and Renoir.

As you tour the museum, look for Matisse's favorite motifs—including fruit, flowers, wallpaper, and sunny rooms—often with a window opening onto a sunny landscape. Another favorite subject is the *odalisque* (harem concubine), usually shown sprawled in a seductive pose and with a simplified, masklike face. You'll also see a few souvenirs from his travels, which influenced much of his work.

Chagall Museum

Chagall, Song of Songs IV

The Riviera's Art Scene

The list of artists who have painted the Riviera reads like a *Who's Who* of 20th-century art. Pierre-Auguste Renoir, Henri Matisse, Marc Chagall, Georges Braque, Raoul Dufy, Fernand Léger, and Pablo Picasso all lived and worked here—and raved about the region's wonderful light. Their simple, semi-abstract, and—most importantly—colorful works reflect the pleasurable atmosphere of the Riviera. You'll experience the same landscapes they painted in this bright, sun-drenched region, punctuated with views of the "azure sea." Try to imagine the Riviera with a fraction of the people and development you see today.

A collection of modern- and contemporary-art museums dot the Riviera, allowing art lovers to appreciate these masters' works while immersed in the same sun and culture that inspired them. Many of the museums were designed to blend pieces with the surrounding views, gardens, and fountains, thus highlighting that modern art is not only stimulating, but sometimes simply beautiful.

Cost and Hours: Covered by €10 Nice museum combo-ticket; Wed-Mon 10:00-18:00, mid-Oct-mid-June from 11:00, closed Tue year-round, 164 Avenue des Arènes de Cimiez, tel. 04 93 81 08 08, www.musee-matisse-nice.org.

Getting There: Take a cab (€20 from Promenade des Anglais). Alternatively, hop bus #15, direction: Rimiez, from the east end of Galeries Lafayette (from train station, catch #17, direction: Cimiez Hôpital). Get off at the Arènes-Matisse bus stop (look for the crumbling Roman arena that once held 10,000 spectators), then walk 50 yards into the park to find the pink villa.

▲RUSSIAN CATHEDRAL (CATHEDRALE RUSSE)

Nice's Russian Orthodox church—claimed by some to be the finest outside Russia—is worth a visit. Five hundred rich Russian families wintered in Nice in the late 19th century, and they needed a worthy Orthodox house of worship. Dowager Czarina Maria Feodorovna and her son, Nicholas II, offered the land for the construction, which began in 1903. Nicholas underwrote much of the project and gave this church to the Russian community in 1912. (A few years later, Russian comrades

who *didn't* winter on the Riviera assassinated him.) Here in the land of olives and anchovies, these proud onion domes seem odd. But, I imagine, so did those old Russians. The park around the church stays open at lunch and makes a nice setting for picnics.

Cost and Hours: Free; daily 9:30-17:30 except during services, chanted services Sat at 18:00, Sun at 10:00; no tourist visits during services, no shorts, Avenue Nicolas II, tel. 04 93 96 88 02, www.sobor.fr.

▲CASTLE HILL (COLLINE DU CHATEAU)

This hill—in an otherwise flat city center—offers sensational views over Nice, the port (to the east, created for trade

The view from Castle Hill is worth the climb.

Matisse "cutout" painting

Russian Cathedral

and military use in the 15th century), the foothills of the Alps, and the Mediterranean. The views are best early, at sunset, or whenever the weather's clear.

Nice was founded on this hill. Its residents were crammed onto the hilltop until the 12th century, as it was too risky to live in the flatlands below. Today you'll find a playground, a café, and a cemetery—but no castle—on Castle Hill.

Cost and Hours: Park is free and closes at 20:00 in summer, earlier off-season.

Getting There: You can get to the top by foot, by elevator (free, daily April-Sept 9:00-19:00, until 20:00 in summer, Oct-March 10:00-18:00, next to beachfront Hôtel Suisse).

See the "Promenade des Anglais Walk" for a pleasant stroll that ends near Castle Hill.

Experiences

MEDITERRANEAN CRUISE

To see Nice from the water, hop this one-hour ▲Trans Côte d'Azur cruise in a comfortable yacht-size vessel to Cap Ferrat and past Villefranche-sur-Mer, then return to Nice with a final lap along Prom-

enade des Anglais (€18, covered by French Riviera Pass, Tue-Sun 2/day, no boats Mon or in off-season). Boats leave from Nice's port, Bassin des Amiraux, just below Castle Hill—look for the ticket booth *(billeterie)* on Quai de Lunel.

NIGHTLIFE

The city is a walker's delight after dark. Promenade des Anglais, Cours Saleya, Vieux Nice, Promenade du Paillon, and Place Masséna are all worth an evening wander. I can't get enough of the night scene on Place Masséna and around the adjacent fountains.

Most activity focuses on Vieux Nice. Rue de la Préfecture and Place du Palais are ground zero for bar life, though Place Rossetti and Rue Droite are also good targets. **Distilleries Ideales** is a good place to start or end your evening, with a lively international crowd, a *Pirates of the Caribbean* interior, and a *Cheers* vibe (lots of beers on tap, where Rue de la Poissonnerie and Rue Barillerie meet, happy hour 18:00-21:00). **Wayne's Bar** and others nearby are happening spots for the younger, Franco-Anglo backpacker crowd

(15 Rue Préfecture). Along the Promenade des Anglais, the classy Le Relais bar at **Hôtel Negresco** is fancy-cigar old English with frequent live jazz. To savor fine views over Nice, find **Hotel Aston La Scala**'s seventh-floor bar/terrace, which is a good spot for a drink any night, but offers jazz and blues on Thursdays and Fridays and a DJ on Saturdays (daily 17:00 to late, on Promenade du Paillon at 12 Avenue Félix Faure, tel. 04 92 17 53 00).

Eating

My favorite dining spots are in Vieux Nice. It's well worth booking ahead for these places. If Vieux Nice is too far, I've listed some great places handier to your hotel. Promenade des Anglais is ideal for picnic dinners on warm, languid evenings or a meal at a beachside restaurant. For a more romantic and peaceful meal, head for nearby Villefranche-sur-Mer. Avoid the fun-to-peruse but terribly touristy eateries lining Rue Masséna.

In Vieux Nice

$$$ Le Safari is a fair option for Niçois cuisine, pasta, pizza, and outdoor dining. This sprawling café-restaurant, convivial and rustic with the coolest interior on Cours Saleya, is packed with locals and tourists, and staffed with hurried waiters (daily noon to late, 1 Cours Saleya, tel. 04 93 80 18 44, www.restaurantsafari.fr).

$$ Acchiardo is a homey-but-lively eatery that mixes loyal clientele with hungry tourists. The food is delicious and copious, and the house wine is good and reasonable (Mon-Fri 19:00 until late, closed Sat-Sun and Aug, reservations smart, indoor seating only, 38 Rue Droite, tel. 04 93 85 51 16).

$ Chez Palmyre, your best budget bet in Vieux Nice, is tiny and popular, so book ahead (a week is advised). The ambience is rustic and fun, with people squeezed onto shared tables to enjoy the home-style cooking. Philippe serves everyone the same three-course, €17 *menu,* which changes every two weeks (closed Sat-Sun, 5 Rue Droite, tel. 04 93 85 72 32).

$$$ Olive et Artichaut is a sharp bistro-diner with a small counter, black-meets-white floor tiles, and a foodie vibe. It's a good choice to dine on carefully prepared Mediterranean dishes with creative twists (closed Mon-Tue, 6 Rue Ste. Réparate, tel. 04 89 14 97 51).

$$ Koko Green is a sweet little haven for vegan and raw-food types and is run by a delightful Franco-Kiwi couple (open Thu-Sun for lunch, Sat for lunch and dinner, 1 Rue de la Loge, mobile 07 81 63 14 88).

Rick's Tip: Nice's **dinner scene converges on Cours Saleya,** *which is entertaining enough in itself to make the generally mediocre food a good deal. It's a fun spot to compare tans and mussels—and worth wandering through even if you eat elsewhere.*

In the City Center

$$ Le Luna Rossa is a small neighborhood place serving delicious French-Italian dishes. Owner Christine and her staff welcome diners with enthusiastic service and reasonable prices. Pasta dishes are copious and served in cast-iron pans, and the *assortiment* main course is a great sampler dish. Dine inside or outside on a sidewalk terrace (closed Sun-Mon, just north of parkway at 3 Rue Chauvain, tel. 04 93 85 55 66).

$ L'Ovale offers an unpretentious and local café-bistro experience. Owner David serves traditional dishes from southwestern France (rich and meaty). Dining is inside only. Consider the cassoulet, the hearty *salade de manchons* with duck and walnuts, or the €18-23 three-course *menus* (daily, 29 Rue Pastorelli, tel. 04 93 80 31 65).

$$$ Les 5 Sens ("The Five Senses") is a lively and dressy restaurant serving classic French fare at higher-end prices that justify the cost for discerning diners (daily, 37 Rue Pastorelli, tel. 09 81 06 57 00).

The Riviera's Cuisine Scene

While many of the same dishes served in Provence are available in the Riviera, there are differences, especially if you look for anything Italian or from the sea. When dining on the Riviera, I expect views and ambience more than top-quality cuisine.

A **salade niçoise** makes the perfect introduction to the Riviera's cuisine. Surprisingly, the authentic version contains no potatoes or green beans but consists of ripe tomatoes, plenty of raw vegetables (such as radishes, green peppers, celery, and perhaps artichoke or fava beans), as well as tuna (usually canned), anchovy, hard-boiled egg, and olives. This is my go-to salad for a tasty, healthy, cheap (€14), and fast lunch. I like to spend a couple of extra euros and eat it in a place with a nice ambience and view.

For lunch on the go, look for a **pan bagnat** (like a *salade niçoise* stuffed into a crusty roll drizzled with olive oil and wine vinegar). Other tasty bread treats include **pissaladière** (bread dough topped with caramelized onions, olives, and anchovies), **fougasse** (a spindly, lace-like bread sometimes flavored with nuts, herbs, olives, or ham), and **socca** (a thin chickpea-and-olive-oil crêpe, seasoned with pepper and often served in a paper cone by street vendors).

The Riviera specializes in all sorts of fish and shellfish. **Bouillabaisse** is the Riviera's most famous dish; you'll find it in seafront villages and cities. It's a spicy fish stew based on recipes handed down from sailors in Marseille. This dish often requires a minimum order of two and can cost up to €40-60 per person. Far less pricey than bouillabaisse and worth trying is the local **soupe de poissons** (fish soup). It's a creamy soup flavored like bouillabaisse, with anise and orange, and served with croutons and *rouille* sauce (but has no chunks of fish).

Other fishy options include **fruits de mer** (platters of seafood—including tiny shellfish, from which you get the edible part only by sucking really hard), herb-infused mussels, stuffed sardines, squid (slowly simmered with tomatoes and herbs), and tuna *(thon)*. The popular *loup flambé au fenouil* is grilled sea bass, flavored with fennel and torched with *pastis* prior to serving.

Do as everyone else does: Drink **wines** from Provence. **Bandol** (red) and **cassis** (white) are popular and from a region nearly on the Riviera. The only wines made in the Riviera are **Bellet** rosé and white, the latter often found in fish-shaped bottles.

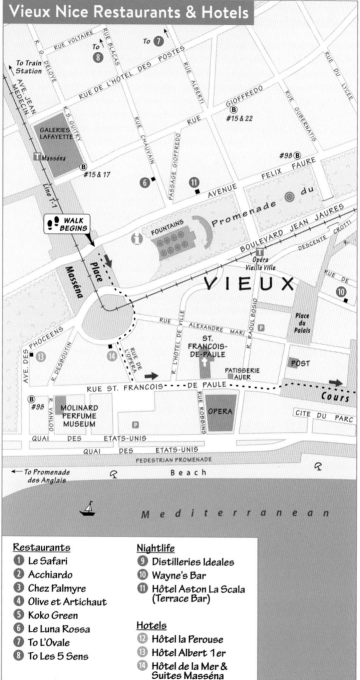

Vieux Nice Restaurants & Hotels

Restaurants
1 Le Safari
2 Acchiardo
3 Chez Palmyre
4 Olive et Artichaut
5 Koko Green
6 Le Luna Rossa
7 To L'Ovale
8 To Les 5 Sens

Nightlife
9 Distilleries Ideales
10 Wayne's Bar
11 Hôtel Aston La Scala (Terrace Bar)

Hotels
12 Hôtel la Perouse
13 Hôtel Albert 1er
14 Hôtel de la Mer & Suites Masséna

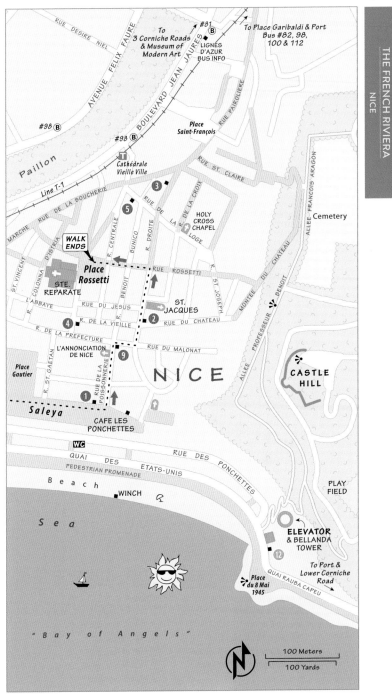

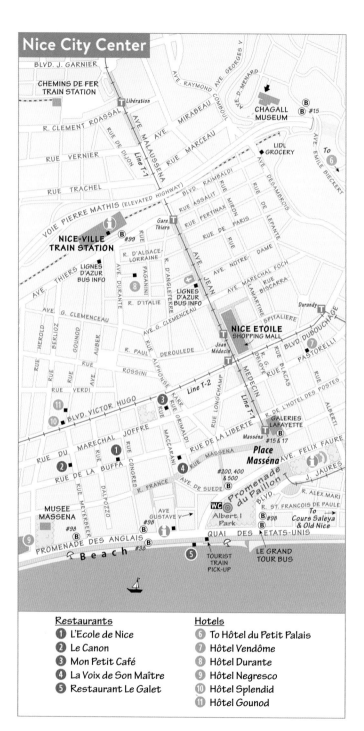

Nice City Center

BLVD. J. GARNIER

CHEMINS DE FER
TRAIN STATION

AVE. RAYMOND COMBOUL

AVE. GEORGES V

AVE. D. MENARD

CHAGALL
MUSEUM

Ⓑ #15

LIDL
GROCERY

AVE. EMILE BIECKERT

To
6

Libération

Line T-1

AVE. MALAUSSENA

R. CLEMENT ROASSAL

RUE DE DIJON

RUE VERNIER

AVE. MIRABEAU

RUE MARCEAU

AVE.

BLVD. RAIMBALDI

RUE ASSALIT

RUE PERTINAX

RUE DE PARIS

RUE MIRON

RUE DESAMBROIS

RUE DE LEPANTE

RUE TRACHEL

VOIE PIERRE MATHIS (ELEVATED HIGHWAY)

Gare
Thiers

AVE. JEAN

AVE. NOTRE- DAME

AVE. MARECHAL FOCH

RUE
DISCARRA

Durandy

NICE-VILLE
TRAIN STATION

Ⓑ #99

RUE D'ALSACE-
LORRAINE

PAGANINI

R. D'ANGLETERRE

AVE. DURANTE

LIGNES
D'AZUR
BUS INFO

LIGNES
D'AZUR
BUS INFO

AVE. THIERS

8

R. D'ITALIE

AVE. G. CLEMENCEAU

AVE. G. CLEMENCEAU

SPITALERIE

BLVD. DUBOUCHAGE

7

PASTORELLI

HEROLD

BERLIOZ

GOUNOD

AUBER

RUE
ALPHONSE
KARR

R. PAUL DEROULEDE

NICE ETOILE
SHOPPING MALL

Jean
Médecin

RUE G.
DELOYE

RUE BACAS

RUE DE L'HOTEL DES POSTES

ALBERTI

RUE

RUE

RUE
VERDI

ROSSINI

Line T-2

RUE GRIMALDI

MEDECIN

Line T-1

RUE DE L'HOTEL DES POSTES

GALERIES
LAFAYETTE

Ⓑ #15 & 17

11

10

BLVD. VICTOR HUGO

3

RUE DE LA LIBERTE

Masséna

Place
Masséna

AVE. FELIX FAURE

RUE DU MARECHAL JOFFRE

1

RUE

MACCARANI

RUE MASSENA

J. JAURES

2

RUE DE LA BUFFA

RUE
CONGRES

R. FRANCE

4

AVE. DE SUEDE

#200, 400
& 500
Ⓑ

Promenade
du Paillon

R. ALEX.MARI

BLVD.

R. ST. FRANÇOIS DE PAULE

MUSEE
MASSENA

#98
Ⓑ

AVE
GUSTAVE V

#98

Ⓑ

WC
Albert I
Park

Ⓑ #98

To
Cours Saleya
& Old Nice

9

PROMENADE DES ANGLAIS

Beach #98

5

QUAI DES ETATS-UNIS

TOURIST
TRAIN
PICK-UP

LE GRAND
TOUR BUS

Restaurants
1 L'Ecole de Nice
2 Le Canon
3 Mon Petit Café
4 La Voix de Son Maître
5 Restaurant Le Galet

Hotels
6 To Hôtel du Petit Palais
7 Hôtel Vendôme
8 Hôtel Durante
9 Hôtel Negresco
10 Hôtel Splendid
11 Hôtel Gounod

Pick an outdoor table in Nice and try the socca *(thin chickpea crêpe).*

$$ L'Ecole de Nice brings wine-shop decor to a cozy-but-modern restaurant, and serves a limited selection of delicious dishes complimented by a vast selection of wines. The set-price *menu*—less than €30 for three courses—is a swinging deal (closed Sun, 16 Rue de la Buffa, tel. 04 93 81 39 30).

$$$ Le Canon is a fine-if-trendy choice, run by two friends intent on serving top-quality and inventive dishes that emphasize the region's local, fresh, and in-season ingredients (closed Sat-Sun, 23 Rue Meyerbeer, tel. 04 93 79 09 24).

$$$ Mon Petit Café delivers fine, traditional cuisine to appreciative diners in a warm, candlelit interior or on a pleasant front terrace. Book ahead for this dressy place and expect top service and mouth-watering cuisine (closed Sun-Mon, 11 bis Rue Grimaldi, tel. 04 97 20 55 36, www.monpetitcafe-nice.com).

$ La Voix de Son Maître is a handy *creperie,* with seating on a broad terrace or inside (closed Sun, on Place Grimaldi, tel. 04 93 82 28 47).

On the Beach
$$$ Restaurant Le Galet is your best eat-on-the-beach option. The city vanishes as you step down to the beach. The food is nicely presented, and the tables feel elegant, even at the edge of the sand. Arrive for the sunset and you'll have an unforgettable meal (open for dinner May-mid-Sept, 3 Promenade des Anglais, tel. 04 93 88 17 23). Sunbathers can rent beach chairs and have drinks and meals served literally on the beach (lounge chairs-€16/half-day, €19/day).

Sleeping
Don't look for charm in Nice. Seek out a good location and modern, reliable amenities (like air-conditioning). For parking, ask your hotelier.

In the City Center
The train station area offers Nice's cheapest sleeps, but the neighborhood feels sketchy after dark. The cheapest places are older, well-worn, and come with some street noise. Places closer to Avenue Jean Médecin are more expensive and in a more comfortable area.

$$$$ Hôtel du Petit Palais**** is a little belle-époque jewel with 25 handsome rooms tucked neatly into a residential area on the hill several blocks from the Chagall Museum. It's bird-chirping peaceful and plush, with tastefully designed rooms, a garden terrace, and small pool. You'll walk 15 minutes down to Vieux Nice (or use bus #15), free street parking is usually easy to find (17 Avenue Emile Bieckert, tel. 04 93 62 19 11, wwww.petitpalaisnice.com, reservation@petitpalaisnice.com).

$$ Hôtel Vendôme** gives you a whiff of the belle époque, with pink pastels, high ceilings, and grand staircases in a man-sion set off the street. The modern rooms come in all sizes; many have balconies (limited pay parking—book ahead, 26 Rue Pastorelli at the corner of Rue Alberti, tel. 04 93 62 00 77, www.hotel-vendome-nice. com, contact@vendome-hotel-nice.com).

$ Hôtel Durante** rents quiet rooms in a happy orange building with rooms wrapped around a flowery courtyard. All but two rooms overlook the well-maintained patio. The rooms have adequate comfort (mostly modern decor), the price is right, and the parking is free on a first-come, first-served basis (family rooms, 16 Avenue Durante, tel. 04 93 88 84 40, www.hotel-du-rante.com, info@hotel-durante.com).

Near the Promenade des Anglais

$$$$ Hôtel Negresco***** owns Nice's most prestigious address on the Prome-nade des Anglais and knows it. Still, it's the kind of place that if you were to splurge just once in your life... Rooms are opulent and tips are expected (some view rooms, *très* classy bar, 37 Promenade des Anglais, tel. 04 93 16 64 00, www.hotel-negres-co-nice.com, reservations@hotel-ne-gresco.com).

$$$ Hôtel Splendid**** is a worthwhile splurge if you miss your Marriott. The pan-oramic rooftop pool, bar/restaurant, and breakfast room almost justify the cost...but throw in plush rooms, a free gym, and spa services, and you're as good as at home (pay parking, 50 Boulevard Victor Hugo, tel. 04 93 16 41 00, www.splendid-nice. com, info@splendid-nice.com).

$$ Hôtel Gounod** is a fine value behind Hôtel Splendid. Because the two share the same owners, Gounod's guests are allowed free access to Splendid's pool, hot tub, and other amenities. Most rooms are quiet, with high ceilings and traditional decor (family rooms, pay parking, 3 Rue Gounod, tel. 04 93 16 42 00, www.gounod-nice.com, info@gounod-nice.com).

In or near Vieux Nice

$$$$ Hôtel la Perouse,**** built into the rock of Castle Hill at the east end of the bay, is a fine splurge. This refuge-hotel is top-to-bottom flawless in every detail—from its elegant rooms (satin curtains, velour headboards) and attentive staff to its rooftop terrace with hot tub, sleek pool, and lovely **$$$$** garden restaurant. Sleep here to be spoiled and escape the big city (good family options, 11 Quai Rauba Capeu, tel. 04 93 62 34 63, www.hotel-la-perouse.com, lp@hotel-la-perouse.com).

$$$ Hôtel Albert 1er** is a fair deal in a central, busy location on Albert I Park, two blocks from the beach and Place Masséna. The staff is formal and the rooms are well-appointed and spot-less, with heavy brown tones. Some have views of the bay, while others overlook the park or a quiet interior courtyard (4 Avenue des Phocéens, tel. 04 93 85 74 01, www.hotel-albert-1er.com, info@hotel-albert1er.com).

\$\$ Hôtel de la Mer** is an intimate, 12-room place with an enviable position overlooking Place Masséna, just steps from Vieux Nice and the beach. Rooms are modern, comfortable, and well-priced (4 Place Masséna, tel. 04 93 92 09 10, www.hoteldelamernice.com, hotel.mer@wanadoo.fr). They also run the **\$\$\$\$ Suites Masséna** in the same building, with seven huge, modern, high-ceilinged rooms—designed for two but with room for three (tel. 04 93 13 48 11, www.lessuitesmassena.com).

Transportation
Getting Around Nice
BY PUBLIC TRANSPORTATION

Although you can walk to most attractions, smart travelers make good use of the buses and trams.

Tickets: Buses and trams are covered by the same €1.50 single-ride ticket, or you can pay €10 for a 10-ride ticket that can be shared (each use good for 74 minutes in one direction, including transfers between bus and tram). The €5 all-day pass is valid on city buses and trams, as well as buses to some nearby destinations (but not airport buses). You must validate your ticket in the machine on every trip. Buy single tickets from the bus driver or from the ticket machines on tram platforms (coins only—press the green button once to validate choice and twice at the end to get your ticket). Passes and 10-ride tickets are also available from machines at tram stops. Info: www.lignesdazur.com.

Buses: The bus is handy for reaching the Chagall and Matisse museums and the Russian Cathedral (for specifics, see listings under "Sights"). Route diagrams in the buses identify each stop.

Trams: Nice has a modern and efficient L-shaped tram line (T-1) that runs to the train station and a new line (T-2) that should connect the city center to the airport in late 2019 (http://tramway.nice.fr). Trams to the train station run every few minutes along Avenue Jean Médecin and

Boulevard Jean Jaurès, and connect the main train station with Place Masséna and Vieux Nice (Opéra stop), the port (Place Garibaldi stop), and buses east along the coast (Vauban stop). Boarding the tram in the direction of Hôpital Pasteur takes you toward the beach and Vieux Nice (direction: Henri Sappia goes the other way). The new T-2 tramway goes from the airport through the city center to Nice's Port Lympia, paralleling the Promenade des Anglais a few blocks inland.

BY TAXI OR UBER

While pricey, **cabs** are useful for getting to Nice's less-central sights (figure €8 for shortest ride, €15 from Promenade des Anglais to the Chagall Museum). Cabbies normally pick up only at taxi stands (*tête de station*), or you can call 04 93 13 78 78. **Uber** works here like it does at home (including your US app and account), though there are fewer cars here, and the price is not much cheaper than a taxi. Still, drivers are often nicer and more flexible, and you usually get a car without much delay.

Getting Around the Riviera from Nice

Nice is perfectly situated for exploring the Riviera by public transport. Trains and buses do a good job of linking towns along the coast, with bonus views along many routes. Have coins handy. Ticket machines don't take US credit cards or euro bills; smaller train stations may be

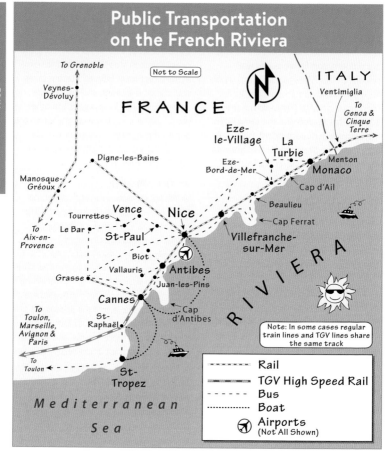

Public Transportation on the French Riviera

Not to Scale

To Grenoble

Veynes-Dévoluy

FRANCE

ITALY

Ventimiglia

To Genoa & Cinque Terre

Eze-le-Village

La Turbie

Menton

Monaco

Digne-les-Bains

Eze-Bord-de-Mer

Manosque-Gréoux

Cap d'Ail

Tourrettes

Vence

Nice

Beaulieu

To Aix-en-Provence

Le Bar

St-Paul

Villefranche-sur-Mer

Cap Ferrat

Biot

Vallauris

Antibes

Grasse

Juan-les-Pins

RIVIERA

Cannes

Cap d'Antibes

To Toulon, Marseille, Avignon & Paris

St-Raphaël

To Toulon

St-Tropez

Note: In some cases regular train lines and TGV lines share the same track

Mediterranean Sea

········· Rail

═══════ TGV High Speed Rail

- - - - Bus

·········· Boat

Airports (Not All Shown)

unstaffed; and bus drivers can't make change for large bills.

BY BUS

Buses are an amazing deal in the Riviera. Regardless of length, most one-way rides on regional buses (except express airport buses) cost €1.50. Tickets are good for up to 74 minutes of travel in one direction, including transfers. To connect to regional destinations, use the following bus lines and stops (see maps in this chapter for stop locations; www.lignesdazur.com).

Eastbound Buses: Due to the new T-2 tram that will end at the port, expect some changes to stop locations for these buses. Trams T-1 and/or T-2 will get you close to

these stops, and transfers are free from tram to bus for all lines but #100.

Bus #100 runs from Nice's port through **Villefranche-sur-Mer** (3-4/hour, 20 minutes), **Monaco** (1 hour). Bus #81 runs from the Promenade des Arts stop to **Villefranche-sur-Mer** (2-3/hour, 15 minutes) and around **Cap Ferrat** (30 minutes to **St-Jean-Cap-Ferrat**).

Westbound Buses: Bus #200 goes to **Antibes** (4/hour Mon-Sat, 2/hour Sun, 1.5 hours). Use the Albert I/Verdun stop on Avenue de Verdun, a 10-minute walk along the parkway west of Place Masséna. You must buy tickets before boarding these buses.

BY TRAIN

Speedy trains link the Riviera's beachfront destinations. Never board a train without a ticket or valid pass—fare inspectors accept no excuses. The minimum fine: €70. See below under "Arriving and Departing" for specific trip information.

Rick's Tip: *The Riviera is awash with* **scenic roads.** *To sample one of its most beautiful and thrilling drives, take the coastal* **Middle Corniche road** *from Nice to Monaco. You'll find breathtaking views over the Mediterranean and several scenic pullouts.*

BY CAR

This is France's most challenging region to drive in. Beautifully distracting vistas (natural and human), loads of Sunday-driver tourists, and every hour being lush-hour in the summer make for a dangerous combination. Parking can be exasperating. Bring lots of coins and patience.

BY BOAT

In summer, **Trans Côte d'Azur** offers scenic trips several days a week from Nice to Monaco (reservations required, tel. 04 92 00 42 30, www.trans-cote-azur.com). The same company also runs one-hour round-trip cruises along the coast to Cap Ferrat.

Arriving and Departing
BY TRAIN

All trains stop at Nice's main station, called Nice-Ville. The TI and bus stops (including #99 to the airport) are straight out the main doors. A nearby tram line zips you to the center in a few minutes (several blocks to the left as you leave the station, departs every few minutes, direction: Hôpital Pasteur). To walk to the beach, Promenade des Anglais, or many of my recommended hotels, cross Avenue Thiers in front of the station, go down the steps by Hôtel Interlaken, and continue down Avenue Durante.

Train Connections from Nice to: **Antibes** (2/hour, 20 minutes), **Villefranche-sur-Mer** (2/hour, 10 minutes), **Monaco** (2/hour, 20 minutes).

BY CAR

Renting a car is easiest at Nice's airport, which has offices for all the major companies. Most companies are also represented at Nice's train station and near the southwest side of Albert I Park. To reach the city center from the autoroute, take the *Nice Centre* exit and follow signs. Ask your hotelier where to park (allow €20-30/day; some hotels offer deals but space is limited—arrange ahead). The parking garage at the Nice Etoile shopping center on Avenue Jean Médecin is near many recommended hotels (ticket booth on third floor, about €28/day, 18:00-8:00). Other centrally located garages have similar rates. On-street parking is strictly metered (usually a 2-hour limit) every day but Sunday, when it is typically free.

You can avoid driving in the center—and park for free during the day (no overnight parking)—by stashing your car at a parking lot at a remote tram or bus stop. Look for blue-on-white *Parcazur* signs (find locations at www.lignesdazur.com), and ride the bus or tram into town (10/hour, 15 minutes, buy round-trip tram or bus ticket and keep it with you—you'll need it later to exit the parking lot; for tram details, see "Getting Around Nice," earlier). As lots are not guarded, don't leave anything of value in your car.

BY PLANE

Nice's easy-to-navigate airport (Aéroport de Nice Côte d'Azur, code: NCE) is literally on the Mediterranean—with landfill runways, a 30-minute drive west of the city center. The two terminals are connected by shuttle buses (navettes). Both terminals have TIs, banks, ATMs, trams, and buses to Nice (tel. 04 89 88 98 28, www.nice.aeroport.fr).

A **taxi into the city center** is expensive considering the short distance (figure €35 to Nice hotels, €60 to Villefranche-sur-Mer, €70 to Antibes, about €5 more at night and on weekends, small fee for bags). Nice's airport taxis are notorious for overcharging. Before riding, confirm your fare. It's always a good idea to ask for a receipt (reçu).

The new **T-2 tramway,** likely operational by the time you visit, will serve both airport terminals and will run frequently into Nice, paralleling the Promenade des Anglais and ending at Nice's Port Lympia. The tram will be handy for those sleeping at hotels near the Promenade des Anglais and Place Masséna.

Two **bus lines** connect the airport with the city center, offering good alternatives to high-priced taxis. Note that these routes may be influenced by the new tram line; check routes before riding. **Bus #99** (airport express) runs to Nice's main train station (€6, 2/hour, 8:00-21:00, 30 minutes, drops you within a 10-minute walk of many recommended hotels). To take this bus to the airport, catch it right in front of the train station (departs on the half-hour).

Bus #98 runs along Promenade des Anglais and along the edge of Vieux Nice (€6, 3-4/hour, from the airport 6:00-23:00, to the airport until 21:00, 30 minutes).

For all buses, buy tickets from the driver. To reach the bus information office and stops at Terminal 1, turn left after passing customs and exit the doors at the far end. Buses serving Terminal 2 stop across the street from the airport exit (information kiosk and ticket sales to the right as you exit).

Airport shuttles work better for trips from your hotel to the airport, since they require you to book a precise pickup time in advance. Shuttle vans offer a fixed price (about €30 for one person, a little more for additional people or to Villefranche-sur-Mer). Your hotel can arrange this, and I would trust their choice of company.

Linking the Airport and Nearby Destinations: To get to **Villefranche-sur-Mer** from the airport, take bus #98 (described above) to Place Garibaldi. From there, use the same ticket to transfer to bus #81. If the new T-2 tram is running, take it to the last stop (Port Lympia). At the port, you can use the same ticket to transfer to bus #81 or buy a separate ticket for bus #100. Allow €60 for a taxi.

To reach **Antibes,** take bus #250 from either terminal (about 2/hour, 40 minutes, €11). Express bus #110 runs from the airport directly to **Monaco** (2/hour, 50 minutes, €22).

NEAR NICE

Day-trip possibilities from Nice are easy and exciting. Villefranche-sur-Mer has a serene setting and small-town warmth. Woodsy Cap Ferrat boasts belle époque mansions and a family-friendly beach. Glitzy little Monaco offers a fancy casino and royal flair. Antibes has sandy beaches, a Picasso museum, and good walking trails. Quick and efficient public transportation gets you where you want to go (see "Getting Around the Riviera from Nice" on page 351).

Villefranche-sur-Mer

In the glitzy world of the Riviera, Villefranche-sur-Mer offers travelers an easygoing slice of Mediterranean life. Sand-pebble beaches and a handful of interesting sights keep visitors just busy enough.

Day Plan

My self-guided walk laces together everything of importance in town. Your biggest decision will be choosing between a beachfront meal or an ice-cream-licking village stroll.

Orientation

Tiny and easy to cover, Villefranche-sur-Mer snuggles around its harbor.

Tourist Information: The TI is located in a park (Jardin François Binon) below the Nice/Monaco Octroi bus stop (daily in season, closed Sun off-season; tel. 04 93 01 73 68, www.villefranche-sur-mer.com).

Getting There

From Nice, **trains** run to Villefranche-sur-Mer twice an hour (10 minutes); it's a level 10-minute walk from the station to the port area. Or take **bus #81** or **#100** from Nice (2-4/hour, 20 minutes); get off at the Octroi stop and walk downhill past the TI to town. From Nice's port, **drivers** should follow signs for *Menton, Monaco,* and *Basse Corniche;* pay lots are just below the TI or near the water (at Parking Wilson).

The beautiful deep-water bay at Villefranche-sur-Mer attracts every kind of boat.

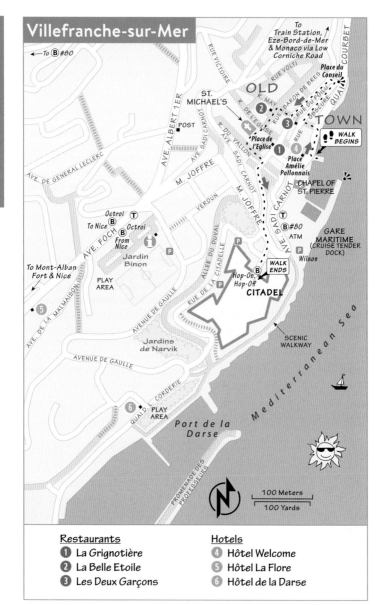

Villefranche-sur-Mer

← To Ⓑ #80

To Train Station, Eze-Bord-de-Mer & Monaco via Low Corniche Road

RUE COURBET

RUE VICTOIRE

RUE VOLTI

Place du Conseil

OLD

R. MAY

RUE BARON DE BRES

RUE DU POILU

QUAI

TOWN

ST. MICHAEL'S

R. DE L'EGLISE

RUE OBSCURE

AVE. ALBERT 1ER

POST

R. DU YALLON

Place de l'Eglise

WALK BEGINS

M. JOFFRE

AVE. SADI CARNOT

Place Amélie Pollonnais

CHAPEL OF ST. PIERRE

AVE. DE GENERAL LECLERC

VERDUN

M. JOFFRE

AVE. SADI CARNOT

Octroi Ⓣ To Nice

Ⓑ Octroi From Nice

ATM

Ⓑ #80

GARE MARITIME (CRUISE TENDER DOCK)

AVE. FOCH

Jardin Binon

AILEE DU DUVAL

Wilson

PLAY AREA

To Mont-Alban Fort & Nice

AVENUE DE GAULLE

RUE DE LA CITADELLE

Hop-On, Hop-Off

WALK ENDS

CITADEL

AVE. DE LA MALMAISON

⑤

SCENIC WALKWAY

Mediterranean Sea

Jardins de Narvik

AVENUE DE GAULLE

QUAI D. L. CORDERIE

⑥ PLAY AREA

Port de la Darse

PROMENADE DES PROFESSEURS

N

100 Meters
100 Yards

Restaurants
❶ La Grignotière
❷ La Belle Etoile
❸ Les Deux Garçons

Hotels
❹ Hôtel Welcome
❺ Hôtel La Flore
❻ Hôtel de la Darse

Rick's Tip: *A fun **bric-a-brac market** enlivens Villefranche-sur-Mer on **Sundays** on Place Amélie Pollonnais by Hôtel Welcome. On Saturday, Sunday, and Wednesday mornings, a market sets up in Jardin François Binon by the TI.*

Town Walk

This quick self-guided walk starts at the waterfront and finishes at the citadel.

• Go to the end of the short pier directly in front of Hôtel Welcome.

The Harbor: At 2,000 feet, this is the deepest natural harbor on the Riviera and the region's most important port until Nice built its own in the 18th century. Today, ships bring tourists rather than pirates. The bay is generally filled with beautiful yachts.

Up on the hill, the 16th-century citadel (where this walk ends) is marked by flags. The yellow fisherman's chapel (with the little-toe bell tower) has a special interior (more on it below). Up the skinny lane just right of the Hôtel Welcome is the baroque facade of St. Michael's Church. The waterfront, lined by fancy fish restaurants, curves to the town beach. Fifty yards above the beach stands the train station and above that, supported by arches, is the Low Corniche road, which leads to Monaco.

• Leave the pier and walk left 30 yards to find a small bronze bust of Jean Cocteau, the artist. A few more steps take you to the...

Chapel of St. Pierre (Chapelle Cocteau): This chapel is the town's cultural highlight. Cocteau, who decorated the place, was a Parisian transplant who adored little Villefranche-sur-Mer and whose career was distinguished by his work as an artist, poet, novelist, playwright, and filmmaker. Influenced by his pals Marcel Proust, André Gide, Edith Piaf, and Pablo Picasso, Cocteau was a leader among 20th-century avant-garde intellectuals (€3 donation, usually closed Mon-Tue, hours vary with cruise-ship traffic and season).

• From the chapel, turn right and stroll the harbor promenade. Immediately after Restaurant La Mère Germaine, a lane leads up into the old town. Walk up a few steps, and turn right into a long tunnel-like street.

Rue Obscure, the Old Town, and St. Michael's Church: Here, under these 13th-century vaults, you're in another age. Walk to the end of Rue Obscure (which means "dark street"), winding up to the sunlight. You'll pass a tiny fountain at Place du Conseil and, a few steps beyond that, you'll reach a viewpoint overlooking the harbor.

Turn around and stroll back past the fountain, straight down the little lane called Rue du Poilu. Notice the homes built under the heavy arches. At Place des Deux Garçons (the square with a namesake restaurant), turn right on Rue May and climb the stepped lane. Take your first left to find St. Michael's Church, facing a delightful square with a single magnolia tree (Place de l'Eglise). The deceptively large church features an 18th-century organ, a particularly engaging crucifix at the high altar, and (to the left) a fine

Chapel of St. Pierre

statue of a recumbent Christ—carved, they say, from a fig tree by a galley slave in the 1600s.

• *Leaving St. Michael's, go downhill halfway to the water, where you'll rejoin Rue du Poilu. Turn right, then curve left, pass the square, and walk up to the...*

Citadel: The town's mammoth castle was built in the 1500s by the Duke of Savoy to defend against the French. When the region joined France in 1860, the castle became just a barracks.

The exterior walls slope thickly at the base, indicating that they were built in the "Age of Black Powder"—the 16th century—when the advent of gunpowder made thicker, cannonball-deflecting walls a necessity for any effective fortification. The bastions are designed for smarter crossfire during an attack.

• *And that concludes our introductory walk.*

Experiences

▲SEAFRONT WALKS

A seaside walkway leads under the citadel and connects the old town with the workaday harbor, Port de la Darse. At the port you'll find a few cafés, France's Institute of Oceanography, and an 18th-century dry dock. This scenic walk turns downright romantic after dark. You can also wander the other direction along Villefranche-sur-Mer's waterfront and continue beyond the train station for postcard-perfect views back to town (ideal in the morning—go before breakfast).

HIKE TO MONT-ALBAN FORT

This fort, with a remarkable setting on the high ridge that separates Nice and Villefranche-sur-Mer, is a good destination for hikers (also accessible by car and bus; info at TI). From the TI, walk on the main road toward Nice about 500 yards past Hôtel La Flore. Look for wooden trail signs labeled *Escalier de Verre* and climb about 45 minutes up to Mont-Alban Fort (interior closed to tourists) and its sensational view terrace. To visit with a much shorter hike, minibus #80 drops you a 15-minute walk away (by Hôtel Fiancée du Pirate).

BOAT RIDES (PROMENADES EN MER)

To view this beautiful coastline from the sea, consider taking a quick **sightseeing cruise** with AMV (€12-22, some stay in the bay, others go as far as Monaco, select days June-Sept, departs across from Hôtel Welcome, www.amv-sirenes.com).

Eating

$$$ **La Grignotière** serves generous and tasty *plats* (daily, 3 Rue du Poilu). $$ **La Belle Etoile** is the romantic's choice, a few blocks above the harbor on a small lane (closed Tue-Wed, 1 Rue Baron de Bres). $$$ **Les Deux Garçons** offers candlelit tables on a quiet square (closed Wed, 18 Rue du Poilu).

Sleeping

Overnighters will find seaview rooms at $$$$ **Hôtel Welcome****** (3 Quai Amiral Courbet, www.welcomehotel.com), $$ **Hôtel La Flore*** (5 Boulevard Princesse Grace de Monaco, www.hotel-la-flore.fr), and $ **Hôtel de la Darse*** (handy for drivers, 32 Avenue Général de Gaulle, www.hoteldeladarse.com).

Cap Ferrat

Cap Ferrat is a peaceful eddy off the busy Nice-Monaco route. You could spend a leisurely day on this peninsula, wandering

Waterfront tables line Villefranche's harbor.

the sleepy port village of St-Jean-Cap-Ferrat (usually called "St-Jean"), touring the Villa Ephrussi de Rothschild mansion and gardens, and walking on sections of the beautiful trails that follow the coast.

Tourist Information: The main TI is near the harbor in St-Jean (closed Sun; 5 Avenue Denis Séméria). A smaller TI is near the Villa Ephrussi (closed Sun, 59 Avenue Denis Séméria, www.saintjean-capferrat-tourisme.fr).

Day Plan

Visit the Villa Ephrussi de Rothschild, then walk 30 minutes, mostly downhill, to St-Jean for lunch (many options, including grocery shops for picnic supplies) and poke around the village. Take the 45-minute walk on the Plage de la Paloma trail (ideal for picnics).

Getting There

From Nice or Villefranche-sur-Mer, **bus #81** (direction: *Port de St-Jean*) runs to Cap Ferrat. For the Villa Ephrussi de Rothschild or the beach, get off at the Passable stop. The return bus (direction: *Nice*) begins in St-Jean.

In high season, late-afternoon buses can be jammed—board bus #81 on the Cap itself, before it gets crowded.

Cap Ferrat is quick by **car** (take the Low Corniche) or **taxi** (allow €30 one-way from Villefranche-sur-Mer, €65 from Nice).

Sights

▲VILLA EPHRUSSI DE ROTHSCHILD

In what seems like the ultimate in Riviera extravagance, Venice, Versailles, and the Côte d'Azur come together in the pastel-pink Villa Ephrussi. Rising above Cap Ferrat, this 1905 mansion has views west to Villefranche-sur-Mer and east to Beaulieu-sur-Mer.

Cost and Hours: Palace and gardens—€14, includes audioguide; mid-Feb-Oct daily 10:00-18:00, July-Aug until 19:00; shorter hours off-season; tel. 04 93 01 33 09, www.villa-ephrussi.com.

Visiting the Villa: Start with the well-furnished belle-époque ground floor. Upstairs, an 18-minute film (with English subtitles) explains the gardens and villa and gives you good background on the life of rich and eccentric Béatrice, Baroness de Rothschild, the French banking heiress who built and furnished the place. Don't miss the view from her private terrace.

Behind the mansion, stroll through the **seven lush gardens** re-created from locations all over the world—and with maximum sea views. An appropriately classy **$$ garden-tearoom** serves drinks and lunches with a view (12:00-17:30).

PLAGE DE PASSABLE

This pebbly little beach, located below the Villa Ephrussi, is a peaceful place, popular with families. One half is public (free, with snack bar, shower, and WC), and the other is run by a small restaurant (€30 includes changing locker, lounge chair, and shower; reserve ahead in summer or on weekends, tel. 04 93 76 06 17). If you were ever to do the French Riviera rent-a-beach ritual, this would be the place.

Getting There: Bus #81 stops a 10-minute walk uphill from the beach, near Villa Ephrussi.

Eating: $$$ Restaurant de la Plage de Passable is your chance to dine on the beach with romance and class (daily late May-early Sept, always make a reservation, tel. 04 93 76 06 17).

Villa Ephrussi de Rothschild

PLAGE DE LA PALOMA LOOP TRAIL

A few blocks east of St-Jean's port, a scenic 45-minute trail offers an easy sampling of Cap Ferrat's beauty. From the port, walk or drive about a quarter-mile east (with the port on your left, passing Hôtel La Voile d'Or); parking is available at the port or on streets near Plage de la Paloma. You'll find the trailhead where the road comes to a T—look for a *Plage Paloma* sign pointing left, but don't walk left. Cross the small gravel park (*Jardin de la Paix*) to start the trail, and do the walk counterclockwise. The trail is level and paved, yet uneven enough that good shoes are helpful. Plunk your picnic on one of the benches along the trail, or eat at the restaurant on Plage de la Paloma at the end of the walk.

Monaco

The minuscule principality of Monaco (less than a square mile) is a special place—it's home to one of the world's most famous auto races and one of its fanciest casinos. The glamorous 1956 marriage of the American actress Grace Kelly to Prince Rainier added to the mystique of this glittering little land of luxury.

Day Plan

The surgical-strike plan is to start with my self-guided walk in Monaco-Ville, then visit the aquarium or gamble away whatever you have left in the Monte Carlo Casino.

Orientation

Monaco-Ville is the oldest part of Monaco, home to the Prince's Palace and all the key sights except the casino. Monte Carlo is the area around the casino.

Tourist Information: The main TI is at the top of the park above the casino (daily, 2 Boulevard des Moulins, tel. 00-377/92 16 61 16, www.visitmonaco.com). Another TI is at the train station.

Getting Around by Local Bus: Buses #1 and #2 link all areas with frequent service (10/hour, fewer on Sun, buses run until 21:00). If you pay the driver, a single ticket is €2, 6 tickets €11, and a day pass €5.50; save by using red curbside machines, where you get 12 tickets for €11. You can split a 6- or 12-ride ticket with your travel partners. Bus tickets are good for a free transfer if used within 30 minutes.

Rick's Tip: *For a* **cheap and scenic loop ride** *through Monaco, ride bus #2 from one end to the other and back (25 minutes each way). You'll need two tickets and must get off the bus at the last stop and then get on again.*

Getting There

If coming by frequent **bus #100** from Nice (1 hour) or Villefranche-sur-Mer (40 minutes), get off at Place d'Armes (at the base of Monaco-Ville) to take my self-guided walk; use the Monte Carlo-Casino stop (in front of the TI on Boulevard des Moulins) if you're headed to the casino.

Trains from Nice (2/hour) stop at the long, entirely underground station in the center of Monaco. From here, it's a 15-minute walk to the casino or the base of the palace.

Drivers should follow *Centre-Ville* signs into Monaco, then watch for the signs to parking garages at *Le Casino* (for Monte Carlo) or *Le Palais* (for Monaco-Ville).

Rick's Tip: *For an official memento of your Monaco visit,* **get your passport stamped** *at the TI.*

➋ Monaco-Ville Walk

This self-guided walk connects Monaco's major sights (except the casino) in a tight little loop, starting from the palace square.

Palace Square (Place du Palais): This square is the best place to get oriented to Monaco. Facing the palace, walk to the right and look out over the city (er... principality). This rock gave birth to the little pastel Hong Kong look-alike in 1215, and it's managed to remain an independent country for most of its 800 years. Looking beyond the glitzy port, notice the faded green dome roof: It belongs to the casino that put Monaco on the map in the 1800s.

The famous Grand Prix runs along the port and then up the ramp to the casino (at top speeds of 180 mph). Italy is so close, you can almost smell the pesto. Just beyond the casino is France again (it flanks Monaco on both sides).

The odd statue of a woman with a fishing net is dedicated to the glorious reign of **Prince Albert I** (1889-1922). The son of Charles III (who built the casino), Albert I was a true Renaissance Man. He had a Jacques Cousteau-like fascination with the sea (and built Monaco's famous aquarium, the Oceanography Museum) and was a determined pacifist who made many attempts to dissuade Germany's Kaiser Wilhelm II from becoming involved in World War I.

• *Head toward the palace, and find a statue of a monk grasping a sword.*

Meet **François Grimaldi,** a renegade sword-carrying Italian dressed as a monk, who captured Monaco in 1297 and began the dynasty that still rules the principality. Prince Albert is his great-great-great... grandson, which gives Monaco's royal family the distinction of being the longest-lasting dynasty in Europe.

•*Now walk to the...*

Prince's Palace (Palais Princier): A

medieval castle once sat where the palace is today. Its strategic setting has had a lot to do with Monaco's ability to resist attackers. Today, Prince Albert and his wife live in the palace, while poor Princesses Stephanie and Caroline live down the street. The palace guards protect the prince 24/7 and still stage a **Changing of the Guard** ceremony with all the pageantry of an important nation (daily at 11:55 in good weather, fun to watch but jam-packed, arrive by 11:30). An audioguide takes you through part of the prince's lavish palace in 30 minutes. The rooms are well-furnished and impressive, but interesting only if you haven't seen a château lately (€8, includes audioguide, €20.50 combo-ticket includes Oceanography Museum; generally daily 10:00-18:00, July-Aug until 19:00, closed Nov-March; www.palais.mc).

• *Head to the west end of the palace square. Below the cannonballs is the district known as...*

Fontvieille: Monaco's newest, reclaimed-from-the-sea area has seen much of the principality's post-WWII growth. Prince Rainier continued—some say, was obsessed with—Monaco's economic growth, creating landfills (topped with apartments, such as in Fontvieille), flashy ports, more beaches, a big sports stadium marked by tall arches, and a rail station.

• *With your back to the palace, leave the square through the arch at the far right (onto Rue Colonel Bellando de Castro) and find the...*

Monaco's classy port

Palace Square

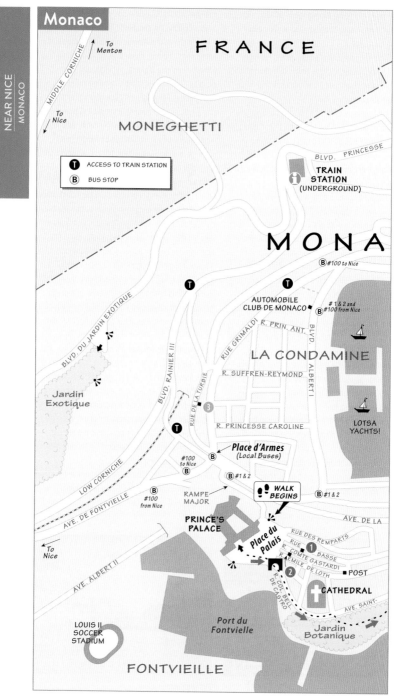

Monaco

F R A N C E

MIDDLE CORNICHE
To Menton

To Nice

MONEGHETTI

BLVD. PRINCESSE

T ACCESS TO TRAIN STATION
B BUS STOP

TRAIN
STATION
(UNDERGROUND)

M O N A

B #100 to Nice

T   **T**

AUTOMOBILE
CLUB DE MONACO

1 & 2 and
B #100 from Nice

BLVD. DU JARDIN EXOTIQUE

RUE GRIMALDI   R. PRIN. ANT.

LA CONDAMINE

BLVD. RAINIER III

BLVD. ALBERT I

RUE DE LA TURBIE

R. SUFFREN-REYMOND

Jardin
Exotique

LOTSA
YACHTS!

3

R. PRINCESSE CAROLINE

T

LOW CORNICHE

Place d'Armes
(Local Buses)

#100
to Nice
B

B

B #1 & 2

B #1 & 2

RAMPE
MAJOR

B
#100
from Nice

**WALK
BEGINS**

AVE. DE FONTVIELLE

PRINCE'S
PALACE

AVE. DE LA

To
Nice

**Place du
Palais**

RUE DES REMPARTS

RUE

R. BASSE

1

R. COMTE GASTARDI

AVE. ALBERT II

R. EMILE DE LOTH

POST

2

R. COL. BEL.
DE CASTRO

CATHEDRAL

AVE. SAINT-

LOUIS II
SOCCER
STADIUM

Port du
Fontvielle

Jardin
Botanique

FONTVIEILLE

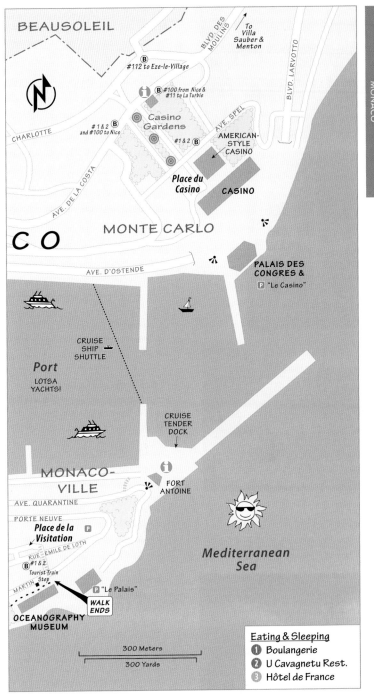

BEAUSOLEIL

BLVD. DES MOULINS

To Villa Sauber & Menton

BLVD. LARVOTTO

B #112 to Eze-le-Village

i **B** #100 from Nice & #11 to La Turbie

AVE. SPEL

Casino Gardens

B #1 & 2 and #100 to Nice

CHARLOTTE

B #1 & 2

AMERICAN-STYLE CASINO

AVE. DE LA COSTA

Place du Casino

CASINO

MONTE CARLO

C O

AVE. D'OSTENDE

PALAIS DES CONGRES & **P** "Le Casino"

CRUISE SHIP SHUTTLE

Port

LOTSA YACHTS!

CRUISE TENDER DOCK

MONACO-VILLE

AVE. QUARANTINE

PORTE NEUVE

Place de la Visitation **P**

RUE EMILE DE LOTH

B #1 & 2
Tourist Train Stop

MARTIN

i

FORT ANTOINE

Mediterranean Sea

P "Le Palais"

WALK ENDS

OCEANOGRAPHY MUSEUM

300 Meters

300 Yards

Eating & Sleeping
1 Boulangerie
2 U Cavagnetu Rest.
3 Hôtel de France

Cathedral of Monaco (Cathédrale de Monaco): The somber but beautifully lit cathedral, rebuilt in 1878, is where centuries of Grimaldis are buried, and where Princess Grace and Prince Rainier were married. Inside, circle slowly behind the altar (counterclockwise). The second tomb is that of Albert I, who did much to put Monaco on the world stage. The second-to-last tomb—inscribed *"Gratia Patricia, MCMLXXXII"* and displaying the 1956 wedding photo of Princess Grace and Prince Rainier—is where the princess was buried in 1982. Prince Rainier's tomb lies next to hers (cathedral open daily 8:30-19:15).

• *Leave the cathedral and dip into the immaculately maintained* **Jardin Botanique**. *In the gardens, turn left. Eventually you'll find the impressive building housing the...*

Rick's Tips: *If you're into stamps, drop by the* **post office** *(on Place de la Mairie), where philatelists can buy from the impressive collection of Monegasque stamps.*

Oceanography Museum (Musée Océanographique): Prince Albert I had this cliff-hanging museum built in 1910 as a monument to his enthusiasm for things from the sea. The museum's aquarium, which Jacques Cousteau captained for 32 years, has 2,000 different specimens, representing 250 species. Don't miss the elevator to the rooftop terrace view café (€11-16, €20.50 combo-ticket includes Prince's Palace; daily 10:00-19:00, longer hours July-Aug, Oct-March until 18:00; www.oceano.mc).

• *The red-brick steps across from the Oceanography Museum lead up to stops for buses #1 and #2, both of which run to the port, the casino, and the train station. To walk back to the palace and through the old city, turn left at the top of the brick steps.*

Ⓐ *Changing of the Guard*
Ⓑ *Cathedral of Monaco*
Ⓒ *Fontvieille harbor*
Ⓓ *Oceanographic Museum*

Experiences
▲MONTE CARLO CASINO (CASINO DE MONTE-CARLO)

Monte Carlo, which means "Charles' Hill" in Spanish, is named for Charles III, the prince who presided over Monaco's 19th-century makeover. In the mid-1800s, olive groves stood here. Then, with the construction of casino and spas, and easy road and train access, one of Europe's poorest countries was on the Grand Tour map—*the* place for the vacationing aristocracy to play. Today, Monaco has the world's highest per-capita income.

The Monte Carlo casino is intended to make you feel comfortable while losing your retirement nest egg. Charles Garnier designed the place (with an opera house inside) in 1878, in part to thank the prince for his financial help in completing Paris' Opéra Garnier (which the architect also designed).

Cost and Hours: Tightwads can view the atrium entry, classy bar/café, and slot-machine room for free; daily 9:00-late. Touring the casino costs €17 (€12 off-season); daily 9:00-12:15; you'll see the atrium area and inner-sanctum gaming rooms with an audioguide, take photos, and have your run of the joint. Gamblers pay €10; daily 14:00 until the wee hours, must be 18 and show ID; no shorts, T-shirts, hoodies, tennis shoes, or torn jeans. Whether you gamble or not, expect lines at the entrance from May through September; tel. 00-377/92 16 20 00, www.montecarlocasinos.com.

Visiting the Casino: Enter through sumptuous **atrium.** This is the lobby for the 520-seat opera house (open Nov-April only for performances). The **first gambling rooms** (Salle Renaissance, Salon de l'Europe, and Salle des Amériques) offer European and English roulette, plus Trente et Quarante, Punto Banco—a version of baccarat—and slot machines. The more glamorous **game rooms** (Salons Touzet, Salle Medecin, and Terrasse Salle Blanche) have those same games and Ultimate Texas Hold 'em poker, but you play against the cashier with higher stakes.

Take the Money and Run: The stop for buses returning to Nice and Villefranche-sur-Mer, and for local buses #1 and #2, is on Avenue de la Costa, at the top of the

Lush gardens lead to Monte Carlo Casino.

park above the casino. To reach the train station from the casino, take bus #1 or #2 from this stop or walk 15 minutes.

Eating and Sleeping

You'll find massive *pan bagnat* (basically *salade niçoise* on country bread) and quiche at the yellow-bannered **$ Boulangerie** (daily, 8 Rue Basse). At **$$ U Cavagnetu,** you'll dine cheaply on pizza and such (daily, 14 Rue Comte Félix Gastaldi).

Centrally located **$$ Hôtel de France**** is comfortable and well run (6 Rue de la Turbie, www.hoteldefrance.mc).

Antibes

Antibes has a down-to-earth, easygoing ambience. Its old town is a warren of narrow streets and red-tile roofs rising above the blue Med, protected by twin medieval towers and wrapped in extensive ramparts.

Day Plan

Antibes is fun to explore. Browse Europe's biggest yacht harbor, snooze on a sandy beach, loiter through an enjoyable old town, and hike along a sea-swept trail. The town's Picasso Museum (closed Mon) shows off its appealing collection in a fine old building.

Orientation

Antibes' old town lies between the port and Boulevard Albert I and Avenue Robert Soleau. Place Nationale is the old town's hub of activity. Stroll above the sea between the old port and Place Albert I (where Boulevard Albert I meets the water). Good beaches lie just beyond Place Albert I, and the walk there leads to fine views.

Tourist Information: The TI is near the train station at 42 Avenue Robert Soleau (daily, closed Sun in winter, tel. 04 22 10 60 10, www.antibes-juanlespins.com). Hikers should get the free trail map.

Getting Around: Antibes' buses (Envibus) cost €1 and are handiest for carless travelers wanting access to Cap d'Antibes.

Rick's Tip: *Antibes' old-time market hall (Marché Provençal) hosts a vibrant* **produce market daily** *until 13:00 (closed Mon Sept-May). A lively* **antiques/flea market** *fills Place Nationale and Place Audiberti, next to the port (Thu and Sat 7:00-18:00).*

Getting There

Trains and buses run from Nice to Antibes, but the **train** is the better choice—it's faster

Antibes' Plage de la Gravette

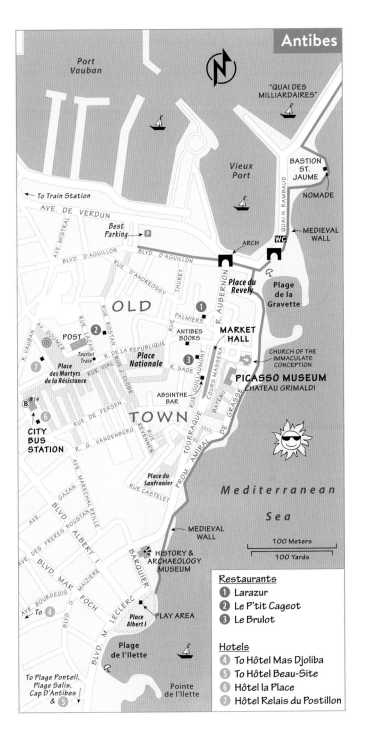

Antibes

Port
Vauban

"QUAI DES
MILLIARDAIRES"

Vieux
Port

BASTION
ST.
JAUME

NOMADE

← To Train Station

AVE. DE VERDUN

Best
Parking → P

ARCH

MEDIEVAL
WALL

WC

BLVD. D'AGUILLON

BLVD. D'AGUILLON

RUE D'ANDREOSSY

THURET

R. AUBERNON

Place du
Revely

Plage
de la
Gravette

OLD

RUE D'ANDREOSSY

RUE PALMIERS

AV. DOUMER

RUE LACAN

RUE RISTAN

POST

ANTIBES
BOOKS

MARKET
HALL

R. VAUBAN

Tourist
Train

R. DE LA REPUBLIQUE

Place
Nationale

R. SADE

RUE GUILLAUMONT

COURS MASSENA

CHURCH OF THE
IMMACULATE
CONCEPTION

Place
des Martyrs
de la Résistance

RUE VIAL

RUE J. CLOSE

ABSINTHE
BAR

BATEAU

DE GRASSE

PICASSO MUSEUM

CHATEAU GRIMALDI

B #14

RUE DE FERSEN

RUE REVENNES

TOWN

RUE TOURRAQUE

PROM. AMIRAL

CITY
BUS
STATION

R. G. VANDENBERG

Place du
Sanfranier

RUE CASTELET

Mediterranean

Sea

AVE. MARECHAL REILLE

GAZAN

BLVD. ALBERT I

AVE. DES FRERES ROUSTAIN

BLVD. MAR

BARQUIER

MEDIEVAL
WALL

HISTORY &
ARCHAEOLOGY
MUSEUM

100 Meters

100 Yards

MAIZIERE

BLVD. G. FOCH

AVE. BOURGEOIS

To ④

BLVD. M. LECLERC

Place
Albert I

PLAY AREA

Plage
de l'Ilette

To Plage Ponteil,
Plage Salis,
Cap D'Antibes
& ⑤

Pointe
de l'Ilette

Restaurants
① Larazur
② Le P'tit Cageot
③ Le Brulot

Hotels
④ To Hôtel Mas Djoliba
⑤ To Hôtel Beau-Site
⑥ Hôtel la Place
⑦ Hôtel Relais du Postillon

and won't get you stuck in traffic (2/hour, 20 minutes).

To walk from the station to the port, the old town, and the Picasso Museum (15 minutes), cross the street in front of the station, skirting left of the café, and follow Avenue de la Libération downhill as it bends left. At the end of the street, head to the right along the port.

Day-trippers coming **by car** should follow signs to *Centre-Ville,* then *Port Vauban.* The easiest place to park is the underground lot located outside the ramparts near the archway leading into the old town.

Sights
▲▲PICASSO MUSEUM (MUSEE PICASSO)

Sitting serenely where the old town meets the sea, this compact three-floor museum offers a manageable collection of Picasso's paintings, sketches, and ceramics. Picasso lived in this castle for part of 1946, when he cranked out an amazing amount of art (most of the paintings you'll see are from this short but prolific stretch of his long and varied career). The resulting collection (donated by Picasso) put Antibes on the tourist map.

Cost and Hours: €6; Tue-Sun 10:00-18:00, July-Aug Wed and Fri until 20:00, closed Mon year-round; tel. 04 92 90 54 20).

Terrace at the Picasso Museum

Rick's Tip: *You can tour star-shaped* **Fort Carré,** *on the headland overlooking the harbor, but there's little to see inside. It's only worth a visit for fantastic views over Antibes.*

▲BEACHES (PLAGES)
Good beaches stretch from the south end of Antibes toward Cap d'Antibes. They're busy but manageable in summer and on weekends, with cheap snack stands and good views of the old town. The closest beach is at the port (Plage de la Gravette), which seems calm in any season.

Hikes
These two hikes are easy to combine by bus, bike, or car.

▲▲CHAPELLE ET PHARE DE LA GAROUPE HIKE
The territorial views—best in the morning—from this viewpoint more than merit the 20-minute uphill climb from Plage de la Salis. You can see from Nice to Cannes and up to the Alps.

Getting There: Take bus #2 or #14 to the Plage de la Salis stop and find the trail a block ahead. By car or bike, follow signs for *Cap d'Antibes,* then look for *Chapelle et Phare de la Garoupe* signs.

▲▲CAP D'ANTIBES HIKE (SENTIER TOURISTIQUE DE TIREPOIL)
Cap d'Antibes is filled with exclusive villas and mansions protected by high walls. But all the money in the world can't buy you the beach in France, so a thin strip of rocky coastline forms a two-mile long, parklike zone with an extremely scenic, mostly paved but often rocky trail (Sentier Touristique de Tirepoil). At a fast clip you can walk the entire circle in just over an hour. Don't do the hike without the tourist map (available at hotels or the TI). You can do it in either direction.

Getting There: Drivers will find parking easier at the trail's eastern end (Plage de la

Cap d'Antibes' seaside walk

Garoupe), though some street parking is available at the trail's western end. Pedestrians should start at the western end: Take bus #2 from Antibes for about 15 minutes to the La Fontaine stop at Rond-Point A. Meiland.

Eating

Antibes' **Market Hall** (Marché Provençal) has great ambience and is popular with budget-minded diners each evening after the market stalls close. **$$$$ Larazur** is relaxed yet elegant (book ahead, closed Mon-Tue, 8 Rue des Palmiers, www. larazur.fr). The chef at **$$ Le P'tit Cageot** makes delicious Mediterranean cuisine (closed Wed and Sun, 5 Rue du Docteur Rostan). **$$ Le Brulot** is known for its

Provençal and meat dishes, most cooked over an open fire (come early or book ahead, closed Sun, 2 Rue Frédéric Isnard, www.brulot.fr).

Sleeping

Consider the tasteful **$$$ Hôtel la Place*** (1 Avenue 24 Août, www. la-place-hotel.com) or mellow **$ Hôtel Relais du Postillon**** (8 Rue Championnet, www.relaisdupostillon.com).

Outside the town center and convenient for drivers are **$$ Hôtel Mas Djoliba,**** a traditional manor house (29 Avenue de Provence, www.hotel-djoliba. com), and cozy **$$ Hôtel Beau-Site,**** on Cap d'Antibes (141 Boulevard Kennedy, www.hotelbeausite.net).

Burgundy

If you're looking for quintessential French culture, you'll find it in Burgundy. This is a calm, cultivated, and serene region, where nature is as sophisticated as its people. Its luscious landscapes are crisscrossed with canals and dotted with quiet farming villages. Both the soil and the farmers who work it are venerated. Its rolling hills give birth to superior wine and fine cuisine.

The town of Beaune is the transportation funnel for eastern France and makes a convenient stopover for travelers (car or train), with easy access north to Paris or Alsace (Colmar), east to the Alps (Chamonix), and south to Provence. Burgundy is a joyride for drivers. Without a car, take a bike, minibus tour, or short taxi ride to get from Beaune into the countryside.

BURGUNDY IN 1 DAY

Stay in Beaune. With one day, spend the morning in Beaune and the afternoon exploring the surrounding vineyards and wine villages. If you have a car, or good legs and a bike, the best way to spend your afternoon is by following one of the scenic vineyard drives outlined in this chapter. On summer nights, stroll through Beaune to enjoy the fun light show playing on historic facades.

Getting Around Burgundy

By Car: Drivers enjoy motoring on Burgundy's lovely roads; you'll cruise along canals, past manicured vineyards, and on tree-lined lanes. Navigate using the excellent (and free) map of the region available at all TIs.

By Tour: Beaune offers all kinds of tours—minibus, biking, and walking—of its vineyards and countryside.

Florian Garcenot at **Bourgogne Evasion/ Active Tours** offers walking or biking tours into the vineyards and rents bikes (half-day walks from €20, 6-person minimum; half-day bike tour-€39, full-day bike tour-€137; mobile 09 67 03 40 59, www.burgundybike-tour.com).

Chemins de Bourgogne runs tours with an SUV to get you off the beaten path (€60-70/half-day, €135/day, mobile 06 60 43 68 86, www.chemins-de-bourgogne. com).

Safari Wine Tours has four itineraries (€45-60, tour #2 is best for beginners; tours depart from TI, tel. 03 80 24 79 12, www.burgundy-tourism-safaritours.com, or call TI to reserve).

Kelly Kamborian guides walking tours as well as driving tours of the region (€250/half-day, €380/day, mobile 06 63 41 21 10, kellykamborian@gmail.com).

For vineyard and history tours, try **Stephanie Jones** (RS%: €65-115/half-day, €125-210/day; prices are per person,

BURGUNDY AT A GLANCE

In Beaune

▲▲▲**Hôtel Dieu des Hospices de Beaune** Colorfully decorated medieval charity hospital that's now a fine museum. **Hours:** Daily April-mid-Nov 9:00-18:30, shorter hours off-season. See page 377.

Museum of the Wine of Burgundy Folk museum featuring the history of the vine. **Hours:** Wed-Mon 10:00-13:00 & 14:00-18:00, closed Mon off-season, closed Dec and Tue year-round. See page 379.

Vineyard Loops near Beaune

▲▲**South Vineyard Loop** Beautiful route from Beaune to Château de la Rochepot with wine-tasting opportunities—best by car. See page 384.

▲**North Vineyard Loop** This route connects wine villages from Beaune to Savigny-lès-Beaune—good by car or bike. See page 387.

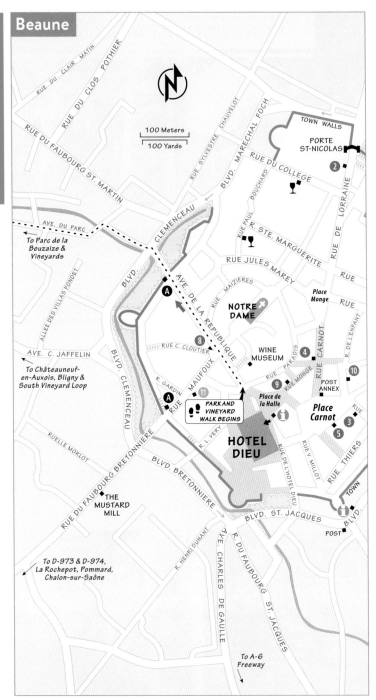

Beaune

TOWN WALLS

PORTE
ST-NICOLAS

2

To Parc de la
Bouzaize &
Vineyards

AVE. DU PARC

RUE DU CLAIR MATIN

RUE DU CLOS POTHIER

RUE DU FAUBOURG ST. MARTIN

RUE SYLVESTRE CHAUVELOT

BLVD. MARECHAL FOCH

RUE DU COLLEGE

RUE PAUL BOUCHARD

RUE DE LORRAINE

CLEMENCEAU

BLVD.

AVE. DE LA REPUBLIQUE

RUE R. STE. MARGUERITE

RUE JULES MAREY

RUE

A

ALLEE DES VILLAS FONDET

AVE. C. JAFFELIN

To Châteauneuf-
en-Auxois, Bligny &
South Vineyard Loop

RUE MAIZIERES

NOTRE
DAME ✚

Place
Monge

RUE

RUE

RUE C. CLOUTIER

8

WINE
MUSEUM

4

RUE CARNOT

R. DE L'ENFANT

10

RUE PARADIS

RUE MONGE

RUE MAUFOUX

R. GARDIN

A

11

PARK AND
VINEYARD
WALK BEGINS

Place de
la Halle

9

POST
ANNEX

Place
Carnot

RUE THIERS

3

5

BLVD. CLEMENCEAU

RUELLE MORLOT

R. L. VERY

HOTEL
DIEU

RUE DE L'HOTEL DIEU

RUE V. MILLOT

TOWN

BLVD. BRETONNIERE

RUE DU FAUBOURG BRETONNIERE

♦ THE
MUSTARD
MILL

BLVD. ST. JACQUES

POST

R. HENRI DUNANT

AVE. CHARLES DE GAULLE

R. DU FAUBOURG ST. JACQUES

To D-973 & D-974,
La Rochepot, Pommard,
Chalon-sur-Saône

To A-6
Freeway

100 Meters

100 Yards

To D-974,
Route des Grands Crus,
Savigny & Dijon

To Gigny,
Chorey-les-Beaune
& Aloxe-Corton

R. DU F. ST. NICOLAS

RUE DE CHOREY

RUE PASTEUR

Jardin
Anglais

Recommended route for
bikers to Aloxe-Corton.

P Pavillion
du Jardin
Anglais

BLVD. MARECHAL JOFFRE

RUE JACQUES COPEAU

RUE OUDOT

RUE J. BELIN

R. MARIE FAVART

RUE MORIMONT

RUE E. SPULLER

POOL

BLVD. DE L'ARQUEBUSE

15

RUE COLBERT

R. DESLANDES

RUE

DES TONNELIERS

A

RUE DU CHATEAU

RUE THIERS

12

AVE. DU 8 SEPTEMBRE 1944

R. DU TRIBUNAL

7 14

**TRAIN
STATION**

A

D'ALSACE

WALLS

BLVD. JULES FERRY

RUE EMILE GOUSSERY

16

RUE PIERRE JOIGNEAUX

1

PERPREUIL

6

*Place
Madeleine*

RUE DU FAUBOURG MADELEINE

13

RUE DU FAUBOURG PERPREUIL

R. PIERRE GUIDOT

Restaurants
1 Caveau des Arches
2 La Ciboulette
3 Les Pôpiettes
4 Brasserie le Carnot
5 Aux Hospices
6 Le Bistro des Cocottes
7 Le Tast'Vin

Wine Bars
8 Maison du Columbier
9 Le Bistrot Bourguignon
10 Bistrot du Coin

Hotels
11 Hôtel le Cep
12 Hôtel des Remparts
13 Hôtel de la Paix
14 Hôtel de France
15 Hôtel La Villa Fleurie
16 Hôtel Rousseau

A Wall Access
🍷 Wine Tasting

2-person minimum; mobile 06 10 18 04 12, www.burgundywinetours.fr).

By Bike: Pedaling a rental bike from Beaune takes you within minutes into the world-famous vineyards of the Côte d'Or. You can follow my south and north vineyard loops (later in chapter). Bourgogne Randonnées offers excellent rental bikes of all types, as well as maps and itineraries (daily, near Beaune train station at 7 Avenue du 8 Septembre, tel. 03 80 22 06 03, www.bourgogne-randonnees.fr).

BEAUNE

You'll feel comfortable right away in this prosperous, popular, and perfectly French little wine capital, where life centers on the production and consumption of Burgundy's prestigious Côte d'Or (Gold Coast) vintages.

Beaune's real charm is the town itself, which is especially vibrant on Saturday, when colorful market stands fill the main square, Place de la Halle. The one must-see sight is the medieval hospital—Hôtel Dieu des Hospices de Beaune. Stroll the squares and pedestrian lanes to enjoy the town's ambience. Try a wine-tasting in town, or bike or drive through nearby vineyards.

Orientation

Beaune's ring road (with a bike path) follows the foundations of its medieval walls. All roads and activities converge on the town's two squares, Place Carnot and Place de la Halle. At night, the city's monuments are beautifully lit, ideal for a post-dinner stroll.

Tourist Information

The **main TI** is located across from the post office on the ring road's southeastern corner (look for the *Porte Marie de Bourgogne* sign above the doorway; daily June-Sept 9:00-19:00, April-May and Oct until 18:30, Nov-March 9:00-12:30 & 13:30-18:00, closes earlier Sun year-round; tel. 03 80 26 21 30, www.beaune-tourisme. fr). A small **TI annex** (called "Point-I") is in the market hall, across from Hôtel Dieu (daily 9:30-13:00 & 14:00-18:00).

Helpful Hints

Market Days: Beaune hosts a smashing Saturday market and a meager Wednesday market. Both are on Place de la Halle and run until 12:30. The Saturday market is worth planning ahead for.

Supermarkets: Supermarché Casino has several small shops in Beaune, a store in the town center (next to 10 Rue Carnot), and a mothership store through the arch off Place Madeleine (daily 8:30-19:30, closed Sun afternoon).

Laundry: Beaune's lone launderette is open daily 7:00-21:00 (65 Rue Lorraine).

Taxi: Call 06 11 83 06 10 or 06 09 35 63 12.

Beaune Greeters: The TI can arrange to have an English-speaking local show you their city for free, in hopes of helping travelers better appreciate their Burgundian home.

Park and Vineyard Walk

Stroll to a pleasant Impressionist-like park and into Beaune's beautiful vineyards. This walk is ideal for those lacking a car, families (good toys in park), and vine enthusiasts. The vine-covered landscape is crisscrossed with narrow lanes and stubby stone walls and provides memorable early morning and sunset views.

Follow Avenue de la République west from the center, cross the ring road, stay parallel to the stream along a few grassy blocks for about five minutes, and then veer right into the serene Parc de la Bouzaize (opens at 8:00 and closes a bit before sunset). Walk through the park alongside the pond and pop out at the right rear corner (find the path to a small opening in the iron fence behind the kids' play area). Turn left on the small road and keep left, hugging the stone wall, then enter the Côte de Beaune vineyards. Find the big poster showing how the land is sliced and diced among different plots (called *clos*, for "enclosure"). Each *clos* is named; look for the stone marker identifying the area behind the poster as Clos Les Teurons (*1er cru*).

Poke about Clos Les Teurons, noticing the rocky soil (wine grapes need to struggle). As you wander, keep in mind that subtle differences of soil and drainage between adjacent plots of land can be enough to create very different-tasting wines—from grapes grown only feet apart. *Vive la différence.* A perfectly situated picnic table awaits under that lone tree up Chemin des Tilleuls.

Sights

▲▲▲HOTEL DIEU DES HOSPICES DE BEAUNE

This medieval charity hospital is now a museum. The Hundred Years' War and the plague devastated Beaune, leaving three-quarters of its population destitute. Nicholas Rolin, chancellor of Burgundy (enriched, in part, by his power to collect taxes), had to do something for "his people" (or, more likely, was getting old and wanted to close out his life on a philanthropic note). So, in 1443 Rolin paid to build this place. It was completed in just eight years and served as Beaune's hospital until 1971, when the last patient checked out. You'll notice Hospices de Beaune on wine labels in fine shops—they are Burgundy's largest landowner of precious

vineyards, thanks to donations made by patients over the centuries (and today). Besides its magnificently decorated courtyard, Hôtel Dieu is famous for Rogier van der Weyden's superb *Last Judgment* altarpiece, which Rolin commissioned. It's also wonderfully animated from the outside during Beaune's summer light show.

Cost and Hours: €7.50, €11.30 combo-ticket with Museum of the Wine of Burgundy, includes audioguide, daily 9:00-18:30, mid-Nov-March 9:00-11:30 & 14:00-17:30, last entry one hour before closing, on Place de la Halle; tel. 03 80 24 45 00, www.hospices-de-beaune.com.

❷ Self-Guided Tour: Tour the rooms, which circle the courtyard, in a clockwise direction (following *Sens de la Visite* signs). Allow an hour.

• *To start, enter the courtyard and find the stone bench.*

Courtyard of Honor: Honor meant power, and this was all about showing off. The exterior of the hospital and the town side of the courtyard are intentionally solemn, so as not to attract pesky 15th-century brigands and looters. The dazzling inner courtyard features a colorful glazed tile roof, establishing what became a style recognized in France as typically "Burgundian." The sturdy tiles, which last 300 years, are fired three times: once to harden, again to burn in the color, and finally for the glaze.

• *Now enter the hospice from the courtyard on the left side (follow* Salle des Pôvres *signs).*

Paupers' Ward (*Salle des Pôvres*): This grandest room of the hospital was the ward for the poorest patients. Rolin, who believed every patient deserved dignity, provided each patient with a pewter jug, mug, bowl, and plate. A painting on an easel at the left shows patients being treated in this room in 1949, 500 years after the hospital's founding. During epidemics, there were two to a bed.

• *Enter the chapel.*

Chapel: The hospice was not a place of hope. People came here to die. Care

Hôtel Dieu des Hospices de Beaune

St. Hugue Ward was for wealthy patients.

was more for the soul than the body. The stained glass shows Nicolas Rolin (lower left) and his wife, Guigone (lower right), dressed as a nun to show her devotion. Notice the action on Golgotha. As Jesus is crucified, the souls of the two criminals crucified with him (portrayed as miniature naked humans) are being snatched up—one by an angel and the other by a red devil. At the bottom, Mary cradles the dead body of Christ.

• *Exit right to the next room...*

St. Hugue Ward: In the 17th century, this smaller ward was established for wealthy patients (who could afford Cadillac insurance plans). They were more likely to survive, and the decor displays themes of hope, rather than resignation: The series of Baroque paintings lining the walls shows the biblical miracles that Jesus performed.

St. Nicolas Room: Originally divided into smaller rooms—one used for "surgery" (a.k.a. bloodletting and amputation), this room now holds a model of the steep roof support and tools of the doctoring trade (amputation saws, caulking gun-size syringes, pans for bloodletting, and so on).

• *Continue to the kitchen.*

Kitchen: Notice the 16th-century rotisserie. When fully wound, the cute robot would crank away, and the spit would spin slowly for 45 minutes. The 19th-century stove provided running hot water, which spewed from the beaks of swans.

Pharmacy: Inside the pharmacy, strange and wondrous concoctions were mixed, cooked, distilled, and then stored in pottery jars. The biggest jar (in the second room, by the window) was for *theriaca* ("panacea," or cure-all). The most commonly used medicine back then, it was a syrup of herbs, wine, and opium.

• *Continue to the St. Louis Ward, which provides access to the Last Judgment.*

St. Louis Ward: A maternity ward until 1969, this room is lined with fine 16th- and 17th-century tapestries illustrating mostly Old Testament stories. Dukes traveled with tapestries to cozy up the humble places they stayed in while on the road. The 16th-century pieces have better colors but inferior perspective.

Rogier van der Weyden's *Last Judgment*: This exquisite painting, the treasure of Hôtel Dieu, was commissioned by Rolin in 1450 for the altar of the Paupers' Ward. He spared no cost, hiring the leading Flemish artist of his time. The entire altarpiece survives. The back side (on right wall) was sliced off so everything could be viewed at the same time. The painting is full of symbolism. Christ presides over Judgment Day. The lily is mercy, the sword is judgment, the rainbow promises salvation, and the jeweled globe at Jesus' feet symbolizes the universality of Christianity's message.

The intricate detail, painted with a three-haired brush, is typical of Flemish art from this period. While Renaissance artists employed mathematical tricks of perspec-

Van der Weyden, Last Judgment

Medieval wine cellar

tive, these artists captured a sense of reality by painting minute detail upon detail.

Except for Sundays and holidays, the painting was kept closed and people saw only the panels that now hang on the right wall: on top, the Annunciation—the beginning of man's salvation; and at the bottom, Nicolas and Guigone piously at the feet of St. Sebastian, invoked to fight the plague, and St. Anthony, whom patients called upon for help in combating burning skin diseases.

MUSEUM OF THE WINE OF BURGUNDY (MUSEE DU VIN DE BOURGOGNE)

From this well-organized folk-wine museum, which fills the old residence of the Dukes of Burgundy, it's clear that the history and culture of Burgundy and its wine were fermented in the same bottle. Wander into the free courtyard (beautifully illuminated during summer light shows) for a look at the striking palace, antique wine presses, and a concrete model of Beaune's 15th-century street plan (a good chance to appreciate the town's once-impressive fortified wall). Inside the museum, you'll find rooms devoted to the region's topography, tools of the trade, barrel making, traditional wine festivals, and more. English explanations are posted in every room.

Cost and Hours: €5, €11.30 combo-ticket with Hôtel Dieu; Wed-Mon 10:00-13:00 & 14:00-18:00 except closed Mon off-season, closed Dec and Tue

year-round; in the Hôtel des Ducs on Rue d'Enfer, tel. 03 80 22 08 19, www.musees-bourgogne.org.

Getting There: With your back to the cathedral, turn left down the cobbled alley called Rue d'Enfer ("Hell Street," named for the fires of the Duke's kitchens once located on this street), keep left, and enter the courtyard of Hôtel des Ducs. There's also an entrance off Rue Paradis, opposite Le Petit Paradis restaurant.

LES CHEMINS DE LUMIERES LIGHT SHOW (PATHWAY OF LIGHTS)

Nightly from June through early September, and off-season on holiday weekends, Beaune puts on an entertaining light show accenting the exteriors of many buildings in the town center and along its ramparts walk. The main attractions are seven razzle-dazzle light shows (lasting about five minutes each) highlighting Beaune's most historic buildings. The most centrally located are Hôtel Dieu, Collégiale Notre-Dame church, the Museum of the Wine of Burgundy courtyard, and the bell tower at Place Monge (behind the Notre-Dame church). The lights start when daylight ends, making this ideal for an after-dinner event (TIs have maps with all the details).

THE MUSTARD MILL (LA MOUTARDERIE FALLOT)

The last of the independent mustard mills in Burgundy opens its doors for guided

Burgundy's Wines

Burgundy is why France is famous for wine. From Chablis to Beaujolais, you'll find great fruity reds, dry whites, and crisp rosés. The three key grapes are chardonnay (dry white wines), pinot noir (medium-bodied red wines), and gamay (light, fruity red wines, such as Beaujolais). Sixty percent of the wines are white, thanks to the white-only impact of the Chablis and Mâcon regions.

The Romans brought winemaking knowledge with them to Burgundy more than 2,000 years ago; medieval monks perfected the art a thousand years later. Those monks determined that pinot noir and chardonnay grapes grew best with the soil and climate in this region, a lesson that is followed to the letter by wine-makers today. The French Revolution put capitalists in charge of the vineyards (no longer a monkish labor of love), which led to quantity over quality and a loss of Burgundy's esteemed status. Phylloxera insects destroyed most of Burgundy's vines in the late 1800s, and forced growers to rethink how and where to best cultivate grapes in Burgundy. This led to a return of the monks' approach, with the veneration of pinot noir and chardonnay grapes, a focus on quality over quantity, and a big reduction in the land devoted to vines.

In Burgundy, location is everything, and winery names take a back seat to the place where the grape is grown. Every village produces its own distinctive wine, from Chablis to Meursault to Chassagne-Montrachet. Road maps read like fine-wine lists. If the wine village has a hyphenated name, the second half usually comes from the town's most important vineyard (such as Gevrey-Chambertin, Aloxe-Corton, and Vosne-Romanée).

Burgundy wines are divided into four classifications: From top to bottom you'll find *grand cru, premier cru* (or *1er cru*), *village,* and *Bourgogne.* Each level allows buyers to better pinpoint the quality and origin of the grapes in their wine. With *Bourgogne* wines, the grapes can come from anywhere in Burgundy; *village* identifies the exact village where they were grown; and *grand cru* and *premier cru* locate the precise plots of land. As you drop from top to bottom, production increases—there is far more *Bourgogne* made than *grand cru.* In general, the less wine a vine produces, the higher the quality.

tours in French (with a little English). They offer two tours: one with a hands-on focus on production (Découvertes tour) and another that highlights the history of mustard (Sensational Experience tour). The tours are long yet informative—you'll learn why Burgundy was the birthplace of mustard (it's about wine juice), and where they get their grains today (Canada).

Cost and Hours: €10, daily at 10:00 and 11:30, also on summer afternoons, call to reserve or book online—space is limited; free mustard tasting—daily 9:30-18:00, except closed at lunch in winter and Sun afternoon year-round; across ring road in the appropriately yellow building at 31 Rue du Faubourg Bretonnière, tel. 03 80 22 10 10, www.fallot.com.

Rick's Tip: *It costs about* **€15 per bottle to ship a case of wine home,** *though you'll save about 20 percent on the VAT tax—so expensive wines are worth the shipping cost. The simplest solution for bringing six or so bottles back is to pack them very well and check the box on the plane with you.*

Burgundy's Cuisine Scene

Arrive hungry. Considered by many to be France's best, Burgundian cuisine is peasant cooking elevated to an art. Entire lives are spent debating the best restaurants and bistros.

Several classic dishes were born in Burgundy: *escargots de Bourgogne* (snails served sizzling hot in garlic butter), *bœuf bourguignon* (beef simmered for hours in red wine with onions and mushrooms), coq au vin (rooster stewed in red wine), and *œufs en meurette* (poached eggs in a red wine sauce, often served on a large crouton), as well as the famous Dijon mustards. Look also for delicious *jambon persillé* (cold ham layered in a garlic-parsley gelatin), *pain d'épices* (spice bread), and *gougères* (light, puffy cheese pastries). Those white cows (called Charolais) dotting the green pastures are Burgundian and make France's best steak and *bœuf bourguignon*.

Native cheeses are **Époisses** and **Langres** (both mushy and great), and my favorite, **Montrachet** (a tasty goat cheese). **Crème de cassis** (black currant liqueur) is another Burgundian specialty; look for it in desserts and snazzy drinks (try a *kir*).

WINE TASTING IN BEAUNE

Here are two good places to learn about Burgundy wines without leaving Beaune. **Patriarche Père et Fils** is home to Burgundy's largest and most impressive wine cellar, where you'll explore some of their three miles of underground passages and try Burgundian classics (€17 for 10 wines, daily 9:30-11:15 & 14:00-17:15, 5 Rue du Collège, tel. 03 80 24 53 78, www.patriarche.com). **Sensation Vin** offers informative wine classes in the comfortable wine bar/classroom and learn while you taste (book ahead, €35 for 1.5-hour class with 7 wines, daily except closed Sun in winter, 2 Rue Paul Bouchard, tel. 03 80 22 17 57, www.sensation-vin.com, contact@sensation-vin.com). Ask about their intimate tastings-in-the-vineyards class for two.

Eating

$$$ Caveau des Arches is a reliable choice for Burgundian specialties, with romantic stone cellars and fine table settings (€26 *menu* with the classics, €36 *menu* with greater choices, and a €58 *gourmand menu*, but portions can be small; closed Sun-Mon and Aug, impressive wine list, where the ring road crosses Rue d'Alsace—which leads to Place Madeleine—at 10 Boulevard Perpreuil, tel. 03 80 22 10 37, www.caveau-des-arches.com).

$$$ La Ciboulette, intimate and family-run, offers fine cuisine that mixes traditional Burgundian flavors with creative dishes and lovely presentation. It's worth the longer walk—and you can do your laundry next door while you dine (indoor seating only, closed Mon-Tue; from Place Carnot, walk out Rue Carnot to 69 Rue Lorraine; tel. 03 80 24 70 72).

$$ Les Pôpiettes is a lively place that's popular with locals and foodies. The chef-owner produces cuisine that's an eclectic blend of delicious and inventive—though limited in choice—such as risotto and snails (inside dining only, closed Tue-Wed, 10 Rue d'Alsace, tel. 03 80 21 91 81, www.les-popiettes.com).

$$ Brasserie le Carnot is a perennially popular café with good inside seating and better exterior tables in the thick of the pedestrian zone. It serves pizza, salads, and pasta dishes as well as the usual café offerings (open daily, 18 Rue Carnot where it meets Rue Monge, tel. 03 80 22 32 93).

$ Aux Hospices, on the main square, serves simple, light meals at bargain prices. You'll get a fun outdoor experience, but there's good inside seating, too (daily, 32 Place Carnot, tel. 03 80 24 99 01).

$ Le Bistro des Cocottes is a warm place where locals go for top regional cuisine at good prices. Interior tables buzz with regulars while terrace tables seem popular with tourists (closed Sun-Mon, 3 Place de la Madeleine, tel. 03 80 24 02 60).

$$ Le Tast'Vin, across from the train station at the recommended Hôtel de France, has a tasty €26 *menu* and fun cheeseburgers with Burgundian cheese (closed Sat and Mon for lunch and all day Sun, 35 Avenue du 8 Septembre, tel. 03 80 24 10 34, www.hoteldefrance-beaune.com).

Wine Bars: Good choices include **$$ Maison du Colombier** (delicious tapas, *tartines,* and *plats,* closed Sun, 1 Rue Charles Cloutier), **$$ Le Bistrot Bourguignon** (15 types of *vin* by the glass, light dinners, closed Sun-Mon, on pedestrian street at 8 Rue Monge), and **$$ Bistrot du Coin** (limited seating, wine only—no food, Tue-Fri 17:00-24:00, Sat 10:00-24:00, closed Sun-Mon, 2 Place Ziem).

Sleeping

$$$$ Hôtel le Cep**** is *the* venerable place to stay in Beaune, if you have the means. Buried in the town center, this historic building comes with fine public spaces inside and out, and 65 gorgeous wood-beamed, traditionally decorated rooms in all sizes (family rooms, fitness center, spa, pricey pay parking, 27 Rue Maufoux, tel. 03 80 22 35 48, www.hotel-cep-beaune.com, resa@hotel-cep-beaune.com).

$$ Hôtel des Remparts,*** a peaceful oasis in a rustic manor house built around a soothing courtyard, comes with attentive service, Old World comfort, big beds, and a few good family suites (RS%, laundry service, bike rental, pay garage parking, just inside ring road between train station and main square at 48 Rue Thiers, tel. 03 80 24 94 94, www.hotel-remparts-beaune.com, hotel.des.remparts@wanadoo.fr, run by the formal Epaillys).

$$ Hôtel de la Paix,*** a few steps off Place Madeleine, is a top choice. In the main building (with reception, breakfast room, bar, and comfy lounges) are 30 three-star, handsome, well-appointed rooms, including several good family rooms and "apartments" sleeping up to six. In a nearby annex are seven good-value, comfortable two-star rooms and two family rooms (good breakfast, pay parking, 45 Faubourg Madeleine, tel. 03 80 24 78 08, www.hotelpaix.com, contact@hotelpaix.com).

$ Hôtel de France*** is a simple but good place with fair prices and updated rooms that's easy for train travelers and drivers. It's run by fun, English-speaking owners Nicolas and Virginie (family rooms, bar, good bistro, pay garage parking, 35 Avenue du 8 Septembre, tel. 03 80 24 10 34, www.hoteldefrance-beaune.com, contact@hoteldefrance-beaune.com).

$ Hôtel La Villa Fleurie, an adorable 10-room refuge, is a solid value (a 15-minute walk from the center). First-floor-up rooms are wood-floored, plush, and *très* traditional; second-floor rooms are carpeted and cozy. Most rooms have queen-size beds, and all have big bathrooms (family rooms, easy and free parking, 19 Place Colbert, tel. 03 80 22 66 00, www.lavillafleurie.fr, contact@lavillafleurie.fr). From Beaune's ring road, turn right in front of the Bichot winery.

¢ Hôtel Rousseau is a good-value frumpy old manor house that turns up its nose at Beaune's sophistication. Cheerful, quirky, and elusive owner Madame Rousseau, her pet birds, and the quiet garden will make you smile, and the tranquility will help you sleep. Rooms are spotless and filled with big wood armoires and heavy wood bed frames (family rooms, includes continental breakfast, cash only, no air-con, Wi-Fi in reception only, free and easy parking, email reservations preferred, 11 Place Madeleine, tel. 03 80 22 13 59, www.hotel-rousseau.com, hotelrousseaubeaune@orange.fr).

Transportation
Arriving and Departing
BY CAR

Driving provides the ultimate flexibility for touring the vineyards. To reach the center of Beaune, follow *Centre-Ville/Place de la Madeleine* signs and park for free in Place Madeleine (turnover is quick). The free Parking du Jardin Anglais at the north end of the ring road usually has spaces, and there are free parking spots all along the ring road. Parking inside Beaune's ring road is metered from 9:00 to 12:30 and 14:00 to 19:00; there's a convenient pay parking garage next to the main TI on the ring road.

Car Rental: ADA is close to the train station (Mon-Sat 8:00-12:00 & 14:00-18:00, closed Sun, 26 Avenue du 8 Septembre, tel. 03 80 22 72 90). **Hertz** is outside the center at 52 Route de Serre (tel. 03 55 87 05 50). **Europcar** is also on the outskirts (53 Route de Pommard, tel. 03 80 22 32 24).

BY TRAIN

To reach the city center from the train station (no baggage storage), walk straight out of the station up Avenue du 8 Septembre, cross the busy ring road, and continue up Rue du Château. Follow it as it angles left and pass to the left of the mural, veering right onto Rue des Tonneliers. A left on Rue de l'Enfant leads to Beaune's pedestrian zone, Place Carnot, and the TI annex.

From Beaune by Train to: Paris Gare de Lyon (nearly hourly, 2.5 hours, most require reservation and easy change in Dijon; more via Dijon to Paris' Gare de Bercy, no reservation required, 3.5 hours), **Colmar** (10/day, 3 hours via TGV between Dijon and Mulhouse, reserve well ahead, changes in Dijon and Mulhouse or Belfort), **Arles** (hourly, 5 hours, transfer in Lyon), **Chamonix** (7/day, 7 hours, several changes), **Amboise** (6/day, 6 hours, transfer at Nevers and/or St-Pierre-des-Corps; more with multiple connections).

NEAR BEAUNE

VINEYARD LOOPS

These drives combine great scenery with some of my favorite wine destinations (before heading out, read the section on Burgundian wines on page 380). Certain segments are doable by bike depending on your fitness and determination.

If time is tight and you have a car, drive the beautiful **"South Vineyard Loop"** to Château de la Rochepot. The last part is a tough ride on a bike (unless it's electric), so bikers should only do the first section of this route (ideally to Puligny-Montrachet and back—an easy, level ride). My **"North Vineyard Loop"** takes you through Aloxe-Corton to Savigny-lès-Beaune and is good by car or by bike (manageable hills and distances).

Vineyard Tips: Along these routes, I avoid tasting at famous wine châteaux (such as those in Pommard and Meursault) and look for smaller, more personal places. Although you can drop in unannounced at a wine château or a *caveau*, at private wineries it's best to call ahead and arrange an appointment (ask your hotelier for help). At free tastings, you're expected to buy at least a bottle or two unless you're on a group tour.

South Vineyard Loop

Take this pretty, peaceful route, worth ▲▲, for the best approach to La Rochepot's romantic castle, and to glide through several of Burgundy's most reputed vineyards. Read ahead and note the open hours of wineries and sights along the route (you can also do this loop in reverse). There are good picnic spots along the way; one is just before entering Puligny-Montrachet from the north (turn right, pass the first picnic spot, and continue 100 yards farther to one closer to the hills). The entire loop is 28 miles.

Bikers can follow the first part of this route to Puligny-Montrachet, along Burgundy's best bike path (connects the wine villages of Pommard, Volnay, Meursault, and Puligny-Montrachet for a level, 18-mile loop; allow two hours round trip). Only power riders or those with e-bikes should tackle the hills to La Rochepot.

⊃ *From Beaune to Château de la Rochepot*

By Car: Drivers leave Beaune's ring road, following signs for *Chalon-sur-Saône* (often abbreviated *Chalon-s/ S.,* first turn-off after Auxerre exit), then follow signs to *Pommard/Autun.* When you come to Pommard, you'll pass several lunch and wine-tasting opportunities, including **Domaine Lejeune** (free tasting, Mon-Sat 9:00-12:00 & 14:00-18:00, best to call ahead, behind the church, tel. 03 80 22 90 88, www.domaine-lejeune.fr).

South of Pommard, the road gradually climbs past Volnay and terrific views. From here, follow signs into **Meursault** (*centre-ville* signs lead to its fine square, bakeries, grocery shops, and good restaurants).

Drivers just passing through Meursault follow *Toutes Directions* to the lower end of the village, then turn right on D-113b,

Vineyards line the roads between Beaune and the Château de la Rochepot.

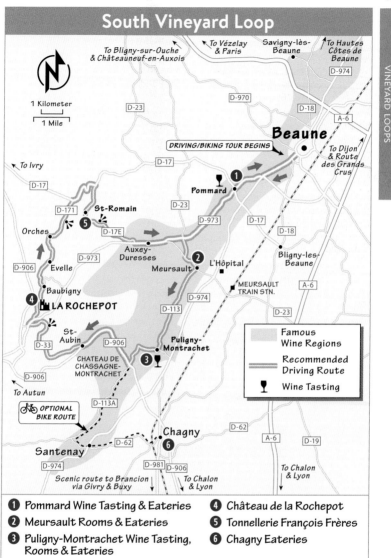

South Vineyard Loop

To Bligny-sur-Ouche
& Châteauneuf-en-Auxois

To Vézelay
& Paris

Savigny-lès-
Beaune

To Hautes
Côtes de
Beaune

D-974

To Vézelay
& Paris

D-970

D-23

D-18

A-6

Beaune

DRIVING/BIKING TOUR BEGINS

To Dijon
& Route
des Grands
Crus

1 Kilometer

1 Mile

To Ivry

D-17

D-17

Pommard ❶

D-171 St-Romain ❺

D-23

D-973

D-17

D-18

Orches

D-17E

Auxey-
Duresses

D-973

Evelle

Meursault ❷ L'Hôpital

Bligny-les-
Beaune

D-906

Baubigny

MEURSAULT
TRAIN STN.

A-6

❹ LA ROCHEPOT

D-974

D-113

D-23

St-
Aubin

D-33

D-906

Puligny-
Montrachet

CHATEAU DE
CHASSAGNE-
MONTRACHET

D-906

❸

To Autun

D-113A

OPTIONAL
BIKE ROUTE

Chagny

D-62

Santenay

D-62 ❻

A-6

D-19

D-974

D-981 D-906

Scenic route to Brancion
via Givry & Buxy

To Chalon
& Lyon

To Chalon
& Lyon

Legend:
Famous
Wine Regions

Recommended
Driving Route

Wine Tasting

❶ Pommard Wine Tasting & Eateries
❷ Meursault Rooms & Eateries
❸ Puligny-Montrachet Wine Tasting,
Rooms & Eateries
❹ Château de la Rochepot
❺ Tonnellerie François Frères
❻ Chagny Eateries

and follow signs for *Puligny-Montrachet*. Pass through low-slung vineyards south of Meursault, then enter **Puligny-Montra-chet**—with good picnic spots on the right as you enter. At the big roundabout with a bronze sculpture of vineyard workers, find the **Caveau de Puligny-Montrachet** and a chance to sample from vines that produce "the world's best whites" (€20/6 wines, can ship to the US; daily 9:30-13:00 & 15:00-19:00, closes at 18:00 in winter; tel. 03 80 21 96 78, www.caveau-puligny. com). A block straight out the door of the *caveau* leads to a small grocery and the town's big square (Place du Pasquier de la Fontaine), with **Hôtel-Restaurant Le**

Montrachet and **Café de l'Estaminet des Meix.**

Go back to the roundabout and follow signs to *Chassagne-Montrachet* and *St. Aubin* (D-113a), leading through more manicured vineyards.

Continue on to **Château de la Rochepot** by making a hard right on D-906 to St-Aubin and following *La Rochepot* signs onto D-33. After heading over the hills and through the vineyards of the Hautes-Côtes (upper slopes), you'll come to a drop-dead view of the castle (stop mandatory). Turn right when you reach La Rochepot, and follow blue *Le Château* signs to the castle).

You can visit **Château de la Rochepot** if it's open. Splendid both inside and out, construction of this pint-size, very Burgundian castle began during the end of the Middle Ages (when castles were built to defend) and was completed during the Renaissance (when castles became luxury homes). So it's neither a purely defensive structure nor a palace—it's a bit of both (€8.50; July-Aug daily 10:00-18:00; March-June & Sept-Nov Wed-Sun until 17:00 and closed Tue; closed Dec-Feb; www.larochepot.com).

Returning to Beaune: When leaving the castle, turn right out of its parking lot. You'll crest the hill, then turn left following signs into Baubigny and track the D-17 through Evelle and rock-solid Orches. After Orches, climb to the top of Burgundy's world—keeping straight on D-17, you'll pass several **lookouts** on your right (simple dirt pullouts with exceptional views, the best is about 50 yards before the steel guardrail). Get out of your car and wander cliffside for a postcard-perfect Burgundian image. The village of St-Romain swirls below, and if it's really clear, look for Mont Blanc on the eastern horizon.

Next, drive down to **St-Romain**, passing Burgundy's most important wine-barrel maker, **Tonnellerie Francois Frères** (it's above the village in the modern building, www.francoisfreres.com). Inside, well-stoked fires heat the oak staves to make them flexible, and sweaty workers use heavy hammers to pound iron rings around the barrels as they've done since medieval times. The workshop is closed to the public, but discreet travelers can take quick peeks through the glass doors to the far left.

Château de la Rochepot

Next, follow signs for *Auxey-Duresses*, and then *Beaune* for a scenic finale to your journey.

By Bike: Take the vineyard bike path by leaving the ring road toward Auxerre, and turning left at the signal after Lycée Viticole de Beaune (look for bike-route icons and *Voie Verte Beaune-Santenay* signs). **Pommard** has lunch and wine-tasting stops (listed earlier). South of Pommard, follow bike icons along the bike-only path, then ride into **Meursault** (restaurants and more). Follow more bike icons out of town through low-slung vineyards to reach **Puligny-Montrachet** (wine tastings).

From Puligny-Montrachet, double back to **Beaune** or continue on the bike path to **Santenay,** then ride along the canal to **Chagny,** and take the train back to Beaune (2/hour weekdays, 1/hour weekends, ask for *la gare* in Chagny—it is poorly signed). Continuing to **Château de la Rochepot** is not recommended without an e-bike.

North Vineyard Loop

For an easy and rewarding spin by car— or ideally by bike—through waves of vineyards that smother traditional villages, follow this relatively level 10-mile

loop from Beaune, worth ▲. It laces together three renowned wine villages— Aloxe-Corton, Pernand-Vergelesses, and Savigny-lès-Beaune—connecting you with Burgundian nature and village wine culture.

With stops, allow a half-day by bike or 1.5 hours by car. Bring water and snacks, as there is precious little available until the end of this route. Your tour concludes in Savigny-lès-Beaune, where you'll find a café-pizzeria, wine tastings, a small grocery, and a unique château.

⊙ *From Beaune to Savigny-lès-Beaune*

Start out by heading to Aloxe-Corton by car or bike.

By Car: From Beaune's ring road, drivers take D-974 a few blocks north toward Dijon. Follow Savigny-lès-Beaune signs left at the signal, then quickly turn right. On the outskirts of town you'll cross over the autoroute, then veer right, following the second signs you see to Pernand-Vergelesses (D-18). Turn right at the first Aloxe-Corton sign, and glide into the town. Make a hard left at the stop sign and climb uphill to find a small parking area with several recommended wine-tastings close by.

By Bike: From Beaune's ring road, turn right on Rue de Chorey after passing the public pool, following signs for Gigny (just before D-974 to Dijon). Continue following signs toward Gigny into Chorey-les-Beaune. In Chorey-les Beaune, veer left onto Rue Pavelot, pass through two stop signs, then follow the lane as it enters the vineyards and eventually curves left. Cross busy D-974, go straight up the tree-lined road, veer right at the fork, then make a left at the stop sign and climb uphill into Aloxe-Corton.

Aloxe-Corton: This tiny town, with a world-class reputation among wine enthusiasts, is packed with top tasting opportunities (but no cafés). The easygoing **Domaines d'Aloxe-Corton** (small fee for tasting, Thu-Mon 10:00-13:00 & 15:00-

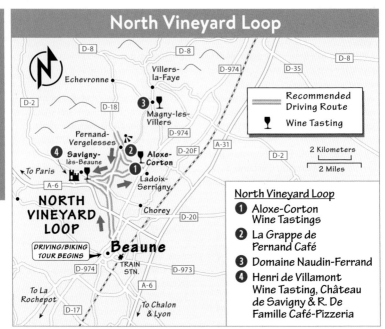

North Vineyard Loop

Recommended Driving Route
Wine Tasting

North Vineyard Loop
1 Aloxe-Corton Wine Tastings
2 La Grappe de Pernand Café
3 Domaine Naudin-Ferrand
4 Henri de Villamont Wine Tasting, Château de Savigny & R. De Famille Café-Pizzeria

19:00, no midday break on high-season weekends, closed Tue-Wed, tel. 03 80 26 49 85, http://aloxe.corton.free.fr) and more upscale **Domaine de Senard** (lunch Tue-Sat 11:30-13:30, €69 with 4 wines; tastings—€28 for first person, €15/person after that; Tue-Sat 10:00-11:30 & 14:00-17:30, closed Sun-Mon; reserve ahead by phone, 1 Rue des Chaumes, tel. 03 80 26 41 65, www.domainesenard.com, table@domainesenard.com) offer different kinds of tastings.

• *Drivers and bikers leave Aloxe-Corton and head up the hill on Rue des Chaumes, following signs for Pernand-Vergelesses (you'll pass a* **good picnic spot** *on the left in about 300 yards, just after passing a house). At the T-intersection with D-18, most bikers will want to turn left and pick up the directions for leaving Pernand-Vergelesses (below). Otherwise, turn right and head into...*

Pernand-Vergelesses: As you enter the village, look for a cute little café called **$ La Grappe de Pernand** (follow the umbrellas down to the right and find

reasonably priced food and drink, closed Mon in off-season and Tue year-round).

Drivers and strong bikers should consider two worthwhile detours from Pernand-Vergelesses: Climbing well above the village leads to one of the best vineyard panoramas in Burgundy. To get there, enter Pernand-Vergelesses, turn right at the roundabout and head up into the village, turning right on Rue du Creux St. Germain, and then continuing straight and up along Rue Copeau. Curve up past the church until you see small *Panorama* signs. Drivers and bikers wanting to extend their ride can follow signs (just after passing the church, en route to the panorama) to **Magny-les-Villers** and track a scenic and hilly wine lane for about two miles to one of my favorite wineries, **Domaine Naudin-Ferrand** (by appointment only—call or email, free for short tasting, fee for elaborate tasting; Mon-Fri 9:00-12:00 & 13:30-17:30 except closed Wed afternoon, Sat 14:00-18:00, closed Sun, Rue du Meix-Grenot—carefully track faded signs, tel. 03 80 62 91 50, mobile 06 87 76 85 42, www.naudin-ferrand.com, julie@naudin-ferrand.com).

• *Leaving Pernand-Vergelesses, bikers and drivers both follow the main road (D-18) back toward Beaune, and turn right into the vineyards on the first lane (at the Pernand-Vergelesses Premier Cru sign, about 400 yards from Pernand-Vergelesses). Keep left at the first fork and rise gently to lovely views. Drop down and turn right when you come to a T, then joyride along the vine service lanes (bikers should watch for loose gravel). The lane dumps you in the center of...*

Savigny-lès-Beaune: A left leads to **Henri de Villamont** winery (free tasting,

hours vary but generally Tue-Sat 10:00-12:30 & 13:30-18:00, best to call ahead for tasting, Rue du Dr. Guyot, tel. 03 80 21 52 13, www.hdv.fr), and a right leads to the village center and the **R. De Famille** café-pizzeria (closed Mon).

• *From Savigny-lès-Beaune, drive or pedal following signs back into Beaune. To avoid busy D-18 into Beaune, bikers can take a slightly longer route following D-2a from Savigny, tracking signs to D-974, then crossing it and taking the first right in Chorey-les-Beaune (along the stone wall), and then following* Route de Beaune *signs. Turn right at the* "do not enter" *sign, then take your first left to reach Beaune's ring road.*

BEST OF THE REST

The bountiful vineyards, classic villages, and hearty cuisine of eastern France extend well beyond Burgundy. Get acquainted with alpine vistas in the picturesque resort town of Chamonix, nestled at the foot of Europe's mighty Mount Blanc. Enchanting Colmar, in the Alsace region, is the ultimate Franco-Germanic blend, with old burghers' houses, colorful tiled roofs, and cobbled lanes.

Chamonix

Surrounded by snow-capped peaks, powerful—if receding—glaciers, and richly rewarding hiking trails, Chamonix (shah-moh-nee) is France's favorite alpine resort. Ever since tourists eclipsed cows as the town's economic base a couple hundred years ago, Chamonix's purpose has been to dazzle visitors with some of Europe's top alpine thrills.

Day Plan

If you have one sunny day, spend it this way: Start with the Aiguille du Midi lift (go very early—by 8:00 at the latest, reservations possible and recommended July-Aug), take a lift all the way to Pointe Helbronner (Italy), then double back to Aiguille du Midi.

From Aiguille du Midi, take the lift back down to Chamonix, but if you're a hiker, consider getting off halfway down (at Plan de l'Aiguille) to hike to Montenvers and its Mer de Glace (with good shoes and snow level permitting), explore there, then take the train down to Chamonix.

End your day with a hearty dinner and well-deserved drink at a view café in town.

Orientation

The frothy Arve River splits Chamonix in two, with mountains (Mont Blanc and the Aiguilles Rouges peaks) towering on either side. The thriving pedestrian zone forms Chamonix's lively core.

Tourist Information: Visit the TI to get the mountain weather forecast, pick up the free town and valley map and the "panorama" map of all the valley lifts, and maybe the €5 Carte des Sentiers hiking map (daily, closed Sun off-season; tel. 04 50 53 00 24, www.chamonix.com).

Getting There

Bus and train service to Chamonix is surprisingly good. Some train routes (such as from Paris and Colmar) pass through Switzerland to reach Chamonix. The **train** station is east of the town center: Walk straight out of the station and up Avenue Michel Croz three blocks to reach the center. The long-distance **bus station** is south of town (234 Avenue de Courmayeur, a 15-minute walk to the center).

By **car**, take the Chamonix Nord turn-off and follow signs to *Centre-Ville*. Most parking is metered; your hotel can direct you to free parking. From mid-July to late August, plan ahead or arrive before 10:00 to get a spot.

Rick's Tip: *The* **Multipass lift ticket** **allows unlimited access** *to all the lifts and trains in Chamonix (except the Helbronner gondola to Italy). It's sold online (www.montblancnaturalresort.com), at participating lift stations, and at some hotels.*

Sights

▲▲▲AIGUILLE DU MIDI

The Aiguille du Midi (ay-gwee doo mee-dee) is the most spectacular mountain lift in Europe—and the most popular ride in the valley. If the weather's clear, the price doesn't matter. Take an early lift and have breakfast above 12,000 feet. Remember,

it's freezing cold up there and you'll need sunglasses.

Cost: From Chamonix to Plan de l'Aiguille—round-trip-€33 (one-way-€18); Aiguille du Midi—round-trip-€62 (one-way-€50, not including parachute). Tickets for the Panoramic Mont Blanc *télécabines* from Aiguille du Midi to Pointe Helbronner (Italy) are sold at both base and summit lift stations with no difference in price (round-trip-€30; as conditions can change, I wouldn't buy the Helbronner ticket until I'm at the top).

Hours: Lifts generally run daily July-Aug 6:30 or 7:00-18:00, late May-June and Sept 8:10-16:30, and Oct-mid-May 8:10-15:30, closed mid-May-late May and Nov-mid-Dec. Hours can change with the weather, among other reasons. Always confirm plans locally. The last *télécabine* departure to Pointe Helbronner is about 14:30, and the last train down from Montenvers (for hikers) is between 17:00-18:00, depending on the season.

Crowd-Beating Strategies: To beat the hordes and clouds, ride the Aiguille du Midi lift (up and down) as early as you can. To beat major delays in summer, leave no later than 8:00.

You can reserve at the information

Chamonix with Mont Blanc in the background

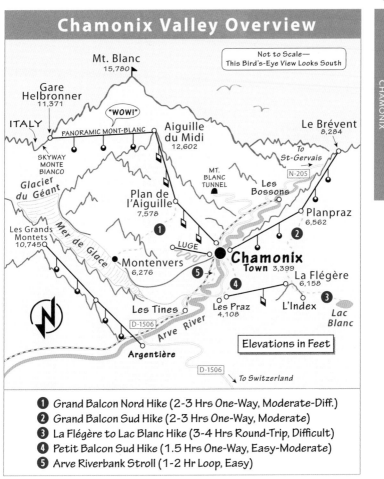

Chamonix Valley Overview

Not to Scale—
This Bird's-Eye View Looks South

Mt. Blanc
15,780

Gare Helbronner
11,371

ITALY

"WOW!"

PANORAMIC MONT-BLANC

Aiguille du Midi
12,602

Le Brévent
8,284

To St-Gervais

N-205

SKYWAY MONTE BIANCO

MT. BLANC TUNNEL

Les Bossons

Glacier du Géant

Plan de l'Aiguille
7,578

Planpraz
6,562

Les Grands Montets
10,745

Mer de Glace

LUGE

Chamonix
Town 3,399

Montenvers
6,276

La Flégère
6,158

L'Index

Lac Blanc

Les Tines

Les Praz
4,108

D-1506

Arve River

Elevations in Feet

Argentière

D-1506

To Switzerland

1 Grand Balcon Nord Hike (2-3 Hrs One-Way, Moderate-Diff.)
2 Grand Balcon Sud Hike (2-3 Hrs One-Way, Moderate)
3 La Flégère to Lac Blanc Hike (3-4 Hrs Round-Trip, Difficult)
4 Petit Balcon Sud Hike (1.5 Hrs One-Way, Easy-Moderate)
5 Arve Riverbank Stroll (1-2 Hr Loop, Easy)

booth next to the lift, online at www. montblancnaturalresort.com, or in person at this or other lifts (reservations are non-refundable). Reservations are not possible for the *télécabines* to Helbronner.

Visiting the Aiguille du Midi: At the top, you'll find several gift shops, cafeterias, view terraces, and many nooks and crannies to explore. A **skybridge** leading from the station past an information kiosk (which sells tickets for the Helbronner lift) deposits you in the **main building** with an elevator to the summit. Before riding the elevator up, visit the mountain-

eering exhibits, then follow *Vallée Blanche* signs to a drippy **"ice tunnel"** where skiers and mountain climbers make their exit. The views are sensational if you can get close (only skiers/climbers allowed past a certain point).

The highlight of your ascent is riding the elevator to **the summit** (signed *Terrasse 3842*)—12,602 feet above sea level (pose with the much-photographed altitude sign). From this platform, the Alps spread out before you. Use the orientation posters to identify key peaks: You can see the main Swiss and Italian summits

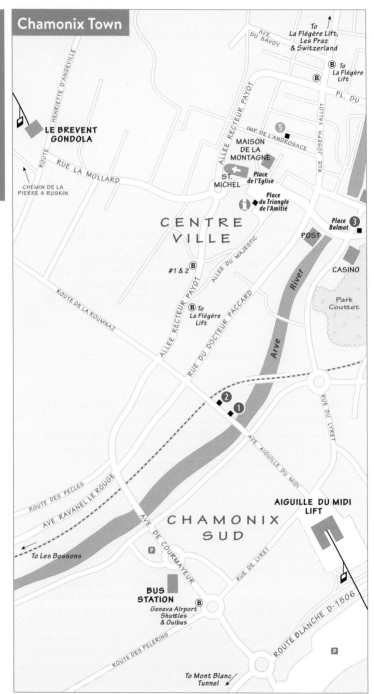

Chamonix Town

To La Flégère Lift,
Les Praz
& Switzerland

AVE. DU SAVOY

B To La Flégère Lift

B

PL. DU

RUE JOSEPH VALLOT

ROUTE HENRIETTE D'ANGEVILLE

ALLEE RECTEUR PAYOT

LE BREVENT GONDOLA

RUE LA MOLLARD

IMP. DE L'ANDROSACE

5

MAISON DE LA MONTAGNE

ST. MICHEL

Place de l'Eglise

CHEMIN DE LA PIERRE A RUSKIN

CENTRE VILLE

i

Place du Triangle de l'Amitié

Place Balmat

3

POST

ALLEE DU MAJESTIC

#1 & 2

B

CASINO

Park Couttet

ROUTE DE LA ROUMNAZ

ALLEE RECTEUR PAYOT

B To La Flégère Lift

RUE DU DOCTEUR PACCARD

Arve

River

RUE DU LYRET

2

1

AVE. AIGUILLE DU MIDI

ROUTE DES PECLES

AVE. RAVANEL LE ROUGE

AVE. DE COURMAYEUR

AIGUILLE DU MIDI LIFT

CHAMONIX SUD

RUE DE LYRET

P

To Les Bossons

P

BUS STATION

Geneva Airport Shuttles & Ouibus

B

ROUTE DES PELERINS

ROUTE BLANCHE D-1506

P

To Mont Blanc Tunnel

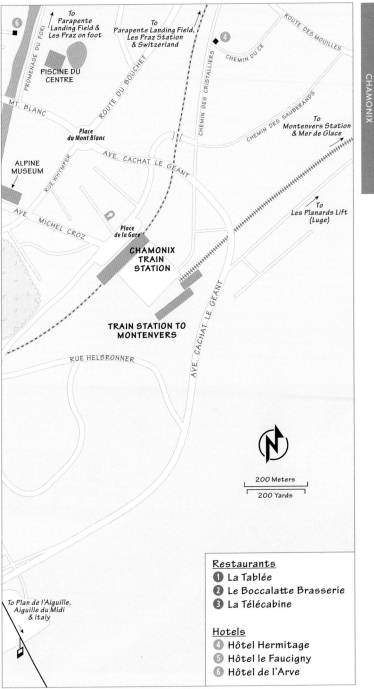

To Parapente Landing Field & Les Praz on foot

To Parapente Landing Field, Les Praz Station & Switzerland

ROUTE DES MOUILLES

CHEMIN DU CÉ

PROMENADE DU FORI

PISCINE DU CENTRE

ROUTE DU BOUCHET

CHEMIN DES CRISTALLIERS

CHEMIN DES SAUBERANDS

To Montenvers Station & Mer de Glace

MT. BLANC

Place du Mont Blanc

AVE. CACHAT LE GÉANT

ALPINE MUSEUM

RUE WHYMPER

To Les Planards Lift (Luge)

AVE. MICHEL CROZ

Place de la Gare

CHAMONIX TRAIN STATION

TRAIN STATION TO MONTENVERS

AVE. CACHAT LE GÉANT

RUE HELBRONNER

200 Meters

200 Yards

To Plan de l'Aiguille, Aiguille du Midi & Italy

Restaurants
1 La Tablée
2 Le Boccalatte Brasserie
3 La Télécabine

Hotels
4 Hôtel Hermitage
5 Hôtel le Faucigny
6 Hôtel de l'Arve

rising above 13,000 feet. If it's clear, you can see the bent little Matterhorn—the tall, shady pyramid listed in French on the observation table as "Cervin—4,505 meters" (14,775 feet). And looming on the other side is Mont Blanc, the Alps' highest point, at 4,810 meters (15,780 feet).

At the summit, the "Step Into the Void" glass box offers a chance to stand in what feels like midair. (They'll take your photo for a fee.)

Taking the Gondola to Italy: Embark on the little red Panoramic Mont Blanc *télécabine* and sail south to Pointe Hel-bronner, the mountaintop Italian border station (typically open late June-early Sept). In a gondola for four, you'll dangle silently for 40 minutes as you glide over glaciers and past a forest of peaks to Italy. Return by gondola to Aiguille du Midi.

Returning to Chamonix via Plan de l'Aiguille: To get from Aiguille du Midi to Chamonix, you'll need to change gondolas at **Plan de l'Aiguille.** Take some time here on your way down. Gondolas depart every few minutes, and those boarding

here never have to wait. At Plan de l'Aiguille you'll find a scenic café and rocky perches for sunbathing. It's a great place to just relax. But the best reason to get off here is to follow the wonderful **trail to the Mer de Glace,** then catch the cogwheel train back into Chamonix (for details, see "Chamonix-Area Hikes," later).

▲▲▲MER DE GLACE (MONTENVERS)

From Gare de Montenvers (the little station over the tracks from Chamonix's main train station), the cute cogwheel Train du Montenvers toots you up to tiny Montenvers (mohn-tuh-vehr). Sit on the left-hand side as you go up for good views among pine trees over the valley. There you'll see a dirty, rapidly receding glacier called the Mer de Glace and fantastic views up the white valley (Vallée Blanche) of splintered, snow-capped peaks.

Cost and Hours: Round-trip-€33, one-way-€28, family rates available, prices include gondola and ice caves entry, daily 8:30-17:00, July-Aug 8:00-18:00, 2/hour, 20 minutes, confirm first/last trip times with TI or call 04 50 53 12 54.

Riding the gondola to Aiguille du Midi

Visiting the Glacier: Find the **view deck** across from the train station. France's largest glacier, at eight miles long, is impressive from above and below. The swirling glacier extends under the dirt about a half-mile downhill to the left. Use an **orientation table** as you look up to the peaks. The path to the right (as you face the glacier) leads to a fine view café and a reconstruction of a crystal cave.

The glacier's **ice caves** are beneath you (and are skippable for most). Take the free, small gondola down and prepare to walk about 500 steps each way. (Several years ago, it was 280 steps.) This glacier is beating a hasty retreat—as you walk down you'll pass signs that bring this point home by showing the extent of the glacier over the years. The ice cave, a hypnotizing shade of blue-green, is actually a long tunnel dug about 75 yards into the glacier.

▲▲▲LIFTS TO LE BREVENT AND LA FLEGERE

Though Aiguille du Midi gives a more spectacular ride, the Le Brévent and La Flégère lifts offer worthwhile hiking and viewing options, with unobstructed panoramas across to the Mont Blanc range and fewer crowds. The Le Brévent (luh bray-vahn) gondola is in Chamonix; the La Flégère (lah flay-zhair) lift is in nearby Les Praz (lay prah). The lifts are connected by a scenic hike or by bus along the valley floor; both have sensational view cafés. Both lifts are closed from late April to mid-June and again by mid-September (reopening when ski season starts, usually in Dec).

Chamonix-Area Hikes

The **Maison de la Montagne** service center is a good first stop for serious hikers (located across from the TI, first-floor WC). On the second floor, the **Office de Haute-Montagne** (High Mountain Office) can help you plan your hikes and tell you about trail and snow conditions (daily 9:00-12:00 & 15:00-18:00, www.chamoniarde.com).

For your hike, bring sunglasses, sunscreen, rain gear, water, snacks, and maybe light gloves. Pack warm layers (mountain weather can change in a

Mer de Glace

of the crowds that the Aiguille du Midi lift draws. While you'll start at 1,900 meters (6,230 feet) and end at 2,000 meters (6,560 feet), there's a lot more than just 100 meters (330 feet) of climbing between the La Flégère and Planpraz lift stations. While it's possible to hike the trail in either direction, it's better to start in La Flégère.

▲▲LA FLEGERE TO LAC BLANC

This demanding trail climbs steeply and steadily over a rough, boulder-strewn path for 2 hours to snowy Lac Blanc (pronounced "lock blah"). Some footing is tricky, and good shoes or boots are a must. The destination is a snow-white lake framed by peaks and the nifty Refuge-Hôtel du Lac Blanc, which offers good lunches (and dinners, if you stay the night, summers only). The views on the return trip are breathtaking.

▲PETIT BALCON SUD TO CHALET DE LA FLORIA AND LES PRAZ

This trail runs above the valley on the Brévent side from the village of Les Houches to Argentière, passing Chamonix about halfway, and is handy when snow or poor weather make other hikes problematic. No lifts are required—just strong thighs for the climb up and down. The highlight of the trail is flower-covered Chalet de la Floria snack bar (allow one hour each way from Chamonix).

ARVE RIVERBANK STROLL

For a level, forested-valley stroll, bike ride, or jog, follow the Arve River toward Les Praz. At Chamonix's Hôtel Alpina, follow the path upstream past the middle school and red-clay tennis courts, and find the green arrow to *Les Praz*. You'll cross a few bridges to the left, turn right along the rushing Arve River, and then follow Promenade des Econtres. Several trails loop through these woods; if you continue walking straight, you'll reach Les Praz in about an hour—an appealing destination with a number of cafés and a pleasing village green.

moment) and wear good shoes (trails are rocky and uneven).

▲▲PLAN DE L'AIGUILLE TO MONTENVERS-MER DE GLACE (LE GRAND BALCON NORD)

This three-hour hike (including breaks) is the most efficient way to incorporate a high-country adventure into your ride down from the valley's greatest lift, and check out a world-class glacier to boot. The spectacular, well-used trail rises but mostly falls (dropping 1,500 feet from Plan de l'Aiguille to Montenvers and the Mer de Glace) and is moderately difficult, provided the snow has melted (generally snow-covered until June). Note the last train time from Montenvers-Mer de Glace back to Chamonix, or you'll be hiking another hour and a half straight down.

▲▲LA FLEGERE TO PLANPRAZ (LE GRAND BALCON SUD)

This lovely hike traverses for 2.5 hours above Chamonix Valley, with staggering views of Mont Blanc, countless other peaks, glaciers, wildflowers, and a fraction

Other Activities

▲ LUGE (LUGE D'ETE)

Here's something for fun-seekers: Ride a plastic sled on rails up the hill, and then scream down a twisty, banked slalom course. Young or old, hare or tortoise, any fit person can manage a luge. *Freinez* signs tell you when to brake.

Cost and Hours: One ride–€7, six rides–€40, ask about double sleds, kids under 8 must ride with adult, generally July-Aug daily 10:00-18:30, mid-April-June and Sept-Oct Sat-Sun and select weekdays 13:30-18:00, check website for hours; 15-minute walk from town center, over the tracks from train station and past Montenvers train station; www.chamonixparc.com.

▲▲▲ PARAGLIDING (PARAPENTE)

When it's sunny and clear, the skies above Chamonix sparkle with colorful parachute-like sails that circle the valley like birds of prey. For €110-120 plus the cost of the lift up to Planpraz (Le Brévent ski area) or Plan de l'Aiguille, you can launch yourself off a mountain in a tandem paraglider with a trained, experienced pilot and fly like a bird for about 20 minutes (true thrill-seekers can launch from Aiguille du Midi, €280, 40-minute ride). **Sean Potts** is English (no language barrier), has been paragliding in Chamonix for 25 years, and is easy to work with (www.fly-chamonix.com). You can also try Summits Parapente (smart to reserve a day ahead, open year-round, www.summits.fr).

Eating

To dine well with a view, consider these places: **$$ La Tablée** has good *menu* deals (daily, 75 Avenue de l'Aiguille du Midi). **$$ Le Boccalatte Brasserie** serves meals in a casual interior and on a big view terrace (daily, 59 Avenue de l'Aiguille du Midi). **$$ La Télécabine** delivers a classy, peaceful experience (daily, 27 Rue de la Tour).

Sleeping

$$$ Hôtel Hermitage**** is a gorgeous chalet hotel (63 Chemin du Cé, www.hermitage-paccard.com); **$$ Hôtel le Faucigny****** is a tranquil retreat (118 Place de l'Eglise, www.hotelfaucigny-chamonix.com); and **$$ Hôtel de l'Arve****** offers a contemporary alpine feel (60 Impasse des Anémones, www.hotelarve-chamonix.com).

Colmar

A fantasy of steeply pitched roofs, pastel stucco, and wooden half-timbers, Colmar feels made for wonderstruck tourists. Antique shops welcome browsers, homeowners fuss over their geraniums, and locals seem genuinely proud of Alsace's most beautiful city. Located near the German border, Colmar has a hybrid culture: Natives who curse do so bilingually, and the local cuisine features sauerkraut and escargot.

Day Plan

Take my self-guided Old Town walk, which delivers you to the Unterlinden Museum, home to the powerful Isenheim Altarpiece. Then seek out one of the many places specializing in *tarte flambée* ("Alsatian pizza").

Colmar

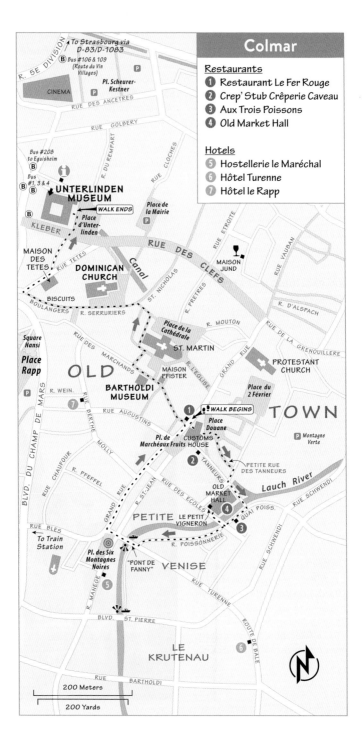

Colmar

Restaurants
1. Restaurant Le Fer Rouge
2. Crep' Stub Crêperie Caveau
3. Aux Trois Poissons
4. Old Market Hall

Hotels
5. Hostellerie le Maréchal
6. Hôtel Turenne
7. Hôtel le Rapp

Orientation

There isn't a straight street in Colmar's historic center—count on getting lost. Thankfully, most streets are pedestrian-only, and it's a lovely town to be lost in. Navigate by church steeples and the helpful signs that seem to pop up whenever you need them.

Tourist Information: The efficient TI is next to the Unterlinden Museum on Rue Unterlinden (daily, closed for lunch in winter, tel. 03 89 20 68 92, www.tourisme-colmar.com).

Getting There

The best **train connections** to Colmar are via Paris and Reims via TGV service (10-12/day, 2-2.5 hours). It's a 15-minute walk from the station into town: Exit straight out of the station past Hôtel Bristol, turn left on Avenue de la République, and keep walking. Or hop any Trace bus from the station and ride to the Champ de Mars stop (Place Rapp) or the Théâtre stop, next to the Unterlinden Museum (€1.30). Taxis charge €7 for any downtown ride.

Drivers should follow signs for *Centre-Ville*, then *Place Rapp* (where there's a huge underground garage, first hour free, €21/24 hours).

BEST OF THE REST

COLMAR

Rick's Tip: For a fun in-town wine-tasting experience, visit **Maison Jund.** *The family own 44 acres of vineyards and grow all seven of the Alsatian grapes (€6, call for appointment, 12 Rue de l'Ange, tel. 03 89 41 58 72, www.martinjund.com).*

---

❷ Colmar Old Town Walk

This self-guided walk—good by day, romantic by night—is a handy way to link the city's most worthwhile sights in about an hour (more if you enter sights).

• *Start in front of the Customs House (where Rue des Marchands hits Grand Rue). Face the old...*

Customs House (Koïfhus): Colmar is so attractive today because of its trading wealth. And that's what its Customs House was all about. The city was an economic powerhouse in the 15th, 16th, and 17th centuries because of its privileged status as a leading member of the Decapolis, a trading league of 10 mostly Alsatian cities founded in 1354.

Customs House

This "Alsatian Big Ten" enjoyed special tax and trade privileges, including the right to build fortified walls and run their internal affairs. As "Imperial" cities, they were ruled directly by the Holy Roman Emperor rather than by one of his lesser princes.

Delegates of the Decapolis would meet here to sort out trade issues, much like the European Union does in nearby Strasbourg today. Note the plaque above the door to the right with the double eagle of the Holy Roman Emperor—a sign that this was an Imperial city.

Walk under the archway to Place de l'Ancienne Douane and face the Frédéric-Auguste Bartholdi statue of General Lazarus von Schwendi—arm raised (Statue of Liberty-style) and clutching a bundle of local pinot gris grapes. He's the man who brought that grape from Hungary to Alsace.

• *Follow the statue's left elbow and walk down Petite Rue des Tanneurs (not the larger "Rue des Tanneurs"). The half-timbered commotion of higgledy-piggledy rooftops on the downhill side of the fountain marks the...*

Tanners' Quarter: These 17th- and 18th-century rooftops competed for space in the sun to dry their freshly tanned hides, while the nearby river chan-

nel flushed the waste products. When the industry moved out of town, the neighborhood became a slum. It was restored in the 1970s.

At the street's end, carry on a few steps, and then turn back. Notice the openings just below the roofs where hides would be hung out to dry. Stinky tanners' quarters were always at the edge of town. You've stepped outside the old center and are looking back at the city's first defensive wall. The oldest and lowest stones you see in the buildings are from 1230, now built into the row of houses.

• *Walk with the old walls on your right to the first street, Rue des Tanneurs. Turn left, and enter the...*

Old Market Hall: Colmar's historic market hall is where locals have come since 1865 to buy fish, produce, and other products (originally delivered by flat-bottomed boat). You'll find picnic fixings and produce, sandwiches and bakery items, wine tastings, and clean WCs. Several stands are run like cafés, and there's even a bar (Tue-Sat 8:00-18:00, Sun 10:00-14:00, closed Mon).

• *Exit the market from its far side, onto the flower-bedecked Rue des Ecoles bridge, leading to...*

Petite Venise

Petite Venise: This neighborhood, a collection of Colmar's most colorful houses lining the small canal, lies between the town's first wall (built to defend against arrows) and its later wall (built in the age of gunpowder). Medieval towns needed water. If they weren't on a river, they'd often redirect parts of nearby rivers to power their mills and quench their thirst. Colmar's river was canalized this way for medieval industry.

• *Turn right and walk along the flower-box-lined canal to the end of Rue de la Poissonnerie.*

Half-Timbered Houses: As you stroll, notice the picturesque houses. The pastel colors are just from this generation—designed to pump up the cuteness of Colmar for tourists. But the houses themselves are historic and real as can be.

Enjoy the creaky houses toward the end of Rue de la Poissonnerie, as the lane narrows into a sort of alleyway. When you emerge, on your right is "Pont de Fanny," a bridge so popular with tourists for its fine views that you see lots of fannies lined up along the railing. Walk to the center of the bridge, and add yours to the scene.

• *Cross the bridge, walk a short block, and take the second right onto Grand Rue, then walk for several blocks to the Customs House where this walk began. With your back to the Customs House, walk uphill on Rue des Marchands for a couple of blocks, and you'll come face-to-face with the...*

Maison Pfister (Pfister House): This richly decorated merchant's house dates from 1537. Here the owner displayed his wealth for all to enjoy (and to envy). The external spiral-staircase turret, a fine loggia on the top floor, and the bay windows were pricey add-ons. The painted walls, depicting biblical, historical, and allegorical scenes, indicate that the owner was one of those liberal elites with a taste for Renaissance humanism.

• *As you move past the spiral staircase, check out the attached building (at #9).*

Meter Man: The man carved into the side of this building was a drapemaker; he's shown holding a bar, Colmar's local measure of about one meter (almost equal to a yard). In the Middle Ages, it was common for cities to have their own units of length; it's one reason that merchants supported the "globalization" efforts of their time to standardize measuring systems.

Two doors farther up the street on the left is the ▲**Bartholdi Museum,** located in the home of the famous sculptor Frédéric-Auguste Bartholdi, creator of the Statue of Liberty (€6, March-Dec Wed-Mon 10:00-12:00 & 14:00-18:00, closed Tue and Jan-Feb, www.musee-bartholdi.fr).

• *A passage opposite the Bartholdi Museum leads you through the old guards' house to the...*

Church of St. Martin: The city's cathedral-like church was erected in 1235 after Colmar became an Imperial city and needed a bigger place of worship. Colmar's ruler at the time was Burgundian, so the church has a Burgundian-style tiled roof.

Walk left, under three expressive gargoyles, to the west portal. Facing the front of the church, notice that the relief over the main door depicts not your typical Last Judgment scene but the Three Kings

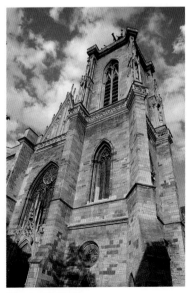

Church of St. Martin

who visited Baby Jesus. The Magi, whose remains are nearby in the Rhine city of Cologne, Germany, are popular in this region.

• *Continue past the church, go left around Jupiler Café, and wander up the pedestrian-only Rue des Serruriers ("Locksmiths Street") to the...*

Dominican Church: Compare the Church of St. Martin's ornate exterior with this simple ▲▲ Dominican structure. While both churches were built at the same time, each makes different statements. The "High Church" of the 13th century was fancy, while monastic orders preached a simpler faith and way of life. In the style of St. Dominic and St. Francis, they tried to get Rome back on a Christ-like track. This church houses the exquisite *Virgin in the Rosebush* (1473) by Martin Schongauer; if the church is open, pop in to see this mesmerizing medieval masterpiece.

• *Continue straight past the Dominican Church, where Rue des Serruriers becomes Rue des Boulangers ("Bakers Street"). Stop at #16.*

Skyscrapers and Biscuits: The towering green-and-brown house, dating from the 16th century, was one of Colmar's tallest buildings in that age. Notice how it contrasts with the string of buildings to the right, which are lower, French-style structures—likely built after a fire cleared out older, higher buildings.

As this is Bakers Street, check out the one right here at #16. Maison Alsacienne de Biscuiterie sells traditional biscuits (cookies), including boxed Christmas delights year-round.

• *Turn right on Rue des Têtes (notice the beautiful swan sign over the pharmacie at the corner). Walk a block to the fancy old house festooned with heads (on the right).*

Maison des Têtes ("House of Heads"): Colmar's other famous merchant's house, built in 1609 by a big-shot winemaker (see the grapes hanging from the wrought-iron sign and the happy man at the tip-top), is playfully decorated with about 100 faces and masks. On the ground floor, the guy showing his bellybutton in the window's center has pig's feet.

Look four doors to the right to see a bakery sign (above the big pretzel), which shows the *boulangerie* basics in Alsace: croissant, *Kugelhopf (a coffee bread),* and baguette.

Isenheim Altarpiece

• *Continue another block to a peaceful square where a canal runs under linden trees. Our walk is over, but the venerable church and convent on your left house Colmar's top attraction.*

Unterlinden Museum: This museum, rated ▲▲▲, is Colmar's touristic claim to fame. Its extensive yet manageable collection ranges from Roman Colmar to medieval winemaking exhibits to Monet and Renoir, and from traditional wedding dresses to paintings that give vivid insight into the High Middle Ages.

But its highlight is one of the most unforgettable masterpieces of medieval Europe: Matthias Grünewald's gloriously displayed **Isenheim Altarpiece** (c. 1515). Designed to help people in a medieval hospital endure horrible skin diseases— long before the age of painkillers—this complex work is a polyptych, a series of two-sided paintings on hinges that pivot like shutters. As the church calendar progressed, priests would change which parts of the altarpiece were visible by opening or closing these panels. The museum has disassembled the altarpiece so that visitors can view all the individual panels. To understand how the altarpiece was originally put together, see the models on the side walls (€13, Wed-Mon 10:00-18:00, until 20:00 first Thu of month, closed Tue, www.musee-unterlinden.com).

Rick's Tip: Colmar puts lots of creative energy into its **floodlit cityscapes,** *making* **evening strolls** *memorable. You could retrace the route of this chapter's guided walk simply to enjoy the lights and architecture.*

Route du Vin

France's smallest wine region is long (75 miles) and skinny (just over a mile wide on average). Peppering the landscape are villages full of quaint half-timbered architecture corralled within medieval walls and welcoming wineries featuring crisp, dry white wines.

By Car or Bike: Drivers and energetic bikers (bikes rentable at Colmar's train station) can pick up a detailed map of the wine road (Route du Vin) at any area TI.

Be advised that after seeing two or three towns, they start looking the same. Two villages work well for most. Distances are short; you can lace together what you like. Focus on towns within easy striking range of Colmar. The most picturesque are Eguisheim, Kaysersberg (Mon morning market), Hunawihr, Ribeauvillé (Sat morning market), and the *très* popular Riquewihr.

By Minivan Tour: Two companies that run wine road tours from Colmar are **Ophorus Tours** (www.ophorus.com) and **Alsascope** (www.alsascope.fr); their prices are roughly the same (€125/day, €75/half-day).

Eating

$$ Restaurant Le Fer Rouge, facing the Customs House, serves Alsatian classics (daily, 52 Grand Rue). **$ Crep' Stub Crêperie Caveau** is my favorite for crêpes (closed Mon, 10 Rue des Tanneurs). **$$$ Aux Trois Poissons** offers a traditionally French menu (closed Sun-Mon, 15 Quai de la Poissonnerie).

For quick, inexpensive, and memorable lunch options, grab a bite in the **$ Old Market Hall** in Petite Venise.

Sleeping

$$$ Hostellerie le Maréchal**** holds Colmar's most characteristic rooms (4 Place des Six Montagnes Noires, www. le-marechal.com). **$$ Hôtel Turenne*****is less central but offers very comfortable rooms (10 Route de Bâlewww.turenne. com). **$$ Hôtel le Rapp*****has rooms for many budgets (1 Rue Weinemer, www. rapp-hotel.com).

France: Past and Present

French History in an Escargot Shell

About the time of Christ, Romans "Latinized" the land of the Gauls. With the fifth-century AD fall of Rome, the barbarian Franks and Burgundians invaded. Today's France evolved from this unique mix of Latin and Celtic cultures.

While France wallowed with the rest of Europe in medieval darkness, it got a head start in its development as a nation-state. In 507, Clovis, the king of the **Franks**, established Paris as the capital of his Christian Merovingian dynasty. Clovis and the Franks would eventually become Louis and the French. The Frankish military leader Charles Martel stopped the spread of Islam by beating the Spanish Moors at the Battle of Poitiers in 732. And **Charlemagne**, the most important of the "Dark Age" Frankish kings, was crowned Holy Roman Emperor by the pope in 800. Charles the Great presided over the "Carolingian Renaissance" and effectively ruled an empire that was vast for its time.

The Treaty of Verdun (843), which divided Charlemagne's empire among his grandsons, marks what could be considered the birth of Europe. For the first time,

a treaty was signed in vernacular languages (French and German), rather than in Latin. This split established a Franco-Germanic divide, and heralded an age of fragmentation. While petty princes took the reigns, the Frankish king ruled only Ile de France, a small region around Paris.

Vikings, or Norsemen, settled in what became Normandy. Later, in 1066, these **"Normans"** invaded England. The Norman king, William the Conqueror, consolidated his English domain, accelerating the formation of modern England. But his rule also muddied the political waters between England and France, kicking off a centuries-long struggle between the two nations.

In the 12th century, **Eleanor of Aquitaine** (a separate country in southwest France) married Louis VII, king of France, bringing Aquitaine under French rule. They divorced, and she married Henry of Normandy, soon to be Henry II of England. This marital union gave England control of a huge swath of land from the English Channel to the Pyrenees. For 300 years, France and England would struggle over control of Aquitaine. Any enemy of the French king would find a natural ally in the English king.

In 1328, the French king Charles IV died without a son. The English king (Edward III), Charles IV's nephew, was interested in the throne, but the French resisted. This quandary pitted France, the biggest and richest country in Europe, against England, which had the biggest army. They fought from 1337 to 1453 in what was modestly called the **Hundred Years' War.**

Regional powers from within France actually sided with England. Burgundy took Paris, captured the royal family, and recognized the English king as heir to the French throne. England controlled France from the Loire north, and things looked bleak for the French king.

Enter **Joan of Arc,** a 16-year-old peasant girl driven by religious voices. France's national heroine left home to support Charles VII, the dauphin (boy prince, heir to the throne but too young to rule). Joan rallied the French, ultimately inspiring them to throw out the English. In 1430, Joan was captured by the Burgundians, who sold her to the English, who then convicted her of heresy and burned her at the stake in Rouen. But the inspiration of Joan of Arc lived on, and by 1453 English holdings on the Continent had dwindled to the port of Calais.

By 1500, a strong, centralized France had emerged, with borders similar to those of today. Its kings (from the Renaissance François I through the Henrys and all those Louises) were model **divine**

monarchs, setting the standards for absolute rule in Europe.

Outrage over the power plays and spending sprees of the kings—coupled with the modern thinking of the Enlightenment (whose leaders were the French *philosophes*)—led to the **French Revolution** of 1789. In France, it was the end of the *ancien régime,* as well as its notion that some are born to rule, while others are born to be ruled.

The excesses of the Revolution in turn led to the rise of **Napoleon**, who ruled the French empire as a dictator. Eventually, *his* excesses ushered him into a South Atlantic exile, and after another half-century of monarchy and empire, the French settled on a compromise role for their leader. The modern French "king" is ruled by a constitution. Rather than dress in leotards and powdered wigs, the president goes to work in a suit and carries a briefcase.

The **20th century** spelled the end of France's reign as a military and political superpower. Devastating wars with Germany in 1870, 1914, and 1940—and the loss of her colonial holdings—left France with not quite enough land, people, or production to be a top player on a global scale. But the 21st century may see France rise again: Paris is a cultural capital of Europe, and France—under the EU banner—is a key player in unifying Europe as a single economic power. And when Europe becomes a superpower, Paris may yet be its capital.

France Today

Today, the political issues in France are the economy, terrorism, its relationship with the European Union, and immigration.

French unemployment remains high (about 9 percent, even higher for youth) and growth has flatlined. France's public spending—at 56 percent of GDP—chews up a bigger chunk of output than any other eurozone country. The challenge for French leadership is to address its economic problems while maintaining the

Top French Notables in History

Madame and Monsieur Cro-Magnon: Prehistoric hunter-gatherers who moved to France (c. 30,000 BC), painted cave walls at Lascaux and Font-de-Gaume, and eventually settled down as farmers (c. 10,000 BC).

Vercingétorix (72 BC-46 BC): This long-haired warrior rallied the Gauls against Julius Caesar's invading Roman legions (52 BC). Defeated by Caesar, France fell under Roman domination, resulting in 500 years of peace and prosperity. During that time, the Romans established cities, built roads, taught in Latin, and converted people to Christianity.

Charlemagne (742-814): For Christmas in 800, the pope gave King Charlemagne the title of Emperor, thus uniting much of Europe under the leadership of the Franks ("France"). Charlemagne stabilized France amid centuries of barbarian invasions. After his death, the empire was split, carving the outlines of modern France and Germany.

Eleanor of Aquitaine (c. 1122-1204): The beautiful, sophisticated ex-wife of the King of France married the King of England, creating an uneasy union between the two countries. During her lifetime, French culture was spread across Europe by roving troubadours, theological scholars, and skilled architects pioneering "the French style"—a.k.a. Gothic.

Joan of Arc (1412-1431): When France and England fought the Hundred Years' War (1337-1453), this teen—guided by voices in her head—rallied the French troops. Though Joan was captured and burned as a heretic, the French eventually drove England out for good, establishing the current borders. Over the centuries, the church upgraded Joan's status from heretic to saint (canonized in 1920).

François I (1494-1547): This Renaissance king ruled a united, modern nation, making it a cultural center that hosted the Italian Leonardo da Vinci. François set the tone for future absolute monarchs, punctuating his commands with the phrase, "For such is our pleasure."

Louis XIV (1638-1715): Charismatic and cunning, the "Sun King" ruled

high level of social services that the French people expect from their government.

France also has its economic strengths: a well-educated workforce, a robust service sector and high-end manufacturing industry, and more firms big enough to rank in the global Fortune 500 than any other European country.

The French believe the economy should support social good, not vice versa. This has produced a cradle-to-grave social security system of which the French are proud. France's poverty rate is half of that in the US, proof to the French they are on the right track. On the other hand, if you're considering starting a business in

France, think again—taxes are daunting (figure a total small-business tax rate of around 66 percent). And a job-security entitlement makes it difficult for employers to find motivated staff.

French voters are notorious for their belief in the free market's heartless cruelty. France is routinely plagued with strikes, demonstrations, and slowdowns as workers try to preserve their hard-earned rights in the face of a competitive global economy.

Another ongoing issue French leaders are working to address is immigration, which is shifting the country's ethnic and cultural makeup in ways that challenge French society. Ten percent of France's

Europe's richest, most populous, most powerful nation-state. Every educated European spoke French, dressed in Louis-style leotards and powdered wigs, and built Versailles-like palaces. Though Louis ruled as an absolute monarch (distracting the nobility with courtly games), his reign also fostered the arts and philosophy, sowing the seeds of democracy and revolution.

Marie-Antoinette (1755-1793): The wife of Louis XVI came to symbolize (probably unfairly) the decadence of France's ruling class. When Revolution broke out (1789), she was arrested, imprisoned, and executed—one of thousands guillotined on Paris' Place de la Concorde as an enemy of the people.

Napoleon Bonaparte (1769-1821): This daring young military man became a hero during the Revolution, fighting Europe's royalty. He went on to conquer much of the Continent, become leader of France, and eventually, rule as a dictator with the title of emperor. In 1815, an allied Europe defeated and exiled Napoleon, reinstating the French monarchy—though future kings and emperors (including Napoleon's nephew, who ruled as Napoleon III) were somewhat subject to democratic constraints.

Claude Monet (1840-1926): His Impressionist paintings captured the soft-focus beauty of the belle époque—middle-class folk enjoying drinks in cafés, walks in gardens, and picnics along the Seine. At the turn of the 20th century, French culture reigned supreme while its economic and political clout was fading, and was soon shattered by World War I.

Charles de Gaulle (1890-1970): This career military man helped France survive occupation by Nazi Germany with his rousing radio broadcasts and unbending faith in his countrymen. He left politics after World War II, but after France's divisive wars in Vietnam and Algeria, he became president of the Fifth Republic in 1959. De Gaulle shocked allies by granting Algeria independence, blocking Britain's entry into the Common Market, and withdrawing from the military wing of NATO. Student riots in the late 1960s eventually led to his resignation in 1969.

population is now of North African descent, mainly immigrants from former colonies. Many immigrants are Muslim, raising cultural questions in this heavily Catholic society with a history of official state secularism. In 2011, the government (quite controversially) made it illegal for women to wear a full, face-covering veil in public. Debates continue about whether banning the veil enforces democracy—or squelches diversity.

A series of terrorist attacks in France in recent years has battered the nation's self-confidence. Locals have had to adjust to life with armed soldiers patrolling rail stations and streets. Many of the attackers were immigrants—and French citizens. Each attack raises serious questions about immigration, policing, class divisions, and what it means to be French.

France is part of the European Union, the "United States of Europe" that has successfully dissolved borders and implemented a common currency, the euro. France's governments have been decidedly pro-EU and critical to the EU's success. But many French are Euro-skeptics, afraid that EU meddling threatens their job security and social benefits.

What is clear is that, regardless of the shifting winds of politics, France has a social structure that stretches back 1,000 years.

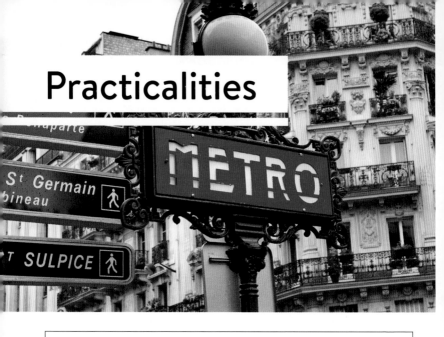

Practicalities

TOURIST INFORMATION

The French national tourist office is a wealth of information. **Before your trip,** scan their website—http://us.france. fr. It has particularly good resources for special-interest travel and plenty of free-to-download brochures. Paris' official TI website, www.parisinfo.com, offers practical information on hotels, special events, museums, children's activities, fashion, nightlife, and more.

In France, a good first stop is generally the tourist information office (abbreviated **TI** in this book). TIs are in business to help you enjoy spending money in their town, but even so, I still make a point to swing by to confirm sightseeing plans, pick up a city map, and get information on public transit, walking tours, special events, and nightlife.

HELP!

Emergency and Medical Help: For any emergency service—ambulance, police, or fire—call **112** from a mobile phone or landline. If you get sick, do as the locals do and go to a pharmacist for advice. Or ask at your hotel for help—they'll know the nearest medical and emergency services.

Theft or Loss: To replace a passport, you'll need to go in person to an embassy or consulate. If your credit and debit cards disappear, cancel and replace them. (See "Damage Control for Lost Cards," page 411). File a police report, either on the spot or within a day or two; you'll need it to submit an insurance claim for lost or stolen rail passes or travel gear, and it can help with replacing your passport or credit and debit cards. For more information, see www.ricksteves.com/help.

US Embassy in Paris: Tel. 01 43 12 22 22 (2 Avenue Gabriel, to the left as you face Hôtel Crillon, Mo: Concorde, https://fr.usembassy.gov).

US Consulate in Marseille: Tel. 01 43 12 48 85 (Place Varian Fry, 13286 Marseille, https://fr.usembassy.gov/embassy-consulates).

Canadian Embassy in Paris: Tel. 01 44 43 29 00 (130 Rue du Faubourg Saint-Honoré, Mo: Saint-Philippe-du-Roule, www.canadainternational.gc.ca/france).

Canadian Consulate in Nice: Tel. 04 93 92 93 22 (10 Rue Lamartine, nice@international.gc.ca).

TRAVEL TIPS

Time Zones: France, like most of continental Europe, is generally six/nine hours ahead of the East/West Coasts of the US. The exceptions are the beginning and end of Daylight Saving Time: Europe "springs forward" the last Sunday in March (two weeks after most of North America), and "falls back" the last Sunday in October (one week before North America).

Business Hours: You'll find much of rural France closed weekdays from 12:00 to 14:00 (lunch is sacred). On Sunday, most businesses are closed (family is sacred), though some small shops such as *boulangeries* (bakeries) are open until noon, special events and weekly markets pop up, and museums are open all day (but public transportation options are limited). On Mondays, some businesses are closed until 14:00 and possibly all day. Smaller towns are often quiet and down-

Avoiding Theft

Pickpockets are common, but fortunately, violent crime is rare. Thieves don't want to hurt you; they just want your money and gadgets.

My recommendations: Stay alert and wear a money belt (tucked under your clothes) to keep your cash, debit card, credit card, and passport secure; carry only the money you need for the day in your front pocket.

Treat any disturbance (e.g., a stranger bumps into you, spills something on you, or tries to get your attention for an odd reason) as a smoke screen for theft. Be on guard waiting in line at sights, at train stations, and while boarding and leaving crowded buses and subways. Thieves target tourists overloaded with bags or distracted with smartphones.

When paying for something, be aware of how much cash you're handing over (state the denomination of the bill when paying a cabbie) and count your change. For advice on avoiding big-city scams and pickpockets, read page 30 of the Introduction chapter.

There's no need to be scared; just be smart and prepared.

right boring on Sundays and Mondays, unless it's market day.

Watt's Up? Europe's electrical system is 220 volts, instead of North America's 110 volts. Most newer electronics (such as laptops, battery chargers, and hair dryers) convert automatically, so you won't need a converter, but you will need an adapter plug with two round prongs, sold inexpensively at travel stores in the US.

Discounts: Discounts for sights are

generally not listed in this book. However, seniors (age 60 and over), youths under 18, and students and teachers with proper identification cards (www.isic.org) can get discounts at many sights—always ask. Some discounts are available only to European citizens.

MONEY

Here's my basic strategy for using money in Europe:

- Upon arrival, head for a cash machine (ATM) at the airport and withdraw some local currency, using a debit card with low international transaction fees.
- Save money by minimizing your credit and debit card exchange fees. The trend is to pay for bigger expenses with your credit card, and use cash for smaller purchases and tips.
- Keep your cards and cash safe in a money belt.

What to Bring

I pack the following and keep it in my money belt.

Debit Card: Use this at ATMs to withdraw local cash.

Credit Card: Handy for bigger purchases (at hotels, shops, restaurants, travel agencies, car-rental agencies, and so on), payment machines, and ordering online.

Backup Card: Some travelers carry a third card (debit or credit; ideally from a different bank), in case one gets lost or simply doesn't work.

A Stash of Cash: For an emergency reserve in most of Europe, bring dollars. But in France consider bringing €200 in €20-50 bills (because dollars can be hard to change in France).

Before You Go

Know your PIN: Make sure you know the numeric, four-digit PIN for all your cards, both debit and credit. Request it if you don't have one and allow time to receive the information by mail.

Report your travel dates. Let your bank know that you'll be using your debit and credit cards in Europe, and when and where you're headed.

Adjust your ATM withdrawal limit. Find out how much you can take out daily and ask for a higher daily withdrawal limit if you want to get more cash at once. Note that European ATMs will withdraw funds only from checking accounts; you're unlikely to have access to your savings account.

Ask about fees. For any purchase or withdrawal made with a card, you may be charged a currency conversion fee (1-3 percent) and/or a Visa or MasterCard international transaction fee (1 percent).

In Europe

Using Cash Machines: European cash machines have English-language instructions and work just like they do at home—except they spit out local currency instead of dollars, calculated at the day's standard bank-to-bank rate.

In most places, ATMs are easy to locate—in France ask for a *distributeur* (dee-stree-bew-tur). When possible, withdraw cash from a bank-run ATM located just outside that bank.

Exchange Rate

1 euro (€) = about $1.20

To convert prices in euros to dollars, add about 20 percent: €20 = about $24, €50 = about $60. (Check www.oanda.com for the latest exchange rates.) Just like the dollar, one euro (€) is broken down into 100 cents.

If your debit card doesn't work, try a lower amount—your request may have exceeded your withdrawal limit or the ATM's limit.

Avoid "independent" ATMs, such as Travelex, Euronet, Moneybox, Cardpoint, and Cashzone. These have high fees, can be less secure than a bank ATM, and may try to trick users with "dynamic currency conversion" (see below).

Exchanging Cash: Avoid exchanging money in Europe; it's a big rip-off. In a pinch you can always find exchange desks at major train stations or airports—convenient but with crummy rates. Banks generally do not exchange money unless you have an account with them.

Using Credit Cards: US credit cards no longer require a signature for verification, but don't be surprised if a European card

reader generates a receipt for you to sign or prompts you to enter a PIN (it's important to know it for each of your cards). After entering your PIN, you may need to press "validate," usually shown as a "V" on the keypad or touch screen. If a cashier is present, you should have no problems.

In France, self-service payment machines (transit-ticket kiosks, parking, autoroute tollbooths, etc.) can be a headache, as US cards may not work in unattended transactions even if you know the PIN (though this is rare with updated cards). If that happens, look for a cashier who can process your card manually—or pay in cash.

Drivers Beware: Be aware of potential problems using a US credit card to fill up at an unattended gas station, enter a parking garage, or exit a toll road. Carry cash in bills under €50 and be prepared to move on to the next gas station if necessary. When approaching a toll payment plaza, look for coin icons (meaning cash) or a green arrow.

Dynamic Currency Conversion: If merchants offer to convert your purchase price into dollars (called dynamic currency conversion, or DCC), refuse this "service." You'll pay extra for the expensive convenience of seeing your charge in dollars.

Damage Control for Lost Cards: If you lose your credit or debit card, report the loss immediately to the respective global customer-assistance centers. Call these 24-hour US numbers collect: Visa (tel. 303/967-1096), MasterCard (tel. 636/722-7111), and American Express (tel. 336/393-1111). In France, to make a collect call to the US, dial 08 00 90 06 24, then say "operator" for an English-speaking operator.

For another option (with the same results), you can call these toll-free numbers in France: Visa (tel. 08 00 90 11 79), MasterCard (tel. 08 00 90 13 87), and American Express (tel. 08 05 54 05 24). You can generally receive a temporary card within two or three business days in Europe (see www.ricksteves.com/help for more).

Tipping

Tipping (*donner un pourboire*) in France isn't as automatic and generous as it is in the US. For special service, tips are appreciated, but not expected. As in the US, the proper amount depends on your resources, tipping philosophy, and the circumstances, but some general guidelines apply.

Restaurants: At cafés and restaurants, a service charge is included in the price of what you order, and it's unnecessary to tip extra, though you can for helpful service. For details on tipping in restaurants, see "Eating," later.

Taxis: For a typical ride, round up your fare a bit (for instance, if the fare is €13, pay €14).

Services: In general, if someone in the tourism or service industry does a super job for you, a small tip of a euro or two is appropriate...but not required. If you're not sure whether (or how much) to tip, ask a local for advice.

Getting a VAT Refund

Wrapped into the purchase price of your French souvenirs is a Value-Added Tax (VAT) of about 20 percent. You're entitled to get most of that tax back if you purchase more than €175 (about $210) worth of goods at a store that participates in the VAT-refund scheme.

Get the paperwork. Have the merchant completely fill out the necessary refund document, called a *bordereau de détaxe*. You'll have to present your passport. Get the paperwork done before you leave the store to ensure you'll have everything you need (including your original sales receipt).

Get your stamp at the border or airport. Process your VAT document at your last stop in the European Union (such as at the airport) with the customs agent who deals with VAT refunds. Arrive an additional hour before you need to check in to allow time to find the customs office—and wait.

Collect your refund. You can claim your VAT refund from refund companies, such as Global Blue or Premier Tax Free, with offices at major airports, ports, or border crossings (either before or after security, probably strategically located near a duty-free shop). These services (which extract a 4 percent fee) can refund your money in cash immediately or credit your card (within two billing cycles).

Customs for American Shoppers

You can take home $800 worth of items per person duty-free, once every 31 days. Many processed and packaged foods are allowed, including vacuum-packed cheeses, dried herbs, jams, baked goods, candy, chocolate, oil, vinegar, mustard, and honey. Fresh fruits and vegetables and most meats are not allowed, with exceptions for some canned items. As for alcohol, you can bring in one liter duty-free.

To bring alcohol (or liquid-packed foods) in your carry-on bag on your flight home, buy it at a duty-free shop at the airport. You'll increase your odds of getting it onto a connecting flight if it's packaged in a "STEB"—a secure, tamper-evident bag.

For details on allowable goods, customs rules, and duty rates, visit http://help.cbp.gov.

SIGHTSEEING

Sightseeing can be hard work. Use these tips to make your visits to France's finest sights meaningful, fun, efficient, and painless.

Plan Ahead

Set up an itinerary that allows you to fit in all your must-see sights. Given how precious your vacation time is, I recommend getting reservations for any must-see sight that offers them (see page 29). Many museums are closed or have reduced hours at least a few days a year, especially on holidays such as Christmas, New Year's, and Labor Day (May 1). A list of holidays is near the end of this chapter; check online for possible museum closures during your trip.

At Sights

Here's what you can typically expect:

Entering: Several cities offer sightseeing passes (listed in this book) that can be worthwhile values. You may not be allowed to enter some sights if you arrive less than 30 to 60 minutes before closing time. And guards start ushering people out well before the actual closing time, so don't save the best for last.

Many sights have a security check, and some are fairly rigorous. Allow extra time for these lines. Some sights require you to check daypacks and coats. (If you'd rather not check your daypack, try carrying it tucked under your arm like a purse as you enter.)

At churches—which often offer interesting art (usually free) and a cool, welcome seat—a modest dress code (no bare shoulders or shorts) is encouraged though rarely enforced.

Photography: If the museum's photo policy isn't clearly posted, ask a guard. Generally, taking photos without a flash or tripod is allowed. Some sights ban selfie sticks; others ban photos altogether.

Expect Changes: Artwork can be on tour, on loan, out sick, or shifted at the whim of the curator. Pick up a floor plan as you enter, and ask museum staff if you can't find a particular item.

Audioguides and Apps: Many sights rent hand-held audioguides, which generally offer worthwhile recorded descriptions in English. Increasingly, museums and sights offer apps—often free—that you can download to your mobile device (check their websites).

EATING

The French eat long and well. Relaxed and tree-shaded lunches with a chilled rosé, three-hour dinners, and endless hours of sitting in outdoor cafés are the norm. Here, celebrated restaurateurs are as famous as great athletes, and mamas hope their babies will grow up to be great chefs. Cafés, cuisine, and wines should become a highlight of any French adventure: It's sightseeing for your palate. Even if the rest of you is sleeping in a cheap hotel, let your taste buds travel first-class in France.

You can eat well without going broke—but choose carefully: You're just as likely to blow a small fortune on a mediocre meal as you are to dine wonderfully for €20. Read the information that follows and consider my restaurant suggestions in this book.

In Paris, restaurant lunches are a great value, as most places offer the same quality and similar selections for far less than at dinner. If you're on a budget or just like going local, try making lunch your main meal, then have a lighter evening meal at a café.

Breakfast

Most hotels serve an optional breakfast, which is usually pleasant and convenient (generally €10-20, price rises proportionately with room cost). They almost all offer a buffet breakfast (cereal, yogurt, fruit, cheese, ham, croissants, juice, and hard-boiled eggs). Some add scrambled eggs and sausage. Before committing to breakfast, check to see if it's included in your room rate; if not, scan the offerings to be sure it's to your liking.

If all you want is coffee or tea and a croissant, the corner café or bakery offers more atmosphere and is less expensive (though you get more coffee at your hotel).

Picnic Dining and Food to Go

Whether going all out on a perfect French picnic or simply grabbing a sandwich to eat on an atmospheric square, dining with the town as your backdrop can be one of your most memorable meals.

Picnics

Great for lunch or dinner, French picnics can be first-class affairs and adventures in high cuisine. Be daring. Try the smelly cheeses, ugly pâtés, prissy quiches, and minuscule yogurts. Shopkeepers are accustomed to selling small quantities of produce. Get a succulent salad to go, and ask for a plastic fork. If you need a knife or corkscrew, borrow one from your hotelier (but don't picnic in your room, as French hoteliers uniformly detest this). Though drinking wine in public places is taboo in the US, it's *pas de problème* in France.

Visit several small stores to put together a complete meal. Shop early, as many shops close from 12:00 or 13:00 to 15:00 for their lunch break. Say *"Bonjour madame/ monsieur"* as you enter, then point to what you want and say, *"S'il vous plaît."*

To-Go Food

You'll find plenty of to-go options at

crêperies, bakeries, and small stands. Baguette sandwiches, quiches, and pizza-like items are tasty, filling, and budget-friendly (about €5).

Sandwiches: Anything served *à la provençale* has marinated peppers, tomatoes, and eggplant. A sandwich *à l'italienne* is a grilled *panini* (usually referred to as *pannini*). Here are some common sandwiches:

Fromage (froh-mahzh): Cheese (white on beige)

Jambon beurre (zhahn-bohn bur): Ham and butter (boring for most but a French classic)

Jambon crudités (zhahn-bohn krew-dee-tay): Ham with tomatoes, lettuce, cucumbers, and mayonnaise

Fougasse (foo-gahs): Bread rolled up with salty bits of bacon, cheese, or olives

Poulet crudités (poo-lay krew-dee-tay): Chicken with tomatoes, lettuce, maybe cucumbers, and always mayonnaise

Saucisson beurre (saw-see-sohn bur): Thinly sliced sausage and butter

Thon crudités (tohn krew-dee-tay): Tuna with tomatoes, lettuce, and maybe cucumbers, but definitely mayonnaise

Quiche: Typical quiches you'll see at shops and bakeries are *lorraine* (ham and cheese), *fromage* (cheese only), *aux oignons* (with onions), *aux poireaux* (with leeks—my favorite), *aux champignons* (with mushrooms), *au saumon* (salmon), or *au thon* (tuna).

Crêpes: The quintessentially French thin pancake called a crêpe (rhymes with "step," not "grape") is filling, usually inexpensive, and generally quick. Crêpes generally are *sucrée* (sweet) or *salée* (savory). Technically, a savory crêpe should be made with a heartier buckwheat batter, and is called a *galette*. Standard crêpe toppings include cheese (*fromage;* usually Swiss-style Gruyère or Emmental), ham (*jambon*), egg (*œuf*), mushrooms (*champignons*), chocolate, Nutella, jam (*confiture*), whipped cream (*chantilly*), apple jam (*compote de pommes*), chestnut cream (*crème de marrons*), and Grand Marnier.

Restaurant and Café Dining

To get the most out of dining out in France, slow down. Give yourself time to enjoy meals at a French pace, engage the waiter, show you care about food, and enjoy the experience as much as the food itself.

French waiters probably won't overwhelm you with friendliness. To get a waiter's attention, try to make meaningful eye contact, which is a signal that you need something. If this doesn't work, raise your hand and simply say, *"S'il vous plaît"* (see voo play)—"please."

This phrase also works when you want to ask for the check. In French eateries, a waiter will rarely bring you the check unless you request it. If you're in a hurry, ask for the bill when your server comes to clear your plates or checks in to see if you want dessert or coffee.

Note that all café and restaurant interiors are smoke-free. Today the only smokers you'll find are at outside tables, which—unfortunately—may be exactly where you want to sit.

Tipping: At cafés and restaurants, a 12-15 percent service charge is always included in the price of what you order (*service compris* or *prix net*), but you won't see it listed on your bill. Unlike in the US, France pays servers a decent wage (a favorite café owner told me that his waiters earn far more than some high school teachers). Because of this, most locals only tip a little, or not at all. If you feel the service was good, tip a little—about 5 percent; maybe 10 percent for terrific service. To tell the waiter to keep the change when you pay, say *"C'est bon"* (say bohn), meaning "It's good." If you are using a credit card, leave your tip in cash—credit-card receipts don't even have space to add a tip. Never feel guilty if you don't leave a tip.

Cafés and Brasseries

French cafés and brasseries provide user-friendly meals and a relief from sight-seeing overload. They're not necessarily cheaper than many restaurants and bistros, and famous cafés on popular squares can be pricey affairs. Their key advantage is flexibility: They offer long serving hours, and you're welcome to order just a salad, a sandwich, or a bowl of soup, even for dinner. It's also OK to share starters and desserts, though not main courses.

Cafés and brasseries usually open by 7:00, but closing hours vary. Unlike some restaurants, which open only for dinner and sometimes for lunch, many cafés and all brasseries serve food throughout the day, making them the best option for a late lunch or an early dinner (though small-town cafés often close their kitchens from about 14:00 until 18:00).

Check the price list first, which by law should be posted prominently (though I see fewer posted every year). There are two sets of prices: You'll pay more for the same drink if you're seated at a table (salle) than if you're seated or standing at the bar or counter (comptoir).

Ordering: A salad, crêpe, quiche, or omelet is a fairly cheap way to fill up. Each can be made with various extras such as ham, cheese, mushrooms, and so on.

Sandwiches, generally served day and night, are inexpensive, but most are very plain (boulangeries serve better ones). To get more than a piece of ham (jambon) on a baguette, order a sandwich jambon crudités (garnished with veggies). Popular sandwiches are the croque monsieur (grilled ham-and-cheese) and croque madame (monsieur with a fried egg on top).

Salads are typically meal size and often can be ordered with warm ingredients mixed in, such as melted goat cheese, fried gizzards, or roasted potatoes.

The daily special—plat du jour (plah dew zhoor), or just plat—is your fast, hearty, and garnished hot plate for about €14-22. At most cafés, feel free to order only entrées (which in French means the starter course); many people find these lighter and more interesting than a main course. A vegetarian can enjoy a tasty, filling meal by ordering two entrées.

Restaurants

Restaurants open for dinner around 19:00 and are most crowded about 20:00 (21:00 in cities). The early bird gets the table. Last seating is usually about 21:00 (22:00 in cities and on the French Riviera; possibly later in Paris).

Tune into the quiet, relaxed pace of French dining. The French don't do dinner and a movie on date nights; they just do dinner. The table is yours for the night.

Ordering: In French restaurants, you can choose something off the menu (called the carte), or you can order a multicourse, fixed-price meal (confusingly, called a

menu). Or, if offered, you can get one of the special dishes of the day (plat du jour).

Two people can split an entrée or a big salad (small-size dinner salads are usually not offered á la carte) and then each get a plat principal. At restaurants, it's inappropriate for two diners to share one main course. If all you want is a salad or soup, go to a café or brasserie.

Fixed-price **menus**—which usually include two, three, or four courses—are always a better deal than eating à la carte, providing you want several courses. With a three-course menu you'll choose a starter of soup, appetizer, or salad; select from three or four main courses with vegetables; and finish up with a cheese course and/or a choice of desserts.

French Cuisine

The following list of items should help you navigate a typical French menu. Galloping gourmets should bring a menu translator. The Rick Steves French Phrase Book & Dictionary, with a menu decoder, works well for most travelers.

First Course (Entrée)

Crudités: A mix of raw and lightly cooked fresh vegetables, usually including grated carrots, celery root, tomatoes, and beets, often with a hefty dose of vinaigrette dressing.

Escargots: Snails cooked in parsley-garlic butter.

Foie gras: Rich and buttery in consistency—and hefty in price—this pâté is made from the swollen livers of force-fed geese (or ducks, in foie gras de canard).

Huîtres: Oysters, served raw any month, are particularly popular at Christmas and on New Year's Eve, when every café seems to have overflowing baskets in their window.

Oeuf mayo: A simple hard-boiled egg topped with a dollop of flavorful mayonnaise.

Pâtés and **terrines:** Slowly cooked ground meat (usually pork, though game, poultry liver, and rabbit are also common) that is highly seasoned and served in slices with mustard and *cornichons* (little pickles). Pâtés are smoother than the similarly prepared but chunkier *terrines*.

Soupe à l'oignon: Hot, salty, filling—and hard to find in Paris—French onion soup is a beef broth served with a baked cheese-and-bread crust over the top.

Salads (Salades)

With the exception of a *salade mixte* (simple green salad, often difficult to find), the French get creative with their *salades*. Here are some classics:

Salade de chèvre chaud: This mixed-green salad is topped with warm goat cheese on small pieces of toast.

Salade de gésiers: Salad with chicken gizzards (and often slices of duck).

Salade composée: "Composed" of any number of ingredients, this salad might have *lardons* (bacon), Comté (a Swiss-style cheese), Roquefort (blue cheese), *œuf* (egg), *noix* (walnuts), and *jambon* (ham, generally thinly sliced).

Salade niçoise: Greens topped with ripe tomatoes, raw vegetables (such as radishes, green peppers, celery, and perhaps artichoke or fava beans), tuna (usually canned), anchovy, hard-boiled egg, and olives.

Salade paysanne: Potatoes (*pommes de terre*), walnuts (*noix*), tomatoes, ham, and egg.

Main Course (Plat Principal)

Duck, lamb, and rabbit are popular in France, and each is prepared in a variety of ways. You'll also encounter various stew-like dishes that vary by region. The most common regional specialties are described here.

Bœuf bourguignon: A Burgundian specialty, this classy beef stew is cooked slowly in red wine, then served with onions, potatoes, and mushrooms.

Cabillaud: Cod cooked in many ways that vary by region, but most commonly with butter, white wine, and herbs.

Confit de canard: Duck that has been preserved in its own fat, then cooked in its fat, and often served with potatoes (cooked in the same fat). Not for dieters.

Coq au vin: This Burgundian dish is rooster marinated ever so slowly in red wine, then cooked until it melts in your mouth.

Daube: Stew made with beef, but sometimes lamb.

Escalope normande: This specialty of Normandy features turkey or veal in a cream sauce.

Gigot d'agneau: A specialty of Provence, this is a leg of lamb often grilled and served with white beans.

Poulet rôti: Roasted chicken on the bone.

Saumon and **truite:** Salmon, usually from the North Sea, most commonly served with a sorrel (*oseille*) sauce. Trout (*truite*) is also fairly routine on menus.

Steak: Referred to as *pavé* (thick hunk of prime steak), *bavette* (skirt steak), *faux filet* (sirloin), or *entrecôte* (rib steak), French steak is usually thinner and tougher than American steak and is always served with sauces (*au poivre* is a pepper sauce, *une sauce roquefort* is a blue-cheese sauce). Because steak is usually better in North America, I generally avoid it in France (unless the sauce sounds good). By American standards, the French under-

French Wine Tasting 101

France is peppered with wineries and wine-tasting opportunities. For some, trying to make sense of the vast range of French wines can be overwhelming, particularly when faced with a no-nonsense winemaker or sommelier. Do your best to follow my tips, and don't linger if you don't feel welcome.

Visit several private wineries or stop by a *cave coopérative* or a *caveau* to taste wines from a number of local vintners in a single, less intimidating setting. (Throughout this book, I've tried to identify which vineyards are most accepting of wine novices.) At wineries, you'll have a better experience if you call ahead to let them know you're coming (even if it's open all day; ask your hotelier for help). Avoid visiting places between noon and 14:00: Many wineries close midday, and those that don't are staffed by people who would rather be at lunch.

While Americans commonly like a big, full-bodied wine, most French prefer subtler flavors. The French enjoy sampling younger wines and divining how they will taste in a few years, allowing them to buy bottles at cheaper prices and stash them in their cellars. Americans want it now—for today's picnic.

At tastings, vintners and wine shops are hoping you'll buy a bottle or two (otherwise you may be asked to pay a small tasting fee). They understand that North Americans can't take much wine with them, but they do hope you'll look for their wines when you're back home. Some places will ship wine—ask.

Here are some phrases to get you started when wine tasting:

Hello, sir/madam.
Bonjour, monsieur/madame.
(bohn-zhoor, muhs-yur/mah-dahm)

cook meats: Their version of rare, *saignant* (seh-nyahn), means "bloody" and is close to raw. What they consider medium, *à point* (ah pwan), is what an American would call rare. Their term for well-done, or *bien cuit* (bee-yehn kwee), would translate as medium for Americans.

Steak tartare: Very lean, raw hamburger served with savory seasonings (and topped with a raw egg yolk).

Cheese Course (Le Fromage)

The cheese course is served just before (or instead of) dessert. Some restaurants will offer a cheese platter *(plateau de fromages),* from which you select a few different kinds. A good platter has at least four cheeses: a hard cheese (such as Cantal), a flowery cheese (such as Brie or Camembert), a blue or Roquefort cheese,

and a goat cheese. To sample several types of cheese from the cheese plate, say, *"Un assortiment, s'il vous plaît"* (uhn ah-sor-tee-mahn, see voo play).

Dessert (Le Dessert)

To have coffee with dessert, ask for "café avec le dessert" (kah-fay ah-vehk luh day-sayr).

We would like to taste a few wines.
Nous voudrions déguster quelques vins.
(noo voo-dree-ohn day-goo-stay kehl-kuh van)

We would like a wine that is _____ and _____.
Nous voudrions un vin _____ et _____.
(noo voo-dree-ohn uhn van _____ ay _____)

Fill in the blanks with your favorites from this list:

English	French
red	*rouge* (roozh)
white	*blanc* (blahn)
rosé	*rosé* (roh-zay)
light	*léger* (lay-zhay)
full-bodied	*robuste* (roh-bewst)
fruity	*fruité* (frwee-tay)
sweet	*doux* (doo)
dry	*sec* (sehk)
sparkling	*pétillant* (pay-tee-yahn)

Baba au rhum: Pound cake drenched in rum, served with whipped cream.

Café gourmand: An assortment of small desserts.

Crème brûlée: A rich, creamy, dense, caramelized custard.

Crème caramel: Flan in a caramel sauce.

Fondant au chocolat: A molten chocolate cake with a runny (not totally cooked) center.

Fromage blanc: A light dessert similar to plain yogurt, served with sugar or herbs.

Glace: Ice cream.

Ile flottante: Islands of meringue floating on a pond of custard sauce.

Mousse au chocolat: Chocolate mousse.

Profiteroles: Cream puffs filled with vanilla ice cream, smothered in warm chocolate sauce.

Riz au lait: Rice pudding.

Sorbets: Fruity ices, sometimes laced with brandy.

Tartes: Open-face pie, often filled with fruit.

Tarte tatin: Caramelized, upside-down apple pie.

Beverages
Water, Juice, and Soft Drinks

The French are willing to pay for bottled water with their meal (*eau minérale;* oh mee-nay-rahl) because they prefer the taste over tap water. Badoit is my favorite carbonated water (*l'eau gazeuse;* loh gah-zuhz) and is commonly available. To get a free pitcher of tap water, ask for *une carafe d'eau* (ewn kah-rahf doh).

Coffee and Tea

The French define various types of espresso drinks by how much milk is added. To the French, milk is a delicate form of nutrition: You need it in the morning, but as the day goes on, too much can upset your digestion. Therefore, the amount of milk that's added to coffee decreases as the day goes on. The average French person thinks a *café au lait* is exclusively for breakfast, and a *café crème* is only appropriate through midday.

Café (kah-fay): Shot of espresso

Café allongé, a.k.a. **café long** (kah-fay ah-lohn-zhay; kah-fay lohn): Espresso topped up with hot water—like an Americano

Noisette (nwah-zeht): Espresso with a dollop of milk

Café au lait (kah-fay oh lay): Espresso mixed with lots of warm milk

Café crème (kah-fay krehm): Espresso with a sizable pour of steamed milk

Grand crème (grahn krehm): Double shot of espresso with a bit more steamed milk

Décaféiné (day-kah-fee-nay): Decaf—available for any of the above

Thé nature (tay nah-tour): Plain tea

Thé au lait (tay oh lay): Tea with milk

Thé citron (tay see-trohn): Tea with lemon

Infusion (an-few-see-yohn): Herbal tea

Alcoholic Beverages

The legal drinking age is 16 for beer and wine and 18 for the hard stuff—at restaurants it's *normale* for wine to be served with dinner to teens.

Wine: Wines are often listed in a separate *carte des vins.* House wine is generally cheap and good (about €3-8/glass). At a restaurant, a bottle or carafe of house wine costs around €10-15. To order inexpensive wine at a restaurant, ask for table or house wine in a pitcher, rather than a bottle. Finer restaurants usually offer only bottles of wine.

Here are some important wine terms:

Vin de table (van duh tah-bluh): House wine

Verre de vin rouge (vehr duh van roozh): Glass of red wine

Verre de vin blanc (vehr duh van blahn): Glass of white wine

Pichet (pee-shay): Pitcher

Demi-pichet (duh-mee pee-shay): Half-carafe

Quart (kar): Quarter-carafe (ideal for one)

Beer: Local *bière* (bee-ehr) costs about €5 at a restaurant and is cheaper on tap (*une pression;* ewn pres-yohn) than in the bottle. France's best-known beers are Alsatian; try Kronenbourg or the heavier Pelfort (one of your author's favorites). Craft beers (*bière artisanale*) are gaining in popularity; Brittany produces some of the best, though all regions seem to be making craft beers these days. *Une pinte* is a British pint.

Aperitifs: For a refreshing before-dinner drink, order a *kir* (pronounced "keer")—a thumb's level of *crème de cassis* (black currant liqueur) topped with white wine. Pastis, the standard southern France aperitif, is a sweet anise (licorice) drink that comes on the rocks with a glass of water. Cut it to taste with lots of water.

SLEEPING

Extensive and opinionated listings of good-value rooms are a major feature of this book's Sleeping section. Rather than list accommodations scattered throughout a town, I choose hotels in my favorite neighborhoods that are convenient to your sightseeing.

Book your accommodations as soon as your itinerary is set, especially if you want to stay at one of my top listings or if you'll be traveling during busy times. Reserving ahead is particularly important for Paris—the sooner, the better. Wherever you're staying, be ready for larger crowds in May and September and during holiday periods. See page 440 for a list of major holidays and festivals in France.

Sleep Code

Hotels in this book are ranked according to the average price of a standard double room without breakfast in high season.

$$$$	**Splurge:** Most rooms over €250
$$$	**Pricier:** €190-250
$$	**Moderate:** €130-190
$	**Budget:** €70-130
¢	**Backpacker:** Under €70
RS%	**Rick Steves discount**

Unless otherwise noted, credit cards are accepted, hotel staff speak basic English, and free Wi-Fi is available. Comparison-shop by checking prices at several hotels (on each hotel's own website, on a booking site, or by email). For the best deal, book directly with the hotel. Ask for a discount if paying in cash; if the listing includes **RS%**, request a Rick Steves discount. **Asterisks (*)** in the listings refer to the French hotel rating system, ranging from zero to five stars.

Rates and Deals

I've categorized my recommended accommodations based on price, indicated with a dollar-sign rating (see sidebar). The price ranges suggest an estimated cost for a one-night stay in a standard double room with a private toilet and shower in high season, don't include breakfast, and assume you're booking directly with the hotel (not through a booking site, which extracts a commission).

Booking Direct: To get the best deal, contact hotels directly. When you go direct, the owner avoids the commission paid to booking sites, thereby leaving enough wiggle room to offer you a discount, a nicer room, or a free breakfast. If you prefer to book online or are considering a hotel chain, it's to your advantage to use the hotel's website. French hotels recently won the right to undercut Booking.com and Hotels.com prices on their websites; virtually all offer lower rates if you book direct. If the price they quote is higher than the offer on a booking site, let the hotel know, and they'll usually adjust the rate.

Getting a Discount: Some hotels extend a discount to those who pay cash or stay longer than three nights. And some accommodations offer a special discount for Rick Steves readers, indicated in this guidebook by the abbreviation "RS%." Discounts vary: Ask for details when you reserve.

Room Taxes: Hotels in France must charge a daily tax (taxe du séjour) of about €1-4 per person per day (based on the number of stars the hotel has). Some hotels include it in their prices, but most add it to your bill.

Types of Accommodations
Hotels

The French have a simple hotel rating system based on amenities and rated by stars (indicated in this book by asterisks, from * through *****). The number of stars does not always reflect room size or guarantee quality. One- and two-star hotels are less expensive, but some three-star (and even a few four-star) hotels offer good value, justifying the extra cost. Unclassified hotels (no stars) can be bargains...or depressing dumps.

Most French hotels now have queen-size beds—to confirm, ask, *"Avez-vous des lits queen-size?"* (ah-vay-voo day lee queen-size). Some hotels push two twins together under king-size sheets and blankets to make *le king-size*. If you'll take either twins or a double, ask for a generic *une chambre pour deux* (room for two) to avoid being needlessly turned away.

The EU requires that hotels collect your name, nationality, and ID number. When you check in, the receptionist may ask for your passport and may keep it for anywhere from a couple of minutes to a couple of hours. (If not comfortable leaving your passport at the desk for a long time, ask when you can pick it up.)

Hotel lobbies, halls, and breakfast rooms are off-limits to smokers, though they can light up in their rooms. Still, I seldom smell any smoke in my rooms. Some hotels have nonsmoking rooms or floors—ask.

Most hotels offer breakfast, but it's rarely included in the room rates—pay attention when comparing rates between hotels (though some offer free breakfast to Rick Steves readers or with direct booking—ask). Some hoteliers, especially in resort towns, strongly encourage their peak-season guests to take *demi-pension* (half-pension)—that is, breakfast and either lunch or dinner. By law, they can't require you to take half-pension unless you are staying three or more nights, but, in practice, some do during high season.

Hoteliers uniformly detest it when people bring food into bedrooms. Dinner picnics are particularly frowned upon: Hoteliers worry about cleanliness, smells, and attracting insects. Be tidy and considerate.

Even at the best places, mechanical breakdowns occur: sinks leak, hot water turns cold, toilets may gurgle or smell, the Wi-Fi goes out, or the air-conditioning dies when you need it most. Report your concerns clearly and calmly at the front desk.

To guard against theft in your room, keep valuables out of sight. Some rooms come with a safe, and other hotels have safes at the front desk. I've never bothered using one.

For more complicated problems, don't expect instant results. Above all, keep a positive attitude. Remember, you're on vacation. If your hotel is a disappointment, spend more time out enjoying the place you came to see.

Modern Hotel Chains: France is littered with ultramodern hotels, providing drivers with low-stress accommodations and often located on cheap land just outside town. Though hardly quaint, these can be a good value (look for deals on their websites), particularly when they're centrally located.

Bed & Breakfasts

B&Bs (*chambres d'hôte,* abbreviated "CH") generally are found in smaller towns and rural areas. They're usually family-run and a good deal, offering double the cultural intimacy for less than most hotel rooms. While you may lose some hotel conveniences—such as lounges, TVs, daily bed-sheet changes, and credit-card payments—I happily make the trade-off for the personal touch

Making Hotel Reservations

Requesting a Reservation: For family-run hotels, it's generally cheaper to book your room directly via their website, email, or a phone call. For business-class hotels, reserve directly through the hotel's official website (not a booking website). For complicated requests, send an email. Almost all my recommended hotels take reservations in English.

Here's what the hotelier wants to know:

- Type(s) of rooms you want and size of your party
- Number of nights you'll stay
- Your arrival and departure dates, written European-style as day/month/year (18/06/20 or 18 June 2020)
- Special requests (en suite bathroom, cheapest room, twin beds vs. double bed, quiet room)
- Applicable discounts (such as a Rick Steves reader discount, cash discount, or promotional rate)

Confirming a Reservation: Most places will request a credit-card number to hold your room. If you're using an online reservation form, look for the *https* or a lock icon at the top of your browser. If you book direct, you can email, call, or fax this information.

Canceling a Reservation: If you must cancel, it's courteous—and smart—to do so with as much notice as possible, especially for smaller family-run places. Cancellation policies can be strict; read the fine print before you book. Many discount deals require prepayment, with cancellation refunds.

Reconfirming a Reservation: Always call or email to reconfirm your room reservation a few days in advance. For B&Bs or very small hotels, I call again on my day of arrival to tell my host what time to expect me (especially important if arriving late—after 17:00).

Phoning: For tips on how to call hotels overseas, see page 426.

and lower rates. And though your hosts may not speak English, they will almost always be enthusiastic and pleasant.

Gîtes

Countryside *gîtes* (pronounced "zheet") are usually urbanites' second, countryside homes, rentable by the week, from Saturday to Saturday. For more information, visit www.gites-de-france.com (with the most rentals) or www.gite.com. Also check sites like Airbnb and HomeAway/VRBO.

Short-Term Rentals

A short-term rental—whether an apartment, house, or room in a local's home—is an increasingly popular alternative, especially if you plan to settle in one location for several nights. For stays longer than a few days, you can usually find a rental that's comparable to—and cheaper than—a hotel room with similar amenities. Aggregator websites such as Airbnb, FlipKey, Booking.com, and the HomeAway family of sites (HomeAway, VRBO, and VacationRentals) let you browse properties and correspond directly with European property owners or managers.

Hostels

A hostel (*auberge de jeunesse*) provides cheap beds in dorms where you sleep alongside strangers for about €35 per night. Travelers of any age are welcome if they don't mind dorm-style accommodations and meeting other travelers. Most hostels offer kitchen facilities, guest computers, Wi-Fi, and a self-service laundry. Family and private rooms are often available.

Independent hostels tend to be easygoing, colorful, and informal (no membership required; www.hostelworld.com). You may pay slightly less by booking directly with the hostel. **Official hostels** are part of Hostelling International (HI) and share an online booking site (www.hihostels.com). HI hostels typically require that you either have a membership card or pay a bit more per night.

STAYING CONNECTED

One of the most common questions I hear from travelers is, "How can I stay connected in Europe?" The short answer is: more easily and cheaply than you might think.

The simplest solution is to bring your own device—mobile phone, tablet, or laptop—and use it just as you would at home (following the tips below). For more details, see www.ricksteves.com/phoning. For a practical one-hour talk covering tech issues for travelers, see www.ricksteves.com/mobile-travel-skills.

Using a Mobile Phone in Europe

Sign up for an international plan. To stay connected at a lower cost, sign up for an international service plan through your carrier. Most providers offer a simple bundle that includes calling, messaging, and data. Your normal plan may already include international coverage (T-Mobile's does).

Use free Wi-Fi whenever possible. Unless you have an unlimited-data plan, you're best off saving most of your online tasks for Wi-Fi (pronounced *wee-fee* in French). You can access the internet, send texts, and even make voice calls over Wi-Fi.

Using Online Services to Your Advantage

From booking services to user reviews, online businesses are playing a greater role in travelers' planning than ever before. Take advantage of their pluses—and be wise to their downsides.

Booking Sites

Booking websites, including Booking.com and Hotels.com, offer one-stop shopping for hotels. To be listed, a hotel must pay a sizeable commission. When you use an online booking service, you're adding a middleman. To support small, family-run hotels whose world is more difficult than ever, book direct.

Short-Term Rental Sites

Rental juggernaut Airbnb and other short-term rental sites allow travelers to rent rooms and apartments directly from locals. Airbnb fans appreciate feeling part of a real neighborhood as "temporary Europeans."

Critics view Airbnb as creating unfair competition for established guesthouse owners. As a lover of Europe, I share the worry of those who see residents nudged aside by tourists. But as an advocate for travelers, I appreciate the value and cultural intimacy Airbnb provides.

User Reviews

User-generated review sites and apps such as Yelp and TripAdvisor can give you a consensus of opinions about everything from hotels and restaurants to sights and nightlife. But a user-generated review is based on the limited experience of one person, while a guidebook is the work of a trained researcher who visits many restaurants and hotels year after year.

Both types of information have their place, and in many ways, they're complementary. If something is well reviewed in a guidebook and it also gets good online reviews, it's likely a winner.

Minimize the use of your cellular network. Even with an international data plan, wait until you're on Wi-Fi to Skype, download apps, stream videos, or do other megabyte-greedy tasks. Using a navigation app such as Google Maps over a cellular network can take lots of data, so do this sparingly or use it offline. Disable automatic updates so your apps will only update when you're on Wi-Fi. Also change your device's email settings from "auto-retrieve" to "manual" (or from "push" to "fetch").

Use Wi-Fi calling and messaging apps. Skype, WhatsApp, FaceTime, and Google Hangouts are great for making free or low-cost voice calls or sending texts over Wi-Fi. With an app installed on your phone, tablet, or laptop, you can log on to a Wi-Fi network and contact friends or family members who use the same service. If you buy credit in advance, with some of these services you can call or send a text anywhere for just pennies per minute.

Without a Mobile Phone

It's possible to travel in Europe without a mobile device. You can make calls from your hotel, and check email or browse websites using public computers.

Most **hotels** charge a fee for placing

How to Dial

To make an international call, follow the dialing instructions below. Drop an initial zero, if present, when dialing a European phone number—except when calling Italy. I've used the telephone number of one of my recommended Paris hotels as an example (tel. 01-45-51-63-02).

From a Mobile Phone

It's easy to dial with a mobile phone. Whether calling from the US to Europe, country to country within Europe, or from Europe to the US—it's all the same. Press zero until you get a + sign, enter the country code (33 for France), then dial the phone number.

▶ To call the Paris hotel from any location, dial +33-1-45-51-63-02.

From a US Landline to Europe

Dial 011 (US/Canada access code), country code (33 for France), and phone number.

▶ To call the Paris hotel from your home phone, dial 011-33-1-45-51-63-02.

From a European Landline to the US or Europe

Dial 00 (Europe access code), country code (1 for the US, 33 for France), and phone number.

▶ To call my US office from France, dial 00-1-425-771-8303.
▶ To call the Paris hotel from Germany, dial 00-33-1-45-51-63-02.

For a complete list of European country codes and more phoning help, see www.howtocallabroad.com.

calls—ask for rates before you dial. Pre-paid international phone cards (*cartes international*) are not widely used in France, but can be found at some news-stands, tobacco shops, and train stations. Dial the toll-free access number, enter the card's PIN code, then dial the number.

Public computers are not always easy to find. Some hotels have one in their lobby for guests to use; otherwise you may find one at a public library (ask your hotelier or the TI for the nearest location). On a European keyboard, use the "Alt Gr" key to the right of the space bar to insert the extra symbol that appears on some keys. If you can't locate a special character (such as @), simply copy and paste it from a Web page.

Mail

You can mail one package per day to yourself worth up to $200 duty-free from Europe to the US (mark it "personal purchases"). If you're sending a gift to someone, mark it "unsolicited gift." For details, visit www.cbp.gov, select "Travel," and search for "Know Before You Go." The French postal service works fine, but for quick transatlantic delivery (in either direction), consider services such as DHL (www.dhl.com).

TRANSPORTATION

France's bigger cities are well connected by train, and a snap to visit by public transportation. But in France, many of your destinations are likely to be small,

Tips on Internet Security

Make sure that your device is running the latest versions of its operating system, security software, and apps. Next, ensure that your device and key programs (like email) are password- or passcode-protected. On the road, use only secure, password-protected Wi-Fi hotspots. Ask the hotel or café staff for the specific name of their Wi-Fi network, and make sure you log on to that exact one.

If you must access your financial info online, use a banking app rather than accessing your account via a browser. A cellular connection is more secure than Wi-Fi. Avoid logging onto personal finance sites on a public computer.

Never share your credit-card number (or any other sensitive information) online unless you know that the site is secure. A secure site displays a little padlock icon, and the URL begins with *https* (instead of the usual *http*).

remote places far from a station, such as Mont St-Michel, the D-Day beaches, Loire châteaux, Dordogne caves, and villages in Provence and Burgundy. For these far-flung spots, a car is a good way to go. Those without a car should consider signing up for one of the excellent minibus tours I recommend in these regions.

For more detailed information on transportation throughout Europe, see www.ricksteves.com/transportation.

Trains

France's SNCF rail system (short for Société Nationale Chemins de Fer) sets the pace in Europe. Its high-speed trains (TGV, tay zhay vay; *Train à Grande*

Vitesse—also called "InOui") have inspired bullet trains throughout the world. The TGV, which requires a reservation, runs at 170-220 mph. The TGV has changed commuting patterns throughout France by putting most of the country within day-trip distance of Paris.

Any staffed train station has schedule information, can make reservations, and can sell tickets for any destination. For more on train travel, see www.ricksteves.com/rail.

Rick's Tip: *Going on strike* (en grève) *is a popular pastime in France.* **Train strikes** *generally last no longer than a day or two, and you can usually plan around them. Your hotelier will know the latest (or can find out).*

Schedules

Schedules change by season, weekday, and weekend. Verify train times and frequencies shown in this book—online, go to www.bahn.com (Germany's excellent all-Europe schedule site), or check locally at train stations. The French rail website is www.sncf.com; for online sales, go to https://en.oui.sncf/en. If you'll be traveling on one or two long-distance trains without a rail pass, it's worth looking online, as advance-purchase discounts can be a great deal.

Bigger stations may have helpful information agents roaming the station (usually in bright red or blue vests) and at *Accueil* or *Information* offices or booths.

Rail Passes

The single-country Eurail France Pass can be a good value for long-distance train travelers. Each day of use of your France Pass allows you to take as many trips as you want on one calendar day (you could go from Paris to Beaune in Burgundy, enjoy wine tasting, then continue to Avignon, stay a few hours, and end in Nice—though I wouldn't recommend it).

Be aware that France's fast TGV and international trains require paid seat reservations (up to €20 within France and more for international, especially if your pass doesn't cover both ends of travel). Particularly on international trains, places for rail-pass holders can be limited—which means trains may "sell out" for pass holders well before they've sold out for ticket buyers. Reserving these fast trains at least several weeks in advance is recommended (for strategies, see "Reservations," later).

For very short trips in France, buy second-class point-to-point tickets. Longer rides are where you can really save money with either a rail pass or advance-purchase ticket discounts.

For more detailed advice on figuring out the smartest rail-pass options for your train trip, visit www.ricksteves.com/rail.

Buying Tickets

Online: Buy well ahead for any TGV you cannot afford to miss. Tickets go on sale as far as four months in advance, with a wide range of prices on any one route. The cheapest tickets sell out early and reservations for rail-pass holders also go particularly fast.

To buy the cheapest advance-discount tickets (up to 60 percent less than full fare), visit https://en.oui.sncf/en three to

---

French Train Terms and Abbreviations

SNCF (Société Nationale des Chemins de Fer): The Amtrak of France, operating all national train lines

TGV (*Train à Grande Vitesse;* also called "InOui"): SNCF's network of high-speed trains that connect major cities (reservations required)

Intercité: Trains just below the TGV in terms of speed and comfort (reservations required)

TER (Transport Express Régional): Trains serving smaller stops within a region (no reservations needed)

Paris Region

RATP (Réseau Autonome de Transports Parisiens): Subways and buses within Paris

Le Métro: Subway lines serving central Paris

Le Train (RER): Commuter rail and subway system linking central Paris with suburban destinations

Transilien: Similar to Le Train system, but travels farther, serving the Ile-de-France region around Paris (covered by rail passes)

---

four months ahead of your travel date. Otherwise, US customers can order through a US agency, such as at www.ricksteves.com/rail, which offers both etickets and home delivery, but may not have access to all the cheapest rates; or Trainline (www.trainline.eu).

In France: You can buy train tickets in person at SNCF Boutiques or at any train station, either from a staffed ticket window or from a machine. While most machines accept American chip cards if you know the PIN code, be prepared with euro coins and bills just in case.

Rail Pass or Point-to-Point Tickets?

Will you be better off buying a rail pass or point-to-point tickets? It pays to know your options and choose what's best for your itinerary.

Rail Passes

A Eurail France Pass lets you travel by train in France for one to eight days (consecutively or not) within a one-month period. France is also covered (along with most of Europe) by the classic Eurail Global Pass. Discounted rates are offered for seniors (age 60 and up) and youths (ages 12-27). Up to two kids (ages 4-11) can travel free with each adult-rate pass (but not with senior rates). All rail passes offer a choice of first or second class for all ages. Rail passes are best purchased outside Europe (through travel agents or Rick Steves' Europe). For more on rail passes, including current prices, go to www.RickSteves.com/rail.

Point-to-Point Tickets

If you're taking just a couple of train rides, look into buying individual point-to-point tickets, which may save you money over a pass. Use this map to add up approximate pay-as-you-go fares for your itinerary, and compare that to the price of a rail pass. Keep in mind that significant discounts on point-to-point tickets may be available with advance purchase.

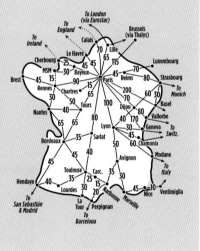

Map shows approximate costs, in US$, for one-way, second-class tickets on faster trains.

Reservations

Reservations are required for any TGV or Intercité train, *couchettes* (sleeping berths) on night trains, and some other trains where indicated in timetables. You can reserve any train at any station any time before your departure or through SNCF Boutiques. If you're buying a point-to-point ticket for a TGV or Intercité train, you'll reserve your seat when you purchase your ticket.

It's wise to book well ahead for any TGV, especially on the busy Paris-Avignon-Nice line. If the TGV trains you want are fully booked, ask about TER trains serving the same destination, as these don't require reservations.

Rail-pass holders can book TGV reservations directly at French stations up to departure, if still available, or book etickets at www.raileurope.com. Given the possible difficulty of getting TGV reservations with a rail pass, I recommend making those reservations online before you leave home.

For trains other than the TGV and Intercité, reservations are generally unnecessary, but are advisable during busy times (for example, Friday and Sunday

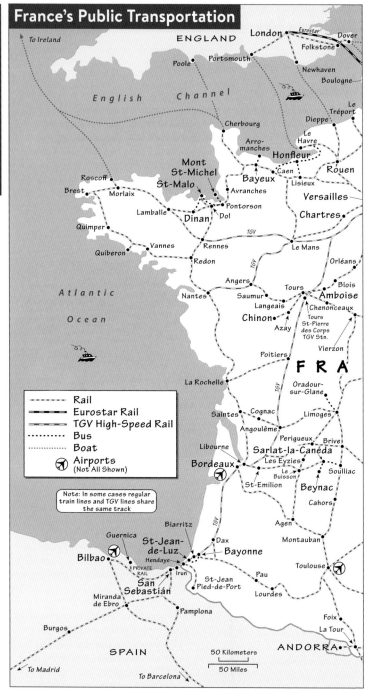

France's Public Transportation

To Ireland

ENGLAND

London — Eurostar — Dover
Folkstone

Poole   Portsmouth
Newhaven
Boulogne

English   *Channel*

Le
Tréport
Cherbourg   Dieppe
Le
Arro-   Havre
manches   Honfleur
Caen   Rouen
Mont
St-Michel   Bayeux   Lisieux
St-Malo   Avranches   Versailles
Roscoff   Pontorson
Brest   Morlaix   Dinan   Dol   Chartres
Lamballe
Quimper
Vannes   TGV
Quiberon   Rennes   Le Mans
Redon   Orléans
Angers   Tours   Blois
Atlantic   Nantes   Saumur   Amboise
Langeais   Chenonceaux
Ocean   Chinon   Tours
Azay   St-Pierre
des Corps
TGV Stn.
Vierzon
Poitiers

F R A

La Rochelle   Oradour-
sur-Glane
Cognac   Limoges
Saintes
Angoulême
Perigueux   Brive
Libourne   Sarlat-la-Canéda
Bordeaux   Les Eyzies
St-Emilion   Le   Soulliac
Buisson
Beynac
Cahors

Biarritz   Agen
Guernica   St-Jean-   Dax   Montauban
de-Luz   Bayonne
Bilbao   Hendaye   Toulouse
PRIVATE
RAIL   Irun   Pau
San   St-Jean   Lourdes
Sebastián   Pied-de-Port
Miranda
de Ebro   Pamplona
Foix
Burgos   La Tour

SPAIN   50 Kilometers   ANDORRA
50 Miles
To Madrid   To Barcelona

Legend

········· Rail
▬▬▬ Eurostar Rail
▬▬▬ TGV High-Speed Rail
·········· Bus
·········· Boat
✈ Airports
(Not All Shown)

Note: In some cases regular
train lines and TGV lines share
the same track

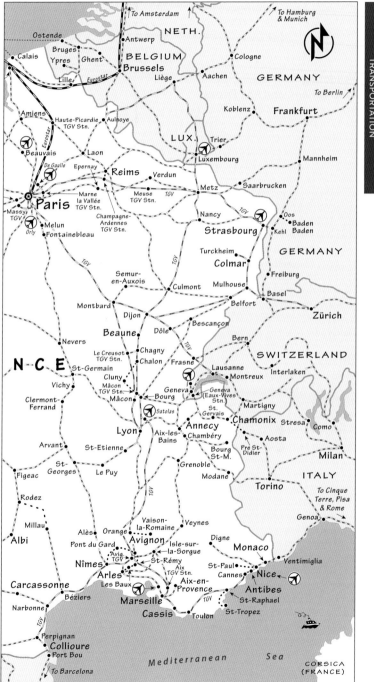

afternoons, Saturday mornings, weekday rush hours, and holiday weekends; see "Holidays and Festivals" near the end of this chapter).

Validating Tickets, Reservations, and Rail Passes

At major stations (including all Paris stations) you'll need to scan your ticket at turnstiles to access the tracks. Smaller stations continue to use the old system of validating your ticket in yellow machines near the platform or waiting area. Print-at-home tickets and etickets downloaded to your phone don't require validation.

If you have a rail pass, get it activated at a ticket window before using it the first time (don't stamp it in the machine). If you're traveling with a pass and have a reservation for a certain trip, you must activate the reservation by stamping it. If you have a rail flexipass, write the date on your pass each day you travel (before or immediately after boarding your first train).

Buses

Buses usually provide the cheapest transportation between European cities. Eurolines is the old standby, but two relative newcomers—Ouibus and FlixBus—are cutting prices drastically while offering speedy service, snacks for purchase, Wi-Fi, easy booking, and lots of destinations in France. All of these companies usually provide service between train stations or between train stations and airports within France, as well as to international destinations.

Ouibus has routes mostly within France, but serves some other European cities as well (toll tel. 08 92 68 00 68, www.ouibus. com). German-run **FlixBus** connects key cities within France and throughout Europe, often from secondary airports and train stations (handy eticket system and easy-to-use app, tel. 01 76 36 04 12, www. flixbus.com). **Eurolines'** buses depart from Paris' Gare Routière du Paris-Gallieni station in the suburb of Bagnolet (28 Avenue du Général de Gaulle, Mo: Gallieni, toll tel. 08 92 89 90 91; from the US, dial 011 33 1 41 86 24 21, www.eurolines.com).

Train stations usually have bus information where train-to-bus connections are important—and vice versa for bus companies.

The bus company websites I've listed in this book are usually in French only. Here are some key phrases you'll see: *horaires* (schedules), *en semaine* (usually Monday through Saturday, sometimes through Friday), *samedi* (Saturday), *dimanche* (Sunday), *jours fériés* (holidays), *LMMJV (Monday, Tuesday, Wednesday, Thursday, Friday)*, *année* (bus runs all year on the days listed), *vac* (runs only during summer vacations), *scol/scolaire* (runs only when school is in session), *ligne* (route or bus line), and *réseau* (network—usually all routes).

Renting a Car

Most of the major US rental agencies (including Avis, Budget, Enterprise, Hertz, and Thrifty) have offices throughout Europe. Also consider the two major Europe-based agencies, Europcar and Sixt, and the French agency, ADA (www. ada.fr). Consolidators such as Auto Europe/Kemwel (www.autoeurope. com—or the sometimes cheaper www. autoeurope.eu), compare rates at several companies to get you the best deal.

Wherever you book, always read the fine print. Ask about add-on charges—such as one-way drop-off fees, airport surcharges, or mandatory insurance policies—that aren't included in the "total price."

Rental Costs and Considerations

Figure on paying roughly $250 for a one-week rental for a basic compact car. Allow extra for supplemental insurance, fuel, tolls, and parking.

Manual vs. Automatic: Almost all rental cars in Europe are manual by default—and cars with a stick shift are generally cheaper. If you need an automatic, request one in advance. When selecting a car, don't be tempted by a larger model, as it won't be as maneuverable on narrow, winding roads or when squeezing into tight parking lots.

Age Restrictions: Some rental companies impose minimum and maximum age limits. Young drivers (25 and under) and seniors (69 and up) should check the rental policies and rules section of car rental websites.

Choosing Pickup/Drop-off Locations: Always check the hours of the locations you choose. Except at airports and major train stations, most rental offices close from midday Saturday until Monday morning and, in smaller towns, at lunchtime. Wherever you select, get precise details on the location and allow ample time to find it.

Picking Up Your Car: Before driving off in your rental car, check it thoroughly and make sure any damage is noted on your rental agreement. Rental agencies in Europe tend to charge for even minor damage, so be sure to mark everything. Find out how your car's gearshift, lights, turn signals, wipers, radio, and fuel cap function, and know what kind of fuel the car takes (diesel vs. unleaded). When you return the car, make sure the agent verifies its condition with you. Some drivers take pictures of the returned vehicle as proof of its condition.

Car Insurance Options

When you rent a car in Europe, the price typically includes liability insurance, which covers harm to other cars or motorists—but not the rental car itself. To limit your financial risk in case of damage to the rental, choose one of these options: Buy a Collision Damage Waiver (CDW) with a low or zero deductible from the car-rental company (roughly 30-40 percent extra), get coverage through your credit card (free, but more complicated), or get collision insurance as part of a larger travel-insurance policy.

For more on your car-rental insurance options, see www.ricksteves.com/cdw.

Navigation Options

If you'll be navigating using your phone or a GPS unit from home, remember to bring a car charger and device mount.

Your Mobile Phone: The mapping app on your phone works fine for navigation in Europe, but for real-time turn-by-turn directions and traffic updates, you'll need mobile data access. And driving all day can burn through a lot of very expensive data. The economical workaround is to use map apps that work offline. By downloading in advance from Google Maps, Apple Maps, Here WeGo, or Navmii, you can still have turn-by-turn voice directions and maps that recalibrate even though they're offline.

You must download your maps before you go offline—and it's smart to select large regions. Then turn off your data connection so you're not charged for roaming. Call up the map, enter your destination, and you're on your way. Even if you don't have to pay extra for data roaming, this option is great for navigating in areas with poor connectivity.

GPS Devices: If you want the convenience of a dedicated GPS unit, consider renting one with your car ($10-30/day). These units offer real-time turn-by-turn directions and traffic without the data requirements of an app. The unit may come loaded only with maps for its home country; if you need additional maps, ask. Also make sure your device's language is set to English before you drive off.

Maps and Atlases: Even when navigating primarily with a mobile app or GPS, I always make it a point to have a paper map. It's invaluable for getting the big picture, understanding alternate routes, and filling in when my phone runs out of juice. Buy a better map before you go, or pick one up at European gas stations, bookshops, newsstands, and tourist shops.

Driving

Road Rules: Seat belts are mandatory for all, and children under age 10 must be in the back seat with a special seat. In city and town centers, traffic merging from the right (even from tiny side streets) may have the right-of-way (*priorité à droite*). So even when you're driving on a major road, pay attention to cars merging from the right. In contrast, cars entering the countless suburban roundabouts must yield (*cédez le passage*).

Be aware of typical European road rules; for example, many countries require headlights to be turned on at all times (in France, they must be used in any case of poor visibility), and nearly all forbid handheld mobile-phone use. Ask your car-rental company about these rules, or check the "International Travel" section of the US State Department website (www.travel.state.gov, search for your country in the "Country Information" box, then click "Travel and Transportation").

Speed Limits: Because speed limits are by road type, they typically aren't posted, so it's best to memorize them:
- Two-lane D and N routes outside cities and towns: 80 km/hour, 90 km/hour if the road has a divider separating the lanes.
- Two-lane roads in villages: 50 km/hour (unless posted at 30 km/hour)
- Divided highways outside cities and towns: 90-110 km/hour

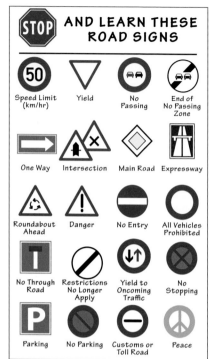

AND LEARN THESE ROAD SIGNS

STOP

Speed Limit (km/hr) · Yield · No Passing · End of No Passing Zone

One Way · Intersection · Main Road · Expressway

Roundabout Ahead · Danger · No Entry · All Vehicles Prohibited

No Through Road · Restrictions No Longer Apply · Yield to Oncoming Traffic · No Stopping

Parking · No Parking · Customs or Toll Road · Peace

- Autoroutes (toll roads): 130 km/hour (unless otherwise posted)

Road speeds are monitored regularly with cameras—a mere two kilometers over the limit yields a pricey ticket (a minimum of about €70). The good news is that signs warn drivers a few hundred yards before the camera and show the proper speed. Look for a sign with a radar graphic that says *Pour votre sécurité, contrôles automatiques.*

Pulling to the Side of the Road: All rental cars are equipped with a yellow safety vest and triangle. You must wear the vest and display the triangle whenever you pull over on the side of the road (say, to fix a flat tire). If you don't, you could be fined.

Fuel: Gas (*essence*) is expensive—about $7 per gallon. Diesel (*gazole*) costs less—about $6.50 per gallon. Know what type of fuel your car takes before you fill up. Many Americans get marooned by filling with unleaded in a diesel car. Many

Driving in France

ENGLAND
To London
Dover
Calais
Lille
BELGIUM
GERMANY
LUX.
English Channel
Arromanches (D-Day Beaches)
Honfleur
20m .5h
45m .75h
55m 1h
Mont St-Michel
Bayeux
80m 1.5h
Caen
80m 1.5h
Rouen
80m 1.5h
180m 2.75h
140m 2.25h
Paris
90m 1.5h
Reims
Verdun
75m 1.25h
150m 2.75h
Strasbourg
305m 4.5h
50m 1h
Colmar
Dinan
195m 3h
Chartres
285m 5.5h
Amboise
225m 4.5h
85m 2h
140m 2.25h
155m 2.5h
Semur-en-Auxois
50m .75h
Chinon
50m 1.25h
270m 5.5h
250m 4h
165m 2.5h
Beaune
145m 2.5h
SWITZ.
FRANCE
Oradour-sur-Glane
135m 3h
95m 1.5h
Lyon
85m 1.5h
Annecy
55m 1h
Chamonix
Atlantic Ocean
360m 5.25h
220m 4.5h
700m 2.25h
260m 5h
St. Emilion
80m 2h
Sarlat-la-Canéda
30m 1.25h
Rocamadour
140m 2h
235m 5h
ITALY
155m 2.5h
225m 2.5h
Albi
25m .5h
Avignon
160m 2.5h
Monaco
10m .5h
St. Jean-de-Luz
20m .5h
210m 4.75h
170m 3h
70m 1.75h
Arles
80m 1.25h
105m 1.5h
Nice
10m .5h
San Sebastián
250m 3.5h
Carcassonne
150m 2.25h
165m 2.5h
95m 1.5h
Cassis
Antibes
SPAIN
ANDORRA
Collioure
Mediterranean Sea

m = miles
h = hours

Note: Travel times may vary based on traffic, construction, and road conditions.

rentals are diesel; if yours is one of them, use the yellow pump. Fuel is most expensive on autoroutes and cheapest at big supermarkets. Your US credit and debit cards may not work at self-serve pumps—so you may need to find gas stations with attendants (all autoroute stations have them, as do most countryside stations during business hours)—and be sure to know your card's PIN (explained earlier, under "Money").

Plan ahead for Sundays, as most gas stations in town are closed. I fill my tank every Saturday. If stuck on a Sunday, use an autoroute, where the gas stations are always staffed.

Autoroutes and Tolls: Autoroute tolls are pricey, but the alternative to these super-"feeways" usually means being marooned in countryside traffic—especially near the Riviera. Autoroutes save enough time, gas, and nausea to justify the cost. Mix high-speed "autorouting" with scenic country-road rambling.

You'll usually take a ticket when entering an autoroute and pay when you leave. Cash (coins or bills under €50) is your best payment option as some US credit

French Tollbooths

For American drivers, getting through the toll payment stations on France's autoroutes is mostly about knowing which lanes to avoid—and having cash and a chip-and-PIN credit card on hand. Don't assume that your US credit card will work even if it has a chip—have cash as a backup.

When approaching the tollbooths, slow down to study your options (and pull off to the side if you need time to consider your choices). Skip lanes marked only with a lowercase "t"—they're reserved for cars using the automatic Télépéage payment system. Follow green arrows to get a ticket (green-arrow lanes are sometimes combined with Télépéage lanes).

When exiting the autoroute, follow the coins icon (usually in white), meaning cash or chip-and-PIN cards are accepted. If you don't see these icons, take the green-arrow lane. Avoid the "t"-only (Télépéage) lane or the credit-card-only lane. Exits are entirely automated (if you have a problem at the tollbooth, press the red button for help). Even machines that take cash usually have a credit card slot—give it a try (know your PIN). Have smaller bills ready (payment machines won't accept €50 bills). Shorter autoroute sections have periodic tollbooths, where you can pay by dropping coins into a basket (change is given for bills, but keep a good supply of coins handy to avoid waiting for an attendant).

To estimate how much cash to have on hand for tolls, use the planning tool at ViaMichelin.com.

---

cards won't work (for more on paying at tollbooths, see the sidebar).

Autoroute gas stations are open on Sundays and usually come with well-stocked minimarts, clean restrooms, sandwiches, maps, local products, cheap vending-machine coffee, and Wi-Fi. Many have small cafés or more elaborate cafeterias with reasonable prices. For more information, see www.autoroutes.fr.

Highways: Roads are classified into departmental (D), national (N), and autoroutes (A). D routes (usually yellow lines on maps) are often slower but the most scenic. N routes and important D routes (red lines) are the fastest after autoroutes (orange lines on maps). Green road signs are for national routes; blue are for autoroutes. Some roads in France have had route-number changes (mostly N roads converting to D roads). If you're using an older map, the actual route name may differ from what's on your map. Navigate by destination rather than road name...or buy a new map. There are plenty of good facilities, gas stations (most closed Sun), and rest stops along most French roads.

Parking: Finding a parking place can be a headache in larger cities. Ask your hotelier for ideas, and pay to park at well-patrolled lots (blue P signs direct you to parking lots in French cities). Parking garages require that you take a ticket with you and pay at a machine (called a *caisse*) on your way back to the car or at a machine at the exit. American chip cards should work in these machines; otherwise, use euro coins (some accept bills, too). If your credit card does not work and you don't have enough coins, find the garage's *accueil* office, where the attendant can help or direct you to a nearby shop where you can change bills into coins.

Metered parking is strictly monitored in France. At parking machines, prepare to enter your car's license plate number and the amount of time you need, then

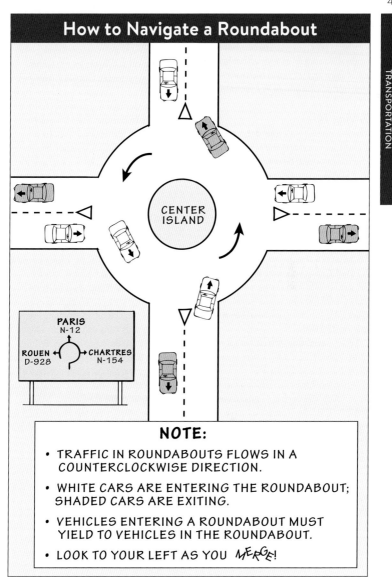

How to Navigate a Roundabout

NOTE:

- TRAFFIC IN ROUNDABOUTS FLOWS IN A COUNTERCLOCKWISE DIRECTION.
- WHITE CARS ARE ENTERING THE ROUNDABOUT; SHADED CARS ARE EXITING.
- VEHICLES ENTERING A ROUNDABOUT MUST YIELD TO VEHICLES IN THE ROUNDABOUT.
- LOOK TO YOUR LEFT AS YOU MERGE!

take the receipt and place it on your dash. While the first 30 minutes is often free, you still need to input your license number and get a ticket. Metered parking is sometimes free 12:00-14:00 and usually free 19:00-9:00 and on Sunday (varies by city and parking area). Look for a small machine selling time (called an *horoda-* *teur,* usually one per block), and plug in a few coins or your credit card. Avoid spaces outlined in blue, as they require a special permit.

Theft: Theft is a problem, particularly in southern France. Thieves easily recognize rental cars and assume they are filled with a tourist's gear. Try to make your car look locally owned by hiding the "tourist-owned" rental-company decals and putting a French newspaper in your back window. Be sure all of your valuables are out of sight and locked in the trunk—or, even better, with you or in your room.

Driving Tips

France is riddled with **roundabouts**—navigating them is an art. The key is to know your direction and be ready for your turn-off. If you miss it, take another lap (or two).

At intersections and roundabouts, French **road signs** use the name of an upcoming destination for directions—the highway number is usually missing. That upcoming destination could be a major city, or it could be the next minor town up the road. Check your map ahead of time and get familiar with the names of towns and cities along your route—and even major cities on the same road beyond your destination.

When **navigating into cities,** approach intersections cautiously, stow the map, and follow the signs to *Centre-Ville* (city center).

When **leaving** or just passing through cities, follow the signs for *Toutes Directions* or *Autres Directions* (meaning "anywhere else") until you see a sign for your specific destination. Look also for *Suivre* signs telling you to follow (*suivre*) signs for the (usually more important) destination listed.

Driving on any roads but autoroutes will take longer than you think, so allow **plenty of time** for slower traffic (tractors, trucks, and hard-to-decipher signs all deserve blame). First-timers should estimate how long they think a drive will take...then double it. I pretend that kilometers are miles (for distances) and base my time estimates accordingly.

On **autoroutes,** keep to the right lanes to let fast drivers by, and be careful when merging into a left lane, as cars can be coming at high speeds.

Keep a stash of **coins** handy for parking and small autoroute tolls.

Flights

To compare flight costs and times, begin with a travel search engine: Kayak.com is the top site for flights to and within Europe, easy-to-use Google Flights has price alerts, and Skyscanner.com includes many inexpensive flights within Europe.

Flights to Europe: Start looking for international flights about four to six months before your trip, especially for peak-season travel. Depending on your itinerary, it can be efficient and no more expensive to fly into one city and out of another. If your flight requires a connection in Europe, see our hints on navigating Europe's top hub airports at www.ricksteves.com/hub-airports.

Flights Within Europe: Flying between European cities has become surprisingly affordable. If you're visiting one or more French cities on a longer European trip—or linking up far-flung French cities (such as Paris and Nice)—a flight can save both time and money. Before buying a long-distance train or bus ticket, first check the cost of a flight on one of Europe's airlines, whether a major carrier or a no-frills outfit like EasyJet, Vueling, or Ryanair. Also check Air France for specials. Be aware of the potential drawbacks of flying with a discount airline: nonrefundable and nonchangeable tickets, minimal customer service, time-consuming treks to secondary airports, and stingy baggage allowances (also an issue on major airlines).

Flying to the US and Canada: Because security is extra tight for flights to the US, be sure to give yourself plenty of time at the airport. It's also important to charge your electronic devices before you board because security checks may require you to turn them on (see www.tsa.gov for the latest rules).

Resources from Rick Steves

Begin Your Trip at www.RickSteves.com

My mobile-friendly **website** is *the* place to explore Europe in preparation for your trip. You'll find thousands of fun articles, videos, and radio interviews; a wealth of money-saving tips for planning your dream trip; travel news dispatches; a video library of my travel talks; my travel blog; and my latest guidebook updates (www.ricksteves.com/update).

Our **Travel Forum** is a well-groomed collection of message boards where our travel-savvy community answers questions and shares personal travel experiences—and our well-traveled staff chimes in when they can be helpful.

Our **online Travel Store** offers bags and accessories that I've designed to help you travel smarter and lighter. These include my popular bags (rolling carry-on and backpack versions, which I helped design...and live out of four months a year), money belts, totes, toiletries kits, adapters, guidebooks, and planning maps.

Our website can also help you find the perfect **rail pass** for your itinerary and your budget.

Guidebooks, TV Shows, Audio Europe, and Tours

Small Group Tours: Want to travel with greater efficiency and less stress? We offer more than 40 itineraries reaching the best destinations in this book...and beyond. You'll find European adventures to fit every vacation length. For all the details, and to get our tour catalog, visit www.ricksteves.com or call us at 425/608-4217.

Books: This book is just one of many books in my series on European travel, which includes country and city guidebooks, Snapshots (excerpted chapters from bigger guides), Pocket Guides (full-color little books on big cities), and my budget-travel skills handbook, *Rick Steves Europe Through the Back Door*. A more complete list of my titles appears near the end of this book.

TV Shows and Travel Talks: My public television series, *Rick Steves' Europe*, covers Europe from top to bottom with over 100 half-hour episodes (watch full episodes on my website for free). Or, to raise your travel I.Q., check out the video versions of our popular classes (covering most European countries as well as travel skills).

Radio: My weekly public radio show, *Travel with Rick Steves*, features interviews with travel experts from around the world. It airs on 400 public radio stations across the US, or you can hear it as a podcast. A complete archive of programs is available on my website.

Audio Tours on My Free App: I've also produced dozens of free, self-guided audio tours of the top sights in Europe. For those tours and other audio content, get my free **Rick Steves Audio Europe app,** an extensive online library organized into handy geographic playlists. For more on my app, see page 29.

HOLIDAYS AND FESTIVALS

This list includes selected festivals in major cities, plus national holidays observed throughout France. Many sights and banks close on national holidays—keep this in mind when planning your itinerary. Before planning a trip around a festival, verify the dates with the festival website, France's national tourism website (http://us.france.fr), or my festival web page at RickSteves.com.

Here is a sampling of events and holidays:

Jan 1	New Year's Day
Feb–March	Carnival (Mardi Gras) parades and fireworks, Nice (www.nicecarnaval.com)
March/April	Easter weekend (Good Friday-Easter Monday)
April–Oct	International Garden Festival, Chaumont-sur-Loire (www.domaine-chaumont.fr)
May 1	Labor Day
May 8	VE (Victory in Europe) Day
Mid-May	Cannes Film Festival, Cannes (www.festival-cannes.fr)
Late May	Monaco Grand Prix auto race (www.grand-prix-monaco.com)
40th Day after Easter	Ascension
May/June	Pentecost Sunday/Monday
June 6	Anniversary of D-Day Landing, Normandy
June 21	Fête de la Musique (music festival), free concerts and dancing in the streets throughout France
July	Tour de France, national bicycle race culminating on the Champs-Elysées in Paris (www.letour.fr)
July 14	Bastille Day (fireworks, dancing, and revelry all over France)
Aug 15	Assumption
Nov 1	All Saints' Day
Nov 11	Armistice Day
Late Nov–Dec 24	Christmas Markets, Strasbourg, Colmar, and Sarlat-la-Canéda
Early Dec	Festival of Lights (celebration of Virgin Mary, candlelit windows), Lyon
Dec 25	Christmas Day
Dec 31	New Year's Eve

CONVERSIONS AND CLIMATE

Numbers and Stumblers

- Europeans write a few of their numbers differently than we do: 1 = 1, 4 = 4, 7 = 7.
- In Europe, dates appear as day/month/year; Christmas is 25/12.
- Commas are decimal points and decimals are commas. A dollar and a half is $1,50, one thousand is 1.000.
- When counting with fingers, start with your thumb. If you hold up your first finger to request one item, you'll probably get two.
- What Americans call the second floor of a building is the first floor in Europe.
- On escalators and moving sidewalks, Europeans keep the left "lane" open for passing. Keep to the right.

Metric Conversions

A **kilogram** equals 1,000 grams (about 2.2 pounds). One hundred **grams** (a common unit at markets) is about a quarter-pound. One **liter** is about a quart, or almost four to a gallon.

A **kilometer** is six-tenths of a mile. To convert kilometers to miles, cut the kilometers in half and add back 10 percent of the original (120 km: 60 + 12 = 72 miles). One **meter** is 39 inches—just over a yard.

Clothing Sizes

When shopping for clothing, use these US-to-European comparisons as general guidelines (but note that no conversion is perfect).

Women: For pants and dresses, add 32 in France (US 10 = French 42). For blouses and sweaters, add 8 for most of Europe (US 32 = European 40). For shoes, add 30-31 (US 7 = European 37/38).

Men: For shirts, multiply by 2 and add about 8 (US size 15 = European 38). For jackets and suits, add 10. For shoes, add 32-34.

Children: Clothing is sized by height—in centimeters (2.5 cm = 1 inch), so a US size 8 roughly equates to 132-140. For shoes up to size 13, add 16-18, and for sizes 1 and up, add 30-32.

France's Climate

First line, average daily high; second line, average daily low; third line, average days without rain. For more detailed weather statistics for destinations in this book (as well as the rest of the world), check www.wunderground.com.

Paris

J	F	M	A	M	J	J	A	S	O	N	D
43°	45°	54°	60°	68°	73°	76°	75°	70°	60°	50°	44°
34°	34°	39°	43°	49°	55°	58°	58°	53°	46°	40°	36°
14	14	19	17	19	18	19	18	17	18	15	15

Nice

J	F	M	A	M	J	J	A	S	O	N	D
50°	53°	59°	64°	71°	79°	84°	83°	77°	68°	58°	52°
35°	36°	41°	46°	52°	58°	63°	63°	58°	51°	43°	37°
23	22	24	23	23	26	29	26	24	23	21	21

Packing Checklist

Whether you're traveling for five days or five weeks, you won't need more than this. Pack light to enjoy the sweet freedom of true mobility.

Clothing

☐ 5 shirts: long- & short-sleeve
☐ 2 pairs pants (or skirts/capris)
☐ 1 pair shorts
☐ 5 pairs underwear & socks
☐ 1 pair walking shoes
☐ Sweater or warm layer
☐ Rainproof jacket with hood
☐ Tie, scarf, belt, and/or hat
☐ Swimsuit
☐ Sleepwear/loungewear

Money

☐ Debit card(s)
☐ Credit card(s)
☐ Hard cash (US $100-200)
☐ Money belt

Documents

☐ Passport
☐ Tickets & confirmations: flights, hotels, trains, rail pass, car rental, sight entries
☐ Driver's license
☐ Student ID, hostel card, etc.
☐ Photocopies of important documents
☐ Insurance details
☐ Guidebooks & maps

Toiletries Kit

☐ Basics: soap, shampoo, toothbrush, toothpaste, floss, deodorant, sunscreen, brush/comb, etc.
☐ Medicines & vitamins
☐ First-aid kit
☐ Glasses/contacts/sunglasses
☐ Sewing kit
☐ Packet of tissues (for WC)
☐ Earplugs

Electronics

☐ Mobile phone
☐ Camera & related gear
☐ Tablet/ebook reader/laptop
☐ Headphones/earbuds
☐ Chargers & batteries
☐ Phone car charger & mount (or GPS device)
☐ Plug adapters

Miscellaneous

☐ Daypack
☐ Sealable plastic baggies
☐ Laundry supplies: soap, laundry bag, clothesline, spot remover
☐ Small umbrella
☐ Travel alarm/watch
☐ Notepad & pen
☐ Journal

Optional Extras

☐ Second pair of shoes (flip-flops, sandals, tennis shoes, boots)
☐ Travel hairdryer
☐ Picnic supplies
☐ Water bottle
☐ Fold-up tote bag
☐ Small flashlight
☐ Mini binoculars
☐ Small towel or washcloth
☐ Inflatable pillow/neck rest
☐ Tiny lock
☐ Address list (to mail postcards)
☐ Extra passport photos

French Survival Phrases

When using the phonetics, try to nasalize the <u>n</u> sound.

English	French	Pronunciation
Good day.	Bonjour.	bohn-zhoor
Mrs. / Mr.	Madame / Monsieur	mah-dahm / muhs-yur
Do you speak English?	Parlez-vous anglais?	par-lay-voo ahn-glay
Yes. / No.	Oui. / Non.	wee / nohn
I understand.	Je comprends.	zhuh kohn-prahn
I don't understand.	Je ne comprends pas.	zhuh nuh kohn-prahn pah
Please.	S'il vous plaît.	see voo play
Thank you.	Merci.	mehr-see
I'm sorry.	Désolé.	day-zoh-lay
Excuse me.	Pardon.	par-dohn
(No) problem.	(Pas de) problème.	(pah duh) proh-blehm
It's good.	C'est bon.	say bohn
Goodbye.	Au revoir.	oh vwahr
one / two	un / deux	uhn / duh
three / four	trois / quatre	twah / kah-truh
five / six	cinq / six	sank / sees
seven / eight	sept / huit	seht / weet
nine / ten	neuf / dix	nuhf / dees
How much is it?	Combien?	kohn-bee-an
Write it?	Ecrivez?	ay-kree-vay
Is it free?	C'est gratuit?	say grah-twee
Included?	Inclus?	an-klew
Where can I buy / find...?	Où puis-je acheter / trouver...?	oo pwee-zhuh ah-shuh-tay / troo-vay
I'd like / We'd like...	Je voudrais / Nous voudrions...	zhuh voo-dray / noo voo-dree-ohn
...a room.	...une chambre.	ewn shahn-bruh
...a ticket to _____.	...un billet pour _____.	uhn bee-yay poor _____
Is it possible?	C'est possible?	say poh-see-bluh
Where is...?	Où est...?	oo ay
...the train station	...la gare	lah gar
...the bus station	...la gare routière	lah gar root-yehr
...tourist information	...l'office du tourisme	loh-fees dew too-reez-muh
Where are the toilets?	Où sont les toilettes?	oo sohn lay twah-leht
men	hommes	ohm
women	dames	dahm
left / right	à gauche / à droite	ah gohsh / ah dwaht
straight	tout droit	too dwah
When does this open / close?	Ça ouvre / ferme à quelle heure?	sah oo-vruh / fehrm ah kehl ur
At what time?	À quelle heure?	ah kehl ur
Just a moment.	Un moment.	uhn moh-mahn
now / soon / later	maintenant / bientôt / plus tard	man-tuh-nahn / bee-an-toh / plew tar
today / tomorrow	aujourd'hui / demain	oh-zhoor-dwee / duh-man

For more user-friendly French phrases, check out *Rick Steves' French Phrase Book and Dictionary* or *Rick Steves' French, Italian & German Phrase Book*.

In a French Restaurant

English	French	Pronunciation
I'd like / We'd like...	Je voudrais / Nous voudrions...	zhuh voo-dray / noo voo-dree-oh<u>n</u>
...to reserve...	...réserver...	ray-zehr-vay
...a table for one / two.	...une table pour un / deux.	ewn tah-bluh poor uh<u>n</u> / duh
Is this seat free?	C'est libre?	say lee-bruh
The menu (in English), please.	La carte (en anglais), s'il vous plaît.	lah kart (ah<u>n</u> ah<u>n</u>-glay) see voo play
service (not) included	service (non) compris	sehr-vees (noh<u>n</u>) koh<u>n</u>-pree
to go	à emporter	ah ah<u>n</u>-por-tay
with / without	avec / sans	ah-vehk / sah<u>n</u>
and / or	et / ou	ay / oo
special of the day	plat du jour	plah dew zhoor
specialty of the house	spécialité de la maison	spay-see-ah-lee-tay duh lah may-zoh<u>n</u>
appetizers	hors d'oeuvre	or duh-vruh
first course (soup, salad)	entrée	ah<u>n</u>-tray
main course (meat, fish)	plat principal	plah pra<u>n</u>-see-pahl
bread	pain	pa<u>n</u>
cheese	fromage	froh-mahzh
sandwich	sandwich	sah<u>n</u>d-weech
soup	soupe	soop
salad	salade	sah-lahd
meat	viande	vee-ah<u>n</u>d
chicken	poulet	poo-lay
fish	poisson	pwah-soh<u>n</u>
seafood	fruits de mer	frwee duh mehr
fruit	fruit	frwee
vegetables	légumes	lay-gewm
dessert	dessert	day-sehr
mineral water	eau minérale	oh mee-nay-rahl
tap water	l'eau du robinet	loh dew roh-bee-nay
milk	lait	lay
(orange) juice	jus (d'orange)	zhew (doh-rah<u>n</u>zh)
coffee / tea	café / thé	kah-fay / tay
wine	vin	va<u>n</u>
red / white	rouge / blanc	roozh / blah<u>n</u>
glass / bottle	verre / bouteille	vehr / boo-tay
beer	bière	bee-ehr
Cheers!	Santé!	sah<u>n</u>-tay
More. / Another.	Plus. / Un autre.	plew / uh<u>n</u> oh-truh
The same.	La même chose.	lah mehm shohz
The bill, please.	L'addition, s'il vous plaît.	lah-dee-see-oh<u>n</u> see voo play
Do you accept credit cards?	Vous prenez les cartes?	voo pruh-nay lay kart
tip	pourboire	poor-bwahr
Delicious!	Délicieux!	day-lee-see-uh

INDEX

MAP INDEX

Start your trip at

Our website enhances this book and turns

Explore Europe

At ricksteves.com you can browse through thousands of articles, videos, photos and radio interviews, plus find a wealth of money-saving travel tips for planning your dream trip. And with our mobile-friendly website, you can easily access all this great travel information anywhere you go.

TV Shows

Preview the places you'll visit by watching entire half-hour episodes of Rick Steves' Europe (choose from all 100 shows) on-demand, for free.

ricksteves.com

your travel dreams into affordable reality

Radio Interviews

Enjoy ready access to Rick's vast library of radio interviews covering travel tips and cultural insights that relate specifically to your Europe travel plans.

Travel Forums

Learn, ask, share! Our online community of savvy travelers is a great resource for first-time travelers to Europe, as well as seasoned pros.

Travel News

Subscribe to our free Travel News e-newsletter, and get monthly updates from Rick on what's happening in Europe.

Classroom Europe

Check out our free resource for educators with 300+ short video clips from the Rick Steves' Europe TV show.

Audio Europe™

Rick's Free Travel App

Get your FREE Rick Steves Audio Europe™ app to enjoy…

- Dozens of self-guided tours of Europe's top museums, sights and historic walks
- Hundreds of tracks filled with cultural insights and sightseeing tips from Rick's radio interviews
- All organized into handy geographic playlists
- For Apple and Android

With Rick whispering in your ear, Europe gets even better.

Find out more at ricksteves.com

Pack Light and Right

Gear up for your next adventure at ricksteves.com

Light Luggage

Pack light and right with Rick Steves' affordable, custom-designed rolling carry-on bags, backpacks, day packs and shoulder bags.

Accessories

From packing cubes to moneybelts and beyond, Rick has personally selected the travel goodies that will help your trip go smoother.

Shop at ricksteves.com

Rick Steves has

Experience maximum Europe

Save time and energy

This guidebook is your independent-travel toolkit. But for all it delivers, it's still up to you to devote the time and energy it takes to manage the preparation and logistics that are essential for a happy trip. If that's a hassle, there's a solution.

Rick Steves Tours

A Rick Steves tour takes you to Europe's most

great tours, too!

with minimum stress

interesting places with great guides and small groups of 28 or less. We follow Rick's favorite itineraries, ride in comfy buses, stay in family-run hotels, and bring you intimately close to the Europe you've traveled so far to see. Most importantly, we take away the logistical headaches so you can focus on the fun.

travelers—nearly half of them repeat customers—along with us on four dozen different itineraries, from Ireland to Italy to Athens.

Is a Rick Steves tour the right fit for your travel dreams? Find out at ricksteves.com, where you can also request Rick's latest tour catalog.

Join the fun

This year we'll take thousands of free-spirited

Europe is best experienced with happy travel partners. We hope you can join us.

See our itineraries at ricksteves.com

A Guide for Every Trip

BEST OF GUIDES

Full color easy-to-scan format, focusing on Europe's most popular destinations and sights

Best of England
Best of Europe
Best of France
Best of Germany
Best of Ireland
Best of Italy
Best of Scotland
Best of Spain

COMPREHENSIVE GUIDES

City, country, and regional guides with detailed coverage for a multi-week trip exploring the most iconic sights and venturing off the beaten track

Amsterdam & the Netherlands
Barcelona
Belgium: Bruges, Brussels, Antwerp & Ghent
Berlin
Budapest
Croatia & Slovenia
Eastern Europe
England
Florence & Tuscany
France
Germany
Great Britain
Greece: Athens & the Peloponnese
Iceland
Ireland
Istanbul
Italy
London
Paris
Portugal
Prague & the Czech Republic
Provence & the French Riviera
Rome
Scandinavia
Scotland
Sicily
Spain
Switzerland
Venice
Vienna, Salzburg & Tirol

THE BEST OF ROME

ome, Italy's capital, is studded with man remnants and floodlit-fountain uares. From the Vatican to the Colosm, with crazy traffic in between, Rome onderful, huge, and exhausting. The wds, the heat, and the weighty history

of the Eternal City where Caesars walked can make tourists wilt. Recharge by taking siestas, gelato breaks, and after-dark walks, strolling from one atmospheric square to another in the refreshing evening air.

ired **Pantheon**—which rgest dome until the narly 2,000 years old day over 1,500).

l of Athens in the **Vat**bodies the humanistic ance.

n, gladiators fought another, entertaining 0.

POCKET GUIDES

Compact, full color city guides with the essentials for shorter trips

Amsterdam	Munich & Salzburg
Athens	Paris
Barcelona	Prague
Florence	Rome
Italy's Cinque Terre	Venice
London	Vienna

SNAPSHOT GUIDES

Focused single-destination coverage

Basque Country: Spain & France
Copenhagen & the Best of Denmark
Dublin
Dubrovnik
Edinburgh
Hill Towns of Central Italy
Krakow, Warsaw & Gdansk
Lisbon
Loire Valley
Madrid & Toledo
Milan & the Italian Lakes District
Naples & the Amalfi Coast
Nice & the French Riviera
Normandy
Northern Ireland
Norway
Reykjavík
Rothenburg & the Rhine
Sevilla, Granada & Southern Spain
St. Petersburg, Helsinki & Tallinn
Stockholm

Rick Steves books are available
from your favorite bookseller.
Many guides are available as ebooks.

CRUISE PORTS GUIDES

Reference for cruise ports of call

Mediterranean Cruise Ports
Northern European Cruise Ports

Complete your library with...

TRAVEL SKILLS & CULTURE

Study up on travel skills before visiting "Europe through the back door" or gain insight on European history and culture

Europe 101
Europe Through the Back Door
European Christmas
European Easter
European Festivals
Postcards from Europe
Travel as a Political Act

PHRASE BOOKS & DICTIONARIES

French
French, Italian & German
German
Italian
Portuguese
Spanish

PLANNING MAPS

Britain, Ireland & London
Europe
France & Paris
Germany, Austria & Switzerland
Iceland
Ireland
Italy
Spain & Portugal

PHOTO CREDITS

Avalon Travel
Hachette Book Group
1700 Fourth Street
Berkeley, CA 94710

Text © 2019 by Rick Steves' Europe, Inc. All rights reserved.
Maps © 2019 by Rick Steves' Europe, Inc. All rights reserved.

Printed in China by RR Donnelley
Third edition, first printing October 2019

ISBN 978-1-64171-109-8

For the latest on Rick's lectures, guidebooks, tours, public radio show, and public television series, contact Rick Steves' Europe, 130 Fourth Avenue North, Edmonds, WA 98020, 425/771-8303, www.ricksteves.com, rick@ricksteves.com.

RICK STEVES' EUROPE
Special Publications Manager: Risa Laib
Managing Editor: Jennifer Madison Davis
Assistant Managing Editor: Cathy Lu
Project Editor: Suzanne Kotz
Editors: Glenn Eriksen, Tom Griffin, Rosie Leutzinger, Jessica Shaw, Carrie Shepherd
Editorial & Production Assistant: Megan Simms
Graphic Content Director: Sandra Hundacker
Maps & Graphics: David C. Hoerlein, Lauren Mills, Mary Rostad
Digital Asset Coordinator: Orin Dubrow

AVALON TRAVEL
Editorial Director: Kevin McLain
Senior Editor and Series Manager: Madhu Prasher
Editors: Jamie Andrade, Sierra Machado
Copy Editor: Kelly Lydick
Proofreader: Patrick Collins
Indexer: Stephen Callahan
Interior Design & Layout: Tabitha Lahr
Cover Design: Kimberly Glyder Design
Maps & Graphics: Kat Bennett

PHOTO CREDITS
Front Cover Photos: Front cover photos: top, left: French Baguettes © Pipa100 | Dreamstime.com; top, middle: Lavender in South of France © Beatrice Preve | Dreamstime.com; top, right: Kayaking on the river Dordogne © Buurserstraat386 | Dreamstime.com; bottom: The Louvre, Paris © Dennis Dolkens | Dreamstime.com
Back Cover Photos: Left: Sully-sur-Loire © Scaliger | Dreamstime.com; middle: French Craquelin © Svetlana Day | Dreamstime.com; right: Etretat, Normandy © Valentin Armianu | Dreamstime.com

Let's Keep on Travelin'

Your trip doesn't need to end.

Follow Rick on social media!